P9-DGJ-181

HISTORY OF THE ART OF WAR

CONTRIBUTIONS IN MILITARY HISTORY

History of the Art of War

Within the Framework of Political History

By Hans Delbrück

Volume I

Antiquity

Translated from the German

by Walter J. Renfroe, Jr.

Contributions in Military History, Number 9

GREENWOOD PRESS

Westport, Connecticut ● London, England

Library of Congress Cataloging in Publication Data

Delbrück, Hans, 1848-1929.
    History of the art of war within the framework of political history.

    (Contributions in military history; no. 9)
    Translation of Geschichte der Kriegskunst im Rahmen der politis-
chen Geschichte.
    Includes bibliographical references and index.
    CONTENTS: v. 1. Antiquity.
    1. Military art and science—History. 2. Naval art and science—
History. 3. War—History. I. Title. II. Series.
U27.D34213   355'.009s [355'.009]   72-792
ISBN 0-8371-6365-X

Maps drawn by Edward J. Krasnoborski

English language edition copyright © 1975 by Walter J. Renfroe, Jr.

Originally published in German under the title *Geschichte der Kriegskunst im Rahmen der politischen Geschichte*.

All rights reserved. No portion of this book may be reproduced, by
any process or technique, without the express written consent of
the publisher.

Library of Congress Catalog Card Number: 72-792
ISBN: 0-8371-6365-X

Translation first published in 1975

Greenwood Press, a division of Williamhouse-Regency Inc.
51 Riverside Avenue, Westport, Connecticut 06880

Manufactured in the United States of America

Table of Contents

BOOK VII
Caesar

List of Illustrations

Translator's Foreword

This translation into English of the first volume of Hans Delbrück's *Geschichte der Kriegskunst im Rahmen der politischen Geschichte* is based on the third edition of that volume, which was published in Berlin in 1920. I have endeavored to adhere as closely as possible to the original, both in spirit and in style, and I have assumed that those using this book will be familiar enough with military history and the political history that Delbrück used as his background to eliminate any need for supplementary explanations on the part of the translator. In those very rare cases where it was felt necessary to point out an obvious error or oversight appearing in the German version, this has been done within the body of the text. No notes have been added by the translator.

Delbrück's frequent use of Greek and Latin citations has created a problem in translating the text into English at this time, more than fifty years after the appearance of his third edition and over seventy years since the first edition was published in 1900. Although it could be assumed that the scholar of Delbrück's day would be familiar with both Greek and Latin, such an assumption can no longer be made, especially with respect to Greek. In a few cases, where Delbrück has cited a Greek or Latin word parenthetically, without using it as a central point in the development of his argument, I have taken the liberty of omitting it completely. In most cases, however, Greek expressions have been translated into English and are given in quotation marks, followed by an asterisk. In a few cases, where Delbrück expounds at some length on the meaning of a Greek word, an English transliteration of the word is shown. For obvious reasons of economy no use has been made of the Greek alphabet. In the case of Latin, the cited passages are shown in the original, followed in most cases by the English translation in parentheses.

I am indebted to Assistant Professor Bruce Taggart of the Department of Classics, Boston University, for his translations of the Greek and Latin citations.

In his statement of distances Delbrück varied between the use of German miles and of kilometers. Where he gives such figures in kilometers, the same unit of measure has been retained; where he uses German miles, his figures have been converted into English miles.

Finally, I wish to express my own appreciation and that of the publisher, Greenwood Press, to Frau Helene Hobe-Delbrück, daughter of Hans Delbrück, for kindly granting permission for this translation.

But I say that we ought to
judge that the writer's
authority be taken not
necessarily as worth nothing,
but, again, not as final;
readers ought to make judgments
from the facts themselves.
Polybius 3.9

Preface
to the First Edition

The constantly progressing specialization in knowledge is developing in two ways in the field of history, by periods and by phenomena. Some persons study all phases of a specific time, whereas others seek to trace a special aspect through the various —and where possible, through *all*—periods. One sees specialized histories of art and literature, the history of religion, the history of the constitutions and of the law, of economic life, of finances, and even of individual institutions, such as marriage, for example. All individual branches of history flow together in universal history and cross-fertilize one another. No one branch is to be dispensed with without harming the knowledge of the whole. And so universal history is also in need of a history of the art of war. Wars, which form and destroy nations, occupy such a broad part of the total of history that one cannot bypass the challenge, not simply to recount them event by event as reported in the sources, but to examine them critically and to develop a technically correct presentation. The best means of doing this, according to the law of the division of labor, is through a specialized history.

For the historian, the difficulty of each such specialized history lies in the mastery of sufficient technical knowledge. If one is to believe that the literary historian is capable of plunging himself completely into the process of literary production, then it is all the more difficult for the art historian to master completely the techniques of painting and sculpture, the economic historians those of agriculture, handworking skills, and commerce. Certainly one does not demand of them that they should personally paint madonnas, build cathedrals, guide the plow, or found colonies; but although one does not demand these things, nevertheless the persons who

11

have these practical skills, who are familiar with these things or actually practice them, do have a certain advantage over the historian and tend to regard him with a certain mistrust. Achilles owes his fame to Homer—but one wonders if he might not have cried out at this or that verse: "It's easy to see that you are a poet and never personally hurled a spear, standing at the head of the Myrmidons!"

The scholar who writes a history of strategy and tactics is in an even worse position. It is already a considerable advantage if he has had the good fortune to become acquainted with the realities of war through service in the lowest ranks. But he must seek to make himself master of everything at a higher level on a purely theoretical basis, and he may not later embellish his account with poetic license. Technical accuracy is the prerequisite of success. Just as the artist or the military man who wishes to describe the past deeds of his particular field must adapt himself to carrying out methodical source studies, so too must the historian who wishes to recount wars, and especially the history of the art of war itself, study the objective conditions, the technical possibilities of the events, as long as is necessary to let him master them with complete certainty.

In principle, this requirement is in no way new, and from the very start one should eliminate the idea that, in the case of a work such as the present one, some different scientific method is to be used than applies in other areas of historical research. True enough, one may speak of critical analysis based on objective considerations in contrast to analysis based on the written word, but those are not opposites, only different tools of the same unified, scientific criticism. No philologist, no matter how strong the mastery he might feel that he possesses in strict, literal interpretation, will for that reason discard in principle the objective observation of the subject; no expert, even if he is able to demonstrate the practical context with experimental certainty, will for that reason deny that the basis of all historical knowledge is the passing down of source-based facts. The only difference is that the one, by virtue of his own studies and personal viewpoint, finds his strength principally in the philological method, the other more in the objective one. The one is subject to the danger of restating a false set of facts, since he is not capable of perceiving their objective impossibility; the other runs the danger of attributing to the past certain events taken from the reality of the present, without paying sufficient attention to the difference in circumstances. In order, therefore, to assure the accuracy of the research, the philological and the objective approaches must go hand in hand in every step and every observation, must constantly enlighten and control one another. There is no true objective analysis without a philologically accurate base of source material, and there is no true philological study without objective analysis. Only in this way can one arrive at the full rigor of the method whose essence is the exclusion of all whim, both in the acceptance and in the discarding of the inherited accounts. Polybius has already expressed this idea pointedly in the citation that I have placed as my epigraph.

If this book signifies a step forward in our knowledge of the past, which is such a profound need of the human mind, this result does not, therefore, rest on the application of a new method, but rather on the practical and systematic application of long known and theoretically recognized principles. It is therefore of the essence of this book—and I ask the reader's indulgence in allowing me to speak about it—how I myself was led to realize that in this field scholarship was once again faced with a task, and how unusually favorable circumstances combined to make possible for me precisely the study of the art of war.

Quite soon after leaving the university I did some study of the history of the art of war, without really remembering how I first became interested in this. In the spring of 1874 I had a maneuver to do in Wittenberg; I obtained from the regimental library Rüstow's *History of the Infantry* (*Geschichte der Infanterie*), and from that time on I never again lost sight of this subject.

In 1877, through the good offices of Countess Hedwig Brühl, I was charged with completing the biography of Gneisenau, the Countess's grandfather, which had been left unfinished by George Heinrich Pertz. As I plunged into the history of the wars of liberation, I experienced in the strongest possible degree the need to be able to arrive at a realistic appraisal of the events, and my studies toward this end had to be expanded all the more broadly in that, at that time, two different basic strategic viewpoints—one represented by Archduke Karl, Schwarzenberg, and Wellington, and the other by Napoleon and Gneisenau—were in conflict with each other and had to be tested historically.

Goethe spoke once of the great step forward that one can sometimes experience through a single significant word, and another time he said that one learns best not from books, but through a living exchange of ideas, through contact with wise people. The truth of these pronouncements I learned for myself at that time.

In those years I was the tutor of the youngest son of Kaiser Frederick, Prince Waldemar, who died in 1879 at the age of eleven. In this position I had not only the opportunity to gain a certain direct understanding of how the decisions of an army commander originate psychologically, through the stories of the then Crown Prince himself and of Field Marshal Count Blumenthal, but I could also, through a question at any moment, clarify and fill out my studies, starting with Clausewitz, whose works the Crown Prince presented to me. I can still remember today points where my understanding had come to a stop, so to speak, and where a lucky expression, an appropriate word, carried me over the obstacle, and I cannot help thinking in gratitude, now, after almost twenty-five years, of the names of those gentlemen to whom I am indebted for this instruction. Included are the names of General von Gottberg, who died as commanding general of the I Army Corps; General von Winterfeld, recently commanding general of the Guard Corps; General von Mischke; Colonel von Dresky; the late General von Unruh, whose last assignment was as commander of the Alexander Regiment; but, above all, the then Lieutenant Colonel (and military tutor of Prince Frederick Leopold) von Geissler, who died as a lieutenant general. Herr von Geissler was pedagogically inclined and, while our two young gentlemen were playing under our supervision on the exercise area of the New Palace or on the Böttcherberg near Glienicke, he took pleasure in replying to my eager questioning with entire lectures on military subjects, which, being of excellent, understandable clarity, furthered my knowledge greatly. In the same connection I should like also to mention two other high-ranking officers: General von Fransecky, who in 1870 was commanding general of the II Army Corps, later of the XI, and finally governor of Berlin; and the then Major of the General Staff, Boie, who died as the governor of Thorn. General von Fransecky had once, as a young General Staff officer, begun a biography of Gneisenau; through that I came into contact with him and often visited him and discussed that subject with him. Major Boie turned over to me the notebook for the campaign of 1814 which he himself had worked up from the original documents for a lecture at the War College, and we used to discuss in detail individual problems of this campaign.

When, in January 1881, after I had completed the Gneisenau biography, I joined the faculty of the University of Berlin, my first lecture was about the war of 1866. Then I gave (in the summer of 1881) "History of Military Concepts and of the Art of War since the Introduction of the Feudal System" ("Geschichte der Kriegsverfassungen und der Kriegskunst seit der Einführung des Lehnswesens"). I did not yet venture to introduce antiquity into this lecture. I had not yet worked it out myself from the original sources, and I felt, even though I had already started to harbor the idea that the prevailing belief about the development of Roman tactics (*Quincunx-Stellung*) could not possibly be right, that I was still not in a position to offer some other concept as a substitute. Not until two years later, in the summer of 1883, did I dare to announce the lecture "General History of Military Concepts and of the Art of War from the Persian Wars up to the Present." I then gave this lecture many times; and I also spoke on the "War of 1870," "Selected Chapters from Strategy and Tactics, for Historians," "The Principal Battles of Frederick and Napoleon," and finally (in the winter of 1897-1898) "Concerning the Economic Prosperity of Nations in its Interplay with their Military Posture and their Military Deeds." I published works based on original sources on the Persian Wars, the strategy of Pericles, on Thucydides and Cleon, the Roman manipular tactics, the pre-Germanic nation and district, the First Crusade, the Swiss and Burgundian battles, the bases of the strategy of Frederick and Napoleon; and at my urging, younger scholars did other works dealing with the most varied periods of military history, from Hannibal to Napoleon.

In and through these lectures and special studies there has gradually been created the book of which I am now bringing out the first volume, and in doing so I ask the reader to bear in mind that this is only the first volume and that, from the personal viewpoint of the author, his point of departure rests, not in this period, but in the most recent period of world history.

An essential prerequisite that made my work possible was the painstaking working out and ordering of the source material in its philological, antiquarian, and political science aspects, as provided by the present state of our knowledge. At this point I would have to name countless precursors if I wished to list all those to whom thanks are due concerning this work, and to say that Mommsen stands at their head is so obvious that respect perhaps forbids more strongly than it demands that this point receive special mention. For this reason I shall content myself with the general statement of this indebtedness. *One* book I should like to mention expressly, since it forms, so to speak, a spiritual parallel to my own. It is *The Population of the Greco-Roman World* (*Die Bevölkerung der griechisch-römischen Welt*), by Julius Beloch (1886), which, just as I have done with the art of war, traces the population statistics through all antiquity, based not just on the philological method, but principally on the objective method as it has been practiced and refined in recent times. The more I consulted this book, the greater I learned to prize it. If it turns out that I myself seek at times to establish not only individual extensions but even a few not insignificant variations from Beloch's figures, I should like to make it clear from the start that Beloch himself indicated that such variations and corrections were very likely possible. The small differences in carefully verified points of individual detail only prove concurrence and confirmation for the whole and the essential aspects.

Without Beloch's preceding work, many parts of the present book could hardly have been written; in fact, the strengths of the armies will play such an important role that one could perhaps conclude that my research was based squarely on them. That was not the case, however, but I must confess that, to my astonishment, in the course of each individual bit of research I arrived again and again at this same point. Perhaps the most important conclusion of the whole book for the following volumes, as for history, is the establishment of the numerical relationships in Caesar's Gallic War and the logical deductions therefrom, and on that point, as I must acknowledge, I myself did not arrive at a clear understanding until my last reworking of the material. Here, it is true, an historical work means no more than anywhere else the following-through to it's logical conclusions of an idea that has occurred to one in a fortunate moment of intuition, but it rests, rather, on empirical research that progresses from point to point, and only slowly do the thoughts struggle free from the matrix of the deeply rooted account passed down to one.

The purpose of my book, like its guidelines, is indicated accurately enough, I believe, by its title. I do not claim to have written a complete and all-inclusive "History of the Art of War"; to such a work would belong also the study of ancient relics; the details of drill, with its commands; the technique of weapons; the training and handling of horses; fortifications; siegecraft; and finally also the whole matter of seafaring—things about which I would have nothing new to recount or which I do not even have knowledge of. In this light, there still remains the task of writing a "History of the Art of War," somewhat in the sense of a practical manual. One has to believe that there is such a value inherent in the history of warfare, for the great captains have often said so. Napoleon, especially, laid down again and again the requirement that he who wished to become a strategist should study the great deeds of the past, and Clausewitz set up as an ideal the teaching of war purely by way of historical examples. This book, however, does not pretend to such high aims. Whatever practical contribution history might make lies in the field of the military man; the orientation of my own mind is not in that direction. I am only a historian and wanted to write a book for friends of history and a manual for historians in the spirit of Leopold Ranke.

4 June 1900

HANS DELBRÜCK

Preface
to the Second Edition
of the First Two Volumes

The first two volumes of *History of the Art of War* have already been out of print for a number of years now without my having found the time to prepare the new edition, occupied as I was with my work on the third volume. A number of fine new detailed studies had appeared in the meantime and had to be tested and worked into the old text, and in addition small points had to be corrected here and there, and an important part, the oldest Roman organization for war, had to be completely remolded. But in the final analysis, these corrections required the least work and would not have held up the new edition so long; the real effort and time-consuming aspect of the new edition were necessitated by something else. In a review of the first volume, General of Infantry von Schlichting, author of *Tactical and Strategic Principles of the Present Day*, (*Taktische und strategische Grundsätze der Gegenwart*), expressed the hope that the present work would "bring an end to the military dilettantism that has heretofore reigned in the writing of history." These words express in the precisest possible way the goal on which I have based my work and toward which my hopes were directed. But this hope has not only not been fulfilled, but the exact opposite has taken place. I venture to say that hardly ever in any previous period has so much of a distorted and confusing nature been published in the field of military organization and the military art through unmethodical and dilettantish scholarship as precisely in this last decade. There are not only historians and archaeologists involved in this but also military men, who are inclined to believe much too quickly and with far too much self-assurance that, with the concepts they have gained in practice, often only in peacetime service, they can critically master the conditions of earlier military periods. And so not only have there been developed and published false interpretations of the sources, concerning which there can and always will be different opinions, but also constructions that are objectively and physically impossible, and they have greatly obscured the clear historical events. The greater part of my work on this second edition of these first two volumes has therefore consisted of dispelling and rebutting these impossibilities through both critical examination of the sources and objective analysis. That is by no means an easy and simple task, as we shall also see further on, for in history the long period that separates us from the events themselves allows even the most foolish ideas to take on a certain varnish of verisimilitude; it requires broad-ranging and thorough presentations to destroy such false concepts and, since we cannot resort to experiments, to clarify verbally what is physically possible and what is impossible. Sometimes this kind of discussion leads to the advantage of shedding more light on the subject itself, and then one feels rewarded for his pains. Generally, however, one does not reap such a harvest but finishes with the irritated feeling of having wasted time and effort that could better have been applied to something else.

How much I would have preferred to have gone ahead with the preparation of the fourth volume!

As for the first volume, the reception that it found among critical scholars evoked in many quarters, even where it was otherwise welcomed in friendly fashion, concern as to whether I had not exceeded the right of objective critical analysis and moved farther away from the written sources than could be justified. At no place has my reworking of the material shown me that there is a sound basis for this concern. On the contrary, I may say that the objectively analytical changes that I have now made have stemmed from recognition of the fact that in the first edition I had not yet moved sufficiently away from the viewpoints passed down to us. It really is true that not the Persians but the Greeks were numerically superior; that Alexander did not march out with a small band to conquer the Persian world empire but with an army perhaps twice as large as that of Xerxes had been; that in Rome levies were never made according to classes of wealth; that the barbarian armies that threatened the civilized world were always quite small; that the Romans won their victories over the Gauls and the Germanic tribes chiefly by numerical superiority; that the knightly manner of warfare already existed before the feudal system and did not grow out of the latter.

The belief in the opposite tradition on all these points is almost as firm as it is ancient, and not only reasons but also time will be required to overcome it and to establish a better recognition in its place. The best reinforcements in this war, however, will be the continuation of the present work itself.

The historian of antiquity who reads only the first volume, the legal historian who only compares the origin of the feudal system with the attitudes that he has received from the sources, the historian of the Crusades who only reads how small the number of knights was and how little of an original nature this great military period is supposed to have fostered—I can appreciate the caution and the doubt that they all feel. But I am confident that their doubts will be dissolved and will disappear when the historian of antiquity also becomes familiar with the second and third volumes of this work, when the legal historian realizes the contrast between the individual warrior and the tactical body from the interrelated features of the entire work, and when the historian of the Crusades has become fully aware of the difference between knighthood and cavalry and the opposition of the concepts knighthood and tactics, from a comparison with the preceding and following periods.

Just as this work has grown upon me from my overall observation of the development of the art of war, in the same way only those can derive from it the completely scholarly gain who use it not simply as specialized historians of antiquity, the Middle Ages, or modern times, but who accept it all together as a study in world history.

Berlin-Grunewald, 12 July 1908

HANS DELBRÜCK

Preface
to the Third Edition

Since the appearance of the second edition of this volume in 1908, two great problems of the military history of antiquity have been solved, the battles of Salamis and Thapsus, and I have been able to take them into account in my reworking of this edition. For Plataea and Issus, I have been able to retain the fundamental principles developed in my earlier presentation, but on the basis of new topographic determinations these accounts have been reworked somewhat as to details. The old point of dissension concerning Cannae, as to whether the battle took place on the left or the right bank of the Aufidus, has been definitely settled, but at the same time the underlying bases for the Second Punic War, derived from the source materials, have been strongly shaken by a new and solidly based hypothesis. These are the areas in which, in addition to numerous detailed corrections, this new edition differs from the previous one.

At the same time I have also finally brought the fourth volume to completion and have thus concluded the entire work.

21 July 1920

HANS DELBRÜCK

23

HISTORY OF THE ART OF WAR

Point of Departure

The history of the art of war is a single strand in the braid of universal history and begins with the latter. It is best, however, not to begin one's investigation at the point where the first more or less recognizable events begin to emerge from the twilight of the prehistoric era, but rather at the point where the source material begins to provide a full and valid glimpse into the events. That is the period of the Persian Wars, and not sooner; from that time on, however, right up to our own day, we are able to trace the development with unbroken testimony, and each successive period helps to explain the preceding one. Even for the time before the Persian Wars there is no lack of significant testimony; for the Greeks, Homer is particularly rich, and for the Oriental peoples, such as the Egyptians, we have centuries, even thousands of years of historical sources reaching farther back, but this evidence is still not sufficient to allow directly the formation of a completely certain picture. An historical objective analysis based on much experience in interpreting the events of warfare will facilitate the grouping together into a unified picture of the separate indications. This objective judgment in its highest degree, however, is only to be attained through the study of military history itself, that is, of the later periods. For our first steps we must try to walk on the firmer ground that the accounts of contemporaries offer us. On and with them, the objective analysis can develop to the point of reaching clear perspectives. These perspectives, won in this way, may perhaps later be valid to cast light on the earlier period and to brighten the half-darkness in which it is enveloped.

Even the events of the Persian Wars have been passed down to us with such uncertainty, intertwined with legends, not by a real contemporary writer, but written down only as they came from the mouths of the following generation, so that a Niebuhr despaired of recognizing their special sequence, and whenever, despite his warning, historians time and again present to us all the details of Herodotus' account as history, a great deal of self-deception is involved. No matter how skeptical a position one might wish to assume, however, with respect to the colorful accounts of the father of written history, they do contain a nucleus of accuracy that is suf-

27

ficient for the purposes of a history of the art of war. We recognize
the combat methods of the two armies, we can establish the terrain
on which the fighting took place, and we can understand the
strategic situation. With these things the basic features of the military action are established, and these features, in turn, provide a
very reliable critical measure for the details of the legendary accounts. No older military happenings are laid out before us so
clearly. The Persian Wars, therefore, form the natural point of departure for a history of the art of war.

Excursus

The basis for the scholarly knowledge of the Greek military art is formed, even
today, by two important works:
   *History of Greek Warfare from the Oldest Times to Pyrrhus (Geschichte des griechischen
Kriegswesens von der ältesten Zeit bis auf Pyrrhos)*. Developed from the original sources
by W. Rüstow, former Prussian engineer officer, and Dr. H. Köchly, professor in
ordinary of Greek and Roman literature and language at the University of Zürich.
With 134 woodcuts printed in the body of the text and 6 lithographed tables. Aarau:
Verlags-Comptoir, 1852.
   Greek Military Authors (Griechische Kriegsschriftsteller). In Greek and German with
critical and explanatory notations by H. Köchly and W. Rüstow. Two parts, in three
volumes. Leipzig, 1853-1855.
   Newer works include the following:
   *Army Organization and Conduct of War by the Greeks (Heerwesen und Kriegführung der
Griechen)*, by Dr. H. Droysen, gymnasium professor and dean at the Royal University
of Berlin. With one table and seven illustrations in the text (in K. F. Hermann's
Manual of Greek Antiquities (Lehrbuch der griechischen Antiquitäten). Freiburg im Breis-
gau, 1888-1889. Akademische Verlagsbuchhandlung von J. C. B. Mohr (Paul
Siebeck). (Discussed by me in the *Literarisches Centralblatt* 1888, No. 16.)
   Ancient Greek Military Periods (Die griechischen Kriegsaltertümer), by Dr. Adolf Bauer,
professor of ancient history at Graz University (in *Handbook of Classical Knowledge of
Antiquity [Handbuch der klassischen Altertumswissenschaft]*). Nördlingen (now in
Munich): C. H. Beck, 1886; 2d ed. 1892. An excellent work, which contains a very
clear presentation of the source evidence. I should also like to point out here, once
and for all, that Bauer's bibliography shows a very careful and thorough treatment.
   The Military Organization of the Ancients (Das Kriegswesen der Alten), with particular
consideration of strategy, by Dr. of Philosophy Hugo Liers, professor in the Gymnasium of Waldenburg, Breslau, 1895, is a stimulating and scholarly book based on
comprehensive and independent readings of the old authors, which made me take
full notice of many a significant passage. As a whole, however, the work is unfortunately faulty; the individual accounts are grouped systematically, but they are far
from having been tested enough as to the degree of their credibility, and particularly there is a lack of sufficient distinction between the individual periods of the
development.
   In the *Historische Zeitschrift*, Vol. 98, 1907, Ben. Niese published an article entitled
"On the Organization for War, the Military Service Obligation, and the Military System of Greece" ("Ueber Wehrverfassung, Dienstpflicht und Heerwesen Griechen-
lands") that does not contain anything new on the subject.
   I myself treated the military-historical problem of the Persian Wars in a monograph: *The Persian Wars and the Burgundian Wars (Die Perserkriege und die*

Burgunderkriege). Two combined military-historical studies with a supplement on the Roman manipular tactics. Berlin: Walther and Apolant (now Hermann Walther, Successor), 1887.

Of the general works on Greek history, the most meaningful ones for our consideration are those of Busolt (2nd ed.), Beloch, and Duncker, and here and there also the works of Grote.

Throughout all the volumes of the present work, right up to modern times, we shall be accompanied by the following book, despite the shortcomings and superficiality in its execution, which is ingeniously organized: *History of the Infantry* (*Geschichte der Infanterie*), by W. Rüstow. Two volumes. Gotah, 1857 and 1858 (and later reprints).

We shall also adhere to the following work, particularly valuable in the later volumes: *History of Military Science, Principally in Germany* (*Geschichte der Kriegswissenschaften vornehmlich in Deutschland*), by Max Jähns. (From the *History of Learning in Germany* [*Geschichte der Wissenschaften in Deutschland*]). By special authority of His Majesty the King of Bavaria, published by the Historical Commission of the Royal Academy of Sciences.) Munich and Leipzig, 1889-1891.

BOOK I

The Persian Wars

Chapter I

Army Strengths:
Introductory Material

Wherever the sources permit, a military-historical study does best to start with the army strengths. They are of decisive importance, not simply because of the relative strengths, whereby the greater mass wins or is counterbalanced by bravery or leadership on the part of the weaker force, but also on an absolute basis. A movement that is made by an organization of 1,000 men without complications becomes an accomplishment for 10,000 men, a work of art for 50,000, and an impossibility for 100,000. In the case of a larger army, the task of providing rations becomes a more and more important part of strategy. Without a definite concept of the size of the armies, therefore, a critical treatment of the historical accounts, as of the events themselves, is impossible.

Since there still persist numerous false ideas on this very point, and reported numbers, without realization of the extent of the conclusions that would have to be drawn from them, are simply repeated, it appears helpful, in order to sharpen one's critical perception, so to speak, to indicate at once in a few examples how easily and to what a great extent false strengths become established in the historical accounts.

In the older German works on the wars of liberation, in Plotho, who was senior aide-de-camp of Frederick William III and during the war personally gathered his information at the supreme headquarters; in the biography of Radetzky by an Austrian veteran; and again in the older editions of the much read and deserving work of Beitzke, *German Wars of Liberation* (*Deutsche Freiheitskriege*), the French Army, at the beginning of the fall campaign of 1813, is given as 300,000 to a maximum of 353,000. The allies had at their disposal at that time more than 492,000 men and would therefore have had a crushing superiority. In fact, aside from the garrisons

33

of the fortifications in the theater of war, Napoleon had 440,000 men and was therefore numerically almost equal to the allies.[1]

E. M. Arndt estimated in 1814 the total casualties of all the Napoleonic Wars together at 10,080,000 men; a closer check brings the number considerably below 2 million, of which a fourth would be on the French side,[2] and exact statistics would still lead to a considerably smaller figure.

Even in newer scholarly presentations of the wars of liberation one finds that, in the meeting engagement at Hagelsberg, the home guards of the Mark bashed in the skulls of 4,000 Frenchmen with their rifle butts. In reality, it was about 30.

In the 1897 work of the Austrian General Staff Captain Berndt, *Numbers in War (Die Zahl im Kriege)*, the strength of the French at the Battle of Orléans (3 and 4 December 1870) is given as 60,700, whereas other researchers have estimated it at 174,500 and even higher.

According to the same book, 75,000 Austrians fought at Aspern against 90,000 French, and the latter are said to have lost 44,380. In reality, on the first day some 105,000 Austrians fought against 35,000 French, and on the second day the same Austrians (with allowance made for casualties) fought against some 70,000 French and the latter supposedly lost some 16,000 to a maximum of 20,000 men.

The army of Charles the Bold at Granson was estimated by Swiss contemporaries at 100,000 to 120,000 men; later, at Murten, he is supposed to have had a strength triple this number. Actually, in the first battle he had some 14,000 men, and in the second a few thousand more. The Swiss, who claim to have fought against an immeasurable superiority, had a considerable numerical superiority in both battles.

Even at Granson they claim to have killed as many as 7,000 of the Burgundians, whereas in reality it was 7 knights and just a few private soldiers.[3]

The Hussite armies, which cast terror over all of Germany and were portrayed as endless masses, were some 5,000 men strong.

It is probably not just the general tendency to hyperbolic concepts, a lack of feel for numbers, boastfulness, fear, apology, or other similar human weaknesses that lie at the base of the gigantic exaggerations, but it must probably also be considered that it is very hard, even for a practiced eye, to estimate accurately rather large masses, even on one's own side, where one has a free opportunity to observe them; in the case of the enemy, it is as good as impossible. An excellent example of this is provided by a recently published account of Frederick William III concerning the defeat suffered under his own command at Auerstadt.[4] The King says that during the battle one could no longer deceive himself as to the fact that he was facing a very superior force. The French, he reported, as was possible with their greater strength in infantry, had quite often replaced their fighting battalions with fresh troops. Since the Prussians had a strength of 50,000 men, the French would therefore have to be estimated at 70,000 to 80,000. Actually, they were only 27,000 strong,[5] and that Frederick William really had been mistaken and was not perhaps merely trying to excuse the defeat is apparent from a later annex, which the King soon thereafter added and in which he says that, from the French documents and other information, he has become convinced "that—be it said to our shame—the enemy opposing us was no stronger than 30,000 men."

Let it be noted that it is not always a question simply of overestimates and exaggerations; the opposite occurs, too, and with full intent I also introduced a few examples of that kind above.

The army that Xerxes led into Greece is given by Herodotus as numbering exactly 4,200,000 men, including the trains. An army corps of 30,000 men covers, in the German march order, some 14 miles, without its supply train. The march column of the Persians would therefore have been 2,000 miles long, and when the head of the column was arriving before Thermopylae, the end of the column might have been just marching out of Susa, on the far side of the Tigris. A German army corps is accompanied by artillery and ammunition caissons, which take up much room, and in this regard an ancient army would require less space. On the other hand, a Persian army certainly had only a very loose march discipline, that quality which can only be attained through a very exact articulation of the army organization, with constant attention and effort. Without march discipline columns very quickly stretch out to double or triple the normal length. Persian troops may therefore, even without artillery, be compared approximately with modern troops in their marching space needs.

After the departure of Xerxes with his large army, Mardonius is supposed to have remained behind with 300,000 men, but even this figure has no claim to credibility. According to Herodotus' account, Mardonius, when he had destroyed Athens for a second time, marched back from there via Decelea to Tanagra, and on the following day, farther. No army of 300,000 men can march in this way. Even if a part of the Persian army had remained behind in Boeotia and not only the pass of Decelea but all the passes over the mountains were used at the same time, the army cannot have numbered more than some 75,000 warriors, including the allied Greeks.

But this whole method of gradually reducing the figures has only a preparatory value; it does not really lead us to our goal.

We must convince ourselves and very definitely hold fast to the idea that we are deceiving ourselves if we place reliance on numbers like those of Herodotus. Even if one might, in any way whatever, prove a specific number that is no longer impossible, one that even, in fact, appears quite possible—even in doing this nothing is really won. The true and only reliable historical method is not the method by which one, when he has no reliable information, contents himself with the unreliable and acts as if it were acceptably trustworthy, but rather, that method by which one distinguishes sharply and definitely between what can be regarded as accurately passed down, and what is not. Perhaps we can still find some basic point or other that will allow us to express an approximate estimate of the strength of the Persian army. First of all, however, it must be established that the Persian strengths claimed by the Greeks merit no credence whatever, not even the slightest—that they are in no way more trustworthy than the claims of the Swiss concerning the armies of Charles the Bold, so that we cannot determine from them, therefore, whether the numerical superiority lay on the side of the Greeks or the Persians.

If we now turn toward the Greeks, we seem to be treading on firmer ground. For the Battle of Plataea, Herodotus gives a specific listing of the various contingents: 8,000 Athenians, 5,000 Spartiates, 5,000 Perioeci, etc., for a total of 38,700 hoplites. Since the Greeks would no doubt have known their own strength, these numbers could perhaps be trusted, and most researchers have simply accepted them. But that is a methodological error. We do not have the slightest guarantee that some informant or the other of Herodotus did not draw up the list by a completely arbitrary estimate, and there is at least one place in the list that shows up the feel of the original writer for numbers in quite an unfavorable light. Every Greek hoplite was normally accompanied by a serving man; therefore, in order to account for the full strength of the army, Herodotus doubles the number. Every Spartiate, however, according to him, had seven Helots with him; one must therefore count an additional 35,000 men for this group. A ratio of 35,000 noncombatants to 5,000 combatants, considering both movement of

the army and its supply, is an absurdity. It probably had its origin
in the fact that the Greek thought of the Spartiate as an eminent
man, who always went into the field with several servants. Seven
servants seemed to be a very acceptable number and was therefore
multiplied, without further reflection, by the supposed number of
Spartiates. The same kind of thing is sometimes done by modern
historians. In Philippson's *History of the Prussian State* (*Geschichte des
Preussischen Staatswesens*), 2:176, one reads that the Prussian army
under Frederick the Great, in 1776, took precisely 32,705 washwomen along into the field. The author does not even hesitate to
give his source, Busching's *Reliable Contributions to the Governmental
History of King Frederick the Second of Prussia*, (*Zuverlässige Beyträge z.
d. Reg.-Gesch. König Friedrichs II. v. Preussen*), a source that does
indeed, for the most part, contain reliable material, and since in reality a number of canteen women and soldiers' wives did accom-
pany Frederick's army, it is still more readily possible for an army
of 200,000 men to have 32,705 washwomen than for 5,000 Spartiates to have 35,000 Helots; and a modern, methodically trained
historian deserves more credence than does the naïve Herodotus.
But in the final analysis we shall discard both bits of information. A
brief analysis of the character of Frederick the Great and of his
army is enough to convince us that the army was certainly not accompanied into the field by washwomen, and that consequently
Büsching fell victim to some misunderstanding or other and arrived at his number by counting one washwoman for every tent of
soldiers, and that Philippson simply copied this interesting assertion
without critical analysis. The question of the 35,000 Helots of
Herodotus probably came about in the same way. In total,
Herodotus' estimate of the Greek army leads to a strength of some
110,000 souls. The historians who copied this number did not reflect sufficiently on the question of what it means to feed 110,000
men in one spot for a rather long time. We shall have much more
to say about this in the later periods, where we have at our disposal
more certain strengths from the original sources.[6] The number
passed down to us is obviously untrustworthy. We must content
ourselves with the fact that we do not possess a figure for the
strength of the Greeks at Plataea on which we can base any
conclusions.[7]

The figures of the later Greek sources, too—to the effect that the
Athenians were 10,000 men strong at Marathon—are completely
unverified. They can be characterized straight off as an arbitrary
estimate by the fact that the strength of the allied Plataeans, either

included in that total or in addition to it, is given as 1,000 men. Plataea was a very small spot and could not possibly have furnished a tenth or a ninth of the number of Athenians. If historians, for the most part, have accepted the number of 10,000 up to now, that is because, from a practical viewpoint, it seemed quite reasonable; it has no validity, however, through any kind of evidence.

Despite the lack of reliable direct-source evidence, we can arrive at an idea of the strength of the Greek armies in the Persian Wars. We have at our disposal, in addition to the events themselves, which we must first become acquainted with, conclusions from later Greek history and from the population that was at hand; the population can be determined, in turn, to a certain degree from the size and the fertility of the country.

The result for the richest city state, Athens, is that the tiny country, the peninsula of Attica, in the year 490 B.C. probably counted some 100,000 free souls, and thus, since the slave population at that time was undoubtedly still moderate, at the most 120,000 to 140,000 persons, or 115 to 140 per square mile (about 50 to the square kilometer). That is approximately the same as today.

How many of these Athenians actually bore arms in the battles of the Persian Wars we still do not know, and we must see if the sequence of events themselves offers us a lead for an estimate.

EXCURSUS

ON THE POPULATION OF ATTICA AND OF THE OTHER GREEK STATES.

Greece has a number of areas from which we can be very sure she drew no supply whatever of foodstuffs or only a very small amount—Boeotia, Arcadia, Lacedaemon, Messenia. We have no definite measure for the degree of fertility of the agriculture in these areas at the time of the Persian Wars. But we shall be able to estimate a certain maximum of self-support capability of these areas nevertheless, by analogy with known relationships, and when that is done, we can further conclude that this maximum was more or less attained. Thebes cannot have been such a very small city, and in addition to Thebes, Boeotia counted also quite a number of other cities. On the other hand, Lacedaemon cannot have been, relatively, so very much less densely populated than the other Greek regions; otherwise it would not have been able to play such an important role for such a long time.

On these basic principles, with help from the figures passed down historically, Beloch estimated, in his *The Population of the Greco-Roman World* (*Die Bevölkerung der griechisch-römischen Welt*),[8] for Laconia and Messenia together a population of 230,000 souls, or 27 to the square kilometer; for the Peloponnesus, 800,000 to 900,000 souls, or 36 to 40 per square kilometer, because the commercial cities of Corinth, Sicyon, Troezen, Epidaurus had a comparatively larger population. It cannot have been so very great, however, since the importation of grain to these cities by sea was almost completely blocked during the Peloponnesian War. They therefore had to live from the sparse supply of grain that could be brought to them by land.

For Boeotia, Beloch estimates in the first half of the fourth century B.C. 60 persons to a square kilometer, of whom about a third were slaves. This number of slaves for a region with nothing but country towns seems very high to me; from what source would the Boeotians have drawn so many slaves, and with what would they have paid for them? A slave population perpetuates itself only to a small degree and requires constant reinforcement to maintain itself. For the fifth century B.C. Beloch also accepts the fact that Boeotia was a country of free labor, and therefore with some 40 souls to the square kilometer. This number stands in a correct relationship with the Peloponnesus, since Boeotia was, it is true, much more fertile; in the Peloponnesian trading cities, however—Corinth, Sicyon, etc.—there were many slaves, a fact that tended to balance off the situation.[9]

In his estimates Beloch assumes that the adult men formed approximately a third of the population; he felt that the Greek population was already stabilized as early as the fifth century B.C.,[10] somewhat similar to present-day France. I cannot agree with this opinion.

Athens, Megara, Corinth, and many other cities actually grew greatly in the fifth century B.C. through the immigration of metics, and if Laconia, Messenia, Arcadia did not also grow, that was because of internal migrations. I also prefer to estimate the number of children somewhat higher than Beloch and therefore count the adult males as less than a third of the population. In Germany today (1898) the males over eighteen years old account for 28 to 29 percent of the population. But the difference is not so great that Beloch's end results would be significantly affected by it.

The German Empire today (1898) has some 97 souls per square kilometer but is not able to feed them all, being obliged to rely on imported grains for more than a quarter of its consumption and on the average to import almost exactly a quarter of all agricultural and forest products. It therefore feeds, with the help of potatoes and all modern means of agriculture, some 74 persons to the square kilometer or about 190 to the square mile.[11]

It is impossible to draw any conclusions as to the population of Attica from the land and area relationships, since Athens had already been importing much grain from abroad long before the Persian Wars. Nevertheless, we have a whole series of reliable figures from the second half of the century, which also permit a conclusion as to the population at the time of the Persian Wars. Since I differ here from Beloch quite significantly, we must go into a special analysis.

At the beginning of the Peloponnesian War, in 431 B.C., Thucydides has Pericles saying in a speech (2. 13) that Athens has 13,000 hoplites and also 16,000 garrison troops from the oldest, the youngest, and the metics who were performing hoplite service; also 1,200 mounted men, 1,600 archers, and 300 triremes. ("There were 13,000 hoplites, not counting the men who were stationed in the forts or who manned the city walls. For this many men were engaged in defense at the first when the enemy invaded, and they were made up of the oldest and youngest men as well as such metics as were themselves heavily armed.")*

This report, definite as it may seem, unfortunately cannot be accepted at face value. The oldest and youngest, with the metic-hoplites, cannot have amounted to 16,000 men when the field army was only 15,800 men strong. With the Athenians the field service obligation lasted from the twentieth to the forty-fifth or even the fiftieth year; the number of service-qualified men under twenty and over forty-five or fifty must therefore have been much smaller than the number eligible for field service. Furthermore, there is lacking any estimate of the crews of the 300 triremes; with full crews the latter would have required no fewer than 60,000 men. Did there exist in Athens, outside the field army, any such numbers of men as these? Why then was the field army so small? Was it composed only of the upper classes of citizens? Where was the dividing line? Why did they not reach down lower?

People have sought to shed light on these uncertainties through the most diverse hypotheses. Beloch had no solution for it but to change the 16,000 garrison hoplites to 6,000 and to add, on the other hand, 12,000 citizens as ships' crews—a desperate resort and only too characteristic of the condition of the accounts passed on to us: that we are obliged to distort in this way, in order to make it understandable, the only passage in all of Greek literature that to a certain extent claims to report completely and systematically on Greek levies. This procedure is further complicated by the fact that Ephorus already read this passage approximately as it stands in the manuscripts today; Diodorus, who copied from him, sets the field army at 12,000, the garrison troops at 17,000—a confirmation, but at the same time a variation (12,000 instead of 13,000; 17,000 instead of 16,000), which again underlines the uncertainty of our sources.

Recently, in *Klio* 5 (1905): 341, Beloch expressed the supposition that the number 16,000 was not to be changed to 6,000, but rather was to be completely disregarded as the addition of an editor.

Under these conditions of uncertainty of its own content, the Thucydides citation will be useful for us only on the condition that we find some other estimate that provides us a key for the interpretation and at the same time a reliable control.

As a matter of fact, I find in Thucydides a piece of information that has never before been appreciated, not even by Beloch, and which, I believe, can help us.

Twice Thucydides describes for us an unusual levy of the Athenians, each of which, in its way, appears to be the largest and is indicated as their maximum effort. In the fall of the first year of the war, 431 B.C., they made an incursion into Megaris with 13,000 hoplites, while 3,000 were in position before Potidaea. At the same time they had a fleet of 100 ships at sea (and also possibly a few ships at Potidaea). A hundred ships mean crews of 20,000 men; that gives a total of 36,000 men, with the hoplites. Since, however, Thucydides adds that a not insignificant group of "light troops"* was also on hand, nothing definite can be concluded from this point as to the total strength of the Athenians.

It is different in the second citation (3. 17), where Thucydides describes the armament of the Athenians after the revolt in Lesbos in 428 B.C. They have at that time 70 ships at sea (40 at Lesbos, 30 at the Peloponnesus) and 1,000 hoplites before Mytilene. This makes the Spartans believe that they have no further capabilities, and so they plan an attack on Athens by land and sea. In order to show them how mistaken they are, the Athenians then man 100 more ships from the two lower tax classes of their citizenry.

Thucydides compares this accomplishment with that of the first year of the war; he says it is similar and on an even larger scale. For in this year (431 B.C.), 100 ships had guarded Attica and Euboea, 100 had blockaded the Peloponnesus, and some 50 more were at Potidaea and other places, so that there was a total of 250. The 100 ships that guarded the homeland were naturally not continuously at sea, for which there was no immediate necessity, but they were fully outfitted reserve ships whose crews were assigned and ready, so that they could put to sea at any moment, and from among them, from time to time, the individual ships undoubtedly made test and practice cruises to check their readiness. For this reason, the accomplishment of the year 428 B.C., when 170 ships actually were in action at the same time, was in a certain respect greater than that of 431 B.C., when a total of 250 could be counted, of which, however, only 150 were really fully active at the same time. According to Pericles' account, the Athenians had 300 triremes. We shall have to understand this as meaning, however, that at the outbreak of the war, the Athenians were capable of actually manning 250 ships, whereas 50 were left over as reserve replacements. They manned the 170 ships in 428 B.C., as Thucydides expressly adds, by calling up also the citizens of the third tax class, who otherwise normally did hoplite duty.

And now we have a basis for an estimate of the Athenian citizenry in the year 428 B.C. One hundred seventy ships required crews of 34,000 men; and in addition there were 1,000 hoplites, together with their serving men. In addition to these 36,000 men there remained in Athens a garrison for the defense of the city and of a few forts, which we may estimate at some 4,000 to 6,000 men. From this number we must make a reduction in that the manning of the 100 suddenly outfitted ships was probably not complete, and at the least the *epibatae* either were included in the rowers or were missing entirely, so that the crews amounted to some 18,000 men instead of 20,000. Then, too, in the fleet before Lesbos and the fighting fleet there was certainly a large number of mercenaries,[12] and finally there is doubt as to how many slaves were possibly included among the oarsmen. Despite these numerous uncertain factors in our estimate, it still gives us a certain maximum and minimum limit. It is certain that a considerable number of mercenaries and probably also of slaves were in the fleet; it is also certain, however, that the predominant character of the whole was that of an Athenian citizen levy.[13] If everything had been at full strength, we would reach a figure of 42,000 men. It is probable, however, that there were only 38,000, and of these we can consider that at least 10,000 were mercenaries and slaves. This number could even have been as high as 18,000. The total of militarily qualified Athenian citizens and metics in the year 427 B.C. must therefore be found somewhere between 20,000 and 32,000.

The writing of Thucydides does not allow us any greater leeway. To judge from the entire character of Athenian policy, however, 20,000 is considerably too small a figure; we may with certainty set the minimum at 24,000. On the other hand, if Athens had had in the year 428 B.C. considerably more than 32,000 militarily qualified citizens and metics, it would be impossible to understand why the other Hellenes should have considered that city as being almost exhausted as a result of the expedition against Lesbos, which required only 10,000 men, and certainly a good half of them mercenaries; and again, the following outfitting of the 100 ships must have required practically the rest of the men fit for service.[14] The basic figures 30 + 40 + 100 = 170 ships and 1,000 hoplites we may take at face value from Thucydides; an error on his part is practically impossible, and the manuscript report, too, is verified by comparison with the other figures from the year 431 B.C.

In 424 B.C. the Athenians marched out "with the whole body of the city drawn up as an army"* (battle of Delium) and had 300 mounted men, 7,000 hoplites, and "many more than 10,000 'light troops'*"; there were, consequently, altogether 20,000 to 25,000 men. Furthermore, they had 70 to 80 ships at sea with 14,000 to 16,000 men. Grand total: 35,000 to 40,000 men. That is about the same as in 428 B.C., only as a military effort much lower, by virtue of the fact that almost a half were "light troops,"* who accompanied the army not to fight but to build hasty entrenchments.[15] We may accept, then, as completely verified, that Athens had in 428 B.C. between 24,000 and 32,000 citizens and metics qualified for military service. And based on this we can specify the number at the outbreak of the war. Up to that point Athens had had very light combat losses, but very many had died of the plague, "from the ranks"*—4,400 hoplites and 300 mounted men. The 4,400 hoplites do not give us any definite measure, since we do not know to which group we should relate them—whether only to the field hoplites, or also to the metics and garrison hoplites. The 300 mounted men, however, are undoubtedly in relationship to the 1,200 mounted men in the speech of Pericles. Of the city inhabitants, it is possible that a somewhat larger proportion of the lower classes died, but on the other hand many of them were outside the city as farm cleruchs and less exposed to the hazards of the plague. We may therefore establish for this group also an average death rate of 25 percent. If Athens therefore still had in 428 B.C. 24,000 to 32,000 service-qualified citizens and metics, then in 431 B.C. it had 30,000 to 40,000 of them; and if we add 25 percent old men and disabled veterans, then Athens had at that time a total of 37,500 to 50,000 citizens and metics, of whom we may list 30,000 to 40,000 as citizens, and of their number 22,500 to 30,000 qualified for service. The most extreme possible lower limit hardly comes into consideration. If, on the upper side, we add 1,000 to 2,000 men qualified for service, it is only to pacify the strongest skeptic and forestall any objection.

Now we have found a number forming a standard against which the passage in Pericles' speech may be measured (Thucydides 2. 13). Pericles estimates: 13,000 field hoplites, 16,000 garrison hoplites, 1,200 mounted men, 1,600 archers, for a total of 31,800 armed men. Included therein (according to 2.31) are 3,000 metic hoplites; that leaves, therefore, 28,800 citizens.

Previously this number was somewhat doubtful because of uncertainty as to whether it included the entire service-qualified Athenian citizenry or whether, since it literally seemed to be a question of *land troops* only, the entire group of ships' crews had to be added. In addition to metics, mercenaries, and slaves, at least 15,000 Athenian citizens, then, had to be estimated for this service, possibly even 25,000. We would therefore arrive at completely different dimensions for the service-qualified Athenian citizenry. All of their accomplishments would show up in another light, and the analysis of their campaigns and operations becomes something quite different if it is possible that we might be dealing with, instead of scarcely 30,000, some 50,000 or more service-qualified citizens. All of this confusion is now eliminated. The figures from the year 428 B.C., which have led us to a maximum figure of something over 30,000 service-qualified men, give us complete assurance that Pericles, in his figure of 28,800 service-qualified men, did not omit from consideration any such large figure as the Thêtes or the entire group of ships' crews—that is, some 20,000 souls—but that, on the contrary, he meant the entire citizenry.

On mature reflection, this concept is, too, the only logical one. We may expect Thucydides to tell us which financial resources, how many warships, and how many service-qualified citizens the state of Athens had all together, and these numbers, in the last citation including also the metics who were obligated for hoplite service, he did in fact give us in the speech of Pericles.

The number of citizens one might wish to outfit with hoplite equipment, aside from those who provided their own equipment, was a simple matter of money, which, in a rational survey of the available combat forces, must not be confused with the personal capabilities of the people. Precisely for this reason, it is impossible that Pericles would have included in his estimate any foreign mercenaries whatever.

The total strength of the levy in the fall of 431 B.C. is consistent with this total. We estimated it above at 36,000 men and in addition a considerable number of "light troops."* All in all, then, there may have been 45,000 to an absolute maximum of 50,000 men under arms. Athens was fully capable of this, since, in addition to the 28,800 service-qualified citizens and 3,000 metic hoplites, there were also some 5,000 nonhoplite metics, and the remainder can be reckoned as mercenaries and slaves.

Now that we have established a definite base through a determination of the total number of the Athenian citizenry, we may attempt to dispel the remaining haziness enveloping the figures given in Pericles' speech.

We have already seen that Thucydides' report must contain some kind of error, for it estimates the field army at 15,800 and the garrison troops at 16,000, while expressly saying of the latter, however, that they were composed of the oldest, the youngest, and the metic hoplites. This forms an impossible ratio. Since we are told elsewhere that the metic hoplites numbered 3,000 men, there would then have remained 13,000 from the oldest—that is, the men from fifty or forty-five years of age to sixty—and the eighteen- and nineteen-year-olds. It is impossible, however, that these year-groups—17 at most—would number almost exactly as many men as the 25 or 30 year-groups of the field army.

But this is not the only questionable point. The 16,000 men over and above the field army, Thucydides says, would have garrisoned the long walls and the strongholds whenever the enemies attacked. Just at this time, however, the largest part of the field troops were also at home, and the field hoplites were, in any event, called up very seldom and for a short time or, in the case of distant expeditions, only in small numbers. Is it conceivable that precisely this best part of the army performed no duty at all when the enemy invaded the country, and that the fifty- to sixty-year-olds were ordered to the long walls while the twenty- to fifty-year-olds stayed at home? Furthermore, it is striking that Thucydides' account seems to indicate that the garrison of the Athenian walls was composed entirely of hoplites. For the possible defense of the walls the heavy armor with shield was superfluous and even an impediment. Cover was provided by the battlements, from behind which one would repel the enemy by shooting arrows, hurling javelins, and throwing stones. Hoplites had to be held in reserve for the contingency of close combat against those who broke through.

There is, consequently, no doubt that there is an error somewhere in Thucydides' report. To assume that it is not a question of an error by Thucydides himself, but rather an error in the figures of a writer who copied him, is, as we have proved, impossible. The figures are sufficiently specified and verified by the numbers given elsewhere in Thucydides. Beloch's most recent explanation, that Thucydides himself did not make the error but that the publisher of his work created the confusion by adding the number 16,000, can, of course, neither be proved nor disproved. As a matter of general principle, however, one will always prefer, as long as it is possible, the milder and less incisive means of correcting obvious errors in the historical accounts. It therefore seems to me that my hypothesis—that the master himself, for once, made an error here—still detracts much less from the authority of the entire work, as we know it, than would be the case if we imagined that the publisher irreverently made corrections without even applying the proper care and reflection. We shall see at once how small the slip actually is, in the final analysis, which we attribute to Thucydides, and no matter how gladly I normally count myself among the admirers of Thucydides, I cannot agree that this possible solution is completely out of the question. That even the most careful critical brain can, precisely in the matter of establishing numbers, for once fall into an error which, once it is clarified, hardly seems possible—for this we have a very illustrious example from the most recent time. No less a person than Moltke, in his history of the war of 1870, estimated the number of Germans in the Battle of Gravelotte-St. Privat at some 50,000 men too small, by forgetting all the officers, the cavalry, and the artillery, categories that *are* counted in arriving at the enemy's total. One recognizes the origin of the error at once by comparing the appropriate page in the *General Staff Work* (*Generalstabswerk*) (2:234, Appendix), which he had in front of him as he wrote, with the passage in his work (p. 63); and it is not a question of a cursorily given number, but rather, a number that serves as the basis for a highly important conclusion. If this happened with Moltke—who was, to be sure, at an advanced age—then we are not being too unfair to Thucydides by attributing a similar error to him when, for once, the figures given by him are absolutely impossible.

The error stems from characterizing the garrison troops as being composed of the "oldest and youngest and the metic hoplites." Missing here is a category that, in keeping with the overall context, cannot be dispensed with, namely, the service-qualified citizens who were not assigned to hoplite duty.

If we subtract the 3,000 metics from the 16,000 garrison troops, there remain 13,000 citizens, or exactly as many as the citizen field hoplites. That is hardly pure coincidence. Rather, we may be permitted to assume that it was specified that at any given time half of the service-qualified citizenry was to be trained and equipped for hoplite duty. The two recruit year-groups ("guards"*) were assigned to the garrison of the forts and were at the same time undergoing training. It was therefore said in Athens—and Pericles, too, in his speech, may have expressed himself in this way —that even if the entire field army of 13,000 hoplites had marched out, there would still remain just as many men for the defense of the long walls and in the forts—and 3,000 metic hoplites in addition. In adding these figures, Thucydides named only the youngest and the oldest and the metics but forgot to mention the others.

The modern reader, then, in order to understand the passage correctly and completely, must be in the clear as to the following:

The 13,000 field hoplites are not only the citizens of the higher classes, who provide their own equipment (which would put the total citizenry of Athens at much too high a figure), but in addition to them also those Thêtes who are outfitted by the state for hoplite service.

The 16,000 garrison troops are not those who actually garrisoned the walls when the enemy came into the country, but those who would still have been available for the defense of the walls if the whole field hoplite army had been engaged elsewhere.

These 16,000 men include 3,000 metics who were assigned to hoplite service; the recruits; the older year-groups, from age forty-five or fifty up to sixty; the half-invalided ones; and finally all those Thêtes who were not designated for field hoplite service.

Furthermore, Thucydides did not include in his estimate the metics who were not hoplites. For us, this latter omission is almost the most sensitive one, but for Thucydides, as we shall still see (2. 3), a completely logical omission.

In this number that we have estimated as 36,000 Athenian citizens are included the cleruchs. These colonists were and remained Athenian citizens, but they lived, in part, quite far away, for example on the islands of Lemnos, Imbros, Skyros. They formed their own communities there, and Thucydides later always mentions their contingents in the campaigns separately from the Athenians; moreover, Thucydides gives the strength for the campaign of 431 B.C. as 16,000 hoplites, consequently the same number as Pericles. It must be assumed, however, that the distant cleruchs were not called in for this campaign.

One might conclude from this, as Beloch did (p. 82), that Pericles, too, omitted them from his count. The following, however, contradicts this: We have seen that Pericles claims to give the total number of service-qualified Athenians. It would be completely incomprehensible if, in doing so, he had omitted such a large segment as the entire cleruch communities, which Beloch estimates probably too high at 10,000 citizens, and which were located partly quite far away, but in part also quite near, as in Salamis and Oreos on Euboea. The account of Thucydides from the year 428 B.C. positively excludes any leeway for such a high estimate of the Athenian armed forces. The estimate that 13,000 hoplites attacked Megara in 431 B.C., while 3,000 were in position before Potidaea, can be explained without difficulty. It is true, of course, that the more distant cleruchs were certainly not called up for this campaign, but there was, nevertheless, surely a contingent of them with the fleet, and Thucydides by no means gives a specific number for this special case, but simply repeats the number given in Pericles' speech without venturing further into a special accounting as to how many, possibly by chance, prevented by whatever reasons, might have been missing. It is highly probable, therefore, that not only more distant cleruchs, but also a rather large number of Athenians, who were always away on commercial undertakings, were missing without Thucydides' having made allowance for them.

I should like finally also to explain on what points and for what reasons I have now modified the estimates to which I had come in my *Persian and Burgundian Wars*. In that book, following an idea of Duncker, I sought to solve the contradiction in Thucydides, 2. 13, in such a way as to have all the field-service-qualified Thêtes counted in with the hoplites, and the more distant cleruchs with the garrison troops. Strictly speaking, this solution agrees best with the wording of Thucydides, since the distinction between field troops and garrison troops is rigorously observed and maintained.

But it has now become clear to me that the characterizing of the 16,000 men as garrison troops cannot possibly have been meant literally; it now becomes entirely impossible to support the otherwise very desirable concept of the cleruch communities as garrisons. Moreover, it would be very illogical if Pericles, on the purely theoretical possibility of making hoplites of all the field-service-qualified Thêtes, had actually shown them as such while, on the other hand, omitting the cleruchs, who performed real hoplite service.

I have therefore proposed, so to speak, an exchange between cleruchs and Thêtes, and in this way the final total has become higher by 2,000 citizens. This is because at that time, in order to be consistent, I had to omit from the number given by Thucydides a number of metic garrison hoplites also, which I estimated at 1,500. Now that is no longer necessary, since this whole concept has been discarded. The number of service-qualified citizens is thereby increased by 1,500 and with a 25 percent addition for the militarily unfit, the overall total is increased by 2,000.

Whereas I have gone up from 34,000 to 36,000 citizens, Beloch, in his *Greek History (Griechische Geschichte)* (which appeared in 1893, 1:404, footnote), went down from 45,000 to 40,000 Athenian citizens (30,000 living in Attica and 10,000 cleruchs). Consequently, we have approached each other so closely that our difference now amounts to only 4,000.

My list is now:

1,200 mounted men
1,600 archers
13,000 hoplites, including the cleruchs
13,000 service-qualified Athenian citizens (including cleruchs), nonhoplites
7,200 militarily unqualified

Total: 36,000 Athenian citizens.
In addition, some 6,000 to 8,000 metics.

From these figures we can still draw no conclusion as to the total population of Attica in 431 B.C., since we have no basis for the number of slaves. We can only say that this number was, in any case, quite high.

For the almost purely agricultural state of Sparta, Beloch correctly estimated that it had a quite stable population; the increase was lost through emigration. That did not apply to Athens. Emigration, aside from the cleruchs, was certainly very small, whereas on the other hand, in the period in which Athens was flourishing, the metics increased greatly in the course of the fifth century and in 490 B.C. were present only in rather small numbers. As to the rate of the natural increase, we unfortunately have no indication at all. Normally, under favorable circumstances, a population can be expected to double in sixty years. We may not assume that rate for the Athenians, who in the meantime also suffered very heavy war casualties (for example, in the campaign in Egypt). The principal increase is no doubt to be attributed to immigrating metics and slaves. Nevertheless, the citizenry probably did not remain stable, so that, if there were 28,800 service-qualified citizens on hand in 431 B.C., we may be allowed to assume some 18,000 to 26,000 for the year 490 B.C.; and in addition possibly 2,000 metics.

From the first edition of the second volume (pp. 1 ff.) I transpose to this position still another difference of opinion, with Eduard Meyer, over the same subject.

Shortly before the printing of the first volume of this work, the second volume of *Studies in Ancient History (Forschungen zur alten Geschichte)* by Eduard Meyer appeared, but it did not come to my attention soon enough to permit my using it. On the basic questions of Greek history of the fifth century B.C. we are completely in agreement. On two points, however, we came to opposite conclusions.

The first is the interpretation of Thucydides 2. 13 as to the population of Attica at the outbreak of the Peloponnesian War. On this point Meyer (II:149) proposed a new solution that results in exactly the double of my estimate. When one remembers what importance the figures have in my research and how much one number is always used to check the other, how one figure is built up on the other, then one can measure the range of our difference. I would, of course, like to think that the new solution that I, for my part, have proposed, is so persuasive in itself that a special refutation of Meyer's concept is no longer necessary; but since such an outstanding Hellenic scholar as Adolf Bauer, in the *Historische Zeitschrift* 86:286, on the contrary, accepted Meyer's solution as the right one, I cannot avoid a specific explanation. According to my concept, the worth of Thucydides as an historian and of Pericles as a statesman actually depends on this statistical question. For I have not simply suggested, as Bauer claims, but have stated very positively, and I stand solidly behind it: "The authority of the greatest of all historians is irrevocably destroyed, a pillar of Greek literature is thrown over, if somebody proves that Athens had 60,000 citizens in 431 B.C. For if Thucydides has falsely judged Pericles and his statesmanship, then we may in no way ever again trust his judgment." Since such a recognized scholar as Meyer, who agrees with me on the basic points of the method as well as of the concept in general, has actually undertaken that proof, then one can see that there is something at stake and that a reexamination is not unjustified.

Meyer, too, proceeds from the assumption that the figure as it stands in Thucydides—13,000 hoplites in the field army, 13,000 citizen hoplites in the garrison troops, consisting of the oldest and the youngest—is logically impossible, since the few year-groups of the men unqualified for field service but qualified for garrison duty could not possibly have been as strong as the approximately 30 year-groups of those unqualified for field service [*sic*: "Nicht-Felddienstfähigen," obviously an error—*Translator's note*]. Whereas I assume (dropping an older hypothesis) that Thucydides neglected—expressly in this case—to mention the Thêtes who had been called in for other than hoplite service along with the oldest and the youngest, Meyer claims that from the field-service-qualified year-groups a large number (5,400) of the weaker men were assigned to the home guard (*Landsturm*) and were not mentioned by Thucydides. According to Meyer, Thucydides, therefore, left completely out of consideration the number of nonhoplite Thêtes, and we must try to determine their number through other figures. In doing so, Meyer arrives at 20,000 and for the metics at 14,000 at least, so that Athens had at her disposal more than 70,000 grown free men without the cleruchs. I, on the other hand, came to a figure of some 40,000 (36,000 of them citizens), including the cleruchs, and consequently almost exactly half of Meyer's figure.

The following considerations contradict Meyer's estimate:

1. He counts 33,000 zeugitae as compared to 20,000 Thêtes. That is an impossible ratio. Meyer did not take into consideration the fact that, insofar as hoplite service through one's own means was concerned, not only the lowest stratum of the population belonged to the Thêtes class, but necessarily also very many sons of middle-class landowners. It was absolutely impossible, when a father who had several grown sons was rated among the zeugitae, to burden the sons as well with the obligation of hoplite service, for, indeed, in most cases there was normally just one set of hoplite equipment in a family. If Athens had had 33,000 citizens who could provide their own equipment, and in addition 2,500 mounted men, then she would have had to have at least 40,000 to 50,000 Thêtes.

Meyer is also in error in his idea (p. 158) that "the Thêtes were prevented by their trade from attaining the full military and physical training of the hoplites." That gives a completely false picture of the duties of a hoplite, who needed physical training as little as did a Roman legionary. The great majority of the hoplites, who were very moderately fixed farmers and craftsmen, probably had no athletic training at all, and their military training certainly required less drill than the training of a thranite.

2. In Thucydides 3. 17, we are told that the Spartans considered Athens to be exhausted when, in 428 b.c., she had 70 ships and 1,000 hoplites in action. The Athenians, however, by straining their resources, still brought 100 more ships to sea.

This account would be senseless if Meyer's estimate were correct. For, of the approximately 14,000 men manning the 70 ships, there were at the very highest —cleruchs excluded—5,000 to 7,000—with the hoplites, 8,000—Athenians. Even if we assume that the plague had cost Athens 15,000 service-qualified men (Thucydides gives "4,400 hoplites 'from the ranks'* and 300 mounted men"), the city would still have had some 40,000. How then could the Spartans have possibly believed that Athens was exhausted by the sending forth of some 8,000 citizens? And it would have been just as unlikely, with such a supply of citizens, for the outfitting of 100 ships to be an unusual accomplishment; 18,000 men were sufficient for these ships, and at that, the larger half could have been slaves, or foreign sailors who happened to be in Athens at the time.

On the other hand, there is close agreement between Thucydides' account and the estimate that Athens did not have more than some 40,000 adult citizens and metics in 431 b.c. In this case we could arrive at the following accounting:

a. Citizens and metics in 431 b.c.		about 44,000
b. Losses from the plague		about 12,000
	Remainder:	32,000
c. Nonservice-qualified and absent		8,000
	Remainder:	24,000
d. Serving at sea on the 70 ships		7,000
	Remainder:	17,000
e. Aboard the 100 ships (smaller half of the combined crews)		8,000
	Remainder:	9,000

These 9,000 men, with the addition of partially qualified men from category "c," were enough to man and guard the forts and city walls, although one must still deduct a certain figure to account for the more distant cleruchs.

We may shift the individual figures in this accounting up or down by 1,000 or 2,000 men, but the two limiting factors, which are given in Thucydides' account—i.e., that Athens, on the one hand, was thought to be exhausted by the dispatch of 70 ships and 1,000 hoplites, and that, on the other hand, 100 more ships could be manned and the necessary city garrison left behind—these two limiting factors may not be violated, and therefore Meyer's accounting is not reconcilable with that of Thucydides.

For the defense of the city of Athens itself and the long walls, a few thousand men were sufficient. On page 154 Meyer states the opinion that even 6,000 men would not have been enough for this purpose, since the circumference of the walls amounted to 26,000 meters and therefore, with 1/6 of the total, or 1000 men, on post at any one time, there would have been only one double sentry every 52 meters. The assumption underlying this reckoning, however, is false. Not enough distinction is made between *observation* and *defense*. Only a large enemy army could venture to attack a city like Athens, and a large enemy army cannot approach unnoticed. Consequently, as long as no enemy army was reported nearby, a few watchtower sentries sufficed. But if an enemy army actually did move toward the walls, they were not evenly manned with double sentry posts, but on the contrary, were principally put under good observation, and an alert force was moved to whatever position might be threatened. Certainly there was never a situation with evenly spaced double sentries posted all the way around, and with particular regard to the year 428 B.C., the fleet of 100 ships had naturally been back in the harbor quite a long time before a Peloponnesian army could appear before the long wall. Only for protection against a possible surprise attack by a highly mobile task force was it necessary for a small garrison to remain at home. In fact, under conditions like those of 431 B.C., when the Athenian field army moved out against Megara, even this was unnecessary, since the army, by its position, covered the city against any attack by land. Furthermore, the Boeotians would not have risked an undertaking against Attica, since they would have been cut off.

3. Like me, Meyer recognizes that Pericles' war plan was the right one. If at that time, however, Athens had counted 80,000 free men, including the cleruchs, this war plan would have been wrong. Since the financial power and the trading centers of her entire great sea alliance stood at the disposal of Athens, she would have been able to turn on the Peloponnesians not with a strategy of attrition, but with a strategy aimed at victory. The invading army of the Peloponnesians can hardly have been stronger than 30,000 men. The Athenians would therefore have been able to meet them squarely in the open field, and the isthmus offered the possibility of splitting the enemies and defeating the Boeotians and Peloponnesians separately. The possibility of raising the estimated population of the other Greek city-states in comparison with that of Athens is ruled out, since they were blockaded for many years and existed with practically no imports. Consequently, even Corinth can have been only a moderately sized city.

The statement of Adolf Bauer (*Historische Zeitschrift* 86:288), "With a field army of 13,000 hoplites Athens could not risk a great decisive battle against the vastly superior armed forces of the Peloponnesian League, and her additional manpower was available only on a very limited scale," misses the mark. Why were not more than 13,000 men available, if Athens had more than 80,000 citizens, cleruchs, and metics, and, in addition, the money to hire very many mercenaries? Rome, in the Second Punic War, made much greater efforts without help from her allies. Nothing would have been more illogical than to hold troops and ships constantly at hand and thereby keep them from engagement in the main battle, as Bauer believes was the case, because of the possibility of insubordination on the part of her allies. On that point one should read again what Clausewitz says about the error of holding out a strategic reserve in a strategy of all-out victory. The best way to reassert the authority of the leading state was to conquer Sparta, Corinth, and Thebes. Now, since there is ample evidence at hand that Athens was not remiss in her efforts—for example, that even the metics donned hoplite equipment and that Socrates, at the age of forty-seven, still had to do field service as a hoplite, and on the other hand it is specifically reported that, when the force moved out "with the whole body of the city drawn up as an army"* in 424 B.C., it had a strength of only 7,000 hoplites—it is impossible that there would have been 70,000 free men on hand in Attica in 431 B.C.

4. At the outbreak of the Peloponnesian War Athens had 300 triremes; even if one agrees with Meyer when, for reasons not completely clear to me, he raises this number to 400, nevertheless Athens never had more than 170, or at the very most 250, triremes in service at the same time (see p. 40 above). Corinth, however, sent out 90 triremes in 433 B.C. (Thucydides 1. 46). According to Beloch's estimate, Corinth did not have more than some 10,000 free adult men, and it is impossible to increase this number significantly, since we could not account for the possibility of feeding any larger number than this during the long blockade of the Peloponnesian War. If Athens had had seven times as many inhabitants as Corinth, not only would its sea strength appear very small but it would also be incomprehensible how Corinth could have entered such a serious and protracted rivalry with such a hugely superior neighbor.

This becomes even clearer if we go back to the period of the Persian Wars. Meyer assumes that, even then, Attica had approximately the same population as in 431 B.C. That is not really demonstrable; but even if we come close to this estimate, we are faced with impossibilities. At Artemisium and Salamis, Corinth is supposed to have had 40 ships, Athens 123 and 180 respectively. The last figure is probably too high. But even if it were correct, it is clear that Athens could not be anywhere near seven times as large as Corinth, since, according to historical records and the situation, she had mounted not a relatively smaller fleet than her neighbor, but a relatively larger one. Only a few years previously, however, Athens had had to borrow 20 triremes from Corinth and was, consequently, still by no means a highly developed commercial center, a situation that is inconceivable without warships. If, then, she was not yet a highly developed trading center and was consequently not attracting a very important level of imports, it follows that she cannot yet have had such a large population. The report that Athens had needed to import grain ever since the time of Solon does not, of course, contradict our conclusion—insofar as the size of the importation is concerned, much depends on whether not a tenth or a twentieth of the population, but a third or even half lived on imported grain. At a time when Athens was only starting to become a sea power, such can not yet have been the case.

We may also be permitted to reach the following conclusion. If Athens at that time had already been a very populous trading center, Corinth would have had a strong sensitivity vis-à-vis this increasing commercial rivalry and would not have provided a benefit to her rival through the loan of ships. If Athens was at that time, however, still so little developed as a city that she incited no significant envy in Corinth, she can by the same token not possibly have already had seven times as many citizens fifty years later.

The size of Corinth, then, establishes indirectly a certain limit for the size of Athens, and the size of Corinth can, in turn, be verified by that of Sparta. See below, Chapter III, note 3.

5. Even though I reject the results of Meyer's investigation, it still makes, like every serious scholarly study, an important indirect contribution. The crux of the controversy over the account of Thucydides 2. 13 is really whether the Thêtes are included or not. Up to the present the advocates of the opinion that the Thêtes were not counted in this number have never made a clear and consistent estimate as to how high a figure one could reach for the total population of Athens, and by adhering to a somewhat vague middle line have made the accounting appear to be more or less possible from a practical viewpoint. Not until Meyer showed indisputably that this interpretation would necessarily lead to a figure of some 70,000 free adult men in Attica (consequently without the cleruchs)—and even this number would still be too small—did he also make possible the equally inevitable counterproof that this number is, from a practical viewpoint, absolutely impossible. We must therefore look for another interpretation of Thucydides 2. 13, and here the one proposed by me can at any rate have the advantage of providing no contradiction either with the figures passed down in other accounts or with the actual accomplishments of Athens. Since the Athenians waged a not insignificant portion of their wars with mercenaries, they were no doubt in a position, even when they numbered only 36,000 citizens and 6,000 to 8,000 metics, to fight simultaneously on the mainland and in the Aegean Sea, on Cyprus and in Egypt.

The way to the correct interpretation and filling out of the numbers given by Thucydides has been obscured by considering them in combination with the breakdown of the various classes of Athenians, a breakdown of which Thucydides makes no mention here and which has nothing at all to do with his accounting. From another point of view as well, it is most important to dissolve this connection that has falsely been injected into the interpretation. It has created confusion in many places. The whole concept of Roman political history has been distorted by the erroneous idea of the significance of the division of the people into classes. By eliminating the classes in Thucydides 2. 13, and interpreting the figures correctly, we arrive simultaneously at a correct concept of the Athenian constitution and, indirectly, of the Roman one.

NOTES FOR CHAPTER I

1. Beitzke, *History of the German Wars of Liberation* (*Geschichte der deutschen Freiheitskriege*), Vol. 1, Appendix. Bernhardi, *Memorable Events in the Life of Toll* (*Denkwürdigkeiten aus dem Leben Tolls*), Vol. 3, Appendix.

2. Pertz-Delbrück, *Life of Gneisenau* (*Leben Gneisenaus*), large ed., Vol. 4, Appendix; small ed., 2d printing, 2:19.

3. Delbrück, *Persian and Burgundian Wars* (*Perser- und Burgunderkriege*), p. 157.

4. P. Bailleu in the *Deutsche Rundschau*, December 1899.

5. von Lettow. *The War of 1806 and 1807* (*Der Krieg von 1806 und 1807*).

6. Compare "Mind and Mass in History" ("Geist und Masse in der Geschichte"), *Preussische Jahrbücher* 147 (1912): 193.

7. R. Adam, in his dissertation "De Herodoti ratione historica quaestiones selectae sive de pugna Salaminia atque Plataeensi" (Berlin, 1890), shows that the army strengths and number of ships given by Herodotus are based on an estimate table that removes from them any residual element of credibility.

8. In the *Wochenschrift für klassische Philologie* 12 (1895): 877, Beloch defended himself well, in a review, against several unfounded attacks.

9. Kromayer claimed, in the article "Studies on the Military Power and Military Organization of the Greek States, particularly in the Fourth Century" ("Studien über Wehrkraft und Wehrverfassung der griechischen Staaten, vornehmlich im 4. Jahrh."), *Klio*, Vol. 3, 1903, that the population and the levies were considerably higher, but he was contradicted by Beloch, *Klio*, Vols. 5 and 6, 1905, 1906, in the essay "Greek Levies" ("Griechische Aufgebote").

10. In his *Greek History* (*Griech. Gesch.*), 1:403, Beloch dropped this viewpoint and assumed that even in the fifth century the population was sharply increasing.

11. According to P. Voigt, "Germany and the World Market" ("Deutschland und der Weltmarkt"), *Preussische Jahrbücher* 91: 260.

According to a more recent estimate of Max Delbrück, "German Agriculture at the Turn of the Century" ("Die deutsche Landwirtschaft an der Jahrhundertwende"), *Preussische Jahrbücher*, February 1900), one must consider on the other hand the fact that our population enjoys a large proportion of meat foods, which makes for very great production costs. With a primarily vegetarian diet, a country can support more people.

By way of comparison I cite also the following figures:

	STATE	INHABITANTS PER SQUARE KILOMETER
1890	Prussia	86
	Mecklenburg-Strelitz	33
1888	Switzerland	71
	Graubünden	13
	Schwyz	55
	Uri	16
	Wallis	19
1889	Greece	34
	Laconia	30
	Messenia	55
	Euboea	24
	Attica and Boeotia	41

12. As early as in the preparations for the Peloponnesian War, Thucydides mentions with decisive emphasis that the Athenians fought their wars partly with mercenaries (1. 121; 1. 143); after the plague the remaining citizens in business, on the farm, and in industry were even more indispensable than otherwise, and the number easily to be spared smaller, so that the number of mercenaries was certainly unusually large.

13. That the Athenian fleet and army at that time, despite a certain reinforcement by mercenaries and slaves, were still manned principally by Athenian citizens themselves, follows from the political situation of the state. The ancient authors are agreed on this point, and especially the older "Constitution of the Athenians,"* which, in my opinion, comes down to us from no less a person than Thucydides himself, bears full witness to the fact that the democracy rested on naval service. If the fleet had been manned completely or predominantly by mercenaries and slaves, it would have been rather an instrument of the rich merchants, who paid the mercenaries or could buy slaves, as was the case with other great trading cities (Carthage, Venice, Amsterdam). Aristotle, too, in his *Politics* 5. 5. 5, says: "And then again the naval people, having been the cause of the victory at Salamis, and therefore, of the hegemony of Athens because of her power at sea, made the democracy

stronger."* The Corcyraeans' fleet at Sybota was for the most part manned by slaves. Thucydides 1. 55. Compare with Book II, Chapter II, Excursus, below.

14. The fact that, for short expeditions, a Greek canton once sent out what amounted to all its men fit for service follows from the account of Thucydides 1. 105, where Myronidas moves out against the Corinthians with "the oldest and the youngest, because the regular army was engaged elsewhere," and in 5. 56, where the Argives (in 418 B.C.) believe they can take Epidaurus by surprise, since the men are off at war.

15. The march out to Delium took place "with the whole body of the city drawn up as an army."* It might consequently seem strange that Athens brought up only 7,000 hoplites, whereas the speech of Pericles gives 13,000 + 3,000 metics, or a total of 16,000. If, however, we subtract the losses from the plague, consider that, in the fleet, not only the *epibatae* but also a number of citizens were serving, men whose names appeared on the hoplite list at the same time, and finally that the number 16,000 gives the payroll roster, from which, in reality, many are absent—sick, traveling, or otherwise indispensable elsewhere—then the two numbers are quite consistent with each other.

Chapter II

Greek Arms and Tactics

At the time of the Persian Wars the great mass of a Greek army was composed of armored foot soldiers with a thrusting lance about two meters long,[1] the hoplites. The protective equipment consisted of helmet, harness,[2] greaves, and shield. A short sword was an auxiliary weapon.

The hoplites form a tight tactical unit, the phalanx. The phalanx is a continuous linear arrangement composed of several ranks.[3] The depth varies; very often we hear of an 8-man depth, which seems to be regarded as a kind of normal formation; but we also hear of 12-man and even 25-man depths.[4]

In such a phalanx two ranks at most can participate in the actual combat, with the second rank stepping into the holes of the first at the moment of contact. The following ranks serve as immediate replacements for the dead and wounded, but they exercise principally a physical and moral pressure. The deeper phalanx will defeat the more shallow one, even if on both sides exactly the same number of combatants actually manage to use their weapons.

But for the advantage of this pressure, it would be much better to lengthen the line, outflanking the enemy and enveloping his two flanks at the moment of shock. But with equal opposing forces such an envelopment can only take place at the expense of the depth of the formation, and although it requires only a few minutes from the first contact of the two lines until the envelopment has been completed, nevertheless in this time the deeper of the opposing phalanxes would presumably already have overrun the shallow center of the opponent and would thereby have broken up the whole formation.

Therefore, in any consideration of the phalanx two principles stand diametrically opposed: depth, which gives weight, and length, which facilitates envelopment. It is up to the commander to determine the depth and length of his phalanx from the circumstances

53

of the situation, the strength of the armies, the quality of the troops on both sides, and the form of the terrain. A very large army is more strengthened in the dimension of depth than in the dimension of length, because it is extremely difficult to move a long line forward in a fairly aligned and well-ordered way, whereas the formation of a deep column is not so easily disrupted.

Since the rearmost ranks of the phalanx almost never arrive at the point of using their weapons, it might appear superfluous to supply complete protective armament to all the warriors from about the fourth rank back. Nevertheless, we have no account from the Greeks to the effect that such a distinction was ever made. An unarmored person is not capable of really fighting against an armored one. The forming up of several ranks of unarmored men behind the armored ranks would therefore have been not much more than a kind of pretense. The realization that they could not really expect to receive any true support from these rear ranks would have seriously weakened the drive, the forward thrust of the foremost ranks, in which, of course, the value of the rearmost ranks normally lies. If, at any section of the line, it really happened that, by some possible chance splitting of the phalanx, the armored enemy penetrated into the unarmored rearmost ranks, the latter would have had to give ground at once, and the flight in this one area would easily have pulled the entire army back with it.

Least of all, then, would it have been desirable to put possibly unreliable men, slaves, in the rearmost ranks of the phalanx. They would do no good there but would be able, through premature, perhaps even malicious, flight, to create a panic quite easily, even among the hoplites.

This explanation does not eliminate, of course, the opposite proposition, that when one has some men less well armed, they are placed in the rearmost ranks. Such lightly armed or only partially armed men can also be useful by helping friendly wounded soldiers and by killing or taking prisoner those enemy wounded over and around whom the battle is being waged. Those are only secondary services, however, and the phalanx as such presupposes the most completely armed warriors possible throughout all the ranks.

Of the utmost importance in this kind of combat is the type of men who stand in the first rank. Again and again, in his war songs, Tyrtaeus praises the men of the forward battle, "among those fighting in front."* The later theoreticians recommend to army commanders that the most reliable men be placed in the first and last ranks, in order to hold the entire phalanx together. An accused

Athenian citizen brought out in his defense in a trial the fact that he had voluntarily had himself placed in the first rank in a dangerous battle.[5]

In Lacedaemon the Spartiates and the Perioeci took to the field equally as hoplites, but the Spartiates, as professional warriors, were considered much more valuable than the Perioeci, who were usually occupied in their civilian profession. This superiority is probably most evident in the fact that the Spartiates predominantly formed the first ranks of the phalanx.[6]

Missile-type weapons played only a very small role in connection with the hoplite phalanx. With the Greeks the bow was a traditionally respected weapon; the national hero, Hercules, was an archer. In the case of the Athenians, a special archer corps is mentioned in the campaign of Plataea. But since the time the phalanx was formed of spear-carriers, the bow was pushed into the background, since the two arms, even if not mutually exclusive, can be combined only with great difficulty. One can picture the archers, sling men, and javelin-throwers in front of, beside, and behind the phalanx. Whenever they were deployed forward of the front line, they must have disappeared before the clash of the two phalanxes, and therefore would necessarily have withdrawn around the flanks. If they attempted to push back through the phalanx itself, the resulting disorder and delay would cause much more damage than the advantage from the losses that they might have inflicted on the enemy. In order to be sure of passing around the two flanks, the sharpshooters would have to begin their withdrawal while the phalanxes were still several hundred paces apart. If the enemy had no sharpshooters and we sent out marksmen against him, to fire on him continuously during the approach march, that could of course cause him serious disruption. If both sides had sharpshooters, however, these two forces would, for the most part, only shoot at each other and would have no influence at all on the decisive phalanx battle. Firing obliquely on the approaching enemy from the two flanks of the hoplite phalanx, a number of marksmen could exercise an influence on the progress of the battle. But we find no recognizable traces of this kind of action, even in the later Greek battles.

Finally, if sharpshooters were stationed behind the phalanx, they could shoot out their volley from that position shortly before the clash. Fired in an arching trajectory, however, without real aiming, this could not be very effective, especially when, as is usually the case, our own phalanx was moving toward the enemy at the assault

pace. Consequently, although we find such an employment of projectiles fairly often recommended in theory,[7] nevertheless, from a
practical viewpoint, it was used only infrequently, as, for example,
in the battle that Thrasybulus fought against the thirty Tyrants in
the streets of Piraeus. (Xenophon, *Hellenica* 2. 4). There, however,
the troops of Thrasybulus stood only ten men deep, on a rise of
ground, and waited for the enemy, who advanced up the street
with a fifty-man depth. Under these special conditions the projectiles fired from above onto the thick mass were able to do very
good service. Generally speaking, however, the marksmen formed
only an auxiliary arm. The real combat force of the Greeks in the
Persian Wars consisted only of hoplites.

Nevertheless, Herodotus estimates for every hoplite in the Persian Wars one unarmored man ("lightly armed soldier")* and
counts these unarmored persons in his estimate of the army's
strength. The later Greek historians also mention quite often, it is
true, great masses of unarmored men, but they do not really count
them as warriors, and as we have seen, rightly so, since they were
as good as worthless for the battle itself. We are faced here with a
difficulty that will confront us again quite often, especially in the
knightly armies of the Middle Ages. The sharp distinction between
combatants and noncombatants that today appears quite natural to
us cannot be traced through so strictly. The Greek hoplite had a
heavy load of equipment to carry and was responsible, for the short
time that the campaigns usually lasted, for his own supplies. Most
of them were men of property, no longer youths. Consequently
they could hardly get along without a helper to act as porter, for-
ager, cook, and in case of their being wounded, nurse. Each hoplite
had to have a second man with him, whether it be a son, brother,
neighbor, or even only a trustworthy slave. This companion was
not completely unarmed; he had at least a dagger in his belt or a
hand-axe, and perhaps also a light spear. If it came to laying the
enemy's land to waste, when the enemy refused to join battle, the
unarmored men could do that task better than the heavily burdened hoplites. In the battle a part of them could move along on
the flanks of the phalanx, in order to harass the enemy with stones
and javelins as he moved out. Another part of them might follow
the phalanx, in order to pick up and care for the wounded at once
and to capture or kill enemy soldiers who fell into their hands.
These unarmored men were therefore not simply supply train
wagoners; they also had certain battle functions. But we nevertheless get a false picture if we simply count them together with the

hoplites in order to arrive at the strength of the army. The correct procedure, rather, is to count only the hoplites and the possibly present mounted men and marksmen who are especially named as such, as the Greeks themselves generally did. In doing so, however, one must keep in mind that approximately the same number of followers were present, who also carried out certain battlefield functions.

As for cavalry, it was not used by the Greeks against the Persians.

The weak point of a hoplite phalanx lay in its flanks. If the enemy should succeed in striking the flank of a phalanx while the front was occupied, all would be lost. The relatively few warriors of the outside columns could hardly hold off an attack, and while they had to stop and wheel against the enemy, they would either force the entire phalanx to stop in like manner, so that all the rearward ranks would be unable to carry out their special mission of pressing forward, or the phalanx would break apart and be rolled up from the flank.

This is described very clearly in a battle at Corcyra in 373 B.C.[8] The Spartans were laying siege to the city and drove back an attempted sortie. At that point other Corcyraeans fell on their flanks from the gates, "lined up eight men deep." Xenophon continues to recount, "The Lacedaemonians believed the flank ("the peak,"* therefore literally the "point") too weak and sought to face around ("they attempted to turn back").* Therefore the last files tried to form in the rear a new front consisting of a line with refused flanks. The enemies, regarding that as the beginning of a flight, drove in all the more strongly, so that the wheeling movement could not be carried out, and one column after the other took to flight.

Of particular danger to the phalanx is cavalry, when, even in small numbers, it attacks the flanks. Then the strength of the phalanx is immediately broken, since it can no longer move forward without falling into disorder.

The scope of this work does not include the origin of the phalanx formation as a tactical body—that is, the way the concept of fighting in a tactical body developed from the multiple single combat concept. We have begun our presentation at a point where the formation of the hoplite phalanx exists beyond any doubt in the Greek states and shows a high degree of effectiveness. I do not wish to deny myself, however, a few remarks on the foregoing subject.

There are numerous indications that the Dorians, who subju-

gated part of the Peloponnesian area, were the first not only to
recognize the value of the closely knit grouping of the fighters but
also to bring this formation into logical and effective practice. The
legendary account of the Messenian wars, as it has been handed
down to us in Pausanias, states (4. 8. 11) that the Lacedaemonians
had not pursued, because it was more important to them to hold
their orderly formation than to kill one or another of the fleeing
enemy.[9] ("It was also an ancient custom with them to pursue
somewhat slowly, keeping it in mind to preserve their formation
rather than killing those who fled before them.")* Almost identical
is an account by Emperor Franz I for his brother Karl of Lorraine,
in the year 1757, concerning the military methods of the Prussians
(Arneth, *Maria Theresia*, 5: 171). "They understood only rarely how
to derive important advantages from a hard-won victory. The
reason is that they dreaded nothing else quite as much as having
their ranks fall into disorder, and so they usually avoided prompt
pursuit."

The oldest record on the origin of the phalanx seems to support
a legend that we find in Polyaenus (1. 10). When the Heraclidae
were fighting against Sparta, they were surprised in the middle of
their sacrifices by their enemies. They did not allow themselves to
panic, however, but ordered their pipers to march forward. The
pipers blew and advanced, but the hoplites, striding forward in
time with the melody and the rhythm, formed their battle ranks
and held the formation solidly, and were victorious. ("The hoplites
marched on accompanied by melody and rhythm and did not
break their ranks; this was how they conquered their enemies.")*
This experience taught the Lacedaemonians always to have the
pipers lead them into battle, and their god promised them that
they would always conquer as long as they fought accompanied by
pipers and not against pipers.

In this context the piper is nothing other than the tactical formation; a group of heroes engaging in individual combat does not
march in step and would, by the irregular noise of their advance,
even drown out the pipers.

EXCURSUS

1. Also Plutarch, *Lycurgus*, Chapter 22, and Thucydides (5. 70) recount that the
Lacedaemonians moved into battle slowly, to the beat and the music of numerous
pipers.

It has erroneously been concluded from this, however (Liers, p. 177), that the
Spartans held this pace until the actual clash and that they made no assault run as

the Athenians did. An approach march with music and in step can be reconciled completely with the fact that the actual attack was finally made on the double, as the nature—one might even say the psychology—of the situation demands.

Polybius, too, reports (4. 20. 6) that the ancient Cretes and Lacedaemonians had introduced in war, instead of the trumpet, "pipe and rhythm,"* that is, a measured piping or flute-playing.

2. On closer examination, one finds in the fragments of the Songs of Tyrtaeus, as Adolf Bauer has already correctly noted (*Ancient Greek Military Periods*, p. 242; 2d ed., p. 304), indications that the singer had a close formation in mind, especially in 10. 15 (Bergk ed.): "They fight while remaining at each other's side."* Other citations point, it is true, more toward individual combat, as in the *Iliad*, for example (the harangue to the Gymnetae at the end of Book 11), but the existence of tactical formations does not exclude single and multiple individual combats.

3. In the citizen's oath of the Athenians there was specifically expressed: "I will not leave a comrade behind with whom I stand in battle."*

To these citations Olsen, in his *Battle of Plataea (Schlacht bei Platää)* (Greifswald Program, 1903), p. 15, added the two following fine quotations: Sophocles' *Antigone*, verse 670, "would stand his ground in the storm of battle";* and Thucydides 2. 11. 9, speech of Archidamus, "Follow wherever any [of your officers] might lead you, reckoning good order and vigilance above everything else . . ."*

4. On the basis of a very careful assembling and comparison of the literary sources with the vase illustrations which have survived, Helbig tried very recently to prove that there existed in Greece (with the exception of Thessaly), until after the Persian wars, no cavalry at all, but that the "Knights,"* which were named and illustrated, were to be considered as mounted hoplites.[10] This question deals principally with a period previous to the start of my own study, but I can nevertheless not fail to remark that Helbig's evidence does not seem compelling to me and that there are numerous important points that can be used to counter his conclusion. Foremost of all, in principle, the concepts of cavalry and infantry are much too modern, that is, much too sharply drawn. In the third volume of this work we shall see that there were warriors on foot and mounted warriors to whom neither the word *infantry* nor *cavalry* applies. Furthermore, Helbig's concept of mounted infantry is for this reason disputable from the very start, and this is not perhaps just a simple contention over words; rather, these basic concepts govern the entire study. Helbig's interpretation of the scenes on the vase paintings, in particular, is repeatedly determined by the idea that, wherever horses and armed men are to be seen, one has only to choose as to whether it is a matter of infantrymen or cavalrymen. Whoever has studied sufficiently the nature of medieval knightly combat will find that the Greek vase illustrations often allow another interpretation than that which Helbig gives them; for example, when he interprets the battle scene in Figure 37, page 255, as showing that two mounted hoplites were ambushed and did not have enough time to dismount in order to fight, I would prefer to believe that they are surprised before they have time to mount up, whether it be for the purpose of fighting on horseback or of fleeing. Also the interpretation on page 188 does not seem acceptable to me, and likewise for several others.

Helbig's idea is that citizens on horseback, even with two horses, were levied for war in order to play the role of hoplites in the phalanx in case of battle, but after the battle they were to mount up and carry out the pursuit. That seems unacceptable to me. It might well have been that a man of means who was called out for service rode his horse in order to avoid marching, and then fought as a hoplite. And it may also have been true that the horse owners, after the decision in the phalanx combat, quickly ran to their horses, mounted up, and pursued the defeated enemy—although the concept of such a pursuit is never clearly shown in earlier Greek history and is hardly compatible with it. It is quite certain, however, that there was not a body of mounted hoplites organized by the state for this purpose.

On most occasions it is clear that the mounted warriors could contribute much more to the decision by not dismounting but attacking on horseback the enemy phalanx on its flank.

From the application of the modern concept of cavalry Helbig also arrives at the necessity (p. 169) for the riders to form up for common drills, and he is doubtful of the practicability of such drills. Very rightly so. But the pair of riders that each Attic naucrary had to provide definitely did not form a 96-man squadron; rather they were 96 individual riders, or, if one will, knights, who carried out common drills just as little as did the medieval knights.

It is entirely natural that these knights went into the phalanx as hoplites under certain circumstances. Medieval knights, too, often fought on foot, not only when conditions were not suitable for mounted combat, but also to give the other fighters on foot a greater morale boost. Just as such action is credited to the special fame of an Athenian rider,[11] we also find it in praise of knights of the fifteenth century (Vol. III, Book IV, Chapters 2 and 6). In the Persian Wars, where the few Greek mounted men would have been absolutely useless against the superior numbers of the Persians, it is obvious that the prominent Athenians fought in the ranks of the hoplites, and Helbig's conclusion (p. 160) that, since the Greeks at Marathon and Plataea used no cavalry, they did not have any, is not convincing.

To go into the details of Helbig's study is hardly necessary for us, since, though they also fall into our period, they belong more in the area of ancient relics. In this area the last word still awaits a new study. For, if I have not been able to accept Helbig's basic ideas and his positive solution, nevertheless he is right beyond doubt in saying that contradictions exist in the historical accounts, which have up to now remained unnoticed and unchallenged. His raising of the questions, his assembling of the widely spread material, and his perspicacious combining of these sources were in themselves a great service. The final solution, however, is still missing, and the puzzles have remained.

Particularly remarkable for our sensibilities is the statement of Pausanias 1. 18 (Helbig, p. 180) that there were statues of the Dioscuri in an Athenian temple with the masters on foot, their servants on horseback. Today that would be a topsy-turvy world.

NOTES FOR CHAPTER II

1. Adolf Bauer, Section 40, says three meters. On this point, see also below, the study on the *sarissae*.

2. H. Droysen, *Army Organization (Heerwesen)*, p. 24, cites several passages in which the harness is not named as a piece of equipment for the Spartans and considers it possible that they, in contrast to the other Greeks, did not wear any. That would be a far-reaching difference. Nevertheless, this opinion is certainly incorrect. Droysen himself cites a passage from Tyrtaeus in which armor is expressly named, and if one were inclined to conclude from the passage in Xenophon's *Anabasis* 1. 2. 16 that Cyrus' mercenaries wore no armor, that would also have to apply to all the Greeks represented among them.

3. H. Droysen, *Heerwesen*, p. 171, footnote, recommends using the word *phalanx* only with respect to foot soldiers armed with the

sarissa, whose particular combat position consisted in the "closeness of their formation in comparison with those in the rear."* I believe in holding fast, however, to the expression that has become quite common, which I think I can best establish with the definition given above. The basis therefore will gradually emerge as our study progresses. Droysen himself shows that the Greek usage is very indefinite and has varied.

4. The account of Isocrates (*Archidamus*, p. 99), which says the Spartans had conquered the Arcadians at Dipaea in *one* rank, which Duncker, 8:134, accepted, has been justifiably rejected by Droysen, p. 45, and Adolf Bauer, p. 243 (2d ed., p. 305), as rhetorical exaggeration. Droysen, with equal justification, also rejects the two ranks of Polyaenus 2. 1. 24.

5. Lysias, *Mantitheus* 16. 15. The speaker, Mantitheus, boasts: "There was an expedition to Corinth, and everyone knew ahead of time that it would be a dangerous undertaking. Although some were shirking back, I arranged it so that I might fight our enemies in the front line. And our phyle had the worst luck and suffered the worst losses among its own men. I quit the field later than that excellent man from Steiria who has been accusing everyone of cowardice."* For this fine quotation I am indebted to the book *Warfare of Antiquity* (*Das Kriegswesen des Altertums*), by Hugo Liers, p. 46.

6. Concerning the combination of Spartiates and Perioeci in the same military formation, see Bauer, paras. 18, 19, and 23, and, now at the center of a lively controversy, Kromayer, *Klio* 3 (1903): 177 ff., and Beloch, *Klio* 6:63. On this occasion the following splendid evidence of the importance of the first rank has come to light. Isocrates, *Panathenaicus* 180. 271, writes: "For in the campaign that the king led, they arranged them man by man in rank with themselves, and they also stationed some men in the first rank."*

7. Xenophon, *Cyropaedia* 6. 3. 25. For further information on this point, see below, Book II, Chapter V.

8. Xenophon, *Hellenica* 6. 2. 21.

9. Thucydides, too, reports that the Lacedaemonians, specifically, did not normally carry the pursuit far (5. 73). Helbig, "On the Original Period of the Closed Phalanx" (Über die Einführungszeit der geschlossenen Phalanx") *Sitzungs-Bericht der Bayerischen Akademie 1911*, believes, based on insufficient sources, that the Chalcidians formed the first phalanx.

10. "The Athenian *Hippeis*" ("Les *Hippeis* Athéniens"), by M. W.

Helbig, *Mémoires de l'Académie des Inscriptions et Belles-Lettres*, 1902, p. 37.

See also "Mounted Infantry in Antiquity" ("Berittene Infanterie im Altertum"), by Georg Friederici, *Neue Militärische Blätter*, Vol. 67, No. 11/12, 1905.

11. Lysias, *Mantitheus* 16. 13. Helbig, p. 239.

Chapter III
The Greek Army Strengths:
Conclusion

Establishing the tactical nature of the Greek armies gives us new points of departure for estimating their strengths. A panoply is a very expensive set of equipment; not every service-qualified citizen, by far, is in a position to provide himself with one. Each hoplite has, moreover, an unarmored man with him. Consequently, the phalanx was very much smaller than the number of citizens.

In Athens there had existed for a long time four classes categorized by wealth, of which the two higher ones served on horseback and the third—the zeugitae (small farmers), who had an income between 200 and 300 bushels (*metretes*) of grain, wine, or oil—served as hoplites. Before Athens had a fleet, the very significant lowest portion of the citizenry, the Thêtes, therefore, were completely free of any obligation for military service. We may nevertheless assume with certainty that the unarmored man who accompanied the hoplite was normally at that time also a citizen; most of the zeugitae probably did not own any slaves. When the Athenians later created a fleet and simultaneously their wealth in slaves increased, the Thêtes served on shipboard and the hoplites were accompanied by a trustworthy slave. Sparta, with Messenia, had almost twice as many inhabitants, but since only the ruling warrior caste performed military service—with the addition of the citizens, the Perioeci, in urgent situations, but excluding the serfs, the Helots—it did not field any more hoplites than Athens, that is, some 2,000 Spartiates and 3,000 Perioeci. Corinth and Thebes may have been able to put 1,500 to 2,000 in the field. Those are considerably smaller numbers than had been previously estimated, but a careful check of the historical account, taking into consideration all the prevailing circumstances and conditions, warrants our acceptance of the fact that those numbers cannot differ significantly from reality.

1. In view of the numbers that we arrived at in the first chapter, it seems remarkable that the naval service needed and levied so many more men than the army.
Today it is just the opposite. The Athenians at one time had a fleet of 170 ships in
service, requiring a normal force of 34,000 crew members to man them. Their
greatest land levy (in the year 431 B.C.) numbered only 16,000 hoplites—in fact,
quite certainly considerably fewer, since Thucydides gives the number on the levy
list, without any deductions for those falling out or even for the distant cleruchs. We
have seen, however, that a levy of 16,000 hoplites really means that some 32,000
men were moved out. Both levies, therefore, were of almost exactly the same
strength.

Of the 28,800 service-qualified Athenian citizens in the year 431 B.C., 1,200 served
on horseback, 1,600 as archers, 13,000 as field hoplites, and 13,000 remained,
among them two year-groups of recruits.

At the outbreak of the Peloponnesian War, therefore, the field army was made up
of over half of the adult service-qualified citizens. At that time Athens was at the
height of her power and opulence. One cannot assume that, at the time of the battle
of Marathon, her military power was already developed to such an extent. A
panoply was so expensive that even in 431 B.C. perhaps not even half of the citizens
were able to equip themselves in such a way with their own means, but this equipment was, as we shall see later, provided for a portion of the hoplites by the state. It
is not likely that this was already the case in the Persian Wars. We may therefore
assume that at that time only those citizens served as hoplites who were in a position
to provide their own panoply. For this point we have evidence in the class divisions
of the Athenians—the 500-bushel-men, the mounted men, the farmers (zeugitae)
and the day workers (Thêtes). The names indicate that, when these classes were
created the inhabitants of Attica still lived principally from agriculture; we must
nevertheless assume that in the fifth century there were simply four property classes, in which the city population, too, was included according to each man's means.
The classes no longer had any political significance—if they ever had any
otherwise—and they were hardly useful for the paying of taxes; it was in the military organization that they probably had their significance. In our sources no specific
obligation is shown for the highest class as such, but there were certain contributions, especially the outfitting of triremes (the state provided the hull), which were
directly charged to the richest. Since somebody who was not included on the list of
the highest class could certainly not take over such contributions, we will therefore
be permitted to regard this as the special characteristic of this class. In addition to
these contributions, those who were placed in the first class had the obligation, along
with those of the second class, of serving on horseback. The zeugitae had the obligation of maintaining their own hoplite equipment and serving with it. My assumption
that, in the earlier period, the Thêtes went along into the field unarmed is based
on the fact that Athens was already a democracy before she possessed a fleet, and
universal suffrage without universal military obligation is not conceivable. If a hoplite did not bring along his own attendant, be it son, brother, neighbor, or slave, his
precinct probably provided him a citizen as companion. We are to understand clas-
sification in the zeugitae class as meaning that the family was to furnish *one* man,
equipped.[1] It is impossible that the father of a farm family with several grown sons
would have been obligated to provide a panoply for each one. Providing one fully
equipped man meant sending not one, but two men.

If this concept is correct, then an Athenian hoplite army in 490 B.C. cannot have
included a half of the service-qualified Athenian citizenry, as in the year 431 B.C.,
but hardly a third, and probably only a fourth or fifth. Including the metics, therefore, the Athenians at Marathon had at the very most 8,000 hoplites, and probably
only some 5,000, accompanied by the same number of unarmored men.

The extent of the service obligation of the metics is uncertain. For our purposes that does not matter, since they were in any event called out in case of emergency and for home defense, and our estimate is concerned only with the possible maximum achievement.

Schenkl, in his "On the Attic Metics" ("De Metoecis Atticis"), *Wiener Studien* 1 (1879): 196, expressly rejects the opinion of Hermann, that citizens and metics had the same military service obligation. Thumser, too, in *Wiener Studien* 7 (1885): 62, claims that the metic hoplites before the time of Demosthenes, except in very unusual cases, were employed only in defense of the Attic homeland. And likewise Busolt, III:53.

2. The population of Laconia and Messenia has been estimated by Beloch at 230,000 persons— to wit, 9,000 Spartiates, 45,000 Perioeci, 176,000 Helots. I prefer to estimate the number of individuals somewhat higher, since I assume the relative number of adult men to be somewhat smaller than does Beloch. Furthermore, there always exist a greater number of men of an age for military service than actually move out into the field or are capable of moving out. In other respects, however, I agree completely with Beloch's estimate and can refer the reader to him for the details. Sparta was, according to him, capable of sending into the field a hoplite army of some 2,000 Spartiates and 3,000 Perioeci;[2] the unarmored men for this army came from the Helots.

These calculations fully validate a number from the sources handed down to us—a number that up to now has always been treated very cursorily. In the year 490 B.C., according to Herodotus 6. 120, the Spartans sent 2,000 men to the aid of the Athenians. That would, however, have been remarkably few if they had really had at Plataea, in addition to the ships' crews, 5,000 Spartiates and 5,000 Perioeci as hoplites. Now we realize that it was really the entire Spartiate levy that came to the aid of the Athenians and that Spartans, consequently, took the war very seriously. Of course, since Herodotus' strength estimates have no credibility in themselves, it may be that it is simply a question of coincidence here. It is also possible, however, that precisely the number 2,000, which was probably reported officially to the Athenians, was maintained in the oral tradition, whereas the number of Athenians and of Plataeans who marched out "with the whole body of the city drawn up as an army"* found no place in the legend. Later, perhaps in reply to a question by Herodotus, the total number may have been estimated so inaccurately by somebody or other having no knowledge of the situation, that a relatively much higher accomplishment is attributed to the village of Plataea than to Athens itself.

3. The resulting total for Sparta is mutually supported by our estimate for Athens. At that time Sparta was considered among the Greeks as clearly the strongest state militarily.[3] The Spartiates were warriors by profession and therefore qualitatively certainly superior to the citizen levies of the other areas. If at the time of the Persian Wars, however, Athens had already been capable of sending into the field 10,000 hoplites, exactly double the strength of the Spartan army, Sparta would not have been able to claim such unquestioned superiority. The assumption that the numbers were about equal and that the superiority of the Spartans lay in the excellence of the reigning warrior caste removes every difficulty. If Athens and Sparta were unable to raise more than 5,000, or at most 6,000, hoplites, then Corinth or Thebes, which controlled only very small land areas, certainly had no more than 1,500, or at most 2,000.

Notes for Chapter III

1. That seems to be proved by Plato in *Menexenus*, where it is indicated that the family decides which one shall go to war.

2. Adolf Bauer does not draw up any total figure, but does estimate (although he, too, considers the figures of Herodotus to be too high) that at Mantinea in 418 B.C. there were 3,584 Spartiates alone, for a total of about 4,300 field-service-qualified men (para. 23; 2d ed., p. 312). I cannot agree. It is true that Thucydides' figures are contestable, especially the *pentecostys* of 128 men; if one accepts them, however, it seems to me that there is no doubt that Thucydides intends to give the total strength of the Lacedaemonians and not just that of the Spartiates. But he does not indicate this limitation in any way; nor is there any conceivable reason why the ephors should have left all the Perioeci, except the Scyrites, at home at a time of such grave danger.

3. Thucydides 1. 18, "The Lacedaemonians were the leaders of their Hellenic allies, because their strength was superior."*

Chapter IV

The Persian Army

The Persian army was of a type completely opposite that of the Greek army; it was composed of mounted men and archers. Aeschylus, the only contemporary whose report on the Persian Wars is directly available to us, sings and speaks again and again (in his drama *The Persians*) of the combat of the spear against the bow.[1]

Even the Persian mounted men were armed with the bow.

The swords or short spears that are mentioned served only as auxiliary weapons.

Since the bow formed the principal weapon, the protective armor was only light—for the dismounted troops, probably only a shield of woven straw that the archer could place in front of himself while firing. "With pants and hats they go into battle," Aristagoras said of the Persian warriors in describing them to the Spartans. In another passage scale armor is mentioned,[2] but it was probably worn by only a portion of the mounted men.

It is not only the difference in arms, however, that distinguishes the Persians from the Greeks. The power of the phalanx rests, in addition to the courage and equipment of the individual soldier, on the steadfastness of the whole of the tactical formation. We have seen that, even when one side has a much larger number of warriors, they influence the decision not by their weapons, but through the fact that in the rear ranks of the phalanx they exercise a physical and moral pressure. The Persians do not form a tactical body; marksmen lend themselves but little to it. By their very nature they tend to spread out rather than to form a unit. Only a particularly highly developed skill can, consequently, make an intrinsic unit of them. Primarily, however, everything depends on the skill, the vigor, and the courage of the individual.

Marksmen cannot be employed in large masses against hoplites. If they are drawn up in a deep formation, the rearward ranks no longer have the capability of shooting effectively. If they spread out, before long their arrows will no longer be able to reach the enemy.

The Persian Empire was composed of the Persian national nucleus and the numerous subject peoples. The Persian kings drew no warriors from these latter groups. The Mesopotamians, Syrians, Egyptians, and inhabitants of Asia Minor were, for them, the unwarlike, tribute-paying masses, with the exception of the Phoenician and Greek sailors, who naturally manned the fleet. When Herodotus enumerates the huge mass of peoples who appeared in the Persian army, we consider that as pure fantasy. Persia itself, embracing present-day Persia, Afghanistan, Baluchistan, and large portions of Turkestan, was and still is today, for the most part, steppes and desert, with numerous small or fairly large oases and a few very large ones. Persians, Medes, and Parthians are branches of the same people, somewhat as Saxons, Franks, Swabians, Bavarians in medieval Germany. What held them together was not just their nationality but also their common religion, the revelation of Zarathustra. The truly warlike element was naturally the nomadic branches rather than the agricultural ones. It was probably with the nomads that the empire was originally established. As the Persians became masters of distant and rich civilized lands, they were gradually transformed from warlike shepherds to warlike rulers, or knights. We shall have to imagine that all the satraps from the Black Sea to the Red Sea were accompanied by large retinues of warlike, national Persian bodyguards, with whom they surrounded themselves and occupied important strongholds. With the help of tribute and goods which they received, they not only retained these groups, but they also added to them, according to the circumstances, with mercenaries from warlike tribes that in many instances had remained in the limits of the realm but were still half or even entirely independent. From Persia itself, however, more from the nomads than from the farmers, it was always possible to levy, recruit, and send out replacements and reinforcements.

The Persian Empire, in its foundation as in its structure, has its parallel 1,200 years later in the world empire that sprang up from another oasis land, that of the Arabian Bedouins, who, like the Persians, were held together by a new religion. The Persians in their time had as little tendency to form mass armies as did the Arabs later, for large masses cannot be moved over such great distances as are to be found in empires of such breadth. The Arabs, like the Persians, formed quality armies. To form an idea of the character of the Persian army, one would do well to supplement the reports of the Greek sources by considering the analogy of the Germanic and knightly military system: the Franks under the Merovingians, who occupied the rich Roman areas of Gaul with small units, while the main part of their people remained in place in the areas they had inherited, and the German knights, with whom the Saxon, Salic, and Hohenstaufen kings took Italy and held it under their rule. Any other differences that may have existed between the oriental and occidental political systems do not come into consideration here; what we have to consider is the character of the military profession, which with very small numbers is nevertheless able to maintain very extensive dominion.[3]

The work of each and the differences between the two armies are meaningfully described in the conversation that the Greeks report taking place between Xerxes and the banished Spartan King, Demaratus. The king of kings boasts that he has men in his bodyguard who can take on three Greeks at the same time. Demaratus, however, replies that the individual Spartans are just as courageous as other men but that their real strength lies in their joint steadfastness and that the law commands them to conquer or die standing together in rank and column. We stress this point specifically: the Greek hoplites form a closed tactical body, the Persian warriors do not.

The historical accounts of the Greeks concerning the Persians contain a basic contradiction. On the one hand the Persians are pictured as gigantic but very unwarlike masses that must be driven into battle with whiplashes. Then again, they appear as extremely brave and skillful warriors.[4] If both of these points—the mass as well as the warlike skill—are correct, the repeated victories of the Greeks would be inexplicable. Only one of the two can be right, and here it is clear that the superiority of the Persians is to be found not in numbers, but in quality.

The victory of the citizen armies over the professional army has been distorted in the Greek legend, which is our only source, into the victory of a small minority over a gigantic majority. This is a national psychological aberration that one finds again and again. The criterion of quality is too fine for the mass, which transforms it into the criterion of quantity. That is legend but not falsehood. For everybody who understands the difference between a professional army and a citizen army, the victory of the Greek citizens over the Persian knights is no less praiseworthy than is the victory of the few over the many in the legend. For the proper understanding from the viewpoint of military history, however, everything in this passage depends on the difference between legend and history. The concept of a Persian mass army is to be rejected completely. Nothing forces us to assume that the Persians had numerical superiority at all at Marathon and Plataea; it is completely possible, in fact even probable—in my opinion, certain—that the Greeks were stronger.

The Persians were professional warriors. Even the men who perhaps, for such a large war as this one against the Greeks, were levied from the shepherds and peasants of Persia to fill out the essentially knightly army were, after all, no popular levy, but rather the more warlike ones from the mass of the people. The Greeks, with the exception of the Spartiates, represented citizen levies that did not even have a strong military tradition. The heroic period was already long past, and the last generations had, it is true, seen many a quarrel between neighbors but had nevertheless brought up the mass of the people for peaceful occupations, as farmers, sailors, merchants, and artisans.

When I stated this opinion for the first time in my *Persian and Burgundian Wars*, it was rejected by many a scholar with a simple "impossible," without any further reason given, and it is of course only natural that a concept so deeply rooted as that concerning the strength of Xerxes' army is not given up easily. Because I foresaw this, I linked my study of the Persian Wars with that on the Burgundian Wars between Charles the Bold and the Swiss. Here we have exactly the same sequence of events. In repeated battles the army of citizens and farmers conquered the army of professional warriors (knights and mercenaries), but the popular accounts transformed that into a victory of the small minority over the great majority. From Granson and Mutter, however, a few army muster rolls for both sides have been handed down to us, and so we can prove from original sources that the supposed many hundred thousands of Charles the Bold were actually considerably fewer than the Swiss. By no means, therefore, can one banish such a changed concept with an "impossible." There is no reason for assuming that Herodotus and the Greeks should be given any more credence than the solid Swiss chroniclers, who have also been believed for centuries. Whoever doubts my evidence I request to reserve judgment until he has tested the proof of the Swiss legend. We have a Swiss account, that of Bullinger, which was written just about as long after the events as was that of Herodotus after the Persian Wars and therefore had remained unprinted. I copied the passage in question in my *Persian and Burgundian Wars* from the manuscript, so that one can study from it the character and the reliability of such an account. Just as I myself, by this methodological preliminary work, first came to complete certainty in dealing with the Greek accounts, I advise every scholar who wishes to plow further in this field to adopt this instrument before he entrusts his seeds to rocky soil. Unfortunately, I have not yet noticed, as I will add in this new edition, that any scholar has followed this advice.

NOTES FOR CHAPTER IV

1. Verse 25:   "Those who subdue with the bow, and the horsemen"*

Verse 82:   "He leads spear-subduing Ares against men famed for the spear."*

Verse 133:   "Whether it is the drawing of the bow or the strength of the spear-headed lance that has prevailed."*

Verse 226:   "Is it the bow-stretching arrow that is strong in their hands? Not at all: they have lances for close fights and shields to use as armor."*

Verse 864:   "Those who subdue with the bow."*

Herodotus says the same thing in 9. 18 and 9. 49. Also a consecration formula of Simonides (fragment 143, Bergk) states: "These bows which are now finished with tearful warfare lie under the roof of Athena's temple; often, mournfully, in the melee, they were bathed in the blood of the man-destroying horsemen of Persia."*

Likewise, fragment 97, Bergk, p. 452. Colonel Billerbeck in his study "Susa" calls attention to the fact that the reliefs show the principal weapon of the Iranians to have been not the bow, but the lance. Not only the specific statements of the Greeks, but also, as we shall see, the course of events, point indisputably to the bow. We must leave it to the specialists to clarify the reliefs.

2. Herodotus 7. 61 and 9. 22.

3. The nature of the Persian Empire as a feudal nation has recently been studied and described still further by Georg Husing in an essay "Porusatis and the Achamandish Feudal System" ("Porusatis und das achamanidische Lehenswesen"), *Berichte des Forschungs-Instituts für Osten und Orient in Wien*, Vol. 2, 1918.

4. "The Persians were not inferior in either courage or bodily strength, but being unarmed and untrained, they were not the equals of their enemies in respect to skill"* (Herodotus 9. 62, on the battle of Plataea).

Chapter V

The Battle of Marathon

On the basis of the previously discussed relationships, we estimate the Persian army in 490 B.C. at about the same strength as the Athenians or perhaps somewhat smaller—that is, at about 4,000 to 6,000 warriors, including 500 to 800 mounted men. And in addition, as with the Greeks, there was a large number of unarmored men. This estimate may at first seem arbitrary, but one must realize that the strength of one army always permits a certain conclusion as to the strength of the other, as soon as one has an idea of the quality of the warriors on the two sides, and the march of events will soon give us still more evidence. The Persian army came across the Aegean Sea on a large fleet, first took and destroyed the small city of Eretria on Euboea, and then crossed over to Attica. The Athenians still had no fleet that could have stood up to the Persian one, and so they could meet the Persian attack only on land.

The mission of the Persian commanders Datis and Artaphernes was, first, to debark the army at some point on the Athenian coast, and then to attack and conquer the city of Athens itself. If an Athenian army should appear in the open countryside, then it would first have to be defeated and driven back.

Under the guidance of Hippias, the former ruler of Athens, who had been banished twenty years earlier, the Persians chose the plain of Marathon for their debarkation area. It is at a distance of about nineteen miles from Athens and was unguarded, since the Athenians could not know where the Persians would land. If the Athenian army was already assembled, it was in any event in or near Athens. Even though the Athenians had a very careful lookout organization and the start of the debarkation was immediately reported to the city, it still necessarily took at least eight hours before the army had arrived at Marathon, drawn up for battle, and prepared for the attack. In this time the Persian army, too, was able to ready itself for battle. Furthermore, the Marathon plain was

72

surrounded by mountains and had only a few approaches, which the Persians were able to occupy easily with the first archers to be debarked, in order thereby to delay still longer the entry of the Athenians onto the plain.

In Athens there is said to have been doubt as to whether they should give battle against the enemy outside the city or else allow the situation to lead to a siege. The majority opinion, that a battle should be risked, won out. Word was sent to Sparta, asking for a reinforcing expedition.

The high command was entrusted to Miltiades, a man from a rich patrician family, who, like the Venetian noblemen in the fourteenth and fifteenth centuries, as an Athenian citizen possessed a principality in the land of the foreigners, on the Thracian Chersonese, and had gotten to know the Persians there. He had even been a subject of the Persian King and had had to flee before him to Athens.

We know what the superiority of the Persians consisted of. If it came to a battle in the open country, then there was no doubt that the Persian mounted men, placed on the wings, would attack the Athenian phalanx on its two flanks, while the archers showered arrows on them in the front. Unable to make a well-ordered attack on the archers because of the flank attack, the phalanx, hardly coming to a real battle, would have had to succumb to the combined arms of the enemy. The mission of the Athenian leadership was to offset this tactical weakness of the single-arm Athenian army. If one studies the terrain of Marathon and compares the reports of the battle with it, one can recognize with certainty just how Miltiades succeeded in carrying out his mission.

Cornelius Nepos, who drew his information from Ephorus, tells us in his *Life of Miltiades* that the Athenians had drawn up in a narrow area at the foot of the mountains, where they had felled trees so that they would be protected, both by the mountains and by the trees, from being surrounded by the enemy mounted troops.[1]

This description corresponds so closely to the circumstances that we would have to imagine something similar, even if it had not come down to us in such a positive way. Even the place in the small plain of Marathon that corresponds best to the Nepos/Ephorus account can be detected without difficulty on a special map by an eye practiced in matters of military history; it is the entrance to a small side valley that is today called Vrana. This valley is about 1,000 meters wide at a distance of 150 meters from its entrance. For a

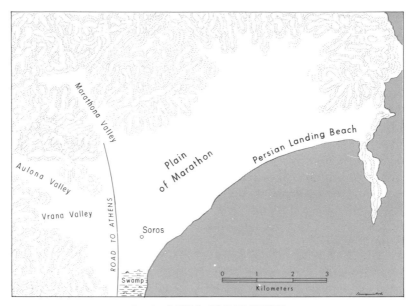

Fig. I   BATTLE OF MARATHON

hoplite phalanx of some 6,000 men, that is too wide; however, the space was narrowed down further by the cuttings. A trail passable for infantry leads from Athens over the mountains directly into this valley. The Vrana valley forms a flanking position for the highway, the only one that leads into the plain of Marathon, so that the enemy army could not march against Athens without first having driven the Athenian army out of the Vrana valley.

Herodotus tells us that the Athenians drove down on the enemy with a charge of 8 *stadia* (4,800 feet, or 1,500 meters). Such a run is a physical impossibility: a heavily equipped unit can cover at the most 400 to 500 feet (120 to 150 meters) at a run without completely exhausting its strength and falling into disorder. Individual trained runners and primitive peoples are, of course, capable of covering very great distances at a run, even when burdened, but the Athenians at Marathon were no longer a primitive people but a bourgeois-farmer general levy. According to the Prussian regulations, running with full field equipment is not permitted for more than two minutes, or 330 to 350 meters. The Athenian army, however, did not even consist of troops who were in training or of youths who exercised in the gymnasium, but of the mass levy of citizens, farmers, charcoal burners, and fishermen, up to the age of forty-five or fifty; and a closed mass runs with much more difficulty than an individual person. When a modern historian uses the expression, the Athenians "supposedly" ran 8 *stadia*, that is just the same as if he repeated a source report to the effect that, in one day, they "supposedly" marched 60 miles. When another one states the opinion that the immense excitement of the battle allows a completely different effort of the nerves and muscles than the normal practice on the drill field, that is very true, but it still does not make it possible for a phalanx to run almost a mile.

A battle from more modern military history may provide us an example of this. In the Danish war of 1864 a Prussian detachment that had been pushed far forward, under Captain von Schlutterbach near Lundby in Jutland, was attacked by a superior force of Danish infantry (3 July). The Prussians took up a defensive position. At a distance of 400 paces the Danes, with a loud "hurrah," took up a run. "But," the account of the battle states,[2] "a body of troops cannot continue for 400 paces at a forced speed that spontaneously develops into a full run, in a situation leading to hand-to-hand combat with the enemy. The individual runs out of breath, and after 100 paces the company is forced to halt. The ensuing minutes, until they can again move forward, are most painful."

"The fabulous run should not bother anybody; Artemis has given them the strength for the 'running with a shout'* and as a token of their gratitude receives the sacrifice of a live goat," a philologist has explained, and he warns against rejecting, through lack of understanding and of goodwill, the fact that simple trust in God and in one's own virtue has given the victory, contrary to all predictions stemming from little faith. This viewpoint, too, is correct in its way; particularly in the Middle Ages, in the lives of the saints and the accounts of the Crusades, the world, and consequently war also, are full of miracles, and one would be very loath, too, to cast aside the romantic style of recounting history. But whoever wishes to explore the history of the art of war in a critical fashion may implore for himself the assistance of Saint George, or even, if he prefers, that of the divine Artemis and of Apollo—but he must banish them from his research. This running pace is the decisive point for the historical understanding of the battle on which Greek freedom, and with it all of modern culture, rests. Through the "8 *stadia*" the location of the battle and with it also the tactical development and the bases for victory and defeat must, first of all, necessarily be established. We must therefore consider ourselves lucky to have here a point on which a simple objective test can give us complete certainty, independently of all doubtful witnesses and untrustworthy chroniclers. The objective test shows, however, that neither a Greek phalanx nor any other close-order battle line ever ran 1½ kilometers or was able to run that distance.[3] Herodotus' account rests on some misunderstanding, and this misunderstanding will not even remain a puzzle for us but will soon be explained.

In the middle of the plain of Marathon rises an artificial hill, the "*Soros*," which has been established, through modern excavations, as being the grave of the Athenians killed at Marathon. Thucydides (2. 32) tells us explicitly that, on other occasions, the Athenians had buried their fallen warriors at home but that, because of the special honor involved, the dead of Marathon were buried on the battlefield. There is no doubt that Herodotus himself stood beside or atop this burial mound, about 12 meters high, and observed the battlefield from that position. Exactly 8 *stadia* from this mount, in the ring of mountains enclosing the Marathon plain, is the mouth of the Vrana valley.

It is hard to consider as a simple coincidence the fact that on the terrain here we actually find exactly the 8 *stadia* that are also mentioned in Herodotus' account. The Athenians stood in the Vrana valley; 8 *stadia* beyond the valley lies the mound with the remains of their dead; according to the battle of Herodotus, they stormed forward 8 *stadia*. The battle, then, extended up to this point. The Athenians did not carry their dead back to the position where the first clash occurred, but brought them forward to the point where the last one of the dead lay, to the point to which the pursuit had gone, where the victory was completed. Here, in the middle of the plain, visible from all sides, they erected the high burial mound. Here, too, Herodotus looked over the field and had the account of the battle given to him: Up to this point, 8 *stadia* from that valley, the Athenians stormed forward—as he understood it, in the attack; as it was really meant, through the battle and in the pursuit.

Herodotus goes on to tell us how the Athenians and Persians had stood opposing each other for three days before the actual battle started. The Athenians who gave him that information had not been able to give him a reason for it, or rather, they had only too good a reason: Miltiades did not bear the real high command; it was borne in common by the then *strategoi*, who, according to the law, commanded in turn, each for a day. They were agreed, however, to turn the high command over voluntarily to Miltiades; nevertheless, he waited, in order to receive the full honor of the victory, for the day on which the command fell to him by the law.

We have here again a psychological trait that we shall encounter
again and again in the process of our research into military history.
The factual motives are too fine, too hard to understand, too unin-
teresting for the legend, which replaces them by personal motives.
For us, however, the factual relationships are not difficult to recognize. What we may accept from the legend without hesitation
—something which did not need to be invented—is the fact that the
enemy armies stood facing each other for several days before joining battle. In doing so the Athenians lost nothing; they were able to
supply themselves in their own country without difficulty, they increased their countrymen's courage when these soldiers saw that
the Persians did not dare to attack them, and they were expecting
reinforcements from the Spartans. It was completely impossible
that Miltiades should order the start of the battle of his own free
will without awaiting the arrival of the Spartans. It is therefore out
of the question that the attack should have been launched by the
Athenians; it must have been initiated by the Persians.

Now, I think, the overall picture of the battle becomes recognizable. As soon as the news had arrived that the Persians had landed
on the plain of Marathon, Miltiades put the Athenian army in
march and led it into the Vrana valley, which has a direct connection over the mountains with the capital. Here in the Vrana valley,
a short distance behind the mouth of the valley, in such a manner
that the mountains still covered the two flanks and with the additional protection provided by abatis, he drew up his army, or had
it pitch camp in such a way that it could take up position at the
first report of an enemy approach march. Since the valley was still
too wide for the small Athenian army, despite the abatis,[4] Miltiades
was not able to give the phalanx the desired depth throughout, but
made the center weaker and the two wings stronger, so that, even
when they moved out from their covered position, they would be
able to oppose possible flank attacks from the Persian cavalry. The
best and most courageous of the unarmored men were presumably
sent out onto the heights on the right and left, in order to put
pressure on the Persian cavalry with arrows, stones, and javelins.
The high ground covering the left flank rises only very slightly, as
I was able to see for myself during a visit in 1911, but it is so covered with scattered boulders as to be completely impassable for
mounted men. The actual road from the plain of Marathon toward
Athens goes southward rather close to the beach and along a
swamp, paralleling the front of the Athenian formation at a short
distance. The Persians could not move out of the plain of

Marathon without first having driven off the Athenians. They could not march along the actual highway, where the Athenians would have driven into their columns from the flank. They were also unable to use one of the paths leading out toward the north, and not even the lateral valley of Marathona, since they would always be running the risk that, when a part of their army was engaged in the mountains, the other part would be attacked by the Athenians while in march.[5] The Marathona valley was, furthermore, supposed to be blocked by the Athenians at a narrow spot in order to prevent the Persians from being able by this route to fall upon their rear in the Vrana valley. The Persians therefore had only the choice of either giving battle to the Athenians on terrain chosen by the Athenians or of embarking again and attempting a landing at another place. This too, however, would have been very dangerous. Being as close as they were, the Athenians were in a position to fall on the Persian army during the embarkment; and if they did perhaps successfully accomplish a landing once again in another place, could not the Athenians once more find a position in their so highly compartmented terrain that would offer them similar advantages for the battle as did the Vrana valley? The Persian generals must have fallen into strong doubt and perhaps quarreled with one another as to what they should do, since it does seem to be true that they deliberated for several days. The decision that finally prevailed was to attack the Athenians where they stood, at least before the Spartans, too, should have arrived.

This decision would have been extremely absurd if, as is usually accepted, the Persians had been numerically very superior to the Greeks. In this case the thing for them to do would have been to divide their army in order to fix the Athenians in the Vrana valley with half of it, while with the other half, covered by the first, they enveloped the Athenians either by land or, with the help of the fleet, by sea, thereby maneuvering them out of their position. This expedient for use in the face of too strong an opposing position is so obvious that one is forced to conclude, by the same token, that the Persians' failure to do so means they were too weak. What we formerly decided in an overall way from the general circumstances—namely, that the Persians could not possibly have been significantly stronger than the Athenians numerically—is borne out here by the positive train of events. Against a superior army the position of the Athenians in the Vrana valley would have been useless; numbers and position always have a mutual effect on each other. The Persians took the bull by the horns, because there was nothing else for them to do. Up to that time the Greeks had never yet been able to stand up against the Persian warriors. Consequently, one could risk it. Miltiades allowed the enemy to approach his defensive position, and at the moment when the storm of arrows was becoming effective—that is, at 100 to 150 paces[6]—the entire hoplite phalanx surged forward and hurled itself on the enemy at the double.

The running pace had the double purpose of strengthening the weight of the impact, both physically and from the morale point of view, and of outrunning the rain of arrows. The weak center, it is true, where the rear ranks did not exercise sufficient pressure, wavered under the hail of Persian arrows and fell back, but the two deeper flank columns stayed at the run and were face to face with the enemy even before the Persian cavalry was able to hold them up by a flanking attack. Presumably the protective terrain obstacles stretched out so far on the right and the left of the Athenians that only a very short space remained to be covered on the open plain. The speed of the approach and the depth of the formation supplanted what may have been lacking in the way of natural flank protection, and as soon as the Athenian hoplites were in hand-to-hand contact with the Persian archers, the latter, with their much less effective protective armor, were lost. Although as brave men they may have fought on for a certain time, they were not able to withstand the weight of this attack for long. Even the archers in the center, victorious initially, could do nothing more when they were pressed from both sides, and once they had turned tail, as the rush of the general flight poured out onto the open plain, then the cavalry no longer possessed the capability, even in the open field, of redressing the battle. One might imagine that well-organized, disciplined squadrons under skillful leaders might still have been able to bring the battle to a standstill by a resolute charge, but the continuation of this study will show—the battles of Charles the Bold against the Swiss are particularly instructive in this connection—that knightly mounted men, as the Persians were, are not capable of this. He who hesitated too long was surely lost. Everybody rushed toward the ships. Since the northern corner of the bay, where the Persian ships undoubtedly lay at anchor, is about two miles from the battlefield, the mass of the Persians did, in fact, succeed in reembarking. The pursuit, as we may conclude from Herodotus, extended 8 *stadia* from the Vrana valley, almost a mile, as far as the *Soros*. Then Miltiades assembled his army again and led it forward against the ships. We are told of a battle beside the ships. Between the two combat actions there must have been a considerable pause, during which the Persians were able to launch and board their ships, for the Greeks were able to seize and hold only seven triremes. We hear nothing of numerous prisoners or horses that might have fallen into their hands. If the Athenians had pursued the Persians up to the ships without a break, the spoils would have had to be much greater. But it is extremely difficult after a victory to assemble troops again and move them out in such an immediate pursuit. It is a brilliant proof of the personal strength and effectiveness of Miltiades that there was a second battle, at the ships, at all. The losses of the Athenians amounted to 192 killed, to which number we shall have to add several hundred wounded, since men who were so well armored as the Athenian hoplites were no doubt seldom killed outright by the Persian arrows. The casualties of the Athenians in killed and wounded, by our present-day estimates, may therefore have still amounted to something like 1,000 men, an indication that Marathon was no mere skirmish but a very hard-fought battle.

Concerning the losses of the Persians we have no reliable figure.

The figure of Miltiades as a field commander stands giant-like in the early annals of world military history. The most complete and rarest form of battle leadership that the art of war has evoked up to the present day, the defensive-offensive combination, is found here, in the simple lines of the classical work of art of the first great military event in our study. What perspicacity in his choice of the battlefield, what self-control in awaiting the enemy attack, what authority over the masses, over a proud, democratic citizens' levy, to be able to hold them fast in the chosen position and then to lead them forward to the attack at the double at the decisive moment! It will not be too rash for us to imagine how Miltiades addressed his fellow citizens before the battle, showing them that they were protected by the mountains against the enemy cavalry, ordering them to stand fast under the Persian arrows until he should give the signal, and how he then placed himself on horseback in the middle of the phalanx, with every eye directed toward him, to choose the moment to raise his arm holding the spear and to call out the command that was then echoed and spread by the trumpet call. Everything was geared to this moment—not a minute too early, for then the Athenians would have reached the enemy breathless and disordered; not a minute too late, for then too many of the enemy arrows would already have struck and the large number of falling and hesitating men would have slowed up and finally broken the power of the assault, which had to fall on the enemy line like an avalanche if it was to give victory.

We shall have further occasion to discuss many a similar situation, but never a greater one.

Excursus

1. The detailed basis for my concept of Marathon is contained in my *Persian and Burgundian Wars*. Since the appearance of that book, however, our information on two important points has either been corrected or enlarged. Only now has it been established that the *Soros* is actually the grave of the Athenians,[7] something that at that time was still so doubtful that I did not risk referring to it. Furthermore, a newer topographical map has shown that the maps I used were inaccurate.[8] That is, on the earlier maps the mouth of the Vrana valley was shown to be so wide that it did not seem to offer the presumed flank protection for a small army, and I had therefore had to place the position of the Athenians farther back in the valley, where a lateral valley (Aulona) branches off. Now that it is established that the Vrana valley, 150 meters from its mouth, is only about 1,000 meters wide, it appears well suited for the position of the Athenians, and it has supporting documentary evidence in the fact that the mouth of the valley is exactly 8 *stadia* distant from the *Soros*. I made this correction in the *Historische Zeitschrift*, Vol. 65, 1890. In a few details the overall picture of the battle has become even clearer to me since then. The basic features, however, have remained the same.

2. Herodotus expressly states that the Persians had built for the expedition special ships for the horses and had landed on the plain of Marathon because they thought they could make good use of their cavalry there. That can hardly have been fabricated of whole cloth, and so the Persians did have mounted men. On the other hand, Herodotus makes no mention at all of cavalry in the battle itself, and neither from him nor from later writers do we hear anything at all of captured horses, which, as a prized possession, would certainly have been worthy of mention and would necessarily have been long remembered by the Athenian people by virtue of their offspring.

But since it is very complicated to embark horses aboard ships, it does not appear entirely credible that the Persians should have completely finished doing so before the Athenians arrived at the ships. One might therefore conclude that the Persians, recognizing that they would not be able to use their cavalry against the position of the Athenians, had left them back near the ships and had perhaps embarked them in advance, just in case the outcome of the battle should be unfavorable. Against this concept, however, stands the idea that the Persian leaders cannot have considered an attack by the Athenians from their position as entirely impossible and might well have estimated that the feared cavalry, even if it was kept toward the rear of the plain, behind the archers, would still have a certain morale effect on the Athenians and would serve as a reserve. The surprising and overwhelming weight of the Athenian drive brought this estimate to naught, so that the mounted men had, in fact, no effect on the battle. The fact that the Athenians did not capture any horses is, nevertheless, not inexplicable. Several hours may have passed before they were again formed up and moved out for the attack on the ships, and the Persians may themselves have killed the horses that they could not carry away.

3. Pausanias, 1. 32. 3, reports that there were also burial mounds at Marathon for the Plataeans and slaves: "The slaves fought for the first time."*

This report is probably not very reliable. Nevertheless, it is possible that in many cases the hoplites took with them into the field as helpers not another citizen, but a trusted and skillful house slave, and that also many of these were posted on the mountains and were killed there by Persian arrows.

4. Of great importance in the reconstruction of the battle is the rather long pause between the engagement in the Vrana valley and the fight at the ships, for that is the only explanation for the escape of the rest of the Persians and of most of the ships. One might perhaps contend that only a short time would have been necessary in order to assemble the phalanx, set it in march again, and move three kilometers. Basically this *requires* only a short time—certainly; but it was not so quickly carried out. After the climax of the encounter, the full flight of the Persians across the plain, and with the first stopping for breath, the condition and mood of the Athenians was probably something like the way Frederick described his soldiers, when, after the victory at Soor, he tried for the first time to set a direct pursuit in motion. "My cavalry," he recounted later to Landgrave Charles of Hesse, "halted not far from the enemy rear guard. I hastened forward and shouted: 'March on, forward, at them!' I was greeted with 'Vivat Viktoria' and endless shouts. I continued to shout 'March on,' and nobody wanted to march. I became angry, I beat, I struck, I bawled them out—and I think I know something about bawling men out when I'm angry; but I was unable to move this cavalry a single step forward. They were drunk with joy and simply did not hear me." Miltiades, too, no doubt had great difficulty reassembling the Athenian citizens who, first of all, were concerned either with their dead and wounded, or with the loot from the fallen Persians, or who were completely wrapped up in their jubilation; and without the hope of gaining still more booty at the ships, there would probably have been no chance at all of a second combat. In any event, it is only natural to assume that a rather long pause occurred between the two phases of the battle.

5. A new hypothesis about Marathon has recently been published by W. Schilling in *Philologus* 54 (1895): 253. Schilling bases his theory on the reported massive superiority of the Persians in numbers. Despite their size they did not dare attack the Athenians. But their numerical advantage, according to Schilling, allowed them to reembark by posting in the middle of the plain, for the protection of the embarkment, a corps which was still twice as strong as the Greeks, i.e., 20,000 men, but without cavalry. This covering force was the formation that the Athenians attacked at the place where the *Soros* was later erected, defeating them and killing 6,500 of their number.

Even if this assumption were correct, it still would not explain why the Persians left their covering force in the plain without cavalry. If one has cavalry, one places it where it can best be used, and nowhere could it have been of such good use to the Persians as precisely here.

The only objectively reliable conclusion is the opposite one: since it is expressly reported that the Persians chose the plain of Marathon for their landing because of their cavalry, and since this report seems credible in relation to what is known of the Persians' tactics elsewhere, the presence of a cavalry force must form one of the basic assumptions for the reconstruction of the battle. If the Persians had cavalry, however, then the battle cannot have taken place in the plain, since the Athenian phalanx would have had great difficulty in winning it and there would necessarily be some mention of the cavalry action. Consequently, the battle took place on terrain that was not passable for the mounted men.

A further weakness in the Schilling hypothesis is the fact that one cannot understand why the Persians reembarked a portion of their army. If they drew up a covering force at the *Soros*, nothing would have been simpler than to have the force that was disengaged move directly forward on the road through the Mesogaea toward Athens. Then the Athenians would have had to move out immediately from their flanking position in the Vrana valley.

6. A certain relationship with the Schilling hypothesis is shown in another, which was published at the same time by N. W. Macan in his *Herodotus* (London, 1895) and with which E. B. Bury agreed in the *Classical Review*, Vol. 10, 1896. Macan agrees with the opinion of Duncker and Busolt (the latter has, however, in the meantime,

in the second edition of his *Greek History* [*Griechische Geschichte*], published in 1895, changed his concept and accepted mine), but he modifies it in one important respect.

Macan claims that the Persians, recognizing that the Athenians could not be attacked in the Aulona valley, intended to march off toward Athens through the southerly pass and that they were attacked on the plain by the Athenians during this movement. The *Soros* was then erected at approximately the place where the Athenian center gave way. He thinks that the Persians were not attacked on the flank, however, or not even really struck by surprise, but that they had prepared themselves for the possibility of an attack and had also had enough time to establish an orderly formation. According to him, this southerly part of the plain was not suitable for cavalry, and the Persians had also perhaps reembarked most of their mounted men, since they would have been of no use to them on the overland march. And it was for this reason that the cavalry played no role in the battle.

The following points can be argued against this theory:

(a) If the Persians were prepared for the possibility of a battle, why did they embark a portion of their troops? If they considered them superfluous for a victory, why had they brought them along?

(b) It would be doubly incomprehensible that the Persians would have embarked their cavalry, of all things. Their strength lay in their cavalry; they had to make a flank march over an open plain across the enemy front. If ever cavalry was needed, it was precisely here.

(c) Why the terrain here is supposed to have been unfavorable for cavalry is completely inconceivable and it is, moreover, neither substantiated nor explained with a single word by the author. The fact that there is a brook on the right flank, and a swamp on the left, does not come into consideration, since the space between the two obstacles still amounts to more than three kilometers.

(d) If the Persians had risked a flank march along the front of the Athenian position, the Athenians would certainly have attacked them and would probably have conquered them, even if they sought to have their cavalry cover them. The Athenians would naturally have delayed the attack until the main body of the Persians was already engaged in the pass, since this portion of the army was certainly a sure prey to them after they had first overcome and destroyed the last third, with the cavalry. For this very reason it is completely unthinkable that the Persians should have made such a movement and, what is more, have moved away their cavalry in advance. They were no longer in a position to reembark without danger, since the Athenians were so close, and under no circumstances could they leave the plain by land without first having driven the Athenians out of their position. Consequently, after some hesitation, they decided on the direct attack.

7. Later I learned of the book *Herodotus, Historian of the Median Wars* (*Hérodote, Historien des guerres médiques*), by Amédée Hauvette (Paris, 1894), which forces us to a renewed investigation of the run of 8 *stadia*. My explanation rests on the assertion that such a run is a physical impossibility, and in arriving at that conclusion I based my case on the provisions of the Prussian regulations. Hauvette (p. 261) counters my argument in the following manner:

"These provisions, which are no doubt very useful when it is a question of training young soldiers, also exist in our army; but they are far from corresponding to what one can ask of men who are strong and well trained, as the Athenians were. The proof of this lies in the fact that Captain of Artillery de Raoul—adopting, it is true, a new method of marching and of double time—recently obtained extraordinary results: the platoon that he commanded in the large-scale maneuvers of the XI Army Corps in 1890 managed to cover as much as 15 kilometers at double time, with arms and equipment. See an article by Dr. Felix Regnault in the periodical *La Nature*, No. 1052, 29 July 1893."

If one compares these two statements, the contradiction appears irreconcilable. I assert: Such a large, closely ordered mass of hoplites as the one that fought at Marathon cannot run any farther than 100 to 150 paces (double-time paces—i.e., 150 to 200 marching paces) without becoming exhausted and disorganized. Hauvette replies: "Captain Raoul, with his platoon, covered 15 kilometers (that is, 24,000 marching paces) at a run with weapons and equipment." That is not the only thing, however, that separates us. Basically, Hauvette rejects the objective-type analysis with the help of which I have sought to check the historical account of the Persian Wars. A considerable portion of his book is directed against my *Persian and Burgundian Wars*. Hauvette does not recognize the proof that I claimed to adduce from an analogy with the Swiss popular account, particularly the Bullinger report on Granson and Murten, to the effect that an account like that of Herodotus is worthy of only very little credence. On the contrary, Hauvette considers Herodotus both subjectively and objectively as generally trustworthy and sees the task of the scholar as consisting only of correcting possible individual errors, mistakes, and contradictions that have crept into the account. He applies these principles with consummate erudition and great perspicacity, and although he by no means completely rejects objective considerations, nevertheless he puts less trust in them than in the written word of the historical account.

In this respect, it is correct that objective-type analysis easily leads one into error. It is a very difficult procedure, even in simple questions, since even the expert is seldom familiar with all the circumstances that, in other periods and among other peoples, exerted or could have exerted an influence on events, to say nothing of the fact that experts are very often prejudiced in their various theories and consequently arrive at different, even opposite, conclusions.

The basis for all historical knowledge always remains the positive statements of contemporary sources or of sources close to the contemporary ones. But the farther the art of historical interpretation has progressed, the more it has become convinced that even contemporary reports are often falsified and clouded by fantasies of every type, and that in cases where the available material is not sufficient to permit checking one source against the other, objective-type interpretation remains the last resort. It is only a matter of following through thoroughly and of acquiring so much special knowledge of the subject that one can be certain of not being led astray by a simple false analogy. Even Hauvette, in fact, exercises objective interpretation by citing Raoul/Regnault against the Prussian regulations, but in doing so he falls into a basic paradox. He rejects the objective-type interpretation carried out as a matter of basic principle, while applying it himself with respect to the facts that he has adopted so casually and coincidentally. This kind of half-objective interpretation naturally serves no useful purpose, but only leads one into error. In this case it would be better simply to repeat the sources naïvely. In Hauvette's case particularly, this point can be made clearly. Consequently, I shall take up, below, several more of his statements. First of all, the question of the 8-*stadia* run.

Hauvette refers to an article by Regnault in the popular journal *La Nature* of 29 July 1893. Since then a book on this subject, *Methods of Marching* (*Comment on marche*), by Regnault and de Raoul, with an introduction by M. Marey (Paris: Henri Charles-Lavauzelle, 188 pp.) has appeared, thoroughly treating the whole subject.

In this book Major Raoul claims that, in the winter of 1889-1890, he trained a platoon of the 16th Infantry Regiment so thoroughly in three months that it covered 20½ kilometers in 1 hour and 46 minutes and, after a rest of 2 hours, returned over the same route in 3 hours and 5 minutes. Each man was carrying his rifle, his saber, 100 rounds of ammunition, and rations. The route was not level. General Fay inspected the platoon; it showed no fatigue.

Two days later the same platoon covered 11 kilometers cross-country with field equipment under the eyes of General Colonieu in 80 minutes. Immediately after their arrival the soldiers carried out target practice and beat all their rivals.

In other units this training was imitated, and a Captain Fay wrote to Raoul that on the ninth day he had already covered with his company 7 kilometers in 45 minutes.

Raoul is of the opinion that an army that goes about its marching flexibly and gradually can attain on a good road the rate of 5 minutes to the kilometer from the third kilometer on and can maintain this pace for several hours.

The Prussian double-time, which I used as a point of departure, is based on 165 to 175 meters per minute, and consequently some 6 minutes to the kilometer. Raoul's running pace is still a sixth faster and equals the speed of a horse at a brisk trot.

If it is possible for modern soldiers to run at this pace for several hours, why should the Athenians not have been able to do so for 9 minutes?

Why, however, does the Prussian physical exercise regulation prescribe that troops may not run more than 2 minutes under full pack?

First of all, the results attained by Captain Raoul are to be accepted with a certain degree of skepticism.

He himself points out of what immeasurable importance it would be for the conduct of war in the future if troops were capable of the running and marching accomplishments promised by him. It has often been said, and with good reason, that wars are won with the legs. The invention of modern rifles would be less significant for the revolution of the art of war than soldiers who could cover more than 4½ miles in three-quarters of an hour and could continue at such a pace for many hours and days. All the governing concepts of the present concerning strategic operations would have to be completely revised if Raoul's idea is correct. Why then, does the French army not introduce the Raoul march method? It would mean certain victory over every enemy. The tests were made as far back as 1890 and are supposed to have proved themselves before the eyes of generals. The suspicion arises that, after all, certain self-delusions are at play in Major Raoul's case, illusions that can so often be observed with inventors. His results are not verified for us by neutral third parties, but only by himself and his colleagues.

Captain Raoul's unit was no regiment, not even a company, but a single platoon of thirty-four men, presumably selected men from the entire regiment. The training period was three months.

The possible performance of such an elite unit establishes absolutely no standard for the capabilities of a large mass. It is not, however, simply a matter of running but also of the necessity for the phalanx to reach the enemy in perfect order, with the fighting strength of the men undiminished—and therefore not out of breath. The performance of the group is not dependent on the best runners, but on the worst ones. If the running pace were carried so far that even a few individuals lost their strength and fell back, even that would not only create disorder but would also be extremely dangerous from the morale point of view.

Aristophanes tells very graphically in his *Peace*, 1. 78n. 1171 ff., of the warrior who marched out to battle and was found without arms in the nearest bush, or of the general who passed off his purple garment as fine Sardis dye, which he had, however, himself dyed when he urinated in it and took to his heels, a deserter. In every army there are such men of little courage, and once breathlessness gives an excuse for falling back and a few men do so, that quickly has an infectious effect. In that respect the Athenians were no different from other people, and if Hauvette believes they were in better condition than modern soldiers, it is easy to show that it was the opposite situation that prevailed. The Athenian army at Marathon was made up of the popular levy, men from twenty to about forty-five years old, of whom certainly only a very small fraction had ever exercised on an athletic field. Most of them did not live in the city of Athens but at a distance of one to two days' march, and outside the city there was hardly any type of gymnastic exercise. Men who have to work throughout the day to earn their daily bread, like the Attican farmers, fishermen, charcoal burners, potters, sculptors, normally have neither the time nor

the strength to spare to keep themselves in running condition, and least of all into a
more advanced age. Even the outstanding youths, who were exposed to athletic education in the schools, are hardly to be compared in the strenuousness of their physical training with modern soldiers, who are subject, through strict discipline for several years, to living exclusively a life of physical and military training and must devote their whole way of life to that regime, who do not carouse at night and may in
no way allow themselves to let up. Even if one wishes, however, to think of the physical training in the Hellenic gymnasium as being at a very high level, that really had
little significance for the mass levy of the militia; in order to judge the capabilities of
the militia, one may in no way count on special training.

The true objective interpretation of the run at Marathon can, consequently, lead
to no other conclusion than I reached in my *Persian and Burgundian Wars* (p. 56).
The Prussian regulations, "Rules for the Conditioning of Infantry" ("Vorschriften
über das Turnen der Infanterie") prescribes (p. 21):

"The following running times may not be exceeded in training at the double-time:

"Without equipment: 4 minutes at a run, 5 minutes at a walk, 4 minutes at a run.

"With field equipment: 2 minutes at a run, 5 minutes at a walk, 2 minutes at a
run.

"The speed amounts to 165 to 175 paces per minutes.[9] That gives as a maximum
of distance that may be covered at a run with equipment 350 paces, and the director
of the Military Central Physical Training School was kind enough to tell me personally that he considered 2 minutes, or 300 to 350 paces, as the maximum that a
march column with field equipment might run and still arrive before the enemy
with undiminished combat strength. And in that connection, the total burden of a
Greek hoplite was very considerably heavier than that of a Prussian infantryman (for
the latter, 58 pounds; for the former, 72),[10] and in a single mass of perhaps 10,000
men, running is much more difficult than for a smaller detachment."

As positive proof that even the best-trained soldiers of antiquity were not capable
of a greater accomplishment, let us consider Caesar's account of Pharsalus (*Bell. Civ.*
3. 92-93). Pompey had commanded his soldiers to stand fast in the face of the attack
by Caesar's troops, so that the latter, by virtue of their doubly long assault—that is,
600 to 700 feet, according to *Bell. Civ.* 1. 82—would become tired and breathless.
Caesar's battle-tested soldiers noticed this intention, however, made a short halt at
the halfway point to catch their breath, and then resumed the attack. Compare
History of Julius Caesar, the Civil War (*Histoire de Jules César, guerre civile*), by Colonel
Stoffel, II:339.

8. The deeper formation of the two wings and the more shallow one of the
center, which, according to Herodotus, was ordered by Miltiades, is of course not to
be regarded as a special stratagem, but rather as an expedient necessitated by the
width of the Vrana valley, which was somewhat too large for the Athenian strength.
In and of itself, it would naturally have been better to make the center just as strong
as the flanks. Perhaps it should also be especially pointed out that the deeper formation of the flanks would possibly not have sufficed to repel the Persian cavalry in a
battle on the open plain. To be sure, a deeper column cannot be rolled back so simply by a flanking attack as can a shallow phalanx, but it can be brought to a standstill, and that is enough to ruin it when, as at Marathon, it is faced in the front by
archers. For it is defenseless against their fire if it does not close with them. The
deeper formation of the flanks, therefore, is only to be considered as an adjunct of
the real flank protection, which was sought in the terrain; and no matter how cleverly it was conceived, we can never determine whether it served the Athenians at
Marathon more as an advantage or a disadvantage, from a practical viewpoint, since
we do not know if it really contributed to the defense against the Persian cavalry,
whereas it is certain, on the other hand, that the highly dangerous weakening and
penetration of the center was a result of it.

9. Eduard Meyer, in the third volume of his *History of Antiquity* (*Geschichte des*

Altertums), which was completed so soon after the appearance of the first edition of this volume that my work could only be mentioned in its foreword, took in general, with respect to the Persian Wars, a position that was formulated in my *Persian and Burgundian Wars*, published in 1887. As to details, however, certain important points of difference are to be noted from case to case. I call attention to the following in Meyer's presentation of Marathon (transposed here from the second volume of my first edition).

Meyer states, "A national army, which could have contested the Persians' landing in Attica, was not available." No army can contest a landing—only a fleet can. The coast of Attica is so long that an enemy fleet can always appear with surprise effect at a given point and, with the simple construction of ancient ships, debark its soldiers before the defender can be in position. For this reason Miltiades rightly did not consider this kind of operation at all, but only a battle under favorable conditions with the disembarked enemy.

It appears to Meyer "completely inconceivable" that the Athenians should have taken up a position before the battle from which they could not see the enemy. This is not at all inconceivable. It is not necessary that the encamped army be able to see the enemy—but only that reliable lookouts who are in quick and sure communication with the army command see him.

The principal difference between Meyer and me insofar as the battle itself is concerned has to do with the terrain. I assume that the Athenians had a position at the mouth of a valley, where the mountains covered their two flanks. Meyer has them encamped on the slope of the southerly mountain (Agrieliki) and moving out from there for the counterattack against the approaching Persians on the open plain. Why the Persians, in this case, did not attack the Athenian phalanx from one or both flanks with their cavalry is not explored. It is only stated that the Persians, who on their side forced the joining of the battle and moved forward, deployed, against the Athenians, had, to be sure, fought bravely with their infantry, but their cavalry, "surprised and uncertain, was not able to enter the battle." Why they were surprised, why uncertain, and why unable to intervene in the battle, is not stated.

We can pass up the question whether this presentation is false, for it suffers from a much more serious error; it gives the appearance of a logical interrelationship where actually there is none. When a phalanx fights with hand weapons on a plain against an army of archers and mounted men, the decision depends on whether the cavalry attacks the phalanx in its flank. The question whether or why that did not occur must necessarily form the central issue of every historically and militarily sound description of this battle. It is possible for the question to remain unanswered, for our sources to be insufficient, or for the explanations that are given not to enlighten the author. If Meyer, therefore, had added to his account of Marathon the sentence, "The tactical events and overall picture of the battle have not been passed down to us and cannot be surmised," that would be a concept that one would have to accept as valid. But Meyer does not do that at all; rather, he completely fails to pose the question why the Persian mounted men accomplished nothing. He even explains (p. 333) that the battle offers no points of difficulty at all, that it is completely understandable in the light of the Persian manner of fighting—that is, the problem that the battle presents is not only not solved, either rightly or wrongly, but it is not even recognized and not pointed up at all.

Even worse, it is a veritable mockery of the laws of strategy that Meyer repeats the marketplace rumors of the Athenians to the effect that the Persians, even after their defeat, sailed around Sunium, still intending to capture the capital.

10. I. A. Munro, in "Some Observations on the Persian Wars", *Journal of Hellenic Studies*, 1899, p. 185, formulated a new Marathon hypothesis, related to that of Schilling (see No. 5 above), based on the points that, first of all, the Persians had a marked superiority, and second, that they had a strong faction in Athens itself. Both of these points appear, it is true, in Herodotus' report, but they cannot, for that

reason, be regarded as verified, and the conclusions Munro draws from them are in general so artificial and forced that I believe I can dismiss the idea of a refutation in detail.

NOTES FOR CHAPTER V

1. The passage reads: "Sub montis radicibus acie regione instructa non apertissima proelium commiserunt, namque arbores multis locis erant rarae, hoc consilio, ut et montium altitudine tegerentur et arborum tractu equitatus hostium impediretur, ne multitudine clauderentur." ("The line was drawn up at the base of a mountain, where the plain was not totally open—for there were trees here and there in many places—and they joined battle. Their plan was to protect themselves by the height of the mountains, and to keep the enemy's cavalry back, impeded by the scattered trees, so that they themselves would not be overcome by the enemy's superior numbers.") Instead of "arbores rarae," A. Buchner (*Corn. Hepotis vitae cum Augusti Buchneri commentario*. Francof. a. Lipsiae, 1721) has proposed that one should read "stratae," which is actually more appropriate, but is no longer necessary, since one reads, instead of "nova arte, vi summa," "non apertissima."

2. Lieutenant General von Quistorp, *Supplements to the Military Weekly (Beihefte zum Militär-Wochenblatt)* 1897, p. 186.

3. Even a phalanx of professional soldiers, such as the mercenaries of Cyrus, is incapable of moving forward in orderly fashion for a considerable distance at a run. "They shouted to one another not to run headlong, but to pursue the enemy in order,"* Xenophon tells us in *Anabasis* 1. 8. 19.

Caesar, in *Bell Gall*. 2. 18 ff., recounts how the Nervii, suddenly attacking his soldiers, rushed 200 paces down a hill, across the 3-feet-deep Sambre, and then stormed up a hill. That is a very great accomplishment, but it does not permit a comparison with Marathon, since (1) the Gauls were not, under any circumstances, as heavily armored as the Athenian hoplites, (2) the run was broken up by the fording of the river, (3) the entire distance is not mentioned at all, and (4) the Gauls, falling on the Romans as they were digging in, did not need to rely on their own tactical alignment.

In *Bell Gall*. 3. 19, the Gauls suddenly attack a Roman camp and cover 1,000 paces—8 *stadia*—with a great run ("magno cursu"). They arrive so exhausted and breathless that they cannot cope with the Romans, who make a sally, and they immediately take flight. Of itself, however, this incident is not conclusive, since the run was uphill and the Gauls were carrying fascines. One might also well question whether the 1,000 paces were covered at an uninterrupted, actual run, since it was not a question of an ordered phalanx, in which all must move at the same tempo if no disorder is to occur, but rather of an unaligned mass, in which a man who runs short of breath can slow down for a while.

4. A brook divides the Vrana valley into two parts. Although it is not really deep even today, it nevertheless necessarily had a considerably disruptive effect on the advance of a closed and well-ordered phalanx. Possibly Miltiades did not have the valley narrowed on both sides by abatis, but blocked off one side completely, from the mountain to the brook.

5. Cyrus speaks as follows in the *Cyropaedia* 5. 4. 44. "To move forward and to move laterally are not the same. For the man moves forward who is of such a mind as to believe that he is best able to fight—on the other hand, one has to move by laterally with an extended column of wagons and a long-drawn-out pack train. The whole formation, however, must be covered by armed men and the pack train must never appear to the enemy to be unprotected. Necessarily, then, in such a movement the armed part of the formation is disposed thinly and weakly."

6. In Polyaenus 2. 2. 3, there is a description of how Clearch led the Greeks into the attack at Cunaxa: "He led the phalanx at the march to a point opposite the troops, astonishing the barbarians with their good order. And when he was almost within range of the missiles, he gave orders for the men to run, so that they would not be hit by the missiles."* And similarly Diodorus. The fact that this description is not at odds with that of Xenophon, according to which the phalanx spontaneously broke into a run, is effectively presented by G. Friedrich, *Neue Jahrbücher für Philologie* 151:26. Paul Reichard, writing in *Deutsche Rundschau* 12 (September 1890): 426, reports that Stanley claimed in his book to have shot far beyond 200 meters with an African bow. Reichard goes on to say that that was, at the least, an exaggeration. He himself had once engaged in a contest with Watusis, the best bowmen of East Africa, in which the strongest one had shot only 120 meters, or 160 paces, while he, Reichard, had shot seven paces farther. In like manner, Lieutenant Morgen once reported, in a lecture about Cameroons, that the arrow shot from a bow reached in certain conditions a distance of 150 to 180 paces. Nevertheless, the Asiatic bows, according to the research of Luschan ("On the ancient bow" [Über den antiken Bogen,"] *Festschrift für Benndorf*, 1898, and in the

Verhandlungen der Berliner anthropologischen Gesellschaft, Session of 18 February 1899), were much better than the African ones, and the very best ones, the making of which required many years, shot an unbelievably long distance. Strabo, 14. 1. 23, reports that Mithridates shot an arrow from the roof of the temple of Ephesus and decreed that the free area of the temple, which up to that point extended a *stadium*, would extend thenceforth to the range of this shot, which, as Strabo says, went a little farther. At any rate, Mithridates had the best bow and was an excellent marksman, and if he did not considerably exceed a *stadium* in distant—that is, high-angle—shooting, then a low-trajectory shot certainly did not exceed 200 to 240 paces. A recently published epigram from Olbin praises the archer Anaxagoras for having been able to shoot 280 *klaster*, or 521.6 meters (*Literarisches Centralblatt* [1901], Column 887). Naturally, for a large army only a performance of lesser quality comes into consideration. Vegetius estimates 600 feet; Jähns, *History of the Development of Ancient Offensive Weapons* (*Entwicklungsgeschichte der alten Trutzwaffen*), p. 281, "up to 250 paces for low-trajectory shooting, 400 for high-angle shooting." More modern investigation by Paul Reimer, "The Bow" ("Der Pfeilbogen"), *Prometheus*, No. 944, 20 November 1907.

7. *Mitteilungen der archäologischen Institut in Athen*, 1890.

8. *Maps of Attica*. Edited by officers and officials of the Royal Prussian Superior General Staff. With explanatory text by E. Curtius and I. A. Kaupert. 1889. (*Karten von Attika*. Aufgen. d. Offiziere und Beamte d. K. preuss. Gr. Gen.-Stabes. Mit erl. Text v. E. Curtius u. I. A. Kaupert. 1889.)

9. The reference is to running paces—1 meter; the French running pace is only 80 centimeters long.

10. Droysen, *Military Organization* (*Heerwesen*), p. 3, footnote, now rejects—perhaps justifiably—the special figures of Rüstow/Köchly, which I have accepted here, as being arbitrary; the fact of being heavily burdened, however, can, in general, not be questioned.

Chapter VI

Thermopylae

The battle of Marathon had taught the Persians that they would have to muster stronger forces in order to overcome the Hellenes.

For the new campaign, then, a much larger army was outfitted—so large that it could hardly be transported on a fleet, and since, at any rate, the campaign was to be designed for the conquest of all of Greece, it appeared desirable to choose the land route and, as the army moved forward, to force all of the independent peoples along the route to acknowledge the Persian hegemony. A large fleet accompanied the land army in order to furnish provisions, to overpower the Greeks at sea also, and to facilitate detours by sea for the land army in cases where such movement by land was perhaps not feasible.

We are able to draw for ourselves a much less certain picture of the course of this war than that of the first campaign. At Marathon the events are so simple that, once the legendary exaggerations such as the gigantic mass of the Persian army and the one-mile run of the Greeks are put aside, the indications of this historical account suffice to make the overall picture recognizable. The second war is more complicated. The political considerations and relationships, not only of Athens and Sparta, but also of the middle states, come into interplay with the strategy; and the leadership of the land army and that of the fleet interact with one another. These various forces and counterforces are, by their nature, continuously crossing back and forth among themselves. Under such circumstances, it is impossible to work out again from a purely legendary account the real historical base of the whole. What is important for us, however—to recognize the status of the art of war in this decisive moment of world history—will still be possible, even if the motives for the individual strategic moves can, for the most part, only be conjectured.

The logical idea of the Greeks was, first of all, to block from the

91

approaching enemy land army the passes that, in only a few places, lead from the north over the mountains into Greece proper. The first, more northerly one, the Tempe pass, was given up, however, since it was recognized that there were other passes farther inland and since, furthermore, a few of the peoples on this side of the pass had allied themselves with the Persians. The second one is the pass of Thermopylae, between Mount Oeta and the sea, which was occupied by an army under the command of Leonidas.

At this point there arises the general question whether this is, in fact, the best way to utilize a mountain chain for the defense of the country, and whether the Greeks already possessed an insight into certain laws governing the strategic use of mountains and stemming from the nature of warfare.

Modern, carefully conceived strategy does not use mountains in the same way as Leonidas did for the defense of a country. Over a mountain range—and therefore also over Mount Oeta—there is always more than one route, whether it be nearer or farther, easier or more difficult. It is hard to occupy all of them, and one can never succeed in defending them all.[1] The enemy will always find a place where he either breaks through, thanks to his great superiority, or where he happens to come upon an unguarded place, where, through some ravine or other, even though it be pathless, he takes a defensive position from the rear. Once the line is penetrated at one place, then the garrisons of all the other passes are endangered to an extreme degree. If they are not promptly informed and do not withdraw as quickly as possible, they can lose their line of retreat, and even if they succeed in escaping without losses, they are still, initially, separated from one another and can perhaps reestablish contact only with difficulty.

The villainy of a traitor, Ephialtes, impossible to imagine in advance, was therefore not necessary to open the pass of Thermopylae to the Persians. Even in enemy territory a guide can always be found, whether by means of kindness or force, reward or punishment, and the idea of a detour is in no way just a product of modern military theory, but it has been common with military commanders from the most ancient times. As early as in their saga of the battles of Astyages and Cyrus, the Persians have an example of the overcoming of a courageously defended pass by means of an envelopment. In close proximity to Thermopylae, there leads over the mountain range that same footpath on which the Persians, according to Herodotus, outflanked the defenders of the pass in 480 B.C., and where the Gauls in 278 B.C. and the Romans in 191 B.C.

also carried out successful outflanking movements. Leading out from Trachis, where this footpath begins, there is still another route directly over the mountain toward Doris, and it was even used by a detachment of the Persian army. A few miles farther on, in the year 191 B.C., the consul M. Acilius Glabrio moved over the mountain with his army, along Mount Corax; although it is true that the march was very difficult and costly, it still succeeded.[2] Xerxes was strong enough to have all of these crossings attempted at the same time; his army was at any rate already divided up into three forces marching abreast on parallel roads and therefore would have taken the defenders of Thermopylae from the rear sooner or later under any circumstances, if it was not able to overcome them by frontal attack.

The defense of mountain passes is effective only when one does not intend to stop the enemy completely, but only to cause him to lose time and to force him into costly skirmishes. If you wish to utilize the mountain chain really to repel a superior invading force, then the tactical theory requires you to take a position with your concentrated forces opposite the defile, or one of the defiles, from which the enemy is about to debouch. Then you attack him at the moment when he has just taken the defile with a portion of his troops. If you succeed in defeating these troops while they are still relatively weak numerically and not deployed, they cannot avoid suffering heavy losses. They are forced to move back into the narrow pass, and some detachments are perhaps driven off separately, getting completely lost. If the enemy has undertaken the crossing simultaneously at several places, you can now strike with your entire force at another column, thus always defeating the enemy in detail with your concentrated power. This stratagem is so simple that we find it used in a similar manner even in the oldest legendary account of battle. The first great conquering people in the legendary accounts were the Assyrians under King Ninus, and when he, according to the saga, moved out against the Bactrians, the king of the Bactrians allowed a part of the Assyrians to move down into his country through the passes and then attacked and defeated them. Ninus was so strong, however, that those of his troops who had advanced through other passes were still sufficient to conquer the Bactrians in the end.[3]

We may therefore say that the theoretical insight into the strategic exploitation of a mountain range was already known in the oldest times but that the Greeks, in the year 480 B.C., were not in a position to apply this knowledge. They would have had to concentrate all their forces beside Mount Oeta and wage an offensive battle at that point. First of all, that was impossible from a political viewpoint; one must not expect a conglomerate of small republics to send their entire forces so far from home and to expose them to the danger of an offensive battle before their own territory is directly threatened, and moreover a large fraction of the whole, particularly the Athenians, was occupied with the fleet. Principally, however, they were tactically not in a position to wage an offensive battle, in view of the Persian cavalry. Victory had come at Marathon only by virtue of the ingenious defensive position with its covered flanks. If one should once again seek such a position, the Persians would certainly not attack it again but would bypass it, with the help of their fleet if necessary, and would seek battle in open terrain.

A later account has it that Themistocles, whom the Athenians chose as general,[4] wanted from the very start to renounce any kind of defense by land and as far as possible oppose the Persians with the fleet. That would, in fact, have been the best plan at that time. Under any circumstances, sooner or later there had to be a sea battle; if they succeeded in defeating the Persian fleet, they would thereby have created more favorable chances for the decision by land. A larger number of men from the ships' crews could go ashore, don hoplite equipment, and reinforce the land army, and the Persians, in their strategic maneuvers, would no longer have the alternative of a detour by water.

Many an obstacle, however, may have arisen to interfere with such a plan. The various contingents of the Greek fleet would only with great difficulty have all been ready and assembled soon enough to make the long voyage to the area of the Hellespont. The risk was very great, and the Persian ships held back cautiously until the land army had arrived at the borders of Greece.

This probably explains why the Greeks finally chose a compromise solution: they decided on blocking the pass at Thermopylae, while the fleet awaited the enemy ships nearby, at the north end of Euboea near the foothills of Artemisium. The Athenians, who had already strongly participated in the occupation of Tempe pass, had now changed their minds, devoted all their strength exclusively to the fleet, and had sent no contingent to the army of Leonidas. The occupation of Thermopylae was therefore only a secondary, auxiliary move for the real strategic plan, that is, to wage a sea battle in the open water north of Euboea. To assemble the various fleet contingents still farther northward was impossible; they were, in fact, not completely assembled even near Artemisium. Farther southward, one would have given up middle Greece to the Persian army, since Thermopylae was the only point where one could hope to stop that army, if and as long as the fleet protected the sea flank.

It has often been asked why the Greeks did not make the army of Leonidas stronger. Even if we may not rely on the reported numbers, one thing is still sure: although the total contingent of Spartiates amounted to some 2,000 men, Leonidas nevertheless had only 300 of them with him. From this it follows that most of the other states, too, had probably sent only a few or even no troops at all. That can probably be explained very easily, however. The dangers inherent in a mountain defense were not unknown to the Greeks. If the blocking action should fail, then not only the position itself but also a large part of the army would be lost, a part that would be all the larger, the larger the army itself was and the more it hindered itself in any withdrawal. The Persian cavalry and archers were particularly dangerous pursuers for a retreating army. Even a small army was enough for the actual defense of the pass; it was not because of too weak a garrison but because of a lack of alertness that the Greeks actually lost the battle in the end. Thermopylae, however, even though I have treated it first here, was only the secondary action, the auxiliary operation in the strategic concept of the Greek defense. The definite hope they had in occupying the position was that the Greek fleet might succeed in beating the Persian fleet at Artemisium, whereupon the land army would give up its operation and withdraw. Of itself, the defense of Thermopylae was as good as hopeless; observed without regard to other events, it was an heroic attempt but one in which they were not willing to stake everything simultaneously. As a matter of form, it could also be said that it was a mistake from the physical-military point of view, but it was of morale significance and of inestimable value in its fulfillment, in that the entrance into Greece proper was not to be handed to the barbarians without a fight.

Leonidas was a man who understood and knew how to carry out this aspect of his mission. When the bypassing by the Persians was reported, he had the main body of his army start the withdrawal; he himself, however, stood fast with the Spartiates, in order at the same time to cover the withdrawal and to bring to full fruition the concept of the battle that was entrusted to him. The defeat of the Spartiates represents not just a sacrificial death and not simply a covering action, but both at the same time.

The critics say that Leonidas should have withdrawn. One thing is certain—the critics would have withdrawn. This statement by Heinrich Leo may also well be repeated in this military-historical study as the best characterization of the encounter at Thermopylae.

Just as Miltiades showed us in his defensive-offensive action at Marathon that the Hellenes had already mastered the basic concepts of all generalship, so does Leonidas embody for us the morale element in war, its importance and its value; not only the knightlike, personal courage, the heroic death, but heroism in the organic context of warfare as a conscious military action.

Testimony to the fact that the Greeks were conscious of this idea is given us by the poet who, in words as classical as the event itself, set forth its meaning for all ages:
"Traveler, if you come to Sparta, tell them there that you have seen us lying here, as the law has commanded."

EXCURSUS

1. The more clearly one realizes that the Greeks were not able to accept a land battle with the Persians before they had defeated the Persian fleet, the more noteworthy it is that the Athenians first sent a large land army to Tempe pass, and under the command of Themistocles at that, who, among all the Greeks, was thought to have the fullest insight into the strategic situation.

The following explanation appears to be a possibility. When the Greeks were moving toward Tempe, they still had at their sides not only the Boeotians but also the Thessalians, both of whom, and especially the Thessalians, had excellent cavalry. Therefore Themistocles may have had the plan—not to defend Tempe, something which was completely hopeless, since the Persians could bypass it, not only by land, but also by sea—but, with the help of the Thessalian cavalry, to give battle against the Persians as they were debouching from Tempe. That proved to be impracticable, particularly since one could not depend on the Thessalians, and the other Greeks did not appear to be numerous enough. Only then did Themistocles lead the Athenians over to the other route, to fight first against the Persian fleet, sending no more troops to Thermopylae.

And so Thermopylae was from the very outset (unless the Persians should first lose a sea battle and thereupon turn about) a position that was as good as lost, and Leonidas was given the mission of dying with honor in order to provide an example for the Greeks.

2. In Diodorus 11. 4 there is (according to Ephorus) an account that nobody has been willing to believe up to now, but one that, nevertheless, in keeping with the foregoing, might very well come close to the truth. According to this story, Leonidas wished to take along only 1,000 men from Lacedaemon, and when the ephors offered him more, he is reported to have said that that was a small number to block the passes, but that in reality he was not blocking the passes with them but was leading them to their death. And if he were to march there with the entire population, then Lacedaemon would go down completely. We need not belabor the number 1,000 in this account, nor the report that the ephors offered the king a larger number. They undoubtedly knew just as well as Leonidas himself what was at stake. The important thing is that here, in popular form, the correct strategic concept is

actually preserved for us. For Marathon, too, we found the popular legend of the correct military concept in Ephorus.

3. According to Herodotus' account, Leonidas also kept with him 700 Thespians who volunteered for that duty, and the Thebans. The Thebans surrendered to the Persians, and the Thespians fell with the Spartiates.

If the sacrifice of the Spartiates, who form a warrior class, is a deed of eternally memorable heroism, then the voluntary participation of the citizen militia of a small city seems to surpass human capabilities. That an entire city could be inhabited by such heroes—a small city like Thespia could not possibly have had more than 700 hoplites—cannot be accepted on the strength of a legendary account. The logical explanation could be that the Persians caught up with the Thespians in their withdrawal and annihilated them there, since they offered resistance, whereas the Thebans offered to surrender and were taken prisoner.

4. In opposition to my concept of Leonidas' deed, it has been objected (Busolt, p. 686, footnote) that Leonidas, if he wanted to cover the withdrawal of the others, could always have gone back so far as to have the Persian enveloping column again in front of him, since still farther back on the route there were narrow passes that lent themselves to a defense. This objection does not hold up. The Persians had, after all, established outposts and would have begun immediately to press on as soon as they noticed the evacuation of the pass. Then the Greeks would first of all have suffered considerable casualties from the pursuers' arrows, only to be bypassed again at their new position, possibly still saving in the end a small number of the Spartiates while sacrificing, however, the entire morale value of the battle. Both points are closely bound together and may not be separated: the sacrificial death with its morale significance, and the military purpose.

5. (Second Edition.) In my presentation of Thermopylae as it appeared in the first edition I have changed nothing of importance, although Grundy, in his excellent topographical studies (*The Great Persian War and its Preliminaries; a study of the evidence, literary and topographical*, London, 1901), questions the passability of the mountains near the pass at Thermopylae and denies especially the existence of the road from Trachis to Doris in ancient times. Even if it were not a road, however, it definitely was a path, according to Munro, *Journal of Hellenic Studies* 22 (1902): 314, who has so generally limited and corrected the statements of Grundy that my theory can still hold true. Which path the enveloping Persians took in the end is a simple topographical question that, for us, can be left out of consideration.

Notes for Chapter VI

1. Because of the most recent enlargement of armies, this thesis must be modified. With the gigantic masses of the standing armies that are now available, even long mountain ranges can be so closely occupied that they cannot easily be penetrated. In this way we succeeded for a long time in the winter of 1914-1915 in holding the Carpathians against the Russians.

2. Livy 36. 30.

3. Diodorus, 2. 6, from Ctesias.

4. Plutarch, *Themistocles*, Chapter 7.

Chapter VII

Artemisium

At about the same time as the engagements at Thermopylae, the two fleets were fighting for three days running at Artemisium.[1] In the later popular accounts Artemisium is treated as a victory. According to the account of Herodotus, the battle was about even, but the Greeks, because of the damage to so many of their ships, had decided to start a withdrawal and had no sooner begun it than the news of the catastrophe of Leonidas arrived.

It seems basically that this account has to be accepted as the admission of a defeat. For the withdrawal of the fleet from the northern point of Euboea meant sacrificing Thermopylae, and that sacrifice meant the evacuation of all of middle Greece and Attica. The people may have imagined, as Herodotus recounts, that one would move back only as far as the Euripus and that a Greek land army would once again face Xerxes farther southward. The commanders, however, must have known that, if they had not even been able to hold Thermopylae, there was no position farther southward that the Persians could not have bypassed, and consequently the Spartans would not take up the defense until they were on the isthmus. It was no minor decision, especially for the Athenians, to withdraw from Artemisium; their country and their city were thereby lost. Only absolute necessity—consequently, a defeat—seems to explain such a decision.

On the other hand, it is very remarkable that the Persians allowed them to withdraw unpursued. The Persian admirals knew that their land army was fighting before a narrow pass; they knew what great merit they would earn if they drove off the Greek ships and thereby facilitated the envelopment of Thermopylae by water. Nevertheless, they reportedly did not sail out again to combat on the fourth day, after the three-day battle; instead, only after receiving the report that the Greeks had sailed away did they move out from their anchorage at the entrance of the Gulf of Pagasae. After a complete victory the Persians would certainly not have been so hesitant.

It appears, therefore, that the Greeks gave a good account of themselves in the three-day battle. It is perhaps a false account that the withdrawal was already decided before the arrival of the report of Thermopylae. At any rate, the circumstances would appear to be much more understandable if one assumes that it was only this news that swung the balance (Plutarch had already conceived it in this way) and brought the final decision to withdraw, whereas at first possibly only a few voices had demanded that action.

However that may be, it appears certain that the Greek fleet showed itself the equal of the Persian fleet on the open sea and that it could not be defeated in a three-day fight.

From this we may conclude that the two fleets were quite equal in strength. When the Greeks try to explain away the contradiction (that on the one side the Persians were supposedly three times as numerous and still could not win) by the fact that the enemy ships, because of their size and number, had become mixed up and damaged each other, that is patent fable. The principal part of the Persian navy consisted of Phoenicians and Ionian Greeks, both excellent sailors, who also knew how to control the ships they built. The crews presumably were composed exclusively of professional sailors, whereas the Greek ships must have been manned partly, it is true, by excellent sailors, but also partly by citizens with little seagoing experience. Herodotus himself points out repeatedly the technical superiority of the opponents (7. 179; 8. 10) and also has Themistocles say expressly (8. 60) that the ships of the Greeks were less maneuverable. Later naval history—for example, the superiority of the Athenians in the Peloponnesian War—teaches us how much difference it makes for a fleet when its crews are professionally trained. The crews of the Athenian fleet in 480 B.C., however, were composed in very large part of Attic farmers, charcoal burners, and artisans, who could only have had emergency training in the fleet, which itself had been developed in only the two preceding years.[2] The Greeks therefore would not possibly have been able to hold out in the three-day battle on the open sea if the enemy, professionally superior and well led, had in addition enjoyed a great numerical superiority. The Greeks themselves claim to have had 271 triremes on the first day of battle; the Persians, therefore, certainly did not have more than 200 to 300. Supposedly they had lost very many ships in a heavy storm a few days earlier. Even if these losses were exaggerated and they had not had more than 200 to 300 triremes from the very start, it is nevertheless probable that Xerxes believed he could sweep all the Greeks from the sea with such a fleet. Of the total of Greek ships, 127 were Athenian. Only a few years earlier the Athenians had borrowed 20 ships from the Corinthians in order to wage a war against Aegina. Only then, on the proposal of Themistocles, was the great fleet of 483-482 B.C. built, and at the Persian court they certainly had no concept of what an extraordinary effort the small state had made at the last moment. There appears, therefore, not only to be no internal reason for assuming that the Persian fleet was more numerous than the Greek one, but also in fact the course of the battle of Artemisium, at least after the losses through shipwreck, definitely eliminates this possibility.[3] That the Persians may have moved up to attack before all of their fleet was present is naturally also out of the question.

If all of this is correct, then the withdrawal of the Greeks becomes quite understandable. According to Herodotus, the Athenians were further reinforced at Artemisium by 53 additional Athenian triremes. This reinforcement has, with good reason, been questioned by Beloch; Athens certainly did not have the personnel to man 200 triremes. There can be no doubt, however, that it was not until Salamis that a considerable portion of the smaller contingents joined the fleet. Herodotus takes pains to point out expressly that the reinforcing of the Greeks was matched by reinforcements on the part of the Persians. For the Persians, however, they consisted of a few ships of the island Greeks, while for the Greeks Herodotus gives the figure 55 triremes (in addition to the 53 Athenian ones). By withdrawing from Artemisium, then, they were going back for reinforcements, and they could also again repair the many damaged ships very quickly in the home ports, something that was much more difficult for the Persians. If the Greeks had already acquitted themselves with honor at Artemisium, then they could also look forward with good prospects to a second battle in the Saronic Gulf. The price to be paid was admittedly very high, since the Athenians had to leave their country and their city to the mercy of the enemy, but since they had not initially succeeded in defeating the enemy fleet at Artemisium, they had no alternative.

Excursus

1. Herodotus recounts that the Greeks had already moved back once, before the battle, from their position at Artemisium to the Euripus and had not moved up again to Artemisium until they received news of the Persians' heavy losses in the shipwreck. This report deserves no credence, since, in that event, Leonidas would also have had to evacuate Thermopylae. It is simply an expression of the fear in which the Greeks lived over the arrival of the Persians and of the help which the gods sent them in wind and weather. The greater the losses of the Persians in the shipwreck, the larger the fleet had been originally.

2. With the establishing of the strength of the fleet, there disappears once and for all the fable that the Persians had sent 200 ships around Euboea in order to cut off the withdrawal of the Greeks, and that they had all foundered in a storm. In order to cut off the Greek fleet—if indeed the Persians could get along without these ships in the battle—they did not need to send them around Euboea but simply across the water into the left flank of the Greeks, while the main fleet was rowing up for the battle. This account, too, is an auxiliary theme of the legend, aimed at explaining the contradiction between the gigantic true size of the Persian fleet and its actual appearance in the battle.

3. I sought earlier to explain the paradox that the Persian fleet was supposed to be many times larger than the Greek and yet the latter supposedly held its own in a three-day battle on the open sea; my explanation was that there was really no battle at all at Artemisium. This solution, however, is untenable, not so much because of the Greeks' account—legend often invented entire battles—but because of the combat actions at Thermopylae. The Persian fleet cannot possibly have remained unengaged while the king was fighting here, but it must have moved in with all its power to drive off the Greek fleet and take the position of Leonidas from the rear. Since the decision at Thermopylae did not take place until the seventh day after the king's arrival in front of the pass, it is clear that the land army simply awaited the action of the fleet. The fleet was reportedly held up for three days by bad weather. These accounts of Herodotus may be regarded as correct, even though the details of chronological reports in a narrative after such a long time are always subject to strong suspicion and Herodotus also contradicts himself.

Notes for Chapter VII

1. Plato, *Menexenus* 11. Aristophanes, *Lysistrata*, verse 1250. Later they also placed on the foothill a victory monument whose inscription has come down to us through Plutarch.

2. Concerning the construction of the triremes, see Hauck *Zeitschrift des Vereins deutscher Ingenieure*, 1895; A. Tenne (engineer), *Warships in the Days of the Ancient Greeks and Romans* (*Kriegschiffe zu den Zeiten der alten Griechen und Römer*), 1916. Review by Voigt, *Die Literarische Zeitung*, 29 (1917): 932.

3. It is perhaps well to recall that not only large land armies but also large fleets are hard to maneuver. The complete fleet with which the Athenians moved to Sicily in 415 B.C. was 134 triremes

and 2 penteremes strong, and had in addition 131 cargo ships and a number of volunteer trading vessels. This fleet did not sail as a single squadron, but was divided into three divisions, "so that they might not, by sailing together, be wanting water and ports and provisions when they landed, and so that they might, in other matters, be more orderly and easy to control, being assigned to a commander according to set divisions"* (Thucydides 6. 42).

Chapter VIII

Battle of Salamis

When the word reached Athens that the citizens were to leave the city and give it up to the enemy, they refused in dull despair to follow this advice, and even the interpretation of the oracle concerning the wooden walls was of no avail. Finally it turned out that the Holy Snake of the Citadel had not eaten its monthly sacrificial cake. One was therefore forced to conclude that even it had moved out. Now at last even the Athenian citizens no longer hesitated to follow such a godly example.

The population was moved partially to the Peloponnesus, but partly also only over to Salamis. Presumably the means at hand were not sufficient to transport the large number of people with their movable possessions all together to the Peloponnesus. The farming population probably fled to the mountains. The island of Salamis, by providing a refuge for the citizens of the city, tied the fleet to this place. Nevertheless, according to the legendary account, a great quarrel is supposed to have occurred between the field commanders as to whether one should accept battle against the Persian fleet near Salamis. We are not in a position to know with certainty the nature of this quarrel, and it is completely unmethodical to pass on as history an account like that of Herodotus, even when it is possible to eliminate obvious impossibilities and contradictions. Perhaps this whole story of a quarrel between the leaders is a fable with only a small nucleus of truth in the fact that the reasons for deciding to fight at Salamis or elsewhere were carefully weighed in a council of war. Precisely this distortion, as strong as it might seem, is to be found quite often in military history, even in more modern times. I would simply refer here to the Bullinger chronicle of the battle of Murten and of the similar alleged dispute between Frederick and Schwerin before the battle of Prague. Certain portions of Herodotus' account correspond so closely, it is true, to the nature of the matter, that we can well accept them; but whether or not other motives, unknown to us and perhaps of a much stronger nature, played a role in the situation, we do not know.

First of all, it must be recorded that it was only a question of *where*, and not *whether*, the sea battle was to be fought. If they had not had the courage to risk the sea battle, then Greece would have had to bow to the Persians. Without the opposition of the fleet, the Persians would have enveloped the isthmus, which was barred by a wall, and we know already that the land army did not have the self-confidence to give battle to the Persians in the open countryside. If, then, the battle was fought between Salamis and the mainland and was lost, the losers were, for all practical purposes, cut off, and only a few ships would have been able to save themselves through the Sound of Megara, assuming that the Persians did not block this one, too. A battle in open water therefore had the advantage of not pushing the danger to its highest point. But for the outcome of the war, that point did not come into consideration; a defeat of the fleet, even if somewhat less complete, would have been decisive under any circumstances, since after all, without the fleet, the land army, too, was incapable of resistance. Furthermore, by withdrawing to the isthmus they would be giving up to the enemy not only Salamis and the Athenians who had taken refuge there, but also Aegina and Megara. That seems completely convincing, and one is at first at a loss for any passably rational reason that the advocates of a further retreat must nevertheless have proposed. Indeed, the legend is content with an explanation of simple stupidity and cowardice. In reality, things did not come about that way, and it is completely certain that the Spartan King Eurybiades and the leader of the Corinthians, Adeimantus, whom his compatriots celebrated as a hero and hailed as the real conqueror of Salamis, brought forth still other reasons for their plan than Herodotus passed on. In fact, we now find in Herodotus' account another fact that has remained completely unnoticed until now but that could give us the sought-after solution, if there is any reality at all underlying the account.

We are told that a fleet of 60 Corcyraean triremes had already arrived at the southern point of the Peloponnesus. The Greeks later expressed the suspicion that the Corcyraeans, who reportedly were held up by unfavorable winds, had intentionally held back in order to await the outcome and to join the victors. It does not seem impossible, however, that in the council of the Greek commanders their arrival was expected from one moment to the next and therefore one was willing, even under the hardest sacrifices, to withdraw another step farther and thus make the victory still more certain by virtue of their help.

Themistocles is supposed to have forced the decision with the entire weight of his personality by feigning treason and informing King Xerxes himself of the split among the Greeks, thereby inveigling him into an immediate attack. As to the contents of the message that Themistocles sent to the King, the Greeks were not in agreement. In Aeschylus (*Persians*, verse 336) it is said that a man reported to Xerxes that the Greeks would flee during the night and scatter, in order to save their lives. To this Herodotus adds that the Greeks would fight among themselves if the Persians sailed up. Diodorus (probably quoting Ephorus) has the messenger say that the Greeks intended to sail to the isthmus in order to join the land army there. Similarly, and probably from the same source, Plutarch. The reason for the transformation is clear: there were some people to whom it did not occur that the King should have had an interest in preventing the Greeks from splitting up their forces. For if things had reached that point, then the Persian fleet would not only easily have overwhelmed each Greek fleet division, to the extent that it dared at all to stay at sea, but would also have determined the land victory by landing a part of the Persian army at some place on the Peloponnesus, thereby maneuvering the Greeks out of their last unenvelopable position behind the isthmus wall. On this basis, then, we find in Herodotus the addition that the Greeks would fight among themselves and consequently a part of them would go over to the Persians—which makes the Persian attack understandable, at least to a certain extent. But Ephorus recognized that even this did not suffice, and since there was not another positive account on hand, introduced, instead of the disbandment of the fleet, a simple withdrawal to the isthmus and contact with the land army. Later writers, like Nepos, Justin, Frontinus, turned back to the original legend and would have the King informed: "The Greeks are about to disband; you should therefore act quickly in order to catch them all together." No fairy tale could have a haughty king duped more splendidly. A real soldier like Themistocles, however, would probably have said to himself that Xerxes would answer him as follows: "That is a very cheering bit of news; then I can do away with them one at a time without any danger." The message would probably appear most credible if it ran somewhat like this: "There are still sixty Corcyraean triremes on the way, so the Persians should therefore seek battle before their arrival."

Up to this point I have been able to let my presentation in the two first editions stand as it was. The following, however, is new. Surprisingly enough, careful philological research has succeeded in discovering a completely new fact that places the events of Salamis, both from a tactical and a strategic viewpoint, on a completely different basis from the one formerly taken for granted. All the studies on Salamis proceeded from the assumption that the island of Psyttalea, which was occupied during the battle by Persian warriors who, after the victory, were cut off and destroyed, was identical with the present-day island of Leipsokutali, which still lies in front of the entrance into the sound. Endless pains have been taken to reconcile Aeschylus' and Herodotus' battle reports with each other and with this topography. Now Julius Beloch has established the fact that people have been led astray by the superficial resemblance of Psyttalea and Leipsokutali, that the two names have nothing at all to do with each other, and that the island of Psyttalea, near which the battle must have taken place, is rather the island Hagios Georgios, which lies considerably farther to the north in the sound. This is an occurrence similar to that in the battle of Murten, where the topography and, as a consequence, also the tactical-strategic context of the battle were distorted by virtue of an unfounded tradition, which indicated as "Battle Chapel" a chapel which was quite distant from the real battlefield. With Beloch's work in hand, I walked along the beach of the sound in 1911 and at that point the scales fell from my eyes as I realized that the battle could not have taken place in this sound at all, because there is far too little space in it. Only on the far side of the narrows, in the Bay of Eleusis, could the battle have taken place.

On this basis the source accounts were once again worked over by one of my students, Gottfried Zinn, and resulted in an irreproachable picture of the battle, both tactically and strategically.[1] All the reports from the original sources, which seemed to be so much at odds that one was convinced the situation could be remedied only through textual changes, some here and some there, now stand in perfect harmony.

The Persians allowed a good fourteen days to slip by after they had occupied Athens before they forced a decision (occupation of the city, about 10 September; battle, 28 September). Despite all their previous successes, the situation was difficult for them, and it was not easy to decide how they could best go at it. The Greek fleet lay on the north coast of the island of Salamis, where the necessary sand beach was present (almost the entire east coast is rocky). Since the island had too little water to provide for the whole fleet (some 300 ships, with combined crews of 50,000 to 60,000 men), it is probable that a portion of the ships lay off the Megaran coast. One can easily imagine that Xerxes must have pondered the question whether he should perhaps, at the same time he attacked with the fleet, move forward by land on the road leading from Athens to Megara. Since, however, no information has been handed down on this subject, let us just establish the fact that the Persians did not at any rate go as far as Megara[2] and therefore probably did not feel themselves strong enough to do so, so that they limited themselves to a fleet attack, which required a careful, rather long reconnaissance. In order to come up with the Greeks, the Persian fleet had to move either through the rather winding Sound of Salamis, dotted with islands and rocks, or through the still narrower passage on the other—the Megara—side of the island, Trupica Bay. It was finally decided to attack the Greeks simultaneously from both sides; victory would mean the loss and complete destruction of the Greek fleet. Both parts of the fleet started out during the night, in order to move into the Bay of Eleusis on both sides at the same time the next morning.

As soon as their approach was reported, the Greeks also made their preparations, divided their fleet likewise, and moved out against the enemy. Themistocles allowed himself the time to give another stirring address before the engagement. His intention was not to prevent the enemy from sailing into the more open bay, but to attack him while he was still involved in deploying out of the narrow passage. The foremost Greek ships, probably the same ones that had observed and covered the entrance to the sound, first rowed a certain distance toward the rear. Then the attack started, with the Greeks trying, as Herodotus quite correctly reports, to envelop the right wing of the Persians, that is, the one that was moving in the direction of Eleusis. The Persians fought back most courageously, but the strait allowed their ships to move out only slowly, whereas the Greeks could immediately exert their power, superior under any circumstances. Thus the Phoenician-Ionian ships, in spite of their superior maneuverability, had to yield, and they were pushed back again into the sound. Since the retiring ships came up against those that were still striving to move forward, the greatest confusion resulted, and heavy losses ensued.

Nothing has been told us of the combat in the opposite strait, near Megara. We can nevertheless assume with certainty that it took place in a very similar way, since the Athenians reported to Herodotus that the Corinthian ships had moved off toward that side (as they believed, in flight), and the Corinthians celebrated their leader, Adeimantus, as victor.

All the distortions that made the account so incomprehensible up to this point have now disappeared.

It could not be understood up to the present why the narrowness of the water passage should have been disadvantageous precisely for the Persians, as Aeschylus particularly emphasizes, since, after all, the Phoenicians and Ionians were undoubtedly better sailors than the Athenian militia crews. Now, however, it becomes clear how the strategic genius of Themistocles was able to arrange the battle in such a way that the strait helped the Hellenes, while the enemy, with all his nautical ability, could not be effective. For the pass is not directly related to the battle itself, but to the approach into the battle.

The contradiction that the Greeks fought successfully in open water at Artemisium and here supposedly sought out, intentionally, a narrow battle area with their increased number of ships, is now dispelled, since it was not the battle area itself but only the approach to the battle area that formed the narrow strait.

Parallel to the popular account that Xerxes observed the battle from a hill beside the Sound of Salamis is another report, from Plutarch, that he erected his throne on a hill at the border of Megaris. How could such an account develop, when the battle took place at the southerly entrance of the Sound of Salamis, 10 to 12 kilometers distant from that point? Now it is, to be sure, probably not accurate, but quite reasonable.

Finally, too, the necessary space for the battle has been found. The orienting of the Persian right flank on Eleusis, as reported by Herodotus, and the conduct of the Corinthians are clarified.

On the other hand, there is present in the overall source accounts not a single point that might contradict Zinn's reconstruction of the battle.

The Greeks had won, but their victory was not so great that they might have pursued the foe far out into the sea. In fact, they expected the attack to be renewed. But Xerxes had become convinced that he was not capable of conquering the Greeks at sea, especially if the Corcyraeans now came up also. He therefore sent the fleet homeward, feeling that, if it could not overcome the Greeks, it had no further role to play.

This fact did not at all mean, however, that the war was lost. True enough, there was now nothing more to be attempted against the isthmus position, but the Persians were, nevertheless, holding central Greece and Attica, and the Greeks did not dare risk meeting them head-on by land. Thus, if the land army remained in Greece and lived off the subjugated countryside, it could be assumed that the Greeks, especially the Athenians, would not be capable of defending their country against repeated incursions and would in time become weary of it all. After all, they could not evacuate their city and flee across the water each year.

The war, therefore, had to be planned now on a long-term basis. For the Great King there was now nothing more to be done in Hellas; his presence would have called for great, brilliant deeds, which, for the time being, were no longer to be expected. On the contrary, it was even correct, from the political and military points of view, that Xerxes himself should return to Asia. The weak point in the Persians' situation was the but slight degree of trustworthiness of the Ionian Greeks. If they should by chance defect, the Persian army in Hellas would be separated from the mother country in a dangerous manner. Since he did not have at his disposal many additional troops, the best way to retain the obedience of the Ionian Greeks was through the personal authority of the King. Xerxes therefore turned the high command over to Mardonius and returned to Sardis, where he remained for a while.[3] Mardonius withdrew to northern Greece, where he was not exposed to any sudden attack and his army could be supplied in the occupied countryside. From here he was in a position to take up the offensive again at any opportune moment.

NOTES FOR CHAPTER VIII

1. Berlin dissertation, 1914. R. Trenkel, publisher.
2. By the nature of Herodotus' account, it is naturally not impossible that a large portion of the overall account has been lost without leaving any trace. Nevertheless, it is very unusual that we hear nothing at all about why the large Persian army, during the fourteen days it camped in Attica before the battle, did not also occupy Megara, which, after all, lay in front of the isthmus and its wall. A logical explanation would be that the Spartiates, with the army of

the Peloponnesians, to the extent that they were not digging in on the isthmus, were occupying the passes leading from Attica to Megara and that Xerxes, unlike his action at Thermopylae —precisely because of his experience at Thermopylae—did not attack because he wanted to do away with the fleet first. Under those circumstances, it is all the more likely that a part of the Greek fleet could have been on the beach at Megara. It is, of course, obvious that this construction is in direct contradiction to the historical narrative.

3. All kinds of conclusions have been proposed as a result of the fact that Xerxes returned by land, while sending his children home with the fleet. For such details, however, so many varied reasons are imaginable that there is little purpose in going deeply into the matter.

Chapter IX

Battle of Plataea

The leaders of the Hellenes were not unaware of where and how they should carry out their counterattack against a Persian offensive that had withdrawn only a step and might be renewed at any moment. As early as the period immediately after the battle of Salamis Themistocles is supposed to have proposed that the fleet sail to the Hellespont and destroy the Persian bridges; this proposal, in a form that could be understood by the masses, was a plan for a campaign into Thrace and Asia Minor in order to encourage the Greeks in those areas to defect from the barbarians. Themistocles would not have needed to take this trouble just for the purpose of destroying the Hellespont bridge; wind and weather took care of that without any help from the Greeks.

Themistocles' plan evoked no enthusiasm from his compatriots; they were supposed to move off to a distant place while the large Persian army was laying waste to their homeland? Even in the following spring Themistocles so failed to put over his idea that the Athenians chose as commanders in place of him—the victor of Salamis—his political enemies Aristides and Xanthippus.

Themistocles was better appreciated by the Spartans —quite naturally, since, if the plan succeeded, Mardonius would have to abandon Greek soil, and the land battle that the Spartans feared so greatly would be unnecessary.

With this difference existing between the two leading city-states, nothing at all occurred at first. The Athenians demanded that the Peloponnesians move forward with their full forces and help cover Attica against an invasion by the Persians. The Spartans insisted on the sea expedition. Each side tried to force the other to accept its plan. The Spartans did not move out, and the Athenians, as Mardonius approached, had to give up their city and country for a second time and flee across the water. They thereupon threatened the Spartans that they would negotiate with the Persians, would make

111

peace and even an alliance, if they received no help from the Peloponnesus.

Finally a compromise was reached. From the Ionians there came one message after the other, saying they were ready to defect. Consequently, the entire fleet was no longer needed, but only a part of it, to make the expedition a worthwhile risk. Through this step the bulk of the Athenian hoplites became available for the land war. Whereas at Salamis, according to the most modest estimate, 310 Greek triremes were reported to have been in the fight, requiring a combined manning of 50,000 to 60,000 crew members, now only 110 triremes crossed over the sea, with perhaps 20,000 men, under the command of the Spartan King Leotychides and the Athenian Xanthippus. The Peloponnesian hoplite army, however, under Pausanias, assembled on the isthmus, and as Mardonius abandoned Attica, in order not to have to fight with a reversed front, took up a position on Mount Cithaeron near Plataea, covering Attica. But it remained here, and the Persians camped opposite, on the plain. Neither attacked the other.

Up to this point we have been able to unfold the account without going into a special study of the size of the two armies. One thing is clear: the Persians believed themselves to be tactically superior to the Greeks, and the latter did not dare to give battle in the open field. Since the previous year the circumstances for the Greeks had become much more favorable in that a part of the combined fleet crews that had fought at Salamis was now serving on land, especially contingents from the Athenians, the Megarans, Aeginetans, and Corinthians. For this reason they were now capable of taking up the position near Plataea covering Attica, something they would not have felt capable of doing a year earlier. In view of the fact that parts of the ships' crews were still needed, but that simultaneously the most strenuous efforts were made to strengthen the land forces, we may assume that the Spartans and Athenians each had some 5,000 hoplites, and all the others together had about the same combined number there; the entire army was therefore about 20,000 hoplites strong, and with the same number of unarmored men, formed a mass of 40,000 men. The Persians, with the Greeks who were subject to them, probably approached the same strength. If Mardonius had had a significant or even a twofold superiority, he would not have remained quietly on the Asopus but would have enveloped the Greeks through one of the eastern passes of Mount Cithaeron with half of his army and would have cut their supply lines or attacked them from the rear, while holding them fixed from the front with the other half.

Even with a more modest numerical superiority, Mardonius would probably have been able to carry out, and would actually have carried out, the enveloping maneuver without concern that the separate portions of the army could be attacked individually and defeated. For, being at least the equal of the Greek militia in military quality, the Persian army was so very superior to its enemy in maneuverability, through its combination of the various arms, that even an isolated force could not so easily be forced into a battle against its will. By virtue of their reinforcement by the Greek communities, the Persians now had hoplites also, in addition to their cavalry and archers. The fact that they remained quietly by the Asopus can therefore only be satisfactorily explained if we assume that Mardonius was only barely the equal of the Greeks in numbers, perhaps more likely weaker by a few thousand or perhaps even by quite a few thousand men.

From the strength of Mardonius' army we may now belatedly conclude that Xerxes, too, a year earlier, had had about the same number of warriors. The casualties and the troops that escorted him back and remained with him were undoubtedly richly compensated by the contingents of the subject Greeks and by some sailors from the fleet.[1] The supply train of his army, judging from the many aristocratic elements composing the army, was probably relatively stronger than that of the Greeks and can easily have amounted to some 40,000 to 50,000 persons, so that the entire force formed a mass of 50,000 to 70,000 souls, a multitude that seemed innumerable to the Greeks, so that they indulged in the most extreme numerical fantasies on that score.

The popular account of Plataea, as it appears in Herodotus, is thorough and rich in details, but full of contradictions, which up to the present have not lent themselves to unraveling. Whoever wishes to get a correct concept of how far legend can vary from the real truth in a single generation should, I suggest, refer once again to the history of the Burgundian Wars by Bullinger. It is also extremely interesting from the viewpoint of national psychology to see how similarly the folk fantasy has worked with peoples who are nevertheless so different as Hellenes and Swiss, and how it has fashioned almost identical pictures and types, without any indication of imitation or copying.

But although every single point, every single account must be considered as not truly proven and therefore subject to doubt, nevertheless an attempt at reconstruction is not so completely hopeless. However unreliable the legend may be in all its details, a few facts do still appear in it that cannot very well have been invented and that give us the possibility of establishing with certainty what is really important, the typical, the principal elements of the outcome of the battle. But we may be led even further by the topography. In his work, which was already referred to, Grundy presented an extremely careful study and identification of the terrain of Plataea, which was still unknown to me when I was writing the first edition of this work, but which provided for one of my students, Ludwig Winter,[2] the basis for what appears to me to be a very successful reconstruction.

Through a correlation with the admittedly very few definite points, it was possible to fix on the terrain all the names of passes, bays, hills, temples, which Herodotus wrote of in profusion and to see if the movements of the two armies could be reconciled with them. It is the same situation as with Marathon and Salamis. The terrain on which a battle is fought is such an important element of the event that, as soon as this is clarified, the military-history picture, too, loses its veil.

As soon as the Greeks debouched from the Cithaeron pass onto the northern side of the mountain, the Persian mounted archers fell upon them. The Megarans, who formed the point, were hard pressed until the Athenians came to their aid with their archers. Gradually more and more Greeks came welling out of the pass, and since they did not push farther down the mountain but held fast on the slope, the Persians broke off the battle without committing their foot soldiers.

Pausanias showed here that he had understood the lessons of Marathon and intended to be guided by them. That was not so simple, however. His army consisted of the militia of some twenty independent communities, people who were anxious to get home again in order to get on with their normal lives, and who did not understand the reason for the delaying strategy of their commander. Pausanias knew what he was about. He had a prophet come to him to whom he gave enough insight into the tactical situation to allow him to recognize from the omens that the Hellenes would conquer if they remained on the defensive and did not cross the Asopus, the small river in front of them. Although there was finally a serious lack of provisions in the Greek ranks, they still held fast in their position.

After a few days Pausanias moved his position farther forward, onto the last hill at the edge of the plain, directly at the foot of which the Asopus flows. This maneuver was obviously intended to lure the enemy to attack. They extended the position just as far out as possible without completely giving up the advantage of the defensive position, covered as it was on the right and the left.

But Mardonius knew just as well as Pausanias what this tactic demanded of him and what the worth of a good prophet was. He, too, had a soothsayer come to him who saw from the omens that the Persians did not dare to cross over the Asopus.

Instead of attacking the Greeks on their hill, Mardonius with his archers prevented them from drawing water from the Asopus, and his cavalry even rode around the hill and stopped up the spring (Gargaphia) on the rear of the hill and intercepted their supplies.

In this way he brought the Greeks to such distress that Pausanias finally had no other recourse but to withdraw. He intended to take up a position somewhat farther to the rear, close to the city of Plataea, where neither water nor supplies could be cut off from the army. The withdrawal was not so simple, since, with the Persian army so close, they could easily be attacked while on the march. It was therefore decided to withdraw in the night, dividing the army into three columns. The Spartans remained until the end. Herodotus tells of the leader of a *lochus*, Amompharetus, who had hesitated to withdraw, had quarreled with the King over that point, and had finally laid a stone with both hands at the King's feet. But since Amompharetus after all did finally follow the others, it appears that the story should be interpreted as follows: the captain was in no way opposing the King but, on the contrary, had sworn to him to hold out on the hill like that stone, and to cover the withdrawal.

When the Persians discovered in the morning that the Greeks had withdrawn, they moved out at once and took up their pursuit. They caught up with them before the Greeks had joined forces again, and it was undoubtedly this division of the Greeks that moved Mardonius to discount his oracle and to order the attack.

At one point, in the area of the Megarans and the Phliasians, the Persians were victorious. This may be because the Megarans and Phliasians, after the outcome of the battle was already decided, ventured carelessly and in poor order onto the plain, as Herodotus recounts, or—since we cannot rely too strongly on the account as such—because other advantageous circumstances favored the success of the cavalry attack. The Athenians, in their area, fell upon the Greek allies of the Persians and defeated them in a steady, but probably not very stubborn, hoplite battle. The real and characteristic combat, however, was waged by the Spartans and the Tegeans, who were attached to them.

When the Persians moved up into the attack against the Spartans, Herodotus tells us, they literally smothered them with arrows. Many of them were killed and wounded, but they took the losses and stood fast, because the omens were not yet favorable. Finally, when Pausanias invoked the aid of the Hera of Plataea, whose temple was visible from the Spartans' position, the augury became favorable, the Spartans charged against the enemy, and the Persians, without sufficient defensive weapons, could not withstand the massed storm of the ironclad men.

Pausanias knew how to make use of prophets and priests. As long as the forward elements of the Persians were only shooting at the phalanx from a distance, probably to lure the Greeks into a premature attack, he had his men stand fast. Not until the mass of the Persians had come closer, onto the spot that he had chosen, did Pausanias raise his hands in prayer to the goddess, and the understanding priest immediately saw this and announced that the augury had become favorable, whereupon Pausanias gave the signal for the attack.

Although right up to this moment we had been hearing continuously of the Persian cavalry, who were pressing the Greeks, we now hear nothing of their moving into the Greek flanks during this attack; they only cover the withdrawal. Pausanias managed, therefore, to fight the battle on terrain where the Persian cavalry could not attack the phalanx in the flank, and Winter has now been able to establish this position correctly. The analogy with Marathon is complete. One might question all the details, but this much can still be accepted with certainty: the Persians finally risked the attack, and the battle took place in a manner similar to that of Marathon, just as Pausanias had planned it from the very beginning. Without Marathon we would not be in a position to detect any kind of historical nucleus in the account, but Marathon provides the key to the understanding of the battle, and from this point on I have no hesitation in moving still one step farther and declaring the account of the steadfastness of the Spartans under the hail of Persian arrows, of the unfavorable augury, and of the prayer of Pausanias to be verified historical facts. There are undoubtedly few examples in history in which we can so clearly recognize the core of the historical happening within the wonderful embellishment of the popular legend.

It seems to me not at all impossible that, in Mardonius' decision to force the issue by battle, a certain role was played by a strategic consideration of which there is no trace in the account, but which seems logical by the nature of the situation.

If we observe in an isolated way the Boeotian theater of operations, it seems that it would have been the Greeks who had to push for a decision. Mardonius had indeed resorted to a war of attrition; he was having his army supplied by the subjected Greeks and was threatening Attica with renewed desolation. But Boeotia is only a part of the theater of operations. It cannot have escaped Mardonius' notice—the Greeks themselves undoubtedly saw to it that he knew—that their fleet had sailed off to Ionia and that they hoped to incite rebellion in that area. It would, indeed, not be too bold to assume that Xerxes himself recognized the danger in Sardis and sent a message to Mardonius to hasten to bring on a decision in Hellas and send back a part of his troops to protect Ionia and hold it in subjection. Consequently, Mardonius now had the stronger reason for seeking a decision, and this would explain why, despite his reasonable recognition that it would be more favorable for him tactically to remain on the defensive and await the Greek attack on the plain, he nevertheless finally moved to attack first.

It still remains unexplained why a force of Persians under the command of Artabazus did not, according to Herodotus' account, take part in the battle. Presumably it simply arrived too late.

The fact that the Greeks divided their forces and, while moving against Mardonius, simultaneously sent off a great fleet, appears on the face of it to be a great error. Why did they not first strike Mardonius with their assembled forces and then move out across the sea? In this case, as we shall often see later, strategy is seen to be dependent on tactics. Even 10,000 more hoplites would not have enabled the Greeks to move down onto the Boeotian plain and attack the Persians at a favorable spot in the open field. They had no choice but to offer them a defensive battle on terrain covered against their cavalry and to seek to lure them into attacking. This was accomplished by the sea expedition and perhaps also by the repeated shifting of position that Pausanias ordered. Is anybody willing to believe that there was only coincidence in all these connected events, only the effects of blind superstition in the soothsaying and sacrificial auguries? Such an opinion could not be disproved, but I have enough confidence in Themistocles and Pausanias to believe that, as the Greeks picture them to us, they knew what they were doing. Side by side with Miltiades and Leonidas, what men these were, men who knew how to combine a strategic understanding and heroism with the cleverness and skill of the superior mind, to understand the overall situation from afar, and to resort to the most extreme means, the appearance of treachery, the utilization of the superstition of the masses, in order to arrive at their high goals!

Excursus

1. At the same time as the battle of Plataea the Greeks were also winning in Asia Minor at Mycale. Here, where there is no mention of Persian cavalry, the Greeks were supposedly the attackers. During the battle the Ionians defected to them. Since the hoplite contingents of the Greek fleet were under any circumstances only very small, the Persian army, too, at least after the withdrawal of the Ionians, must have been very small—another bit of testimony that Xerxes did not have huge masses of warriors at his disposal. Otherwise, it would not have been hard for him to assemble a new army in the interval of almost a year since Salamis. The military efficiency of the Persians was not yet broken; even some twenty-five years later they defeated an important Athenian army in Egypt and completely destroyed it.

2. The same ingenious soothsayer who had guided the Spartans so well at Plataea was also with them when they conquered the Arcadians in a hard-fought battle at Dipaea somewhere around 467 B.C. During the night before this battle an altar embellished with shining equipment had erected itself spontaneously in the Spartan camp, and around it could be seen the tracks of two steeds. From these signs the warriors realized that the godly Dioscuri had come to their aid, and they were inspired with such courage and such enthusiasm that they overcame the enemy, who was far superior to them in numbers. The enlightened Greek who passed this story on to us, however, explains that King Archidamus had the altars erected and the horses led around them in order to strengthen the courage of his warriors. (Herodotus 9. 35; Polyaenus, *Strategica* 1. 41).

3. At this point I come back once again to Hauvette's book.

Hauvette believes in the 2,100,000 warrior strength of the Persian land army. He admits that the number might be exaggerated by some 100,000 men, but specifically the 80,000 cavalrymen seem to him an entirely credible number (pp. 311–12). My objection, to the effect that the Persian army, under modern conditions, would have reached from Berlin to Damascus, and, even if reduced to one-third of the space required by a modern army, would have been so long that, when the head of the column was arriving before Thermopylae, the tail could have been just marching out of Sardis—this objection makes no impression on Hauvette, since the conditions governing ancient armies, of course, were completely different from those of modern armies. Modern armies march only in four-man ranks, so that half of the road may remain open, and furthermore a considerable interval is always maintained between companies, battalions, regiments, and divisions. According to Hauvette, the Persians knew nothing of all this. Xenophon in the *Cyropaedia*, on one occasion, has a cavalry unit of 10,000 men forming a square 100 men wide by 100 deep. The Persians of Xerxes could have marched in a similar formation.

The width of a marching troop column depends on the width of the road. If the road is too narrow for the column, even at only a few places, that still creates a march disruption that builds up progressively toward the rear and finally becomes completely intolerable. The troops who are marching farther toward the rear are forced to wait for hours and use up their strength in so doing, or, if they are not well disciplined, they fall out of formation. The foremost troops extend out in the same manner, and the column falls completely apart. Every good commander therefore considers it of the highest importance to avoid march jam-ups, or, since with large masses that is hardly ever attained, to reduce them to a minimum. For this reason intervals are established between the various units, so that the smaller hold-ups can immediately be absorbed, and the higher leaders are constantly concerned with maintaining the intervals. If, as Hauvette believes and is certainly possible, the Persians did not take these steps, their march columns must have stretched out relatively still farther than the modern ones. Modern troops also see to it very deliberately that half of the road remains as open as possible. In the case of every marching column it is absolutely necessary, especially in enemy territory, that movement and communication be possible alongside the column for high-ranking officers, liaison officers, messengers, and under certain circumstances also for quickly moving forward a special unit, such as cavalry. That cannot have been any different with the Persians. On the long route from Sardis to the Hellespont and from the Hellespont to Attica there are numerous rivers to be crossed, mountainous land to pass through, passes to overcome. At many places the bridges, fords, and mountain paths were undoubtedly not broader but narrower than those with which modern armies have to contend. The Persians must have marched with a column, not 100 men wide, certainly often not even 4 men wide, but only 2 men in width, using quite naturally at the same time, wherever possible, several parallel roads.

In the handwritten account by a general of the Prussian Guard Corps, which on 18 August 1870 marched forward under special orders with a wider than usual front, I have found a rather long comment to the effect that, in the experience of the author, such a march with a broad front on a road does not attain its purpose, but "rather was very tiring because of frequent stops, holdups, and resumptions of the march, and quite naturally for such a long march, caused breaks to develop in the column, which showed up as a lack of good order."

The difference between Hauvette's estimate (something like 1,700,000 warriors) and mine (at the most 25,000, but probably more like 15,000 to 20,000 warriors) is very great, but it gives a quite appropriate indication of the differences of methodology of our respective research. The differences are so great that any kind of reconciliation seems impossible. Every single fact in the Persian Wars, every attempt at a causal explanation of the relationships, necessarily appears different, depending on which of the two army strengths one accepts, or whether one can even come close to one of them. I therefore believe that it is no use going further into details, and I give up the idea of contradicting other false concepts in this book, once again pointing out that Hauvette is in no way weak in either scholarship or intelligence, but that our methods are different—naturally different only from the point of view of their application. In principle, Hauvette, too, does not reject the objective approach. He too has cited practical, objective considerations, for example, in the question of the run at Marathon, in connection with march intervals, and so on. But he does not follow through with them, and he exposes himself to the illusion that, where an eye with exclusively philological training sees no impossibilities, none are actually present.

4. Whatever mass the army of Xerxes formed and whatever it was by my estimates, one can best understand by imagining the army on the march. Twenty thousand warriors, or with the great supply train, in all perhaps some 70,000 souls strong, with many horses, little march discipline, roads that were often narrowed down, uneven, impaired by inclines, washouts, and other natural obstacles—we must imagine this whole contingent as forming a column at least 73 kilometers long (where parallel roads could not be used). If the situation was not critical, the point

would normally not set out before five o'clock in the morning and the tail of the column would not arrive in camp later than six o'clock in the evening. If one plans to march 15 kilometers, or the equivalent of four hours, then the last troops must start the march at two o'clock in the afternoon—that is, half the army does not yet reach the march objective on the first day, or, in other words, for more than two days the inhabitants see new troops continuously marching by, and even on the third day still some further troops march by, and presumably even on the next few days still many stragglers. It is not surprising that under these circumstances one gives up counting.

NOTES FOR CHAPTER IX

1. Herodotus 9. 32.
2. Berlin dissertation, 1907.

BOOK II

The Greeks at Their Height

Chapter I

Greek Tactics up to the Peloponnesian War

Through the entire fifth century the hoplite phalanx, which had defeated the Persians, remained the basic formation of Greek tactics.

The hoplite phalanx is the logical tactical formation for a military citizens' militia. The demands on the individual are all very simple and require only little drill. Each man learns how to move in his heavy equipment, how to manipulate his spear, how to stay in file and maintain his direction. No elaborate drills are necessary. The ensemble forms a single, closed formation that marches straight ahead and takes up the run for the attack a short distance in front of the enemy. According to Herodotus, this approach run is supposed to have been done for the first time at Marathon.

In a normal hoplite battle it usually happened that both sides moved somewhat to their right and the left flank hung somewhat behind, because each individual man was aware that his right, unshielded side was less protected and for that reason sought to come at the enemy from the right. Each side, therefore, easily overlapped the other from the right, won this flank from him, and consequently had the better of it at this spot. Then the two victorious right wings had to fight, for the second time, often with their front reversed, against each other, and it was not until this second act of the encounter that the battle was decided.

Nevertheless, no kind of tactical conclusions whatever have yet been drawn from this peculiarity; the basic character of the combat remains that of a parallel battle without articulation.

These tactics were retained, even though their weaknesses were realized and had already been known before the Persian Wars. As early as 511 B.C. the Spartans suffered a defeat at the hands of the

123

Thessalonian cavalry on the plain not far from Athens (Herodotus 5. 63), and the entire course of the Persian Wars was marked by the Greeks' fear of the Persian cavalry. Even in the battle of Plataea some of the Greek contingents suffered very heavy losses by being caught by the Theban cavalry.

And yet we hear nothing of any attempts to guard themselves in principle against this weakness by means of new tactical formations or battle tactics. The cavalrymen, archers, and other lightly armed men remained simple auxiliary arms beside the hoplite phalanx, perhaps under certain circumstances exercising a strong influence, but not yet considered capable of being an important, organic part of the army. Even as early as the Persian Wars this was basically true. If in these wars we hear nothing about cavalry on the Greek side, that is not to be understood as meaning that they had previously not had any at all, but only that their few cavalrymen could not risk riding out against the Persians, and consequently presumably most of the mounted men left their horses at home and took their places in the hoplites' ranks.

Neither in Sparta nor in Athens were the conditions favorable for forming a truly strong cavalry,[1] even though in the campaign of the Athenians on Sicily, for example, the cavalry did play quite an important role.[2]

As with the cavalry, so too must the Athenian archers, in my opinion, be regarded as an elite corps.[3] Even though their equipment was less expensive than that of the hoplites, nevertheless an archer required much more intensive training in order to be really effective. A hoplite was very quickly sufficiently trained to allow his being incorporated in the mass, by which he was swept up and carried along. The archer not only had to be an expert shot but also very quick and coordinated, in order to be able to approach close to the enemy and yet, when he himself was attacked, to be able to withdraw again quickly. He therefore had to have self-reliance, alertness, judgment, and presence of mind. In nations with a warlike tradition, such characteristics are imparted from an early age through the training of the youth. In highly civilized states, such as the Athens of that day, they are produced in the higher classes, who have enough time and leisure to devote themselves to practice. I look for the archers, therefore, in the class of Athenian citizenry whose sons were not rich enough to maintain a horse but who could, nevertheless, spend somewhat more time and effort in military training than the great mass of the citizens. Moreover, a truly good bow was also an expensive weapon.

In the ranks of sharpshooters, besides the archers, there were also the slingers and the spear-throwers. The manipulation of the sling involves a great skill, which is only attained in places where the youth, in keeping with a local tradition, practice at it from an early age. On Rhodes, for example, such a tradition existed, and Rhodes slingers were consequently much in demand as mercenaries.

The spear-thrower cannot stand up to either the bow or the slinger if, like the latter, he has no defensive arms. But his weapon does not exclude the possibility of a light protective equipment. And so, first of all, there were formed among the northerly, half-Greek strains, where one did not have the means for the construction of many sets of complete armor, a special combat branch made up of spear-throwers, the peltasts. They were equipped with a light round shield, a hat, generally probably also a stiff cape made of leather or quilted linen, several spears, and a sword. The present-day Bantu and Sudan Negroes can throw the spear to a distance of forty paces.

Naturally, the peltasts could not risk a direct clash with hoplites in equal numbers, but it was easy to organize a larger number of them,[4] and under difficult terrain conditions they could move more easily and operate very effectively against flanks or rear of a hoplite phalanx. Under such circumstances the archer and the slinger were even more dangerous for the hoplites, but in case of emergency the peltast had the advantage of joining in the hand-to-hand combat. Both hoplite and archer were to a high degree narrowly limited in their performance; the peltast could be used for anything. He threw his spear from a distance, moved with ease forward and to the rear, and by virtue of his shield he had just enough protection to enable him to participate in close combat, too.

The unarmored men who accompanied the army as servants or supply train drivers retained the same character they had in the Persian Wars. Quite similar to the manner in which the Athenians, according to the description in Aeschylus' *Persians* (verse 441), crossed over to the island of Psyttalea after the decision at Salamis and first bombarded the isolated Persians with stones until they fell on them with cold steel—so, in Thucydides 1. 106, the Athenian hoplites blocked the route of a Corinthian unit that was cut off, and the "lightly armed men"* killed them with stones. We might be seeing here a change, to the extent that, in Athens at any rate, more and more slaves were taken along into the field as servants. Whatever purely military weakening was caused by this was counterbalanced by the broadened contribution of specially trained lightly armed men.

In battle formation, cavalry and unarmored men, as well as the peltasts, were placed on the flanks of the hoplite phalanx.

Under favorable circumstances, now and then cavalry or the lightly armed units were successful in supporting the hoplites very effectively in the fight and in bringing about the decision or even in defeating a hoplite force on their own.

Simple as the tactical formations of the combat of the Peloponnesian War may seem, the methods of fortification and siegecraft were still more primitive. They built simple walls, and although they were just sufficiently guarded, they seem to have been invincible. Even with immeasurable superiority in numbers, the besiegers neither knew how, nor dared, to undertake an attack by force but sought to starve out the besieged place.

EXCURSUS

1. The Greek word *psiloi* covers in general all those who have no protective equipment, and consequently both the train attendants, who only occasionally exercised a combat function, and also the real fighters, archers, slingers, spear-throwers. For that reason I have translated it as "unarmored."

In Thucydides 1. 60, the Corinthians send 1,600 hoplites and 400 "lightly armed men"* to Potidaea. Obviously it is not meant that these 400 were train attendants but actual warriors.

In 2. 79, Thucydides obviously also counts the peltasts among the "lightly armed men."*

On the other hand, in 4. 93, at Delium he makes a distinction and names first 10,000 "lightly armed men"* and then also particularly 500 peltasts.

In 4. 94, it reads: "Regular lightly armed troops, equipped and armed."* This sentence is not very easy to understand. Thucydides distinguishes "lightly armed men"* in the sense of the armed train, which had accompanied this army in large numbers but which had already moved out on the withdrawal, from "regular lightly armed men,"* that is, warriors who were equipped as such but had no defensive weapons—consequently, archers, slingers, and perhaps peltasts. But now when he says that the city did not possess that kind of unarmored men, this stands in contradiction to the speech of Pericles, in 2. 13, where it is expressly said that the city had 1,600 archers. The explanation probably is that Thucydides was not thinking here of archers, who formed a special arm, but was considering under "regular lightly armed men"* lightly armed men of the type of the peltasts. At any rate, this passage shows that by plain "lightly armed men"* Thucydides was not thinking of any real fighting men, since they were not "regular,"* that is, intentionally, systematically, and specifically equipped with weapons.

CHARACTERISTIC BATTLES OF THIS PERIOD
2. At Potidaea in 432 B.C. (Thucydides 1. 1. 2 ff.) both sides—the Athenians and their allied opponents, the Chalcidians and the Corinthians—had, in addition to their hoplites, several hundred cavalry. The cavalry were detached however, and on both sides held back at some distance from the battle, so that only the hoplites

fought against each other. Each side was victorious on one of the flanks; the allies then broke off the contact and, massed together tightly, quickly moved past the victorious Athenians and withdrew into the city of Potidaea.

3. In the battle of Spartolus in 429 B.C. (Thucydides 2. 79) the Chalcidian hoplites were defeated by the 2,000-strong Athenian hoplites. The Chalcidian cavalry and unarmored men, including peltasts, on the other hand, defeated the Athenian cavalry and unarmored men. Encouraged by this success, the Chalcidian cavalry, peltasts, and other unarmored troops (apparently very superior in numbers) now attacked the Athenian hoplites, constantly drawing back as soon as the latter attacked and then moving forward again as soon as the Athenians halted or turned away, and shot at the Athenians from afar. In this way they finally drove them into flight, pursued them, and killed 430 hoplites of the total of 2,000, including all the leaders.

4. In the year 426 B.C., in Aetolia, the Athenians, under the command of one of their best generals, Demosthenes, suffered a defeat very similar to that at Spartolus. As long as their archers still had arrows, they held off the enemy spear-throwers; but when their arrows had all been shot, the lightly armed enemy, constantly attacking and then withdrawing, pushed in on the hoplites from all sides, wore them down, and finally annihilated the majority of them. In this wooded, hilly area cavalry played no part in the battle.

5. In the same manner the Athenians overcame the 420 Spartans isolated on the island of Sphacteria in 424 B.C. (Thucydides 4. 27-29). Small as the band of Spartan hoplites was, the Athenians still did not wish to attack them directly, in order to avoid the heavy losses associated with an obstinately fought hand-to-hand combat against skillful and despairing warriors. They therefore held back their hoplites and released against the Spartans a huge mass of unarmored men, ranging from archers all the way down to the oarsmen of triremes, who threw stones. To these overwhelming numbers, swarming on them from all sides, the Spartans finally succumbed, without the Athenians having suffered any significant losses. Of special note in this case was the fact that the noise of the mass prevented the Spartans from understanding their leaders' commands.

In the second volume of the first edition of this work I added supplementary comments to the foregoing passage, which might now better be moved to this position.

I did not introduce into my account in this work the taking of the Spartans as prisoners on Sphacteria in the year 425 B.C., for, interesting as this event is in itself, it still has no place in a history of the art of war. A history of the military art is not a general military history; I should also like, incidentally, to point this out to Adolf Bauer, who is surprised that I treated the history of the Diadochi so briefly (*Historische Zeitschrift* 86: 285). I am not willing to recognize this as an error until somebody has proved that in this period a change took place in the art of military command—a change that escaped my notice.

With the stipulation, however, that it really does not belong here, I still wish to introduce a few words on Sphacteria, because Eduard Meyer (2:333) has declared that he does not agree with a study I published earlier on this subject ("The Strategy of Pericles clarified through the Strategy of Frederick the Great," Annex [Die Strategie des Perikles erläutert durch die Strategie Friedrichs des Grossen]), but his polemic is based entirely on misunderstandings, and I would like to protect other readers from these errors. I shall not hesitate to state in advance, however, that I consider the present question, the description of Thucydides and his judgment of Cleon in this matter, as the most difficult theme and the finest psychological problem in all of world military history. Thucydides is unconditionally, exclusively, and completely right; whoever is not willing to be satisfied, however, with simply accepting his judgment but wants to form his own conclusion in independent analysis, should not risk this until he has studied Clausewitz through and through and has become so familiar with his psychology of strategy that he is able to apply it with completely independent certainty.

Here I shall simply list the misunderstandings and errors of Meyer's study.

I stated that the landing of the Athenians on the island succeeded essentially because the Spartans were not on guard. I pointed out that the island was not even four kilometers long; that if the Spartans had established posts all around and had set up a signal system, then a half-hour after the Athenians' approach had been observed—consequently before the landing was really completed and the landing force formed up in order—the main body of the Spartans could have been on the spot and have thrown the landing force back into the sea. Meyer finds it "understandable" that the beleaguered troops did not act in this way. Not once in the two months since the end of the armistice had the Athenians attempted an attack. "So it is not surprising that the Spartans were not expecting an attack and were not exhausting their strength through strenuous guard duty." This excuse for the Spartans is undoubtedly all the less satisfying in that there could be no question of "strenuous guard duty." After all, what does a beleaguered garrison have to do except to maintain its observation posts?

Thanks to an excellent topographical study by the Englishman Grundy (*Journal of Hellenic Studies*, Vol. 16, 1896) we have recently been put in a position to examine the tactical question still more definitely, and my earlier conjectures, based more on theory, have thereby gained important reinforcement.

The island of Sphacteria rises up from the sea on all sides with steep slopes and cliffs to a height of several hundred feet. It is quite narrow (500 to 750 meters) and some 2 miles long. Only at seven locations is a landing possible, and of these seven sites, one is at the northern point and all the others are in the middle or at the south end. The northern approach, however, immediately rises up steeply, and it was therefore not usable for the landing and deployment of a rather large force. The landing sites of possible usefulness for the Athenians were the central and southerly ones, where steep slopes do not rise up immediately from the beach but a more gradual, broader slope leads upward between the cliffs. The mission of the Spartan leader Epitadas should have been to have all of these landing sites kept under observation.

The posting at each of the seven sites of two Spartiates and a dozen Helots, relieved daily, could hardly be called a great effort. But, according to Meyer, even if the Spartans had done that, it would not have changed the situation very much. The Athenians would at any place have overcome the weak outposts and would have established a foothold before reinforcements arrived. This is, from every point of view, a false concept of the military situation. There can be no question of "overcoming" the outposts, since they would naturally not have allowed themselves to be drawn into combat. Their only mission was to give the signal promptly and to dispatch a runner. It was a question of nothing else but the proper functioning of this warning system. The landing of several thousand men (hoplites and lightly armed soldiers) in a narrow space does not take place so quickly. Furthermore, no point on the island was more than two kilometers distant from the Spartan camp in the middle of the island. In fact, since the landing sites that really called for a close watch were all in the one general area, the Spartans, by camping not exactly in the middle but still somewhat farther to the south, could have been on the scene even faster. If the Athenians landed at the northerly point, the Spartans would have taken somewhat longer to arrive there, but they would nevertheless still have certainly arrived before the Athenians had mounted the cliff. The site where the Athenians actually landed, according to Grundy, is not more than 1,200 meters distant from the place where the Spartans were encamped, near the spring in the middle of the island. And here we must point out something that is at least very questionable: we doubt that the Athenians would have been in battle order before the Spartans, if they were only alerted at once, were already in the attack; moreover, in view of the awesome respect that the Spartan phalanx still enjoyed, a large number of already debarked but still unordered troops would hardly have been inclined even to stand up to the attack. It is not mistakenly that Grundy states that Thucydides' account of the battle of the huge superior force of the Athenians against the small Spartan phalanx gives the impression of a pack of snarling dogs surrounding a dying lion but afraid to approach him.

If it were really true that, as Meyer says, "such an extended position as that of Sphacteria cannot be defended against a surprise attack"—in other words, if a failure was as good as impossible in view of the great numerical superiority of the Athenians, then it must certainly be clear that all the Athenian leaders who were not willing to move into action are stamped as some kind of blockheads. But even Meyer cannot avoid admitting, later, that "the attack on the island [was] nevertheless a risky undertaking," since the enemies could by chance be warned or by chance be very alert. If we assume, instead of a chance alertness, a constant and continuous watchfulness, then we are in agreement. It is completely false to conclude, however, that the realization of the danger of the undertaking made it inadvisable.

When Meyer misconstrues me by saying that I am "inclined to agree with the judgment," as Nicias perhaps may have had it, "that the landing was the purest dilettantism and flies in the face of the first rules of correct, methodical leadership," this only proves how completely he has misunderstood me. From the same misunderstanding there arises also the reproach that I had left out of consideration the fact that the Athenian position would become untenable if the blockade dragged on into the winter. I did not indulge in this speculation, because there is nothing in the world more certain than that the Athenians had the highest possible interest in overcoming the beleaguered troops before the winter.

Since Meyer considers the landing on Sphacteria to be a rather easily accomplished affair, as a matter of consistency he rejects as inappropriate the reference I made, by way of illustration, to the abortive landing on Alsen. He states that at Alsen the Danes had dominated the sea and the Prussians had landed under the fire of the Danish canister. Here, then, the operation was, to be sure, very difficult and dangerous. The difference is obvious, but it is compensated by other circumstances. Alsen is an island 15 kilometers long, broken by steep-banked bays, so that it was possible that many hours might pass before the main Danish force appeared at a point on the coast taken by surprise attack. Sphacteria is a very small island, on which the garrison, at any point, if it but made the correct preparations and maintained a sharp lookout, could be on the spot in almost a moment. The common denominator therefore is the fact that in both cases success depended exclusively on surprise. Finally, I should like to add that Meyer confuses the landing attempts at Alsen. The one of which I spoke is not supposed to have taken place at the same location as the one that was actually carried out later under the fire of the Danish cannon, the one of which Meyer speaks. At Ballegaard, where the first attack was to take place, the bay is so wide that the interval from one echelon to the arrival of the next was necessarily two hours; on the other hand, however, the position is also very distant from Sonderburg. Satrup, where the crossing was actually carried out three months later, is situated quite close to Sonderburg, but there the bay is only very narrow.

Although Meyer pictures the landing on Sphacteria as an operation that could hardly fail, in his opinion the significant accomplishment, a purely technical one; is attributed to Demosthenes as the commanding general.

"Cleon's role consists only of the fact that he made the operation possible and took upon himself the moral responsibility for it." It is impossible to misunderstand more strongly than this the nature of strategy. Great as the accomplishment of Demosthenes in the execution of the plan was, the real deed is still that of the man who made the overall decision and bore the responsibility for it and who, in addition, had enough understanding and knowledge of human nature to call into his service the most outstanding military technician and to turn over to him the practical execution of the plan. Not until one becomes completely aware of the full meaning of Cleon's act can one also recognize the full difficulty of the problem: that this same man, nevertheless, is supposed to have been an upstart, brutal demagogue. From Grote to Lange the solution has been sought by exalting Cleon's personality and declaring Thucydides' judgment unjust. Meyer, who agrees with me in the conclusion that Amphipolis shows the complete nullity of Cleon, seeks to establish the consistency of his personality by downgrading his accomplishment at Sphacteria. The one solution is as false as the other. Cleon really accomplished a great deed at Sphacteria, and it is in no way my opinion, as Meyer seems to indicate (p. 333), that he succeeded only because of the favorable circumstances.

If the matter were so simple, why would Thucydides not have told it in that manner? Why does he not simply attribute the accomplishment to Demosthenes, as Aristophanes did? Why does he confuse us by first calling Cleon's demands "crazy" and then immediately afterward recounting their brilliant execution? Before one criticizes Thucydides, one should seek to understand him, and I am glad that Meyer, too, decisively rejects all the errors of false modern scholarship, which claims to judge Pericles' strategic plan or the events of Amphipolis more wisely than the master. But the point about Cleon and Sphacteria must also be held firmly. Thucydides knew very well what he was doing when he in no way diminished the objective accomplishment of the demagogue and at the same time showed us the man himself as a worthless poltroon.

It is precisely this paradox that makes Cleon primarily the political type, a role in which he lives on—and deservedly so—in history. Thucydides would hardly have considered it worth the trouble to picture this repulsive person for us so carefully if his intervention had been of so little importance, or if the fruits of Sphacteria had been so easily plucked. Yes, one may even go one step farther and say that not only Cleon but all of Athens, in the period between the death of Pericles and the ascendancy of Alcibiades, loses all political interest for us, if the city was at that time so poor in political virtue, character, and intelligence as Meyer would have us believe. But it was not at all like this. The task confronting Athens was, rather, so great and so difficult, that only a very great man could have done justice to it in all respects. Such a man was not at hand, and so it happened that Cleon was able not only to win a position but also, for once, to accomplish a truly great deed. In no other way may Thucydides be interpreted, and whoever still has doubt in his soul and does not feel satisfied with my commentary in the above-mentioned pamphlet—to him I can only give a single piece of advice: Study Clausewitz, again and again, until you have understood Thucydides. (Compare also the following chapter, excursus 6.)

6. At Olpae in 426 B.C. Demosthenes defeated an Ambraciot and Peloponnesian army, although his numbers were smaller, by laying an ambush that fell on the enemy from the rear as the battle was beginning. Very seldom do we find such a maneuver.

7. The description that Thucydides (4. 93–96)[5] gives of the battle of Delium (424 B.C.) seems to be a preview of a later period. Both sides, Athenians and Boeotians, had the same strength in hoplites, 7,000 men. In addition, the Boeotians had 10,000 unarmored men, the Athenians only a few, since the mass of this type that they also possessed had already marched off. The Boeotians had, further, 1,000 cavalrymen; the number of Athenian cavalry is not given, but it was under any circumstances considerably less than that of the Boeotians. At that time Athens had all together hardly more than 900 mounted men, and of these there were naturally a considerable number who were not participating in the campaign, and 300 cavalry had been left behind at Delium in order to operate from that base against the Boeotians' rear; they were, however, held in check by the Boeotian cavalry.

The entire mass of the Boeotian unarmored men had no effect at all in the battle, since forest streams prevented them from closing with the enemy—probably an indication that the warlike zeal of the unarmored men was very slight. The battle was fought, as usual, by the hoplites. The Athenian hoplites stood uniformly 8 men deep, and therefore had a front of some 880 men. The Boeotians stood in varying depth in the different contingents; specifically, the main body, composed of the Thebans, was no less than 25 men deep. The Boeotian battle line must therefore have been considerably shorter than the Athenian. This was counterbalanced, however, by the superiority of the Boeotian cavalry.

There is no account of an actual cavalry combat. The Athenians were victorious on their right flank and then swung around, surrounding the Boeotians who stood farther toward the middle, who suffered heavy losses. But in the meantime the deep Theban battle mass, covered on its flank by the cavalry and perhaps also by the terrain, had pushed back the opposing left wing of the Athenians, and when the combat went well for the Boeotians at this point, the Theban commander, Pagondas, sent two cavalry detachments to the aid of the other wing. Their sudden appearance spread terror among the Athenians, and here, too, the battle was decided in favor of the Boeotians. In the pursuit of the fleeing Athenian hoplites, in addition to the cavalry, the numerous Boeotian unarmored men also proved effective and killed very many of the enemy.

8. In the annex to my book *The Strategy of Pericles* (*Die Strategie des Perikles*) I gave a thorough treatment of the battle of Amphipolis (422 B.C.). The Athenians lost the battle because of the lack of ability of Cleon, who, in his insolent thoughtlessness, exposed the army to an attack just as it had gone from battle formation into march formation. The Lacedaemonian hoplites of Brasidas were supported by lightly armed men and cavalry.

9. In the battle of Mantinea (418 B.C.) the Spartan army probably had a total strength of some 7,000 to 8,000 men,[6] and was slightly stronger than the opposing Mantineans, Argives, and Athenians. Of this battle in particular, Thucydides reports for us the characteristic pulling toward the right. King Agis of Sparta wanted to prevent the envelopment of his left wing and so ordered it to cut away from the center and move to the left. Two overlapping units were supposed to move into the gap from the right wing. But the commanders of the two units did not want to give up their good locations, and so they refused to obey. Thus the left wing remained separated from the main body, and it was enveloped from both flanks and defeated. The right wing, however, won in the same manner, and since this latter victory was won over a much larger portion of the enemy army, it proved decisive; the right wing of the Mantineans and Argives did not dare take up the battle again when Agis turned against it, and it abandoned the battlefield.[7]

Thucydides points out that the losses of that wing of the Argives and Athenians that was defeated first would have been much greater if the Athenian cavalry had not come to their aid. The Spartans, too, had cavalry, but we hear nothing about any cavalry combat. There is also no mention of lightly armed troops.

10. In Thucydides 6. 64, Nicias refuses to march by land from Cantania to Syracuse, for the Syracusan cavalry would have inflicted great damage on the "lightly armed men"* and the "mass"* on the way. The Athenians were without cavalry.

At Syracuse they took up a position where the cavalry could not do them much harm. "They were protected," says Thucydides, "by walls, houses, trees, swamps, and cliffs."

11. Thucydides' report (6. 67) on the first battle of Syracuse is very unclear. The Athenians reportedly placed only half of their army in the actual battle line, forming the other half in a square farther to the rear, in the middle of which was placed the baggage; this second half was also ordered to go to the aid of the first half if necessary. Both phalanxes were 8 men deep. How are we to picture the square with the baggage in the middle? Why was the defense of the baggage not left to the large force of lightly armed men who were available from the ships' crews? As it was, the army was weak in its number of hoplites in comparison with the total levy of the Syracusans.

The Syracusans had a phalanx twice as deep as the Athenians—16 men—and they also had 1,200 cavalry. Nevertheless, the Athenians were victorious. The enemy cavalry accomplished nothing except to slow the pursuit.

The historians Grote and Holm in *History of Sicily in Antiquity* (*Geschichte Siziliens im Altertum*), 2:26, have, so far as I can see, simply repeated Thucydides' account without looking into the questions it leaves unanswered.

Despite his victory, Nicias turned back to Catania, since he supposedly could do nothing without cavalry.

The fact that the Syracusan cavalry, even if it accomplished nothing in the battle, did block the pursuit seems to place it above the Persian cavalry, which did not succeed in doing that at Marathon. The reason probably is that the Syracusans were assured of a definite means of retreat, whereas the Persian horsemen at Marathon, when the foot soldiers broke into flight, were overcome by the feeling that whoever did not get quickly aboard ship was surely lost. At Plataea, supposing that part of the Persian army was detached, the great numerical superiority of the Greeks must be considered, and we do not know whether the Persian cavalry, nevertheless, succeeded somewhat in slowing the pursuit.

12. When Gylippus came, he quickly discovered how the Syracusans should utilize their superiority in cavalry. He sent the cavalry with all his spear-throwers (Thucydides 7. 6) against the flank of the Athenians while he attacked them frontally with hoplites, and the Athenians were defeated.

13. Diodorus' account (13. 72) on the march of King Agis against Athens in 408 B.C. contains so much that is incomprehensible or unbelievable that it can hardly be used from an historical point of view. Agis' army supposedly was 14,000 hoplites strong, 14,000 "light-armed men,"* and 1,200 cavalry. The phalanx was 4 men deep and 8 *stadia*—1,500 meters—long. According to those figures, therefore, there was only 43 centimeters of front per man. At the same time, however, the army was supposed to have surrounded two-thirds of the wall of Athens. In that case it must, therefore—quite contrary to the highly compressed formation of the phalanx—have stretched out over some 30 *stadia* (some 5,600 meters) through the entire plain north of the city and on over the foothills of the Lycabettus. The Athenians reportedly sent out their cavalry, numerically the equal of the enemy, to fight him, and it was victorious. Is it conceivable that Athens could, as late as the year 408 B.C., suddenly send out 1,200 battle-ready mounted men in front of her gates? On the following day the Athenian army was reportedly drawn up so close under the walls that it was protected by the missiles being fired over its heads from above. How many hoplites was Athens actually able to form up at that time, while a great fleet was abroad under Alcibiades? Did the Spartans, who after all must have been numerically much stronger, actually hesitate to dash over the short area covered by the hail of arrows and spears in front of the wall in order to achieve the certain defeat of the Athenian hoplites, pressed as they were against the wall? As soon as they closed in hand-to-hand combat, the launching of projectiles from above surely caused them little more damage than it did the Athenians, if the wall garrison did not, indeed, stop firing altogether, in order to avoid hitting their own men.

14. The thorough account that Thucydides gives us of the siege and the starving-out of Plataea in the Peloponnesian War, has been challenged by Müller-Strübing in the *Jahrbücher für Philologie*, Vol. 131, on the basis of the topographical conditions, but it has nevertheless been fully revalidated by Hermann Wagner in the *Curriculum for the Gymnasium of Dobberan* (*Programm des Gymnasiums von Dobberan*), 1892 and 1893.

NOTES FOR CHAPTER I

1. Not until the Peloponnesian War did the Spartans create cavalry and archer units, in order to defend their land against the

Athenians, who would quickly attack from the sea, now here and now there. (Thucydides 4. 55.)

2. See Bauer, Section 52.

3. Wernicke, in *Hermes* 26 (1891): 51, states the opinion that the Athenian citizens who served as "bowmen"* had come from the poorer classes.

4. Xenophon, *Hellenica* 1. 2. 1. Thrasylus is sent out with a fleet and equips five thousand of his sailors as peltasts.

5. Diodorus' divergent account, as Grote has already correctly pointed out, cannot be compared with that of Thucydides.

6. Beloch, *Population (Bevölkerung)*, p. 140, counts 4,234 Lacedaemonians; and with them the Neodamodeis, Brasidians, and allies. That there were exactly 400 cavalrymen here, too, is hardly to be concluded from Thucydides 4. 55. (Compare note 2, Chapter III. Book I.)

7. In Thucydides' account (4. 67 ff.) there is a contradiction, in that he first indicates that the Lacedaemonians had drawn up their units one behind the other in the center, and on the extreme right flank "but few Lacedaemonians" had stood with the Tegeans, but then, nevertheless, two whole units (*lochi*), apparently Lacedaemonians, are called away from this flank. Busolt, in *Hermes* 40 (1895): 399, seeks to solve the contradiction in this way: the two units had not formed the extreme right wing but were supposedly drawn out from the right flank of the center; the resulting interval could be filled again by a sliding toward the right on the part of the other Lacedaemonian units. That may not be impossible, but I would nevertheless prefer not to take a definite stand on this. The word "almost,"* as used by Thucydides, can have a rather broad radius of meaning, as for example when he says a short time earlier (5. 66. 4) that "almost the whole army"* of the Lacedaemonians consisted of commanders. It might therefore be only a case of a certain carelessness of expression, where it is first said that the Lacedaemonians had drawn up their units "one behind the other,"* and we later hear that the "few" who were separated from the others by foreign contingents and who had been on the right flank had been two whole *lochi* (of seven). The expression "few" could not possibly have meant individual warriors separated from their units, but tactical units must have been intended; that is, therefore, at least *one lochus* and possibly also two.

Nor am I ready to accept the idea that the disobedient *polemarchs* in this battle were not the commanders of the units, but, as Busolt states (on p. 418), staff officers of the King. Only one would have been needed for the delivery of the order, and the insubordination of one such staff officer is on the one hand hardly understandable, on the other too easily disposed of by the dispatch of a second officer. The story is consequently only understandable in the sense that the *polemarchs* were the commanders of the units.

Chapter II

Strategy: Pericles

As we have seen, tactics changed but little in the period from the Persian Wars to the Peloponnesian War. Nevertheless, the latter war offers us a completely different point of view from the former. The Persian War is significantly dominated by the dissimilarity of the opponents in arms and tactics. In the Peloponnesian War Greeks were fighting against Greeks; their arms and tactics were the same, but the peculiar characteristic is that the one side had a superiority on the sea just as great as the other had on land. This situation established a completely new problem of a strategic nature. The Persian War was based on great decisive battles; it had to end in one of two ways—either the King of Kings defeated and subjected the Greeks within a short time, or he himself suffered a massive defeat. The Peloponnesian War dragged on for twenty-seven years, brought about perhaps a few land battles but no important decision, and did not actually come to its close until special circumstances made it possible for the Spartan side, too, to develop into a sea power comparable to that of the Athenians.

When the war broke out, neither side could have had an idea of how this would develop. They lived exclusively with the thought that the superiority on land on the one side and at sea on the other was so great that the weaker side could not risk a great tactical decision, a battle like Salamis or Plataea. Consequently, an unusual new aspect of strategy had to be faced: war without decision, through simple attrition.

What we encounter here is one of the most complicated but most frequent phenomena of world history. In the normal course of events, the concept of war calls for one opponent to seek to come to grips with and subdue the other one in order to submit him to his will. All the forces are gathered for a great blow, a battle that is supposed to bring on a decision or which is followed by others until the decision is reached. The task of strategy is to prepare this decision and to bring it about under the most favorable possible conditions. But here we have a war—and from now on we shall encounter this type time and again—that, for the most varied reasons, eliminates the possibility of such a decision. Nevertheless, means are to be found to bend the will of the enemy and to attain the political goal of the war.

Just as at Marathon, Thermopylae, Salamis, and Plataea, here again we find that the Greek people produced a man who grasped the new task in its deepest meaning and accomplished it with classical certainty.

Pericles, the Athenian, recognized that his city was not the equal of the Peloponnesian-Boeotian League on land, and from this fact he drew the inexorably logical conclusion that the entire countryside of Attica had to be evacuated and left to the mercy of the enemy army. "If I thought that I could persuade you, I would demand that you lay waste your land yourselves," he told the Athenians. The country dwellers had to move back into the city and between the long walls that joined the city with its ports, Piraeus and Phalerum. The damage the enemies now wreaked on the Attican countryside, however, was compensated through the Athenian fleet's blockade of the enemy coasts, destruction of the trade of all the enemy cities, and landing first here and then there and suddenly appearing, bringing to the enemy countryside the same or even greater destruction than the enemy was accomplishing in Attica. What could result from such a conduct of war, which might almost be called a "nonconduct of war"? An overwhelming decision, never. Everything depended on who first reached the point of no longer being able to bear the pain, who first became exhausted. One could have devised a way of conducting the war without any bloodshed; but after all, it was not so completely out of the question that strong blows be struck at some point, blows that could contribute greatly to softening the enemy's will. With careful forethought and wise awareness, Pericles added to the foregoing points, as he explained his war plan to the Athenians, the fact that one had to seize "the opportunity that does not wait." The strategy of attrition, which by its very nature renounces the possibility of an absolute decision, is accompanied by the danger that the commanders may become entirely too cautious. Each war creates crucial situations that must be exploited with bold courage. But whether this will succeed is a question depending on fate. The commander never knows exactly how strong the enemy actually is or whether circumstances are involved that he cannot perceive. While one hesitates, estimates, studies the situation further—the opportunity has once again slipped away. And the commander then finds it twice as hard—even ten times as hard—to decide to act if he constantly has hanging over him as the basic principle of the war the belief that the outcome is to be arrived at not through great decisions with their risks, but through gradual attrition. Only the continuation of our theory into more modern times (where we shall see time and again how often commanders have been prey to this temptation of attrition strategy to avoid risky decisions) will bring us to a complete understanding of how important was that statement of Pericles that despite the general principle of an exclusive warfare of attrition, "the opportunity that does not wait" must be exploited.

The Athenians reckoned that Pericles had won nine victories as a commander. Of these victories we know too little to be able to conclude from them anything as to Pericles' strategic talent, but the structure of the Peloponnesian War, together with the reports of numerous battle victories, obliges us to give him a position not simply among the great statesmen, but also among the great military leaders of world history. It is not his war plan as such that bestows this right on him (for the fame of the commander is gained not by word, but by deed), but rather the gigantic power of decision that accompanied it, not to halt with a half-measure, but to plunge in wholeheartedly and give up completely what had to be sacrificed, the entire Attican countryside, and in addition the strength of personal authority that was able to make such a decision understandable to a democratic national assemblage and to gain their approval. The execution of this decision is a strategic deed that can be compared favorably with any victory. In 480 and 479 B.C., at the approach of the Persians, the Athenians had evacuated not only the countryside but also the city—a decision that, in itself, was even more magnificent, but of a completely different nature. It was a deed of desperation, when no other possibility remained if they were not to be conquered. The battle in which the homeland was to be won back was to follow immediately. In the Peloponnesian War it was also a question of an inevitable necessity, but not one that was immediately obvious. On the contrary, it was clear only to the reflective strategic judgment, and it was not a matter of only a momentary evacuation, but of an action that gave promise of being repeated year in, year out, over a long period. Even today one occasionally encounters scholarly prigs who deny the necessity for such an act and thereby furnish new proof of the power of mind of

Pericles, who was able to persuade the sovereign Athenian citizenry to adopt a strategy that was so hard to grasp.

Pericles' war plan was carried out by Athens over a long period; in the first year and a half, or as long as Pericles was leader of the city, the plan was carried out with wise and energetic application of individual details, so that the various undertakings were well coordinated; and even after the fall and death of Pericles this was continued with no less energy, but without the coordination of details, in a sporadic way, prompted by the fortuitous pressures of the moment, in keeping with the ideas of this or that speaker. Nevertheless, Athens maintained an obvious superiority over its opponents. Even the frightful ravages of the plague, which robbed the city of a fourth of its citizens, did not break its strength, and finally the continuing guerrilla war even provided the opportunity for a great blow. Four hundred twenty Lacedaemonians were cut off on the island of Sphacteria; a portion of the group was killed and the remainder, 292 men, including 120 Spartiates, were taken prisoner.

With this success, five years after the death of Pericles, his war plan was accomplished. One should not, of course, assume as the objective of the war the subjection of all of Greece by Athens, in the manner in which Rome later subjected Italy. Neither Pericles nor any other Athenian statesman had thought of this; Athens was much too weak. To do this would have required not only the victorious conduct of great land battles but, finally, also the siege and capture of the enemy cities of Thebes, Megara, and Corinth. In this war, as in modern European wars, the task facing Athens was only the assertion of her position of importance, the maintaining of a balance of power, and a greater or lesser expansion of her sphere of influence.

The lack of a capable, influential statesman after the death of Pericles caused Athens to miss the moment and the favorable situation for an advantageous peace settlement. But even after Athens had suffered a defeat at the hands of the talented Spartan commander Brasidas, at Amphipolis, she was still able to conclude a peace in which her position was completely recognized, and basically anything beyond this was not at all necessary.

Eight years later the war broke out again, and this time the Athenians lost it, because they had completely ignored Pericles' advice on one important point. Pericles had warned "not to make any new conquests during the war."

As early as the year 424 B.C., inflated over the success at Sphacteria, they had planned a big operation by land and had suffered a very heavy defeat (Delium); they lost no fewer than 1,000 hoplites. After the conclusion of peace, however, which was actually still only an armistice, they undertook the subjection of Sicily and lost some 6,000 citizens[1] in that venture, together with a great fleet and its equipment. That brought the turning point. Now the Ionians risked breaking away from Athens, and the Peloponnesians appeared on the sea and made an alliance with the Persian King. Athens was not the equal of this coalition; she was finally defeated at sea and had to give in.

EXCURSUS

1. The basic question in passing judgment on the Peloponnesian War is, of course, whether Pericles' plan was right, and the answer depends, not in its least important aspect, on the statistics involved. If it were true that Athens had at that time 60,000 citizens, while it is accepted that Lacedaemon numbered no more than 2,000 to 3,000 Spartiates and 9,000 Perioeci-citizens, then Athens would undoubtedly have been able to risk a policy and a conduct of the war in the manner of Rome. One can see here the basic importance of the verification of these dry data. On them depends our judgment of Pericles and on the latter, again, that of Thucydides. The authority of the greatest of all historians is irreparably destroyed, a pillar of Greek literature is overturned, if someone can prove that Athens had 60,000 citizens in the year 431 B.C. In this case Thucydides has falsely judged Pericles and his policies, so that we can no longer trust his judgment in any way.

Fortunately, there can be no question of such a possibility. The fact that the Athenians moved out at Delium "with the whole body of the city drawn up as an army"* and still were only 7,000 hoplites strong, taken in conjunction with all the other numbers that have been reported, is an irrefutable proof that Athens can never have had 60,000 citizens.

One may assume that, aside from the 15,800 men mentioned by Pericles in his speech, from the Thêtes and metics Athens could still perhaps have drawn 8,000 men and provided them with hoplite equipment. In addition, she could have called on a few allies and could have organized a great mass of mercenaries as hoplites. If one estimates what troops were necessarily left behind in the form of garrisons and that a certain number of triremes always had to remain in service, too, Athens could perhaps have put into the field, through the maximum possible effort, an army of 25,000 hoplites. The army with which the Peloponnesians invaded Attica has been estimated by Beloch (p. 152) at 30,000, and more recently at 27,000 hoplites.[2] It would therefore seem that a victory in an open battle was not completely out of the question for the Athenians. But what purpose would it have served? "Even if we win," Pericles told the Athenians (Thucydides 1. 143), "we would still have to fight again soon against just as strong an enemy." The large Athenian army could remain in the field only a few days, or at most weeks, since the citizens had to return to their work. There could be no question of a pursuit of the enemy into his own country, a siege of Thebes or of Corinth. Not even any of the later popular leaders, at the height of the success on Sphacteria, ever had any such idea. Therefore a victory would have brought the Athenians nothing but a momentary respite; a defeat could have cost them half of their citizens, and in any case such a campaign would have made such inroads on their finances that they would have been completely incapable of further campaigns. We shall have occasion to return very often to the law of economy of force, which made itself felt so clearly here. In the fourth volume of this work, which has now (1920) been published, this basic principle of strategy is treated thoroughly.

2. In my book *The Strategy of Pericles, illustrated through the Strategy of Frederick the Great* (1890) (*Die Strategie des Perikles, erläutert durch die Strategie Friedrichs des Grossen*), I have studied the problem of the Periclean strategy in all its details. Almost simultaneously with that book there appeared the study by Nissen, "The Outbreak of the Peloponnesian War" ("Der Ausbruch des Peloponnesischen Krieges"), *Historische Zeitschrift*, Vol. 63. The objections he raised against Thucydides' account are not justified, in my opinion, but in one significant point we have nevertheless come to the same conclusion—that is, that Athens wanted to concentrate on a positive objective in this war, it had to be the incorporation of the Megaris.

3. Later there also appeared "A Chronological Contribution to the Historical Prelude of the Peloponnesian War" ("Ein chronologischer Beitrag zur Vorgeschichte des Peloponnesischen Krieges"), by W. Kolbe (*Hermes*, Vol. 34, 1899). Kolbe places the battle of Sybota as early as the fall of 433 B.C. (I estimated May of 432); from that we derive no conclusions concerning my concept of the policies of Pericles.

4. In his study "On the War Plan of Pericles" ("Zum Kriegsplan des Perikles") (*Festschrift* offered to Ludwig Friedlander by his students, 1895) Busolt took the position of those who regard this war plan as theoretically correct, "but in its execution there was a lack of energetic action and aggressive spirit." He notes particularly the failure in the first years of the war to occupy enemy coastal sites like Pylos and the island of Cythera. "An energetic application of power in the framework of the war plan could undoubtedly have shortened the duration of the war and led more quickly to the exhaustion of the enemy." Nevertheless, one cannot put forth this claim quite so strongly as "undoubtedly." Busolt himself, in this very treatise, correctly stressed more than had previously been the case how important the blockade of the Peloponnesus was. Even if it was not carried out to the point of hermetically sealing off the peninsula, it still reduced the trade and the almost indispensable grain shipments for the larger coastal cities in an extremely effective manner. The longer it lasted, the harder was the effect of this pressure. It certainly cannot be said that the Athenians, if they had brought to bear on their enemy right in the first year all the damage that they could have caused, would thereby have won the peace. The length of suffering, the psychological factor of time had to play their roles. We are faced here with a problem that arises time after time in the history of warfare. When a statesman-commander like Pericles establishes a war plan that is supposed not to crush the enemy but to wear him out gradually, there is no definite indication of how much is to be undertaken each year, or to what extent the safeguarding of one's own strength is to be given consideration. In the strategy of annihilation there is such a measure—that is, the combat forces of the enemy. One must either commit *all* the forces that are in any way available, or at least so much that one can count with certainty on victory. If that does not come about, an error has been made. In the strategy of attrition, the standard is more subjective. To concentrate all one's forces at the same time would be wrong and would contradict one's own plans. No matter what takes place, it is always possible for a critic to come along and say that, in addition, this or that should also have been done. On page 116 of my *Strategy of Pericles* I explained the reasons why more was not done in the first year and a half, as long as Pericles was in power. In the second year, instead of occupying Cythera, as Busolt calls for, he undertook something much greater, that is the conquest of Epidaurus, a venture in which, of course, he failed. The fact that, after this failure, the move against Cythera was not undertaken cannot, at any rate, be attributed to Pericles, since he was dismissed. It is completely understandable, however, for the reasons I presented on page 130 of my aforementioned work.

5. Pericles' statement concerning the "opportunities in warfare that do not wait" (Thucydides 1. 142) is first said of the opponents, who are not able to exploit the opportunities because of a lack of ready means and because of the loose treaty of

alliance. Implicit in this, however, is naturally also the opposite—that the Athenians, namely, are in a position to do it and should seize the opportunities.

6. In an annex to my above-named book I treated the question of the importance of Cleon. Again and again scholars appear who cannot understand that anyone who has carried off such a brilliant success as Cleon did at Sphacteria is supposed to have been in every respect a negative personality. Nowhere outside the military field is the temptation greater to allow oneself to be carried away by success and to consider someone who has won a victory as a great strategist. Nowhere, however, is it more important to free oneself from a worship of success and to test impartially whether a reputation is deserved or whether it falls on one by chance. The case of Cleon lends itself quite especially to the development of one's power of judgment and to practice in criticism. A very interesting and, in many respects, downright striking analogy to Cleon's leadership is provided by the great victory that the demagogue General l'Echelle won over the Vendéens, which I suggest be read in the excellent book of General von Boguslawski, *The War of Vendée against the French Republic* (*Der Krieg der Vendée gegen die französische Republik*) (1894).

7. After one has become convinced that, in its cardinal points, concerning the judgment of Pericles and his war plan, as well as that of Cleon, the concept of Thucydides is the only completely right one, one is not only justified in trusting this author but also obliged to do so, even in those points where a strict verification is not possible with our faulty knowledge of the facts. The account of the history of this period is built on this base.

The complaints that some have wished to make against Thucydides as a strategist, based on his own account, are devoid of any basis and arise solely from the incorrect tactical concepts of the critics.

8. Herodotus, in 3. 9, has Mardonius say to Xerxes: "As I have come to understand it, the Greeks have been accustomed to wage their wars most senselessly because of their foolishness and folly. When they declare war against each other, they discover the fairest and most level ground, and proceeding to it, they have their battles in the place. The result is that the victors come away without much harm; but about the vanquished I shall say nothing at all, for they are completely destroyed."*

They ought preferably to understand and tolerate each other peacefully, "speaking the same language . . . and if it was at all necessary to fight against each other, they would have to discover the place where each one's strength lay, and try it out there"*—"where victory is most difficult for both sides," the translation reads. Father Herodotus was not able to express what he meant or what was told him; the meaning is apparently that *each side* should seek to exploit the terrain for its own benefit.

One must recognize that such points were taken into consideration in Periclean Athens.

9. In arriving at the population estimates for Attica, I assumed that the Athenians had also called on slaves for duty with the fleet. Niese has declared this assumption to be "completely untenable" and has documented his opposing view thoroughly in an annex to his essay in *Historische Zeitschrift*, Vol. 98 (see also p. 28, above). The question has no significance in our statistical estimate, since on the one hand it is established that the main portion of the fleet personnel consisted of Athenian citizens, and on the other hand that the noncitizens were essentially mercenaries, so that in any case there remains but little room for the slaves that were possibly there. Whether, in any case, we term the but roughly estimated contingent of noncitizens as "mercenaries" or as "mercenaries and slaves" really makes no great difference in the results. When Böckh (*National Economy* [*Staatshaushault*], 1:329, 3d ed.) states that "a large portion of the oarsmen were slaves," he may have gone somewhat too far. I expressed myself more cautiously by writing (page 145, below): "When there was to be a levy in Athens for a campaign—so we may assume—enough men, Athenians or foreigners, always volunteered for fleet service, or slaves were taken for this pur-

pose. Therefore, in Athens, fleet service, aside from the expeditions 'with the whole body of the city drawn up as an army,'* became a purely mercenary duty very shortly after the Persian Wars." These words seem to me to say clearly enough that I should not regard the supplementary number of slaves on the Athenian fleet as something important, but as an auxiliary means, whenever the citizens and mercenaries were not numerous enough, and therefore probably in the cases of the unusual levies, which I use as a basis for my statistical estimates. Consequently, Niese expresses my viewpoint too sharply when he repeats it in these words: "Hans Delbrück has said in his *History of the Art of War*, p. 110, that the Athenians had *regularly* called on slaves for the manning of their warships."

Niese adduces for his theory first of all several *argumenta ex silentio*, to which a certain weight can no doubt be attributed, so long as they are directed against Böckh's opinion that "a large portion of the oarsmen were slaves," but not against me, since the slaves play such a secondary role with me that they could easily be overlooked in enumerations.

It has been proved on numerous occasions that slaves were used for rowing duty in other Greek states. When Niese claims (pp. 496, 501, 505), "There is sufficient proof that the slaves in Athens . . . were aboard only as servants for their masters who were serving with the fleet," he unfortunately neglected to state this proof in his discussion, which is otherwise abounding in scholarly references, but laid himself open to the suspicion of having only very vague ideas of the conditions on an ancient trireme. It is difficult for us to understand that there could possibly be enough room on such a ship for 200 men—to say nothing of slaves as servants. Except possibly for the captain and mate? And the masters would have rowed, with the slaves looking on?

The positive pieces of evidence that in the Athenian fleet, too, slaves did appear as crewmen are as follows: in Thucydides 7. 13. 2, Nicias writes home from Sicily that there were people who, by bribing the captains, placed Hyccaran slaves in their places and thereby nullified the established order of seafaring ("And there are some who, being themselves commercial travelers, have persuaded the trierarchs to take on board Hyccaran slaves in their stead, and so have robbed the navy of its discipline,"*). Hyccara is a Sicilian city that was taken by the Athenians immediately after their arrival and whose inhabitants they had enslaved. Nicias, then, finds the error not in the fact that slaves were placed in the rowing crew, but rather in the fact that slaves of such an origin, basically hostile, were smuggled in for rowing duty, without practice or training. If he had intended to indicate that it was unheard of that slaves should have been mixed in at all with the oarsmen, then he would not have added the word "Hyccaran."

In Thucydides 8. 73. 5, it is said of the *paralus*, the ship of state, that she was manned only by freemen; therefore this was not the case with other ships. Niese (p. 501, footnote) claims that this explanation, generally accepted up to now, is a misunderstanding; he seems to want to understand the Greek word *eleutheroi* as "inclined toward freedom"—an interpretation for which I see no basis.

Xenophon, in *Hellenica* 1. 6. 24, reports how, in the year 406 B.C., the Athenians assigned freemen and slaves in order to man their fleet. The same procedure is also mentioned in Aristophanes and in the commentaries, cited in Böckh, 1:329.

In his speech on peace (8. 48), Isocrates mentions that the Athenians formerly had foreigners and slaves serve as sailors, the citizens as hoplites aboard ship. (See Niese, p. 501, note 3.)

All these bits of evidence seem to me to leave no doubt that my account is correct—which, to repeat, does not actually differ so fundamentally from that of Niese as the force of his polemics might suggest. For even Niese admits that, at least as an exception (in the case of 406 B.C.), slaves were incorporated in the fleet crews, and in my work they play such an incidental role that I, too, could have used the expression "by way of exception" without changing anything in the statistics.

NOTES FOR CHAPTER II

1. Athens lost 4,450 hoplites and citizen-cavalrymen; in addition, on each trireme at least a few Athenian citizens as officers. The entire expedition, with all its logistical support, can be estimated at 60,000 men.

2. *Klio* 6 (1906): 77.

Chapter III

Mercenaries

In the Persian War the Greek armies consisted of citizen levies; as the Peloponnesian War approached its end, this no longer held true.

The general citizen levy, the mass taking to the field "with the whole body of the city drawn up as an army,"* had actually occurred only very seldom. As a normal thing it would be decided to send out an army or a fleet of a certain strength, and the draft for this purpose, as it took place in Athens, we must picture somewhat as follows. The citizenry was divided up into ten tribes, and each of these was split into three trittyes—one in the city, one on the coast, and one in the interior—which, in turn, included a variable number of demes. The total strength to be levied was divided up among these units and would have had to be filled, according to the rules, in alternation by the men who were so obligated. Such a regular alternation would, however, have led to serious inequalities. The individual expeditions were very different in length and difficulty; hoplite service, which was performed by the men of means, came up much less often than fleet service. The citizens had provided for the short campaigns of earlier days out of their own means, and they were not so completely disrupted in their professional and commercial life by the campaigns. The long wars, often fought abroad, had created completely different conditions. In order to make longer campaigns possible, the practice had been initiated of paying wages, and in fact very high ones.[1] The means of doing this were provided by the Athenian allies, who were thereby exempted from military service or at least much less heavily burdened with it.[2] The Athenian citizens did their military service for them, and it was precisely in doing so that they had attained such a high degree of military ability. Although they remained citizens, they had nevertheless taken on, to a certain degree, the characteristics of professional soldiers and were also completely aware of this.

144

Before the first battle of Syracuse their commander, Nicias, reminded them that they were quite different warriors from the citizen levy of their opponents.[3] Consequently, whenever there was to be a levy in Athens for a campaign, we may assume that always enough volunteers, Athenians or foreigners, enrolled for service with the fleet, or slaves were taken for this purpose. By all appearances, no special list was kept of men obligated for sea duty. In cases of emergency, all those who were not engaged were called to the ranks.[4] In the case of hoplite service it was a different matter; this was, of course, not only a form of personal service but also a kind of tax payment, since the hoplite had to provide his costly equipment personally. Consequently, there was an appraisal procedure for hoplite service and a muster roll, called "Catalog," was kept on eligible men, in addition to the general citizen list. Nevertheless, we may assume that it was not so very difficult to find a replacement if one did not wish to take the field himself,[5] and the state could not object to a suitable replacement. In taking this viewpoint, the state spared the citizens in their normal work, and military efficiency did not necessarily suffer from this exchange but could even improve. As it was, hoplite service was, of course, by its very concept not a strictly personal duty; rather each house provided one man, with his servant. From the start, then, it was probably considered as an internal family matter whether it was the father or the son, one brother or the other, or instead even possibly a distant relative or a neighbor, who donned the hoplite equipment and undertook the service. In order to be able to reinforce the hoplite levy, the state, too, had equipment at the outbreak of the Peloponnesian War and equipped a number of Thêtes with it.[6] If for the Sicilian expedition 1,500 hoplites from the Catalog were embarked and 700 Thête hoplites, this means that either no more than 1,500 men from the upper classes had reported for the campaign or, what is probably more likely, it was not desired to ship so many citizens of means so far away, and therefore no more than 150 were taken from each tribe, and in addition to them 700 Thêtes who had likewise reported as volunteers were armed at the expense of the state.

Fleet service in Athens, therefore, except for the mass levies, became a purely mercenary service as early as the period shortly following the Persian Wars, and in the course of the Peloponnesian War hoplite service, too, gradually became more and more a mercenary service.

A similar development took place in the other states. In the first years of the Peloponnesian War the allies, for the most part, did nothing other than to invade Attica with two-thirds of their citizen hoplites, plunder and lay waste the country for a few weeks, and return home again. Soon it became apparent that they were not wearing Athens out in this way, and finally the Spartan Brasidas moved out to Thrace with an army, in order to attack Athens through her colonies and her allied cities. This army could no longer be composed of citizens who were leaving their business for a short time and were supplying themselves. But it did not consist, say, of Spartiates, who had always prided themselves on having no civilian profession but were exclusively warriors. Such a campaign at a distance with half or even only a fourth of the Spartiates qualified for military service (and that would actually have been no more than 500 to 600 men) completely contradicted the character of the state organization and the point of view of the Spartans. Rather, they called out robust farm boys who were in bondage, Helots, and trained them as hoplites. Naturally, they had to be given their rations and also a certain pay, in order to bind them to the colors. And so, because of the internal necessities of carrying out the war, Sparta proceeded in the same manner as Athens.

Excursus

1. Thucydides 5. 67, reports that the Argives, in addition to the general levy, had an elite unit of 1,000 men who received special training at the expense of the state (". . . a thousand picked men of the Argives, for whom the state for a long time had provided training at the public expense in the arts of war").* Presumably these 1,000 were not only especially trained, but they had to be ready to participate in the more distant expeditions that from time to time were necessary and that would have torn the average citizen too much away from his business and would have harmed him economically. For this they received regular pay.

2. When Agesilaus needed cavalry in Asia in 391 B.C., he levied the rich Asia Minor Greeks for that purpose and allowed them to provide substitutes. (Xenophon, *Hellenica* 3. 4. 15.)

3. The shift to a mercenary army naturally also wiped out in Athens the old division into classes. As early as in his speech of the year 431 B.C. Pericles took no further heed of this division, since the state was actually outfitting the Thêtes, who did not have the means to do it themselves. *A potiori*, however, it still was commonly said by the people that the citizens of the lowest class "did not wage war."* Usener (in the *Jahrbücher für klassische Philologie*, 1873, p. 162) states the opinion that the bar had fallen definitively in 412 B.C.; the speech of Lysias on the restoration of the democracy shows that the hoplite service of the Thêtes was normal at that time, whereas at the time of the staging of Aristophanes' *Banqueters* in 427 B.C. that was not yet understood in the same way.

4. In Book I, Chapter II we established the fact that Thucydides informed us in Pericles' speech of the number of Athenian citizens and of metic hoplites, but not the number of metics who were not hoplites. We see now that, as far as Thucydides was concerned, there was actually no reason for doing so. The nonhoplite metics

came into consideration in the Athenian military situation only as fleet oarsmen, crews that could also be filled out with slaves. Even if a list was kept of all the metics, nevertheless the poorer among them were a mass that was too unsettled to be counted in the substance of the state. Those who were well-to-do enough to be appraised for hoplite service were also, however, because of their means, also more closely bound to the state of Athens and were therefore included.

NOTES FOR CHAPTER III

1. Böckh, *National Economy* (*Staatshaushalt*), 1: 152, 340 (3d ed.). The wages varied between 4 obols and 1 drachma (6 obols) per man; for the hoplites, therefore, 2 drachmas, 1 for the warrior and 1 for his servant, including ration money. When the humorist Theopomp says that a man could feed a wife on 2 obols and that he could be completely happy on 4, he probably means the base pay aside from the ration allowance, which was, where needed, provided by 2 additional obols. At the time of Aristotle the Athenian *ephebi* received 4 obols daily, their instructors 1 drachma. *State of the Athenians* (*Staat der Athener*), Chapter 42.

2. Nöthe, *Federal Council, Federal Taxes, and Military Service of the Delhi League* (*Bundesrat, Bundessteuer und Kriegsdienst der delischen Bündner*), Magdeburg Program, 1880. Gülde, *Military Procedures of the First Athenian League* (*Kriegsverfahren des ersten athenischen Bundes*), Neuhaldensleben Program, 1888.

3. Speech of Nicias, Thucydides 6. 68: ". . . Against men that meet us in a mob and are not picked men as we are, and even against Sicelots, who, on the one hand, despise us, but yet do not stand their ground against us, because their skill is less than their daring."*

4. Xenophon, *Hellenica* 1. 6. 24. The Athenians decided to move out with 110 ships, "putting aboard every one of military age, whether they were slave or free. Even many of the knights went on board."*

5. According to a report contained in Polyaenus 3. 3, Tolmidas, when he was once supposed to move out with 1,000 hoplites, was joined by 3,000 volunteers. Two passages in Aristophanes seem to contradict this. In *The Knights*, verse 1369, Demos expresses the wish that men will no longer be excused from hoplite service by favoritism, and in *Peace*, verse 1179, an individual is very unhappy because he finds that he is suddenly once again called up for service, and he complains that in general the country people are oppressed in this regard, while the city dwellers are given the preference. It is clear, therefore, that at that time (424 and 421 B.C.) the

army levy had not yet become a purely voluntary, reimbursed service.

6. In Aristotle, *On the State of the Athenians*, Chapter 24, where he explains that the mass of Athenians lived from the state (by virtue of the taxes of the allies), it is also said that the city maintained 2,500 hoplites. It is not easy to say how we should interpret this. There can be no thought of a standing army. The *peripoloi*, who had a strength of about 2,000, can hardly be meant here. Perhaps there existed an arrangement whereby 2,500 men were to keep themselves in a special degree of readiness at any given moment, were occasionally assembled, had to drill, and received a small reimbursement. It can hardly have been otherwise, at any rate, with the 1,200 cavalrymen and 1,600 archers whom Aristotle mentions in the same line. Beloch, in *Klio* 5: 357, expressed the conjecture that it must simply have been 12,500 instead of 2,500, and, in the end, that seems to me to be the most logical solution.

Chapter IV

Refinement of the Existing Tactical System in the Fourth Century

As long and oscillating as the Peloponnesian War was, it still did not produce new forms of the art of war. The one new aspect it did bring to Greece was the professional military status. Much earlier Greece had already become familiar with professional soldiers as mercenaries; the tyrants, like Polycrates of Samos and Pisistratus of Athens,[1] had bodyguards on which their hegemony rested. Polycrates is even supposed to have had a small army of 1,000 archers.[2] The kings of Egypt and Lydia had an army of Greek mercenaries. But, after all, those are not decisive sizes, and the real mercenary system, which became a significant factor of the life of the Greek people and of Greek history, was basically a product of the Peloponnesian War. But it is not only the mass of private soldiers that comes into consideration, but more importantly the completely new position of the mercenary leaders, the professional officers who now appear.

This transition is provided by the Athenians Demosthenes and Lamachus, the Spartans Brasidas, Gylippus, and Lysander. When, shortly after the close of the Peloponnesian War, the Persian Prince Cyrus, viceroy of Asia Minor, rebelled against his brother, King Artaxerxes, he was able to enlist in his pay an army numbering no fewer than 13,000 Greek soldiers under nothing but experienced military leaders of higher and lower rank.

The gradual transition from citizen armies to mercenary armies certainly had as a result a refining and a more intensive application of drill; in other words, the drill discipline of the Spartans was extended to the other Greek armies. The army of the Spartans,

149

Thucydides says (6. 66), consists almost entirely of commanders ("rulers of rulers"*), and the author of *State of the Lacedaemonians* reports that Spartan drill is based on the principle that each man follows his platoon leader (*enomotarch*); this made the most complicated formations easy. The individual steps in the development of this drill are not recognizable for us, but the development lies in the nature of things, and a few individual indications on the retreat of the Ten Thousand show us clearly that there had been progress. The administrative lower echelons of the army were capable, under certain circumstances, of moving as small independent tactical units, and their cohesiveness—which can only be attained through drill—was so strong that the hoplites once in a battle with Pharnabazus had the self-confidence to move forward on the offensive against Persian cavalry, even though they themselves had only a very few mounted men to cover their flanks. (*Anabasis* 6. 3. 30.) As a substitute for cavalry, a few detachments of 200 hoplites each were placed 30 meters behind the phalanx (6. 3. 9). The increase in cavalry that we have observed was therefore balanced by improvement in the military quality of the infantry.

On one occasion we also find a completely new combat formation employed. The Colchians blocked the route of the Ten Thousand by occupying a broad mountain in front of them. An attack in the usual closed phalanx was not feasible, for the phalanx on this very irregular terrain would necessarily have broken during the forward movement and would have fallen apart. And so, on the advice of Xenophon, they formed 80 smaller columns of about 100 men each, which were drawn up in great depth—probably about 20 men deep and 5 men wide—and which left moderate intervals between them. In this way each column could seek its own route, and the exterior ones outflanked the enemy. The peltasts moved forward in three groups, assigned to the two wings and the middle, with the hoplites. Against a Greek phalanx they would not have been able to move forward in this way; completely aside from the fact that the peltasts were in the middle among the hoplites, the separated hoplite columns would also not have been able to withstand a shock encounter with a closed hoplite phalanx: the head of each of the individual columns would have been taken at the moment of impact simultaneously from the right and the left and would have been crushed, and so all the columns of the center would have been beaten before the outflanking phalanxes might have been able to exert any effect on the flanks of the enemy phalanx. Naturally, a massive, closed front is stronger than one with intervals. Against barbarians, however, who depended more on protection by their mountains than on their own weapons, and who did not have sufficient leadership to make a coordinated offensive blow at the right moment against such an enemy, on such terrain—against such an enemy the small, deep columns with intervals were the best-suited tactical formation. The Colchians did not dare to push into the intervals, because they feared that they would then be attacked in the rear by the neighboring columns and cut off. And so this inspired improvisation fulfilled its purpose, but it neither was nor did it become, as some have claimed, a step toward a further theoretical development of the Greek tactics.

The peltast arm benefited particularly from the mercenary establishment. More was necessary for a capable peltast than for a hoplite. The fixed framework of the phalanx carries along with it even the moderately trained man and the moderately brave man; it binds him and increases his worth. But that peltast who is not a completely capable warrior has basically no worth at all. Whenever he is forced to withdraw before the better armament of the hoplite, the peltast must move forward again at the right moment; everything depends on this. In order to do that, each individual must have a very strong inner drive, and the leadership must enjoy the highest confidence of the men and must have them securely in hand. The commander who attains that can do a great deal with it, and such leaders, formed through practice and constantly training their men, now appear on the scene.

The Athenian mercenary commander Iphicrates is particularly famous for great accomplishments with his peltasts. He transformed this arm, which theretofore had been considered as half barbarian, into the arm truly representative of Greek military professionalism, by concurrently improving weapons and equipment. The long sword instead of the short sword, and a long spear in addition to the shorter javelin, both of which made the peltasts more capable of engaging in close combat with the hoplite, were supposedly introduced by Iphicrates. The main stress, however, should not be placed on these inventions, which, strictly speaking, are not inventions at all, but rather on the excellent disciplinary system that, according to Nepos, Iphicrates introduced among his troops. This is what enabled him to employ so effectively the light infantry, which had previously been held in low esteem. Xenophon tells us (*Hellenica* 4. 4. 16) that, for fear of the peltasts of Iphicrates, the Arcadian hoplites had not dared to move out from behind their city walls. In the face of the Lacedaemonian hoplites, however, who had their younger age groups swarm out against them, the peltasts, in turn, were afraid and were unwilling to move within javelin range. The younger Lacedaemonian hoplites were, consequently, so strong in their running training that they were able to overtake the peltasts despite their heavy equipment.

But on one occasion when a Lacedaemonian *mora* with excessive self-confidence moved across in front of Corinth, it was suddenly attacked near Lechaeum by Iphicrates with great superiority and was crushed, while the peltasts continuously fired on the marching men and then, as the enemy attacked, fell back on their following hoplites. A cavalry group that then came to the aid of the Lacedaemonians was apparently too weak and accomplished nothing. Xenophon reproaches them for having been too lackadaisical (*Hellenica* 4. 5).

At Abydos Iphicrates won a similar victory to that at Lechaeum with his peltasts by falling suddenly on the Lacedaemonian hoplites while they were descending a mountain, stretched out loosely in a long line (*Hellenica* 4. 8. 37).

When, shortly thereafter, Agesilaus was attacked in a similar way in Acarnania, he succeeded in a resolute attack, with the support of his cavalry, in inflicting heavy losses on the enemy peltasts and driving their reserve of hoplites to flight, so that he was able to continue the march freely (*Hellenica* 5. 6).

The Thracian or Northern Greek peltasts, who appeared in the earlier period as mercenaries, were probably not uniformly armed and equipped. It was left to the individual whether he would provide himself with a longer or shorter sword and whether he wore greaves or boots or simple sandals. The use of uniform military arms and equipment was probably first established in the regular mercenary service under Greek leaders like Iphicrates.

Whether or not the cavalry, too, made any progress in this period cannot be determined. Cavalry was appreciated principally by the Boeotians, who also developed the mixed combat concept by attaching to the cavalry swift-footed light infantrymen, the *hamippen*.[3] Agesilaus realized, Xenophon tells us, that in his war in Asia he could do nothing in the open field without cavalry, and he therefore formed a cavalry unit.[4] Xenophon himself devoted two of his works to this arm. What we have to say on this subject is best treated in the discussion of the Macedonians in the next book.

The progress the Greeks made during this period in the art of siegecraft is very significant. As far back as on the original wall paintings and reliefs of the Egyptians and the Assyrians one can recognize siege engines. The Greeks, however, were still quite inept in their use, even in the Peloponnesian War. Pericles had already, it is true, had siege machines built at the investment of Samos, and the Peloponnesians made some attempts during the siege of Plataea to subdue the town by means of an embankment that was built up, a battering ram, or fire, but failing to achieve their goal by any of these means, they finally contented themselves with surrounding the wall, thus shutting in the city and starving the inhabitants. The Greeks seem to have learned the real art of siegecraft first of all on Sicily from the Carthaginians, who attacked and took Selinus, Himera, Acragas, and Gela with mines, towers, and battering rams[5] (409–405 B.C.). Dionysius the Elder, tyrant of Syracuse, was a great machine builder, and this art spread from Sicily to ancient Greece.

Around this time the construction of cannon, catapults, and *petrobols* was also invented in Syracuse, and the triremes were enlarged into penteremes. As Diodorus recounts,[6] Dionysius gathered in Syracuse the most expert technicians from the whole world, personally concerned himself with the workers, spurred them on, rewarded the industrious and capable ones, and invited them to his table. So they bent every effort and devised new kinds of projectiles and machines.[7]

EXCURSUS

1. Among the Spartans we find a very thorough, precise organization, but it was changed so often that we cannot determine its details with certainty. The *lochi* were divided into *pentecostys*, the *pentecostys* into *enomotys*, which numbered from 32 to 36 men.[8] Undoubtedly drills were also conducted in these smallest units.

2. Nepos recounts the work of Iphicrates in such a way as to give the impression that the latter had transformed hoplites into peltasts and had, in fact, been the first one to invent the peltast branch. That may be correct for Athens, which up to this time had had no peltasts, since they were considered a barbaric arm. By virtue of a systematic development this arm was raised so high that even Athenian citizens were willing to serve in it. Nevertheless, the description Nepos gives of Iphicrates' peltasts is unsatisfactory. He makes no mention of the throwing weapons but only of the long spear and the long sword. From this account one would be forced to believe that it was a question of a close-in fighter, and Rüstow and Köchly did, in fact, feel obliged to believe that they should understand Iphicrates' changes in this way, that he had created a new type of medium infantry. This concept, however, has already been rejected, and rightly so, by Bergk and also by H. Droysen (p. 26) and Adolf Bauer (Section 42). Nowhere in the accounts of military actions does such a type of infantry appear; the decisive arm continued to be the hoplites. The only doubtful point is to what extent the lengthened spear and the longer sword, used in conjunction with the light protective equipment (burlap armor; boots instead of the "Iphicrates greaves") were inventions of Iphicrates or were already the regular equipment of the peltasts before his time.

NOTEWORTHY BATTLES OF THIS PERIOD

3. With the battle of Cunaxa, as with all the Persian battles, one must first undertake a trimming-down of the numbers involved. The Greeks had become so accustomed to the idea that Persian armies, in keeping with the huge size of that empire, had to be gigantic, that even a sober, clearheaded thinker and practical soldier like Xenophon simply passes on the current fables as if hypnotized. At Cunaxa Artaxerxes is supposed to have had four army corps of 300,000 men each, three of which were on the scene.[9] Even the number of 100,000 men that Cyrus was supposed to have had with him, in addition to the 13,000 Greeks, is the object of well-founded doubts, as L. Hollaender has shown, in the *Annex to Annual Report of the Cathedral Gymnasium of Naumburg, 1793* (*Beilage zum Jahresbericht des Domgymnasiums zu Naumburg, 1793*). Presumably this was only a rather unimportant corps.

In the battle the Persian cavalry under Tissaphernes charged down on the Greek peltasts, who were in position beside the hoplite phalanx. The peltasts gave way before the attack, allowed the Persian horsemen to pass through, and shot at them from both sides as they plunged through. The cavalry did not risk charging into the phalanx, although they could now have attacked it from behind and, after the Persians of Cyrus had taken flight, also from the flank, where Cyrus' men had been. The Greeks were concerned about such an attack and therefore wanted to make such a maneuver as to provide cover for their rear and flank, that is, to form up with their rear to the Euphrates, which up to this point had been on their right flank. They would therefore have had to make a full 90-degree wheeling movement, a maneuver that is most difficult to carry out for a deployed long line. The movement, the logic and possibility of which are not clear to us,[10] seems nevertheless not to have been executed.

The Persians assembled in their old position, and the Greeks—whether it be that the Persians were threatening an attack or not[11]—made at them once again and threw them back. Presumably the Persians did not follow through seriously in this second action, because their infantry had already left the battlefield. Otherwise, it would be impossible to explain why the cavalry did not attack the Greeks on their flank.

It is obvious how greatly the conditions had changed in comparison with Marathon and Plataea. The Greek phalanx, composed of mercenaries with professional officers, had a very much stronger cohesiveness than the Athenian citizen militia. Corresponding to this awareness and the morale superiority that the events of the century had given the Greeks, their phalanx went into battle with much greater self-confidence, the Persians with correspondingly less. Finally, the phalanx was being supported by an excellent auxiliary arm with projectile weapons. And so the Greek infantry was now capable of meeting the Persians in the open field.

All of this also explains the possibility of a withdrawal. The Persians would probably have been able to overwhelm the Greeks, but they probably wanted to spare their own blood and hoped that the Greeks, without their intervention, would collapse in the Carduchian mountains. It does not follow from this that there was a positive superiority of the Greek infantry over the Persian cavalry. Even the 50 men whom the Greeks had mounted as cavalry cannot have frightened the Persians back in such a way. Xenophon himself recounts, in *Hellenica* 3. 4. 15, as already mentioned above, that Agesilaus, in the war against Tissaphernes, recognized that cavalry was indispensable if he was to be able to hold his own against the Persians in the open field.

Dr. Marie Pancritius, in her *Studies on the Battle of Cunaxa* (*Studien über die Schlacht bei Kunaxa*) (Berlin, Alex. Dunker, 1906), successfully disproves many of the distorted points that have recently been put forward by scholars concerning Xenophon and the Ten Thousand, but she does not facilitate the insight into the strategic and tactical circumstances, since she proceeds from false assumptions.

4. Xenophon, in *Hellenica* 3. 4. 23, tells of a combat action of Agesilaus against Persian cavalry. He wanted to support his own, obviously weaker cavalry with his

infantry. For this purpose he sent the ten youngest classes of hoplites ahead, then the peltasts, and then the main body of the phalanx. The purpose of this separation was to allow not only the peltasts but even the hoplites to move against the enemy horsemen, and since the main body of the phalanx, with many older men, was too slow for this, the younger men, who could continue running for a longer time, were sent out ahead.

5. On the battle of Corinth, in 394 B.C., we have, it is true, an account by Xenophon (*Hellenica* 4. 2) and a few bits of information, but they are not enough for a true understanding. On both sides the right wing triumphed by outflanking the enemy left wing, thanks to the pulling to the right, and taking the enemy from the flank. The Lacedaemonians then swung to the left with their victorious corps and beat the enemy contingents that were returning from the pursuit, one after the other.

From this account we must therefore assume that the excellent discipline and good order of the Spartans, which did not let up after the victory and made possible the difficult maneuver of the 90-degree wheel (with 6,000 men), proved to be the decisive factor. Many of the details, however, still remain obscure.

According to Xenophon the allied Corinthians, Boeotians, and Athenians had 1,550 horsemen, the Lacedaemonians only 600; and the former, moreover, had numerical superiority in light infantry. How was it possible for the Lacedaemonian hoplites to envelop the Athenian flank if at that point there was a superior force of cavalry with a larger number of light infantrymen? According to a remark in Plato's *Menexenus* (cited in Grote), the Athenians are supposed to have attributed their defeat to the bad terrain ("since they were making use of rough ground"*). Perhaps this explains why the cavalry did not intervene—but why then did they fight on terrain where the superiority of their cavalry could not be exploited?

According to Xenophon, the allies are supposed to have had also 24,000 hoplites, the Spartans only 13,500. The latter achieved their first partial victory with 6,000 men against 3,600 Athenians (6 tribes), while the rest of their army, with the exception of a small detachment, was being defeated. Consequently there were now 20,400 victorious opponents facing the 6,000 victorious Lacedaemonians—and the allies were then supposedly all defeated, one after the other. That sounds, however, quite unlikely, especially if we remember also the cavalry and the fact that we do not know where it remained. What is more, if we now observe from Diodorus (14. 82. 83) that another report gave the two sides 500 horsemen each, but the Spartans 23,000 men on foot against 15,000, it seems clearly best to conclude that we know too little of a definite nature concerning the course of this battle to enable us to analyze its details.

6. A few weeks after the battle of Corinth the army that was defeated there had to take to the field again in order to block, at Coronea, the route of Agesilaus, who was approaching from Asia. This time the opposing strengths were quite equal, even according to Xenophon. Again we learn nothing of the activity of the horsemen and the light infantry, and again the right flank is victorious on both sides. But contrary to the previous battle, the two victorious wings now took up the fight in earnest, turning to face each other, and they fought it out with the greatest obstinacy. The Thebans finally forced Agesilaus' soldiers aside and so gained a means of retreat, but suffered very heavy losses. Xenophon says that the battle was "*such as no other during our times.*"* That is probably attributable to the unusually energetic execution of the second combat, since it was otherwise normal for one side to give way immediately after the clash of the phalanxes. In *Agesilaus* there is a description of how, the next day, the ground was seen soaked with blood, the dead—friend and foe alike—lying next to each other, splintered shields, broken spears, bared swords on the ground, in bodies, and still in the hands of the dead.

7. In *Hellenica* 4. 2. 5, Agesilaus announces a bounty for "whoever should join the army with the best-equipped force of hoplites, bowmen, and peltasts."*

K. Hartmann, in *On Arrian's Tactics* (*Über die Taktik des Arrian*) (Bamberg Program of 1895), p. 16, understands that as a *lochus* composed of a combination of the three arms. That is hardly correct. It is probably a question of one *lochus* of each arm.

NOTES FOR CHAPTER IV

1. Herodotus 1. 61. The mercenaries of Pisistratus seem, in fact, to have been not Greeks but Scythians. Helbig, *Sitzungs-Berichte der Münchner Akademie* 2 (1897): 259. A military review by Pisistratus or Hippias on a dark-figured bowl.

2. Herodotus 3. 39.

3. Thucydides 5. 57. 2. Xenophon, *Hellenica* 3. 5. 24.

4. *Hellenica* 3. 4. 15: ". . . Unless he procured a sufficient cavalry force, he would not be able to campaign in the plains; he therefore took it to mind that one should be provided, so that he would not have to fight the war shirkingly."*

5. Adolf Bauer, para. 47.

6. Diodorus, Book 10.

7. "On Machines and Their Names" ("Ueber die Konstruktionen und Namen"), Bauer, para. 58.

8. The details are debatable and are described in various ways. Compare Bauer, para. 23; Droysen, p. 68; Beloch, *Population (Bevölkerung)*, p. 131. Busolt, in *Hermes* 40 (1905): 387, seeks to explain the contradictions in the accounts by proving (successfully, in my opinion) that there were many changes.

9. Reuss, in *Neue Jahrbücher für Philologie* 145: 550, has made it appear probable that Xenophon is innocent in the matter of these numbers. It seems that Paragraphs 10 to 13 of Chapter 7, Book 1, are a later insertion. This will serve perhaps to answer the philologists who would like to attack my research with the following conclusion: Xenophon, an eyewitness, truth-loving man, and practical soldier, has the army of Artaxerxes deploy with 900,000 men. Naturally, we cannot imagine how that took place, but a witness of such prestige must be believed. What was possible at Cunaxa was also possible elsewhere—consequently the army of Xerxes also can have been several million men strong. The so-called objective analytical method therefore is not suitable for antiquity; there is nothing else for us to do but to seek out the best account and to repeat it.

10. How the words of Xenophon are to be interpreted has been the subject of very much research, including very recent works by F. Reuss, *Neue Jahrbücher für Philologie* (*NJP*), 1883, p. 817; Bünger, *NJP* 131: 262; and G. Friedrich, *NJP* 151: 19. Scholars always im-

agine the movements of large troop masses as much too easy. Even if the reported numbers of the Persian army are reduced by 95 to 97 percent, there still remain masses that are very difficult to control tactically and absolutely incapable of complicated evolutions. The backward wheel of the Greek phalanx, even if we picture it as a forward wheel, after a face-about, which, as Reuss tells us, they caused to be carried out by only one wing, is an extremely difficult maneuver. See in this connection the special study on Gaugamela below.

11. Diodorus, whose account probably is traceable to Ctesias, the doctor of Artaxerxes, still tells of an attack by the Persians; Xenophon, probably more accurately, does not.

Chapter V

Theory: Xenophon

The progressing technique of warfare also fostered the development of theory. It probably had its start in the observation of the advantages of the various weapons. A special clue as to how the lively Athenians debated the subject is to be found in Euripides' tragedy *Hercules*, in which the author, without actually being forced to do so by his material, but apparently only to delight the public spirit by the poetic echo of his own speeches, has Lycus, who portrays Hercules in a bad light as a simple archer, fight with Amphitryon.

Lycus says (according to Wilamowitz' translation into German):

> What is Hercules after all? A reputation for courage
> Has he won by warring on wild animals.
> In that he may be brave, but nowhere else.
> Never, after all, has there been a shield at his side,
> Nor has he ever touched a spear. His weapons
> Are cowardly arrows, his skill is in flight.
> For manly courage has never been shown by anyone
> As an archer. For that, one must stand fast
> On his two feet and unflinchingly couch his spear.
> He does not step aside. His look is directed on the
> Forest of spears stiffly standing over there—and he
> Moves not a muscle.

Amphitryon thereupon answers him:

> That very logical invention, bow and arrow,
> You, too, reject. So listen now and learn.
> The lance fighter is the slave of his weapon;
> If his point breaks, he is defenseless,

158

For only one weapon protects him;
And if he fights in a rank with poor men,
Then he falls because of his neighbor's cowardice.
On the other hand, he whose hand controls the bow,
He has the advantage (and it is the greatest of all),
Even if he has already fired off a thousand shots,
He still lacks not an arm to protect him.
Even from afar his missile strikes, and the foe,
Feeling himself hit, still does not see by whom.
He, however, stands in a covered place and does not offer
His body to the enemy. This is in war
The greatest skill, independent of chance,
To harm the enemy while sparing oneself.

At just about this time, during the Peloponnesian War, a few Sophists began to conduct lectures on the art of war. Xenophon must be regarded, however, as the first one to analyze systematically the nature of the conduct of war and to present his findings. He already recognized and stressed repeatedly that the conduct of war is not a science, but rather it calls on the whole man, with all his abilities. He has Socrates saying that "tactics are only a very small part of the art of warfare" (*Memorabilia* 3. 1). The field commander must also be aware of everything that has to do with equipment and must be skilled at providing the necessities of life for his soldiers. "He must be ingenious, energetic, careful, full of stamina and presence of mind, loving and tough, straightforward and crafty, alert and deceptive, ready to gamble everything and wishing to have everything, generous and greedy, trusting and suspicious." Nature and education must be blended in his makeup. Another passage (3. 4. 3) states that it is useful for the commander to be eager for glory. The *Cyropaedia* is a textbook on politics and the art of war in the form of a historical novel. Important as the book is in its literary aspect and much as it has been read by practical soldiers, nevertheless, for our purpose, research into the history of the art of war, there is little to be derived from it. The eternal and unchanging elements of the conduct of war, the psychological and morale aspects, were treated admirably by Xenophon, but the historical forms, subject to change, are treated by him only cursorily or even fantastically, so that one must be careful not to take the novel for reality. The forms of warfare in Xenophon's time are so simple that there was not much to be said about them. Xenophon was not the type of creative spirit who would have taken the materi-

al at hand and developed and solved new problems. Wherever he
tries to do so, he obviously fails, and, practical soldier that he is, he
even falls off into impractical theorizing.

Among the problems that must have occupied every Greek
leader was that of the relationship of breadth to depth in the
phalanx. Should one form up, say 10,000 hoplites, preferably 1,000
men wide and 10 men deep, or 500 men wide and 20 men deep?
In the one case one could outflank the enemy, in the other case
one would have a much greater weight for the impact.[1] It is surprising that, in the entire range of ancient literature, we find no
real observations on this question. In fact, we do not even have a
definite report about how deep the phalanxes were normally actually arranged. It is so often a question of an 8-man depth, that we
have tended to regard this number as a kind of normal formation,
and that may be correct. But in individual cases this was varied, not
only because of special need but also arbitrarily. We can hardly understand it when Thucydides reports of the battle of Mantinea that
the various captains had drawn up their detachments in varying
depths, according to their own ideas. In the battle of Delium the
Thebans formed up 25 men deep, while the other contingents were
of varying depth, but in any case very much more shallow.
Xenophon addresses this question in the feigned battle of Cyrus
against Croesus. It was reported to Cyrus that the Egyptians were
drawn up 100 men deep, while his own army stood 12 men deep.
One of his subordinate commanders was concerned about whether
they would be strong enough when faced with such a deep
phalanx. Cyrus replied that, if the phalanx was deeper than the
range of the weapons, then the latter would cause no more
damage—an objection that must be termed unsatisfactory in every
respect. Even with 12 or 8 ranks, more than half of the weapons
can no longer have a direct impact. That the advantage of a deep
formation is its power of impact can, least of all, have been unknown to a man like Xenophon, and he was still to experience it
and to be called upon to recount how this power proved itself and
developed.

Another problem that must have preoccupied Greek military
men is the coordination of the hoplites with the long-distance
weapons. Actually, up to that time each arm conducted its own battle; no tactics of coordinated arms existed. Only infrequently was
there success in using missile weapons effectively against hoplites
and in supporting one arm with another. Xenophon has Cyrus
placing his spear-throwers behind the hoplites and the archers be-

hind the spear-throwers and each shooting over the heads of the ranks in front of him (4. 2). For the sharpshooters, we are told, were not able to hold their own in hand-to-hand combat; but when covered by the hoplites they could hurl their spears and fire over them.

If such a disposition of the arms were possible from a practical point of view, it would naturally be extremely effective, and we would encounter it somewhere in actuality. But it is pure theory. The spears and arrows that are fired off in an arching trajectory over the hoplites can have at best a minimal effect;[2] and they are almost completely unusable when the hoplite phalanx is in the fast motion of its final assault pace. If the projected weapons are seriously to harm and weaken the enemy phalanx before the impact of the hand weapons, then the hail of missiles must start from a considerable distance, or the hoplite phalanx itself must have some kind of firing arm. How could such a practical, clearheaded writer as Xenophon paint such a phantasmagoria as the posting of sharpshooters in the rear ranks of the phalanx? This would be incomprehensible, if it were not for other examples of history showing how easily theory can wander from the firm ground of reality. That eminent practitioner Napoleon I proposed in his observations on the "Seven Years' War" (Remarks 2 to 11 and Chapter 12) giving the men in the third rank of the infantry cork soles 3 to 5 inches thick so that they would be able to shoot over the heads of the other ranks. Were they to buckle on their cork sandals just before firing, or were they to march with their cork soles? This is the precise counterpart to Xenophon's proposal. Not only our friend Homer, but even the greatest generals nod at times.

More realistically conceived seems to be the regulation that military police should be placed in the rearmost positions in order to see to it that nobody straggles and, in extreme cases, to strike down deserters. When one reflects more closely on this, however, this advice, too, shows up as theoretical and we see that it has never yet been carried out in practice by any field commander; for who guarantees the courage of the military police? If they are really men on whose courage one can count with absolute certainty, then they are no doubt better used in the front line than in the rear.

A third problem Xenophon touches on is the organization of a reserve. The Greek hoplite phalanx attacks in a single closed formation. If a portion of this formation is left behind, it is available for special use, but at the same time the force of the initial impact is correspondingly weakened. With his genius for discerning practical necessities, Xenophon had removed a small reserve from the phalanx in the battle against Pharnabazus described above, in order to be able to counter possible flank attacks by the Persian cavalry. A concept of the most far-reaching importance—but we do not find this idea treated in the *Cyropaedia*; at best, one might find an approach to that idea in the positioning of the cavalry in the great fantasy battle (7. 1). Here the cavalry that had been held back was used by Cyrus to take from the flank, in his turn, the outflanking and enveloping enemy cavalry.

The author goes into much more detail, however, in an appraisal of the scythed chariot and proposes (6. 1. 30) having the phalanx followed by high wooden towers occupied by 20 men, to be towed into battle by 16 oxen attached to 8 shafts, and he recounts how a test had shown that they were easily transportable. He explains that in the case of a baggage wagon each team of oxen has 25 *talents* to pull and manages to do so; with these towers, however, each team would have only 15 *talents* of weight, and so it was obviously practicable.

We are abundantly repaid for these trivialities, which one can account for as fiction, by a little story (2. 3. 17), which is supposed to show us what a great superiority close-combat weapons have over projectiles. A taxiarch divided up his men and gave half of them clubs, while he had the other half take clods of earth. Then he had them fight each other, and on the following day the fight was repeated with the weapons exchanged. Cyrus invited the *taxis*, to a meal and asked the men how they had gotten their bumps and how the fight had gone. They were all agreed that they did, indeed, get a few bruises from the clods, but that in exchange they took all the greater pleasure later in beating the clod-throwers with their clubs. According to Xenophon, Cyrus for this reason introduced the type of combat with hand-to-hand weapons, with which one directly attacks the enemy soldiers (2. 1. 7–9; 2. 1. 21; 2. 3. 17). In his time, however, it is said at the end of the work, the Persians had again turned to other customs; they had reportedly again become missile fighters, and although they were armed with sabers, they avoided hand-to-hand combat.

The definite way Xenophon stresses the superiority of the hand-to-hand fighter, who comes directly to grips with his enemy, is to be given all the more weight because in Greece precisely at that time the light branches of the arms, particularly the peltasts, were developed and perfected and had reached such a point as to have defeated the hoplites now and then. One may assume that the introspective and analytical Greeks also frequently argued that the heavy hoplite phalanx could be completely defeated and destroyed in this way.

But the Greeks' tradition did not allow them to forget that the spear had overcome the bow in the Persian Wars, and Xenophon was no more misled on this point than was the Greek practice. The phalanx always remained the backbone of the Greek armies, and all the other branches of the arms, however great the progress that they made, remained as auxiliary arms.

In addition to the *Cyropaedia*, Xenophon has also left us military monographs with many an interesting detail, in his work on the Lacedaemonian state, as in two cavalry-related essays on the art of horsemanship and the cavalry leader.

The first comprehensive work on military theory, free of any poetic trappings and oriented directly toward practical applications, came from the pen of an Arcadian, the Stymphalian Aeneas, who, using Xenophon as a source, wrote around the year 357 B.C. Only one of the various books of his work, that dealing with the defense of a city, has come down to us, and even it does not give us very much information. Most of the book is taken up with precautionary measures against treason, stratagems of war, secret writing, telegraphy, and general observations. Nevertheless, the book contains but little concerning siege machines and countermeasures for the defense, and even this little is possibly a later interpolation.

EXCURSUS

1. Baldes, in *Xenophon's Cyropaedia as a Text on Tactics* [*Xenophons Cyropädie als Lehrbuch der Taktik*] (Birkenfeld Program, 1887), claims that Xenophon had already established the theory for what the Macedonians later put into execution: tactics of the coordinated arms, battle cavalry, pursuit. The description in 3. 2. 5 he conceives of as an echelon formation. I cannot agree. The formation of the Armenians in the face of the Persians seems to me to be a simple description of the battlefield situation, not the embodiment of a special tactical concept. With the first-named items, however, the situation is different; they are actually described, as Baldes brings out, but his account is not of very much consequence, for the thought is just as easy as the deed is difficult. Only in the latter is there true merit.

2. Aeneas was edited by Köchly and Rüstow, and recently by Hug. Furthermore, Hug treats him in the *Gratulationsschrift der Universität Zürich an die Universität Tübingen, 1897 (Congratulatory Volume from the University of Zurich to the University of Tübingen, 1897)*. See also Jähns, *History of the Science of War (Geschichte der Kriegswissenschaft)*, Vol. 1, Section 8, and Adolf Bauer, *Military Antiquity (Kriegsaltertum)*, Sections 2 and 47.

Notes for Chapter V

1. Xenophon, *Hellenica* 4. 2. 13: The allied forces moving out against Sparta in the year 395 B.C. take counsel "into how many (ranks) one ought to order the army so that you do not have to move the hoplites too much while the cities (allies) are surrounding the enemy."* From this it seems as if the individual contingents had the tendency to form up as deep as possible, in order to concentrate as much power as possible, without realizing that this could cause the entire battle line to be too short, or in the hope that the others would be so kind as to line up in a shallower formation.

2. For an exception, see p. 56, above.

Chapter VI

Epaminondas

All the extensions and refinements of the Greek art of war since the Persian Wars that we have studied do not constitute any change or deviation in principle. A fundamental innovation, however, can be attributed to the Theban Epaminondas.

This innovation is related to a purely external, circumstantial phenomenon of the old phalanx tactics, the peculiar movement to the right, which had no very profound significance at all, but was only a consequence of the fact that the shield was borne on the left arm, but it had the further result that the right flank, sometimes on both sides, was normally victorious.

Epaminondas therefore reinforced his left flank, so that it formed a deeper column—at Leuctra 50 men deep—and held back the right flank, which normally tended to be ahead. The enemy right flank, therefore, which was accustomed to winning, encountered here a cleverly reinforced opposition; the left flank, however, also accomplished nothing, since it was at any rate accustomed to approach the enemy somewhat hesitatingly, and thanks to the holding back of the enemy right, the battle on this flank never did develop fully, or only late in the action came into full play.

Reinforcement in depth forces a shortening of the front; in a case of equal opposing forces the enemy right would have been able to outflank the Theban left wing, envelop it, and attack it simultaneously from front and flank. Whether, when the encounter takes place in this manner, the deeper formation is the better one is the big question. If the enemy front holds fast until its overlapping part has carried out the envelopment and the deeper column is now attacked from two directions, the latter will have difficulty holding its own. Therefore an essential complement of the deeper formation on the one flank is the covering of that shortened flank by cavalry. Epaminondas, however, brought the two arms, infantry and cavalry, together in a fruitful organizational blend. For now, since the left wing, despite its shortening, could not be outflanked, it was able with the full weight of its depth not only to withstand the enemy right but to attack it. Like a trireme ramming its opponent, Xenophon says of the battle of Mantinea, the deep column of the Thebans broke through the Spartan phalanx with its mighty impact.

Epaminondas' formation is called the oblique order of battle; even earlier, as we have seen, the phalanxes had moved obliquely against each other, but the oblique formation became a tactical concept only because Epaminondas turned it about, cleverly holding back the right wing, which normally pressed forward, and pushed ahead the left, while at the same time reinforcing it. Earlier both opposing phalanxes had pushed their right flanks forward in identical fashion, so that, despite their oblique formation, they still struck each other with parallel lines. Thanks to Epaminondas' arrangement, they met obliquely, at a sharp angle to each other, so that the older parallel battle became a flank battle. Only the one flank had to carry the offensive shock; the other flank was refused and sought to stay completely out of the fight as long as possible and simply, through its presence and its demonstrations, to occupy and pin down a portion of the enemy force. For this purpose less strength is needed, and the other wing—the offensive one—can be reinforced with the surplus men, thus providing an ingenious superiority on this flank. And when it had once thrown back the right flank with its mass, then the left flank, which considered itself under any circumstances as the weaker one, gave way automatically.

We have already observed the elements peculiar to these tactics, that is, the deep column and the cooperation of the cavalry on both sides of the Thebans in the battle of Delium (Book II, Chapter I, Section 7). The fact that a new concept is embodied in Epaminondas' battle formation is seen in the organization of the flanks. If the Theban commander had adopted the shortening and deepening of the wing on the right, nothing important would have been accomplished thereby; it had already often happened that, first of all, the two right flanks were victorious, and for that no unusual formation was needed. All of this is valuable only because it guarantees one's own left wing the victory over the enemy right.

A new concept, however, normally makes its power felt quickly in several directions. At Leuctra the Boeotian army probably had on its left side a natural flank cover that, well sought out, made any envelopment difficult, and at Mantinea the covering cavalry was, in turn, supported by its own light infantry, the *hamippen*, who were well trained for this.

As an indication of Xenophon's military insight, it is also worthy of mention here that he finds the significance of Epaminondas in no way limited to the latter's discovery of the new tactics, but brings out as particularly admirable "that he had accustomed his army to shy away from no effort, either by day or by night, to avoid no danger, and to maintain its discipline even with the sparsest rations."

EXCURSUS

1. The basic elements of the changes made by Epaminondas are correctly recognized and presented by Rüstow and Köchly. As to details, a few points—and not entirely insignificant ones—are subject to correction. In general it is important to observe that it was not first the Macedonians, but Epaminondas, who conceived the tactics of combined arms.

2. As to detail, it is incorrect to combine the estimate of Diodorus that Epaminondas had 6,000 men at Leuctra with that of Plutarch, who gives the Spartans 10,000 hoplites and 1,000 cavalry, and to conclude from that that the Boeotians had conquered a force twice as large as theirs. It is true that even Diodorus states that the Boeotians had defeated an enemy four times as strong as themselves, but since the same author assures us that the Spartans had lost 4,000 men, the Boeotians only 300, his numerical strengths must be regarded as worthless. From the way the battle went, one cannot assume that one side was very significantly stronger than the other. Adolf Bauer has already correctly remarked that the numbers are unreliable. Grote, too, rejects them, but nevertheless he accepts the fact that the Lacedaemonians were superior in strength. I can see no basis for this. The 6,000 Boeotians are presumably identical with the "one-twelfth of the 70,000 men" mentioned in Chapter 24 of Plutarch's *Pelopidas*.

Rüstow and Köchly, furthermore, have the endangered left flank of the Boeotians covered not so much by the cavalry as by a very complicated maneuver of the infantry: while the Spartans were wheeling with their extreme right wing in order to take the Thebans in the flank, Pelopidas, with his 300-man-strong "Sacred Band," broke out from the tail of the Theban column and, in turn, threatened the flank and the rear of the Lacedaemonians. This account rests on a combination of Plutarch's recital (*Pelopidas*, Chapters 19 and 23) with that of Xenophon (*Hellenica* 6. 4). Adolf Bauer and H. Droysen, too, have accepted this account, the latter with the reservation that nobody knows where Pelopidas was stationed before making his move.

Against this account it can be argued that nothing whatever is to be found in Plutarch about a breaking-out from the column by Pelopidas, much less about a breaking-out toward the flank or an attack on the Spartans' flank. It is only stated that the Theban attack succeeded, while the Lacedaemonians were planning to wheel and therefore were not in good order. It would have been impossible, too, for a small detachment of 300 men who broke loose from the large mass to be able to accomplish such a result. Even in this battle one cannot deny the Spartans the proof of the greatest courage—"all of the dead had been struck in the front." Three hundred men would not have been able to hold up the wheeling maneuver of such a greatly superior number of such men. One can, furthermore, neither assume that it was a question of an improvisation by Pelopidas—for Epaminondas must have taken some precautions against envelopment, in view of the shortness of his front—nor can one assume that this was a prepared maneuver, for in this case Pelopidas' detachment would not have been placed at the tail of the column but would, as a withheld echelon, have been stationed to the side of the column in order to cover its flank. And it follows that, had this been the case, the formation would have had to be expressly reported to us. There seems to me to be no doubt of the fact that Pelopidas with his "Sacred Band" fought at the head of the column and that it is nothing more than Plutarch's rhetorical elaboration that appears to give a special position to his hero with the "Sacred Band." But Rüstow and Köchly believed that what they were observing in this combat must have been the flank protection of the large column, because they quite correctly postulated that such a unit must have been at hand although specific mention of it was missing.

I think, however, that this information is to be inferred from Xenophon without difficulty. The latter, who in any event carries much greater authority for us than does the account in Plutarch, which passed perhaps through many hands and is especially slanted toward Pelopidas—Xenophon, then, places all his stress on the preceding cavalry combat and the fact that the Lacedaemonians were beaten in this encounter. In the wounded pride associated with his prejudice for the Spartans he thoroughly explains how and why their cavalry had been of no avail. Now, after the Laconian cavalry was defeated, the hoplite phalanx was not able to carry out a wheeling move against the flank of the enemy in the presence of the victorious enemy cavalry—but this fact was so obvious to him that he did not make any special mention of it at all. We may (without any hesitation), however, add this point, which is essential for our understanding, instead of reading into Plutarch's lengthy and unclear account the ingenious but still inadequate maneuver of Pelopidas.

According to Xenophon the Lacedaemonian cavalry was drawn up in front of the phalanx of infantry instead of on the flank. Why? Rüstow and Köchly say, "Xenophon's answer to this question—'because the terrain between the two armies was flat'—is no answer," and explain their idea to the effect that, during the approach march of the Lacedaemonians, the cavalry unintentionally got out in front of the infantry. H. Droysen, on page 99 of his work mentioned above, correctly takes issue with this, saying that the specific expression of Xenophon, "proetaxanto," eliminates this interpretion, and he asks, "Did Cleombrotus possibly want to shift his infantry toward the right behind his cavalry, in order to take the Boeotian battle mass in the flank and rear? Was the cavalry perhaps supposed to wait until the infantry had made this move, in order then to attach itself to the infantry on the left (right?), instead of attacking at that time, before the entire army had moved up?"

The simple remark that the terrain between the armies was flat does not, to be sure, explain anything; it appears superfluous, since the Greek hoplite battles were almost always fought out on flat ground. But if we look more closely, we see that Xenophon does not actually give any absolute cause-and-effect relationship. The passage reads:

"Since there was a plain between the armies, the Lacedaemonians placed the cavalry in front of their phalanx while the Thebans also were arranging theirs."*

The "kai" following the "h ate" shows that the "plain between the armies" was only a supporting reason for the formation, not the principal one. If, however, the level ground between the phalanxes attracted the cavalry, it is to be assumed that the terrain on the flank was less passable or even perhaps not at all so.

Epaminondas, then, drew his army up in such a way that his left flank was covered by a natural obstacle. The Spartan line overlapped the Boeotian one but could not envelop it because of the terrain. Then the Spartan cavalry tried to drive off the Boeotian cavalry and for this purpose moved out in front of their own hoplites in order to open up for them a route into the flank of the Boeotian hoplites. If the terrain had permitted an attack by the overlapping cavalry from the flank simultaneously with the advance of the hoplites, such a mistake would be completely incomprehensible. If, however, there was a terrain obstacle on the left flank of the Boeotians, everything is clear. The strange and insufficient reason for the position of the Spartan cavalry, "because the field between the infantry was flat," seems to be the psychological complement of the counteridea that the author had in mind but forgot to express—that is, that the terrain on the left of the Thebans was impassable. Nevertheless, this omission is so striking that a corrupted text, the loss of several words between "hate" and "kai," does not appear to be out of the question.

The account in Plutarch, *Pelopidas*, Chapter 23, that Epaminondas, for his own part, at first tried to envelop the Spartans and take them in the flank, is to be completely rejected as entirely impracticable. With such a movement Epaminondas would have completely lost the cohesiveness of his already shorter front. A deep column such as he had formed can be used only for penetration, not for a flanking movement. This passage shows most effectively that Plutarch's entire account of this battle is unusable.

Busolt, in *Hermes* 40: 455, estimates the army of Epaminondas at some 6,500 hoplites, 600 to 800 cavalry, and an indefinite number of lightly armed men; the Lacedaemonian army at some 9,260 hoplites, at least 600 cavalry, and a few hundred peltasts. Nevertheless, the allies on both sides were said to be unreliable and unwilling; the actual battle, therefore, is based on the combat between the approximately equally strong Thebans and Lacedaemonians, and here the superiority was on the side of the Thebans, since the quality of their cavalry far exceeded that of the enemy.

I do not believe that this correctly characterizes the factors that were decisive at Leuctra. The mighty numerical superiority of the Spartans is supposed to have been counterbalanced by the poor morale of many of their allied contingents. The experience of military history teaches, however, that even politically quite unreliable contingents, once they are incorporated into a larger military organization, have often completely fulfilled their military duty (Rhine Alliance Troops). Disaffection would already have to be imminent; otherwise the battle action itself, the danger and the passion of the battle, the concept of honor are all strong enough to overcome possible political antipathy and even to cause forced allies to fight valiantly. It is for this reason that great commanders have so often been able to risk taking along even unwilling allies into a campaign and using them as reinforcements. The explanation of the victory of the minority over the majority at Leuctra is therefore not to be found in these circumstances and it is not even necessary to depend further on them, since the basis of the estimates is not certain enough to permit a positive claim of the numerical superiority of the Spartans.

Busolt's other military observations in this essay are also not all appropriate; admirable, however, is the rejection of Kromayer's statistical estimates, which Busolt discounts just as sharply as Beloch did at the same time. (See also above, p. 60, note 2.)

3. The account of the battle of Mantinea is also based, in Rüstow and Köchly, on a combination of Xenophon's and Diodorus' reports. From Diodorus the information is taken that the army of Epaminondas had a strength of 30,000 men on foot and 3,000 cavalry, whereas the Spartan army had 20,000 men on foot and 2,000 cavalry. If that were correct, then once again the Boeotian victory would not have been a work of art, but there is not the slightest reason for believing the account of such an unreliable man as Diodorus. The development of the battle gives no indication of any great superiority on the part of the Boeotians, and the fact that Xenophon says nothing of this excuse for the Spartans' defeat tends to contradict it directly.

Concerning the course of the battle itself, Rüstow and Köchly have this to say: "Xenophon really concentrates only on the events on Epaminondas' left wing and, further, tells the story quite inaccurately, despite all his verbosity. Diodorus, on the other hand, restricts himself principally to the combats on the flanks, to the cavalry and the light infantry. And thus the two of them, together, give a tolerably clear picture of the battle." Even from the methodological point of view this basis seems to me incorrect. If, as we must unquestionably believe from Xenophon, the battle on the Boeotians' left flank, with the great column "like a trireme" and the cavalry, brought about the decision, how can we trust an author who, as Diodorus does, recounts practically nothing of this but who, on the other hand, has Epaminondas, in the style of the Trojan heroes (as Grote has already so correctly remarked), fight and fall? Factually, the description of the battle is spoiled by Diodorus' portrayal of a great cavalry battle raging back and forth on the Boeotians' right flank. In this account the "oblique order of battle" does not receive its rightful recognition. In my opinion, not a single point can be accepted from Diodorus' account; presumably (according to Grote) it was just this description of the battle that served as the basis for Polybius' disparaging judgment of Ephorus. The battle of Mantinea may be recounted only as described by Xenophon, who, it is true, makes no secret of his preference for the Spartans and, as at Leuctra, strongly emphasizes the mitigating factors (surprise attack), but who is nevertheless a much too conscientious author, and perspicacious soldier, to give a picture that is not factually correct. According to him, the decisive factor at Mantinea, just as at Leuctra, is the combination of the deep infantry column on the left flank with a superior cavalry. As new factors, there appear here also the support of the Boeotian cavalry by their own lightly armed men (hamippen) and the support of the refused right flank by detached units that threaten the enemy left flank with attacks in the flank and rear and by means of these demonstrations hold it off from attacking long enough for the decision to be reached on the other flank.

4. Epaminondas' strengthening of the left flank and his making it the attacking wing has its basis, as Rüstow has already recognized and I have taken over from him, in the accidental, external circumstance that, in the old phalanx battle, although it was in theory a parallel battle, both right wings normally pressed forward. Kromayer, in *Ancient Battlefields in Greece* (*Antike Schlachtfelder in Griechenland*), I: 79, believes that that is a point of confusion between "movement to the right" and "pressing forward of the right wing," and that only the former was recorded in the sources. This alleged substitution stems only from the inadequacy of Kromayer's study of elementary tactics and of the sources. A phalanx that moves to the right will, even in a simple approach march, "hang up" automatically with its left flank——that is, hold back—and all the more so if the left wing on each side, thanks to the movement to the right, finds itself outflanked and threatened, while on the contrary the right flank, encouraged by the envelopment that now seems likely, pushes energetically on. Moreover, with the Greeks the best troops often were placed on the right wing. Also, the holding-back of the left flank is proved by the sources in the battle of Coronea, in *Hellenica* 4. 3. 15 ff., where the Orchomenians on Agesilaus' extreme left flank await the Thebans' attack while the other contingents move forward to meet them.

Along with Kromayer's false assumption, all his conclusions collapse, too, and it is not worth the trouble to dwell further on this—especially since in his work there is no clear idea at all that Epaminondas actually protected his weaker flank. In Rüstow's concept of the battle the situation is simple and clear; since the enemy left flank customarily moved forward somewhat slowly and cautiously, Epaminondas only needed to order his right to hold back correspondingly, and so he gained the necessary advanced position for his left flank. In place of this clear concept, Kromayer advances indefinite, general observations concerning terrain and pseudo-scholarly erroneous comparisons with the tactics of Frederick the Great. I shall have more to say on this subject when this work treats of Frederick. See also Roloff, *Problems in Greek Military History* (*Probleme an der griechischen Kriegsgeschichte*), pp. 42 ff., where Kromayer is thoroughly rebutted.

Likewise in that work (pp. 12 ff.) Kromayer's reflections on Epaminondas as a "practitioner of the strategy of annihilation" are rebutted, ideas that, once again, originate both in Kromayer's incomplete technical understanding of the difference between all-out-victory strategy and attrition strategy and in his defective source studies. E. von Stern (*Literarisches Central-Blatt*, 1903, No. 24, Column 777), who in other respects often agrees with Roloff, feels obliged to side with Kromayer on this point. Nevertheless, his reasons are not sound.

He misses the express testimony for the fact that Epaminondas had to wait such a long time for the approach of the Peloponnesians, and he believes that it is completely out of the question that such nearby communities as Argos, Megalopolis, and so on, were not on the scene.

But aside from the fact that the passage cited by Roloff (*Hellenica* 7. 5. 9) does, nevertheless, probably mean this—why did Epaminondas actually wait so long before forcing the decision? If all his troops, or even the majority of them, were on the spot, did he not have such an overwhelming superiority as to be able to envelop any position, no matter how strong?

Stern, furthermore, finds it very improbable that the missing contingents should all have arrived, "as if by agreement", within a few days. Why not, after all? And moreover, why not by agreement?

Stern believes also that Epaminondas, when he made his move against Sparta instead of fighting a battle, could definitely have counted on forcing Sparta to peace terms if he succeeded in taking the city by a quick stroke and divesting the women of their young, as well as the men who had remained behind. To this one must answer that Epaminondas would have had to be a rather miserable commander to think in that way; great wars are not decided by sudden strikes against unfortified places. Whether Epaminondas would really have taken so many prisoners is doubtful, for the Spartan women and the others would probably have taken to flight before that. Even if the Thebans had, however, taken such a great booty, why should the Spartans and their allies have then avoided the battle that would actually have brought about the final decision about the disposition of the booty? Quite distortedly Stern reminds us that the Spartans sued for peace after their people had been taken prisoner at Sphacteria. There the conditions were quite different, for they could see no possibility of liberating the prisoners or of otherwise dealing the Athenians a heavy blow. Epaminondas' army, on the other hand, moving but slowly because of its booty, could not avoid a battle with the revenge-thirsty Spartans. There is no doubt, then, that Roloff is right when he sees in this move not a serious plan for the capture of the city, but only a demonstration for the purpose of gaining time for his reinforcements to arrive.

The detailed description of the battle of Mantinea in Kromayer is completely worthless, is full of factual distortions, and does not agree with the sources. In this case even Stern cannot avoid agreeing with Roloff's criticism. Kromayer did not even definitely establish with certainty the topography of the battlefield at the time of his visit, since it did not occur to him until after his return which things really needed to be verified.

The discovery Kromayer claims to have made, to the effect that Epaminondas gave special consideration to the terrain and analyzed it carefully, is also to be rejected. The exploitation of the terrain had already been understood by Miltiades and Pausanias, and the fact that Epaminondas, too, made good use of it is no new discovery but rather something to be taken for granted, and so broadly recognized that it was also quoted in the above presentation.

BOOK III

The Macedonians

Chapter I

The Macedonian
Military System

Epaminondas' tactical concepts were taken up and developed by King Philip II of Macedon. Macedon was a basically agrarian state with open country and very little urban population. The great mass of farmers and shepherds were not sufficiently well-off to provide themselves with hoplite equipment and were also unable, without difficulty, to gather in large units in a single place. In order to arrive at the capital, Pella, which lay more or less in the middle of the country, it took four to five days of marching from the most distant border areas. Consequently a special type of military class, a kind of nobility, had developed, fighting on horseback, while the common folk formed only peltasts, who, fighting without tactical organization, were regarded only as a simple auxiliary arm and were unable to face up to Greek hoplites.

Appropriately, Thucydides (4. 126) once had Brasidas make the distinction for his men between Greek and barbarian methods of warfare. The Spartan commander had to take up a withdrawal in the face of a very superior group of warlike Illyrians, and his soldiers were terror-stricken, but he said to them:

Only the appearance of the barbarians, their numbers, their war cries, the brandishing of their weapons are frightful. But in hand-to-hand combat they are worthless, for they do not remain in formation and feel no shame at falling back out of position. But whenever it is up to each individual whether he should fight or give way, there is never any lack of reasons for withdrawing; for that reason, the barbarians prefer to threaten from a distance rather than engage in hand-to-hand combat.[1]

Since the real Macedonian warrior class, the nobility, on the other hand, could not be very large, the older Macedon was only a very weak state from the military point of view. Only the firm monarchical authority established by King Philip II created from these elements a military system that soon became superior to that of all the neighboring states. The King levied the sums to maintain a standing army of his subordinates in addition to the Greek mercenaries that he took into his service, gave them military training, found new and different battle formations for this army, and drew forth from the art of tactics powers that showed the Greek world a new level of the art of war.

We begin with the cavalry.

CAVALRY

We picture to ourselves the Greek cavalry as rather loose-knit detachments that, provided with protective armor, did on occasion go into combat with cold steel, but which also used the spear still more frequently as a missile than as a thrusting weapon.

Xenophon, from whom we have two works on cavalry, *Concerning Horsemanship* and *The Cavalry Leader*, says that he prefers the set of equipment with two short spears to that with one long one.[2] The latter is, according to him, uncomfortable to carry and fragile; of the short spears, which are easier to carry and stronger, one can throw the one and use the other to thrust out in all directions.[3] In addition to the spears, the cavalrymen also carried a sword or a curved saber; the latter, Xenophon says, is better, since the cavalryman can strike down from above. Xenophon recommends that not only the rider but also the horse be provided with armor. He does not provide the rider with a shield. Stirrups were not yet invented; cavalrymen rode on firmly tied blankets or cushions. The thrust with the lance, therefore, had to be made much more with the strength of the arm than is the case today, when the rider can put the whole weight of his body and the momentum of his steed into the thrust. In the numerous designs on vases that portray battle scenes and have been preserved to our time, I have never found the lance carried as is prescribed today for our cavalry (pressed between the upper arm and the body). On the mosaic that presumably portrays the battle of Issus, Alexander carries the very long lance free in his hand.

In its armament and equipment the Macedonian cavalry was similar to the Greek. The cavalry force made up of the Macedonian nobility was called the companions (*hetairoi*) of the king. They fought with the spear, which they used as both a missile and a thrusting weapon,[4] and with the sword. The use of armor for the horse, of which Xenophon speaks, does not seem to have been common. On the other hand, the companions did carry shields.[5]

The principal advantage that the Macedonian cavalry probably had over the Greeks lay in the fact that they were disciplined; we may ascribe to their squadrons (*ilai*) such great cohesiveness as to classify them as "tactical units." One may differentiate between "mounted men" and "cavalry" by the fact that the former term indicates groups of individual riders, whereas "cavalry" means riders in disciplined units.

That being the case, the Macedonians would have constituted the first real cavalry. To develop tactical units from riders is, for numerous reasons of which we shall speak later, much more difficult than to form infantry units. It is only natural, then, that the Greek canton republics never went beyond the hoplite phalanx; the monarchical authority of the Macedonian kings, on the other hand, forced even the individualistically inclined horsemen into the firm framework of a unit following the leadership of a single will.

With the Macedonians we find no trace of the mixed troops, the *hamippen*, a fact that also leads to the conclusion that they had more firmly organized tactical units than the Boeotians.

In addition to the companion cavalry, the Macedonians had the "*sarissa*-bearers" armed with the lance, whom many have been inclined to consider as light cavalry. Nevertheless, I cannot find in the sources any basis for this concept. The fact that they were armed with the long *sarissa* would, in fact, more logically lead to the conclusion that they were a heavy cavalry. True enough, it was the companion cavalry (*hetairoi*) that principally waged the hand-to-hand combat; under certain circumstances, however, they even used their lances in the older manner, as missiles. The *sarissa* was too long to be thrown, and so its bearer was even more unconditionally obliged to participate in close-in combat than were the *hetairoi*, a point that again suggests protective armor and therefore leads to the conclusion that they were heavy cavalry. In battle the *sarissa*-bearers seem to have been employed in just the same way as the *hetairoi*, and the latter were also used for reconnaissance and pursuit. It seems, then, that the difference in arms and equipment between the two types of unit was only a small one. Perhaps it lay only in the varied provenance of the men.

During the war against Darius, Alexander also formed, of Asiatics, a force of mounted archers.

THE PHALANX

The Macedonian horsemen had probably always been called the companions (*hetairoi*) of the king. To the newly formed infantry Philip gave the prestigious title of *pezetairoi* or foot companions. They were trained to fight in the phalanx, in a tight tactical formation, in the manner of the Greeks. Nevertheless, there was a certain difference: the Macedonian phalanx was drawn up in tighter formation than was customary with the Greeks, and it was equipped with a longer spear, the *sarissa*, which permitted it effectively to use the spears of several ranks simultaneously. In the same way, Frederick the Great had his infantry drawn up in a closer formation than was customary before that time—four men within three paces rather than within four paces—in order to have more muskets firing at the same time.[6]

We do not know in detail the organization of the *sarissa* phalanx of the classical Macedonian period, and we are ignorant, in particular, of the length of the *sarissa* at that time. I suspect that the first rank or the first two ranks of the phalanx, just as previously, carried the easily handled hoplite spear and that only the ranks farther to the rear carried the long spear, which even at that was probably not so much longer that it could not be manipulated with one hand.[7]

The reasons for this variation from the old Doric order have not come down to us, but can be arrived at from the nature of things.

We may be allowed to assume that the centuries-long experience of the Greeks had taught them to construct their principal weapon, the spear, in such a way—that is, with carefully measured length, thickness, and weight—as to render it most effective for combat: as long as possible, so as to reach the enemy, but not so long that it could not be manipulated effectively with one hand or that the thrust could be parried too easily by the enemy. To judge from the vase figures, the spear was somewhat longer than the height of a man—therefore about 2 meters.[8] Nevertheless, numerous variations may well have occurred. As to what is the best length, even today military men are not in agreement on this point. The lance of the German cavalry is 3.52 meters long; the Russian is 3.16; the French 3.29; the Austrian 2.63 meters.[9] If then the Macedonians exceeded even the longest measure adopted by the Greeks after their experience, it was a disadvantage in a man-to-man combat, and the tight formation accentuated the disadvantage still more by hindering the free movement of the individual soldier. The *sarissa* phalanx, however, was supposed to have had its effect less in man-to-man combat than through the tightly ordered momentum of the whole mass. And if it halted in a defensive stance, it was impossible to penetrate into the many-barbed mass.

Philip probably decided on this combat formation because he was aware that his newly formed troops would not be able to hold their own under similar conditions with the Greek hoplites, who were full of the self-confidence of seasoned warriors. It is also possible that he did not initially have the means of outfitting all the members of his phalanx with the complete, costly hoplite equipment. In the tight formation, which less frequently led to an actual man-to-man combat, the rear ranks could, where necessary, get along without the full protective equipment. That is, however, only a surmise that must remain uncertain. The important point is that the Macedonian phalanx as such is not to be conceived as the invention of a new, more refined battle formation, but as a reduction of the former performance of the infantry. The new phalanx was more cumbersome than the old one, fell more easily into disarray, and was still more sensitive on its flanks. For the kind of individual combat that the warrior is supposed to be able to carry out in numerous assignments outside the mass battle, the *sarissa*-bearer is very awkward. The old Doric hoplite phalanx, which combined the group action of a tactical body with the combat skill of each individual, is, of itself, the higher tactical formation. Nevertheless, at the time of Philip and Alexander this difference was not yet very important. In all the battles of this period of which we have accounts the phalanx moves with such ease and shows so little distinction from the old hoplite phalanx that we could almost disregard the difference if a few reports did not indicate distinctly that the difference that later became very significant—that is, the longer spear and the tighter formation—had already at least started in Philip's time.

An elite corps, the *hypaspists*, was armed entirely in the manner of the old hoplites—perhaps somewhat more lightly—with the certainty that the lighter protective armor would be offset in hand-to-hand combat by increased flexibility. The *hypaspists* form in battle the connecting link between the offensive wing of the cavalry and the great mass of the *sarissa* phalanx, which moves up more slowly.

The Madedonian army was also strong in light infantry, peltasts, archers, and missile-throwers.[10]

TACTICS OF THE COMBINED ARMS

The progress made by the Macedonians lies in the organizational blending of all branches of the arms in a unified cooperation. Epaminondas had paved the way for this, but in such a way that the infantry still remained the principal arm, whereas the cavalry was only a supporting element.

From the very start Philip was much stronger in cavalry than the Boeotians had ever been, and all the more so after he had brought Thessaly under his dominance. Consequently, he was able not only to defeat the enemy cavalry with his own, but also to attack the enemy infantry in the flank. We know from the time of Marathon how sensitive the Greek hoplite phalanx was in this respect.

From now on, therefore, the cavalry is no longer a supporting arm but is of equal importance and even delivers the main blow. It may even be that the phalanx does not close with the enemy until one of his flanks is already beaten and the Macedonian cavalry of the offensive wing is already attacking the main body from the flank. It can also happen that, under the pressure of this blow, the entire enemy army gives up the battle and takes to flight, so that the phalanx does not even enter into the battle.

Rüstow and Köchly have even gone so far as to believe that the cavalry has now become the principal arm, the phalanx only the shadow, no longer the light—the mass and not the nucleus of the army. According to them, the mission of the phalanx was now only to maintain the combat, to form an impenetrable defensive wall until the cavalry had won the decision. A careful analysis of Alexander's battles shows that such a statement goes too far. The heavy infantry, too, *hypaspists* and phalanx alike, play a positive, active role in the victory. The cavalry, in turn, is supported by the mobile light infantrymen, who pave the way and lend general assistance with javelin, arrow, and slungshot.

The close integration of all the individual units is the strength of the Macedonian army organization. The unified concept of the army commander, who is at the same time creator of the army and leader, governs the whole. The Macedonian art of war is a product of royalty.

The peculiar aspect of the Greek phalanx led to the necessity for Epaminondas, when he invented the flank battle and introduced it in place of the parallel battle, to assign the offensive action to the left wing and to hold back the right. Philip no longer needed to adhere to this scheme. He was able to place his cavalry on whichever flank was the more appropriate in view of the terrain conditions. The fact that, in the battle accounts that have been handed down to us, the cavalry of the right flank almost always delivers the decisive offensive blow is not fundamental to the nature of the situation but is to be regarded rather as a development of the older Greek tradition or as pure coincidence.

Another result of a military system centralized in a single hand and a single head is the fact that the Macedonians took up and developed the means for advanced siegecraft. As late as the middle of the century little was known in Greece of the inventions of Dionysius of Syracuse; Philip carried out two great sieges, at Perinthus and Byzantium, using every method of this technique.

We shall not go into the details of a technical nature. The fact itself, however, is of the greatest importance in the coherent development of the art of war. Alexander's strategy would not have been feasible if he had been able to overcome Halicarnassus, Tyre, and Gaza only by means of an interminable starving-out, instead of by an attack in force pitting skill against skill.

Excursus

1. King Philip's military reforms have to be envisaged principally from the conduct of war and battle by Alexander, which is in agreement with the little information we have concerning Philip himself. Philip's first battle against the Illyrians, in 359 B.C., is recounted by Diodorus (16. 4) as follows: Philip had his cavalry on the right flank; he had them attack the barbarians from the flank, and the double attack, from front and flank, and finally from the rear, too, eventually overcame them, but only after the most courageous resistance.

"Philip, commanding the right wing—the best of the Macedonians serving under him—gave orders to his cavalry to ride past and attack the barbarians on their flanks, while he, falling frontally on the enemy, began the bitter battle."*

Also, speaking of the battle in Thessaly in the year 353 B.C., Diodorus expressly makes the point (12. 35) that it was decided in Philip's favor by the cavalry.

2. We have only very incomplete reports on the battle of Chaeronea. From both Diodorus (16. 86) and Polyaenus (6. 2. 2 and 7), however, we learn enough to know that it was likewise a flank battle. The King was in command of the wing opposing the Athenians, which he held back, while his son Alexander was in command of the offensive wing against the Boeotians, which won the decision. If Diodorus has the King moving into the attack only after he has seen the victory of his son, because he does not wish to leave all the glory to him alone, or if Polyaenus, without taking into account the cooperation of the two Macedonian wings, has Philip, after first giving way, suddenly overcome the fiery Athenians with all his force, these are popular accounts which do not penetrate to the real reasons for the decision.

Since the above words were written, Kromayer has studied the topography of the battlefield and, based on that study, has attempted to make a more exact reconstruction of the battle in the above-cited work. His reconstruction effort, however, completely failed, as Roloff has proved in the work already cited and E. von Stern has also recognized, for the attempt is based not only on completely insufficient and unreliable source materials, but also on the monstrous idea that Philip's phalanx pulled back 600 meters "without making a turn" (p. 167, note). An individual man can hardly move backwards 600 meters, on a good road, without stumbling; a phalanx that tried to do that in the open field would very quickly end up with its men lying on the ground, one on top of the other. When a unit moves backward on the drill field, it can go only a few feet in the strictest drill formation of the back step. It is particularly characteristic that Kromayer's idea of an orderly backstep movement by a close mass formation of 15,000 men is not just a possible accidental slip, but the author sought to justify his grotesque concept in detail in the *Historische Zeitschrift* 95: 20. Whoever cannot find the rebuttal himself is referred to the *Preussische Jahrbücher* 121: 164.

Roloff and Stern at least believed that they could recognize Kromayer's service in describing the battlefield. But even this contribution has not stood up under investigation. G. Sotiriades, in *Mitteilungen des königlichen deutschen Archeologischen Instituts*, in Athens, 28 (1903): 301 and 30 (1905): 113, has published detailed topographical studies of the battlefield that point up a series of mistakes in Kromayer's observations and upset his basic points. Kromayer has admitted the decisive point, the position of the Macedonian burial mound, in *Historische Zeitschrift* 95: 27. On the other objections, he has justified himself in a single point: he actually had not stated that the wall remnants of the Turkish *Chans* were antique, a point on which Sotiriades (p. 326) had reproached him and which I had referred to thereafter in *Preussische Jahrbücher* 116: 211, but he had only brought up, and left unanswered, the question whether it was the remains of an ancient building. The other errors, however, remain, particularly the lack of mention of the ravine of Bramaga, through which, according to Sotiriades (p. 328), there leads a path that is no worse than the one leading through the Kerata pass, a point that was of great importance for a withdrawal on that side.

3. The prevailing opinion is that the *sarissa* phalanx, in the form in which we meet it later in the battles of the Macedonians with the Romans and in which it has been described by Polybius, is identical with the one that already existed in the time of Philip and Alexander. But H. Droysen had already been impressed (*Untersuchung*, p. 64) with the great flexibility with which Alexander's phalanxes moved, and I myself have gradually arrived at the conviction that a later progressive development must have taken place. For the sources and factual basis of this opinion, see below, Book VI, Chapter I.

4. Rüstow and Köchly, in *Greek Military Historians* (*Griechische Kriegsschriftsteller*) (p. 240), picture the *hypaspists* as armed with burlap armor, the small shield of the *pezetairoi*, light footwear, the Macedonian hat, a thrusting lance, and perhaps a long sword. That seems to me, however, much too light a protective equipment for warriors who are not simply to be used in case of emergency, but who are specifically intended for hand-to-hand combat and possess no missile weapons at all, and the above-named authors themselves (p. 241) also add the reservation that the equipment of the *hypaspists* was perhaps not so significantly lighter than that of the hoplites. lites.

On the other hand, H. Droysen has denied them any armor (*Heerwesen*, p. 110). He bases this opinion on the coins of the King of Paeonia, Patraos, who lived at the time of Alexander. A Paeonian horseman is pictured on the point of piercing a fallen warrior. The latter is wearing chiton and broad-brimmed hat, and his weapons are shield and lance. The shield can be recognized as Macedonian by its peculiar type of embellishment, as can be seen on the coins of the later Macedonian kings, and so the warrior is a Macedonian, and specifically not a *pezetairoi*, for his lack of a *sarissa* is immediately noticeable, but a *hypaspist* (*Untersuchung*, pp. 41–42).

Droysen's opinion has also been seconded by Adolf Bauer, who also refers to the illustration of the coin, but I feel that this concept is quite questionable. The Paeonians were obliged in 359 b.c. by Philip of Macedon to recognize his rule, and when they tried to throw off this yoke, they were defeated by him in 358 b.c. and by

Alexander in 335 B.C. Patraos was their prince from about 340 B.C. until 315 B.C. Is it logical to assume that such a vassal prince would dare to show on his coins a picture clearly showing that a warrior of the royal guard of his sovereign was being overcome by a Paeonian? And if the shield decoration really allows us no other interpretation, who can tell us that this is really the picture of a man of the newly formed arm of the *hypaspists*? It may be an imaginary illustration, or it may be a peltast that we see portrayed here. Consequently, nothing can be concluded from this coin, and the utilization of the *hypaspists* leaves no doubt that they formed not a type of light infantry, but heavy infantry with complete protective armor.

NOTES FOR CHAPTER I

1. Thucydides does not mention here the superior protective armor of the Greeks, and perhaps the Illyrians were better equipped in this regard than the Macedonians, who were more accustomed to the agricultural life and therefore, in general, less warlike, although Arrian (1. 1. 12) again specifically characterizes the Illyrian and Thracian barbarians as "ill-equipped allies."* Furthermore, in his speech Brasidas specifically calls the Illyrians the equals of the Macedonians, and we may therefore apply the description to the latter also.

2. "Concerning Horsemanship"* (12. 12), "in place of a spear made of cane."* The meaning of the Greek word *"kamakinon"* is not certain, nor is even the manner of reading it, but judging from the whole context, it is almost impossible that anything but a long spear is meant here.

3. Xenophon's remark may be considered in connection with the cavalry combat in *Hellenica* 3. 4. 13. The account shows, however, that at that time the Greek cavalry carried not the short spear, but the long one.

Furthermore, it is not understandable without further explanation in this account, why the Persians had such a deep formation. They were not able to throw their spears from the rearmost ranks. The explanation lies perhaps in the fact that the Persians were counting on penetrating the Greek line with their deep column and, in doing so, throwing their spears to the right and left.

4. Diodorus 17. 60. Arrian 1. 15.

5. Adolf Bauer, para. 313 (2d ed., para, 433), concludes from Arrian 1. 6. 5 that the companions did not normally carry a shield. I cannot find that the passage necessitates this conclusion; in fact, it hardly permits it. Cavalry shields were naturally much smaller than those of the infantry. Since in Plutarch, *Alexander*, Chapter 16, there is specific mention of the shield that the king carries into

combat, and later, according to Polybius 6. 25. 7, the Macedonian cavalrymen undoubtedly had shields, it seems certain to me that such was also the case in earlier periods.

6. See also below, Vol. IV, Book III, Chapter III.

7. Concerning the discomfort of carrying and the difficulty of fighting with the long spear, see also Vol. IV, Book I, Chapter I.

8. Adolf Bauer, para. 272, estimates 3 meters; among all the vase figures that I have looked through, however, I have never found such long hoplite spears, even where there is no limitation of space.

9. R. Wille, *Text on Arms* (*Waffenlehre*), p. 79.

10. A. Krause, in *Hermes*, 1890, para. 66, proved quite conclusively that Alexander also had slingers in his army and that Arrian intends them to be included in the word "*toxetai*" ("archers").*

Chapter II

Alexander and Persia: The Battle on the Granicus

The army with which Alexander moved out to conquer Asia was estimated at various strengths by his contemporaries, but we may accept as well grounded 32,000 men on foot and 5,100 horsemen.[1] On the Granicus and at Issus some 30,000 men probably took part in the fighting. At Gaugamela Arrian gives a figure of 40,000 men on foot and 7,000 horsemen, while very significant numbers of garrison and line-of-supply troops had remained behind in the conquered areas. Alexander's army was, at any rate, considerably stronger—probably about twice as large—as the army with which Xerxes had formerly set out to conquer Greece.

The Greek authors have engaged in quite the same numerical fantasies concerning the armies that Darius sent against the Macedonians as they had once done concerning the hordes of Xerxes. In a well-balanced progression the sources have the Persians forming up on the Granicus with 100,000 men, at Issus with 600,000, at Gaugamela with 1 million men on foot and 40,000 cavalry.

We can reject these numbers completely; we do not know how strong the Persian armies were that Alexander conquered, and in the first edition of this work I left in doubt the question as to whether the numerical superiority lay on the side of Alexander or of the Persians.

The conclusions of the third volume, the medieval military system, however, turned me back to reconsideration of the Persian Empire and to conclusions that fully destroyed the bases for the concept of the Persian mass armies that was previously commonly held. How gigantic was the expanse of the Persian Empire from the Hindu Kush to the Bosporus, from the Caucasus to the Sahara!

185

It was concluded, therefore, that this empire could also raise gigantic armies. But what armies the German Empire would have had to levy among the Otto dynasty, the Salians, and the Hohenstaufens if armies always corresponded to the mass of the subject peoples —and how small, in fact, were the armies of these emperors! It is not on the mass of the people that the size of the army depends, but on their military concept, and, as we have learned from the history of the Middle Ages, knightly armies were uniformly small. We have already come to know the Persian army under Xerxes as a knightly one, with respect to its organization. The huge mass of subjects of the Achaemenid King was entirely unwarlike. Wars were waged and government was exercised by the Persian national warrior class, whose courage, even in the times of Darius Codomannus, was recognized by the Greeks, whose numbers, however, were very small—so small that the Persian King sought to increase them with foreign mercenaries, primarily with Greeks. The so relatively small areas of Macedon and Hellas produced very many more warriors than the entire Persian Empire as far as India.

One can best understand this by a study of the military events of Europe at the end of the fifteenth century. In circumstances that offer many a point of comparison with those of the Greeks, the inhabitants of the German Alpine region had developed a military system that rested on the warlike orientation of the entire people. And so it came about that the inhabitants of these few valleys were able to send forth armies that struck fear into the surrounding large nations. If we imagine that at that time a single king, himself the master of a capable army of knights and infantry, could have bound to himself the Swiss in the same way that Alexander did the Greeks, then he could have subdued Europe just as the Macedonians did with Asia. Alexander stood at the peak of an empire and a league of completely warlike character. The Persian king, it is true, reigned over a much larger empire, geographically boundless, but only with a very thin military stratum at the top. The campaign of the younger Cyrus, with his 13,000 Greeks, and the campaigns of the Spartan Agesilaus in Asia Minor had already shown how fragile the power of resistance of the colossus actually was. Alexander's last battle against Darius will show that not even at the border of the heartland and from the native Persian population was it possible to assemble a truly mass army.

As a result of the assistance of the Greek mercenaries, the Persian armies were made up of hoplites, archers, and horsemen, just as was the Macedonian army. On the Granicus, says Arrian, the cavalry were at a disadvantage against the Macedonians, since they were fighting with javelins against thrusting lances. He himself recounts, however, in detail, how the Macedonians, too, threw lances and the Persians hacked away with the sword. Consequently, there could not have been any important difference in the equipment and the manner of fighting. The combining of the Persian knightly cavalry and the Persian archers with Greek hoplites had formed an army that was quite similar to the one the Macedonians had on the other side, except that presumably the participation of the different branches of the arms in the two armies was in varying degrees.

An important prerequisite for the campaign was the fact that Alexander's father had bent the Greeks under the hegemony of Macedon. In a solemn statement the Corinthian League declared the war to be a national Hellenic war, and Greek as well as other contingents composed the larger half or even more of Alexander's army.[2] This positive cooperation, however, is not even the most important point. The principal gain lies in the security of the rear, which was achieved through the pacification of Greece. By stirring up a war in Greece itself, the Persians had once forced the Spartan Agesilaus to break off his campaign against them. But Alexander not only had Greece behind him, he was also strong enough to leave behind in Macedon an army of 12,000 men on foot and 1,500 horsemen under Antipater, which relieved him of any concern over the homeland.

BATTLE ON THE GRANICUS

A proof of the complete arbitrariness with which the Greeks judged the strengths of the Persian armies is found in the contradictions in the reports of the battle on the Granicus. The source that Diodorus adopted gives 100,000 infantrymen and 10,000 cavalrymen. On the other hand, Arrian expressly says that the Macedonians were far superior to the Persians in infantry, giving no total number for the Persians at all but mentioning only that they had 20,000 Greek mercenaries and 20,000 horsemen. According to the normal principles of critical analysis, we would have to assume that the lowest estimate, coming from the camp of the enemy, is always the more credible one. But the figures given by Arrian suffer from an inner contradiction: in addition to the Greek mercenaries and Persian horsemen, there must, after all, have been Persian infantry on hand. If, then, the total of infantry is supposed to have been considerably weaker than that of the Macedonians, which was hardly stronger than 25,000 men, the Persians could not have had 20,000 men on the spot from the Greek mercenaries alone. We may only assume as certain the fact that the Persian infantry was in fact weaker than the Macedonian. Which side was superior in cavalry we do not know; probably, however, it was the Macedonians, since the conduct of the Persians does not show any consciousness of superiority, least of all with respect to the cavalry. They did not seek a broad, open plain for the battle, but instead they took up a position with a large obstacle before their front, the Granicus River, to await there the attack of the Macedonians. As it appears, the Granicus was probably fordable at almost any point, but the right bank, on which the Persians were drawn up, was high and steep.

One might suppose that the Persians did not really want to engage in battle here at all but had taken up this position with the expectation that Alexander would not risk an attack on such unfavorable terrain but would have to resort to time-consuming maneuvers. In the meanwhile the Persians would have been able to undertake a diversion toward Europe. But the entire conduct of the Persians, supported by the positive statements of all the sources, leaves no doubt that, in fact, the choice of the battlefield was determined by tactical considerations only. We have here a new phenomenon in the history of war: while the Persians, aware of their weakness, seek aid in the terrain, they choose a frontal obstacle in order to make the attack more difficult for the enemy.

The Macedonian army was drawn up in such a way that the heavy infantry formed the center, while the cavalry and the sharpshooters made up the flanks. Alexander himself was on the right flank with the *hetairoi* cavalry, and next to him toward the middle were the *hypaspists*. This flank—horsemen and sharpshooters, perhaps supported by a detachment of *hypaspists*—crossed the river first and without difficulty drove the Persian cavalry to flight. Although the accounts of the combat incident to the climbing of the river bank are quite detailed, we still cannot arrive at any clear picture of the tactical development, since on the one hand we have no knowledge of the comparative strengths and on the other hand none of the sources reports anything of the activity of the Persian dismounted archers. It is hardly believable that none of them should have been on hand. It is obvious that, under the prevailing circumstances, it is precisely this arm that would be necessary to develop the greatest effectiveness.

According to the Greek sources, however, it was precisely the

arm that was the most inappropriate of all for the defense of a
steep slope, the Persian cavalry, that waged the battle alone. That it
succumbed to the combination of Macedonian sharpshooters and
horsemen was only natural, even if the numerical superiority did
not also lie on the latter side.

The important factors for an understanding of the battle have
consequently escaped us. We can only recognize that the frontal
obstacle was of no use to the Persians—a phenomenon that we shall
have further occasion to speak of quite often—and that the battle
was decided by the combat of the cavalry and sharpshooters on the
right flank. As soon as the Persian cavalry had fled from the field,
the phalanx of Greek mercenaries, which, separated from the
enemy by the river, had stood so long inactive, was attacked by the
Macedonian phalanx from the front, by the cavalry and the
sharpshooters on the flanks, and was chopped up or taken prisoner
without offering significant resistance.

According to the best source, Arrian, the losses of the Macedonians are supposed to have amounted to 85 horsemen and 30 infantrymen killed. This figure would be incredible if the Greek
mercenaries, as the sources would have us believe, had been almost
completely mowed down. These mercenaries were people who sold
their lives dearly. Probably, however, neither their number nor the
slaughter was so very great; the majority of them were probably
spared and taken prisoner. If this was indeed the case, then the
figure for the Macedonian losses appears quite credible. The mass
of the infantry did not fight at all, a fact that explains why three-
fourths of the casualties fell to the lot of the cavalry, and this situation in the loss figures supports the accounts of the events of the
battle. A total of 115 killed leads to an estimate of 500 to 1,000
wounded. Such a casualty figure, it is true, is not great, and it
shows that the resistance by the Persians was not exactly obstinate;
but if, as it appears, the real battle was carried out by no more than
some 6,000 men, then it is easy to reconcile the casualty figures
with the account of the courageous fighting of the Persian knights,
who brought Alexander personally into the most extreme danger.
Of course, one cannot go beyond probabilities here, and we should
not deceive ourselves. If one chooses to accept the idea of the massacre of the Greek mercenaries, and along with it the number that
has been handed down, that they were 20,000 strong, then he can
base this on the same sources that put the losses of the Macedonian
infantry at 30 men. There is no positive proof for rejecting the first
report while accepting the second. One can only say with complete

certainty that the two reports stand in contradiction with one another and one of the two must necessarily be given up.

EXCURSUS

(Added in second and third editions.) I have not undertaken a real study of the battle on the Granicus, since it appeared to me, in view of the status of the sources, to offer too little prospect of a fruitful result and to be unnecessary for the purposes of this work. The important aspects of the art of war in this period will stand out sufficiently in the later battles. In the meanwhile, the material on the battle on the Granicus is greatly improved by a new topographical survey and description of the area in the work, *On the Trail of Alexander the Great. A Trip through Asia Minor* (*Auf Alexanders des Grossen Pfaden*), by A. Janke, Colonel of Reserves (Berlin: Weidmann, 1904). Through this work, which discovers and disposes of a fundamental error in the previous concepts of the terrain on the Granicus, there has been created, actually for the first time, the possibility of a critical treatment of the battle from the military history point of view. Since I cannot personally concur with Janke's description, it seems to me that we have here once again the material for a special study; such a study will necessarily bring to light also the questions of the differences in the sources (Plutarch and Diodorus against Arrian), the peculiar problem of the failure of the Persian infantry to appear, and so on. The focal point of the study, however, is to be sought in the question whether the Persians really intended to fight and to make full use of the frontal obstacle only as a tactical expedient, or whether they intended to maneuver in order to gain time.

Basically, I have had reprinted above without change the observations of the first edition with their significantly skeptical sharpness.

NOTES FOR CHAPTER II

1. That is the result of the careful examination of the sources in W. Dittberner, *Issos* (Berlin: George Nauck, 1908).

2. Bauer, para. 314 (2d ed., 434) even claims that the Macedonians represented not much more than a sixth of the entire army. That is too small under any circumstances. A. Krause, in the passage cited above (*Hermes*, 1890), distinguishes among (1) a field army; (2) an army of occupation; (3) a satrap army, which was formed in the conquered areas by the appointed satraps.

That is fundamentally correct but much too sharply distinguished. Naturally, there were troops that were used primarily for operations and battles, others that were more often assigned to garrisons, and finally the appointed governors did indeed form new military organizations. But according to the circumstances, all of these various troops were naturally used for the various purposes of the waging of war, sometimes in battle, sometimes as occupation forces.

Chapter III

The Battle of Issus[1]

The battle of Issus was fought under the strategically noteworthy circumstances that the two enemy armies first marched past each other through different passes of the same mountain chain and then both faced about and fought the battle with a reversed front. Alexander had marched around the innermost angle of the Mediterranean, the Bay of Iskenderon (Alexandretta), where one turns from Asia Minor to Syria; had moved forward about a day's march toward the south; and now, turning about, took up his front toward the north. Darius, coming from the east, had crossed over the Amanus Mountains behind him, was in position on the coastal plains of Issus, and took up his front toward the south. Alexander's army was probably almost as strong as on the Granicus, since a considerable number of replacements had made up for the casualties and had taken the place of the numerous garrisons that had had to be left behind in Asia Minor.

The Persian army cannot have been so very numerous, since, even with the large train of the Persian court, it had moved through the mountain passes in time and space quite comparable to those of the Macedonian army. If our sources speak of 30,000 Greek mercenaries who fought for the Persian King in this battle, this number is not only completely unconfirmed but also incredible. Of the mercenaries at the battle on the Granicus, only a few had escaped, and even if the Persian fleet was still in the Aegean Sea and was seeking to stir up the Greeks against the Macedonian hegemony and the governors were sending their Greek mercenaries to Darius,[2] one still cannot avoid the question of where their 30,000 men were supposed to have come from. The fact that all the Greek states except Sparta were committed in the league with Alexander and a national war against the Persians had been proclaimed in the most solemn terms, and the allied assembly had declared each Hel-

lene who should bear arms against the allies and the King of
Macedonia to be a traitor—all of this was certainly an obstacle to
recruiting, even in those countries that were already treating once
again with the Persians, and entire fleets supposedly had finally to
stand ready to transport the recruited soldiers to Syria, a point that
was neither in the sources nor is to be believed.

The Greek infantry of Darius, then, cannot possibly have been so
very numerous. On the other hand, we may surmise that here, so
much closer to the heart of the country, the native Persians, cavalry
as well as dismounted archers, and possible contingents of the nations of inner Asia, were much stronger than on the Granicus. In
cavalry, therefore, the Persians may have been superior to the
Macedonians. In infantry they were certainly weaker, especially in
that the fighting arms were organized differently. The hoplites—although in addition to the Hellenes there are also Cardaces mentioned—were fewer, the archers more numerous on the side of the
Persians.[3]

In keeping with these relative strengths, the Persians, when they
heard that Alexander had turned about and was marching toward
them, took up their position.

Alexander could not lead his entire army into the battle, but had
to leave troops behind for the protection of his rear and his camp
at Myriandrus, or at the exit from the Beilan pass, since he could
not know whether Darius had already moved his entire force onto
the plain of Issus or if perhaps a corps was still moving up through
the Beilan pass. For this mission he designated his Greek allies,
who had been the farthest forward when the army suddenly had to
face about and took up the march toward the battlefield.[4]

The Persians moved forward slightly to meet the Macedonians.
They did not remain in the middle of the plain, where it is some
five miles wide, at Issus, along the Deli-Tschai River, but took position farther southward, on the Pinarus River, today the Pajas. On
the plain behind the Deli-Tschai the Persian cavalry could, of
course, have had freedom of movement, and since the Macedonian
army, with fewer than 30,000 men on the spot, could by no means
have been stretched out to a breadth of five miles, it would have
had to accept, in its attack, an outflanking and enveloping movement on either the right or left flank by the Persian cavalry. But
the Deli-Tschai can be forded at most places without significant difficulty; and even where the banks fall off steeply, they are soft.
The Persian infantry, therefore, would have found no protection

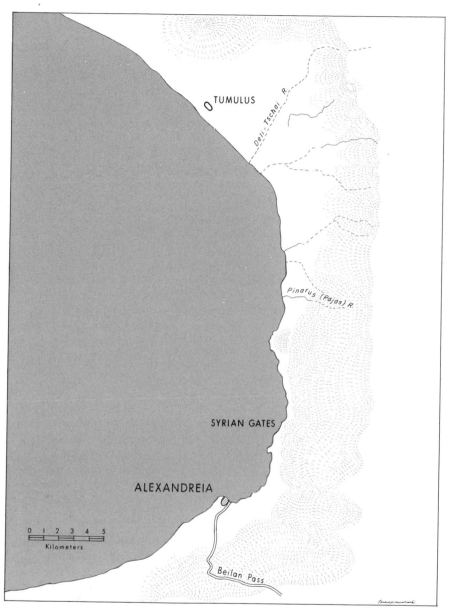

TUMULUS

Deli-Tschai R.

Pinarus (Pajas) R.

SYRIAN GATES

ALEXANDREIA

Beilan Pass

0 1 2 3 4 5
Kilometers

Fig. 2   BATTLE OF ISSUS

from the river against the assault of the stronger Macedonian phalanx. If the superiority of the Persian cavalry had been very great and the prospects of their victory sure and speedy, then the situation by the river would not have mattered; the flank attack of these horsemen would in that event also have brought the Macedonian phalanx to a standstill before it could have become dangerous for the Persian infantry. Since the superiority of the Persian cavalry, however, if it existed at all, was only moderate, the Persian King, whom we must certainly give credit for the best and most discerning ideas, in keeping with the tradition of his people and, furthermore, advised by the Greeks as he was, chose the position on the Pajas, which corresponded to the needs of his army still better than the position in the middle of the plain would have done. Since the description Janke gives of the area still leaves a few doubtful points, I took the trouble to secure a verification, which Senior Engineer Hossbach, who was employed on the construction of the railroad, was kind enough to provide me. I am reproducing it below.

The result is that the upper course of the river is bordered by steep, rocky banks that make it almost impassable. Even the middle portion of the river is not at all passable for cavalry, and passable only with difficulty for infantry. Only the last 1,600 meters, then, are passable for infantry, and the last 500 meters, even though still difficult, passable for cavalry.

Since it is expressly reported that the Macedonian left flank extended to the sea, we can regard these 1,600 meters as the actual battle front. In conformance with the terrain, the Persians had the main body of their cavalry on the right flank, starting at the sea; next came the Greek hoplites, on their left the Cardaces, whose nationality is not certain (perhaps Kurds or even Persians), who were also hoplites. The formation of the Persian archers is not specifically reported in the sources; judging from the type of situation, they were spread along the entire bank of the river in order to take the attacker under fire as he crossed.[5] Also farther up the bank, to the mountains, the places where a crossing seemed possible were probably covered by archers, so that the width of the Persian front was only a relative concept; the front of the articulated, continuous line, infantry or cavalry, was only something over 1,600 meters wide. The line of sharpshooters that formed an extension thereof may have stretched some three kilometers farther.[6]

A rather small detachment of Persians was pushed out on a spur of the mountain that extends out into the small plain, so that it threatened the Macedonians from their right flank as they approached the Persian defensive position, and finally in their rear also.

And so the position of the Persians seemed to be invincible. The infantry, their weaker contingent, was covered by the drop in the ground to its front, but the cavalry was ready to take on the enemy if he should attempt to break through along the seashore and was also in a position to move forward itself.

In this position, which was further strengthened with defensive works here and there, Darius awaited the attack. Each point in the position seemed to be so well defended that the Macedonian attack had no chance of penetrating anywhere along the line. If, however, it was thrown back, then Alexander, cut off from his homeland, would be lost with his entire army. With the help of the Phoenician ships, the Persians dominated the sea. Alexander had used all his strength for his land army and had finally dispersed his fleet, since it was too weak to oppose the Persian one under any circumstances. Once their attack should be thrown back, the Macedonians would have had a very difficult time risking a renewed attack. Consequently, the Persians did not at all need to win an outright victory and drive the Macedonians to flight; they only needed to force them to abandon their attack and to hold fast themselves in their position, in which case their complete success would be assured.

Our sources point repeatedly to how incomprehensible Darius' error was in committing himself on such a restricted piece of terrain that he could not bring his gigantic superiority to bear. They believe that he should have awaited Alexander's attack somewhere on the Syrian plain, so that he could envelop him with his horsemen. Whether this advice would really have been helpful to Darius will be shown in the battle of Gaugamela. There is no doubt of the fact that the situation was spoken of in this way throughout the rank and file of the Macedonian army, stimulated by the headquarters. There could be no more plausible argument to fill the soldiers with the confidence of victory in the coming battle.

Actually, the situation was quite different. If the Persians had actually had a great numerical superiority, they would still have been completely capable of choosing a battlefield appropriate to such strength, as we have seen. The plain of Issus has a width of up to five miles and therefore enough room for an army three and even five times as large as that of the Macedonians. But all of these observations are eliminated for us, since obviously, even if the Persian King had had at his disposal the massive army ascribed to him by Greek popular belief, it could by no means have crossed the

Amanus Mountains so quickly and taken position in the plain of Issus. To what extent Alexander himself was convinced of the Persian mass army we do not know. At any rate, when it was reported to him in Myriandrus (near Alexandretta) that the Persians were suddenly arriving in his rear, he can have been cheered principally by the fact that only a few were at hand and not that the many were unable to find space enough to fight. However this may be, in no case can the Macedonian King have failed to recognize the huge strategic disadvantage at which he was suddenly placed. The Macedonians were cut off from their base, while the Persians were not. The Persians were able, if they were beaten, to withdraw again through the Amanus passes, whence they had come; the Macedonians, if they were defeated, indeed even if the battle was just indecisive, were lost.

The sources tell us how Alexander had his officers assembled and encouraged them and just before the start of the battle rode up to the individual troop units, urged them on, and held up before them the domination of all Asia as the prize for victory over the Great King.

The Persians had won the upper hand strategically, not as the result of any plan but purely by chance, as our sources report, certainly with accuracy. They had believed that Alexander, who had stayed rather long in Cilicia, held up because of illness and other circumstances, would not move up toward Syria for the present, and since the Persian King, with his assembled army, could not possibly remain in Syria for an indefinite period just looking on as the Macedonians made themselves comfortable in conquered Asia Minor, he had finally decided to move forward across the mountains. As chance would have it, however, on precisely the same days Alexander, too, moved forward, and both armies marched by one another through different passes—a situation that then, by the nature of things, worked out to the advantage of the Persians.

It has been asked why the Persians did not simply occupy the passes and cut Alexander off from his homeland. It is not hard to find the answer. We already know from Thermopylae that the blocking of a pass is always a very precarious undertaking, and particularly so here, where the strength of the attacker lay in his infantry, that of the defender in his cavalry. If worse came to worst, Alexander could have left the Persians standing there and could have marched back farther into Syria. If he really was concerned that the Persians could shut the "Syrian Gates" behind him, it was not because he would have been lost by that action, but because the great decision for which he longed would then have been post-poned for an indefinite time. The Persians, therefore, were in no way acting simply negligently by leaving the pass open to the Macedonians and drawing themselves up for a pitched battle in an advantageous position, but were acting in full awareness of the situation. At some moment, sooner or later, the great tactical decision had to be fought out, and the Persians could never have fought under more favorable circumstances than here, where they offered battle, drawn up behind the Pajas, and Alexander took up the challenge.

But it was precisely this physical advantage—which the gods had bestowed on the Persians and which the latter sought to utilize in the best possible way—that worked against them spiritually.

Alexander carefully moved his army out of the Syrian pass, and as the field became wider, gradually had it deploy from march column into linear formation, with cavalry and sharpshooters on the right and left, the hoplites in the middle. Slowly, with pauses, so as not to fall into disorder, the front, 1 to 1½ kilometers wide, moved forward.[7] The main body of the cavalry, under Alexander's personal command, was on the right flank, but when the King noticed that the mass of the Persian cavalry was drawn up on their right flank, beside the sea, he sent the Thessalian cavalry, which had to that point been with him, across behind the phalanx to reinforce his left flank, so that the left was now the stronger flank in cavalry.

Against the Persian detachment stationed on the mountains as a threat to the right flank of the Macedonians, the latter drew up their own flank guard, which drove the enemy higher up the mountains. Then Alexander left only 300 cavalrymen and a number of archers there as a covering force and drew the remainder into his own battle line, which now outflanked the Persians at this point. But since the river was practically unfordable here, that could not harm the Persians.

At some distance farther upstream, however—according to Janke 2½ kilometers from the river mouth, according to Hossbach 3½ kilometers—there is a crossing point. It is here that Alexander with his cavalry must have crossed the river. It is true, of course, that the account in the Macedonian reports, to the effect that he threw back the enemy in a cavalry charge, is impossible, because of the narrowness of the approach, the steep banks, and the stony bottom of the river—and the account must therefore be rejected as an expression of courtly zeal. Nevertheless, it is entirely possible and must therefore be assumed, in keeping with all the circumstances,

that the Macedonian sharpshooters and light infantry did drive the
Persian defenders away from the ford and that the horsemen, too,
then quickly crossed the ford and threw back and pursued the Persian cavalry, which was not very strong on this flank.

In the meantime the main body of the phalanx found itself heavily engaged. While the soldiers of the phalanx scrambled down into
the ravine of the Pajas, they were exposed to the Persians' arrows,
and when they came up over the opposite bank, with their formation broken by the movement forward and the numerous impassable points along the rocky banks, they were attacked by the Greek
hoplites who were in the Persian pay and were thrown back and
downward. The sources repeatedly emphasize the disordered state
of the Macedonian battle formation, and up to now that has been
attributed solely to the natural disruption of the phalanx caused by
the crossing of the river, with its uneven rocky banks. After we
realize, however, that the cavalry of the right flank had not been
able to cross at all in the middle stretch of the Pajas but had been
obliged, for this purpose, to leave its position in the center and
make a wide swing around, then we must take into account, too,
the effect of this uncovering of the left [sic] flank of the phalanx on
the so frequently emphasized disorder. It is not difficult to imagine
how the phalanx soldiers clambered up the far bank, only to be
met there by a counterattack of the Greeks and their flank attack
and to be pushed back into the river.

On the left flank, on the other hand, where the Persian cavalry
was massed, not only was the attack of the Macedonian cavalry
repulsed—if, indeed, it amounted to an attack—but the Persians, in
turn, took up the attack, and crossing to the left bank of the river,
brought the Thessalians into a precarious situation.

The turning point of the battle was determined by the fact that
the Macedonian right wing, which outflanked the enemy line of
battle, came to the assistance of its heavily engaged center. The
King had two *taxis* of the phalanx follow the troops with which he
himself had forced the crossing, right through the same breach,
and while he with his horsemen and the *hypaspists* pursued the
troops who had defended the crossing point or those who, in position beside them, had also taken to flight (Cardaces), those two *taxis*
turned against the left flank of the Greek phalanx. King Darius
himself, who had probably taken position with his staff behind the
Greeks or at the point of contact of Greeks and Cardaces, on seeing his left flank defeated, had given up the battle for lost and
had taken to flight. Under the impact of this flight and of the flank

attack by the soldiers of the phalanx, the Greeks gave up the river bank and began to withdraw.

Almost up to this very moment the balance actually stood almost even, inasmuch as the Persian cavalry of the right flank had just as great an advantage over its opponent—perhaps even a greater one—as the Macedonian right flank had over the Persian left. We can imagine that the victorious Persian cavalry, moving from the shore, might just as easily have fallen on the Macedonian phalanx in its flank as did the Macedonians in attacking the Greek flank from the direction of the mountains. But that did not happen.

The reason is not to be found so much in the personal and tactical superiority of the Macedonians or in the stronger military spirit of Alexander the Soldier, as in the battle concepts of the two sides. The Macedonians waged an offensive battle, the Persians a defensive one. We have seen how the Greeks, too, under the command of Miltiades were forced to wage a defensive battle at Marathon because of the special circumstances, but at the appropriate moment Miltiades went over from defense to attack, and this attack meant victory. The Persians had deliberately planned a purely defensive battle at Issus. They had taken position behind such a formidable frontal obstacle that any attack on their part was impossible from the start. Our sources do not expressly tell us why the Persian cavalry of the right flank, which is credited with a courageous fight, which undoubtedly had numerical superiority, and which even crossed over the river, did not gain a real victory. From the overall situation, we may be allowed to deduce, without hesitation, that that did not take place because it was never intended by the high command. First of all, the account shows that the combat on this flank started considerably later than on the other flank. Alexander had wisely driven forward with his right flank at a point where, once he had crossed the river, he was certain of having the advantage, and he had held up his left flank. Furthermore, as we now know, the river bed is so rocky that forward or backward movements of the cavalry were very difficult. When the battle began on this flank, it was probably already decided on the other one. If the Persians had carried the offensive to the Macedonians with the same energetic offensive spirit as the Macedonians showed against them, it is hard to see why they should not have been just as victorious on the right flank, with their greater numbers, as Alexander was on his flank.

One source (Curtius) speaks of the feigned flight by means of which the Thessalian cavalry managed to hold off their opponents.

That is the account by the horsemen themselves, who considered the success to be of their own doing. The "feigned" flight, however, would very quickly have become a real one if the enemy, for his part, had not held up his pursuit but had continued to pursue relentlessly. But the Persian army had drawn up behind a river and its rocky banks and had even dug some defensive works on the high banks. The battle was planned so as to exploit this advantage. It is no wonder, then, that the cavalry, too, even when it was successful, did not move out very far beyond this line. Naturally, they could not expect any cooperation from other units on the far side of the river. They contented themselves then at best, after their successful attack, with returning again to their position.

For exactly the same reason, in all probability, the flank position of the Persian detachment on the mountains also remained ineffective. In the face of the attack by the Macedonian troops, it had moved back quickly onto the crests of the mountains and had no other alternative. Indeed, if it had accepted combat while the main Persian army stood motionless in its fixed defense, it would have been defeated in its isolated position. Any movement forward again, to attack the Macedonian army from the rear just at the moment when it was becoming engaged with the main Persian army, was prevented by the troops that Alexander had left back as a flank guard. And so the Persian flank detachment was probably waiting for the Macedonians, once they were beaten and being pursued, to have to move by once again in front of them; or at least they were waiting for the situation in the main battle to become favorable for their advance, and since that did not occur, the flank detachment did not move into action at all, and the entire effort turned out to be a useless demonstration, since Alexander did not allow himself to be intimidated by it. To have an isolated force intervene in a battle is an undertaking that succeeds only very infrequently, so that one cannot rightly charge cowardice in this case.

As the Greek phalanx began its withdrawal, the Persian cavalry of the right flank, too, realized that the battle was lost, and it fled the field. The Greeks seemed now to be in a desperate situation. Abandoned by the Persian cavalry, attacked by infantry and cavalry, they had to move at least seven miles back across a plain that in no way offered any strong point for the retreat but, on the contrary, put further obstacles in the way in the form of several deep stream beds crossing the plain. If the Macedonian cavalry should contain them and the phalanx attack them, they would all be lost. They did, indeed, suffer very heavy losses; nevertheless, a large number of them reached one of the mountain passes and escaped. They were veteran, experienced warriors who knew what had to be done, did not break their ranks, but, holding their close formation, were still able to fend off attacks.[8] It probably took long enough for the main body of the Macedonian phalanx to overcome the steep rocky banks of the Pinarus to allow the Greeks to gain a head start. As for Alexander, when he saw that the battle was decided, he prepared to pursue the Persian King himself. That part of the Persian archers that had defended the river bank in front of the Greeks probably withdrew along with the Greeks, and during the retreat warded off the Thessalian and other cavalry that were besetting the march column with missiles and javelins. At the battle of Gaugamela there were still Greeks in the army of the Persian King; the majority of them, however (according to one source—Curtius—8,000; according to the other—Arrian—4,000), gave up their involvement, marched to Phoenicia, and in the city of Tripoli found ships that carried them away.

The Greek report of this battle, according to which the Macedonians lost 150 cavalrymen and 300 infantrymen killed, may, it is true, not be regarded as absolutely accurate, but it is not inconsistent with the nature of the situation and the development of the battle. Furthermore, it is characteristic that the loss of the cavalry is relatively much heavier than that of the infantry. A total of 450 killed leads to an estimate of between 2,000 and 4,000 wounded.

The moderate casualties of the Macedonians lead us back once again to the important question about the strength of the Persian army. We have seen that the sources plainly leave no alternative to the Pajas as the battlefield, and this, in turn, is only acceptable on the condition of a Macedonian superiority of numbers in infantry. The chain of testimony showing that, in fact, the Persians, whose courage even their opponents do not deny, were not numerically the stronger force in the battle, receives a final, closing link in the casualty figures of the victor, which show that his victory in the primary battle was not too hard-won.

As long as the terrain was not so accurately known as it is today, one was both permitted and obliged to classify the battle of Issus, like the other Macedonian battles, under the simple type of the oblique battle formation with the right flank leading. We have seen that this scheme was significantly modified by virtue of the fact that the Macedonian right wing had to make a rather wide-sweeping movement. This swing and the separation of the right flank from the center are not specifically recounted in our sources. This point is, however, very easily explained. We have only second-hand sources, and the authors, especially Arrian, were hardly familiar with the terrain at first hand. The original sources, however, obscured the true overall picture by their exaggerated description of how the King, at the head of his knights, pressed through the hail of arrows to the enemy left flank and drove him to flight. The result of this situation for modern researchers was that, when they learned of the difficulties of the terrain, they declared it completely impossible for the battle to have taken place at this point and concluded that it must have been on another river, the Deli-Tschai. In doing so, however, they encountered, as Dittberner has proved with telling effect, simply unsolvable contradictions, as well with the descriptions of the sources concerning the nature of the terrain as with their very precise accounts of the marches on both sides, and with the strategic situation. The fact must remain that the Pinarus is the Pajas, and if we have to strike out the brilliant cavalry attack under the personal command of the King as the decisive moment of the day, still we gain in turn the deed of the commander. When he recognized the impassable nature of the terrain before his front, with great flexibility of concept he moved the right wing away from the middle, in order to arrive at his goal by a roundabout way, and just as he previously had sent a part of his cavalry from the right flank to the left flank, because it was needed there more urgently, he now moved a part of the heavy infantry to the enveloping flank, in order by means of the flank attack to throw the Greek phalanx from their position, which was unassailable from the front.

It may be said that Alexander adapted the method of the flank battle to the actual circumstances, without violating the concept. His victory was due just as much to the bravery and the number of his warriors as to the efficiency of the army organization that kept the individual units so closely under the control of the commander that he had them with certainty at his disposition at any moment and could direct them according to his will and his insight. Just as important as these factors was his inspired leadership, which controlled the approach with perspicacity, self-confidently ignored the Persian flanking position and the apparently insurmountable difficulties of the terrain, and, wisely deviating from the normal pattern, subsequently reinforced the flank that was normally to be held back and filled the entire army with the spirit of the bold offensive.

EXCURSUS

1. Diodorus, Curtius, and Justin all agree on an estimated loss of 150 cavalrymen, but Diodorus estimates 300 infantrymen, Curtius 32, and Justin 130. It must remain uncertain whether it is a case here of obscuring of the originally uniform number (some 332?), which might very well be true in view of the difference of up to half a millennium between these authors and their original sources and in view of the identical number for the cavalry. At any rate, the highest figures come nearest to the truth, since Arrian gives 120 men as the loss of the phalanx just in the combat with the Greek hoplites.

When Curtius further reckons 504 as wounded, either this number is false or only the seriously wounded are included. In modern reckoning every injury or contusion is counted, even the smallest ones.

2. The actual source study account that I had added to the discussion of the battle in the first edition I have dropped here, since it has been superseded by the more exact topographical verifications in Janke's book and the exhaustive monograph by Dittberner. In order to clarify a few doubtful points that still remained with respect to the topography, I turned to Consul Walter Rossler in Aleppo. He provided me a report by Chief Engineer Hossbach, which I am reprinting below. For all details, I refer the reader to Dittberner. Only the following is repeated here.

Callisthenes' report has come down to us only because Polybius uses it to show how little the author understood about warfare. Remarkably, it now comes about that recent scholars have consistently taken Callisthenes' side and have been inclined to conclude from Polybius' own report that he did Callisthenes an injustice, misunderstood him, and in fact himself committed quite serious oversights. I, too, as highly as I respect Polybius, believe that one may not so unhesitatingly trust his authority—as still is often the case—in that his figures are often sketchy and he himself is more dependent on his sources than it appears; but what he has to say about Issus and Callisthenes is essentially accurate. We cite here only those points that promise to shed some light on the battle itself:

According to Polybius, Callisthenes has said that Alexander gradually had his army deploy as it came out of the narrow pass, finally giving it a depth of 8 men. In this formation it reportedly moved forward 40 *stadia* (about 4½ miles).

Polybius estimates the army at 42,000 foot soldiers and 5,000 cavalry and points out that such a large phalanx in the formation described would have had to have a breadth of 40 *stadia*, whereas Callisthenes asserts at the same time that the plain was only 14 *stadia* wide, that three of these were taken up by the cavalry, and that there was still room left over.

It is not clear how Polybius arrived at the width of 40 *stadia*.[9] With 42,000 men in a formation 8 men deep, allowing 3 feet per man, the result is around 16,000 feet, or 27 *stadia*. One may let the matter drop there, or one may take into account the fact that Polybius, in his eagerness to prove the absurdity of Callisthenes, set the strength of the infantry considerably too high. Nevertheless, he is still right with respect to the principal point, namely, that the phalanx cannot possibly have been formed with a depth of only 8 men.

Bauer has corrected this in the opposite direction and has claimed to prove that that phalanx with a depth of only 8 men fit very well into the terrain and that Callisthenes only erred in estimating the width of the plain at 14 *stadia* (2½ kilometers), which was much too small. Now in this respect Bauer is right; but his concept is impossible, because a phalanx of a depth of 8 men and a width of almost 4½ miles is an absurdity. It would not be able to move 10 steps forward without breaking, and after 100 steps it would be in complete disarray. It would even be absolutely impossible to have it form up or come to a halt uniformly.

The correct solution has already been stated by K. Neumann in "On the Geography and History of Cilicia" ("Zur Landeskunde und Geschichte Kilikiens"), *Jahrbücher für klassische Philologie* 127 (1883): 544, where he points out that in Curtius (going back to Ptolemy) it is stated that the phalanx at Issus had a depth of 32 men. If we assume that the *pezetairoi* and *hypaspists* together were some 20,000 strong, then the phalanx, with its intervals, was less than 1 kilometer, or 4 to 5 *stadia*, wide. To that must be added the cavalry and the light infantry.[10] Callisthenes, who had crossed the area with Alexander's staff a few days before the battle, is perhaps not entirely right, but still partially right, in his topographic description, and consequently, just as Polybius describes, incorrect in his military description. He probably was not a witness to the battle itself, but remained behind with the civilian part of the headquarters in Myriandrus. On the following day he heard how the army had gradually deployed out of the dangerous pass, had drawn up in phalanx formation, and had moved against the enemy. Since he knew that the normal formation of hoplites was 8 men deep, in his rhetorical painting he had the whole mighty phalanx deploy in this formation, and since he remembered that the pass was about 40 *stadia* from the river, he had the phalanx move this distance forward. His military knowledge did not extend far enough to let him know that such an approach march is impossible, that the phalanx of a large army is drawn up deeper than that of a single detachment, and that with the plain's width of only 14 *stadia*, as he himself gave it, the shallow phalanx would not even have fit into the space.

3. In his review of Dittberner's work (*Historische Zeitschrift* 112: 348), Kromayer agrees with us to the extent that he, too, established that the most logical interpretation of the sources leads to the Pajas as the river on which the battle was fought. Nevertheless, he considers the assumption as impossible, since the upper and middle portions of the Pajas are absolutely impassable for troops in close formation, and the break in the upper part of the river bank, which Dittberner describes as 300 meters wide, actually consists only of two small gaps of 50 and 30 meters in breadth. I reply that such gaps are completely sufficient for an operation such as Dittberner and I picture this one to be. The difference, in the final analysis, is again a difference in numbers. If the Persian army had been so large as to form a full, close battle formation extending across and beyond those gaps, then Alexander would have been unable, of course, to penetrate. For a close-order attack by heavy cavalry the gaps are too small and not sufficiently passable. Since travelers who have inspected the battlefield have always approached their study with the preconceived idea of a Persian mass army that was formed up closely along the entire river bank up to the mountains, they have naturally rejected the possibility of a crossing at this point and so from the start have not seriously examined this possibility. Of what use, after all, would a break even as large as 300 meters in width have been for Alexander's cavalry, Kromayer asks, if the phalanx could not cross simultaneously? The answer is: the crossing was so weakly defended that the cavalry with the lightly armed infantry, under such forceful and direct leadership as that of Alexander, could force its way across even without the support of the phalanx. The inadequate defense of the crossing was, on the other hand, the simple result of the weakness of the Persian army, which was drawn up behind the middle and lower sections of the river's course.

4. With respect to Beloch's strange idea that it was not Alexander himself but the chief of his general staff, Parmenio, who was really the great strategist of the Macedonians, let it be noted at this point that this concept cannot be proved in any way, but rather can be directly refuted by the chain of events of the battle of Issus. For the decisive features of this battle—the reinforcing of the cavalry on the left flank while the deployment was still under way, the moving off of the right wing toward the right, its reinforcement first by the troops in the holding position and then by the two *taxis* of the phalanx—all of these can only have been at Alexander's personal direction.

5. In his *Greek History*, 2: 634, Beloch has stated the opinion that it was not by chance but intentionally that Darius passed around the Macedonian army and fought the battle with his front reversed, and as a matter of fact, unanimous as our

sources are, we are still justified in not trusting them unquestioningly on this point. In keeping with the entire manner in which the Persians are presented and characterized, such a bold, even excellent stratagem would have fit too poorly into the picture to be acceptable, even if there had been definite information on this in the Macedonian camp.

Nevertheless, I think that the situation itself and the details of the overall picture eliminate Beloch's assumption.

Darius would not have been able to make the decision to move around the Macedonians until the latter had actually arrived in Myriandrus. If the Persians had not started their march until the Macedonians themselves were on the march between Mallus and Issus, they would have risked colliding with the enemy army directly as they were coming out of the passes, and in doing so they would have fallen into a very poor strategic situation. They could not know until one or two days in advance how long the Macedonians would delay their march. The essential point for the completion of Beloch's hypothesis, then, is that Alexander made a halt of several days in Myriandrus, during which the Persians carried out their enveloping march through the Amanus passes. The fact is that Arrian does not state with absolute clarity how long the Macedonians had already been in Myriandrus when they received the information of the Persians' arrival in Issus. According to the overall tenor of the account, however, this occurred on just the second day, and the report in Curtius, despite its rhetorical exaggerations, that the two armies marched past one another in *one* night also adds weight to the conclusion that the events followed in close succession.

All the Greeks' observations concerning the incomprehensible stupidity of the Persian maneuver of going into the narrow passes with their huge masses we have completely disregarded, since the masses of the Persians were neither so great nor was the plain at Deli-Tschai so small as to prevent any desired maneuvers. But it would nevertheless be hard, for other reasons, to understand the Persians' conduct under the assumption that they already knew of the arrival of the Macedonians in Myriandrus. We have assumed that Darius started his march across the Amanus Mountains in the belief that Alexander would not go beyond Cilicia with his offensive. If he was already in Myriandrus, however, it was also quite certain that he would continue on, and, to be exact, not along the Syrian coast (for by following that coast he would obviously have been voluntarily giving up to the Persians his base of operations and his field hospital in Issus), but across the Beilan pass into the interior, in order to seek out the Persian army. Darius was near Sochi, the exact location of which we do not know; at any rate it was not far from the exit of the Beilan pass. The only logical decision for Darius at the moment when he received the information that Alexander was in Myriandrus would have been to take up position at the exit of the Beilan pass and with his assembled force to fall on the Macedonians as they came out of the pass. The idea of now enveloping the Macedonians would have forfeited this decisive tactical advantage in return for the strategic gain of cutting off the Macedonians' line of withdrawal. This gain was not significant, however, since the Macedonians, if they suffered any defeat at all so far from their homeland, were in any case lost, whether their retreat was cut off from the start or not.

Our concept is therefore as follows: After Alexander had already arrived in Myriandrus, the Persians could no longer logically have decided on the enveloping movement, and consequently there is no reason to reject the sources' report that the marches of the two armies took place simultaneously.

The Persians must therefore have decided on the march while the Macedonians were still in Mallus. But at that time they counted on the fact that the Macedonians would not go any farther forward, for otherwise they would have risked running into the Macedonians as soon as they came out of the Amanus passes onto the plain of the Deli-Tschai. The march was, therefore, not an envelopment march but a simple advance, and it was a simple coincidence that it became an envelopment march because on precisely that same day the Macedonians, too, took up their advance march—exactly as it is reported in our sources.

6. The report that the surviving Greek mercenaries embarked in Tripoli led Dittberner (p. 156) to the idea that they had perhaps completely penetrated the Macedonian phalanx and had escaped via the direct route toward the south. This conclusion, however, is not only not convincing, but it is even completely eliminated because of the other circumstances. The road does lead, to be sure, from the Issus plain across the Amanus Mountains to Phoenicia in a half-circle around the Macedonians, but such a flight around the back of the enemy occurs quite often in military history; for example, in this manner a part of the Burgundian army escaped at Murten in 1476, and a part of the French army from the battle of Novara in 1513.

As is shown in the account by Arrian, the Macedonians naturally did not take up their advance again on the day after the battle. If the Greeks had broken through the Macedonians, they would have moved out on the road on which Alexander had moved up and would therefore have passed through his train and would not have left it undisturbed. Furthermore, Alexander's Greek allies were in position at Myriandrus or at the entrance of the Beilan pass. It is completely impossible that our sources should not have retained the slightest trace of such a prodigious event as the breakthrough itself, the crossing of the Pajas, and all the events that would necessarily have taken place on the withdrawal route.

7. Koepp, in *Alexander the Great (Alexander der Grosse)*, p. 31, believes that the Persians' bypassing action makes the Macedonian reconnaissance units appear in a bad light. Here he underestimates the difficulty of conducting a reconnaissance two days' march away, over mountain passes, in enemy country. Even if Alexander sent out patrols in this direction and they encountered enemy troops who were coming toward them, they still were not able to determine whether it was only a Persian scouting party or actually the whole army that was approaching. Even when Darius was already in Issus, Alexander was still in doubt and before turning about, he first dispatched a ship to take a closer look. Such uncertainties and surprises are inevitable in war and very frequent, and they do not necessarily indicate any laxness.

8. Description of the terrain by Senior Engineer Hossbach in a letter to Consul Rossler dated 21 November 1913:

"After inspecting the Pajas-Tschai in the meantime twice from its mouth up to the point where it breaks out of the mountain, I want to send you today the following complete report of the results:

"1. From its mouth upstream for about 500 meters the river bed is only here and there contained in banks of about 1 to 2 meters in height, but steep. A crossing by cavalry along this stretch is possible, to be sure, but difficult because of the stretches with steep edges and the very stony river bed.

"2. From the 500 meter point to the westernmost (newer) highway bridge (some 1,600 meters from the mouth), the river bed is only about 5 to 15 meters wide, with steep-cut banks. A crossing by cavalry in any numbers is impossible along this stretch, a crossing by infantry possible.

"3. From the 1.6 kilometer point to the easternmost (older) highway bridge (about 3.5 kilometers from the mouth) the river bed is alternately narrower and wider. The banks here have been considerably changed as a result of the later construction in the city of Bajae. Their nature is, however, consistently steep and difficult to take, even for infantry. Along a stretch of about 300 meters the walls consist of from 2- to 4-meter-high conglomerate rock falling off vertically, which makes a crossing almost impossible, even for infantry.

"4. From the 3.5 kilometer point on (that is, directly after the second bridge) there is a place of about 30 (not 300) meters in length, at which a narrow path leads through the river bed, a route that presumably served as a ford earlier—that is, before the construction of the bridges. (At this point, besides the present bridge, there are still at hand the remains of two apparently very old bridges.) On the south side the path leads steeply down into the river bed, and on the north side it rises somewhat more gently along the flattened-off river bank. The attached photograph No. 1 shows this north side with the clearly recognizable footpath, as well as, on the lower left, the edge of the bridge from which the photograph was taken and also, from the center on (behind the white figure), toward the right, the continuous steep banks that start here (compare para. 5, below). The unusually stony river bed is also clearly recognizable.

"5. From about the 3.53 kilometer point on, the river bed is some 15 to 40 meters wide, but on both sides, continuously to the foot of the mountain (that is, for about 1.5 kilometers) enclosed in vertical rock walls varying in height from 3 to 20 meters and completely impassable, even for infantry, unless they should be equipped with scaling ladders, and so on, as are used in our modern maneuvers for attacks on fortresses. Illustration 2 shows the start of this section, that is, about 100 meters from the bridge, where the continuous rocky banks start with a height of about 3 meters. The water forms a small lake here, which accounts for the reflection of the bushes.

"I hope that the foregoing description will give Professor Delbrück a basis for his conclusions on the question of the battlefield of Issus. I was joined on my inspection by two other engineers, both of whom are good horsemen, and we were all in agreement that a crossing by cavalry in battle formation at the point described in paragraph 4 would be impossible."

NOTES FOR CHAPTER III

1. After having had to rework the presentation of this battle for the second edition, I have now once again had to make not unimportant changes. The reason was the same both times—that is, a more correct and more detailed understanding of the structure of the terrain. Even now, however, I have felt obliged to stand by the fundamental fact that the battle took place not on the Deli-Tschai, but on the Pajas. Accordingly, I continue to regard the dissertation of W. Dittberner (Berlin, 1908) as the authoritative work and cannot find that it has been eliminated by Colonel Janke, to whom we are indebted in other respects for the topography (*Klio* 10: 137, "Annex to Petermann's Reports," May 1911 ["Beilage von Petermanns Mitteilungen," 1911, Maiheft]). See also the review of Dieulefoy's study by Dittberner in the *Deutsche Literarische Zeitung*, No. 24, (1912), Column 1525, and the article by Kromayer in the *Historische Zeitschrift* 112: 348.

2. Arrian 2. 2. 1. Curtius 3. 8. 1.

3. An absolute proof for the moderate strength of the Persian army is not to be concluded from the march action, in that, according to Janke, a rather large number of more or less usable passes lead over the Amanus mountain chain into the plain of Issus. Nevertheless it can hardly be assumed that there was an elaborate allocation of forces to various approach roads, and since in the bat-

tle it was almost exclusively the Greeks who played a significant infantry role, then the other infantry contingents on hand cannot have been so very strong.

Kromayer, in the work cited above, believes that the Persian army can be estimated at 50,000 to 60,000 men, since the Seleucids had raised armies of similar strength. The Diadochi states differ, however, from the Achaemenidae Empire precisely in the fact that they had a completely different concept of war, and in any case no comparison is possible in view of the positive factors that exclude the possibility of an army of more than some 25,000 men.

4. Arrian 2. 5. 1 reports that Parmenio had been sent out in advance with the Greeks and other troops from Tarsus in order to secure the Cilician-Syrian passes. Now since the Greeks are not mentioned in the two sources specifying the battle formation at Issus, we can accept the account above with certainty. Köhler, in "The Conquest of Asia" ("Die Eroberung Asiens"), in *Abhandlungen der Berliner Akademie*, 1898, p. 130, believes that Alexander did not need to post troops to cover his rear, since the Persian army was, obviously, in front of him. The flimsiness of this conclusion is evident.

5. Arrian's description, that behind the Persian battle line, which he describes for us, there still stood in useless depth huge numbers of barbarian peoples, has been understood by recent historians as an echelon formation. Aside from the fact that an echeloned formation, as we shall see, means a refinement of tactics that did not occur until a later period, Arrian's report is naturally only the complement of his estimate of the Persian army at a strength of 600,000 men. What the Greeks saw in front of them was only a moderate-sized army; the barbarians, however, were, once and for all, masses—consequently these masses were placed somewhere or other in the rear, drawn up "in unusable depth."

6. Polybius 12. 17. 7, ". . . the peltasts in a line which stretched to the mountains,"* according to Callisthenes. These lightly armed men, who stretched out all the way to the mountains, were probably principally Persian archers. Arrian, in 2. 10. 6, reports specifically that the Macedonians, after moving forward slowly at first in order not to have their battle line become wavy, finally attacked on the run so that they would not suffer too much from the enemy archers.

That the front of the Persians did not extend the length of the river is shown expressly in Arrian 2. 9. 4, where it is said that the Macedonians, after Alexander had drawn the troops from the flank guard positions to him, outflanked the Persian formation. The sentence in 2. 8. 6, "The ground on which they were standing allowed this number of men to be contained in a straight phalanx,"* could be interpreted to mean that the width of the plain would not have contained any more than were formed up, so that the phalanx stretched out from the sea to the mountain. The citation above, however, excludes this interpretation.

7. According to Polybius, Callisthenes estimated that the plain of Pajas was not quite 14 *stadia* (2½ kilometers) wide and that the Macedonian phalanx remained at a considerable distance from the mountains. Arrian reports that their left flank touched the sea. Now the plain is not 2½ but 4 kilometers wide according to Janke, 5 kilometers by Hossbach's estimate—an error of estimation that is not abnormal (see Dittberner, p. 122); nevertheless, we may believe Callisthenes when he says the Macedonian front was considerably less than 2½ kilometers wide. It therefore reached from the sea about the same distance—or perhaps not quite as far—as the river was more or less fordable for infantry.

8. Curtius 3. 11. 18: "Graeci . . . abrupti a ceteris haud sane fugientibus similes evaserunt." ("The Greeks, separated from the rest, had escaped, not at all in the way deserters do.")

9. From all appearances, he initially estimated, in connection with an estimate of Callisthenes, only 32,000 phalanx soldiers, but assumed for each man not the combat width, but the march order width of 6 feet.

10. Polybius 12. 18, estimates 800 horsemen per *stadium* with the deepest normal formation of 8 horses, and therefore 6 feet per horse with intervals. It is also very possible, however, that they were sometimes drawn up deeper and they may very well have been much closer together; 5,000 horsemen, 8 horses deep with 6 feet to a horse would extend, even without intervals, more than a kilometer.

Chapter IV

The Battle of Gaugamela

After the victory at Issus Alexander first subjected Phoenicia and Syria, and then had to carry out two very hard sieges, at Tyre and Gaza. Then he marched on, in order to seize control of Egypt as well. There has been a tendency to criticize this latter campaign and even to find that the expedition can only be explained by taking into consideration the fact that for the Ancients the relative positions of the countries were not clearly understood and Alexander, therefore, could not have been aware of how seriously he was exposing his rearward line of communications toward Babylon when he struck out in this direction.[1]

But I think that Alexander knew very well what he was doing. It could be assumed that the Persians would not yet appear again in Syria in the following year (332 B.C.) with a large army, and if they did so, they would fall a sure prey to him. In order to have a firm base for his forthcoming campaign into the interior of Persia, Alexander needed to have not only the mastery of Syria but also that of Egypt. Certainly it would have sufficed to detach a general with a small force in that direction, but by no means has it been said that it was only for the conquering of Egypt that Alexander held up and left his opponent time to reequip. It is true that the more quickly the Macedonians appeared in Persia, the less time remained for Darius to organize a new army. But Alexander, too, was strengthening himself in the meantime. At Issus he probably had something over 30,000 men with him; from that number were subtracted the losses of the battle and of the sieges and the garrisons that were necessary in Syria. If he had, then, also sent a further detachment to Egypt, he would have crossed the Tigris with hardly more than 20,000—or, assuming that some reinforcements reached him, with some 25,000 to 30,000 men. At Gaugamela, however, he had 47,000 men, and it does not appear that that number was too great. We must therefore praise again, as we did before, the combination of boldness and circumspection that prevented the young King from dashing blindly after his defeated opponent and caused him first of all to assemble the forces necessary for the operation that was to reach out into boundless areas and to fill the interim profitably with the establishment of the Macedonian hegemony in Egypt and the winning over of the cooperation of the Egyptian gods.

Darius did not contest the crossing of the Euphrates and Tigris rivers by his formidable enemy but awaited him on the great plain beyond the twin-river area, not far from the ruins of Nineveh. Greek mercenaries are said to have been with him still at this point, but so few that they play no further role in the battle. It is also reported (Diodorus 17. 55) that the Persian King had had made for his warriors longer spears and swords than they carried previously, because the Macedonians had such weapons. Since the Persians previously fought principally with the bow and javelins (Herodotus, too, mentions the longer spears of the Greeks), this change can probably be interpreted as meaning that Darius intended to form a phalanx with his Asiatics, with the support of his Greek followers; for the long spear is no longer a missile but rather a close combat weapon, and the Persians had no doubt not remained blind to the fact that it was most effective in the tightly ordered phalanx. But whether this report is authentic or not, the fact remains that a tactical body like the phalanx cannot be improvised; it requires drill and military training.

This is reminiscent of the report that Melchior Russ von Luzern, ambassador to King Louis XI of France, sent home in 1480: "The King is reshaping his army and is having manufactured a great number of long spears and halberds of the German type. If he could also manufacture men to handle them, he would no longer need anybody else's services."[2] The art of war has need of weapons, but it is not composed essentially of weapons, and so in the battle of Gaugamela we hear nothing concerning the deeds of a Persian phalanx.

The new weapons by means of which Darius actually sought to break the fearful shock of the phalanx, after the terrain obstacle before his front had proved ineffective at Issus, were the scythed chariots and with them a small number of elephants.

For the rest, the real strength of the Persian army, as was inherent in the nature of things, lay in its cavalry, as at Issus, and certainly it was for this reason that Darius left the river crossings open to Alexander, in order to be able to wait for him on a battlefield of his own choosing, that is, on a broad plain where the Persian cavalry could deploy without hindrance and take full advantage of its superiority. If Alexander had 7,000 cavalry at Gaugamela, as Arrian reports, then it can be assumed that Darius had assembled perhaps 12,000—but certainly no more than that, for 12,000 horsemen in one place is such a large mass that they can hardly be managed and controlled even through a skill of organization, supply, and leadership developed to the point of virtuosity.[3] It is hard to imagine Darius' infantry. Archers—the old arm of the Persians—can only be drawn up a few ranks deep in order to be effective. It was useless to draw up loose-knit groups of an unmilitary people against a hoplite phalanx, and the Persians understood the art of war well enough to know that and to prefer to use all their strength for the reinforcing of the cavalry, instead of involving themselves in insuperable supply difficulties through useless mass levies. If there were any attempts to develop a hoplite phalanx, the battle shows nothing of any success in this area. Consequently it is quite possible that the Persian army, aside from the cavalry, elephants, and scythed chariots, had only a relatively small number of foot soldiers—that is, certainly not more than the Macedonians, and probably fewer. The native Persian cavalry, however, was reinforced by Scythian and presumably Indian mercenaries as well.

Our sources, including even the principal source, Arrian, are a mixture of very accurate, documented reports, especially concerning the formations, and of campfire legends that can, nevertheless, be critically sifted out with reasonable certainty.

The most extreme form of the camp legend has it that the Persians at Gaugamela, just as at Issus and on the Granicus, had sought a frontal obstacle and had on this occasion fabricated one artificially with pitfalls and caltrops. But Arrian himself had already rejected this account, reporting it only as a suspicion on the part of the Macedonians. He claims, in fact, quite to the contrary, that the Persians had artificially cleared the terrain before their front and had removed obstacles in order to open up a clear area for their scythed chariots.

Since we do not hear that any Macedonian soldier whatever fell into the pitfalls or stepped on a caltrop in the battle, we shall eliminate these distortions from the history of the battle. But we may also put aside the idea of artificial smoothing of the field for the scythed chariots, in view of the fact that the Persians, after all, could not know in advance where the Macedonians would attack, and such clearings cannot be effected in a period of a few days. Suffice it to say that the Persians had sought for the battle a generally open plain with only small rises and depressions, where their two principal arms, the cavalry and the scythed chariots, could maneuver unimpeded. If the scythed chariots succeeded in disrupting the Macedonian phalanx and halting its forward movement, while the superior Persian cavalry carried out an enveloping attack against the Macedonian cavalry and drove it off, the victory would be decided in favor of the Persians. It was thus on one earlier occasion (Xenophon, *Hellenica* 4. 1. 19) that the Satrap Pharnabazus had broken up a formation of 700 Greeks with two scythed chariots, falling on them then with his cavalry and cutting them down.[4]

The phalanx, deprived of its own cavalry, would not have been able to ward off the joint attack of the Persian cavalry and archers but would gradually have had to be annihilated.

According to the account of the Greeks, the battle formation of the Persians was found later among the booty, and it has been passed down to us in detail, but it does not really provide us with anything of importance. The only noteworthy point in it is the fact that, from all appearances, not only were the flanks composed of cavalry, but in the center, too, horsemen and foot soldiers were mixed together, another indication that the infantry was not so very numerous.

Alexander was again able at a glance to adapt the normal arrangement of his formation to the circumstances. He did not use the great mass of his infantry to extend the battle line, which would have impeded too much their orderly movement, but instead doubled the depth of his formation and gave his rear elements the command to face about in case of an attack from the rear. Mainly, however, he protected himself against the danger of an envelopment on the part of the superior enemy cavalry in the open plain by means of units of horsemen and light infantry, which were stationed in an angled formation on the two flanks. Consequently these horsemen and light infantry units could follow the advancing line in a deep column from which they could either deploy to extend the battle line (the column behind the right flank had therefore marched off with its left leading) or, swinging into line toward the flank, could form a curved extension to meet an attack from the flank, or, finally, could fill up from the rear any possible breaks in the phalanx that might develop during the advance.

In this formation the Macedonian army moved forward across the plain against the Persians. Assuming that, of the 47,000-man total reported to us, a few thousand men were left behind as camp guards and sick, there still remains a powerful mass, which, once it has formed up, can move forward only with difficulty and slowly without falling into disorder.

The Persian battle plan broke down insofar as the scythed chariots were concerned. Of the elephants we hear nothing at all in the battle. Alexander sent out sharpshooters against the scythed chariots, who, swarming out in front of the phalanx, shot down the drivers of the chariots as they approached, or, running around the chariots, dragged the drivers out. The driverless horses were then, in part, frightened away, and in those cases where they charged down on the phalanx, space was opened up for them, so that only a few men were caught and wounded by the scythes.[5] In the meantime, the cavalry of both sides had tried to win the flanks, the Persians outflanking the Macedonians and the latter deploying against them the troops from the angled formations, and the resulting combat kept flowing back and forth. The outcome was still doubtful when the phalanx, after disposing of the scythed chariots, once again took up its forward movement. The right wing, which had been separated from the left, was in advance, and when it now reinforced the cavalry and drove in on the Persians, they took to flight.

While it is probably true that Persian and Indian cavalry broke through the gap as the phalanx split up during its forward movement, nevertheless the undisciplined units drove for the Macedonian camp instead of attacking the Macedonian army in the rear, so that this incident had no influence on the outcome of the battle.

For a while the left flank of the Macedonians, commanded by Parmenio, was hard pressed, but it was disengaged by the victorious right flank.

Just as had been the case in the two previous battles, Gaugamela, too, was fought as a flank battle with the offensive right flank victorious. Exactly why it was the right flank that was victorious at Gaugamela is not apparent from the account. From the allocation of troops it is not obvious that the right flank was any stronger in cavalry than the left (Rüstow and Köchly have even estimated the opposite), and it is also not clear that the opposing Persian left flank was the weaker.

Diodorus' estimate that the Macedonians had lost some 500 men killed in the battle, along with very many wounded, does not appear to be unreliable.[6]

1. Rüstow and Köchly, and most writers along with them, conceive the Macedonian battle formation differently from that which is described above. They see in the troops formed "into an angle"* a second echelon, which followed both flanks. Objectively that would not be inconceivable; nevertheless, I believe, along with H. Droysen (*Heerwesen*, p. 119), that the Greek for "into an angle"* can be translated in no other way than "hook-shaped," and that which follows allows no other interpretation than this. Arrian tells first of all how on the extreme right flank, starting with the royal squadron, "into an angle"* the troops of Attalus (Agrianians, *peltasts*) were drawn up, and with them those of Briso (archers), and next to them ("having some archers"*) those of Cleander (arm unknown). In the extreme case, that could be interpreted as an alignment in the second echelon. Now, however, Arrian continues: "The front-running cavalry and the Paeonians—Aretes and Ariston were their commanders—were lined up in front of the Agrianians and the archers."* These troops could not possibly all have been placed between the first and second echelons, and Rüstow and Köchly therefore assign to them, with correct perceptiveness, the space *beside* the troops of Attalus and the archers, and consider them as an overlapping portion of the second echelon. If Arrian had intended to say that, he would at least have expressed it very specifically. The matter is completely clear, however, if we imagine the troops of Attalus, Briso, and Cleander as a deep (march) column, at the extreme right flank of the main battle line, forming a right angle with the royal squadron of *hetairoi*; beside them on the right, at a certain interval, the other two columns, first that of Aretes and Ariston; then Menidas'. This word "beside" is expressed by Arrian and his source with "in front of"* since these troops were, of course, formed in a hook shape and consequently had their actual front toward the flank. (See also Dittberner, *Battle of Issus* [*Schlacht bei Iossos*], p. 10.) The difference between my concept and that of Rüstow-Köchly, therefore, is that I picture the troops in question as three parallel, deep (march) columns, whereas Rüstow-Köchly imagine them as already deployed side by side.

The three parallel columns on the right flank had the order "If necessity were to hold him, to fold back or to close up the phalanx."* The expression *"anaptyssein"* (to open up, fold back) has been variously translated as *"explicare"* (to unfold, develop, form up, deploy) or as *"replicare"* (to turn about). As far as the meaning of the word is concerned, both translations are possible. If Arrian intended here the second meaning, the command means: in case of need the troops are to bend around the phalanx—that is, form a hook. They are, of course, already in the position "in an angle"* with respect to the main battle line, but not yet deployed. If there should now be an attack by the enemy on the flank, they are to form a front toward that side by swinging around. They are therefore presumably drawn up with their left leading. Otherwise, they are there to "close", "to close up"* the phalanx—that is, if breaks develop during the movement forward, to move into them or possibly also to extend the front toward the right (a point which, of course, is not directly inherent in the expression).

For anybody who claims that *"anaptyssein"* means "to unfold," the command is to be interpreted: the troops are either to form up beside the phalanx—that is, extend the front—or to "close" the phalanx—that is, to cover it on the flank. The meaning of the two expressions "to open up, roll back"* and "to close up"* could therefore almost be reversed and the sense of the whole would still remain almost the same.

The passages where *"anaptyssein"* is used elsewhere in Greek literature in a military sense permit in some cases both interpretations, in others only one or the other.

In Arrian's own account of the battle of Issus (2. 8. 2), Alexander has his army debouch from the passes, and as it arrives on the plain, "he continued to fold back the wing to the phalanx, leading in more and more the ranks of the hoplites."* This can be translated as follows: he had the march columns deploy into the phalanx and had one *taxi* form up after the other. But one could also say: he had the march columns swing into the phalanx by having one *taxi* deploy after the other.

At Cunaxa the Greek hoplite phalanx is threatened on the left flank (of the original front) by the Persian cavalry, while the right flank is covered by the river. Then the Greeks decide "to fold back the wing so as to have the river at their back."* That can mean: the phalanx first made a swing toward the threatened flank and then marched up into line on this side, or rather, deployed toward this side, since such a deep column would fall into complete disorder during a simple march into line. To complete such a maneuver in good order would require the elaborate form of deployment—that is, right-angled movements of the individual units by command. Opposing this interpretation is the fact that the Greeks would thereby have taken a position 1½ to 2 kilometers away from the river, and would therefore actually have had no further protection from it. For this reason, it has also been claimed that the movement was probably made toward the other flank, so that the Greeks would have turned their backs to the enemy during the movement. But Xenophon could also have meant that the Greeks bent their threatened flank around—that is, they formed a hook. This maneuver, too, would have been hard to carry out, of course, and the new position would have been tactically very unfavorable, since, if either of the two fronts should make an attack, the phalanx would be torn apart.

A third and a fourth time we find the expression "to open up, roll back"* used by Xenophon in the *Cyropaedia* 7. 5, 3 and 5. Cyrus wishes to shorten by half a very long but shallow phalanx and thereby double its depth. For this purpose he orders the hoplites stationed on the flanks to place themselves behind the halted center. This is expressed in this way: "He gave the order that the hoplites should fold back the phalanx from each extremity and move back toward the place where the main body of the army was standing, until the wings on both sides should meet with him in the center."* If the intention here is to relate the "rolling back of the phalanx"* to the already formed phalanx, there is no other way to translate it than by "bend," and that gives a clear, logical meaning. Otherwise, the "phalanx" that is referred to here would not be the one in which the hoplites were formed up, but the one into which they were now supposed to deploy. This would therefore be translated: "He ordered the hoplites from the two flanks to draw up in a phalanx and to march back to a position behind the halted center, until the two leading units met in the middle." The execution of such an order, however, would probably be excessively difficult. Further it goes on to say, "When the phalanx was thus rolled back, it followed that the front ranks and the rear ranks were made up of the best men. . . ."* "When the phalanx was thus rolled back"* can be translated either as "in the case of a phalanx forming up in this way" or as "in the case of a phalanx bent around in this way."

In Plutarch's description of the battle of Leuctra, *Pelopidas*, Chapter 23, the Spartans intend to envelop the Thebans; "they were opening up their right wing and making a circle round about, so as to encircle [them]."* This can probably only be translated as "they inclined their right and moved it around [or, they swung their right around], in order to encircle their enemy."

On the other hand, in Dio Cassius 49. 29, the Romans under Antony in battle with the Parthians formed a thick covering screen with their shields and suddenly broke out in front of it "at the same time they opened up [or rolled back] the whole phalanx."* Here it can hardly be translated as anything other than "deployed the phalanx" or "had the whole phalanx form up."

In Arrian's *Tactics* 8. 3 (Köchly and Rüstow, *Greek Military Authors* [*Griechische Kriegsschriftsteller*], Vol. 2, Part 1, p. 286) the point is made that in an army whose units can always be divided in two, all movements can be executed most easily. In this connection, "to extend [the line] by opening it up [or by rolling it back]"* is also named. Here, too, it is impossible to use a meaning like "bend"; the context with "to extend"* requires the meaning "form up" or "deploy."

Compare in this connection Köchly and Rüstow, *Greek Military Authors* (Vol. 2 Part 2, p. 267), and the observations on Xenophon's *Anabasis* 1. 10. 9 in the editions of

Schneider, Volbrecht, and Krüger, as well as Dindorf's notes to Xenophon's *Cyropaedia* 7. 5. 3. Also Reuss, *Neue Jahrbücher für Philologie (NJP)* 127: 817, and Bünger, *NJP* 131: 262.

3. Just as the formation of troops behind the two wings has been conceived of as a second echelon, so too has the "double phalanx" in the center been pointed out as a formation in two echelons. Reservations concerning this concept were already expressed by H. Droysen in *Heerwesen* (p. 120), and certainly rightly so. Primarily there arises the question of what kinds of troops were posted here; it would after all be extremely curious that they would not be mentioned at all, while otherwise every small unit is named for us, and all the more so in that these troops execute an independent movement—that is, they drive off the enemy forces that have broken into the camp. Niese has surmised that the Greek allies that are not named elsewhere might very well have been stationed here, but it is probable (Köhler, *Sitzungsberichte der Berliner Akademie*, 1898) that these troops did not participate in the battle at all, and the whole idea of a second echelon must be abandoned. We shall have occasion later to discuss the significance and the character of the formation in several echelons; at Gaugamela the use of this formation is not only not adequately proved but is in fact absolutely impossible because of the account of the splitting of the phalanx and the penetration through this breach by the enemy cavalry. The interval between two echelons can probably not amount to less than 100 paces; the two echelons move independently. If the first line breaks, something that can happen very easily, then the second echelon, unless it should by chance happen to break just at the same place, is there to fill the breach or perhaps to take care of those enemy soldiers who break through. A similar function was also supposed to be exercised in case of need by the reserve troops behind the flanks, who fall short of forming a second echelon only in that they are not deployed. In the center, behind the phalanx, however, there was even less chance of the existence of a second echelon; otherwise the enemy horsemen would not have broken through so easily. The double phalanx, consequently, is to be understood only as one that has been doubled in depth, the rearmost units of which have been ordered to face about in case of necessity.

4. According to Arrian's account, at a point when the two armies were already so close to each other that the Macedonians could recognize King Darius on the other side with his retinue, Alexander had his army make a rather long movement toward the right. Rüstow and Köchly repeat that as follows: "Alexander moved by echelons halfway to the right . . . the movement which was calculated to put the whole Macedonian army against the left flank of the Persians." To make such a flank march with a large army presupposes a skill of maneuver that I would, after all, not be willing to attribute to the Macedonians. Furthermore, the movement would be so dangerous that it can be characterized as inconceivable; the enemy would only need to move forward to attack the Macedonian army in a position in which it could hardly defend itself. A flank march so close along the front of the enemy is only feasible when one can be certain that the enemy will remain in his defensive position. But the Persians, whose strength lay in their cavalry and their scythed chariots, were only waiting for the moment when they could charge forward. Somebody might be inclined to recall the flank march of Frederick the Great at Leuthen—but this was done under the cover of a chain of hills, so that the enemy did not notice it promptly, could not observe it sufficiently, and even took the move to be a withdrawal. The Persians, however, are supposed to have had the alleged Macedonian flank march take place directly before their eyes, and, in order to keep pace with it, to have made their own movement toward the flank paralleling the Macedonian move. Not only does such skill of maneuver seem even less likely among Persians than it would among Macedonians, but also the movement is completely incomprehensible. If the Macedonians marched toward the right, they were of course exposing their left flank to the Persians; the latter would therefore only need to move straight ahead (on the terrain that they had presumably cleared in advance) in order to

strike the Macedonians simultaneously on the march, in the flank, and in the rear.

Not until the mutual flank movement had gone on for a while did Darius reportedly realize that it would be best to move to the attack—but probably not because of the unfavorable plight in which the Macedonians found themselves at the moment, but rather so that the armies would not move away from the elaborately cleared terrain onto a rougher area, where the chariots would not be usable.

It is clear that this action cannot possibly have taken place in the manner described by Arrian and analyzed militarily by Rüstow-Köchly. Perhaps the account that has come down to us has confused maneuvers that were carried out during the approach march, before the armies were so close to each other, with the movements on the battlefield itself. A careful critic is not justified in assuming from the action described above anything beyond the fact that the cavalry and the lightly armed infantry of the right flank tried on both sides to get the flanking advantage.

According to Arrian, the breaking of the phalanx during the march forward was related to the flank march. Such a break, however, is not unusual even when no intentional movement at all toward the right has taken place, since it is extremely difficult, in fact almost impossible, to move a widely deployed line straight forward, and in the case of a rather long move forward a break in the line is almost inevitable. If the Macedonian army did move toward the right during the march forward, that certainly was not part of Alexander's plan, since any deviation from the straight line is accompanied by the danger of disorder, but on the contrary, it was an accidental error that the camp legend later characterized as a tactical maneuver.

5. In his report of Engineer Cernik's study expedition (*Supplement No. 45 to Petermann's Geographic Reports* [*Ergänzungsheft Nr. 45 zu Petermanns Geographischen Mitteilungen*] 1876, p. 3), von Schweiger-Lerchenfeld seeks to establish more accurately the location of the battle and finds it in a rich, fertile plain near the town of Keramlais. From the military point of view, there is nothing further of interest in this work.

6. The battle of Gaugamela seems to be the only large battle in world history in which the scythed chariot played a real, though unsuccessful, role. In the *Cyropaedia* (6. 1. 30; 6. 2. 17, 18; 7. 1; 8. 8. 24) Xenophon speaks of them repeatedly and in detail, probably not only because they belonged to the picture of Persian military might, but because the adventurous fearfulness of the weapon appealed to his fantasy. The same point has held true for others after him; Leonardo da Vinci studied the construction of such chariots and made sketches of how they drove into the enemy mass and arms and legs went flying.

As thoroughly as Xenophon treats of the scythed chariots, nevertheless, he too points out where their weakness lies. He states that the horses are protected by armor, and in the battle (7. 1) the drivers suffer heavy losses, and in his concluding chapter he states that the Persians of the time no longer understand how to drive the scythed chariots. While it is true that they start off in the charge, the drivers soon either jump or fall out, and the driverless teams often cause more harm to friend than to foe.

7. Friedrich Hackmann, in *The Battle of Gaugamela* (*Die Schlacht bei Gaugamela*), a dissertation (Halle, 1902), sought to reconstruct the battle in a significantly different form. Nevertheless, I have been able to extract from the undertaking only a few corrections of details; as a whole, it is unsuccessful, since the author was lacking in the necessary knowledge of elementary tactics and their possibilities. See my review in the *Deutsche Literarische Zeitung*, No. 51, 1902, Col. 3229.

NOTES FOR CHAPTER IV

1. Graf York, *A Brief Survey of the Campaigns of Alexander the Great* (*Kurze Uebersicht der Feldzüge Alexanders des Grossen*), p. 32.

2. Reported by Mandrot, *Jahrbuch für Schweizerische Geschichte*, 6 (1881): 263.

3. General von Verdy says, "Twenty-four squadrons (3,600 horses) must be considered as the maximum strength of a cavalry division, since with larger numbers the control of the battle succeeds only with very outstandingly talented leaders, and even with them only under conditions of thorough training of lower commanders and troops."

4. See also *Cyropaedia* 7. 1; also 6. 2 and Book 8, conclusion.

5. Diodorus describes how terrible the wounds caused by these scythes were, but also makes it clear that the number of wounded or killed was only small, a point specifically emphasized by Arrian.

6. Arrian says, "of the men surrounding Alexander,"* at the most 100 men were killed; the expression is very indefinite. If one relates it to the total losses of the Macedonian army, as is usually the case, this small number would contradict Arrian's own description of the battle. Niese claims that it applies only to the actual Macedonians. Still other interpretations are possible, but there is no purpose in accumulating speculations on the subject.

Chapter V

The Battle on the Hydaspes

According to the generally accepted estimates, Alexander is supposed to have undertaken the campaign against India with an army of 100,000 to 120,000 men, consequently with three times the strength that he had against Darius. Nevertheless, the number as passed down to us is not reliable,[1] and it is *per se* untrustworthy, even impossible. The decisive encounter against Porus on the Hydaspes was, according to the specific and unquestionable report of Arrian, fought by 11,000 men (including 5,000 cavalry).[2] It is not logical to assume that, against enemies so incapable of strong resistance, Alexander would have mobilized an army many times larger than the one with which he overcame the gigantic empire of Darius. The army was, moreover, accompanied by a very large train, and even by women and children,[3] and it would therefore, with a strength of 120,000 combatants, have numbered several hundred thousand souls. Such a mass does not move as easily and rapidly as Alexander did, and furthermore the passage over the Hindukush Mountains, over a pass 4,000 meters high, is completely impossible for such masses in one move. Taking as a point of departure the fact that 11,000 men participated in the fight on the Hydaspes and that considerable portions of the army had remained on the other side of the river, but that Alexander, on the other hand, would probably not have accepted a decisive battle without having at least a third of his army on the spot, we may then estimate the entire strength of the army at 20,000 to 30,000 men.

Concerning the strength of Porus' army, the Greek sources have handed down to us the most varied figures, obviously based on completely arbitrary estimates. Diodorus (17. 87) gives him more than 50,000 men on foot in comparison with 3,000 cavalry, over 1,000 chariots, and 130 elephants. Arrian gives him 4,000 cavalry, 300 chariots, and 200 elephants; Plutarch 20,000 men on foot and

2,000 cavalry; Curtius only 85 elephants. It is significant that the sources all agree in giving the Macedonians the numerical superiority in cavalry: 5,000 men against 4,000 (according to Arrian), against 3,000 (Diodorus), against 2,000 (Plutarch). The strength of the Indians lay in the elephants, for which we should probably accept the lowest figure, 85.

Porus did not dare throw down the challenge for a decision in a field battle, believing he could defend himself by denying the Macedonians the chance to cross the full-flowing Hydaspes. That could not possibly succeed, since a reasonably clever and energetic enemy would sooner or later necessarily find the means of getting a part of his army across, upstream or downstream, with surprise effect. Since we hear that another Indian prince was ready to lend Porus assistance, it is always possible that Porus was not caught up in the mistaken idea that the river could serve as an absolute obstacle but was aiming at winning only a few days' time in order to give the reinforcing troops time to arrive.[4]

The decisive encounter came as a result of Alexander's crossing over unexpectedly with 11,000 men 18 miles upstream from the point where the two armies were camped opposite each other, whereupon Porus, after a detached force was defeated, moved to meet him.

Like the Macedonians, Porus divided his cavalry between the two flanks. They were supported by the battle chariots, a designation probably meaning not scythed chariots but light vehicles occupied by archers.

Nevertheless, as we know, the cavalry was not strong; the strength of the Indian army lay in its elephants. They were combined in the center of the battle line with the infantry in a curious formation. The animals, each bearing, besides its mahout, a few sharpshooters in a small tower, were posted at considerable intervals from each other; the infantry was directly behind them, so that foot soldiers even spilled forward somewhat into the intervals between the elephants. Since Arrian expressly says that the infantry had formed a second front, one probably has as little right to say that it was spread out in small groups as that it was posted behind the elephants at a short interval. Rather, the phalanx must have been drawn up at each place behind the elephants more shallowly and between the elephants more deeply. The overall picture, according to the Greeks' report, looked like a city wall with its towers. Porus supposedly expected that the Greeks would not risk moving into the intervals between the elephants. The horses would shy away from the elephants, and the infantry would not risk it either. For if they moved forward in order to attack the elephants from the side, they would have to fear the Indian infantry, and if they moved forward against the latter, they would have to worry about the elephants' turning against them and trampling them.

It is not specifically reported how the Indian infantry was armed. The Greeks call them hoplites; but we cannot assume that we are dealing here with a tightly closed unit intended for close combat, like the Greek-Macedonian phalanx. The deploying of the elephants in front of this infantry seems to indicate that the real decision was expected from the former; in this army still more than in the Persian one, the infantry was a simple auxiliary arm. As the Greeks report, it was supposed to form a kind of cover for the elephants.[5] Nevertheless, the Indian infantry may have been considerably superior in numbers to the 6,000 men whom Alexander brought up.

The Macedonians had their customary formation, with the phalanx in the center, the cavalry on the flanks;[6] the right wing, which moved along the river and which on other occasions had always been commanded by the King himself, was commanded by Coenus. The left wing, which had no geographical feature to tie to and was consequently the more vulnerable, while being the best able to execute the flanking and envelopment movements, was led by Alexander himself. He ordered the phalanx, however, to hold back until he should have thrown the enemy into confusion with his cavalry; for this purpose he ordered the cavalry to attack the enemy not only in the front but, ranging out farther, also quickly in the flank.

Since the Macedonians, as we may certainly assume, were superior to the Indian cavalry even more in tactical training than in numbers, the maneuver succeeded on both flanks. The Indian battle chariots were even less able to withstand the onslaught of the tightly formed Macedonian squadrons than was the cavalry, and the losers fled to positions behind the elephants, followed by the Macedonians. The attack came to a standstill in the face of the elephants, some of which evidently had turned around and passed through their infantry to meet the Macedonians. The horses shied away and could not be pushed up to the huge animals. Since Alexander had already been in the Indian border area for longer than a year and on Indian soil for a number of months and was allied with Indian princes who had brought elephants to him, this battle was in no way a surprise for the Macedonians. Because the horses would shy away from the elephants, Alexander had not risked a crossing over the Hydaspes in the face of the enemy army but had made the envelopment. We might well be surprised that there is no report about whether the Macedonians did not attempt to accustom their horses to the appearance and the trumpeting of the gigantic animals. At any rate, they now were forced first of all to withdraw, and Porus went over into the attack against the Macedonian cavalry and the phalanx opposite him, so that the battle now became general.

The Greek sources vie with one another in describing the fearfulness of this battle: the elephants penetrated into the enemy lines, no matter how closely formed the latter stood, trampled the enemy or seized them with their trunks and threw them into the air or dug their teeth into their bodies, while the sharpshooters on their backs, and especially the mighty King Porus himself, dispatched their missiles.

Nevertheless, the Macedonians were finally victorious. With arrows and javelins they brought down the mahouts from the elephants, leaving the beasts driverless, and most important of all, they wounded the elephants themselves so seriously that the animals finally refused to move farther forward, or they even turned about.

As soon as the elephants slackened their efforts, the Indians were lost. Their infantry, even if supposedly more numerous than that of the Macedonians, was not of the caliber to take advantage of the confusion that the elephants had initially caused and to defeat the Macedonian phalanx in close combat. Moreover, the whole Indian attack was certainly impeded from the very start by the fact that the Macedonian cavalry, following up their initial victory, had come to the rear of the enemy battle line, and even if they had at first recoiled from the elephants, they still remained not only on the battlefield but also in the rear of the elephants and the enemy infantry.

With their great superiority they chased the Indian cavalry, which had again ventured out, back again to the line of elephants. With good foresight Alexander had ordered that his phalanx, shallow as it was, should at first hold back; it could perhaps not have withstood an unimpeded attack of the elephants in conjunction with the Indian infantry. But the continuing cavalry combat in the rear undoubtedly lowered the confidence and the energy of the Indian advance from the start, and once they came to a standstill, they were as good as surrounded and were now gradually squeezed closer and closer together. They were trampled by their own elephants, which turned around and which they could no longer avoid, while the Macedonian infantry near the outer ring gave way before those elephants that were still moving forward, only to drive them back with shots, following them then closely, and so they pushed the enemy army toward the Macedonian cavalry.

A very large part of the Indian army was cut down in this way, and most of the elephants and King Porus himself were captured.

According to Arrian, the Macedonians lost only 310 men killed in this battle, 230 of whom were cavalry. This small number could cause us to question whether the battle was really so terrible and hard-fought as the sources describe it. If we take into consideration, however, the fact that thereafter the Macedonian generals who had taken part in the battle and later, as successors of Alexander, divided his empire and fought over it among themselves, brought more and more elephants into the organization of their armies, we may draw a conclusion from this about the nature of this battle. The Macedonians must have had the impression of great accomplishment and military effectiveness on the part of the elephants, and the victory cannot have been so very easy for them. Therefore, when we read in Diodorus that the Macedonians had lost 280 cavalry and more than 700 infantry, we tend to accept this number in preference to that of Arrian. Almost 1,000 killed and certainly several thousand wounded in an army of 11,000 men indicates a very tough, hard-fought battle. Finally, the Macedonians who crossed over the Hydaspes in the rear of the Indians must have exercised a certain influence, even before they actually attacked. And a part of the casualties may be counted against these troops and therefore deducted from those of the main army, since the former still took part in the pursuit.

EXCURSUS

1. Plutarch's report of the battle is based on a letter from Alexander himself, which his biographer repeats in indirect quotation. The authenticity of this letter has been doubted, and Adolf Bauer especially, in a very fine study (*Publication in Honor of Büdinger* [*Festgaben für Büdinger*], Innsbruck, 1898) adduced the proof that, in those places where this letter differs from Arrian (who again repeats the reports of Ptolemy and Aristobulus, which are essentially in agreement), it is in the sense that everything is said to have happened as the King had foreseen. That applies particularly to the crossing of the Hydaspes with its many incidents, which we have passed over in our account. Now, Bauer continues very correctly, the greatness of a commander consists in no way of his being able to foresee all the possible events, but —and it is precisely this quality that Alexander showed here so brilliantly—in being capable of dealing with the many unforeseeable chance happenings with quick deci-

siveness. The letter, which is intended to flatter Alexander, therefore is the work of a militarily ignorant person. It cannot possibly be from Alexander himself, but was composed by some courtier who was familiar with the reports of Ptolemy and Aristobulus but did not find them sufficient.

If it were really a question of a personal document of Alexander, then it would indeed either have to be rejected as fraudulent or it would constitute a very shabby testimonial for its royal author. A forgery, however, does not seem credible to me, since on the one hand the relationship with the report that we find in Arrian (from Ptolemy) is undeniable and on the other hand the document contains original expressions that point toward a real expert. When, by whom, and for what purpose would the forgery have been made? Did Ptolemy perhaps publish, still during Alexander's lifetime, the account which he later gave in his history, or did someone after all, a whole generation later, wish to flatter the dead King by means of a fraudulent letter?

We avoid all these difficulties if we regard the letter as being, in fact, genuine, but, rather than a personal composition of Alexander, a kind of bulletin that had as its author some secretary from the King's retinue. What Bauer so perceptively noted in the document as characteristic—that is, that it had the King anticipating everything—is precisely the style of official military history writing. On that point one needs only to examine modern general staff works, even though they are written by officers; and also in the *Mémorial de Sainte-Hélène*, for example those passages concerning 1796, and especially in the official French accounts of the campaign of 1800, one finds many an equivalent to this.

That the art of war is so difficult precisely because it must operate in the darkness of ignorance or of half-knowledge and the perspicacity even of the greatest commander can never completely penetrate the darkness—that is a thesis that can never be used to convince the public of a man's greatness but that can at best be cited to forgive his mistakes. The easiest way of making the genius of the commander clear to the public is always to show how he foresaw everything and planned accordingly. Consequently, we are not offending Alexander when we insist that he allowed the bulletin to go out under his name, although it does color the account, as indicated above.

2. Arrian claims that Porus' elephants had been stationed at intervals of a *plethron* (100 feet), and on the strength of this Rüstow and Köchly estimated the length of his entire battle line at some 5½ miles. Alexander, on the other hand, supposedly had only a very short front, reaching as far as the twentieth elephant. His battle plan, therefore, supposedly consisted of defeating, first of all, the one flank—the left—of the Indians. In our sources there is nothing to be found of such a flank battle. It is hard to see why the 180 elephants extending beyond the Macedonian line did not fall on their flank, and in Rüstow and Köchly's own report, too, there is nothing said about the flank battle. But how is the 11,000-man Macedonian army supposed to have been stretched out to a length of over 5 miles?

The solution can only lie in the fact that in Arrian not only is the number of elephants greatly exaggerated but also the interval between the individual animals is much too large. It might very well happen that even a Ptolemy, according to his personal impression (he was present in the battle), estimated the interval at a *plethron* without stopping to realize what the resulting length of the entire battle line would be. Polyaenus (4. 3. 22), in a battle account, which incidentally can serve as an example of and warning against unreliable sources, estimates the distance between elephants at 50 feet.

3. The account I have given of the course of the battle differs significantly from the one normally accepted up to now in its concept of the cavalry combat on the two flanks and in the related attack from the rear. The critical question hinges on solving a point of difficulty in Arrian's account.

Alexander, he says, turned with the main body of his cavalry against the left flank of the enemy. But he sent Coenus with two regiments against the right flank ("as if upon the right wing"*) with the order to attack the barbarians in the rear when they moved against the King. We might well ask: How could Coenus do that if he was stationed at the other flank? He could not very well ride around the entire enemy battle line. Rüstow and Köchly consequently assumed that he was sent not against the enemy right flank, but on the extreme right flank of the Macedonians, and Bauer (loc. cit.) made such an effort to reconcile that with the text that he had the word "right wing"* indeed refer to the Indians, but he explained the whole action as a diversionary maneuver; that is, Coenus set out in that direction but then turned about and supported Alexander. Both these interpretations seem to me absolutely impossible, both objectively and literally. The clear text says that, as Alexander advanced against the enemy left flank, Coenus advanced against the enemy right flank.[7] If Coenus, however, was supposed to attack from the rear the Indian cavalry who were opposing Alexander, he had to hasten and could not first make a diversionary movement that, furthermore, would have had no purpose at all, and Arrian would not have been able to omit that he returned from the feint against the enemy right flank to the real attack against the left one. Furthermore, the Macedonian phalanx must necessarily have had cavalry also on its left flank.

There is nothing left to do but establish the fact that Arrian's account contains an unsolvable contradiction. It can serve no purpose to cover it up halfway with some forced interpretation; rather, we must identify the error and seek to eliminate it. But that is not so very difficult, even without assistance from the other sources.

Alexander necessarily had cavalry on both flanks of his army. The cavalry on one flank was commanded by the King himself, on the other by Coenus. The Macedonians were superior in cavalry on both flanks. Of the right flank, Arrian goes on to relate: the King sent his mounted archers against the enemy; "he himself, with the hetairoi, drove his cavalry sharply against the left wing of the barbarians; the cavalry hastened to attack those who were already in confusion along the wings, before their cavalry was lined up against the phalanx."*

The King, therefore, attacked the Indian cavalry in the flank with his cavalry, while the former were being attacked in their front by his mounted archers.

To this point everything is quite clear. Now, however, Arrian goes on to say that Coenus, too, appeared in the rear of the Indians, and they were forced to form a double front against him and against Alexander. This is the point of confusion. Coenus is, of course, on the other flank, and the Indians already had to form the double front before this, that is, against the mounted archers and against the hetairoi. If Coenus, too, had now come up from the rear, they would have had to fight on three fronts.

There is no other explanation except that Arrian was careless here and misunderstood his sources. Coenus had nothing to do with the fight on this flank. In the source there must have been said something to the effect that, just as on Alexander's flank, Coenus, too, enveloped his enemy and engaged him simultaneously in the front and from the flank (which, if the enemy did not make a countermove at the right time, always means also an attack from the rear). Consequently, the envelopment that Coenus carried out on his flank was attributed by Arrian to Alexander's flank.

If we correct Arrian's account in this manner, it not only becomes clear in itself, but it also moves into agreement with the bulletin. In the latter it is expressly said that Alexander attacked on one flank, Coenus on the other, and that the enemy was defeated on both flanks and fell back to the line of elephants.

This testimony is absolutely decisive; one would otherwise be obliged to declare the bulletin fraudulent, for which, however, there is no basis at all.

Not only can the misconception that Arrian created by confusing the right and left flanks be established, but I believe we can go another step farther and indicate the point at which it originated. The bulletin (in Plutarch's indirect quotation) reports the order of Alexander as follows: "He himself ordered them to attack along the other wing, but Coenus to charge against the right."* If we had only these words, there would be no doubt concerning their meaning; they would be translated: "The King attacked one flank but ordered Coenus to drive against the right [flank]." According to this, then, Alexander himself led the right wing, Coenus the left. Now the entire sentence, however, reads as follows: "Being afraid of the animals and the number of the enemy, he himself ordered an attack along the other wing, but he ordered Coenus to charge against the right."* Therefore, it is the formation of the flanks that is particularly accounted for here; it was not the customary one. "Because of the concern over the elephants and the mass of the enemy"—the King takes over one wing and Coenus the other one. This makes no sense if there was not something unusual in the formation of the flanks. According to the concept of every Greek, however, the king commands the right flank and attacks the enemy left flank. If, instead of that, he wishes to attack the enemy right flank, then that is "the other one," and the words that are used concerning Coenus may very well also be meant in this sense, that is, not that he is to charge against the (enemy) right flank, but that he is to attack with the right flank (his own). Most interpreters, because of the context and the agreement with Arrian, have translated the passage in the first sense, but a few have also adopted the second sense, and there is a quite good objective basis for this latter arrangement. The Indians had their left flank based on the river, so that, if they were defeated here, they had the possibility of withdrawing inland. If, however, they were enveloped and defeated on their right flank, then the main body of their army could be forced back against the river and cut off. Any success at this point would necessarily have the strongest effect at once on the morale of the entire Indian army. Alexander, then, by personally taking over this time the left flank, chose for himself the post that was at the same time the most dangerous and at which he could exercise the greatest influence, and he risked from the start a battle of destruction in which he did then succeed in capturing Porus himself and the most valuable part of his army, that is, almost all of the elephants. Porus himself is supposed to have taken his post on his left, probably in the expectation that the King of the Macedonians would lead his right flank, as usual.

There is still another indication that Alexander actually commanded his left flank in this battle.

According to Curtius, Alexander orders Coenus: "Quum ego Ptolemaeo, Perdiccaque et Hephaestione comitatus in laevum hostium cornu impetum fecero . . . ipse dextrum move et turbatis signa infer." ("When I, accompanied by Ptolemy, Perdiccas, and Hephaestio, shall have made my attack against the enemies' left wing . . . yourself move the right and bring in the standards against them in their confusion.") Later, however, it is said: "Coenus ingenti vi in laevum cornu invehitur." ("Coenus was sent to attack into the right flank with great force.")

Curtius, therefore, contradicts himself. But it is not the first passage, but rather the second one that seems to contain the truth. For it is expressly said that the regiment of Perdiccas, too, belonged to those that the King intended to command. But in the fight that Alexander conducts against one of Porus' detached forces before the actual battle, Alexander sends Perdiccas with his cavalry against the right flank of the enemy (8. 47: "Perdiccam cum equitibus in dextrum cornu hostium emisit"). ("He sent Perdiccas with the cavalry against the right wing of the enemy.") It is not likely that the same horsemen who had already fought on the left flank were later drawn in for the envelopment on the extreme right flank.

Speaking against our interpretation is the fact that the bulletin, to be sure, does not mention in any way the reason we proposed for the exchange of command positions, but only mentions in a general way the elephants and the enemy numbers. But why should the bulletin concern itself specifically with these reasons? To what extent does an effective means against elephants and a large enemy lie in the fact that one general commands one flank and the other general the other flank? One could suppose that Plutarch's reference is inexact and that the unusual aspect of Alexander's formation is to be found in the fact that, as reported by Arrian, both cavalry wings drove forward and the phalanx initially held back. If we take into account, however, the concepts of the Greeks, shared also by the author of the bulletin, then it does not appear impossible, after all, that Plutarch is repeating the content quite correctly. The real strategic reason for Alexander's commanding the left flank this time is too complicated and too fine a point for a bulletin. The principal point, from the author's viewpoint, is to emphasize the impression of the greatest danger and of an extraordinary accomplishment. In a normal battle the King commands the right flank, which, formed of the best troops, usually carries the victory. With the enemy numbers, however, and the dangerous character of the elephants, it could have happened that the enemy, too, might be victorious on his right flank, and therefore the King had to take it upon himself to oppose him in this, the most endangered spot.

It is impossible to draw a definite conclusion here, but perhaps this was the original meaning. Because the words of the bulletin were so indefinite and ambiguous, perhaps the authors became uncertain even at an early time, and so Curtius as well as Arrian became confused. Curtius contradicts himself directly by having the King attack in one passage with the right flank, whereas in another passage it is Coenus. Arrian combines the attacks on the two flanks into a single one—and in doing so he completely omits the left flank.

NOTES FOR CHAPTER V

1. Curtius' figures are worthless. At no place in the *Anabasis* does Arrian give an overall number, but mentions only in the *Indica*, Chapter 19, that the King, when he started his withdrawal, was followed by 120,000 combatants ("fit for battle"*), including many barbarians. Huge levies of Indian, princes, more or less fictitious, may have been included in the count. Even putting that point aside, it is not known what the origin of this number is and whether it is reliable. We may rely on the numbers Arrian gives in the *Anabasis* concerning the Macedonian army, since he is depending here significantly on Ptolemy, but what we find in the *Indica* may have been taken from almost any unclear source. Plutarch, Chapter 66, even puts the army that makes the march through Gadrosia at 120,000 men on foot and 150,000 horsemen.

The computation by Rüstow and Köchly (p. 298) is not sufficiently supported; they claim to estimate the strength of the army concentrated on the Hydaspes at 69,000 men and 10,000 horses. The authors themselves characterize the advance guard force as the one "that really fights the battles." And that is the way it actually is; and here I ask, Why should a commander like Alexander have complicated the conduct of the war by dragging along with him other large masses of troops for which there never appears any need throughout the course of the war?

2. The rest of the army—according to the positive statement of Arrian, which we have no reason to doubt—did not cross over\the

Hydaspes until the battle was decided and therefore may not be counted as participating in the actual combat.

3. Crämer, *Contributions to the History of Alexander the Great* (*Beiträge zur Geschichte Alexanders des Grossen*), Marburg dissertation, 1893.

4. In any event Rüstow and Köchly's idea that this Indian prince, Abisares, moved up to Porus on the right bank of the Hydaspes, is false. There he would have run directly into the hands of the Macedonians and would have been intercepted without being able to receive help from Porus or himself helping Porus. Curtius (8. 47) also says expressly that Porus expected the reinforcements on the left bank.

5. In his essay "The Use of the Elephant for Military Purposes in Antiquity" ("Die Verwendung des Elefanten zu kriegerischen Zwecken im Altertum"), *Jahrbücher für die deutsche Armee and Marine*, Vol. 49, December 1883, Major Ohlendorf states the belief that the infantry had the mission of preventing the elephants from turning around. It is difficult to know how the infantry was supposed to go about that. The concept is apparently founded on a translation error.

6. Alexander had also taken along to the crossing point two *taxis* of *pezetairoi*. Nevertheless, they do not appear in the battle formation; only *hypaspists* and light infantry were involved. The number, too—a total of 6,000 men on foot—eliminates them. Rüstow and Köchly (p. 229) have assumed that they were left behind at the crossing point in order to oppose Abisares in case of need. That would have been an error, even if Abisares was expected here; primarily, it was a question of striking Porus with a combination of all one's forces and of avoiding a fight with Abisares until that was accomplished. An isolated force of light infantry could easily have fallen a victim to him. The reason the *pezetairoi* were not in the battle is probably simply that they had not completed their crossing. To cross a broad river with inflated skins and just a few boats requires a great deal of time.

7. That is also the opinion of Kaerst, *Philologus* 56: 412.

Chapter VI

Alexander as a Military Commander

The Greek city-states .fought countless battles and engagements on land and at sea against one another; all together, so to speak, they had only negative, destructive, or obstructive effects. No great hegemony was established in this way. The defeat of the Athenians on Sicily and the sea battle of Aegospotami ended Athenian dominance but gave Sparta only a leading position, not a dominant one. Sparta's own inner strength was even less sufficient for this than that of Athens earlier. Even a victory like the one Agesilaus won at Coronea had no significant positive results, just as Epaminondas' victories at Leuctra and Mantinea had none, because the armies, like the states, were lacking in the sustained power to follow up the victories on the battlefield to the point of establishing a lasting new order of things. Over and over again we admire the wisdom of Pericles, who did not allow himself to be misled by all the abundant strength of his Athens into a strategy of unconditional victory and conquest and refused to seek useless victories. The gigantic successes of the two Macedonian kings did not become possible until the means for achieving them had been prepared. King Philip waged his wars not only with a hoplite phalanx, Demosthenes told the Athenians,[1] but at the same time with light infantry, archers, and cavalry. It was no longer, he said, like the times of their ancestors, when the Spartans took to the field four or five months in the summer, invaded the country, and then returned home again in winter. He went on to say that, if the Macedonian King did not find his enemy in the open field, he went on to besiege him with his siege machines. He went wherever he wished, and summer and winter were all the same to him. The crux of this whole matter lay in the fact that the professional army had replaced the citizen

230

army. In the uninterrupted work of one generation, pushing forward step by step, King Philip had won and bequeathed to his son a dominion that justified his contemplating the greatest possible accomplishments, and with the growth of the means, of the extensive as well as intensive increase of military power, the conduct of war itself had changed its countenance and taken on other forms. Alexander not only was victorious on the battlefield, but he also exploited his victory. Immediate pursuit destroyed the enemy's fighting force; his strategic-political combination brought the countries under his power that then served as a base for new campaigns. The pursuing rides of the Macedonian cavalry, the marches through mountains and deserts were no less important military accomplishments than the battles themselves and the razing of fortress walls.[2] During the pursuit after Gaugamela many horses collapsed from fatigue.

Alexander was not only a great field commander, but also a commander in the grand manner. But he was still more than that.

He occupies a unique position in that he combined in one person the world-conquering strategist and the unexcelled courageous knightly combatant. Skillfully he led his army toward the enemy, overcame terrain obstacles, had it deploy out of narrow passes, combined the various arms in a different way each time, according to the differing circumstances, for the strongest possible total effect, strategically secured his base and his communications, gave due consideration to his supplies, waited until the preparations and equipping were completed, stormed forward, pursued the victory up to the point of the most extreme exhaustion of his forces—and the same man fought in each battle at the head of his cavalry with sword and spear, drove into the breach at the head of his assault column, or was the first to spring over the enemy wall. It was the only moment in the development of warfare in which the elements of the conduct of war were so close to each other that the commander, following his nature, was at the same time a combatant. The strategic and tactical action was so simple that this unity does not need to be pointed out, particularly in the period from Miltiades and Leonidas up to Epaminondas. With Philip first, and then completely with Alexander, the command of an army developed into an organic function of such magnitude and complexity that it became separated from personal participation in combat. We cannot withhold the highest admiration in seeing that Alexander, in the inexhaustible strength and self-confidence of his personality, still maintained this unity. His genius recognized with unerring acumen all the new requirements and possibilities that were demanded and offered by the new conditions, the organization and size of the armies, as well as the extent and the nature of the conquered lands. It has been repeatedly emphasized, and rightly so, how he recognized and exploited the advantages of the pursuit following a victory, something that had been unattainable at the time of the Greek citizen-commanders.[3] In the Peloponnesian War the Spartans had not been able to consider besieging Athens; Alexander completed the success of his victory at Issus by the skillful seven-month siege and final storming of Tyre. In India he was faced with the problem of fighting the new arm made up of the elephants, and of crossing a stream in the face of this arm. He was able to solve the problem, and in doing so he continuously risked his own person, unconcerned that, if the soldier's fate should befall him in the midst of the melee, his whole work threatened to collapse with him.

Here I wish to indicate at which point the integration of military commander and warrior, which still held true with Alexander, finally had necessarily to be given up: i.e., as soon as the principle of tactical reserves appeared. Alexander might still be allowed to plunge personally into the melee of battle because, with the signal for the attack, the commander's activity is finished; once his troops are engaged in the battle, the commander retains only very limited control over them. It is true that, with Alexander too, we find a certain measure of leadership within the battle; the victorious flank is not supposed to dash blindly after the defeated enemy, but to assemble again and help disengage the flank that is held up, in case the latter is still engaged. Even that, however, is no longer the responsibility of the supreme commander but it falls rather into the sphere of leadership of the individual troop units and can still occur in conjunction with the leader's participation in the battle. Only with the advent of the principle of withheld units whose intervention as to time and place is directed by the commander himself is the latter's regular involvement in the fighting eliminated.

EXCURSUS

1. According to Arrian 7. 23, Alexander, shortly before his end, is supposed to have undertaken a complete reorganization of his army. He created a new phalanx, 16 men deep, in which the first three ranks and the last one were composed of Macedonians with their native arms and equipment, while the twelve interior ranks were made up of Persians with bows and javelins. It is an astonishing proof of the might of the written word that modern scholars have found it possible to continue to copy such an absurdity and to draw up clever hypotheses on the subject of what

Alexander might possibly have had in mind with this formation and how its employment was to be imagined. As an excuse we may point out that of course even Xenophon in his *Cyropaedia*, as we have seen above, describes such an arrangement of combined cutting and thrusting weapons and missiles. Whoever the authors were from whom Arrian may have taken his account, it is clear that here once again we have one of the doctrinaire interpretations that one encounters so often in military history, even with professional military men, despite the fact that, when they are transposed into reality, they can immediately be recognized as invalid and never in any historical battle is there even an attempt at putting them into practice.

It is also stated in Arrian and Aelian's *Tactics* 3. 4. 3 (Köchly and Rüstow, *Greek Military Authors*, Part II, Section 1, p. 270) that the lightly armed troops could shoot over a phalanx of 16-man depth with javelins, slings, and arrows.

Notes for Chapter VI

1. *Against Philip** (*Philippics*) 3. 123. para. 49.

2. H. Droysen, in *Studies* (*Untersuchungen*), p. 66, assembled the accounts of Alexander's forced marches. I would, however, prefer not to repeat the detailed figures concerning time and space. The estimate of distances is very arbitrary, and it is also quite doubtful whether the time is always reported accurately. Schwarz, in his very worthwhile study *Alexander's Campaigns in Turkestan* (*Alexanders Feldzüge in Turkestan*), 1893, which is based on his personal knowledge of the land and the people, has established, probably correctly, that the march that, according to Arrian 4. 6, Alexander made within three days was from Chodschent to Samarkand. Arrian estimates the distance at 1,500 *stadia*, which means 275 kilometers or 170 miles, and the latest measurements actually give 278 kilometers. Such a march in three days, however, exceeds the capabilities of even the best unit.

In 3. 15, Arrian recounts that Alexander reached the Lycus (Zab) on the same evening as the battle of Gaugamela, and Arbela on the following day, which is situated 600 *stadia*—i.e., 68 miles—from the battlefield. We may say with reasonable certainty that the distance was about half that great, but even that is still a tremendous performance.

3. Of course, it is not a completely new idea that a pursuit magnifies and completes a victory. After Plataea the Mantineans wished to pursue the Persians as far as Thessaly, according to Herodotus 9. 77. After the victory at Delium the Boeotian cavalry and light infantry pursued the Athenians until darkness intervened (Thucydides 4. 96). Likewise Alcibiades pursued the beaten Persians with cavalry and hoplites (*Hellenica* 1. 2. 16). Derdas pursued the defeated Olynthians a distance of 90 *stadia* (*Hellenica* 5. 3. 2).

See also other passages in Liers, p. 184. These are nevertheless only exceptional cases and are not to be compared with Alexander's pursuits. In theory, Xenophon, too, in the *Cyropaedia* (5. 3, conclusion), had already recommended pursuit, with the addition that not all the troops should be committed to it but that some should always be kept at hand in good order.

Chapter VII

The Diadochi

From the world empire of Alexander there stem a number of subempires that, founded by his generals, were actually what we call military monarchies, an expression one may not yet use in speaking of Alexander's dominion. The largest of these subempires, Syria, defied any natural, national, or geographical basis. Egypt, even if it had no unified national basis, did at least have a geographical one. Macedon possessed, to a certain extent, the character of a national state.

The armies that held these states together were essentially mercenary armies. The barbarians who came streaming into them in great numbers were more or less assimilated into the Macedonian-Greek system. The quality of the troops may have decreased in that, when the romantic-idealistic glow that enveloped the world conquest and the person of Alexander, and also probably threw its reflection on his whole army, faded away, the conduct of war then sank to the status of a mere occupation in the senseless battles of the subkings among themselves. But mercenary armies with their professional warriors always have the specialized skill of any professionally practiced activity, and there is no reason to deny this quality to the Hellenistic armies of the next century and a half. Drill masters and energetic drilling are expressly attested to.[1] The original warrior élan that the Macedonians brought from their state of half-barbarism, or that they had been imbued with through the inspiration of the two great kings, was replaced by a military artisanship. A portion of these mercenaries formed a standing army.[2]

This period presents us with military history questions in three different areas. First of all, there are the elephants.

This new arm forms the real problem of the period. How were they worked into the traditional organization? How were they combined with the infantry, with the cavalry? To what extent did the repercussions of this new element react on the functions of the

235

older ones? What form did the battle take when there were elephants on both sides?

A second problem lies in the inner development of the phalanx, the gradual lengthening of the *sarissa*.

A third question is the development of the relationship of the arms among themselves. Köchly and Rüstow have voiced the opinion that the cavalry gradually became the only decisive arm; that it had continuously gotten larger; that the phalanx did not really fight any more, but awaited the outcome of the cavalry battle and was governed by that decision. Little is to be extracted directly from the military history of this period. We have, it is true, enough accounts (Diodorus and Plutarch), but they are highly unreliable. There may very well be a good deal of truth in them, but it cannot with certainty be separated from the false material. Just the same, much of it may appear credible enough to warrant our simply repeating it, although it is not credible enough to serve as a basis for conclusions, as our purpose demands.

We plan to discuss the question of the elephants after we have reviewed in turn the other battles in which these animals took part, up to the last one, the battle of Thapsus.

Likewise, we do not intend to discuss the question of the *sarissae* until we reach the point where it faces us in a practical way, in the last battles of the Macedonians with the Romans. King Pyrrhus of Epirus, too, who belongs militarily to the group of Alexander's successors, will best be considered in connection with Roman military history.

The third question, concerning the relationship of infantry and cavalry, we can answer at once simply by bringing it up. That is, if we look carefully at the sources, we see that Rüstow and Köchly's actual assumption does not hold true; the numerical relationship did not change significantly after Alexander.

Aside, then, from the elephants and the lengthening of the *sarissa*, the Macedonian system of warfare did not undergo a change after Alexander, and we can immediately add that the Greek states also, which were asserting themselves in a kind of uncertain independence, copied the Macedonians' perfected art of war, to include finally also the *sarissa*.

It is astonishing that, when the Gauls invaded the country Alexander's successors proved to be incapable of coping with them. This was not because of the individuals involved; rather, it seems unmistakably clear that all their skill in the art of military operations was still not sufficient to withstand the natural power of the warlike spirit of the barbarians. Only the great might of the Syrian King Antiochus I, with his elephants, is supposed to have halted the Gauls. The historical account has preserved his statement: "I am ashamed that we are indebted for our salvation to these sixteen animals." We are not really sufficiently informed, however, on the details of these events.

Excursus

1. The opinion of Rüstow and Köchly to the effect that in this period the cavalry had become still greater in number and importance has already been dropped by Adolf Bauer in his account. The numbers that have come down from the sources (Droysen, p. 134) show in general the same relationship between infantry and cavalry that already existed in Alexander's army—between 5 and 7 to 1. The variations above and below may be conditioned by particular circumstances about which we can hypothesize with a certain degree of probability. In doing so we automatically dispose of the question raised by Droysen (p. 154), and which he was unable to answer, of why, in the later Hellenistic period, the phalanx suddenly again became of such great importance and the cavalry declined.

In order to give a better overall view of the question, I have arranged below in tabular form the figures handed down to us, which, of course, I in no way endorse as completely credible.

Year (B.C.)			Infantry	Cavalry	Elephants
322	Crannon	(Macedonians	43,000	5,000	
		(Greeks	25,000	3,500	
321	Eumenes against	(Eumenes	20,000	5,000	
	Craterus	(Craterus	20,000	2,000	
321	Near Orcynii	(Antigonus	10,000	2,000	30
		(Eumenes	20,000	5,000	
319	Antigonus		60,000	10,000	30
319	Cretopolis	(Antigonus	40,000	7,000	
		(Alcetas	16,000	900	
317	Paraetacene	(Antigonus	28,000 (or a few thousand more)	8,500 (10,300)	65
		(Eumenes	35,000	6,100 (6,200)	114 (125)
316	Gabiene	(Antigonus	22,000	9,000	65
		(Eumenes	36,700	6,050	114
314	Demetrius		13,000	5,000	40
312	Gaza	(Ptolemy	18,000 (and light inf.)	4,000	
		(Demetrius	12,800	5,000	40

Year (B.C.)		Infantry	Cavalry	Elephants
312	Demtrius	15,000	4.000	
306	Antigonus	80,000	8.000	83
302	(Demetrius	56,000	1,500	
	(Cassander	29.000	2,000	
301	Ipsus (Allies	64,000	10,500	400
			(12,000)	(480)
	(Antigonus	70,000	10 000	75
288	Demetrius	98.000	12,000	
222	Sellasia (Antigonus	28,000	1,200	
	(Cleomenes	20,000 total		
217	Raphia (Ptolemy	70,000	5,000	73
	(Antiochus	62.000	6,000	102
197	Cynoscephalae Philip	23,500	2,000	
171	Perseus	39,000	4,000	

2. In the battle of Crannon (Diodorus 18. 17), the Greek cavalry defeated the Macedonian, although the former numbered only 3,500 whereas the Macedonians had 5,000. The Greek infantry, however, only 25,000 strong, was thrown back by the Macedonian, which numbered over 43,000 men. The Greeks, trusting in the skill of their cavalry, are supposed to have stationed them in front of their phalanx ("in front of the phalanx of foot soldiers"*). The Greek phalanx moved back onto higher terrain and in doing so held off the press of the enemy phalanx. The victorious Greek cavalry turned about when they noticed the withdrawal of their phalanx, without, however, intervening further in the battle.

This operation is not clear.

3. Diodorus and Plutarch say that Eumenes wisely provided himself in advance with a large and skilled cavalry arm. With it he first defeated Neoptolemus and also overcame the latter's phalanx when, after it had defeated his own infantry, it fell into disorder. In the second engagement there was no fight with the infantry, since Eumenes, after defeating the enemy cavalry with his preponderance of power (5,000 against 2,000), started negotiations with the enemy phalanx in order to persuade them to come over to his side.

4. From the military history point of view, the engagement near Orcynii cannot be evaluated, since it was decided by treason.

5. At Cretopolis Antigonus had such a great numerical superiority and Diodorus' report is moreover so indefinite that there is nothing to be learned of military history interest from this encounter.

6. Diodorus (19. 27–31) gives us a thorough description of the battle of Paraetacene between Antigonus and Eumenes (317 B.C.); I have serious doubts, however, as to whether one may consider much of it as historical. Without going into the many details, I shall bring up here only those points that, completely aside from the general unreliability of the source, make the whole matter suspect from my point of view.

Diodorus states the overall strength and the individual strengths very exactly, but, as Rüstow and Köchly have already remarked (p. 371, note), the numbers do not agree with each other.

Eumenes is said to have formed up 45 elephants in a curved formation in front of his left flank, with archers and slingers in the intervals. ("He lined up 45 elephants at an angle in front of all of them, along with sufficient archers and slingers in the spaces between the animals."*) Rüstow and Köchly conceive of this line as being curved toward the enemy. That is not impossible, but one cannot see a reason for it. A formation that is curved forward, if it does not have an absolutely secure terrain feature on which to lean, is always vulnerable itself to envelopment by the enemy.

In the center stood the infantry, on the right wing again cavalry, and in front of the infantry and cavalry 80 elephants with lightly armed men. We ask this question: Why were the elephants drawn up in a curve on one flank, while those in the center and on the other flank were in front of the other troops? How was the phalanx supposed to operate behind the 40 elephants that were allocated to it? Were they supposed to follow the elephants and charge the enemy phalanx after the latter had been broken up by the elephants? Antigonus, too, is supposed to have formed elephants in front of his phalanx. In the account of the battle, however, we hear no further word of these elephants on the two sides; the phalanxes advance against each other as usual.

Antigonus is supposed to have observed that the right flank of the enemy was particularly strong because of the presence there of the elephants and the best ("elite"*) of the cavalry. According to Diodorus' own account, however, a large number of elephants and a considerable numerical superiority of cavalrymen were on the other flank.

Antigonus, like his opponents, is said to have formed the elephants of his left flank in a curved line ("along the wing ... making an angle"*). Rüstow and Köchly conceive of this formation as curved to the rear.

Antigonus moved up for the attack in an oblique order of battle with his right flank in advance. Nevertheless, it is not the right, but rather his withheld left flank that supposedly opened the attack. It was composed principally of light cavalry, who, hesitating to move directly against the elephants, sought to take the enemy from the flank. Since Eumenes did not feel capable of opposing them successfully with his heavy cavalry, he moved reinforcements of light cavalry from his other flank.

One wonders why he did not have his elephants, which were immediately at hand, turn against the enemy cavalry, and particularly how he could risk weakening in this manner his left flank, which was obviously most seriously threatened by the enemy offensive flank.

With the help of his reinforcements, while the elephants also cooperate but actually only by following ("followers"*), Eumenes defeats the enemy left flank; likewise, his phalanx, which has a numerical superiority of 35,000 against 28,000, defeats the enemy phalanx.

During this combat the supposedly advanced offensive flank of Antigonus was completely passive. One would think that the victorious army of Eumenes, under his excellent leadership, would have detached a few units and moved them into the flank and the rear of the enemy wing that was still standing fast, in order to complete the victory. Instead, however, Diodorus recounts how Eumenes' victorious troops took no further action than to pursue the defeated units. The left flank, however, stood fast, so that the battle formation broke apart. Into this breach Antigonus charged with his cavalry and defeated that flank of the enemy which had so far been passive and was weakened by the detaching of some of its units. On hearing this, the defeated troops of Antigonus again came to a halt, and Eumenes called his troops back from the pursuit. How it is supposed to be possible that, when eight-ninths of an army is in full flight, a partial victory by the last ninth again stabilizes the battle, is hard to u derstand. With his well-disciplined troops, it certainly would have been possible for Eumenes to call back a few units from the pursuit and use them to finish off Antigonus.

Completely incomprehensible and fantastic, moreover, is Diodorus' account that then follows, showing how the two armies spent half the night marching along at a distance of 400 feet from each other.

7. In the battle of Gabiene (316 B.C.) Eumenes is said once again to have stationed 60 of his best elephants in a curved line ("bent at an angle"*) in front of his left flank ("in front of the whole wing"*) and the remainder, like Antigonus, in advance of his front (Diodorus 19. 40–43).

In the cavalry combat of the left flank, Eumenes, weaker in cavalry and treacherously left in the lurch by one of his corps, was defeated. Nothing is reported of any advantage that he might have gained from his great superiority in elephants. We only hear that the elephants fought against each other and that the leading animal of his side was killed in a battle with an opponent.

In the infantry battle Eumenes' phalanx, which was superior both in numerical strength and in quality, was completely victorious; it killed 5,000 of the enemy without losing a single man of its own. Nothing is said about the elephants and the light infantry that are supposed to have stood in advance of the front line.

We also hear nothing of the battle on the other cavalry flank, which was held back on both sides.

Now a very unusual battle would have had to develop, since on the one side was deployed a very strong and skilled infantry (36,700 men) with many elephants, against cavalry (9,000) with only half as many elephants. The superiority appears to have been unquestionably on the first side, that of Eumenes, and all the more so in that he also still had a portion of his cavalry at hand. The phalanx, forming a square, also repulsed an attack from Antigonus' cavalry, but then suddenly the military action was broken off, as the troops of Eumenes betrayed their commander and delivered him over to the enemy. During the battle Antigonus had had his superior cavalry capture Eumenes' camp, where the women and children of the soldiers were also, and that is supposed to have exerted such an influence on the morale of the soldiers, although it is hard to understand why they did not quickly move to drive off the invaders. The camp was situated at only 1,500 paces behind the battlefield.

8. Gaza (312 B.C.) would be a very interesting battle from the military history point of view, if we had any kind of reliable account of it. According to the only report we have (Diodorus 19. 80–84), Demetrius had the advantage in cavalry (5,000 against 4,000)[3] and in elephants (40), of which the enemy (Ptolemy) had none, whereas Ptolemy was far stronger in infantry (18,000 against 11,000 heavy infantry, "very many" against 18,000 light infantry). We would therefore have to expect something similar to the battle of Gabiene. Concerning a battle between the phalanxes, however, we hear absolutely nothing. The battle took place exclusively between Demetrius' left flank, consisting of cavalry, 30 elephants, and sharpshooters, and Ptolemy's right flank, composed in a like manner, except for the elephants. Under these conditions Demetrius would have had to have the superiority. But Ptolemy found an unusual method of combatting the elephants. He had palisades reinforced with iron and bound together with chains set up in front of his right flank. In what way this stake obstacle was supposed to hold up the animals is not clearly stated. It is impossible to ram in stakes hastily in such a way that they will hold up elephants. Later in the account of the battle, reference is made to the animals' soft feet and to the fact that they impaled themselves on the palisade. This would lead one to think of a kind of foot trap or, as H. Droysen believed, inverted harrows, which were bound together with chains so that they could not be removed. But "charax" has neither this meaning, nor would it help us much from the objective point of view. The emplacing and binding together of the "harrows" took place after

all in full view of the enemy. It appears that the cavalry saw this also, and consequently, since every obstacle of this kind holds up one's own advance as well as that of the enemy, the cavalry combat ensued on the extreme flank and was drawn even farther toward this side by an envelopment by the Ptolemaic forces, thereby avoiding the stake obstacle. Only those for whom it was intended, that is, the elephants, instead of exerting their well-known effect on the enemy horsemen, persisted in moving directly to the point where they were expected. Here they were received by the light infantry with missiles, and the stake or harrow works held them up and wounded them. They were captured, whereupon the courageous and initially victorious cavalry of Demetrius became terrified; they fled, and the battle was lost.

The entire account is a guard room story, not a word of which may be accepted in an historical account.

In the case of the artificial obstacle against the elephants, one could think of what is recounted in Diodorus 18. 71. This is, however, a completely different matter. At the siege of Megalopolis, in order to make a breach impassable for the elephants, Damis had planks laid down through which heavy nails had been driven, and they were lightly covered with earth. Naturally, the elephants could not pass over them, but this was a narrow, limited area in a purely defensive situation, where there was sufficient time for the work and it could be hidden from the enemy.

9. Concerning the battle of Ipsus (301 B.C.), in addition to a few fragments from Diodorus (21. 1), we have only a very short report in Plutarch's *Demetrius* (Chapter 29). Under conditions of approximately equal strength in infantry and cavalry, the allies had a very great superiority in elephants—400 (or 480) against 75. Demetrius first defeated the enemy cavalry and pursued it; when he turned back, the enemy elephants blocked his path, so that he could neither attack the enemy phalanx nor protect the flank of his own. Threatened by the rest of the enemy cavalry, Antiochus' phalanx went partially over to the side of his enemies.

If we could unreservedly trust this report, then Ipsus would have been the first battle that was decided by the elephants. On the Hydaspes, at Paraetacene, at Gabiene, at Gaza, it is always the side that is strong in elephants that loses, and even at Ipsus they did not produce a real tactical decision.

10. Antiochus' victory over the Gauls is recounted in Lucian's *Zeuxis or Antiochus* (Jacobitz edition, 1: 398). The account is quite detailed but not very credible. The Gauls are supposed to have had scythed chariots, whereas the Syrian army is supposed to have consisted principally of light infantry. The victory was decided exclusively by the sixteen elephants, the sight of which was completely new to the Gauls. The horses immediately turned about and raced with the scythed chariots through the ranks of their own men; a general panic seized the barbarians and almost the entire army perished or was captured.

BATTLE OF SELLASIA (221 B.C.)

On this battle between the Spartan King Cleomenes and the Macedonian King Antigonus we have a thorough, well-reasoned report in Polybius (2. 65) and also information in Plutarch's *Cleomenes* and *Philopoemen*. This battle could be very interesting from a military history point of view, since in it the various arms—heavy and light infantry and cavalry—appear to be cleverly combined with a greatly varying terrain and field fortifications in a manner and to a degree unmatched in a battle of antiquity. Nevertheless, in the first edition of this work I treated the battle only peremptorily, since from my analysis of the reports I was unable to discern any sufficiently reliable and clear picture of the events. It seemed to me that Polybius had lacunae in his causal relationships that could be completed only by means of hypotheses of an uncertain type; many of the details in his report even seem to contradict one another.

The situation has been significantly improved since then; Kromayer has given us an accurate topographical description of the battlefield, which brought to light a serious error in the accounts on which I still had to base my study at that time. Furthermore, repeated special studies, too, of other portions of the text have led to a different interpretation of Polybius' report.

Kromayer's own research (*Archeological Clarifications* [*Archäologische Anzeigen*], 1900, p. 204, and *Battlefields of Antiquity* [*Antike Schlachtfelder*], I: 199) is, of course, riddled with so many erroneous military concepts and so much false reasoning that it tends more to confuse and obscure than to clarify and is worthwhile only in a few details. Furthermore, I cannot concur with Lammert's astute reconstruction of the battle (*Neue Jahrbucher fur das klassische Altertum*, 1904, Division 1, Vol. 13, Books 2–4). On the other hand, Roloff, in his *Problems of Greek Military History* (*Probleme aus der griechischen Kriegsgeschichte*), if one fills in his work in *one* important aspect, has probably correctly worked out everything of a positive nature that is to be said about the battle, and he has especially analyzed critically and rejected Kromayer's aberrations.[4] In the main, of course, nothing has really been changed—that is, the battle plays no role in the development of military history and Polybius' report is too incomplete to allow one to recognize the relationships with certainty. Nevertheless, an important step forward has been realized. It is not necessary here to turn back to the details and the controversies; for this, I can refer the reader to Roloff's work. Here I shall give only a general overview and weave into it those particular details that enable me to correct something I said in the first edition [original German edition of 1901], Vol. I, p. 208 and Vol. II, p. 11, or to add still something further of a positive nature to Roloff's position.

Polybius (2. 65) tells us that Cleomenes defended the other approaches to the country by watchposts, ditches, and the felling of trees; but he himself was camped with his army near Sellasia, where he expected the enemy invasion.

These words make it sound as if all the other approaches to Lacedaemon were actually blocked and Antigonus was limited to the road from Sellasia. In reality, a country like Lacedaemon cannot be blocked off in this manner.

This passage should therefore be understood as meaning that Cleomenes had defensive positions prepared on the various approach roads that might come into question, especially in the Eurotas valley, and he moved into the position near Sellasia, 12 kilometers north of Sparta, when Antigonus' approach on this route was reported.

The road to Sparta leads here from the north through a narrow valley; the hills on the two sides are not so easy to pass around. The hill on the right (east) side, the Olympus, has a gentle slope, which Cleomenes occupied with his phalanx; the hill on the left, the Euas, which has at its front and on the left a steep slope, he turned over to light infantry, especially Lacedaemonian home guards (*Landsturm*) under the command of his brother Eucleides. In the valley he placed his small force of cavalry, again with light infantry. Across both hills extended a field fortification system with ditches, a rampart, and palisades. Cleomenes had something approaching 20,000 men, whereas Antigonus had 29,800, including 1,200 cavalry, and was therefore half again as strong.

For me, the indefinite point in this formation was the valley. The installation of the fortifications seemed to apply only to the two hills; Roloff, too, understood it in this way. But in the travel descriptions and available maps, even though they differed considerably among themselves, the valley appeared quite wide. What, therefore, was to prevent King Antigonus from rolling over the small number of horsemen and the light infantry in the valley, thereby piercing through the enemy position in the center, and then rolling up the two flanks? Kromayer's first publication seemed to me to clarify this point through the fact that the valley was very narrow, almost like a ravine, and was therefore dominated on the right and left by the hills. That turned out, however, to be a misunderstanding on my part; even if the actual valley is only 100 meters wide, nevertheless the hills rise so gently on the right and left that there can be no question of dominating the valley from above, and so I cannot agree with Roloff when he says that the penetration of the terrain at this point is impracticable. Rather, the correct solution can only be that which calls for blocking the valley, too, by fortifications. The context of Polybius' work does not rule this out, and Kromayer, too, has already stated that this interpretation is possible, but without drawing the proper conclusions from it.

With this assumption, the dispositions of Cleomenes formed an extremely strong defensive position, and if Polybius praises it by pointing out that the fighting branches were correctly arranged in it and how, as with a clever fencer, nothing was left out of consideration concerning either defensive or offensive possibilities, that statement should be understood as meaning that the Euas with its steep slopes was occupied with light infantry, whereas the Olympus, with its gentle approach, was occupied by the phalanx. It remains to be discovered to what extent the position offered the possibility of an offensive counterattack.

According to Polybius, the battle developed in such a way that Antigonus, since he realized that the position could not be overcome with a simple, direct attack, camped for several days directly in front of the Spartan position and reconnoitered it thoroughly. Then he decided to attack the left flank on the Euas, while he himself marched up on his left flank with his phalanx close to Cleomenes and, without attacking, fixed him there. His center, too, in the valley, where his cavalry was naturally placed, with some heavy infantry, was to hold back until it received the signal for the attack—that is, until the Euas was taken, which automatically effected the outflanking of the Spartans' position in the valley, which we consequently picture as protected by fortifications.

It was not such an easy matter to take the Euas with its steep slopes and the fortifications at its summit. As a reason for its falling after a very short fight, Polybius states that Eucleides, instead of moving out against the attack, as was tactically proper, awaited the attack. This explanation cannot satisfy us, since not a word of consideration is given to the fortifications in this explanation. A fortification consisting of a rampart, a ditch, and palisades (at any rate, the palisades were mentioned on the other hill) is, after all—even if we do not know exactly how high, deep, and strong it was—not so simple to storm.[5] It is also certainly not proper to lead the garrison out against the enemy on the slope, since, if it were pressed back again, it would find the hardest obstacle right up against its own fortification. At the most, it can only be a question of sending out a more or less large number of sharpshooters and particularly agile light infantry for the fight in the forward area. As one reads the account in Polybius, one can hardly avoid the suspicion that this somewhat didactically inclined author, with the tactical rule of the counterattack in mind (which only holds true when there are no real fortifications at hand), momentarily forgot about the fortification. At any rate, his explanation for Eucleides' defeat does not suffice. When we then find it mentioned in Plutarch that the Euas was taken by an envelopment, that forms an additional element that we can hardly reject, even if its validity is not great insofar as its source is concerned.

Kromayer (p. 259) cites by way of clarification of his opinion—"reluctantly," as he says, since it is a question of the obvious—some rather long observations from modern military authors, which provide an excellent example of how dangerous historical analogies become in the hands of a novice. That is, Kromayer did not see at all that the conditions are different for troops with nineteenth-century cannon, firearms, and fieldworks from those applying to troops of antiquity without long-range arms. In antiquity, a modern, short entrenchment would be not only worthless but dangerous, since this trench, with the low effectiveness of the missile weapons, would quickly be enveloped and taken from the rear. Troops of antiquity, therefore, can only use either very long lines or completely enclosed camps with a few narrow openings. This also creates completely different conditions for an advance out of a fortification.

In a modern trench system troops fleeing from the terrain in front of the battle line come back in through the narrow entrance while the fire of the garrison hits and holds up the enemy. In the extended or enclosed entrenchments of antiquity, however, the troops who are being driven back from the forward terrain cannot get in again—unless it be only a few men—since the enemy is following much too closely on their heels. When Kromayer, therefore, adds to his gleanings from modern military authors the advice to transfer these rules analogously to the conditions of antiquity, then his "reluctance" against this whole investigation has tricked him to the point that he himself did not carry through the analogous transposition, and so, despite his study, the problem has remained as it was—that is, Polybius' account as well as his criticism concerning the events on the Euas leaves us with obscurities that we are not in a position to dispel.

The false modern analogies with which Kromayer works tactically are, moreover, almost exceeded by his strategic comparison of Cleomenes' position to Benedek's conduct in Bohemia in 1866. There is not even the slightest similarity between these two, but rather in each and every respect quite the direct opposite.

When the troops of Antigonus had begun their climb up the Euas, the Spartan troops in the center made a sudden sortie and fell on the flank and rear of the attackers. The Macedonian center, awaiting the command of the King, stood passively by, so that the attackers of the Euas might have been easily defeated. The bold initiative of the young Megalopolitan Philopoemen, however, set the Macedonian cavalry in action; their counterattack drove back the Spartan center, which had been followed by its own cavalry as a covering force,[7] and that enabled the attackers to storm the Euas.

The account by Polybius in this episode is completely unobjectionable. It is particularly noteworthy that precisely here Kromayer (p. 238) states very stiffly: "There can be no question of Philopoemen's receiving, as Polybius claims, the credit for the success of the attack against the Euas." In exactly the same way, furthermore, Roloff (pp. 72 ff.) has shown that also in the preceding campaign of the two kings Kromayer rejects precisely those judgments of Polybius the correctness of which cannot be doubted.

In his first account of the battle, Kromayer had claimed that 4,000 men whom Antigonus ordered to follow the attackers as a reserve were supposed to "mask" this attack. I have remarked in that connection (1st ed., Vol. II, p. 14), that I could not conceive of this. To what extent, after all, could the 4,000 men have covered the fact that other units of the great army were undertaking other tasks? Kromayer now says of this point (p. 261) that he could even have considered the entire deployment of the Macedonian army as a masking of the sudden attack on the Euas. I have no objection to make to that, no more so than if Kromayer had written now that, instead of a military absurdity, he could *even* have said something correct. He would even have had many an opportunity to do this.

While the Macedonians were taking the Euas and the valley position, during which on both sides, aside from the cavalry, the fighting was principally by the light infantry, the two phalanxes were in position on the Olympus, deployed opposite each other, and only the light infantrymen assigned to them—who were, it is true, quite numerous—skirmished out in front. Antigonus knew very well how dangerous it would have been for him to storm the Spartan fortification behind which their phalanx stood. Not until his other wing had been victorious and was threatening Cleomenes' flank from the valley and his phalanx from the rear, did the moment for action arrive. But Cleomenes, recognizing the defeat of that half of his army, did not await Antigonus' attack but ordered the palisades to be torn down and moved out over his own fortifications to attack the Macedonians. Despite an initial success, however, he finally could not avoid defeat, since his own phalanx was only 6,000 men strong, whereas the enemy phalanx had 10,000 men.

Here is the real problem of the battle: Polybius says that Cleomenes had been forced to move to the attack ("he was constrained"*) but does not indicate what forced him and to what extent. After all, one can imagine many possibilities. Did he have no route of withdrawal over the mountains? This is what Kromayer claims from his knowledge of the terrain. That, however, would have been such a serious error in the position that Polybius could not possibly have failed to comment on it. After all, how many of his readers could know that? Furthermore, was it impossible to entrust the defense of the palisade to the light infantry, and in the meanwhile to lead the phalanx as quickly as possible into the valley and bring about there, if not a turn in the fortune of battle, at least the possibility of a withdrawal? What did Cleomenes have in mind anyway with his attack? Did he still hope for victory? Or an honorable defeat? In the end he was still able to save himself, although most of the soldiers of his phalanx were killed.

Polybius leaves us no answer to all these questions. From the entire context, Roloff worked out as probable the fact that Cleomenes, when he saw that the valley road, his withdrawal route, was lost, realized that the sudden dash against the enemy phalanx was the only chance of a victory, however slim that chance might be, and in any case the most honorable defeat. If he had waited longer behind his entrenchment, he would soon have been surrounded on all sides. If he had turned down into the valley immediately, that would only have become a disorderly flight and, under the best circumstances, a withdrawal without further hope.

It is quite probable that it happened this way, but nevertheless, as Roloff himself stressed most strongly, no more than an hypothesis. Inasmuch as Polybius does not reveal the subject to us clearly, we cannot arrive at the answer to the principal question: how does a Greek-Macedonian phalanx go about defending a field fortification? In the defense of the Euas Polybius had the defender moving out to meet the attacker in front of his fortifications. Here we are dealing with light infantry, who are able to move back into the fortification relatively fast. Despite this, the whole matter seemed quite doubtful to us, since with a rather large number such a withdrawal is still difficult under any circumstances and can cause heavy losses. Polybius himself knows this difficulty and does not clarify it, but rather makes no further mention of the fortifications, so that the suspicion arises that he expressed a rule that refers to combat without fortifications in a context where, because of the presence of fortifications, it did not apply. Now, on the Olympus, where the men of the heavy phalanx were formed up behind the fortification, Polybius states that they tore down the defenses in order to make their sortie. It seems quite clear that there was no other possibility, if they wanted to attack. The fact that no fewer than 5,000 light infantry are supposed to have fought already in front of the palisades is difficult to understand; but to let the phalanx soldiers out, the palisades had to come down. But what if they now, as is after all the true purpose of a fortification, wanted to defend it instead of destroying it? It would be very interesting to have some information on this from one of our sources. Only then would we be able to understand Cleomenes' battle plan fully and judge its value. Unfortunately, in this respect, too, Polybius leaves us once again in the dark. I would believe, if the phalanx soldiers did not simply defend the wall and the palisades, as the legionaries of Caesar did at the circumvallation of Alesia, that it would probably be the normal thing for the light infantry to defend the fortification and the phalanx to be stationed a few dozen paces behind them, in reserve. If then the enemy drove back the light infantry, stormed the fortification, and in the course of driving into it lost his tactical formation, the phalanx would then move forward and throw him back with an offensive push. In actual fact, however, at Sellasia the light infantry were deployed in front of the fortification, and the phalanx, when it wished to move out to the attack, tore down its own palisades in order to make room for the movement. Tactically, therefore, the fortification served no purpose at all.

Under these circumstances it also remains uncertain whether Polybius, when he praises the position of Cleomenes for being suited to the attack also, had in mind only the possibility of an attack in the valley, or if he also considered this attack of the phalanx out over its own destroyed fortifications. For one can hardly imagine that Cleomenes had had that in mind from the very start. Nevertheless, since the possibility did exist, we may also consider that Polybius included it in connection with his statement. Finally, however, Polybius may also have thought of an offensive drive by the phalanx behind the fortification, after the enemy had overrun it and was still in disorder. Here, too, we cannot go beyond suppositions and possibilities.

Both Polybius and Plutarch say that the Macedonian phalanx was victorious over the courage of the Lacedaemonians because of its tactical uniqueness. Polybius, who has reported previously that the depth of the phalanx was doubled because of the narrowness of the terrain, speaks of the "weight" of the Macedonian formation. Plutarch speaks not only of the mass but also of the type of armament. "through the use of their equipment and the weight of their phalanx of hoplites,"* which gave the Macedonians the preponderance. This observation would be very interesting if it were not subject to suspicion resulting from questionable aspects of the sources. At another place (Chapter 11; see also Chapter 23), that is, Plutarch has told us that Cleomenes had armed and drilled the Spartan hoplites with the sarissa, thereby introducing the Macedonian style of close combat. If they themselves had already accepted it, how could the Lacedaemonians succumb precisely to the uniqueness of the Macedonian art of war? The sources make no mention of their not understanding it sufficiently or of their not yet having trained sufficiently, but seek the reason for the defeat in the differences of the opposing formations.

The contribution of this battle to the history of the art of war is therefore but little. Only in a very general way can we conclude from this how the art of leadership, the combining of weapons, the exploitation of the terrain have been improved and refined. On both sides the number of light infantry, who adapt themselves more readily to the terrain, is very great. A constant and continuing development in this direction does not, however, seem to be imminent. That will be seen in the later collision of the Macedonians with the Romans.

BATTLE OF RAPHIA (217 B.C.)

At Raphia Ptolemy IV of Egypt and Antiochus of Syria fought against each other. In infantry Ptolemy had a small superiority (70,000 against 62,000), but Antiochus had a greater one in cavalry (6,000 against 5,000) and elephants (102 against 73). Polybius' account (5. 86) is very simple, but still not quite irreproachable.

Antiochus was victorious at first on his right flank with his superiority in cavalry and in elephants. Ptolemy's peltasts, who were next in the line, were also involved in this defeat. As reason for the defeat of the Egyptian elephants, Polybius states that the African race of these animals was not up to the quality of the Indian animals; they were afraid of their size and strength and shied from their smell and their cry. Modern naturalists reject this contrast;[8] the African elephant is not only not smaller but actually larger than the Indian, and the two species do not shy away at all from each other but get along very well. There is, therefore, much to be said for the supposition that it was not so much the advantage of the race that led the Indian elephants to victory here,[9] as the greater skill of the Indian mahouts, who had an old tradition in this respect, whereas the Egyptians were only imitating them and had no practice in training.

While Antiochus was winning in this manner on the flank that he himself commanded, on the opposite flank in a similar way the Egyptian cavalry was victorious, in spite of the elephants, which here as on the other flank were assigned to the cavalry wings.

Now Polybius reproaches Antiochus for having driven on in the pursuit following his victory. Demetrius is supposed to have made the same mistake at Ipsus, and we shall encounter this error again quite often, for example at Naraggara (Zama) in 202 B.C. and Mollwitz in 1741. We would not hesitate to attribute the final decision at

Raphia to this point if we were told that the victorious Egyptian cavalry wing on the other flank had attacked the enemy phalanx in the flank instead of falling into this same error. But we hear nothing of the kind; rather, the two phalanxes are said to have fought against each other in quite isolated fashion, with the result that the Egyptian phalanx defeated the Syrian.

The important point that we learn from this battle could be that the elephants were, in general, formed up not in conjunction with the phalanx, but with the cavalry, and that their effect, however, was still not the decisive one.

BATTLE OF MANTINEA (207 B.C.)

Kromayer's accurate topographic description of the battlefield has not changed anything in the historical account. His military history study, closely tied in with the topography, was successful in two places, however, in clarifying points that I had misunderstood in the first edition of this work. But at the same time he once again brought the whole matter into a false light, not simply because of erroneous military reasoning, but also because of repeated translation errors. This has been pointed out by Roloff with excellent clarity and accuracy in his *Problems from Greek Military History* (*Probleme aus der griechischen Kriegsgeschichte*). Consequently I can forgo discussing the controversies in detail here. and I simply repeat what I already said in the first edition, passing over or correcting. as appropriate, those points that have been taken care of or corrected by the two authors named above

Once again we have Polybius' account which has not come down to us in its entirety, however, and also Plutarch, who drew on the other, lost, work of Polybius on Philopoemen.

According to Polybius, Philopoemen formed up the Achaeans behind a trench with both flanks resting on hills. Nevertheless, the Spartans under the tyrant Machanidas moved in against them. A new instrument of war is said to have been employed here for the first time in a field battle: Machanidas had a number of catapults moved up in front of his phalanx, in order to fire on the enemy phalanx. To forestall this, Philopoemen started the battle by having the light cavalry (Tarentines) who were stationed on his left flank and other lightly armed mercenaries move forward.

The logic of this combination is not entirely clear. Philopoemen had taken up a defensive position with an obstacle to his front and is now supposed to have had his own flank move forward over this obstacle.[10] What was supposed to be gained by this? If the Achaean light infantry was victorious, then the question was whether the phalanx should follow or not. If it followed, then it would have to cross over the frontal obstacle of its own choosing in the full view of the enemy; if it did not follow, the victory of the light infantry was useless, and they would have to withdraw before the enemy phalanx. Furthermore, one does not quite understand how the battle of the light infantry on the one flank is supposed to have impeded the work of the catapults in the center, least of all since in that fight the Spartan light infantry was victorious and drove the Achaeans off across the trench in flight.[11]

Now victory would have belonged to Machanidas if he had fallen on the Achaean phalanx in the flank with his victorious right wing, while his own phalanx attacked it simultaneously from the front. The trench would then have been as ineffective in saving the Achaeans as was the Granicus or the Pinarus at Issus in saving the Persians and the Greek hoplites. But Machanidas, instead of making this obvious movement, either did not have his men sufficiently under control or was, as Polybius says, impassioned and childish enough to charge blindly after the fleeing enemy. Philopoemen, on the other hand, assembled as many as possible of the defeated soldiers behind his phalanx and pushed a portion of the phalanx toward the left onto the position that the fugitives had left open, and as the Lacedaemonian phalanx. confident of its victory, now charged forward against his phalanx, Philopoemen led

his phalanx against them at the moment when they were crossing the trench and
had fallen into disorder, and he defeated them.

In opposition to this account there arises a whole series of questions and doubts.

From which place did Philopoemen take the phalanx soldiers who lengthened the
front? According to the text, it was the closest units of the phalanx that
Philopoemen deployed there, and with larger intervals than ordinarily. There was
consequently now a wide breach in the Achaeans' formation. With equal forces, that
would have to be counted as an outright error. Why Philopoemen could risk such a
maneuver, Polybius does not say; in fact, he gives no real reason at all for the entire
maneuver of the voluntary tearing apart of his own battle line. Furthermore, we
have no information about what Philopoemen would have done or planned to do if
the Lacedaemonian phalanx waited to attack until the moment when Machanidas
came back from the pursuit and attacked him from behind.

The logical explanation would be that we picture the Achaeans as being considerably stronger. Unfortunately, on this decisive point, too, Polybius leaves us in the
dark. But he states expressly that Machanidas was the stronger of the two on the
flank where he initially was victorious, not only in the quality of his troops, but also
in the numbers involved. Now since these troops were for the moment at a distance
from the battlefield, we can imagine that Philopoemen had a very considerable
superiority in this short period, which enabled him both to divide his phalanx in two
and to consider taking the offensive. This now seems to be the proper maneuver for
him.

We would normally expect that Philopoemen would now take up the offensive
with his admittedly breached but extended battle line and would seize the
Lacadaemonians in their uncovered flank with his superior wing. That appears all
the more necessary in that at any moment the return of the victorious Machanidas
could be expected. Only some 2,000 paces behind the battlefield lies the city of Mantinea, beyond which the pursuit could not be continued, and Machanidas might even
realize sooner that there was still something to do in the battle. Then he would have
attacked the phalanx in the rear: the assembled stragglers would hardly have held
him up very much.

According to Polybius' account, however, it was not Philopoemen who moved out
in the attack but the Lacedaemonians, and it was not the improvised lengthening of
the flank that gave the decision, but everything can be attributed exclusively to the
frontal obstacle, the trench.

Our suspicions with respect to the unconditional reliability of Polybius' account
that we have at hand are now necessarily increased, however, when we read the
completely different account in Plutarch's *Philopoemen*. That is, we find here precisely what we missed in Polybius: that it was the Achaean phalanx that took up the
offensive and that it was this phalanx that fell on the flank of the enemy, who was
not expecting an attack:

"He straightway led in the Lacedaemonians when he saw that the phalanx had
been left exposed, and he charged, passing over along the flanks, for they had lost
their leader and were unprepared to fight. For they reckoned that they could win
the battle and get the upper hand over the lot of them, when they saw that
Machanidas was in pursuit."*

Efforts have been made in various ways to reconstruct the battle. H. Droysen assumes that Machanidas knew nothing of the existence of the trench and could not
see it during his approach march. That solves only a portion of our difficulties and
is only barely credible in view of the proximity of Mantinea and Lacedaemon. In the
opposite vein, C. Guischard (*Military Memoirs* [*Mémoires militaires*], 10: 159) conjectures that Machanidas assumed from the start that the Achaeans would deploy behind the trench, and for that reason he had had his catapults brought up and put
into play. He further assumes that the report of Polybius has come down to us with
lacunae, and he fills these voids partly from his fantasy, partly from Plutarch—for

example, the contradiction between the lengthening of the Achaean flank for the purpose of an envelopment and the persistence in remaining on the defensive he explains in this manner: Philopoemen saw, at the moment when he himself had planned to go over to the attack, how the Lacedaemonians were already in motion, and now, naturally, first became aware of the advantage of his defensive position and (according to Plutarch) ordered his extended, superior left flank to swing inward and cross over the trench at the moment when the Spartans were seeking to cross.

This is probably correct as to the principal points, but it assumes, as we have said, a considerable superiority on the part of the Achaeans, for without that the commander could not have considered an attack in two separated masses, of which at least one was charged with the difficult trench-crossing.

Polybius also fails to inform us sufficiently concerning the other wing of the Achaeans. On this flank was posted their own assembled cavalry—therefore heavy cavalry. Are we to assume that this unit had no effect against the enemy phalanx; in what way, then, was it hindered from doing so? The failure to mention this unit is all the more noticeable in that Polybius previously described in detail (10. 22–24) the advantages that Philopoemen had acquired precisely as a result of the reorganization of the Achaean cavalry. H. Droysen (p. 182) has conjectured that the cavalry, which could not be employed behind the trench, had probably been held aside for the pursuit. But on the one hand we hear that the trench could be crossed without serious difficulty, and on the other it would have been after all much too gross an error to have the horsemen stationed here and stand fast, while on the other flank they could possibly have prevented the defeat.

For our purpose we are concerned not so much with eliminating the contradictions and lacunae as with identifying them, in order to draw from them the conclusion that one may probably not give much credence to the account in a history of the art of war.

Kromayer's account suffers from the following errors: He either did not recognize or insufficiently filled in the lacunae in Polybius' account, such as we know it; he overlooked the faultiness of concept in splitting a phalanx when the opposing forces are equal; and finally he sought to correct Polybius at the wrong place in the latter's text. We have seen that Polybius expressly points out Machanidas' right, victorious wing as numerically superior. Kromayer sees in this an intentional untruth; according to him, Polybius, in his outspoken preference for the Achaeans, wanted to cover up their not very creditable defeat.[12] Not only is there no basis for such a suspicion of Polybius, but also the false correction eliminates, as we have seen, the most logical (though admittedly only hypothetical) explanation of the battle, for if in fact a considerable number of Achaeans were defeated here by a smaller unit, then there is all the less chance that they still had the superiority for the decisive battle, without which the maneuver of Philopoemen is incomprehensible.

Let it not be said that I am being unduly cautious in declining to make use of this kind of uncertain account of military events for the history of the art of war. For the simple historical account, events that can be reconstructed with a certain degree of probability may suffice, but a history of the art of war demands a more rigorous basis consisting only of events that are completely verified by the sources. It is true that we know much less still about the battles of the Persian Wars than about Sellasia and Mantinea and have nevertheless taken the Persian battles as a point of departure for the whole series of developments. But it is only the principles that we have taken from these battles and, in view of the simplicity of the structures of that period, that is all we *could* extract from them; the positive, detailed points there we have in many cases had to leave in doubt, and we have been able to do so. In the period of Polybius the events are so much more complicated that only very exact reports can satisfy the demands that we must make.

NOTES FOR CHAPTER VII

1. H. Droysen *Studies* (*Untersuchungen*), p. 155. Droysen incorrectly concludes, precisely from the fact of the energetic drilling, that there was a worsening of the soldier material. Rather, one may draw from the energy of the military training the opposite conclusion—i.e., that a strong military spirit existed. The conclusion on p. 132, too, that with the increasing size of the armies the material must have gotten continuously worse, is inadmissible. In the huge area of all the Diadochi empires the militarily qualified material was hardly exhausted even with a few hundred thousand men, and "pirates" can become very excellent soldiers.

2. Athenaeus reports (5. 35. 202–203) about a procession in Alexandria in about 275 or 274 B.C. in which 57,600 dismounted men and 23,210 mounted men had formed the rear units.

Appian reports in *Preface*, Chapter 10, that Ptolemy II had possessed, toward the end of his reign, an army of 200,000 dismounted men, 40,000 cavalry, 300 elephants, 2,000 war chariots, 1,500 warships and 2,000 transport ships.

Paul M. Meyer, in *The Military System of the Ptolemies and the Romans in Egypt* (*Das Heerwesen der Ptolemäer und Römer in Aegypten*), p. 8, accepts these figures. Nevertheless, it is not hard to recognize that they are greatly exaggerated. One need only imagine what a parade of 57,600 dismounted men and 23,210 mounted men through the streets of a city means. Egypt may at that time have had 3 to 4 million inhabitants (Beloch, *Population* [*Bevölkerung*], p. 258); or 7 million, as it was reported and apparently accepted by Ulrich Wilcken, *Greek Potsherds from Egypt and Nubia* (*Griechische Ostraka aus Aegypten and Nubien*), p. 490. This would have made a standing army of 240,000 men amount to 3½ to 7 percent of the population. A fifth of the reported figures would still be quite a large number.

3. According to Chapter 69, Demetrius has 5,000 cavalry; if one adds up those individual troop units that are described in the battle formation, one finds only 4,400.

4. In a review of the Roloff book in *Berliner Philologische Wochenschrift*, 6 August 1904, Column 992, Kromayer states that the differences between his position and that of Roloff are not very important. That is an illusion, as Roloff himself wrote in his reply to the review in the same weekly.

5. Kromayer, p. 237, note 3, states that the fact that Polybius

never again mentions the entrenchments on the ridge is very understandable, since they accomplished no good. Quite right—but why did they accomplish nothing? It is precisely this point that we would have to know in order to understand the battle.

6. Kromayer's statement in the note on p. 234, that there is no basic difference between Polybius' account and Plutarch, is inaccurate. According to Plutarch, we must assume that the Illyrians actually did envelop the Euas and climbed up the height where the fortification no longer extended. The modern reader, with his map before him, can also read that into Polybius' account, but in his text itself one reads only of a frontal attack. This difference between the two sources is very important and in no way simply the use of a *terminus technicus* that one could omit, if he wished, as Kromayer states.

7. Since we must necessarily assume that the valley, too, was blocked by a fortification, then the situation cannot be conceived in any other way than it is presented above. Polybius has the Spartan light infantry move out to the flank attack against the attackers of the Euas and then move back again when their cavalry was attacked by the enemy horsemen. The horsemen, too, therefore must have moved out in front of the fortification (presumably the valley fortification had some kind of gate). Here Kromayer translated erroneously in several respects, as Roloff proves on pp. 108 ff, and thereby he arrives at the false judgment, repeated above, of Philopoemen's deed and at the unwarranted rejection of Polybius.

8. Bolau (director of the Zoological Garden in Hamburg), *The Elephant in War and Peace* (*Der Elefant in Krieg und Frieden*), 1887, pp. 8 and 13.

9. Scharff, *On the Nature and Utilization of African Elephants in Antiquity* (*De natura et usu elephantorum Africanorum apud veteres*), Weimar, Program of 1855.

10. Kromayer believes that the trench did not stretch across the whole plain but came to an end in front of the left flank of the Achaeans. The text of Polybius, however, as Roloff has shown, contradicts this concept. But one can imagine, for example, that it was easier to cross at the east end than in the middle and at the west end. By no means has anything changed with respect to the objection I raised above; even if the trench did not extend to a point in front of the left flank of the Achaeans, one cannot understand what the partial offensive was supposed to accomplish.

11. Fougères, *Bulletin de Correspondence hellenique* 14: 82, seeks to

fill this lacuna by means of the forced correction that the catapults had fired not on the phalanx, as Polybius reports, but on the left flank of the Achaeans.

12. In his review of Roloff's *Problems (Probleme)*, *Berliner Philologische Wochenschrift*, 6 August 1904, Section 995, note 4, Kromayer retracted this charge but did not draw the necessary logical conclusions from the matter.

BOOK IV
Ancient Rome

Chapter I

Knights and Phalanx

If we wished to begin the history of the Roman military system and experience on the same bases that we used for that of the Greeks, we would have to start with the Second Punic War. For it is not until this period that we have accounts that give us a truly reliable and clear picture of the course of a battle and the special character of the Roman methods of combat. But as in the case of Roman history, Roman historiography, too, is of a completely different type from that of the Greeks; we can trace with reliability the development of the Roman political system much farther back than that of the Greeks, and from that there results another procedure for our purpose. The Greek city-states either had in their constitutions something conducive to stagnation, as in Sparta, which is moreover only vaguely known to us, or they plunged from one radical change to another, so that Aristotle was able to count eleven different constitutions for Athens, each of which replaced its predecessor. In all the convulsions that Rome experienced, it still maintained a continuity of development.[1] Even the transition from kingdom to republic, though no doubt a revolution, nevertheless carried on the old political system in its important basic concepts. And so, too, the institutions, even in a much later period, allow in their forms the earlier stages of the development to be recognized and lead us far back into periods for which we no longer possess a direct line of historical source accounts. The voting arrangements of later periods retained some elements of the army organization of primeval times. The real account of the more ancient Roman history is completely legendary; almost nothing but the purely obvious dates of wars and battles or the names of commanders has been passed down with independent certainty. But with the Roman historians of the ancient period there lived a tradition concerning the development of Roman political law and of the military constitution, which was constantly verified in the present and therefore never got completely lost in fantasy and which also "disciplined" the legend from a historical point of view, so to speak.

Historical research would have arrived more easily at verified results if this peculiar legal-political tradition had not been very strongly glossed over with political bias and in important places absolutely falsified. But with the passage of time the historical method has found ways and means of recognizing these falsifications and expunging them. Whereas earlier even critical historians naïvely repeated that the census that King Servius Tullius had carried out resulted in a total of 80,000 citizens, today we know that we can check on such figures through the size of the national area and the city itself, and we eliminate them, with all the results that follow for the history of the constitution.

With these and similar reservations, we can place a certain trust in the reports that have come down to us. Our tools separating the truth from the legendary, the false, the misunderstood, and whatever else has naturally slipped in, are the conditions of that period that we can recognize in the clear light of history, plainly and with certainty. Those bits of information that, as preludes to the historically clear period, arrange themselves in sequence without contradiction must be the right ones: those that can be understood in no way, not even as exceptions, speculations, transitory aberrations or the like, are to be rejected.

Many indications point to the fact that in Italy mounted combat in the ancient times had a greater importance than in Greece. In the first edition of this work I contented myself at this point with this statement and referred to the continuation of the presentation, where I would once again come back to this point. In order to be able to illuminate and make understandable the social significance of the cavalry arm among the economic conditions of the Latin race, I first needed to present to the reader the institution of medieval knighthood in its entire breadth and to develop it genetically. A true insight into the values of these military-social forms is not to be achieved with a few abstract sentences. Since the third volume of this work is now available, I may be allowed to refer to it and to apply to the Roman prehistorical period the conclusions that the medieval forms allow us to draw.[2] It is a matter of taking into consideration the highly developed mounted combat in Italy as a factor contributing to the birth of the patrician class in Rome.

The fact that in the level middle part of Italy cavalry combat was actually much more highly developed in ancient times than in central Greece and in the Peloponnesus is inherent in the nature of things and is contained in the historical accounts. It is true that all the individual combats and fights in the first books of Livy are to be regarded as absolutely mythical, but the general preponderance of cavalry combat stands out so strongly that one can spot in this fact a reflection of reality. If one is not willing to give credence to that and sees in these accounts nothing but fiction composed for the foremost houses in Rome, we nevertheless still have testimony for the history of Capua, which, though indirect, is still very weighty. Of this city which, next to Rome, was the most important one of this whole area, Livy informs us at the very beginning of the Second Punic War that the infantry was lacking in fighting spirit, whereas the cavalry was very competent.[3] He describes an individual combat between two horsemen with the lance, quite like the ones we read about medieval knights. The difference in the development of the two cities probably consisted of this: Capua remained at this stage of possessing a skilled mounted arm but a useless infantry, whereas Rome, through organization, strict military training, and discipline, also developed the mass of her citizens into useful and skilled soldiers. The preponderant and almost exclusive effectiveness of the cavalry had lasted long enough, however, to establish a sharp distinction between the status of those who bore and used their weapons in this manner and the mass of common citizens and farmers. The idea that the patricians had formed the original citizenry and the plebeians were the immigrants—that the difference of classes lay, therefore, in their place of origin—is adopted, it is true, by no less a person than Theodor Mommsen, but it completely contradicts the sources, as he himself admits, and was probably only an expedient, because no other explanation could be found. The key to the correct solution of this problem is given to us by the fact, which we can now take from the history of the Middle Ages, of the uncommon superiority of the knights over bourgeois and peasant infantry before the latter are trained and accustomed to being grouped together in tactical units. There was a time in Rome when the phalanx of legionaries did not yet exist. The idea that Romulus had a legion can be eliminated as a fable without any valid source. At that time the decisive power was the Roman knight. We shall have to regard as the nucleus of this group the old families of clan chieftains, all or most of which gradually had moved their residence to the city, possibly because of a kind of "living together,"* as it is reported in Greece. From the city these families, both rich and warlike, also dominated the countryside. In the city, which was a center of trade, the transition point for sea traffic and the great river region of the Tiber, the economic position of these families developed greatly. They dominated the whole canton, the small peasant residents of the flat land, both through their military skill and their loans. The oldest Roman history is full of the usury practices by which the patricians oppressed the plebeians.

Regardless of how sharp and impassable the division between patricians and plebeians was later on in Rome, the historical accounts nevertheless lead us to believe that, at its origin, the patrician status was not quite uniform. There was a difference between older and younger families. Successful merchants who were also capable of performing military duty and accepted such duty were probably absorbed into the class of the older families, just as we see in the medieval cities the original knightly families being blended into a single class with rising merchants. But in Rome it appears that the element of the old warrior chieftain families was stronger and the commercial element weaker than in the cities of the Middle Ages, and in any case the warrior element was indispensable in the formation of the patriciate. It was evidently not a purely economic development; a ruling class based on a purely economic standard and composed of a few families favored by fortune would not have met with the approval of the mass of the Latin people.[4] But in the joining of warrior superiority and ruthlessly exploited financial power there developed a new aristocratic class stemming from the original group, a class that eventually also disdained marriage with their fellow citizens, the plebeians, and, as a fraternity particularly favored by the gods, demanded and held the dominant position.

The number of military-economic-based aristocratic families that formed the patriciate in the most ancient period of Rome we must regard as very small. External military power was therefore very small, as in the case of the medieval cities. And so it happened, according to one of our sources that we may trust, that Rome came under the domination of neighboring Etruscan princes.

The Latin city freed itself again from this foreign domination and it is entirely possible that this struggle, as it progressed, provided the occasion for the extension and transformation of the previous military organization, based purely on the knighthood. Joining now with the knightly organization came the levy of the entire citizenry and peasant group in a compact mass, in the phalanx. This organization was carried out by a king who was provided with absolute power. These Roman kings were not a hereditary dynasty, nor were they tyrants in the Greek sense, but they were the highest official, invested for their lifetime. From the Greek point of view they would most appropriately be called archons; the clearest understanding would be given us by the title "doge." As with the most ancient Venetian doges, the Roman kings, too, had at hand a council, the Senate, but it hardly limited them, and the desire to make the royal position hereditary may also have created in this period of Roman history inner conflicts as in ancient Venice. The principle of the office, however, was maintained and was developed into the highest power and sternness, since the patriarchal mildness that often accompanies hereditary royalty was missing, and the precarious situation of the nation allowed only the strongest personalities to be entrusted with this office. It was such a ruler who organized the armed levy of the people, the phalanx of infantry.

He divided the Roman canton into 20 tribes, 4 of which were in the city and 16 in the countryside. Each tribe was further divided into 4 centuries, 3 of which were charged with appearing with protective armor, by which, of course, we can hardly assume in this older period full hoplite equipment, but for most men only the most necessary items in the way of shield and head protection. The fourth century was composed of the light infantry, the Greek *psiloi*, who simultaneously were used as orderlies, wagoners, and for secondary military tasks. Since the soldiers provided themselves with weapons, a certain financial position was involved in becoming a hoplite. If proletarians were assigned with them, the state had to give them their weapons.[5]

Whereas in Athens each hoplite was assigned a lightly armed man, in Rome service was so much more austere that three hoplites had to be content with the services of a single lightly armed man, and while this orderly in Athens was often surely a mere slave, in Rome he was also a citizen who could be assigned combat duties.

By the time of the banning of the kings, the area had been broadened somewhat and a new tribe, the 21st, the Clustuminian, was organized, all 4 of whose centuries, however, were set up only for light service, so that now there were 2 lightly armed men for every 5 hoplites, and Rome now had altogether 84 centuries of infantry. In addition to these, there were also, aside from 6 centuries of cavalry, 2 centuries of smiths and carpenters, 2 of trumpeters and buglers, and 1 of quartermaster officials and scribes (*accensi*).

The Roman national area at the time of the elimination of the kings embraced no more than a scant 370 square miles (983 square kilometers), much less than half of Attica. When the phalanx was introduced, it was still somewhat smaller. At a time when the area was still so small, the city, too, cannot yet have been large; otherwise it would have overpowered the surrounding small towns earlier and faster. The country town of Veii, which was situated at only 9 miles from the gates of Rome, was not subjected and drawn into the Roman sphere until more than 100 years later. The area and the population of a city always have a certain relationship to each other. The maximum that one may assume for the Roman nation of that period is probably something over 150 souls to the square mile, and therefore altogether some 60,000 inhabitants, a few thousands of whom must be subtracted as slaves.[6]

With a population not as high as 60,000 free inhabitants, the number of service-qualified men between seventeen and forty-six can be estimated at 9,000 to 10,000, the number of older men and physically unfit at some 5,000 to 6,000, and the total of adult male citizens at 16,000.

From these numbers it is evident that the tribes and centuries were not recruiting areas but were each a division of the general levy; they included all the service-qualified men and corresponded to the name "hundred unit" only if all the men were actually assembled together. For the 9,000 to 10,000 men qualified for field service were divided, as we have seen, among 95 centuries (84 centuries of infantry, 5 auxiliary centuries, 6 centuries of cavalry).

When the last king, whom the historical record calls Tarquinius Superbus, was deposed and banished, the constitution was changed in such a way that, in the place of one superior official with lifetime tenure, there were to be two officials chosen each year, initially called praetors, later consuls. This election was carried out by the people through their army organization, the centuries. From this point on, therefore, the centuries were no longer simply levy organizations but political voting bodies. They remained as such through all the changes of the Roman constitution, and it is because of this that the original military organization of the Roman people is known to us.

In order to use the levy organization for this political purpose, the election of the consuls (praetors), the old men, too, who were no longer service-qualified, had to be organized. Consequently, parallel to the 84 centuries of the *juniores* there were created 84 centuries of *seniores*, and this resulted, either intentionally or by the fortuitous circumstances of the organization, in giving the older citizens a considerably greater voice than the younger ones. The cavalry and the auxiliary centuries were not divided into *seniores* and *juniores*, from which we may conclude that by their nature they were somewhat different from the infantry centuries. The latter were nothing more than the levy organization, and therefore the old men, as long as the military levy was the only purpose, had not belonged. On the other hand, the cavalry centuries should be looked on as mounted societies, to which the old men also had always belonged, who, in keeping with the knightly character, also continued to ride along into battle. In like manner the smiths, carpenters, musicians, and scribes were professional fraternities, guilds if one will, which by their nature also included older men.

This insight into the relationship of the later Roman voting and election procedure with the original military organization has been available for a long time and is not only confirmed for us through the so obviously military allocation principle, but it is also particularly clarified by the reconciliation of the numbers involved. In the first period of the Roman Republic the state was divided into 21 tribes, but the normal strength of the legion—that is, the half of the total levy commanded by each consul—was, as late as the second century B.C., 4,200 men on foot. These two figures have been passed down with consistent certainty and cannot possibly agree with each other by pure coincidence. They can be explained rather in this way: at the founding of the Republic one half of the infantry levy was actually 4,200 men, compared with 300 horsemen, and this number, in itself purely circumstantial, was then retained continuously as the normal strength. The third figure contained in the accounts does not agree exactly with the others—that is, the number of centuries of *juniores* amounted to 85, instead of 84, as we would expect. A very simple explanation has been found for this small deviation, however (see below, comment 1), so that even this figure, despite the error in it, can be regarded as a confirmation of those two others, and consequently of the entire system.

That the *seniores* centuries were not added until later, when the army units were serving as voting bodies, cannot be subject to doubt. An actual levy of the men over forty-six years of age was such a rare event that there certainly did not exist for this purpose a continuing organization with its burdensome registration procedures.[7] The accounts with which authors who lived 200 to 300 years later recorded the wars of Camillus and spoke of the levy of the *seniores* have absolutely no source validity for us.

As the basic principle of the Roman military constitution, as it was already created under the kings and continued in the Republic, we have recognized universal military service, universal service in the sternest imaginable effort and extent.

The Roman military constitution had a much stricter application than the Athenian, even if we take into account the latter's effort at sea, which did not exist for the Romans. For this effort in Athens was, after all, except for individual short periods, mostly accomplished by mercenaries or even slaves.

The Roman military constitution also went deeper than the Spartan. For in Sparta the great mass of the peasants were not free and were neither qualified nor required to do military service until the necessities of the Peloponnesian War broke down this principle.

The military effort of Rome is all the greater in that the pay that was given—and had to be given—to the soldier serving in the field was not obtained from the tribute of some subject people or other, as in Athens, but had to be raised through taxes. The historical accounts connect the beginning of military pay with the siege of Veii; Mommsen believes, probably correctly, that it must be considered as extending farther back. Even in the period when Rome already ruled all of Italy, the leading families prided themselves on the traditional simplicity of their style of life. In this ancient emporium on the Tiber River in the middle of a fertile countryside, there must always have been means of attaining prosperity; but this gain served, not for an easy life, but for the purposes of the state, and this attitude remained alive in the Roman citizenry for a long time after the living conditions had become quite different. The historical legend of the Greeks, too, told of the antiluxury legislation of Lycurgus in Sparta and of the poor but incorruptible Aristides in Athens, but these figures show, after all, only episodes of the Hellenic experience. Cincinnatus, Curius Dentatus, Fabricius are still more characteristic of the national type of ancient Rome.

The two purposes that were combined in the century organization after the year 510 B.C., army levy and voting organization, naturally drifted apart with time. There were some wars in which the entire manpower was not called to the colors, but only a selected group, and the larger the state became, the farther the marches, the longer the campaigns, the less was it possible to take all the men away from home. In the place of the general levy, therefore, there arose the practice of recruiting, and the districts for recruiting were naturally not the small units of the centuries but the regional districts, the tribes. The meaning of the word "century" thereupon split into two concepts, neither one of which any longer had any relationship with the other or with the original meaning of "group of a hundred." On the one side they were the political voting bodies, on the other the subordinate units of the legion. As the Roman national area spread, new tribes were formed—up to 35—and with them also new centuries as election bodies. The 6 original cavalry centuries were at some unknown time (perhaps in the year 304 B.C.) increased to 18.

The combat formation of the ancient Roman army levy we can picture as exactly the same as that of the old Greek hoplite phalanx. We may therefore carry this Greek name, too, over to the Romans. It is true that we do not have any positive historical account of this point; but since both internal reasons and the following development make it impossible for the Romans in the most ancient times to have had combat units armed only with the sword, then the linear formation, or phalanx, fighting with the spear and in heavy protective equipment, appears as the only possible one.

The legion was a military-administrative organization, not a tactical unit. It owed its existence to the chance fact that, at the time of the establishment of the institution of the two consuls, each of whom was to command half of the levy, this half amounted precisely to 4,200 men on foot and 300 cavalry.[8] That was also retained as the regular strength later, when the basic factors of mass and type had completely changed. They did not adhere blindly to the normal figures; often the strength of the unit fell far below, and sometimes the infantry went up to 5,000, finally to be increased, probably by Marius, to 6,000 men, but the basic principle remained, so that with large armies the legions themselves were not indefinitely enlarged, but the number of legions was increased.

The subordinate units of the legion of the older period, the centuries, like the legion, also had in no way a tactical significance but only an administrative one.

When Rome became the capital and leading city of a great alliance and obliged her allies to provide contingents, these units were not formed into legions; that would have served no purpose, since the legions, after all, were only administrative bodies and each allied contingent had to retain a certain administrative organization of its own. The principle was that half of an army always had to consist of Roman troops, half of allies. In general, then, one may double the number of legions in order to determine the strength of a Roman army, although of course in actual practice there were often very strong deviations from the general principle.[9]

In cavalry the allies were called on to provide double the number that the Romans themselves furnished.

The very generous bestowing of Roman citizenship on entire

communities made possible the continuation of this relationship, but this is already taking us into much later periods than we are now studying.

Excursus

1. The identification of the ancient Roman military organization led to the upsetting and reconstruction of the concepts concerning the constitution of ancient Rome in their entirety. Formerly the Servian class division was regarded as fundamental to this constitution. Already in the first edition of this work the class principle was emptied of its real content, since it was apparent from the population estimate that the centuries of the various classes could not possibly have been very different in strength, and that consequently the idea that there had existed in Rome not a strict general military obligation, but only a graduated, limited obligation and in keeping with it a graduated voting privilege according to one's property—this concept had to be reversed. Why then the classes at all? "The only interpretation that remains," I wrote at that time, "for the explanation of the class principle in the framework of the universal equal voting privilege, is the stiff Roman class consciousness." One has the feeling that this interpretation is basically only a last, desperate means to avoid having to give up fully the concept passed down to us. One of my students has finished this off since then; the entire Servian class organization must be eliminated from ancient Roman history. Francis Smith in the book *The Roman Timocracy* (*Die römische Timokratie*),[10] has convincingly proved that the so-called Servian constitution stems not from the sixth, but from the second century. It represents the unsuccessful attempt of a constitutional reform in the sense of Cato's middle-class policy, in order to save the state from the growing danger of ochlocracy in the service of aristocratic corruption. Every probability indicates that this attempt was made in the year 179 B.C. by the Censors Marcus Aemilius Lepidus and Marcus Fulvius Nobilior. (Mutarunt suffragia, regionatimque generibus hominum causisque et quaestibus tribus descripserunt. "They changed the method of voting and constituted the tribes on a regional basis and according to the clans and situations and occupations of the men." Livy 41. 51.) It is probable also that at that time the tribes were divided into 10 centuries each, instead of into 8 each, as formerly. That it must have been 8 originally is to be seen from the concordance of the figures: 21 tribes at 4 centuries of *juniores* each equals 8,400 men or 2 legions of infantry.

In order to make the division according to the new principles acceptable to the people in the year 179 B.C., it was presented as the inherited, truly ancient Roman law, and, like the writings of King Numa Pompilius, so were now also the commentaries of King Servius Tullius supposed to have been found. From Servius Tullius' somewhat disconnected notes the Roman historians then constructed the sections of the Servian constitution (which are so contradictory of each other). This procedure has its parallel in Deuteronomy, in the Priest's Codex, in the Draconian and the Lycurgian constitutions. The falsifiers still knew that Rome had 21 tribes at the time of the banning of the kings, and correspondingly 168 centuries of infantry. In conjunction with their division into classes, they rounded off the total (at least, we may assume so) to 170 (80; 20; 20; 20; 30) and thereby introduced the error that has cost modern scholars so very many headaches, that the army of 8,400 men (2 legions) was now supposed to have had 85 centuries, consequently one too many.

In the matter of the other irregularity—that with 21 tribes in each of which there were 3 centuries of hoplites and 1 century of lightly armed men the legion must have numbered not 3,000 hoplites and 1,200 lightly armed men, but 3,150 hoplites and 1,050 lightly armed men—the historians are obviously innocent. Here there must be an irregularity in the historical development, and one can point it out with a relative degree of probability. It may be assumed as certain that Rome originally counted only 20 tribes; the irregularity must therefore have originated through the addition of the 21st tribe, the Clustuminians. The new tribe members were probably not regarded at the start as completely equal to the others, and since at any rate the ratio of 3 hoplites to 1 lightly armed man was very tight, the Clustuminians were all designated for the auxiliary service, a relationship that in time, as the character of the levy completely changed, disappeared automatically. All of this is, of course, not directly capable of proof, but it may nevertheless be accepted as plausible. As an adjunct to the book by Smith I have developed this whole concept thoroughly in an essay in the *Preussische Jahrbücher* 131 (1908): 87, to which I refer the reader for the details. A series of sections of the first edition have been superseded by this. Let me repeat here only the following.

2. The ancient Roman phalanx is supposed to have had the peculiarity of not having all the ranks identically armed; only the leading ranks wore the full hoplite equipment, then came a rank without body armor, then one that also was without greaves, and the last ones had only spears and finally simply sling stones. Even though not verified, there could nevertheless be a certain degree of truth in this. We have disclosed above (Book I, Chapter III) that it is of no use to the phalanx to have unarmored men follow in the rearmost ranks, but these Roman unarmored men are not to be understood as ranks of the phalanx; rather, they correspond to the Greek *psiloi*, wagoners, orderlies, who also accomplish a certain secondary combat mission as light infantry. With the Romans they are one degree more combat-oriented than with the Greeks, since they consist entirely of citizens, whereas in the more well-to-do Greek cities, especially Athens, the masters often took slaves along into the field, and the Spartans took Helots. The men without body armor and without greaves, that is, with shield and helmet, can on the other hand still be regarded as heavily equipped and can fight in the phalanx. Naturally, there were in the most ancient period very many who were not in a position to provide themselves with the costly armor and greaves. They had to be placed in the rearmost ranks, but it was too much in the interest of the state, as of each of these men himself, that he be provided with complete equipment for this graduated armament arrangement to have been more than a transitional measure. The hoplites marching out to battle must have been equipped with as much armor as was to be found in public arsenals or in private homes. The supposition that it was never really a question of varying armament but only of how much the individual could provide for himself and what the state had to issue to him has something in its favor.[11] The details of the historical reports—that the first class had round metal shields (*clipei*), the second class (because of the lack of body armor) long, rectangular shields (*scuta*), and that the third class was without greaves—are clearly to be recognized as the composition of antiquarians. At a time when the state was not even capable of giving all of its hoplites a complete set of equipment, such fine distinctions could not possibly have been carried out or even prescribed. Whether the shield was metal and round or rectangular, wooden, leather-covered, with iron trim—all of this probably was of little concern to the consuls, and again the greaves were such an insignificant part of the equipment (the later Roman legionaries did not wear them at all), that they are obviously only mentioned in order to allow the demonstration of class differences. The wood of the spear, the sharpness of the point, the temper of the sword were much more important distinctions for the combat capability of the individual than the question of whether a soldier had perhaps wrapped strong leather leggings around his shins instead of wearing metal greaves.

3. The knight centuries obviously had a particular history of their own, differing from that of the infantry, since they originally were called not centuries but tribes. They were not divided into *juniores* and *seniores*, and their number is relatively too large for the most ancient period of the Republic. It is impossible that, at a time when Rome had a total of no more than 9,000 to 10,000 service-qualified citizens at

the most, there should have been 1,800 cavalry among them. The normal adjunct to 8,000 to 9,000 infantry (2 legions) would be 600 horsemen; I therefore accept this as the available number of cavalry at that time.

If one takes into consideration that the 3 oldest and most outstanding cavalry centuries had their individual names—the *Ramnes*, the *Tities*, and the *Luceres*—to which were added the *Ramnes, Tities,* and *Luceres secundi* and then the 12 additional unnamed centuries, there results the supposition that the first-named centuries were ancient societies of the nobility that existed before the mass of the people was organized into centuries. These societies of nobles moved into the field as cavalry, with a certain retinue on foot; since they were, however, more than simple military levies—that is, fraternal organizations, clubs—the older men and the physically disqualified also belonged to them. Now when, after the banishing of the kings, the army units began to function as voting bodies and for that reason the centuries of *seniores* were created, that was not necessary and not possible in the case of the cavalry centuries, because the older men already belonged to them, even if they no longer regularly rode along on a campaign. The outstanding men of Rome never tried to base their power, at any rate, on their voting privilege in the centuries, but rather on influencing the people's vote through the officials and priests.

4. One main proof that the army was the basis for the division into centuries is given by the centuries of musicians and artisans. The smiths are no doubt to be considered principally as weapons artificers who were taken along in order to be able to accomplish the repairs that are always necessary in the field.

In addition to the foregoing, there was also a century of *accensi velati* (supernumerary troops). The Roman antiquarians were themselves very uncertain about what was to be understood by this term (see the passages in Joachim Marquardt, *Roman Political Administration* [*Römische Staatsverwaltung*], 2: 329, note 2). Sometimes they were identified with the scouts; sometimes they were said to be replacements who were to move in for the killed and wounded, taking over the latters' weapons. This is the preferred meaning today. I cannot imagine such men. Did they, until an opening occurred, have no function at all and no weapon? That would have been a waste of strength, since they would nevertheless have had to be fed, like the others. If a hoplite became incapable of fighting, it was of course very important that his costly weapons be saved. The best solution would be to equip another man with them at once. But the 100 *accensi* in an army of 8,400 men would no longer suffice after the first combat. If it was a matter of particular concern that the hoplites remain as close as possible to full strength, the light infantrymen were, after all, there for the purpose of moving into the vacant positions. If that was the case, however, then this small group loses its *raison d'être* as a specific "replacement century." They would be a century of light infantry, as the others were also. Their purpose, since they were after all mentioned as a special unit, must have been something else.

I believe that the inscriptions and passages cited by Mommsen in *Political Administration (Staatsverwaltung)*, Vol. III, Part 1, p. 289, lead to the right clue. Here the *centuria accensorum velatorum* appears as a privileged group, and the individual *accensus velatus* as a respected man, who is proud of this position. This seems to me in no way to agree with the tradition that conceives of the *accensi velati* as the lowest, completely impoverished class of citizens. How is there supposed to have developed from the century of proletarians a society, membership in which was a coveted honor and in which we actually find persons of knightly rank? Mommsen concluded quite correctly that "they must at one time have been active in public affairs." What kind of affairs can that have been? They were related to the army; they were called up for their service. They were, therefore, the people of the army administration, the staff of clerks, accountants, supply officials, and aides, who were needed by both higher and lower leaders. Varro (cited in Marquardt) reports this expressly in various passages. If the army was called up for muster, they too had to join the formation as unarmed men (*velati*), and when the army was divided into voting centuries, they were considered together and organized as a century, just as the trumpeters, buglers, smiths, and carpenters each formed one. The idea that the *accensi velati* were proletarians did not arise until a division of the people by wealth was created in the classes, for the purpose of a timocratic election organization. Here the *accensi* did not fit in by any means; consequently, they were simply placed at the bottom. If it is right that they were also called *ferentarii* (according to Festus and Varro) and that the word is to be traced from *ferre*, and consequently to mean "carrier," then they were originally simple servants, who gradually developed into more important assistants.

5. Such notes as the one in *Athenaeus* 6. 106 ("They borrowed from the Tyrrhenians the practice of fighting pitched battles in phalanxes"*) should not be repeated. It is already a great deal if Cato still knew of a real tradition that the Romans originally fought in the phalanx and did not invent that himself simply from the nature of things. That the Romans, however, took over this method of fighting from some people or other cannot in any way have still been reported in any truly historical account.

And it is just as purposeless to repeat that the *scutum* was, according to Athenaeus, originally a Samnite weapon or, according to Plutarch's *Romulus*, a Sabine weapon, or according to Plutarch's *Camillus*, that it had been reinforced with iron since the time of that commander. All of these are completely arbitrary fantasies and inventions of later antiquarians, full of contradictions among themselves. According to Livy 8. 8, for example, the Romans originally carried *clipei* and did not carry *scuta* until they became *stipendiarii* (paid soldiers), that is, since the time of Camillus.

6. W. Helbig, in "The Castors as Patron Gods of the Roman Cavalry" ("Die Castores als Schutzgötter des römischen Equitatus") (*Hermes*, Vol. 40, 1905) and "On the History of the Roman Cavalry" ("Zur Geschichte des römischen Equitatus"), (*Abhandlungen der königlichen Bayrischen Akademie d. W. I. Kl.*, Vol. 23, 2d Section, 1905.) sought to prove for the Romans, just as he had done for the Greeks (see above, p. 59), that in the older period the *equites* were not to be thought of as cavalry but as mounted hoplites. His Roman study is, however, much more productive than his Greek one, because it is based not so very much on the interpretation of pictures, but on direct sources and evidence. Helbig determines, above all through presentation of all the numerous source passages, how strong the tradition was that in the most ancient period the Romans waged mounted battles and moved out to battle on horseback. In contradiction to this tradition stands the account in the *ineditum Vaticanum* (*Hermes*, 27 [1892]: 118), which probably goes back to Fabius Pictor; according to which it was not until the Samnite Wars that the Romans had created a skilled cavalry. Helbig reconciles these points by explaining that at that time the mounted hoplites, under Hellenic inspiration, had been transformed into real cavalry and he relates this to the parade of the knights through the city, which, according to the tradition, was arranged by Fabius Maximus as censor in the year 304 B.C. (Mommsen, *Staatsrecht*, Vol. III, Part 1, p. 493, note 1).

The error in this study lies, as in the corresponding one on the Greeks by the same author, in the too sharp distinction between infantry and cavalry. Helbig cites the example of the dragoons of the seventeenth century, who represented mounted infantry. These dragoons were for a fact mounted infantry who were given horses of only minimum value so that they could easily put up with their loss. That certainly does not fit in with the *hippeis* and *equites*. The actual analogy to the Roman *equites* is found in the medieval knights, who fought both on foot and on horseback, for whom the horse was by no means simply a means of transportation. Helbig's argument that the *equites* could not have fought on horseback because the shield they carried in the illustrations was too large for that purpose does not ring true; after all, if they wanted to fight on horseback, they may have given up the shield and fought ithout this protection. Even a small shield is a very inconvenient and often dangerous adjunct for the rider, who needs his left hand to control the reins.

To what extent any conclusion can be drawn from the size and shape of the shield concerning the type of combat could probably be learned only from a careful comparison with the combat methods of the medieval knights. The Roman knights of the most ancient period may often enough have fought on foot, and still so even when the legion phalanx was introduced, but most certainly never, as Helbig states on p. 312, as reserve, but rather then as the first rank of the phalanx, as the knights of the fourteenth and fifteenth centuries so often did. "Reserve" is a concept that does not apply at all to the older phalanx tactics.

The contradiction between the surely correct tradition, to the effect that ancient Rome had at her disposal a mounted knightly class, and the *ineditum Vaticanum* is therefore to be eliminated in some other way. The passage reads: "We were not able to ride, and the whole—or almost all—of the Roman force was on foot . . . but we forced them to ride."* Nothing forces us to read into the passage any more than its context states—that is, that in the Samnite Wars the Romans strengthened their cavalry significantly; to wit, they organized 12 new centuries, so that they then had 18. That this took place no earlier than the year 304 B.C. and precisely in that year cannot be considered as definitely proved; just the same, it is not impossible that the formal parade through the city was related to the change.

Of great interest is a stone tablet that is discussed and illustrated in Helbig, dating from the sixth century B.C. and showing Roman knights, one of whom carries a sword and another a battle axe; the third man's weapon cannot be recognized. This mixture of weapons is completely out of keeping with "cavalry" but genuinely consistent with the "knightly" concept.

Whether there is really such a strong case to be made for the honoring of the Dioscuri as the patrons of knighthood, as Helbig undertakes to do, is beyond my judgment.

7. The entire source material as a bibliography of the Roman military system is contained in the second volume of *Roman Political Administration (Römische Staatsverwaltung)*, by Joachim Marquardt; 2d ed., edited by A. von Domaszewski, 1884 (Vol. 5 of the *Handbook of Roman Antiquities [Handbuch der Römischen Altertümer]*, by Joachim Marquardt and Theodor Mommsen). The second edition is in substance only a reprint of the first, with the addition of supplementary material, especially a listing of the newer literature. Consequently the second still presents the concept of the chessboard formation of the maniples in combat, a concept that has almost generally been given up by now.

I myself first treated the problem of the Roman manipular phalanx in the *Historische Zeitschrift*, Vol. 51, 1883, and later in *Hermes*, Vol. 21, 1886, and the *Historische Zeitschrift* 56 (1886): 504 and 60 (1888); 239. The first two essays are presented together in the annex to the *Persian and Burgundian Wars (Perser- und Burgunder-Kriege)*. Other concepts have been developed by F. Fröhlich, *Contributions to the Conduct of War and the Art of War of the Romans in the Period of the Republic (Beiträge zur Kriegführung und Kriegskunst der Römer zur Zeit der Republik)*, 1886; Soltau, *Hermes*, Vol. 20; Bruncke, *Neue philologische Rundschau*, 1888, p. 40; Kuthe in a *Festschrift* dedicated to Director Nölting, 1888; Steinwender, *Program of the Marienburg Gymnasium (Programm des Marienburger Gymnasiums)*, 1877, and *Journal for the Gymnasium System (Zeitschrift für Gymnasiums-Wesen)*, 1878; Giesing, *Program of the Vitzthum Gymnasium (Programm des Vitzthumschen Gymnasiums)*, 1891. All of these works have the common error that they imagine the tactical events, whose highest law is that of simplicity, as much too complicated.

Added to the above now is Edmund Lammert, *The Development of Roman Tactics (Die Entwicklung der römischen Taktik) [Neue Jahrbücher für das klassische Altertum]*, 1902, where on p. 102 the ancient Roman knighthood is presented very well, based on the fragmentary testimony available and on analogies. For the rest, however, the author's inventions are too artificial and have now been overtaken by Smith's book.

Very worthwhile is the article *"Exercitus"* (Army), by Liebenam in Pauly's

Real-Encyklopädie; it contains a carefully worked-out survey of both the entire source material and the newer literature and its points of controversy.

In 1913 there was added Steinwender's *Roman Tactics at the Time of the Manipular Formation (Die römische Taktik zur Zeit der Manipularstellung)*, Danzig: H. Bruning. This study, which is unsuccessful in most of its details, is discussed in a valuable review by Robert Grosse in *Deutsche Literarische Zeitschrift II* (1914): 685.

9. [*sic*] Concerning the meaning of the expressions *classis, infra classem, classes,* Soltau published a study in *Philologus*, 72 (1914): 358 that followed the right track but did not go all the way to the end. My own concept is as follows: *"classis"* means originally the levy; the levy was followed from the beginning by a number of orderlies, light infantrymen, and so on, the *psiloi*, who were called the *"infra classem"*; when these light infantrymen became regularized and 1,200 of them were allocated to each legion, this became a second *"classis."* Thus the word received the meaning "division" and one could now speak of *"classes."*

8. [*sic*] Of decisive importance for the formation of the Roman infantry was naturally the payment of salary that, if not paid from the very start, was nevertheless introduced very early. In this connection it is interesting that Schlossmann (*Archiv für lateinische Lexikographie*, Vol. 14, 1905) determined that *stipendium*, which later meant both soldier's pay and tax, originally meant the tax that was levied especially for the purpose of paying the soldiers.

NOTES FOR CHAPTER I

1. In spite of the contradiction that Eduard Meyer brought up in his *History of Antiquity (Geschichte des Altertums)*, Vol. 2, para. 499, I still feel permitted and obliged to hold to this concept of "the continuity of the development of Rome in its constitutional history." For it is completely clear that the basic principle of the Roman constitutional law, the official power of the magistrature, dates back to a very early time and was gradually divided up and weakened. It is completely impossible that such a strict concept of the power of the official position might not have been formed until the formal sovereign power was already in the hands of the general people's assembly; it is astonishing enough that that strong concept was able to assert itself for so long within the framework of the sovereignty of the people.

Furthermore, it is fully clear that the voting organization of the historical period originally had a purely military and no political basis; consequently, this institution, too, goes back to the period of a very strong monarchy.

One may therefore truly speak of the "continuity of the development of Roman constitutional history," without, of course, taking for more than they actually were the historical changes of outer form—against which, after all, really only the voice of Meyer has apparently been raised.

I can leave aside here all the doubt over the authenticity of the chronology and the historical account in detail. The material in which I am interested for this work is not affected by it.

2. See particularly Vol. III, Book III, Chapters I and II, especially p. 251 [of the German 2d ed., 1923].

3. Livy (23. 46 [215 B.C.]) says of the Capuans: "Sex milia armatorum habebant, peditem imbellem; equitatu plus poterant, itaque equestribus proeliis lacessebant hostem." ("They had 6,000 armed men; the infantry was not inclined to fight, but the cavalry was more capable and so they provoked the enemy into cavalry battles.")

4. The theory that the original inhabitants had become the patricians by means of the income from their land is also opposed by Schmoller, *Basic Outline . . . (Grundriss)*, 2d ed., 1: 497: "If one imagines that capital in itself and its unequal distribution produces big business; if one imagines that, because the heirs of fortunate entrepreneurs in the second and third generations appear primarily as possessors of capital, the possession of the capital had created the financial projects, that is completely false. It is always personal characteristics that create and sustain such ventures."

5. In Gellius 16. 10. 1 there is contained a verse of Ennius, "proletarius publicitus scutisque feroque ornatus ferro." ("The proletarian is armed with shield and sword; armed with sword at the public cost.") Cited by Theodor Mommsen in *Political Law (Staatsrecht)*, Vol. 3, Part 1, p. 29. See also Polybius 6. 21. 7: "They chose the youngest and poorest of the men to be fighters with the javelin."*

6. For Attica we estimated, in the year 490 B.C., 120–145 inhabitants to the square mile; for Boeotia in the fifth century, 110; for Lacedaemon and Messenia 75; for the Peloponnesus 95 to 110. Under the primitive conditions of agriculture, disturbed by the continual warfare with neighboring states, as we must imagine the situation in Italy 2,500 years ago, certainly 120 to 145 is the maximum number that could be fed, even for the fertile soil. As an old trading city, Rome may already have had some grain imports by sea as early as 510 B.C., but surely not yet any great quantity, for if the city had already been large, it would have had a more important position politically. That the city was still small in comparison with the country area is further attested by the fact that only 4 of the 20 tribes were metropolitan ones. The so-called Servian wall, which enclosed a very large area, dates only from the period of the Samnite Wars.

7. A regular, official procedure for maintaining registration lists

appears at first glance to be something quite simple, but if it is to be reliable, it actually is very difficult and demands an extremely careful and energetic control. The advantages and disadvantages that are at stake are very great and the work, by its very nature, is in the hands of clerks who, in addition to the question of carelessness, can also be subject to bribery. In 214 B.C. when every younger man who was not on active duty in the field could not help being noticed in the street, a check-up found 2,000 *juniores* who had avoided military duty. Livy 24. 18. 7.

8. If our assumption is correct, that at the start of the consular regime Rome had 21 tribes and about 8,400 service-qualified infantrymen, the origin of the normal number of 4,200 for the legion is probably to be explained in no other way than that each of the consuls was allocated half the number. If the entire army was assembled and both consuls present, then they each had the command in turn on a daily alternation.

9. Very informative on this point is Theodor Steinwender, *Annual Program of the Marienburg Gymnaisum (Programm des Gymnasiums zu Marienburg)*, 1879.

10. Berlin: Georg Nauck, 1906. See also *Preussische Jahrbücher*, Vol. 131, January 1908.

(Added in the third edition.) A. Rosenberg, too, in *Research into the Roman Century-Organization (Untersuchungen zur römischen Zenturienverfassung)*, 1911, recognizes the indefensible position of Mommsen's constitutional construction and seeks a middle path between Mommsen and me. To try to go into details here on this counterproposal would lead us too far. Rosenberg's basic error is that he did not acquaint himself sufficiently with the population statistics of the canton of Rome.

11. Bruncke, *Philologus*, 1881, p. 368.

Chapter II

The Manipular Phalanx

About the period of the Samnite Wars the original, simple phalanx underwent a change that eventually led to the manipular phalanx.

The individual stages through which the development presumably proceeded can no longer be distinguished, but the result, the organization in which the Romans were still formed when they went into the struggle with Hannibal, is completely clear to us.

The hoplites were now divided into three sections, according to their year groups: the *hastati*, the *principes*, and the *triarii*. The youngest men formed the *hastati*, 1,200 men strong; the middle group made up the *principes*, also 1,200 in number; and the eldest were the *triarii*, numbering 600 men. With this formation the old centuries, the levies by groups of 100, were given up. The name, however, lived on as the designation for the smallest subordinate unit of the legion, which, in the case of the *hastati* and the *principes*, was now fixed at 60 men. Two such centuries together formed a maniple; each section had 10, and so the whole legion counted 30 maniples. The *triarii* maniples, however, had only half the strength of the two younger types.

To each maniple there was assigned an equal number of 40 unarmored men. The old relationship of 3,000 hoplites and 1,200 unarmored men to the legion therefore remained. The fact that the merely 60-man-strong maniples of *triarii* were assigned as many unarmored men as the 120-man-strong maniples of *hastati* and *principes* was naturally related to the orderly character of these unarmored men; the older men of the *triarii* unit were favored with more personal service than the younger *hastati* and *principes*.

The reason for the new formation was a tactical one.

As simple as the phalanx formation was, it still fell easily into disorder. It is extremely difficult with a rather long line even to march straight ahead; suddenly the line is broken at a certain point, while at another there occurs a squeezing together. That happens even on a perfectly level drill field, and if the terrain should have even any kind of irregularity or obstacles, or if the advance should draw off somewhat obliquely to the right or left, then a correct forward movement is simply impossible. On the other hand, it is extremely important to meet the enemy with a reasonable degree of order;[1] for soldiers who are pressed together cannot use their weapons properly, and when there are breaks in the line, the enemy can penetrate; even concern over this in advance produces a faltering of courage, as Xenophon points out on one occasion (*Anabasis* 4. 8. 10). This weakness is supposed to be remedied by the manipular phalanx.

Even with the Greek and Macedonian phalanxes we can assume with certainty that they did not form a completely uninterrupted line, but that from one unit to another small intervals were left, facilitating an orderly approach march, and were filled up automatically at the moment of contact with the enemy, as the ranks farther to the rear welled forward into them. The Romans now arranged for these intervals systematically.

The 10 maniples of the *hastati*, each 20 men wide and 6 men deep in the normal formation, were placed side by side with small intervals. With the small size of the maniples, then, the intervals were very frequent. Behind them the class of the *principes* was formed up as a second echelon, but in such a manner that each maniple covered the interval between two of the *hastati* maniples. And behind them were the maniples of the *triarii*.

The two centuries into which each maniple was divided stood side by side and consequently each had half the breadth of the maniple.

Each maniple stayed in a close-knit formation. If a squeezing occurred at one spot, it was not projected on through the whole phalanx but was taken up in the next interval, or at the latest in the second interval beyond, as these were closed up. The breach that opened on the other side, however, was closed up as soon as it was large enough by having the century or the entire maniple of the *principes* spring forward into the line of *hastati* on the centurion's command. In an extreme case that could even be repeated once again by having the *triarii* maniple, which was of course still in the rear, move into the front line.

The small intervals that might have remained were closed up automatically at the moment of contact.

Both actions, the squeezing and the pulling apart of the phalanx, occurred in a natural alternation. If the soldiers pressed together at one spot, a breach would probably develop at another place. Therefore a cure had to be created for both evils simultaneously. If one divided up the old phalanx and established intervals between the units in order to avoid the squeezing together and the resulting disorder, openings easily developed. The intervals, in fact, tended to exaggerate this situation. It was necessary, therefore, to impose the maximum limitation on these intervals. Numerous intervals could be introduced only by taking at the same time the greatest care to close up any openings that arose, and that was effected by splitting the legion into the three echelons of *hastati, principes*, and *triarii* and positioning the maniples around the intervals. When the phalanx was formed, it had to be aligned simultaneously both crosswise and lengthwise.

The procedure was very simple and yet at the same time ingenious. The Greeks were not capable of accomplishing it. They did not have the prerequisite for it, the Roman discipline. It seemed so simple for each soldier to be taught: the individual, the century, or the maniple moved forward as soon as a breach opened up in front of them. But this simple matter becomes unusually difficult in a combat situation. With the noise and the excitement of combat and under the pressure of imminent mortal danger, such rules are not always followed. But the man in the front line, seeing that a breach has opened up beside him, falls into doubt and uneasiness about which way he should close in. If one meets the enemy without having closed up the breach, the last man is as good as lost, for it is precisely here that the enemy will penetrate and attack him from the side.

The hoplite in the phalanx, as we have heard above from Euripides (2. 5), was not simply dependent on himself and his own courage, but he also leaned heavily on his comrades beside and behind him. Therefore the breach must not only be closed, but the men of the first ranks must be given the certain assurance that this would happen in order to keep their morale up to the point of full effectiveness.

The springing forward of the maniples of the second and third echelons could not, however, be accomplished on the basis of the perspicacity and the goodwill of an individual. One must not move up too soon; a small interval was supposed to remain, and the broadened interval was perhaps only a momentary situation that would quickly pass. At the moment when the breach has become large enough, however, the move forward must take place with unconditional reliability, for if it is delayed, it can lead to loss of the battle. The manipular formation therefore requires an extremely sure and firm leadership of the maniple. The *hastati* must be able to rely on the fact that the centurion of the next *principes* maniple would give the command at the right moment and lead his maniple into the threatened spot. The whole morale of the legion rested on the firm belief of the *hastati* in this movement of the *principes*.

The formation and purpose of the maniple also led the Romans to the invention of battle standards, something that remained foreign to the Greeks. Under no circumstances was the soldier to become separated from his maniple; for this reason each maniple was given a visible, symbolic center, a standard. In the battle itself the ensigns were not exactly of directly significant meaning. Only during the forming-up in line could they serve as an aid for the formation; during the direct approach march it could no longer very well be a question of aligning oneself on the standard; one's whole attention was necessarily directed toward the front. In the middle of the dangerous hand-to-hand combat, the soldier looked exclusively toward the enemy and, at most, cast a glance to the right and left toward his flank men, to see that he did not lose them.

The principal significance of the manipular standard is probably to be sought in peacetime training, in the conditioning of the individual to remain with his maniple under any circumstances. In the course of training for this cohesiveness, the standards were also not simply symbolic during drill, but of practical use for helping to keep the formation.

The manipular formation adheres completely to the basic principle of the phalanx but gives it the possibility of moving with much greater ease, even over unfavorable terrain. Whatever may occur, it does not fall into disorder, it will always reach the enemy with a closed, unbroken front. An articulated unit has taken the place of an almost stiff one. The phalanx has been given joints.

The arrangement of intervals in the phalanx offered still another advantage in addition to speed and good order in the movement forward. We have seen that with the phalanx the light infantry could only be used in very small numbers. Now, the intervals give the possibility of allowing a certain number of sharpshooters to be placed in front of the front line, since they could withdraw through the intervals without creating disorder, even if the hoplites were already quite close together.[2] One must not believe, however, that all 1,200 men of the legion were used in this manner. If the hoplites were drawn up 15 men deep, and consequently 200 men wide, that would have resulted in a forward skirmish line 6 men deep, whereas, after all, 2 ranks at most, one behind the other, could really use their missiles effectively.[3]

According to a note contained in Livy,[4] only 20 men from each *hastati* maniple, consequently altogether 200 men from the legion, were used for this service; presumably also an additional number on the flanks. Another group followed the hoplites in order to care for the wounded; the remainder stayed behind as garrison for the entrenched camp.

With the adoption of the manipular phalanx there was undoubtedly also an associated change in the Roman armament and method of fighting. The older Roman hoplites fought like the Greeks with the spear and had the short sword, a dagger, or a knife as an auxiliary weapon. By this time, the Roman soldiers threw their spears ahead and then charged forward at the assault pace to complete the battle with the sword. Although the spear has the advantage of the greater length, it is an awkward weapon for fighting with an armored opponent.[5] According to the normal method of holding the spear, where the "under-grip" is used (to employ the terminology of the German army),[6] the thrust is very uncertain and not very strong, since the lower arm and the hand must take an unnatural, almost vertical position while making it. This thrust really has its full effect only when made downward from above. The lance thrust, as it is principally practiced by the cavalry today, with "over-grip" and tightly squeezed between the body and the upper arm, was not usable for hoplite combat. It is the thrust of the attacking horseman, who is supposed to strike his opponent only in a general way and also accomplishes his purpose if he strikes the shield or body armor and unseats the man without wounding him. The hoplite, however, must look sharply for an uncovered spot on his armored enemy in order to strike him effectively.

The pointed heavy sword or the short light sword is much more suitable for this purpose than the spear,[7] and it is naturally doubly effective to use both weapons, one after the other, as the Romans made possible by throwing the spear ahead, which for that purpose was suitably constructed as a *"pilum,"*[8] and then breaking into the enemy line, already shaken by this salvo, with the sword. We can assume that the same military authority that articulated the phalanx by means of the manipular formation also ordered and carried out the increased effectiveness in hand-to-hand combat by the combination of the spear and the hand-to-hand battle.

As a normal thing, naturally only the first two ranks executed the spear throw; the others held theirs in their hands. The *triarii*, who hardly ever came to the point of throwing, did not even adopt the *pilum* but retained the old hoplite spear, the *hasta*.[9]

The formation of the manipular organization according to year-groups is also worthy of note. In the older Roman class-phalanxes the best-armed and most reliable men stood in the front ranks. Now the youngest men were placed in the foremost ranks, the oldest in the rearward ranks. This is a sign that in this army the military and the citizenship principles both held true and had been blended. The rearmost ranks of a deep phalanx were only very slightly exposed to danger, they hardly ever came into the hand-to-hand combat, and, except for the case of a general rout, they were hit, at most, by a few stray shots. In a purely citizen army one cannot assign the danger simply according to age, for one citizen is equal to the other. In a purely mercenary army this is even less possible, for each one is staking his life for the same pay. In a militarily organized militia, however, it is the natural thing for the family fathers with long service to have themselves placed in the rear ranks and to say to the young soldiers: "Now it's your turn to move up." It is the same thing as with us, when the *Landwehr* (home guard) is used more for garrison purposes and in the rear area than for open battles. "Res ad triarios venit" ("Now it is up to the *triarii*") has no more the significance that "Now the elite, the most outstanding warriors, must be sent in" than it means for us to say "Die Landwehr kommt" (The home guard is coming). It means no more than: "The situation is urgent." Our *Landwehrmann*, too, has a great military pride as an old soldier vis-à-vis the young lads, but this in no way means that the *Landwehr* is to be considered as an elite troop.

Within the *hastati*, who therefore have to bear the real burden of the battle, selected men were undoubtedly designated to form the foremost ranks, as was the case with the Greeks.

EXCURSUS

1. I have taken 6 men as the normal depth of the maniple; that results for the whole phalanx in 15 men, since the *triarii* were only half the number of the others. We may conclude that from the ratio of the various figures. To each maniple there belong 40 unarmored men, who form the rearmost ranks for the muster. The num-

bers were probably determined in such a way that at full strength there were no blank files. The maniples of the *triarii* undoubtedly had the same depth as that of the other units and so were only half as wide and formed up with very large intervals. Only in this manner could they accomplish their purpose. If they had possibly formed only 3 men deep, their movement up into the front lines would have been of little use, since in hand-to-hand combat such a shallow line does not have enough power to hold fast. The large intervals in the third echelon did no harm, since, during the approach march, the commanders could move over toward those places where the openings were occurring and the pushing forward of the *principes* into the *hastati* line was imminent or was actually being carried out.

The normal width of the maniples must therefore have been such as to be divisible into the three numbers 120, 60, and 40, and the depth such as to be divisible into 120 and 60. That results in a hoplite width of 20 (10 in the case of the *triarii*) and a depth of 6 men, and for the entire phalanx partly 18, partly 12, or an average of 15 hoplites. For the muster, the unarmored men stood 2 men deep behind the two younger units and 4 men deep behind the *triarii*, provided that they were not completely withdrawn from the hoplite phalanx and placed behind the *triarii*. A combination that is also possible from the point of view of the numbers concerned, that the hoplite maniple might have lined up only 3 men deep, is impossible from an objectively considered viewpoint, since the total phalanx would then have been too shallow and the maniple would have been too wide for the purpose of filling in the breaches.

With the Greeks the normal depth was accepted as 8 men. It seems striking that the Romans should have formed almost doubly that deep. But in the first place that is, after all, only a normal formation, which could be changed according to the need; we even hear quite often that the Greeks formed up 12 or even 25 men deep. Moreover, the intervals of the Romans must be taken into consideration. The disadvantage of the deep formation is, of course, the short front, which is vulnerable to envelopment and flanking attack. But the Roman formation was lengthened by means of the intervals, and at the place where the *principes* moved up to the front, the depth decreased to 6 men until the nearest *triarii* maniple moved in behind. A legionary phalanx of an average depth of 15 men would therefore correspond to a Greek one of some 10 to 12 men.

2. In the older legion the light infantry are supposed to have been called "*rorarii*," later "*veliti*." Whether the change of name also meant some kind of physical change is not clear. In Livy 26. 4, it reads for the year 211 B.C.: "Institutum ut velites in legionibus essent." ("It was made the custom to put lightly armed men in the legions.") The sentence reads as if it stems from an old record. The account into which Livy weaves this has the *veliti*, however, appearing as *hamippen*, light infantry who are combined with the cavalry, whereby they would have been taken out of the legions. In other respects, too, the account is subject to serious suspicion—for example, when Livy gives the *veliti* a lance with a point "*quale hastis velitaribus inest*" ("such as are on the spears of the lightly armed troops."). Furthermore, Livy also speaks quite often in the earlier books about *veliti*. (See also Marquardt, 2: 349, note 4.) Perhaps the connection is that not until the year 211 B.C. were the 200 men taken out of the *rorarii*, and from then on specially trained and equipped with special javelins as the men who were to take position in front of the legion. These were named *veliti*, and from them the name was gradually transferred over to all the *rorarii*.

3. THE STANDARDS

The question of the standards in the Roman army is very difficult, and I would not like to risk speaking the last word on this subject. Domaszewski, in his valuable treatise in *Abhandlungen des Archäologischen Epigraphischen Seminars der Universität Wien, 1885*,[10] has at any rate greatly overestimated the practical importance of the field ensigns. He believes (p. 2): "They form during the long hand-to-hand combat the rallying points of the subordinate units, around which the combatants resume their formation, and the commander, by controlling their movements in the battle, succeeds in leading the mass according to a unified plan." He states further on (p. 6) that the commander, controlled the movements of the standard by means of the buglers and the soldiers then followed the standard.

This entire idea is incorrect for the reason that the soldier who is already engaged in hand-to-hand combat can, for all practical purposes, no longer be led, and even if he could, then certainly only through a signal that strikes his ear without his listening for it, but not by means of a standard toward which he would first have to look.

As a result of his concept, Domaszewski assigns the standards their place in the first rank of the maniple, where they can be seen by all the soldiers. Stoffel, in his *History of Julius Caesar* (*Histoire de Jules César*), 2: 329 ff., believes that they were placed in the second rank, and I should like to agree with him on this, with the reservation that this man, too, who is both scholar and soldier, seems to me to place somewhat too high the practical importance of the standard in battle. The *antesignani* (those in front of the standard) are, according to Stoffel's completely plausible presentation, the first two ranks of the maniple. It seems questionable to me, however, as to whether something that applied to the cohort tactics at the time of Caesar may be carried over to the older period. It is, for example, very possible that in the manipular phalanx the expression *antesignani* applied to all the *hastati* and the expression then changed its meaning with the change in tactics. The passages from Livy cited by Domaszewski—8. 11. 7; 9. 39. 7; 22. 5. 7—do not allow at all the interpretation that the standards were placed in the first or second rank, but they make it appear probable that all the standards of the legion had their place side by side during battle, between the *principes* and the *triarii*. Since here once again, however, even in that early period, the standard (*signa sequi*) is said to have been a special symbol of the Roman soldiers and the custom of expressing military movements by means of the movement of the standards (*signa tollere, movere, ferre, efferre, proferre, constituere, inferre, conferre, convertere, referre, transferre, promovere, retro recipere; ad laevam ferre, obicere, signa armaque expedire*), as Domaszewski correctly observes, stems at any rate from an older period, it seems that there is here a contradiction in the sources. Domaszewski (p. 12) sees no other solution than that it was a question of various standards. He assumes that the recollection reported by Pliny in *Nat. Hist.* 10. 16—that the Romans in earlier times had carried as standards, in addition to the eagles, also wolves, minotaurs, boars, and horses—still held true for the Punic Wars and that these symbols had their regular place between the *principes* and the *triarii*, while the field standards that had a tactical purpose, the manipular ensigns, were with each maniple.

I consider still another solution as possible: that the practical use of the manipular standards not only originated on the drill field but that it was limited to that place. In wartime the standards were used only as a guide for forming up and were then brought into the middle of the legion, where they were not endangered and did not limit anybody in the first rank in the use of his weapon. They would have had no practical importance for maintaining good order and alignment in battle anyway, and the lift of morale that a revered standard, carried forward, can give, did not enter into consideration as long as the phalanx moved as a powerful, closely formed mass.

This changed after the introduction of the cohort tactics. For these small tactical units, acting individually, the standards were of much greater importance, especially from the morale point of view. Therefore, they were now given their place in battle, too—not in the first rank, it is true, but nevertheless in the second.

4. Appian (*Celtica*, Chapter 1) reports that the dictator C. Sulpicius ordered in a battle with the Boii that the javelins be thrown by an entire rank simultaneously and that each rank, after throwing, should kneel down in order to allow the next one to throw over them. Since this was told of four ranks and finally, after "all" had

thrown, they were supposed to have gone over to the attack, it has been concluded (Fröhlich, *Caesar's Conduct of Warfare* [*Kriegswesen Cäsars*], p. 146) that the *hastati* were drawn up four ranks deep. I should like to oppose this conclusion as being neither methodical nor objective.

All the battles of the fourth century are accounts of pure fantasy, without any historical validity in their details. The kneeling of the three foremost ranks so close to the approaching, perhaps even assaulting, enemy column is completely impossible. Even as a simple drill under peacetime conditions it is not without danger, since it is all too easy for one man from the first rank to kneel too late or to stand up again too soon or for somebody from the rear rank to throw too soon, with the result that some are wounded. And even if this does not happen, the simple possibility, the necessity for being concerned about it, inevitably brings restiveness and nervous uncertainty to the foremost ranks, a situation that does much more harm than the stepped-up launching of spears can do good.

5. Polybius (4. 22 ff.) gives us a thorough description of the Roman armament, but in his manner, which, with all its breadth, is still often flighty, he forgot the actual construction of the armor. In 6. 23. 14 he says: "The common soldiers wear a brass plate a span square that they place in front of their breasts and which they call their 'heart protector,' and they have it as their last piece of equipment. But those whose property qualification is above 10,000 drachmas have, instead of this 'heart protector,' a coat of chain mail to protect their chests."* According to the sense of this passage one would have to assume that the mass of Roman legionaries had worn no armor at all but only some kind of piece of sheet iron hung about the neck, one span wide and one long, as a "heart protector." There can be no doubt, however, that this heart protector was only an additional piece, a reinforcement to some kind of leather and linen armor. Among the legionaries outfitted in this way there were now supposed to be the citizens of the first class, as it was earlier expressed (those who were assessed as having fortunes over 10,000 *denarii*, as we must now say with Polybius), wearing complete scale armor. (See also Marquardt, 2: 337, note 4, and Fröhlich, *Kriegswesen Cäsars*, p. 68.) It is customary simply to repeat this from Polybius, but what are we to make of this? Are certain men in the middle of the *hastati*, *principes*, and *triarii*, who happened to be well-to-do, supposed to have been placed here and there with completely different armor? The state cannot possibly have had an interest in having individual men in ranks better equipped than were the others.

I think the explanation probably is that the "heart protectors" were the simplest form of body armor that the state had factory-produced and provided. Each individual, however, was free to wear another, better, or more handsome armor, and the very well-to-do procured the complete scale armor for themselves. "Men whose property qualification is above 10,000 drachmas" does not mean here, therefore, that a remnant of the old class formation still held true, but it means nothing more than "the richest," which Polybius has passed on in this misunderstood and erroneous manner.

Likewise, it is an undoubted misunderstanding of Polybius when he gives each legionary two *pila*, a light one and a heavy one (4. 23). Not every legionary is outfitted with two *pila*, but there are two different types of *pilum*; aside from the light one that the legionary takes into the field, there is a still heavier one, which is used for the defense of fortifications.

NOTES FOR CHAPTER II

1. Thucydides (6. 98) tells us how the Syracusans planned to wage a battle against the Athenians and were already drawn up in for-

mation when the commanders noticed that "the army was disordered and did not readily fall into line."* As a result, they led the troops back into the city.

2. Polybius 11. 22. 10.

3. Vegetius, too (1. 20), shows expressly that the number of light infantry who were active in front of the battle line was small and that they moved forward principally from the flanks.

4. In Livy's Chapter VIII of Book VIII, to be discussed in greater detail below (p. 00).

5. Each weapon has certain advantages and disadvantages, and the evaluation remains a subjective one. In Grupp, *Cultural History of the Middle Ages* (*Kulturgeschichte des Mittelalters*), 1: 109, it is said, for example: "The Norwegian Royal Code warns against throwing the spear too soon; in land battle the spear is better than two swords."

6. *Regulations for Drills with Cavalry Weapons* (*Vorschrift für die Waffenübungen der Kavallerie*), Berlin, 1891.

7. It is not known how the original Roman sword was constructed; it was supposedly only a long, strong knife, "Bowie knife," cutlass, or even only the same knife that the man used for cutting meat and wood. In the Second Punic War the *gladius Hispanus* (Spanish sword) was introduced, a straight, two-edged, pointed sword, short and very broad at the top, better suited for thrusting than for hacking.

A. Müller, *Philologus* 47: 541. From Villenoisy's "On the Method of Using Ancient Swords" ("Du mode d'emploi des épées antiques"), *Revue archéologique*, 1894, p. 230, there is nothing important to be gleaned.

8. The *pilum*, which was initially, at any rate, a simple javelin with a very long, thin point, has its own history. For the best discussion of this now, see Dahm, *Jahrbücher des Vereins von Altertumsfreunden im Rheinland*, 1896–1897, p. 226. The surprisingly erroneous construction that Rüstow presented is a proof of how difficult critique is from the objective point of view of the ancient written accounts, even for the experts, and how easily it can go astray. The credit for having reconstructed the correct *pilum* goes to Lindenschmit, and the excavations that Napoleon III had carried out proved also to be very valuable in this matter.

(Added in the third edition.) A. Schulten, *Rhein. Museum N. F.* 66 (1911): 573, points out the probability that the actual *pilum* was perhaps taken over from the Iberians, as late as the Second Punic War. That would, of course, not eliminate the possibility that the

Romans had already long before that adopted the method of throwing the spear ahead and carrying on the actual hand-to-hand fight with knife, dagger, or sword and were indebted to the Iberians only for the final technical improvement in the construction of the javelin. We have no positive testimony about when the Romans introduced the described combination of spear and sword combat, and by the nature of the thing we cannot have such evidence.

9. According to Polybius. In the period of the Empire we find that in the armories the weapons were divided into *"arma antesignana"* and *"arma postsignana"* ("before-the-standard" and "behind-the-standard" arms), which can hardly mean anything other than that the foremost ranks carried the *pilum*, the rear ranks the *hasta*. See also Domaszewski, *Sitzungsberichte der Heidelberger Akademie*, 1910, p. 9.

10. See the supplement to this in *Mitteilungen des Oesterreichischen Archäologischen Epigraphischen Instituts*, Voi. 15, 1892. See also the thorough discussion by Mommsen, in the same periodical, 10 (1886): 1 ff.

Chapter III

Roman Drills, Campcraft, and Discipline

It is impossible to form and move a phalanx without having trained the men who make it up. From the very first day on, after the phalanx idea was conceived, we must imagine that a certain amount of drill took place. There was a systematic training in Sparta and with the Greek mercenaries. The discipline-oriented attitude of the Romans undoubtedly did not allow this excellent means to escape them, and the manipular formation demanded more than the Greek-Macedonian soldiery presumably ever accomplished. On the specialized drill of the manipular phalanx there has come down to us a description that, strongly exaggerated, led the research into this subject astray for a long time, but which, after the erroneous garnishment is removed, may be considered as a very good picture.

The principal mission of the manipular legion was to hold the individual maniples together in a close-knit formation during their approach march, and as soon as openings developed in the leading echelon, to fill these in an orderly way by having a century or a maniple from the second or third echelon move forward. This was drilled in the following manner. The maniples took up, from the start, an interval of one maniple's breadth from each other. Then the formation marched forward, and the centurions had to pay close attention to see that the distances were maintained.

Under battle conditions the intervals between the maniples could, of course, not be made so wide, since each interval offered the enemy a point of penetration.

On the drill field, however, the action of precisely marching straight forward, which is so hard to do, was practiced in this manner. The manipular standards in the first rank of each maniple facilitated the maintaining of the direction, the dressing on the guide, and the interval. Finally the true test was held by having the *principes* maniples spring forward into the *hastati* intervals. Then the *principes* continued to move forward as the first line, and the *hastati* remained behind, in order to fill the openings again, in the same manner, on command. The *triarii*, too, were no doubt put through this drill, although it is not clear how that was done, since they obviously always had either a *hastati* or a *principes* maniple in front of them as long as no breach had opened up as a result of disorder or of losses in a battle situation.

In the matter of campcraft, too, the difference between a Greek and a Roman army was hardly less than that caused by the manipular organization.

Very seldom do we hear anything concerning the Greeks' camps. Xenophon tells us in his description of the Lacedaemonian state (Chapter 12) that they maintained good order in camp and made it circular when the terrain did not dictate otherwise. But whether they regularly fortified it, he does not say. Judging from the overall context, we should almost conclude so, and time and again we hear of fortified camps,[1] but we obviously cannot speak of a standing custom of fortifying their camps, either by the Lacedaemonians, or with even less certainty, by the other Greeks. Even in the case of Alexander the Great and his successors, the fortifying of a camp is mentioned only under special circumstances and it probably was not done otherwise. Polybius says expressly (6. 42) that the Greeks, in order to save themselves the trouble of entrenching, sought out for their campsites areas of terrain with natural protection.[2]

But the Romans already had from very ancient times the firm principle of enclosing every camp, without exception, with a trench and palisaded rampart. However troublesome that was, the many advantages warranted it. The Greeks' habit of seeking cover from the terrain misled them naturally into being satisfied now and then with very mediocre protection and so to expose themselves to surprise attacks. The commander does not like to demand of his troops something that they are not accustomed to doing. The progress of operations is necessarily continuously influenced by this kind of consideration. The Roman commander, who in the training and the habits of his soldiers always and in all places carries his security along with him, is thereby given the capability of much more extended and much longer-lasting operations than was the Greek leader. The gradual, systematic subjection of Italy, on which the Roman national system was based, would not have been possible without the Roman fortified camp. Even after a lost battle the camp offered a temporary refuge.

Of almost as much importance, however, is an indirect result that Polybius brings up. The Greeks, who pitched their camps according to the circumstances, had no fixed forms for them. The Romans had a completely specified plan,[3] in which each unit and each man had a definite place. The camp was rectangular and had four gates; in the middle was the commander's tent. The camp streets were arranged in definite lines and definite symbols showed the directions. Consequently the action of marching in and out took place in a natural order, without disturbance, and even in case of sudden alarms each soldier immediately knew his place.

In Livy (44. 39) Aemilius Paullus delivers a talk to his soldiers before the battle of Pydna, in which he says of the camps:

> Your ancestors considered the entrenched camp as a continuously available haven for the army, from which they could move out to battle, in which, if they were beaten by the storm of the battle, they could find a sure refuge. The camp is a resting place for the victor, a refuge for the loser. This military residence is our second fatherland, the rampart forms the city walls, and for each soldier his tent is his house and hearth.

The burden that the regulations for the fortification of the camp created for the Romans was extraordinarily great. Since there would not always have been time and opportunity to cut the necessary stakes for the fortification on the spot, the soldiers had to carry along with them often enough—in addition to their heavy hoplite equipment, their provisions and tools, axes, spades, and saws—even the stakes themselves.[4]

As we know, each Greek hoplite required an orderly or helper; the Roman legionaries had only two lightly armed men for every five hoplites. The Greeks, Polybius says (18. 18), hardly believed that they could carry their own weapons on the march; for the Romans it was, he says, an easy matter to carry the fortification stakes as well. Caesar (*Bell. Civ.* 1. 78) occasionally mentions that foreign auxiliary troops would not take on the burdens of the legionaries.

It is with good reason that the Roman legend has Camillus saying once (Livy 5. 27. 8) that the factors that enable the Romans to conquer their enemies are *"virtus, opus, arma"* ("courage, work, weapons"). The *opus*, the burdensome, thankless digging, played no less a role in the Roman conquest than courage and weapons.

All the differences between the Greek and Roman military systems can be traced back to the difference in discipline. The Athenian commanders had, it is true, a certain right to mete out punishment, but they nevertheless did not use it, according to the testimony of Aristotle.[5] Even in the case of specifically military crimes, such as refusal to appear at the levy, cowardice, fleeing before the enemy, there was no immediate punishment, but the commanders, after the end of the campaign, made a public accusation in Athens.[6] When, in the Peloponnesian War, Demosthenes hit upon the plan to fortify Pylos, an action which later led to the great victory of Sphacteria, he was initially unable to convince either his fellow commanders or his soldiers to accept it, as Thucydides (6. 4) recounts quite mildly. Not until they had had to remain in place there for a rather long time because of the rough sea, did his soldiers decide, from boredom, to carry out the idea of their commander.

In his recollections of Socrates, Xenophon has Pericles complaining that the Athenians·were obedient to their gymnasium instructors and their choir directors all right, but that the knights and hoplites were refractory vis-à-vis their leaders (3. 5. 19). Wherever possible, the Athenians took pride in acting against higher authority (3. 5. 16). Socrates finds the reason for this in the fact that the commanders themselves understood nothing of the art of war; one should choose men who, through the superiority of their knowledge and ability, would force the voluntary obedience of their units, just like the masters of gymnastics and of choral music.

When Phocion was once asked (Plutarch, *Phocion*, Chapter 23) when he would advise the Athenians to make war against the Macedonians, he replied, "When I see that young men are ready to do their service, rich men to pay their taxes, and speakers to avoid embezzling public funds."

The Spartans were famous for their obedience to authority, and it is certain that this warrior fraternity exercised its domination over its numerous subject peoples through its firm cohesiveness. If one examines the situation more closely, however, it becomes apparent that the Spartan discipline was more of a pedagogical nature, not really the kind we call military discipline. Inherent in the concept of discipline is that it emanates from the command authority. But in Sparta the command authority was very limited. In this complicated political system, command of the army was vested in the hands of the hereditary kings. But these kings did not rule; rather, they had a kind of presiding position within the aristocracy, and in order to prevent their assuming more power through their command of the army, the command authority was very limited. The royal dignity was not just a single position, but a double one; both kings originally held the supreme command jointly in the field as well, and when this practice was abandoned (around 510 B.C.), because of serious disadvantages, other precautions were taken to assure that their power, even in the field, remained tightly limited; otherwise this royalty would have enhanced its position quite differently.[7]

Pausanias is said to have had the experience at Plataea of having one of the Spartiate colonels, Amompharetus, who did not understand his activity, refuse to carry out a command and openly quarrel about it with the King. Later the kings were provided with a council of the ephors in the field. When King Agis in 418 B.C. planned to give battle to the enemy on unfavorable terrain and had already moved up within stone-throwing range, one of the elders called out to him that he was no doubt planning to cure one evil through another, whereupon he led the army back. In the battle of Mantinea, which followed shortly thereafter, two polemarchs refused to obey, failed to carry out a movement that was ordered, and were punished for that, not immediately by the King, but later by the authorities at home, who ordered banishment.

When the Greek mercenary armies came into being, there naturally developed also a different type of discipline from that of the citizen armies. At as early a period as that of the conversation between Pericles and Socrates, Xenophon has Socrates praising the good order of the fleet in contrast to the land army. When the Spartan Brasidas formed his hoplite unit with Helots, which he then led to Thrace, he certainly instilled good discipline in them. Of Clearchus, the most famous soldier of fortune of the Ten Thousand, Xenophon tells us (2. 6. 10) that he had established the principle that the soldier should fear his commander more than the enemy, and he himself wielded the rod whenever he saw one of his men holding back. But when Xenophon himself in a withdrawal once beat a soldier because he had refused to help along a sick comrade, the soldier brought charges against him before the army assembly, and Xenophon was found innocent only after recounting the reason for the punishment.

With the Macedonians, under the assured authority of a royal commander, good discipline no doubt prevailed. In serious cases the king carried out power of punishment with the concurrence of his army.[8] Among the successors of Alexander, too, when the armies were standing mercenary units, the kind of discipline peculiar to this type of soldiery must have prevailed, because without it mercenary armies can neither be used nor held together. Polybius (1. 66) states wisely that a peaceful situation has no value for mercenaries and is but the source of rebellion. Certainly for this reason, too, there was a great deal of drill under the Diadochi. Polyaenus (3. 9. 35) said that Iphicrates always kept the soldiers occupied, so that they would not get the idea of reforms; nevertheless, drilling is not named among these activities, but rather digging, felling trees, moving equipment, and changing position.

If, after all, one cannot say of the Greeks that the basic principles of military discipline were completely unknown to them, nevertheless it was really not until the mercenary army that this concept arose, and according to Polybius' testimony the Greeks never really learned true obedience at all. A completely different atmosphere strikes us as soon as we enter a Roman camp. Only with the Romans were the concept and the power of discipline fully recognized and accomplished.

The strict concept of the right of command was not relaxed with the banning of the kings, but only transferred to the two alternating consuls. Six lictors bearing the fasces walked in front of each of them, as immediate executors of their commands. The citizen inside the city was only partially protected personally from the claws of this official power; but in the field it held unhampered sway over life and death, and it moved about mercilessly. From the consuls it was delegated to the other leaders. Each centurion carried a rod; the later period looked on this as his very special insignia of rank and as such chiseled it into stones.[9] Vegetius describes thoroughly for us (2. 19) how carefully rosters and record books were kept on each and every item in the Roman companies—pay, service, command, leave. In the process of enlisting recruits, care was therefore taken to sign up a few men capable of writing and keeping accounts. We can assume that this administrative exactness went back to very early times, for without such thoroughness there is no order and consequently also no discipline. For this reason, from the early days onward the centurions were also assigned unarmed men (*accensi velati*), that is, clerks.[10] Polybius (6. 36 ff.) tells us that the sentry posts were inspected in the Roman system according to a fixed scheme. If the inspecting officer found a man who was not on his post or was sleeping, on the next day he was court-martialed. The tribune touched with his staff the man who had just been found guilty, whereupon all the soldiers began to beat him or throw stones at him. If he should succeed in escaping from the stoning and fleeing from the camp, he could nevertheless never again return to his home. The same harsh punishment was meted out to the centurions (Polybius says "the officer of the rear and the leader of the troop"*) who did not make their rounds correctly. Insubordination, desertion, and cowardice were punished with death. If entire units were guilty, they were decimated; every tenth man was sentenced to death by lot.

Even high officers of the most outstanding families were sometimes sentenced to corporal punishment.[11]

No account is more famous and more characteristic in the Roman legend than that of the Consul Manlius, who had his own son executed because he had transgressed a command and accepted individual combat with one of the enemy who had challenged him. Stiff with horror, according to Livy's description, the army stared at the terrible execution and did not come to itself again until the head lay separated from the torso and the blood was streaming out—but obedience was assured.

A few years later, the Roman history books go on to relate, it happened that Master of the Horse Quintus Fabius Rullianus waged and won a battle against the command of the dictator L. Papirius Cursor, in the latter's absence. The dictator cited the example of Manlius and summoned the disobedient subordinate before his court. Fabius fled from the camp toward Rome. The Senate intervened. The father of the guilty man, who himself had been dictator and three times consul, appealed to the people and the people's courts. But the courts, for the sake of maintaining the principles of discipline, did not dare to intervene. Not until everybody—Fabius himself, son and father, the Senate, the judges, and the people—had had recourse to entreaties, and the right of command and the law of subordination had thereby been recognized, did the dictator allow himself to relent and turn the criminal over to the Roman people and the power of the courts, because they had made a plea rather than trying to establish a right.

On Greek soil neither the story of Manlius nor that of Papirius would be imaginable. Even in Sparta there never existed such a concept of official power. By means of this official power the aristocratic and democratic elements in Rome were held together and balanced; neither was able to overcome and repress the other completely. In this state of universal equal suffrage, in which the principle of the sovereignty of the people was formally recognized, there existed at the same time, from a practical viewpoint, an aristocracy with the power to rule and actually holding the command. The counteractions of these powers formed the Roman national character; the official power was the root of discipline, and on the tree of discipline grew the fruit of the manipular tactics and of the systematic fortifying of the camps.

EXCURSUS

1. The description from which I believed that I could extract the picture of ancient Roman drills was interwoven by Livy into his account of the Latin War (340 B.C.) and connected with a survey of the entire development of Roman battle methods. In view of the importance of this report, we must treat it in context and try to justify in a sentence-by-sentence analysis the manner in which we have used and evaluated it. Livy (8. 8) says:

"Clipeis antea Romani usi sunt, dein postquam stipendiarii facti sunt, scuta pro clipeis fecere." ("In former times the Romans made use of round shields, but when they later became paid by stipend they manufactured oblong shields in place of the round ones.")

This note is obviously the composition of a Roman antiquarian who imagined that the Romans in olden times must also have had the shield of the Homeric heroes, and (one might say not at all unskillfully) linked the transition to the shield form of the legionary of his time with the introduction of soldier's pay.

"Et quod antea phalanges similes Macedonicis, hoc postea manipulatim structa acies coepit esse, postremo in plures ordines instruebantur." ("Although their line had been drawn up at an earlier time in a way similar to Macedonian phalanxes, it began later to be drawn up in maniples, and, finally, in several ranks.")

This sentence shows that we are dealing with a real expert; it is to be understood as: "The original phalanx was at first formed by maniples and finally divided into several echelons."

The introduction of the echelon formation took place, as we shall find out later, toward the end of the third century B.C., in the Second Punic War. The next stage, the cohort tactics, which was reached toward the turn of the second and first centuries, was not yet mentioned. From this we can conclude that the description is that of an author of the second century and, still more exactly, of the first half of the second century. The writer compares the ancient Roman formation with the Macedonian; he does not mean, naturally, that the Romans had been armed with the *sarissa* in the most ancient times. If he had meant that, he would have had to call the phalanx not simply "similar" but identical to the Macedonian. He can only have meant the closed linear formation with the spear as individual arm—that is, the old Greek hoplite phalanx. The author, presumably Cato, selects for his comparison, however, the Macedonian phalanx instead of the Greek, because at that time, when they were waging war with the Macedonians or had just finished doing so, the latters' phalanx was a very timely concept in Rome.

"Ordo sexagenos milites, duos centuriones, vexillarium unum habebat." ("The *ordo* had 60 soldiers, 2 centurions, and 1 standard-bearer.")

The *ordo*, which had 60 men, was the later century as half of the maniple. The later *ordo*, however, did not have 2 but only 1 centurion, and besides the 60 hoplites there were 40 lightly armed men. Furthermore, it hardly had its own standard-bearer, since it was not the century but the maniple that carried an ensign. Either

Livy was completely confused at this point, and therefore, by reading in his source the word "*ordo*" in the sense of "echelon," thinking of *ordo* in the sense of century, and wishing to give an explanation, he injected his indefinite and slanted recollection at this point—or a later interpolator corrupted the text in this manner. The sentence should therefore be struck out.

"Prima acies hastati erant, manipuli quindecim." ("The first line was made up of the *hastati*, 15 maniples.")

Aside from this we know only of a division of the legion into the 3 echelons of the *hastati*, *principes*, and *triarii*, each of 10 maniples. The 15 maniples Livy reports here may, however, very well be historically accurate. It is conceivable that originally the old phalanx was divided into only 2 echelons, of 15 maniples each, and that a recollection of this was retained in the account. It is true, of course, that Livy does make the mistake of giving all 3 echelons 15 maniples. But a legion of 45 maniples certainly never existed. The original legion of 42 centuries is definitely proved for us by the voting organization of the century elections, and the relationship between this legion and that described by Polybius, in which there are 1,200 lightly armed men allocated to 3,000 hoplites, equaling 42 centuries, is completely clear. This development cannot possibly have been interrupted once by a totally different table of strengths, from which, either by chance or intentionally, they had come back again to the old figures. The consistency of these numbers over several hundred years shows us, rather, how conservatively they thought in the retention of the normal figures, once they were adopted.

"... Distantes inter se modicum spatium. manipulus levis vicenos milites, aliam turbam scutatorum habeat; leves autem qui hastam tantum gaesaque gererent vocabantur. haec prima frons in acie florem invenum pubescentium ad militiam habebat. robustior inde aetas totidem manipulorum, quibus principibus est nomen, hos sequebantur scutati omnes, insignibus maxime armis." ("There was only a small space between them. The light maniple had 20 infantrymen and another squad of troops armed with shields. Those maniples were called 'light' that carried only the spear and the long javelin. This was the front of the line, and it was composed of young men who were new to military service. After them came men of a more mature age in so many other maniples—they were called *principes*—and they were all shield-bearers, whose arms were especially marked.")

Of value in this extract is the note that the maniples of *hastati* were allocated 20 lightly armed men, but those of the *principes* had none. It is not clear why anyone would have made such a statement falsely, and so it is to be regarded as genuine and verifies our interpretation that only a small number of the lightly armed men are to be regarded as real combatants.

"Hoc triginta manipulorum agmen antepilanos appellabant, quia sub signis jam alii quindecim ordines locabantur. . . ." ("They used to call this host or 'battalion' of 30 maniples the *antepilani* because 15 [other] lines were placed behind the standards.")

A special tactical meaning of the "*antepilani*" and of the troops "*sub signis*" is nowhere to be found; furthermore, the word "*antepilani*" can only be explained through the fact that the *triarii* were once called *pilani*, and therefore their first centurion was still called at a later period *primus pilus*. The true meanings of the words *pilus* and *pilani*, however, are not known; as Soltau has correctly pointed out, they are not related to *pilum*. We may, however, also conclude from this passage that in combat the standards were placed between the *principes* and the *triarii*.

"Ex quibus ordo unus quisque tres partes habebat. earum unam quamque primam pilum vocabant. tribus ex vexillis constabat, vexillum centum octoginta sex homines erant. primum vexillum triarios ducebat, veteranum militem spectatae virtutis; secundum rorarios, minus roboris aetate factisque; tertium accensos, minimae fiduciae manum: eo et in postremam aciem reiciebantur." ("Of these, every single *ordo* had 3 parts. The first one of each of them was called the *pilum*; it consisted of 3 units and there were 186 men in each unit. The first unit was formed of the *triarii*, veteran soldiers of proven courage; the second was formed of the *rorarii*, of lesser strength, age, and experience; and the third was formed of the *accensi*, the least reliable unit; for that reason they were placed back in the last line.")

This passage has caused scholars a great deal of trouble. If the 3-by-15 maniples are difficult to explain, then the 3 units, each of 186 men, are absolutely impossible to cope with. They have tried to change the handwritten "*vexillum*" into "*vexilla III*," but that, too, is only an apparent solution. Finally, the entire sequence from "*earum unam quamque*" up to "*octoginta sex homines erant*" was eliminated as being an interpolation. But how is an interpolator supposed to have arrived specifically at the number 186?

All the researchers are now agreed that there are some very serious errors involved. I should like to try to find the solution in the following way. First of all, the 45 maniples of *triarii* are to be eliminated. They came into the picture through the fact that, in Livy's source, it was a question of an earlier period, where there were only 2 echelons in the legion, each of 15 maniples. Livy erroneously attributed this number to the *triarii* as well. After the *triarii* came into existence, each of the echelons had only 10 maniples.

Moreover, the distinction between *triarii*, *rorarii*, and *accensi* according to their military skill is obviously false. The distinction between *triarii* and *rorarii* lay in age, armament, and function. The *accensi*, however, were not soldiers at all.

The formation that Livy describes, therefore, is not the battle formation, but the muster formation, and this results also in the number 186. At the muster, the non-combatants and, where appropriate, the half-combatants, stood behind the combatants, therefore behind the *triarii*. One maniple each of *hastati*, *principes*, and *triarii* belonged together. Behind each *triarii* maniple, which was itself 60 men strong, stood the 3-by-40 *rorarii* of the three maniples and the 6 *accensi* (orderlies, company clerks) of the 6 centuries—that is, 186 men *sub signis* (behind the standard).

The confusion that Livy causes is only that he gives the *rorarii* and the *accensi* their own detachments and that, as is later revealed, he considers the overall formation to be the battle organization. In this sense he exaggerates; his source, however —precisely the controversial number 186 proves the point—was excellent. In Book VI, Chapter I, below, in the battle of Cynoscephalae, we shall become acquainted with an analogy for our author's procedure: in using Polybius, he makes a translation error and then imagines the situation with his own fantasy on the basis of this false translation and invents reasons for it. Since in this case we still possess the original that he translated, his procedure can easily be seen through. The *accensi* of the consuls and the tribunes, of whom there naturally must have been some, did not, as belonging to the staff, form up at musters of the legion.

"Ubi his ordinibus exercitus instructus esset, hastati omnium primi pugnam inibant, si hastati profligare hostem non possent, pede presso eos retro cedentes in intervalla ordinum principes recipiebant. tum principum pugna erat; hastati sequebantur, triarii sub vexillis considebant sinistro crure porrecto, scuta innixa humeris, hastas suberecta cuspide in terra fixas, haud secus quam vallo saepta inhorreret acies, tenentes. si apud principes quoque haud satis prospere esset pugnatum, a prima acie ad triarios sensim referebantur. inde rem ad triarios redisse, cum laboratur, proverbio increbuit. triarii consurgentes, ubi in intervalla ordinum suorum principes et hastatos recepissent, extemplo compressis ordinibus velut claudebant vias, unoque continenti agmine iam nulla spe post relicta in hostem incidebant: id erat formidolosissimum hosti, cum velut victos insecuti novam repente aciem exsurgentem auctam numero cernebant."

("When the army had been drawn up in these ranks, the *hastati* were the first of all to go into battle; if they were not able to overcome the enemy, they fell back and let the *principes* move into the breach, and the fight then became theirs. The *hastati* then followed them, and the *triarii* took their positions under the banners, with their left legs extended, their shields strapped to their shoulders, their spears pushed into the ground and pointing upwards, just as if their battle line were strengthened by a bristling palisade. If the *principes* were also losing the fight, they fell back slowly from the battle line to the *triarii*. From this fact came the saying 'to have come to the *triarii*,' used when things were going badly. The *triarii*, rising up after they had absorbed the *hastati* and *principes* into the intervals between their units, would im mediately draw their units together and close ranks, as it were; then, with no more available reserves, they would charge the enemy in one solid mass. This was incredibly terrifying to the enemy, who, pursuing those whom they thought they had conquered, suddenly perceived a new line rising up, increasing in number.")

Any possibility of an understanding of the development of Roman tactics is out of the question as long as we regard this description, with Livy, as that of a Roman battle. In order for the maniples of *principes* to be able to pass through the maniples of *hastati*, the latter would have had to be formed with intervals equal to the width of a maniple front. That is feasible to a certain extent on a completely level drill field, where the unit moves only a short distance forward and then halts at will to correct errors and become realigned. But this is completely impossible under war conditions, since in the approach march the intervals would all be lost, here becoming too large, there too small. Even if the *hastati* should succeed in reaching the enemy with the correct intervals, that would still result in the most foolish battle formation one can imagine. Each maniple would immediately be enveloped on both flanks and pressed together. Worse yet is the idea that the *hastati* had moved forward, to be sure, with intervals but had then taken up greater intervals between individuals just before making contact with the enemy, in order to close the front in this manner. The most irremediable disorder would result if, just at the moment of the final assault against the enemy, the soldiers first had to direct their attention to taking up a new interval. Only to allow the *principes* to move up, the *hastati* would have to squeeze together, moving in along the enemy front, with the latter constantly slashing at them, into such a tight formation that they could use their own weapons only with difficulty; and before the *principes* would have moved into the intervals, which, after all, could only gradually become wide enough, the enemy would naturally have used these freely offered breaches to penetrate and completely overpower the *hastati* in their helpless, compressed situation. The whole idea, therefore, of the chessboard-shaped formation of the maniples in battle must be thrown out. But it immediately becomes usable and understandable as soon as we conceive of it, as we did above, as simply a drill maneuver. For this purpose it is quite excellently suited. The only point that might be erroneous in Livy's account and which again is to be attributed to pure exaggeration is that the *hastati* were supposed to pull back while the *principes* moved up. To carry out such a movement to the rear in orderly fashion with a company of 120 men is hardly possible and moreover completely purposeless. Rather, the maneuver probably was executed in such a way that the *hastati* stood still and the *principes* continued to move forward. Livy necessarily reversed this, since he imagined the whole action not as a drill but as a combat maneuver and described it accordingly.

The interval between the Roman legionaries, as between Greek hoplites, was much greater than is the case today with us, in order to allow the free use of weapons. The breadth of a file was estimated as 3 feet, whereas the width of a man at the shoulders amounts to only 1½ feet. With the lack of contact, drilling is naturally much harder. The second rank was presumably formed not covering the files of the front rank, but with the men behind the intervals, or at any rate they moved over to this position at the moment of contact with the enemy. For this reason, Vegetius, in 3. 14, estimated not 3 but 6 feet as interval between ranks, that is, from the first to the third, from the second to the fourth, and so on. See also Rudolf Schneider, *Philologische Wochenschrift* No. 20, 15 May 1886, and Book VI, Chapter I, below, "Concerning the *Sarissa* and the Interval between Files."

2. In a very creditable way Steinwender has attempted to establish from the sources the march formation of the Roman army.[12] I myself, however, would prefer not to speak with complete certainty of such details in the present state of our sources. Steinwender's study suffers, moreover, from his mistake in not taking into account the gradual development of Roman tactics from the simple phalanx through the manipular formation to the echeloned series of lines. The manipular formation is treated as if it had been a series of echelons from the start. In a review of this treatise in *Militär-Literaturzeitung* 9 (1907): 336, Major Balck adds: "To judge from the numerous Roman camps with which I am familiar, the *porta praetoria* (general's gate) always had a greater width than the gates on the sides. According to my concept, the movement out of the camp took place by using all the exits (see the citation from Polybius: 'And the entire camp necessarily goes into motion'), in order to shorten as much as possible the time spent deploying from a narrow passage, in such a way that the two legions simultaneously moved out through the *porta praetoria* in two march columns side by side, while the allies left by the two side exits. In expectation of a battle the *'agmen quadratum'*—approach march formation—could then be taken up by means of deployment [Contrary to the author, I understand by this term a march in a shortened march column], or, by controlling the times for marching off, the normal march column, the *'agmen pilatum'* (with a front of four files) was formed."

NOTES FOR CHAPTER III

1. Xenophon, *Hellenica* 3. 2. 2; 4. 4. 9; 6. 2. 23. Plutarch, *Phocion*, Chapter 13.

2. Polyaenus 3. 9. 11: Iphicrates has a fixed point on the terrain in front of the camp occupied, in order to protect the camp. Of course, immediately thereafter it is recounted again (para. 17) that Iphicrates, in enemy territory, also had a trench dug around the camp so that, as commander, he would perhaps not have to say: "I had not thought of that." ("I did not think as befits a general."*) Judging from that, it probably happened more often, after all, than appears in the sources, that at least a trench was dug for the protection of the camp.

3. Polybius calls it four-sided; the later camp description of Hyginus gives the shape as rectangular. The corners were rounded off in the later period, and presumably also from the start. To a certain extent the camp was naturally always laid out in conformity with the terrain, without eliminating the basic shape. Some of the camps of Caesar in Gaul are to this very day so well preserved that Napoleon III was able to have their size and shape very accurately established through excavations.

We cannot go into the details of the Roman camp here. I refer the reader, in addition to Marquardt, to Fröhlich, *Caesar's Military System* (*Kriegswesen Cäsars*), pp. 74 and 220 ff.

4. It is usually assumed (see Marquardt, p. 426), on the basis of a description by Cicero in the *Tusculanae Disputationes* (2. 16. 37), that the legionaries regularly carried along the fortification stakes. Against this viewpoint, Liers (p. 155) properly cited three passages from Livy (8. 38. 7; 10. 25. 6; 25. 36. 5), where it is related as the normal thing that the soldiers did not cut the stakes until reaching the camp site; and he gives a fourth citation (33. 6. 1), where the practice of carrying them along obviously appears as something exceptional.

(Added in the third edition.) Stolle, in *The Roman Legionary and his Equipment* (*Der römische Legionar und sein Gepäk*) (1914), believes, after all, that he must go along with the account that the fortification stake also was included in the soldier's regular equipment; that it was, however, only a rather thin pole, the weight of which he estimates at 1,310 grams. See below, excursus 6 to Book VI, Chapter II.

5. See also Adolf Bauer. *Greek Military Antiquity* (*Griechisches Kriegsaltertum*), para. 39.

6. Gilbert, in *Handbook of Greek National Antiquities* (*Handbuch der griechischen Staatsaltertümer*) (2d ed.), 1: 356, note, states: "The commander has the power of the death sentence in the field" and cites as authority Lysias 13 ("Against Agoratos"*), 67. The passage reads: "He was caught while he was sending secret signals to the enemy and was executed on a plank by order of Lamachus."* There was, consequently, one man who was beaten to death for treason under Lamachus before Syracuse. Under which form of judgment that took place we do not know. It is naturally to be assumed that crimes like treason could, in the field, be immediately punished by death, but how far in this procedure the disciplinary power of the commander came into the picture cannot be seen from the cited passage.

7. Aristotle, in *Politics* 3. 14 (9). 2, says that in combat the Spartan kings had the power of life and death; out of combat this was not the case. This base is too narrow for the formation of real military discipline.

8. Correctly pointed out by Beloch in *Greek History* (*Griechische Geschichte*), 2: 479.

9. For the earlier period this right of the centurions is not directly proved for us, and whoever sees in the Roman citizen army a levy of property owners could harbor the presumption that this kind of

discipline was not introduced until the changeover to recruiting among the masses. As I conceive the history of the Roman military constitution, however, there can be no doubt that the discipline was based from the start on the same principles. Wherever in the highest position the death sentence is handled with such discretionary power, it lies in the nature of things that subordinate officials, too, have broad authority. On the other hand, it also lies in the nature of things that, as long as the centurion felt himself to be a citizen among fellow citizens, he made certain distinctions, and the respected head of a household was not really exposed to the danger of strokes in ordinary service.

Against my concept it would be possible to cite Polybius 6. 37. 8, where tribunes are given the right to punish, to fine, and to lash ("fines, or sureties, or flogging"*), without mentioning the centurions. But Polybius is speaking here of punishment in the framework of formal proceedings, in addition to which there could very well have existed an additional beating by the captains, not specifically provided by the law, in order to maintain good order.

10. See also above, p. 263, and below, p. 292.

11. Livy 29. 9. 4. Valerius Maximus 2. 7. 4. Frontinus, *Strategemetos* 4. 1. 30–31. "Cotta consul P. Aurelium sanguine sibi junctum, quem obsidioni Lipararum, ipse ad auspicia repetenda Messanam transiturus, praefecerat, cum agger incensus et capta castra essent, virgis caesum in numerum gregalium peditum referri et muneribus fungi jussit." ("When the consul Cotta was on the point of going to Messana to take the auspices again, he placed in command of the blockade of the Liparian Islands a certain Publius Aurelius who was related to him by blood. But when the latter's line of blockade was burned and his camp was captured, Cotta ordered him to be flogged, reduced to the ranks, and to perform the tasks of a common soldier.")

12. Theodor Steinwender, professor in the Royal *Gymnasium* in Danzig, *The March Formation of the Roman Army at the Time of the Manipular Organization* (*Die Marschordnung des römischen Heeres zur Zeit der Manipularstellung*) (Danzig: A. W. Kasemann, 1907).

Chapter IV

Pyrrhus

We have developed the most ancient Roman tactics from the accounts handed down to us interwoven with Roman constitutional history; we have received no information, however, on the details of any particular battle. The most ancient Roman battles of which we might know something from the nature of the sources are the battles with Pyrrhus. Although it is true that even then and for a long time thereafter no true historical account was written in Rome, nevertheless the Greeks who took part did not let these noteworthy events pass unnoticed. Pyrrhus himself left his memoirs, which were used in the sources we have at hand, especially Plutarch.

Nevertheless, there is practically nothing to be learned concerning the history of the military art from these accounts. Quite a number of the details of the accounts may well be true, and the historian may be allowed to repeat the accounts without doing any harm. For our particular purpose, however, we must establish a stricter criterion. For us it is a question of establishing the continuing development of a technique, and for this purpose only unconditionally reliable details may be used. But the accounts of the Pyrrhic War, even though they go back to originally valid witnesses, have come to us third-hand, so that there is so little we can do to test their sources and to separate them from the accompanying fables and legends that none of the facts may be considered as completely reliable.

Pyrrhus was the nephew and imitator of Alexander the Great. With full trust in the military system and the art of war developed by the great Macedonians, whose disciple he was, he marched out to conquer the West, as Alexander had subjected the East. By the addition of elephants he had made this military power even more fearful than it had formerly been under Alexander. But he was

297

unable to overcome the tough resistance of the city-state that dominated Italy, with its uniquely structured military system. Though victorious in battle on several occasions, he was still eventually forced to give up the war. We do not know whether he finally suffered a real tactical defeat or if the tactical battle remained undecided and only the impossibility of gaining a reliable political base moved the king–soldier of fortune to give up the struggle as hopeless. At any rate, the Romans were able to hold their own, despite repeated defeats in the field, and that was enough to prevent Pyrrhus from establishing an hegemony from which he could have drawn the means for carrying on the struggle. Without such a dominant position in Italy itself and having to rely solely on supplies from the unimportant Epirus, he was not able to carry on the fight.

EXCURSUS

1. In addition to the general works on Roman history by Mommsen and Ihne, as well as Niese's *History of the Greek and Macedonian States* (*Geschichte der griechischen und macedonischen Staaten*) (see especially the battle of Chaeronea), two monographs are important for a study of Pyrrhus: R. von Scala, *The Pyrrhic War* (*Der Pyrrhische Krieg*), 1884; R. von Schubert, *History of Pyrrhus* (*Geschichte des Pyrrhus*), 1894.

The worthlessness of the Roman accounts for this period is well presented by Schubert, p. 182.

2. **THE BATTLE OF HERACLEA**
The strength of the Romans is estimated by Mommsen as at least 50,000, by Scala at some 36,000 men. The size of Pyrrhus' army is equally unknown to us.

Pyrrhus drew up his army behind the Siris River and is supposed to have wished to avoid battle while awaiting allies. This is improbable in every respect. Pyrrhus was a capable enough commander to know that a small river like the Siris offered no real obstacle. If he was awaiting more allies, the Romans could likewise easily have moved up reinforcements; they were far from being at full strength, reportedly having only a fourth of their army on hand.[1]

It may be correct that a quick decision meant more to the Romans than to the Epirote. The mere fact of his continuing presence on Italian soil was already weakening the authority of the Romans vis-à-vis their subject states, and whatever the Romans lost, Pyrrhus gained. Once the two sides faced each other, however, Pyrrhus would have to accept the tactical decision in order to prove the superiority of his military skill to the anxiously waiting peoples of Italy. Hesitation on his part would have weakened their confidence in him. Pyrrhus no doubt, then, took up his position behind the river not with the idea of avoiding battle but in order to gain the tactical advantage in the expected battle. He did not pitch his camp directly by the river, but at a certain distance, and he observed the crossing only with his cavalry. When the sources report that, on hearing that the Romans had crossed the river, he was at first surprised and confused, that seems to me to be absolutely incredible, for he could not possibly have wished for anything better.

Just as incredible is the report that, now recognizing his advantage and wishing to attack the Romans while they were still in disorder during the crossing, he drove against them with his cavalry alone, leaving his phalanx in place. Why this splintering of his own forces?

When his cavalry gave way, Pyrrhus is supposed to have sent his phalanx into the attack, and after it had fought for a long time without gaining a decision, he finally was able to carry the day by means of his elephants. Every attempt to explain why Pyrrhus supposedly committed his forces individually in such an illogical manner falls flat. Since the crossing of a large army over a river that, as is expressly reported by Plutarch, was passable by infantry only at one ford, takes a long time and Pyrrhus was promptly informed by his cavalry concerning the approach of the Romans, there can be no doubt that he had plenty of time to form his army properly in battle formation and to have it move up in close order. It is impossible to find any reason for holding back the elephants. Pyrrhus would no doubt have truly been wantonly exposing his infantry to heavy losses if, instead of driving off the Roman cavalry with the help of his elephants at the very start and then falling on the flank of the Roman infantry, he had, as Plutarch's source fabricates, first had his phalanx alternate seven times with the Roman legions between flight and pursuit. The King, after all, had complete freedom to choose to avoid battle by taking up a withdrawal before the Romans had crossed the river—or to give battle, whether it be directly at the river or farther to the rear somewhat later. The idea that, in unthinking haste in order to attack the Romans while they were still crossing, he committed his troops piecemeal against the enemy is in itself incredible on the part of a commander of recognized importance, and it is finally quite impossible that the elephants should have come up later than the infantry, which always requires a rather long time to form up.

Even if we are willing to assume that the King initially still did not want to offer battle but by committing his cavalry simply wanted to drive back across the river those portions of the Roman force that had crossed, it would still continue to be incomprehensible that he did not also immediately bring up the infantry and especially that he left the elephants behind.

The account passed down through Zonaras also indicates, it is true, that the battle started as a result of the Romans' crossing the river, and it also has the elephants uncommitted until the end, but in other respects it is very different and is notably lacking in any account of the long, indecisive struggle of the two phalanxes.

The reported numbers of the Roman casualties vary between 7,000 and some 15,000. Since we do not know their overall strength, however, these figures have only very little interest for us. It is noteworthy that in the sources absolutely nothing is said of the difficulties the defeated Romans must have had in withdrawing across the river. Only Zonaras mentions that they had to move back across the river. Pyrrhus is supposed to have called off the pursuit because of a wounded elephant that became wild and frightened the others.

3. BATTLE OF ASCULUM

The reports on this battle are even more uncertain and more contradictory than those on the battle of Heraclea.

There is contained in Dionysius a very exact account of the formation of the two armies; in Frontinus 2. 3. 21 a different one. Schubert (p. 194) has shown that we have here late Roman fantasies, presumably of Claudius Quadrigiarius and of Valerius Antias.

According to Plutarch's source (probably Hieronymus) the battle lasted two days, according to Dionysius only one day.

On the first day the battle is supposed to have taken place on an uneven, swampy piece of terrain, limited by a stream, so that Pyrrhus could not make good use of his cavalry and elephants. According to the accounts of the battle of Heraclea, it was precisely by means of these arms that he finally won; how then is such a competent commander supposed to have come to the point of accepting battle on terrain that was especially unfavorable for him? In his tactical ability he was, after all, certainly superior to the annually changing mayors who commanded the Roman armies. On the second day the battle is said to have been continued on an open plain. Why did the Romans, who on the previous day had arranged the scene so cleverly, go along with this? It is not impossible, of course, that it happened this way, but we know nothing about the circumstances under which this took place and on which everything depends for an understanding of the events.

As at Heraclea, according to both Plutarch and Dionysius, Pyrrhus is said to have brought his elephants up only toward the end of the battle and through them to have gained the victory.

Both armies are reported to have had some 70,000 men on foot and 8,000 cavalry, and Pyrrhus also had 19 elephants. Simply because, by chance, no differing numbers are given, these figures are no more credible than others of this period. It may be correct, however, that Pyrrhus lost 3,505 men killed and the Roman army some 6,000, since this information comes from Pyrrhus' memoirs.

According to Dionysius, Pyrrhus did not fight his way to any victory at all, but the battle remained indecisive, because Pyrrhus himself was wounded. According to Zonaras, it was in fact the Romans who won a complete victory.

4. BATTLE OF BENEVENTUM

Our reports on the battle of Beneventum are completely worthless; we cannot even say whether Pyrrhus suffered a real defeat here or simply was unable to carry out his attack, thus leaving the battle undecided. In this respect I invite the reader's attention to what Niese (2: 52) says. The usual account, which distorts the result of the battle in saying that the Romans had by now learned to defend themselves against the elephants by shooting them with burning arrows and thereby frightening them back against their own men, is found in Eutropius and Orosius. It is contradictory, however, with the relatively best report that we have, in Plutarch, where it is said that the elephants drove the one Roman flank back as far as their camp and only at that point were themselves driven off by the attack and the missiles of the fresh forces of the camp garrison. The use of burning arrows in a battle is probably almost out of the question, since the soldier, when he is so close to the enemy, has no opportunity to set fire to his arrow, and consequently we also hear nothing further of the use of this alleged invention against elephants in later battles. Of course, this use of burning arrows is conceivable from a fixed fortification.

Zonaras shifts the use of fire against the elephants to an earlier date, the battle of Asculum. Special chariots to fight against the elephants and use fire were supposedly built. They were of no use, however, since Pyrrhus perversely refused to have his elephants attack in the area where the chariots had been placed. At Beneventum, according to Zonaras, a wounded young elephant seeking its mother brought disorder into the ranks of Pyrrhus' army and defeat to the King.

NOTE FOR CHAPTER IV

1. Schubert, p. 174.

Chapter V

The First Punic War

The situation with respect to our knowledge of the First Punic War is quite the contrary of that governing the Pyrrhic War. Now a historian of the first rank and a man who had particular interest in the art of war and made very informative explanations of the subject comes into the picture—Polybius. Aside from his account there are practically no independent sources at all, and he has the habit of thinking a situation through objectively, backing it up with his well-grounded authority. Consequently it has always been customary simply to repeat his account. But it is not impossible that there might be a certain delusion in doing so. Polybius did not personally experience the First Punic War, as he did some others, nor was he able to question contemporaries and witnesses concerning the events. His book is based principally on two sources—a Roman one, Fabius Pictor, and a Greek one written from the Carthaginian point of view, Philinus. Polybius was sufficiently critical and well informed to be able to seek verification by balancing the two authors against each other and in this way to create a new and excellently harmonious picture. But precisely by eliminating everything with which he disagreed, he made it impossible for us to recognize what value his sources really had. This worth cannot, however, have been so very great. Fabius Pictor was born about 253 B.C. and probably did not write his work until after the end of the Second Punic War. We know, however, how very much oral tradition distorts the events even in the course of one generation. The skeleton of the basic facts was given by the city diary, but that is not what we are interested in here. The rhymed chronicle of Naevius, which preceded Fabius in the account of the First Punic War, will still hardly strengthen the guarantee for the accuracy of the picture, assuming that Fabius did use it, even though the composer was himself one of the combatants. Philinus probably took part in the war on the Carthaginian side and to that extent was closer to the events than was Fabius,[1] but according to what Polybius himself reports about him, he was not very reliable. From such sources even the greatest master can hardly create a history that is reliable in its details. In Alexander's case, too, no doubt, we do not possess any really primary source, but although Arrian offers us the information second-hand, just as does Polybius, and even though Polybius is the sharper critic of the two, we are nevertheless better off with Arrian, because his original sources were by far the better ones. Ptolemy and Aristobulus, whom he used for the most part, were direct participants, even eyewitnesses of the events from a dominating position. Fabius and probably Philinus, too, were hardly any closer to the events of the First Punic War than was Herodotus to those of the Persian Wars. But with Herodotus we are able to see and to test, with our own eyes, what we should accept and what reject; for the First Punic War we are completely dependent on Polybius' judgment. No matter, then, how highly one might evaluate the critical and historical capabilities of Polybius and particularly also appreciate the fact that he had sources from both sides, nevertheless our knowledge of the battles in and around Sicily and Africa has a less solid basis as to details than that concerning Marathon and Plataea.

The result of this observation, therefore, is that, despite Polybius, we must renounce a closer investigation of the accounts of the First Punic War. What is important and decisive for us, the general aspects, the Roman manipular tactics—this we know already and owe our knowledge partly to this very source; but we may not trust the details sufficiently. To fill in our canvas with probabilities and hypotheses would not increase our knowledge. We therefore pass quickly over this war.

It is incorrect, as has long been recognized, to see in this war the struggle of a purely land power against a sea power. Rome was itself a very old trading city, the market of Latium, and had as its crest the galleon. The alliance, moreover, of which it was the head, included the seafaring cities of Greater Greece from Cumaea and Naples to Tarentum. If up to that time Rome had used all its power for land warfare, that was because its opponents were land powers. And to the extent that such was not the case, as in the oldest times with the other Latin sea powers or finally Tarentum, Rome had waged these battles in league with no other than Carthage,[2] which spared her the trouble of creating a stronger sea power. Not until the struggle against Carthage herself was it neces-

sary to develop further in this direction. Rome built herself the
fleet of five-rowed galleys (or penteremes) that she did not yet possess, a feat that, with her rich variety of materials needed for ship-
building, she was able to accomplish without great difficulty.

It will be useful to note that the famous account that the Romans
had understood absolutely nothing of seafaring, had built their
ships on the model of a stranded Carthaginian pentereme, and had
trained their oarsmen on scaffoldings on land stems from Polybius,
who here clearly fell victim to a monstrous rhetorical exaggeration.

The counterpart to this is that the Carthaginians had to have
themselves instructed in the art of land warfare by the Spartan
Xanthippus. Mommsen considers this account, too, to be the echo
of Greek guard house tales. Nitzsch contradicted him, since one
finds often enough in world history, he says, a narrow-minded lack
of understanding such as the Carthaginians showed here. That is
quite right; Polybius, too, may have thought this when he took the
account possibly from Philinus. But even if it is not such an obvious
fable as the story of the building of the Roman fleet, we certainly
also fail to find anywhere in Polybius' account any guarantee that it
is true.

The war ended with the victory of Rome over Carthage, both on
land and at sea. This superiority that Rome had developed was not,
however, so great; the struggle had lasted for twenty-three years,
until this difference was at last proved, and on land the Carthaginians had held their own up to the end on Sicily. The final decision
came at sea. Whether the invention of the boarding bridge really
contributed as much to giving the Romans the upper hand in the
sea struggle as the accounts would picture it, is probably also to
some extent doubtful. In the later sea battles there is no further
mention of this at all, and the Romans still lost a great sea battle
despite their invention. Their superiority in land warfare did not
guarantee them against the defeat of Regulus in Africa, nor could
they drive the Carthaginians completely from the island of Sicily.
The decisive factor in the Romans' finally winning the upper hand
was not so much the courage and military skill of the legionaries as
the capabilities of the great Italian alliance, united under Rome,
which allowed her again and again, after a certain time, to launch
new fleets in the place of those that were wrecked or were beaten.

Even Carthage could probably still have done that, as the Mercenary War and the war tribute sent off to Rome later showed, but
the continuation of the war offered her no further prospects of
success. She could surely have held out still longer and perhaps

even have been able to win another victory, but the victory would have been in vain. In any case, the Carthaginian land forces were too weak to wrest the cities and forts of Sicily back from the Romans, and, as had already been proved, Rome could not be brought down simply through defeats at sea. Moreover (assuming that our sources are reporting the full truth in this respect), the greatest Roman losses at sea were attributable not so much to the Carthaginians as to wind and weather combined with careless seamanship.

And so the Carthaginians, without being fully defeated, but realizing that no final, positive victory was possible for them, submitted to a peace under tolerable conditions. Even the Romans did not feel strong enough to struggle for more than this peace offered them. To do this they would have had to cross over to Africa—a hopeless undertaking as long as they were not even able to drive Hamilcar Barca out of Sicily.

Excursus

1. In the battle for the relief of Agrigentum (Polybius 1. 19) the Carthaginians are said to have formed their 50 elephants behind their mercenaries. These mercenaries are to be understood at any rate as light infantry, since still other "files"* were formed up with (or behind) the elephants. The mercenaries were thrown back by the Romans, and their flight is supposed to have carried off with it the elephants and all the rest of the army.

2. DEFEAT OF REGULUS IN AFRICA

After the Carthaginians had been beaten in a meeting engagement (Chapter 30) because they accepted battle on terrain that was impassable for their cavalry and elephants, the Spartan Xanthippus is said to have taught them how they had to operate in order to beat the Romans. He chose an open plain for a battlefield, had his 100 elephants in front of the line of infantry, and the cavalry with the light infantry on both flanks. As we know of the action of the elephants from the battle on the Hydaspes, this formation had the danger of having the elephants driven back by the enemy missiles and bringing disorder to their own phalanx, which was aligned behind them. The Romans, who were now familiar with the elephants from the experience of at least four battles and had recently captured a large number of them at Agrigentum, knew how to defend against them. They stationed spear-throwers in the advanced echelon and behind them formed the infantry unusually deep, so that they could not be broken through by the elephants. This formation is praised by Polybius expressly as suited to combat against elephants. Nevertheless, the Romans lost the battle because of the great superiority of the enemy cavalry (4,000 against 500), which, after driving off the Roman horsemen, attacked the phalanx in the rear.

3. Although, according to Polybius' definite statement, it was not the elephants but the cavalry that had brought about the defeat of Regulus in Africa, he says, nevertheless, later in his account (Chapter 39), that fear of the elephants prevented the Romans for two years from allowing themselves to be engaged in a land battle in

Sicily. Finally the Carthaginians, for their part, had enough confidence (Chapter 40) to attack the Romans directly in front of Palermo, on the fortifications of which the latter were basing their flanks. With arrows, javelins, and lances, some of which were shot and thrown from the walls, the Romans wounded the elephants of the Carthaginians so extensively that they drove them back into their own troops, who, swept into confusion, were now beaten by the Romans, who sallied out from the city with fresh troops.

4. The battle in which Hamilcar conquered the mutinous mercenaries (Chapter 76) is incomprehensible. In general, it is repeatedly pointed out that it was with the help of the elephants that the Carthaginians finally seized the upper hand in this dangerous war.

5. Beloch, in *Population* (*Bevölkerung*), pp. 379 and 467, has pointed out that the numbers reported for the First Punic War, and particularly for the huge fleets that both sides are supposed to have outfitted, are subject to the strongest suspicion. Fabius Pictor accepted the reported number of ships, which actually included many small ships, as nothing but penteremes and based the total number of the combined crews on that.

CONQUEST OF THE CISALPINE GAULS

6. The transition from the First to the Second Punic War is formed by the conquest of Gallic upper Italy by the Romans. Polybius gives us a rather thorough account of this, and scholars who have treated Roman military subjects have made much use of this account. Precisely with respect to it, however, we must never forget that Polybius is a distorted source, not at all an original one, and that the sources he used were of greatly varying, generally only small value; therefore, whether it may have been through carelessness or that he was dazzled by the colorful nature of the legend or the piquant quality of discovery, he forgot the critical approach fairly often and reported things that, despite his authoritativeness, we cannot accept as true. The information contained in his second book concerning the battles between the Romans and the Cisalpine Gauls from 238 to 222 B.C. is taken undoubtedly from Fabius Pictor, who was in a position to report on them as a contemporary of the events and quite often an eyewitness. But for me the account inspires very little confidence.

7. In the battle of Telamon the Gallic *Gaesatae* (Transalpine mercenaries who had moved over to join their countrymen in upper Italy) are said to have removed their clothing and to have formed up naked in battle order, through braggadocio and because they were concerned about being caught up in the thorny underbrush and being impeded in the use of their weapons.

As the battle started, then, and the Romans threw their *pila*, the Gauls, who had kept on their coats and trousers, were reportedly protected by them, but the naked *Gaesatae*, who because of their large stature were offered no protection by the Gallic shields, suffered heavily. If it seems surprising that trousers and coat supposedly provided better protection against the Roman javelins than did the shields, then it is completely incomprehensible that the attack with javelins should have taken the *Gaesatae* completely unawares ("unexpectedly"*), since the author states immediately before this that the Romans had attacked according to their custom ("as is usual"*).

According to the apparent meaning of the account (2. 30), we would even have to assume that the *Gaesatae* were defeated simply by the light infantry massed in front of the phalanx. "When the javelin-throwers advanced from the Roman ranks, as is the custom, they threw their javelins with rapid and thick volleys. . . . When the javelin-throwers had withdrawn into the Roman ranks, the Roman maniples attacked."*

8. In the next battle, against the Insubres (Polybius 2. 33), the Roman tribunes are supposed to have urged their soldiers to try a special manner of fighting. They

had become convinced that the Gauls were to be feared principally in the first attack, and that the Gallic swords, under any circumstances good only for hacking and not for thrusting, were so poorly forged that after a blow they bent, both in their width and along their length; for the second blow the soldiers had to put their feet on them and bend them straight again.

In view of this circumstance, the tribunes gave the spears of the *triarii* to the *hastati*. Against these spears the Gauls bent their swords as they struck, and before they could straighten them again, the Romans fell on them with their sharp-pointed swords and thrust them down.

One would think that it would be easy for any well-equipped unit to defeat men armed with such weapons as these Gauls had, and that no particular stratagems would be necessary. But what does the alleged stratagem have to do here with the dangerous aspect of the first assault of the spirited Gauls, and why did they strike their swords crooked against the enemy spears, instead of catching up the spear points with their shields and slashing away directly at the man? For a century and a half the Romans had been fighting the Gauls, and now for the first time they discovered the best way of engaging them? A battle-seasoned people like the Gauls is supposed to have marched into battle with completely useless swords, instead (if the state of their metal-working art was really still so primitive) of providing themselves with the so easily manufactured and so effectively usable spear, topped off with a piece of iron?

If it occurs anywhere, then it is a particularly striking case here of the most palpable guard room tales distorted into serious historical reporting, and if that fact, as soon as it is expressed, should not be perfectly clear in and of itself, then we are also in a position to cite a direct counterproof from our knowledge of antiquity. Formerly it was even assumed that the Germanic tribes, early as was their period, had possessed an effective metal-working technique. This concept had to be given up, as Lindenschmit explains in his treatise, "The Prehistoric Iron Sword North of the Alps" ("Das vorgeschichtliche Eisenschwert nördlich der Alpen") in *Antiquities of Our Prehistoric Pagan Period (Altertümer unserer heidnischen Vorzeit)*, Vol. 4, Book 6:

"The shining light that was attributed to the distant prehistoric period of our country through the assumption of the existence of an independent, highly perfected metal-working technique was extinguished in the face of the realization of the sudden disappearance of the same with the end of the Roman domination." But the Celts had what the Germanic peoples still did not have. In Krain there was a very old forge, concerning which there have come down to us not only many classical references,[3] but also many actual artifacts. The iron has been tested for its quality, and it was found that an excellent steel was produced. Admittedly, with the primitive preparation methods used, the malleable iron was not worked out with complete uniformity; but they took the lower quality for the axes, where it is the mass that is most important, and the best metal went into the swords. When the scholar to whom we are indebted for this research, Müllner-Leubach, adds that perhaps the poorer warriors had to content themselves with swords of poorer metal and in this way clarifies for himself the account in Polybius,[4] it seems to me that it is absolutely unnecessary, in fact is not even permissible, to make this concession to the authority of the written word. Once it is established that the Celts were skilled in iron working, then it was too much in the interest of the whole community as of the individual for them not to have seen to it that every man in the formation should be provided with a usable weapon. If there actually was a shortage of swords, this was certainly not the case with spears. Since we now hear in another place from Polybius himself (Fragment 137 Dindorf, 100 Becker, to the extent that this fragment is derived from Polybius) that the swords of the Celtiberians had been so excellent that the Romans had adopted them from them, and Diodorus, too, (5. 33) praised the Celtiberians as particularly good smiths, it can be seen that all these points actually converge to expose Polybius' account as pure fable.

Finally we read in the same chapter that the Consul Flaminius vitiated the special trait of the Roman system of combat in this battle by forming up the army with its back to a river, so that the maniples had no room to draw back. This criticism naturally has nothing to do with the marching through of the maniples and the relief of the echelons, as it was done on the drill field and as it was earlier thought to have taken place on the battlefield, too, since for this purpose no withdrawal is necessary behind the position of the *triarii*. If the Romans actually did have the river directly behind them in the battle, that would have been, of course, a completely incomprehensible formation—we would have to conclude in this case perhaps that the Consul had in mind raising the courage of his men by removing any possibility of a withdrawal—but this would hold true for any army and has nothing to do with the particular method of combat.

NOTES FOR CHAPTER V

1. Unger, *Rheinisches Museum* 34: 102. von Scala, *Römische Studien* (a complimentary greeting from Innsbruck to the 42d Assembly of German Philologues, 1893), showed that it was probable that Naevius, too, who did not write until he had reached an advanced age, had already used Philinus.

2. Very enlightening on this point is W. Soltau in *Neues Jahrbuch für Philologie* 154 (1896): 164.

3. Collected in L. Beck, *History of Iron* (*Geschichte des Eisens*), p. 510, and from Jähns, *History of Offensive Arms* (*Geschichte der Trutzwaffen*), p. 72.

4. *Korrespondenzblatt der deutschen Gesellschaft für Anthropologie*), 1889, p. 206.

BOOK V
The Second Punic War

Introduction

In the history of the art of warfare the Second Punic War is epochal. We have been able to determine only along general lines the first great change in Roman tactics, or, otherwise stated, the development of the specifically *Roman*, manipular tactics from the general form of the hoplite phalanx, but not really to observe it up to this point in concrete form in definite battles or to fix it chronologically. The Second Punic War shows us the last massive appearance of this battle formation in great battles, its defeat, its inadequacy, and the shift to a new form of tactics, technical skill in which gave the Romans mastery of the world within two generations. Fortune has willed also that we should receive thorough and concrete knowledge of these events. It is the account of these events that won Polybius fame and authority as a great historian. From this point on he was in a position to work with genuine material, so to speak. Fabius Pictor, who served throughout as his principal guide for the Roman side of these accounts, is here reporting as a contemporary and participant in the events; during this war he was a Roman senator. For the Carthaginian side, however, his source is a Greek who, as a member of Hannibal's retinue, recounted the latter's acts; the account of the battle of Cannae is of such quality that it can only have been written by a very great man. I have no doubt that we have at hand here Hannibal's own account, perhaps dictated by him personally.

The reasons for this conjecture will be developed below; it may be nothing more than a conjecture, but even this simple possibility fills us with awe as we glance at these pages: the city of the Carthaginians has been destroyed, and not a stone remains on a stone; the entire nation has been eradicated, and not a monument of its existence, not a document, hardly a sound of its voice has been preserved or has a place in the memories of man. Only history tells of Hamilcar's lion's brood and follows the life of Hannibal from the oath taken by the nine-year-old boy to his death, to the extinction by his own hand of the old man, harassed by the world, tired of living. It is like an enrichment of mankind when we imagine that

311

we are holding in our hand, in the account of his greatest victory, a direct expression of the mind of this hero, the only remaining storm-tossed page from the existence of the once so mighty Carthage as it struggled for world supremacy.

This source breaks down for the last years of this war, but Polybius was still able, in the circle of Scipio the Younger, where he lived, to seize and hold the living account himself. This part of the account is not at the same high level as that of the first part; again we recognize that Polybius was more dependent on his materials than seems to be the case.[1] Nevertheless, despite all the objections that must be raised, the account still remains of such quality that, after careful critical analysis, we can get to the bottom of things.

In their first great struggle Carthage was inferior to the Romans less on land than at sea. So as the Carthaginian patriots, with Hamilcar Barca at their head, considered how they could succeed in a future repetition of the war with Rome, it is easy for us to conclude that it would be the most natural thing for Carthage, the old trading city, to strive for unconditional superiority at sea. But the recently completed war had taught her otherwise. From the start it was impossible for Carthage to gain true superiority at sea against the numerous seafaring cities of Italy united under Rome, and all the more so in that Sicily, too, with its many trading centers and ports, belonged to this alliance; and even if she should succeed temporarily, as had of course happened in the First Punic War, nevertheless little would be accomplished thereby if she were not able to exploit the advantage through land warfare and defeat Rome directly. In order not simply to hold her own but also to be able for once to defeat Rome, Carthage had to create, above all else, a superior land army and use it to attack Rome at the very seat of her power.

To form this army and simultaneously to give Carthage a substitute for her lost hegemony in Sicily, Hamilcar marched off to conquer Spain. As his son, Hannibal was also the heir of his concept, as Alexander of Macedon had been the son and heir of Philip. Hannibal defeated the Romans repeatedly in great battles and brought Rome close to disaster. At sea, however, Rome remained the stronger side, and we shall see how important that became for the final result.

It is not the mission of a history of the art of war to present these events in detail—that would lead to a constantly broadening general military history—but only to examine and to establish which new forms and discoveries the art of war might perhaps show in this period and how the strategic genius of the Carthaginian manipulates and develops the traditional forms of the art. If up to this point we have given our attention to each rather important military action, we were both permitted and forced to do that because the accounts we have received were only just sufficient to let us recognize the development and elucidate it. From here on the sources flow down to us so much more abundantly that it suffices to select individual typical events. Moreover we are obliged to be satisfied with this selective procedure, since now the conduct of war, in a period when very great, similar, and mutually worthy adversaries confront each other, becomes so complicated that the investigation of every single action would lead into a limitless area.

First of all, we must establish the tactical aspects. What was the basis for the superiority that Hannibal's troops showed in battle vis-à-vis the Romans? This tactical factor principally—the confidence in being able to defeat the Romans in open battle—must have dominated Hannibal's strategy. Just as we were able from the tactical relationships to clarify the strategic decisions of Miltiades, Themistocles, Pausanias, and Pericles, so must we seek here the key to Hannibal's actions, his initial victories, and his final lack of success. Consequently, we shall not proceed chronologically but shall seek out first of all that particular military event in which the specific tactical superiority of the Carthaginian army over the Romans is most clearly and fully recognizable. That is the battle of Cannae. The other battles and engagements we need to treat only to the extent that is necessary to establish whether they are in agreement with what we conceive of as the typical aspects of the battle of Cannae. Not until we have established with certainty, through this comparison, the really characteristic element, the tactics of the two sides, will we be able to turn to the investigation of their strategy.

EXCURSUS

In 1912 there appeared the third volume of Kromayer's *Ancient Battlefields* (*Antike Schlachtfelder*), the first half of which contained "Italy," treated by Kromayer, the second containing "Africa," treated by G. Veith. The greatest amount of space is naturally devoted to the Second Punic War. I have been quite critical in my judgment of the earlier volumes of this work, and I must say now that, in relationship to the great expenditure of energy and the great pains taken on the spot in the topographic investigations, the useful results are only minor. Nevertheless, important progress is to be noted with respect to the strategic reasoning; this applies particularly to Kromayer's pamphlet for the general public, *Rome's Struggle for World Hegemony* (*Roms Kampf um die Weltherrschaft*) (Leipzig: B. G. Teubner), which contains much excellent material. The errors are to be found in the tactical aspects, which the author has still not mastered. Even if he has now accepted a number of my conclusions, he has still not arrived at clear perspectives, but by holding to the old philological constructions, he has fallen into inner contradictions. Nevertheless, I have been able to accept gratefully a few individual conclusions.

The *History of the Carthaginians from 218* B.C. *to 146* B.C., (*Geschichte der Karthager von 218 bis 146*), by Ulrich Kahrstedt (3d vol. of the work by Meltzer), 1913, is dedicated almost entirely to the Second Punic War. The book is grandiloquent and vague, the results completely useless. The numerical estimates, whether they be for the city of Carthage or for the strengths of the armies, are, as Kromayer strikingly proved in *Göttingische gelehrte Anzeigen* 8 (1917): 479 ff., not only false but completely lacking in any real perception, when, for example, the author has the Romans send an army of *one* legion to Spain against Hannibal and has the Carthaginians gradually beaten down after Cannae by two Roman legions. I will not conceal the fact that Eduard Meyer praises the book in that it has "significantly furthered our understanding of the war with Hannibal," but I support Kromayer's judgment (p. 467) to the effect that "the entire understanding of the Italian war after Cannae has remained closed" to Kahrstedt.

In the *Reports of the Sessions of the Berlin Academy* (*Sitzungsberichte der Berliner Akademie*), Eduard Meyer has published three "Studies on the History of the Second Punic War" ("Untersuchungen zur Geschichte des zweiten punischen Krieges"), 1913, p. 688; 1915, p. 937; 1916, p. 1068. When he says in the last-cited one, on p. 1069, "Further, Mommsen's judgment, too, on military questions and military history is only too often untenable; apparently these things, by their nature, are alien to him"—one can easily agree. The same thing applies, however, to other historians.

Concerning Dessau's investigation, see below, Book V, Chapter I, Comment 3, "Added in 3d edition."

NOTE FOR INTRODUCTION

1. This opinion has, moreover, already been expressed by another writer, Unger in *Rheinisches Museum* 34: 97.

Chapter I

The Battle of Cannae

The Roman army at Cannae was twice as large as the one that had tried the first time, on the Trebia, to offer Hannibal resistance in pitched battle; it amounted to no less than 8 Roman legions and corresponding allied contingents, or a total of 16 legions—or, after deducting the camp garrison and the *rorarii*, who did not function as combatants, on the order of 55,000 hoplites, 8,000 to 9,000 light infantry, and also 6,000 cavalry. The great mass of hoplites was not used to broaden the front but to increase the depth of the formation. The legions were not formed one behind the other, since they were arranged, of course, according to age classifications, and the young men could not very well be placed behind the fathers of families. The greater depth was therefore arrived at, as Polybius reports, by forming up each individual maniple with much greater depth than width ("making the depth many times as large among the maniples in front"*) and, in keeping with the narrower front, the intervals between maniples were shortened. I assume that the front of the infantry was not any broader than some 800 to 900 meters, estimating the depth of the formation at some 70 men.[1] The consul Terentius Varro, who ordered this formation and is supposed to have pointed out to the Romans in a speech before the battle that they had almost a two-to-one superiority, probably estimated that the longer the front was, the more awkwardly and more slowly the army would move; that, in view of the superiority of the Carthaginian cavalry (a point that his colleague, Aemilius Paullus, repeatedly stressed with great concern), there would be no thought of a possible outflanking and envelopment of the enemy army; so that, finally, everything depended on producing an irresistible shock action with a deep mass.

The cavalry was divided between the two flanks; the right flank rested on the Aufidus River.

The battlefield was formed of a broad plain without any obstacles.

Hannibal was not much more than half as strong as his opponent in infantry, having 32,000 heavily equipped men against 55,000; of about equal strength in sharpshooters, that is, 8,000 men each. But in cavalry he enjoyed just about the same superiority, namely, 10,000 horses against 6,000. He, too, divided his cavalry between the two flanks and formed his phalanx of his Iberians and Celts, something over 20,000 men. He formed his Africans, divided into halves of about 6,000 men each, behind each flank in a manner similar to that of Alexander at Gaugamela, in a deep column, at the point of junction of infantry and cavalry. From such a formation the Africans were in a position to deploy either toward the one side to reinforce and support the center, if that should be necessary, or toward the other to extend the infantry front in order to outflank and envelop the enemy.

Polybius uses a very bold picture for this formation. At first all units formed a straight line: cavalry, Africans, Iberians and Celts, Africans, and cavalry; then the center moved forward and, as it became thinner, the figure of a half-moon was created.

One should be careful not to be taken in too much by the charm of this picture, as Polybius himself was, and to think of this line perhaps as a curved one, or to believe that the center, through its move forward, gradually was thinned out on its own. During an approach march, curved lines form only too easily, it is true, but they are not forms in which one can move tactically, but are rather distortions that cannot be entirely avoided and that one must try to get along with, but which one tries to prevent as much as possible in order to hold a straight line.

If we take Polybius' description literally, the Africans would also have remained between the center and the cavalry, and the latter would have been at the extreme ends of the half-moon, and consequently farthest from the enemy, whereas we hear later that it was precisely the cavalry that had the first fight and therefore must have been closest to the enemy. It was the Africans, however, who outflanked the Roman phalanx. This can be reconciled only through the fact that, as the first shock of contact came, the Africans were in position behind the cavalry. One can best picture the situation as follows: when all the corps were still drawn up in a straight line side by side, they were not yet deployed. The front was therefore formed by the heads of some six columns that had taken such a distance from one another that the deployment could take place in the intervals—the formation that, in the tactics of the eighteenth century, is called the flankwise move into line ("der flügelweise Abmarsch"). But, instead of having all his columns deploy uniformly, Hannibal had only the cavalry and the Iberians and Celts of the center deploy, the latter, however, so shallowly that with their 20,000 men they had the same width as the 55,000 legionaries on the other side. Behind this front, still in column, at the point where the cavalry made contact with the center, the Africans were formed up on both flanks. Today we normally call such a formation "horseshoe-shaped" (borrowing an expression from the cavalry), with the same reservation as in the case of the half-moon image, namely that the lines are not curved but right-angled. Since during an approach march on a broad front the middle easily moves ahead and bends forward, the picture of the half-moon was probably still more appropriate from the point of view of the observer in the middle (from the perspective of the supreme commander, so to speak), than for our tactical analysis, which looks upon the phalanx as a straight front, even when in practice the alignment has been lost.

After the engagement had been started by the skirmishing of the numerous light infantrymen in front of the line on both sides, the cavalry of the Carthaginian left flank under Hasdrubal first moved forward in a decisive attack along the river bank. As it was, Hannibal was of course significantly superior in this arm; in addition, he had concentrated all of his heavy cavalry on this flank.[2] The Roman cavalry was immediately overrun, cut down, pushed into the river, and driven from the battlefield.

In the meantime, on the other flank, the light Numidian cavalry had only been skirmishing with their opponents. Now Hasdrubal sent them reinforcements around behind the Roman infantry, and when the Roman cavalry thereupon took to flight on this side, too, the Carthaginian general led his entire cavalry mass in an attack against the rear of the Roman phalanx.

While the cavalry battle was still going on, the Roman phalanx had made contact with the enemy infantry and, with its huge superiority, 55,000 hoplites against 20,000, had driven the enemy back. But then Hannibal's cavalry attacked from the rear and brought the forward-pressing mass to a standstill. Not that the Iberian, Celtic, and Numidian cavalry could have penetrated into the legions and have broken up the huge mass—but they attacked it with their javelins and soon the Punic light infantry joined them; the hail of spears, arrows, and slungshot which drummed down on the Romans from behind forced the rear ranks to face about and obstructed the further movement forward of the entire phalanx.

Now the Punic center held; the two withheld columns of Carthaginian infantry, the Africans, marched forward and in doing so came into the flank of the Roman phalanx, turned to the right and left, and in this way completed the envelopment, so that the Romans were being simultaneously attacked from all sides.

Although their cavalry had fled the field, the Romans were still considerably superior in total numbers. "Concentric activity against the enemy is not appropriate for the weaker side," says Clausewitz in his work *Vom Kriege*, and in a similar vein Napoleon once said that the weaker side must not simultaneously envelop both flanks. Here the weaker had enveloped on both flanks, up to the point of closing the ring in the rear. If the consuls ordered the maniples to maintain a defensive stance in three directions, they could penetrate on the fourth side, with a mighty push, the but moderately strong ring in their front and roll up the enemy army from the point of breakthrough. But for such a maneuver more is needed than the Roman citizen army could accomplish tactically. The maniples were not independent tactical units; they were only component parts of the one unified tactical body, the phalanx. Nor were the legions tactical bodies, capable of and accustomed to acting independently; they were simple administrative bodies. If the legions had been drawn up two deep, we could perhaps imagine that in this extreme emergency the ones in the rear would have faced about and the flank legions would have turned outward in order to ward off the enemy cavalry and the Africans, while the other six legions would have completely crushed the Iberians and Gauls of the enemy front, whom they were already, of course, pushing back. But the Romans were not drawn up in this way at all, but legion beside legion. No one of them could make a movement on its own without breaking up the entire phalanx. The great depth was achieved—nothing is more characteristic of the state of the Roman tactics—by increasing the depth of each individual maniple, and the three echelons of the maniples, *hastati*, *principes*, and *triarii*, could not be separated from each other. It seems so simple to us for the maniples of the *triarii* to have faced about, in order to hold off Hasdrubal's cavalry with their spears, while the *hastati* and the *principes* continued the attack that had already been started, depending on their great superiority. But no matter how simple they may seem, such tactical shifts cannot be improvised, and the *triarii* were all the less capable of taking up the battle toward the rear in that their maniples were formed with very large intervals (see above, p. 277) and were not capable of forming at once an ordered, closed front. The entire Roman infantry was accustomed to moving forward in closed formation until the enemy gave way and fell back. So now, as soon as the cry rang out "Attack from the rear" and the rearmost ranks had to face about, the forward-driving pressure of the mass stopped, and thereupon the entire phalanx came to a standstill. At this moment they were hopelessly lost. The advantage of numerical superiority was paralyzed. It obviously consisted exclusively of the gigantic physical and moral pressure exercised by the rearmost ranks; the actual use of their weapons is limited in any phalanx to a very small part of the formation. At the moment when an attack from the rear removes this pressure, only the exterior edges of the phalanx still come into consideration as combatants, and they are limited to defensive action only.

With their victory sure and their booty before their eyes, the Carthaginian mercenaries drove in from all sides. It was impossible for any missile hurled into the mass of Romans to miss, and the more the terrified Romans allowed themselves to be pressed together, the less capable were they of using their weapons and the more certain was the harvest reaped by the enemy swords.

In a killing that lasted for hours the entire Roman army was slaughtered; only a few were taken prisoner alive. Not even a fourth succeeded in escaping from the melee.

The decisive factor here was the attack from the rear by the Carthaginian cavalry. There is in this respect a noteworthy discrepancy in Polybius' account: he has Hannibal giving a talk to his soldiers before the battle, showing them how they may expect a sure victory in the plain from their superior cavalry, and Polybius in his own conclusions names this superiority as the basic factor of the Carthaginian victory; nevertheless, in his account, he stresses much more the flanking attack of the Africans. In fact, he does not even have the maneuver of the cavalry appear as the result of an order by Hannibal, but as a spontaneous action on the part of Hasdrubal. The Romans, he says, as they first collided with the protruding center of the Carthaginians and drove it back, had squeezed together toward the middle and in this way had gradually come between the Africans, just as Hannibal had previously calculated. That a certain pressing together of the Romans toward the middle took place is quite natural. Their flank maniples, which probably extended somewhat beyond the flanks of the Carthaginian center, did not swing in against the latter's flanks, since they of course saw in front of them the African columns, which would have moved into their own flanks as the result of such an action. They continued forward, but the enthusiasm of the nearest ones, who still hoped to be able to come to a position where they could slash away directly at the Celts and Iberians, caused them to squeeze toward the middle in doing so. Moreover, the extreme flank maniples no doubt moved somewhat more slowly forward, since the unfavorable course of the cavalry battle that was taking place beside them was a strongly distracting factor. This action, however, is naturally not to be understood as meaning that this squeezing was the cause of the outflanking by the Africans. Nor is it any more likely that it could have been the flanking action of the Africans that brought the attack by the Roman center to a standstill. If there were nothing more to overcoming a courageous, superior army than to make one's own line longer and thinner and lead the flank extensions against the enemy flanks, then this artifice would have been used often. The danger here, however, is that while one is in the process of outflanking the enemy, one's own center, which has to be weakened in order to allow this, can be penetrated. The fact that this did not happen at Cannae is the truly significant element of the battle. The only explanation for it is the Carthaginian cavalry masses' attack from the rear, and therefore it is logical that Polybius, in his concluding observations, finds the decisive aspect in the superiority of the Carthaginian cavalry. Clearly, it was not on his own initiative that Hasdrubal carried out the maneuver, but in furtherance of the battle plan of his commander.

However plausible may be the rule that it is not proper for the weaker side to envelop simultaneously on both flanks, since he must weaken his center too drastically for this purpose—Hannibal nevertheless dared, despite the rule, to encircle completely 70,000 men with 50,000, and he was responsible for their being killed, man by man, in this iron ring. This horrible butchery must have raged for hours. The Carthaginians themselves lost no fewer than 5,700 killed, but of all the Romans, 48,000 dead covered the battlefield, 16,000 escaped, and the rest were taken prisoner.

Everything depended on the fact that the Punic center held fast until their cavalry had driven off the Roman horsemen and had completed their envelopment. Why then did Hannibal not place his more reliable troops, the Africans, in the middle, and why, in addition, did he push his center forward? The longer the center was held back and the later the battle began at that point, the greater was the probability that the cavalry could complete its mission in time and the lesser was the danger that the center might succumb too soon. Why did Hannibal not, on the contrary, push his cavalry forward and place them in front of his two infantry flanks, so that the half-moon, speaking in Polybius' terms, would be turned about?

If we observe the situation correctly, we see that it did indeed happen that way. The pushing forward of the center was not relative to its position vis-à-vis the cavalry; on the contrary, the latter moved forward while the light infantry were still skirmishing out in front. They had to be careful, however, not to ride forward too soon, for in that case the full development of the battle might have been impeded. The Carthaginian commander had to be conscious of the possibility that the consuls, on seeing how their cavalry was being swept away, would lead their infantry as quickly as possible back into the fortified camp. Not until the entire Roman army was so close that it could not possibly withdraw from the battle was the cavalry charge to be unleashed; that is why the cavalry stood on the same line with the infantry, and the Africans, who were to make the enveloping movements, were formed up behind the cavalry.

The precarious period of time during which the weak Carthaginian center was exposed without assistance to the press of the huge mass of the Roman legions was therefore inevitable. This makes it doubly curious that the less reliable allies, the Gauls, were placed in this position.

But in this battle the center was also the position that was susceptible to the heaviest losses; the Gauls left no fewer than 4,000 killed on the field, whereas the Iberians and Africans together lost only 1,500. Hannibal had to be careful about shedding the blood of his most loyal units, who were to form the continuing nucleus of the anti-Roman army in Italy. How strong must have been the thought: Place the Old Guard in the spot where the absolutely reliable resistance has to be provided! How immeasurable would have been the results if at that point, where in the final analysis it was a matter but of minutes, the Romans had penetrated before Hasdrubal tore them back from behind—if the commander had then had to say to himself: "The Africans would have held out for such-and-such a time longer. What an error not to have placed them at that spot!"

In the military art not everything can be calculated, weighed, and measured; in situations defying such calculations, the belief in his own star must govern the commander's decision. In order not to sacrifice the future to the present, Hannibal risked entrusting the critical position to the Gauls, mixing them, for greater security, with his Iberians, and explaining to them in a speech in advance how effective his superior cavalry would be in the broad plain. He put the final seal on their reliability by taking up his own position near them. Alexander had personally engaged in the melee at the head of his cavalry. Hannibal turned the command of his cavalry over to one of his trusted generals and took up his station with his staff,· having his young brother Mago at his side, in the center, in order to be able to conduct the battle from there and to steel the soft iron of the resistance with the force of his personality. Seeing their commander nearby and hearing the shout of his voice gave the Gauls an unshakable confidence in their victory, and they withstood the most difficult of all tests: pulling back before an overwhelming enemy without letting themselves be defeated by him; continuing the battle in the face of the heaviest losses until the promised help appeared from the other side. No description of the battle would be complete without specific attention given to the importance of the position taken by Hannibal. Not only spiritually but also physically Hannibal was the midpoint of the battle—no longer by wielding the sword, like Alexander, nor in such a way that the battle was divided into a series of different actions that the commander himself had to direct (with the deployment and the command to form up, the course of the battle was completely prearranged)—it was the personality as such that in its simple presence at a specified spot exercised the decisive effect in a manner at once passive and active.

The only command that Hannibal had to give after the battle signal had rung out was for the advance of the Africans on the two flanks. Since they initially were still lined up in column, Hannibal had in this connection the idea that, in case of necessity, instead of using them for the envelopment of the enemy phalanx, he could have them deploy in reinforcement of his center, in case the latter might seem incapable of offering sufficient resistance to the press of the Romans, up to the moment when Hasdrubal's envelopment made itself felt. We recognize the similarity of the battle plan to that of Gaugamela. Like Alexander, Hannibal, too, had Greek authors in his headquarters, who were to describe his actions. It is not going too far to suppose that whoever had such men in his retinue also shared in their culture and had learned what Hellas could offer him. Whatever may have been the case with that Spartan, Xanthippus, who is supposed to have taught the Carthaginians in the First Punic War how to defeat Regulus, there is no doubt that Hannibal had studied the Greek-Macedonian art of war, and we must imagine how in the evenings in winter quarters the Greek Silenos read to him King Ptolemy's book concerning the deeds of the great Alexander and the Carthaginian developed his ideas in keeping with the radiant example of the son of Zeus.

At Cannae the Carthaginians were victorious with their barbarian mercenaries because of their superiority in cavalry, because of their officer corps, the generals and staff officers, who had their troops well in hand and knew how to direct them tactically, and because of the commander, who with the unmistakable certainty of genius blended the forces at hand into an organically unified effectiveness.

In my opinion, we are also indebted to this commander for the account of the battle as we read it today in Polybius and in its principal features in Livy as well. This does not show up so much in what is recounted—from that we would be unable to conclude anything, since, excellent as the description may be, nevertheless some other man of talent could have been on the spot—but it stands out in that which is omitted and in its nuances of light and shadow.

The truly decisive point, the attack by the cavalry in the rear, is not particularly stressed; in fact, it appears to be not at all a command of Hannibal but the action of a cavalry general. The entire emphasis of the account is placed on the assignment of the Africans to the two enveloping flanks. The motive for holding out these troops is not mentioned in the account. There is always something painful for the commander when he intentionally exposes certain troops, and especially allies, to greater losses than others. He is hardly willing to admit to himself the fact that he calculates in this way, or at what time he does so. Nevertheless we may be allowed to assume that he had this motive; any third person would have been justified in this assumption and would not have passed over so lightly this transparent motive. Our account, however, says nothing of it but discourses exclusively on the tactical maneuver of the envelopment, for the latter is the original idea of this battle plan. The true deciding feature, the cavalry attack, fades into the background, on the other hand, for this maneuver is nothing unusual for the commander, but is his normal technique. It would have sufficed this time, too, and even more; if Hannibal had not used the Africans for that formation but had simply reinforced his phalanx with them, he would still have had the unconditionally sure victory in his hands. But he did not want simply victory; he wanted the complete destruction of the enemy army. Therefore he dared to make his center thin and to form the Africans in a position of readiness for the envelopment from the two flanks, for the Roman army was not even to be able to take flight in any direction whatever but simply to be encircled. Even in his battle account, therefore, his heart goes out to the Africans, to whom he assigned this mission, and in doing so he holds back on the accomplishment of the cavalry.

The formation is described with impressive completeness—in the illustration of the half-moon and in the narration of the squeezing together of the Romans toward the middle, the swinging in of the Africans from both sides, the shaking up of the thin center, and the exhortation of the commander. Consequently, the reader even today still has a feeling for the particular viewpoint from which the entire picture of the battle is seen and realizes that, in the account that he is reading, the highest priority is given not to what was physically the most important, but rather to what most concerned the commander's mind.

Excursus

1. A strongly argued controversial point is whether the battle was fought on the right or the left bank of the Aufidus. Since it is specifically said that the Roman right and the Carthaginian left rested on the river, with a shift from one side of the river to the other we would also have to turn about the entire position of the armies. I am not reprinting here what I said about this in the previous editions, since that has been overtaken by the investigation of Konrad Lehmann, *Klio* 15 (1917): 162. The status of the research up to that point was that the sense of the sources pointed to the right bank, but nobody was able to find a strategic explanation of how the Romans in this position had their backs toward the sea, and how the Roman fugitives would have saved themselves by fleeing from the battle toward Canusium and Venusia. I have pointed this out in more detail in *Historische Zeitschrift* 109: 502. Konrad Lehmann has now established that even the idea that the source accounts force us to the conclusion that the battle took place on the right bank was in error. He proves, through a comparison between Polybius' statement that Hannibal moved out from Gerunium at the start of the harvest and the actual date of the battle (2 August), that the battle did not take place almost directly after the departure from Gerunium, but that an interval of two months must be assumed. During this time Hannibal was occupied foraging in Apulia south of the Aufidus. The crossings of the river shortly before the battle, which up to now were considered to have taken place from the north to the south, must therefore have started from the south bank and, seen in this light, the interpretation of the sources leads to the conclusion that the battlefield was on the north side of the river.

The strategic sequence can now be established in the following manner. Hannibal marched from Gerunium into the Apulian plain. The Romans followed him, seeking unassailable positions on the bordering heights of the mountainous country. Since they established a supply depot in Cannae and had their provisions moved there from the region of Canusium, they must therefore have had at the end a position that was closer to Cannae than to Canusium and still not in the immediate vicinity of Cannae, since Hannibal, after all, succeeded in taking from them Cannae with its depot. I therefore assume that the camp was in the region of Mount Altino, some 6 kilometers southeast of Cannae, consequently as far forward as possible in order to cover a maximum area of the countryside and yet still be protected by the terrain from a Punic surprise attack. But Hannibal, covered by his strong cavalry, marched from south to north through the plain, passing by the Roman camp, took Cannae with its depot by a sudden stroke, and forced the Romans to withdraw farther into the countryside toward Canusium.

Lehmann now goes on to conjecture that the Romans had chosen as a battlefield a place where, because of the superiority of the Carthaginian cavalry, they had natural terrain features on which their flanks could rest. He finds such a position, some 3 kilometers wide, which is bounded on the right by the river, on the left by a steep escarpment. To this very day the field is called *"pezzo del sangue"* (field of blood). That is probably not at all certain, and in any case I would place the actual battlefield a bit farther on, where the plain becomes narrower, since 3 kilometers seems too broad to me.

2. STRENGTH AND CASUALTY FIGURES

The strength of the Roman army at Cannae is usually given as 86,000 men, 6,000 of whom were cavalry. Ten thousand men remained in the camp, so that 76,000 Romans were defeated by 50,000 Carthaginian mercenaries, 10,000 of whom were cavalry. Polybius, Livy, and Appian are in essential agreement concerning these numbers. The 80,000 infantrymen are accounted for as being composed of 8 Roman legions of 5,000 men each and a similar number of allies.

Only recently has this estimate been contested by P. Cantalupi in *The Roman Legions in the War with Hannibal* (*Le Legioni Romane nella Guerra d'Annibale*), published by Beloch in *Studi di Storia Antica*, Vol. 1.

Cantalupi calls attention to the fact that Livy expressly reported still another source, according to which the Romans had formed in 216 B.C. not 4 new legions, but had only levied 10,000 replacements. When working with figures, one can as a rule always accept the smaller ones as the more likely ones. Cantalupi therefore estimates the Roman army at a strength of only 44,000 men, and whereas Polybius gives the number of killed Romans as 70,000, Cantalupi arrives, after painstaking comparisons, at only 10,500 to 16,000. If these numbers were accepted, the battle picture would therefore be very considerably changed.

But the reasons given by Cantalupi for his estimates are in no way convincing. He believes that it was only through the battle of Cannae itself that Hannibal became the terror of the Romans, the role in which he lives on in history. Previously, according to Cantalupi, the Romans had had no occasion to arm themselves to such an unusual degree. On the Ticinus there had been only a cavalry combat, whereas on the Trebia the Romans had withdrawn without very serious losses. At Lake Trasimene the consul had allowed himself to be attacked by surprise. The dictator Fabius did not have more than 4 legions, and public opinion in Rome demanded that he fight a battle with this force. It was therefore common belief that, with good leadership, such an army was the equal of Hannibal. When the new consuls arrived with the reinforcements, a new camp was established, in addition to the older one, and it was occupied by a legion and 2,000 allies. The reinforcements can therefore not have been very numerous, since, with the exception of this detachment, they all found their places in the older camp.

These arguments are not exactly of great consequence in comparison with Polybius' positive testimony. The fact that Hannibal was considered in Rome as a frightful enemy already for a considerable time before Cannae is proved by the strategy of the dictator Fabius, and if an opposing party demanded of him that he fight, it is still not said that the demand was that he should fight with his 4 legions. The "battle party" might very possibly have added that the dictator should first bring the army up to the necessary strength and then fight. Furthermore, whether the reinforcements found, for the most part, their place in the existing camp is in no way a proven fact; the camp might have been enlarged, and Livy or his source might not have considered it necessary to mention this. Of course, it does remain a curious fact that Livy found widely differing figures and that, as Cantalupi also points out, only the military tribunes of 4 legions are mentioned among those who survived. Critical estimates, however, point inevitably to the fact that the Roman army must have been considerably stronger than 44,000 men.

In order to make his opinion credible, Cantalupi is also obliged to reduce considerably the strength of the Carthaginian army as reported in Polybius. For it is clear from the outset that the Romans, who were not short of manpower, would not have marched out for a decisive battle against Hannibal without considerable numerical superiority. Otherwise the defeat at Cannae would not at all have had such a frightful significance; and the consul pointed out specifically, in the speech that, according to Polybius, he delivered to his officers before the battle, the twofold superiority which the Romans had on their side. The figure given by Polybius, that the Carthaginian army at Cannae consisted of 40,000 infantry and 10,000 cavalry, goes back to the recognized excellent Carthaginian source, Silenos, to whom we owe our overall picture of the battle in general. What reason would Silenos have had for exaggerating the Carthaginian forces? If we had to assume that the 86,000 figure for the Romans also stemmed from him, one might possibly believe, if inclined to be extremely suspicious, that, prompted by the overwhelming impression of the event, he exaggerated equally on both sides. But the 86,000 figure for the Romans stems, as Appian proves, drawing on Roman sources, from their own side, and as we shall establish further below in a closer examination of the composition of the Carthaginian army, no objective reason exists to cause us to doubt the strength of that army.

If then Hannibal's army was 50,000 strong, the Roman army cannot possibly have consisted of only 4 legions. The positive information that it was 8 legions strong and included allies can be considered as undoubtedly correct. At that time a legion numbered 5,000 men; that would bring the number to 80,000 Roman infantry. This number, however, cannot be compared directly to the 50,000 Carthaginian mercenaries. In each legion 1,400 men were the light infantry, who played only a secondary military role. The 8,000 Balearics (slingers) and peltasts of Hannibal were undoubtedly technically trained men, full-fledged warriors; the 22,400 Roman light infantrymen were, completely aside from their lack of technical ability, for the most part not at all usable in battle. On the Trebia we are expressly told (Polybius 3. 72. 2) that 6,000 light infantrymen skirmished in front of the phalanx. Since there were 4 legions present, Sempronius had, including his allies and after deducting his losses, at least 10,000 light infantry. Therefore he had left a part of them in the camp. The hoplite phalanx on the Trebia was probably about 1,000 men wide. If some 2,000 light infantry were stationed on each of the 2 wings, then 2,000 remained for the front—that is, 2 ranks; light infantry could not be drawn up any deeper than that. The front of the phalanx at Cannae was probably not wider—but, taking the most extreme estimate, it could possibly have been some 2,000 men wide—and so it therefore provided room for 2,000, or say, an absolute maximum of 4,000 light infantry in the front. If we estimate 2,000 to 3,000 on each flank, we can say with a certain degree of probability that some 8,000 to a maximum of 10,000 Roman light infantry took part in the battle as combatants. Another group may have followed the phalanx as litter-bearers and for other similar duties. The remainder stayed in the camp.

The camp garrison is supposed to have been, all together, 10,000 men strong, including under any circumstances also a few thousand hoplites, of whom a grand total of 16 by 3,600, or 57,600 men were at hand. According to this, I estimate the Roman army in the battle at 55,000 hoplites, 8,000 to 9,000 combatant light infantry, and 6,000 horsemen, for a total of about 70,000 men.

It is not clear whether Hannibal, too, in addition to his 50,000 men in the battle, had other troops whom he had left behind as camp garrison, or whether we should perhaps make a deduction from the battle strength for this purpose.

The Roman light infantry, which we did not include in the estimate as combatants, are naturally included in the casualty figures. We must therefore consider these from a base of 80,000 men on foot and 6,000 cavalry. According to Polybius, 70,000 men were killed, 3,000 infantry and 370 horsemen escaped, and 10,000 were taken prisoner. The 10,000 prisoners would be those who were left behind in the camp, who had attacked the Carthaginian camp during the battle, and who, later surrounded, surrendered. Polybius' expression is so unclear, however, that one has generally despaired of interpreting it correctly. It even seems possible that he meant that, in addition to those taken prisoner in the camps, another 10,000 men were taken alive by the Carthaginians on the battlefield, and this probably is in agreement with the nature of things. It can hardly be assumed that, after the great majority of Romans already covered the ground, the butchery-sated mercenaries did not prefer to spare the remainder and keep them for sale as slaves or for ransom.

This is of course contradicted by the estimate made by Polybius, who obviously arrived at the figure of 70,000 killed by subtracting some 10,000 prisoners and a few thousand fugitives and stragglers from the original 86,000.

The 70,000 killed figure can in no way be supported, however, for it is definitely established that the Romans formed two full legions from the survivors, and these were specifically *Roman* legions. Besides these, a reasonably corresponding number of allies must also have escaped. Consequently, the number of 70,000 is not based on a real account but on a somewhat flighty and erroneous estimate, and it thereby loses any value it might have had for us.

Now Livy reports that the losses of the Romans amounted to 45,000 infantry and 2,700 cavalry, and even though the authoritativeness of Livy is in general much less than that of Polybius, nevertheless everything points here to the fact that he was passing on a truly reliable official estimate. It is extremely improbable—in fact, impossible—that, as Polybius claims, almost the entire body of Roman cavalry, too, remained dead on the battlefield. After all, they were not surrounded but were driven to flight and were not even pursued very far or very energetically, since the main body of the Carthaginian cavalry quickly turned away from them and turned against the legions. Even a loss of 2,700 killed and 1,500 taken prisoner, as Livy reports, therefore seems very high and it also lends credibility to his figure on the infantry.

According to Livy, some 14,000 infantry were saved; taken as prisoners by the Carthaginians were 3,000 on the battlefield, 2,000 in the village of Cannae, 13,000 in the camp, and 1,500 cavalry.

If we add up the figures and take into consideration that the prescribed strength of 5,000 men per legion was probably not fully reached in every case, we can draw up the following list:

Killed—Infantry	45,500
Killed—Cavalry	2,700
Captured—Infantry	18,000
Captured—Cavalry	1,500
Escaped—Infantry	14,000
Escaped—Cavalry	1,800
Unaccounted for	2,500
	86,000

The original strengths were:

Hoplites in the battle	55,000
Hoplites in the camp	2,600
Rorarii in the battle	8,000
Rorarii serving as orderlies behind the front	7,000
Rorarii in the camp	7,400
Cavalry	6,000
	86,000 men

Of these 86,000 men, therefore, 2,500 should probably be subtracted as missing.

For the figures on Hannibal's army, see Chapter III, below.

3. Since, for Cannae, we are in the exceptionally favorable and very rare position of having a reliable and clear picture of the battle, based on reports from both sides, it is appropriate for us to realize fully from this example how little can be done with battle accounts that are lacking in this quality. Time and again our historians are exposed to the temptation, when good material is lacking, to make use of the bad, and to pass on in their accounts what has been passed down to them, if no other information of a contradictory nature is at hand, throwing out what is obviously false. This procedure, however, is not justified. It might very well be that in such an account everything accurate has fallen out and only the false has remained. Let there serve as proof of this the detailed description of Cannae that has come down to us in Appian's work. If, by chance, this were the only one that had come down to us, it would be absolutely impossible to gain from it an account having even the faintest resemblance to the truth. Since it is so very important that the readers of this book be thoroughly impressed with the truth of this methodological principle, I am copying below the account of Appian, who repeats some Roman account or other, in its entire detail. It reads as follows.

There were elected as consuls Lucius Aemilius, because of the military reputation he had gained for himself in the war with the Illyrians, and Terentius Varro, because of his popularity, in that once again this time, full of ambition as usual, he promised great things. As the two men were marching off, the people accompanied them and asked them to bring the war to a decision by means of an open battle and not to wait until the city was completely exhausted by the long duration of the war, and endless military service, the taxes, famine, and the lying fallow of the devastated fields. The consuls then joined the army of Iapygians to their own, so that they had all together 70,000 infantry and 6,000 cavalry. With these forces they occupied a camp near a village named Cannae, and Hannibal went into camp opposite them. Bellicose by nature and always an enemy of inactivity, Hannibal found himself just at this juncture, because of a pressing shortage of provisions, daily obliged to move out in battle array and in this way to challenge the enemies to battle—all the more necessary because he had to worry at the same time over the possibility that his mercenaries, who were not being paid regularly, would desert to the enemy or scatter to gather food.

The consuls were of different opinions. Aemilius believed that by holding off they should wear Hannibal down and that he would at any rate not be able to resist much longer because of his lack of supplies; and they should not allow themselves to be drawn into a battle with a commander and an army so accustomed to battle and to victory. Terentius on the other hand, as always seeking the approval of the people, said they had to keep in mind the mission that had been given to them by the people as they marched out and should risk a decisive battle as soon as possible. Servilius, the consul of the previous year, who was still with the army, agreed with Aemilius; the opinion of Terentius, on the other hand, was shared by all the senators and the knights who had positions of command in the army.

While the two sides had still not come to an agreement, Hannibal suddenly attacked those Romans who had moved out to seek fodder or wood, pretended that he was beaten, and about the time of the last watch of the night set his whole army in motion, as if he intended to march away. Hardly had Terentius noticed this than he led his army out as if there was nothing else to do but to pursue Hannibal in his flight. It was in vain that Aemilius still tried to dissuade him. But when he refused, Aemilius, according to the Roman custom, had the omens read for himself alone, sent after the other, who had already marched out, and had him told, "The day is of unfavorable omen." Thereupon, out of respect for the omens, Terentius did indeed move back, but in full view of the army he tore out his hair and complained bitterly, saying that the envy of his official colleague had taken victory from his hands. This indignation spread also through the mass of the army.

As soon as Hannibal saw that his attempt had failed, he returned unhesitatingly into his camp, giving obvious proof that his action had only been a pretense. But even this did not make it clear to Terentius that one had to be suspicious of every act of Hannibal's. Rather, fully armed, just as he had come back, he ran into the commanders' tent, where the senators, captains, and highest commanders were still assembled, and accused Aemilius of having taken the omens only as an excuse and of depriving the city of an obvious victory, because he either hesitated through cowardice or he enviously resented the other's fame. These loud and angrily shouted reproaches were heard by the army standing around the tent, and it too now abused Aemilius, who spoke in very conciliatory fashion to those in the tent but whose efforts were in vain. All the others, except Servilius, agreed with Terentius, and so finally Aemilius, too, gave in and on the next day, when he had taken over the high command from Terentius, he led the army out in battle formation. Hannibal saw this, of course, but he did not move out on that day, because he was not yet completely prepared for the battle. Not until the third day did both sides form up down on the plain.

The Romans were drawn up in three battle groups, each of which was formed at a little distance from the next. Each had the infantry in the middle, the light infantry and the cavalry on both flanks. Aemilius commanded in the center, Servilius on the left flank, and Terentius on the right. Each of the three had a thousand selected cavalry at his immediate disposal, whose mission was to hasten to help at any spot where necessity demanded. This was the battle formation of the Romans.

Hannibal, who knew that toward noon there usually sprang up in this area a southeasterly wind that caused the sky to be clouded over, occupied primarily those spots where he had the wind at his back. He then placed his cavalry and his lightly armed men (light troops) on a mountain in a withdrawn position, with wooded growth all around it and cut through with ravines, with the order to attack the rear of the enemy as soon as the battle echelons of the infantry had committed themselves in the attack and the wind had risen. Finally, 500 Celtiberians, in addition to their long swords, were also to strap on shorter swords beneath their underclothing, and they were ordered to await the signal as to when they should make use of the short swords. He then divided his entire army likewise into three groups for battle; the cavalry, however, was placed on the flanks at wide intervals, in order, where possible, to envelop the enemy. He entrusted the command of the right flank to his brother Mago, that of the left flank to his nephew Anno. He himself commanded in the middle, in order to be in position opposite Aemilius, for whose military skill he had great respect. He was surrounded by 2,000 selected cavalrymen, and a unit of 1,000 more, commanded by Maharbal, was designated to speed at a moment's notice to any spot where he might see a dangerous situation. These arrangements taken, he delayed until the second hour of the day, so that the attack would not take place too long before the rising of the wind.

When all the forces on both sides were ready for the battle, the commanders rode about and encouraged their men. The Romans reminded their men of their parents, their children, their wives, and the earlier defeat. They said that the coming battle would be decisive for their situation. Hannibal, on the other hand, reminded his men of the earlier successful actions against this enemy and how shameful it would be to be defeated by men who themselves had already been defeated. Then the trumpets rang out, and the infantry phalanxes raised a shout. The preliminary skirmishing was carried out by the archers, the slingmen, and the stone throwers, who rushed into the middle and attacked each other. After that the phalanxes strode forward into the attack, and both sides fought so courageously that the battle was fierce and the bloodshed extensive. In the meantime, Hannibal gave his cavalry the signal to envelop the enemy's flanks. But the Roman cavalry, although less numerous than the enemy, offered them strong resistance and, even though they had to deploy in a thin line, nevertheless fought with great courage, in the course of which the left flank, on the sea, distinguished itself particularly. Now Hannibal and

Maharbal simultaneously led against them the cavalrymen whom they had with them, uttering an immense barbarian shout in order to terrify their enemies. But even this attack was withstood by the Romans with unshakable coolness.

Because Hannibal had also failed in this attempt, he gave the prearranged signal to the 500 Celtiberians. Suddenly these men abandoned their ranks, went over to the Romans, and, as deserters, offered them their shields, spears, and swords, which they were carrying openly. Servilius praised them, immediately took their weapons from them, and lined them up, wearing only their clothing, as he thought, behind his own ranks. For he did not consider it good to have the deserters tied up within view of the enemy, was not suspicious, since he saw them there with nothing more than their clothing, and under any circumstances had no time in such a heated battle to do anything further about it. In the meantime, a few other units of Libyans pretended that they were fleeing and ran with much shouting to the mountains. This shout was the signal for those who were hidden in the mountain ravines to charge on the pursuing enemy. Suddenly the light infantry and the cavalry appeared from their concealed positions. At the same time, the strong wind arose, obscuring the sky, and it blew so much dust into the faces of the Romans that they could no longer see the enemy at a distance. All the missiles of the Romans, too, were slowed by the opposing wind, whereas those of the enemy, reinforced by the wind, flew much more successfully toward their targets. The Romans could no longer see the missiles coming and therefore could not avoid them; they could not fire off their own effectively and were even hitting each other, so that they were already beginning to fall into great disorder.

This was the moment at which the 500 Celtiberians had already been instructed in advance to draw their shorter swords from under their clothing and to strike down first those Romans in the ranks immediately in front of them. Thereupon they took from the Romans their longer swords, shields, and spears and threw themselves against all the others, cutting them down mercilessly. And the bloodbath which this unit carried out was the most important one, precisely because they were in the rear of the entire (enemy) army. Now the plight of the Romans was critical and complex, as they were hard pressed by the enemy in front, enveloped by the ambushers, and being cut down by the unit which had become mixed with their own ranks. They were unable to turn about against these last, since they were simultaneously beset by the others from the front. Moreover, it was no longer easy to recognize them, since they had Roman shields. Most of all, however, they were so hindered by the dust that they no longer had any idea of what was going on around them. Consequently, as is normally the case with a unit that is in disorder and bewilderment, they imagined everything as much worse, did not realize that the size of the enveloping group was not so great and that the number of "deserters" was only 500, but they thought that their entire army was surrounded by cavalry and "deserters." This caused them to turn around and flee in disorder, at first on the right flank, where Terentius was the first to take flight, and then on the left, from which Servilius, who was in command there, moved quickly to join Aemilius. Around these two men there gathered a mass of brave men, both cavalry and infantry, about 10,000 in number.

Now the commanders, and following their example all those who were still mounted, sprang from their horses and fought on foot against the cavalry of Hannibal which surrounded them. As seasoned warriors and partly through real courage and partly from despair they still accomplished many a brilliant deed, pressing furiously against the enemy. But they were cut down from all sides. For Hannibal rode around them, now encouraging his men and asking them to finish up this last, small task thoroughly, achieving a complete victory, now abusing them and calling it shameful if they could not finish off this small group after their victory over the mass. Nevertheless, the Romans held fast in their ranks as long as Aemilius and Servilius were with them, and they sold their lives dearly. After these leaders had fallen, however, they penetrated with great force through the enemy and, breaking their ranks, fled, some toward the two camps in which those who had fled before them had found refuge—all together, they amounted to 15,000 men, whom Hannibal had surrounded by one of his units—and others, about 2,000 in number, toward Cannae. Later these last 2,000 surrendered to Hannibal. Only a few escaped toward Canusium. The rest spread out individually into the forests.

And thus ended the battle of Cannae between Hannibal and the Romans, after it had lasted from the second hour of the day until two hours before nightfall. Among the Romans it still lives in infamy because of the great defeat they suffered there. For within these few hours 50,000 Romans were killed, and a large number of them were captured in the evening. Many from the Senate, too, who had participated in this campaign, were killed, and in addition to them all the superior officers and captains and the two bravest of the top commanders. Only the cowardly creator of this defeat had fled at the start of the battle. In the two years during which the Romans had been fighting with Hannibal in Italy, they had already lost almost 100,000 men, partly from their own troops, partly from the allies.

And so it was that Hannibal, on one day, had used four stratagems: his taking into account of the favorable wind; the feigned desertion of the Celtiberians; the apparent flight of several units; and the hiding of a reserve in the depths of the ravines. After the brilliant, unusual victory that he had won in this way, he moved around immediately after the battle, looking at the dead. Among these he also saw the bravest of his friends lying on the field. He lamented and said with tears in his eyes that he wished for no such victory. The same statement is supposed to have been made earlier by Pyrrhus, King of Epirus, when he in the same manner, with similar losses, had defeated the Romans in Italy.

Late on the same evening those of the Romans who had fled from the battle who were in the larger camp chose Publius Sempronius as their commander, broke out with force through the dead-tired guards of Hannibal and escaped, 10,000 men strong, at midnight in the direction of Canusium. On the other hand, the 5,000 men in the smaller camp were taken prisoner by Hannibal on the following day. Terentius then assembled the remainder of his army, attempted to renew the vanished courage of his soldiers, gave them one of the tribunes, Scipio, as leader, and hastened to Rome.

Here ends Appian's account.

ADDED IN THIRD EDITION

I have left this chapter unchanged, even though my concept on one point has been shaken. Up to now, it was generally believed that Polybius' account was derived in its principal features directly from a first-rate source from the Carthaginian camp, and this source was believed to be the Greek Silenos, whom we know to have been in Hannibal's entourage. Now H. Dessau, in "On the Sources of our Knowledge of the Second Punic War" ("Über die Quellen unseres Wissens vom zweiten punischen Kriege," *Hermes*, Vol. 51, 3d issue, 1916), has pointed out that this idea rests on very shaky foundations. In two respects Dessau misses the mark, in my opinion. He constantly considers the source that stems from the Carthaginian camp as tantamount to a Carthaginian-biased one, which is, after all, not necessarily so, and absolutely refuses to believe that Hannibal had had Greek scholars with him from the very start. According to him, Hannibal had not established such relationships until he had become master of a number of Greek cities in lower Italy. But that is certainly not true. Greek was at that time the general international language for commerce and culture. Even the Roman Senator Fabius wrote his historical work in the Greek language. We would have to picture Hannibal as a completely uncultured person if he had not spoken and read Greek perfectly, and for this he must have had cultured Greeks around him, even in his camp. I cannot imagine that he did not study Alexander's deeds, and for that purpose he had a need for Greek teachers and readers. And he also needed Greeks for diplomatic negotiations and intelligence services. He therefore undoubtedly also had in his retinue from the start scholars, as Alexander had had, who were supposed to recount his deeds. But I do not want to fall into the same error as Dessau by viewing as provable things that, in the present condition of the material, we can at best speculate about, and so I do not consider it as proven, but in any case as possible, that actually, as Dessau believes, the generally valuable descriptions and figures in Polybius, which we have thought up to now came from Silenos, stem from Fabius Pictor. They would then be only indirectly Carthaginian. Fabius would have drawn them from Carthaginian prisoners or deserters. Dessau points out especially that in 210 B.C. the commander of a Numidian unit, Muttines, deserted to the Romans, won a very important position in Rome, and as late as the year 190 B.C. took part under the Scipios in the campaign against Antiochus. This Punic general could have been that eminent military source from the Carthaginian side whom we take note of and admire in the account of Polybius.

If this conjecture should be accurate, then with it several difficulties with respect to the battle of Cannae are solved very simply. Polybius describes the horseshoe formation of the Punic infantry as "moon-shaped" and conceives of this half-moon as a curved line (*Kyrtoma*: "curved front"*). Researchers are now agreed that that is a tactical impossibility. Such a dilettantish misunderstanding cannot possibly stem from Polybius himself; he must have taken it from his source. There must therefore have been between the original military source and Polybius a middle link on which we can blame such a misunderstanding. This would fit very well with the concept that we have before us the account of an important Numidian general as repeated by the completely unmilitary Senator Fabius. With Silenos, too, who belonged to Hannibal's own staff, this misunderstanding is certainly not out of the question, but it is nevertheless much less probable.

Another striking point in Polybius' account of the battle is the fact that the effect of the cavalry's attack from the rear is given relatively little importance in comparison with the flanking envelopment by the infantry and in the same connection the too strongly stressed squeezing together of the Roman infantry toward the middle. I have attempted above to explain this distortion psychologically from the viewpoint of the headquarters. At least as good, however, and probably better, is the explanation that the account stems from Fabius and that he had received it from one of the leaders of the African infantry, precisely that same Muttines, who was intelligent enough militarily to characterize the importance of the cavalry attack correctly in his reasoning, but who, in his account, praised so greatly the deeds of his own unit that a certain contradiction resulted.

Dessau's investigation receives strong support from the fact that even before him Beloch, in a study of the battle on the Trebia, proved (*Historische Zeitschrift*, Vol. 114, 1915) that Polybius' report did not stem from Silenos but from Fabius. All the many uncertainties concerning the crossing of the Alps, the battle on the Trebia, the crossing of the Apennines, the battle of Lake Trasimeno, which have caused modern investigators so much trouble, would therefore be explainable through the fact that Polybius had at his disposal not the report of a man from Hannibal's staff, but only the account of a Carthaginian general that passed through Fabius.

Dessau, too, once again establishes the fact that Polybius was much more dependent on his sources than is usually believed. Kromayer, in his estimate of Polybius' authoritativeness, swings from one extreme to the other. Whereas he initially appeared as his defender, then in the second volume of *Battlefields* (*Schlachtfelder*) was not willing to credit either his military reasoning or his actual statements of fact (see below "Military Aspects of the Battle of Magnesia" ["Kriegerisches zur Schlacht bei Magnesia"]), he again clothed his account of the battle of Cannae in the garment of adherence to Polybius, in opposition to my criticism, and Kahrstedt (p. 434) explains that, for anybody to undertake "to reject and correct the clear words of the greatest ancient military author up to Caesar, goes beyond my comprehension." One might well accept this. Insofar, however, as the controversy between Kromayer and me with respect to Cannae is concerned, it is primarily a question not of the acceptance or rejection of Polybius, but of how the concept of the curved front of the Carthaginians reported by him and rejected by us all, Kromayer as well as me, can logically be corrected. I have translated the "half-moon" into what we call today "horseshoe-shaped." Kromayer conceives of it as a step-shaped formation, which tactically is just as impossible as a curved line. The second controversy concerns the squeezing together of the Romans, in which I admittedly recognize an actual fact but detect a strong exaggeration, as explained above. According to my concept, the Romans based the battle from the start on a deep mass pressure, which they could not at all have done in any other way in view of their numerically very superior but tactically untrained infantry. Kromayer gives them a completely slack front, which, giving up the traditional Roman style of battle, bunched together toward the middle after the forward movement had started (we would have to assume that they were seized by a kind of mass madness). Let it be noticed, they were not supposed to have been pressed together by some action of the Carthaginian enveloping columns, but they are said to have shortened the front voluntarily so very much during the approach march that the Carthaginians were able to move against their flanks. Foolish as this picture is in itself, it is completely explained by the fact that, under the agreed prerequisites, the Roman flank files would have had to shift sideways no less than 700 meters; since the simultaneous movement forward can only be very short, it really is a question principally of a sideward movement, and one can well imagine what 700 meters of sideward movement by rather large masses within a few minutes would mean.

I have devoted a study of my own, "The Battle of Cannae" ("Die Schlacht bei Cannä"), in *Historische Zeitschrift* 109: 481, to refuting this dance tactics, since it appeared to be supported by good source evidence, or at any rate referred to such sources. Furthermore, Kromayer, in his booklet published in 1912, *Rome's Struggle for World Hegemony* (*Roms Kampf um die Weltherrschaft*), came very close to my own reconstruction of the battle, in that he too now stresses very much that the Romans, from the very beginning, had stayed "as close together as possible." With him, as with me, the later, additional narrowing of the front therefore becomes something of secondary importance. Seriously considered, there is in fact no longer any difference between us, since a formation "as close together as possible" obviously excludes the possibility of fighting with *quincunx* intervals and, too, the step-shaped formation of the Carthaginians has become superfluous.

TICINUS. TREBIA. TRASIMENO.

4. We need not study in detail the battles and engagements of this war that preceded and followed the battle of Cannae, but we only need to establish that they are in agreement with the conclusions on the Roman and Carthaginian tactics that we have derived from Cannae.

On the Ticinus the Carthaginian cavalry defeated the Roman cavalry. The Roman light infantry that accompanied their cavalry did not even manage to get off one discharge of their missiles but took flight, because they feared being ridden down by the charging enemy horsemen.

5. On the Trebia, in a very similar way to that at Cannae, the Romans were enveloped on both flanks by the Carthaginian cavalry and light infantry and were finally attacked from the rear. An ambush that Hannibal is supposed to have laid is believed to have strengthened this rear attack still further. Such an ambush is a tactical impossibility; either it lay just about on the route on which the Romans were moving—and in that case these 2,000 men, in the very likely case that the Romans discovered them, were lost. Or, on the other hand, the ambush lay considerably off to the side, in which case it was useless, since the Carthaginians made their encirclement move much faster by enveloping the Roman flank. I therefore consider it certain in this case that Polybius fell prey to a Roman fable. At Cannae the Roman pride tried to console itself through a very similar little story (which is still repeated by quite a number of historians). The principal point is that the Romans, although

they were entirely surrounded as later at Cannae, succeeded in breaking out in several directions and in saving the greater part of the army. Why they escaped so much more successfully here than at Cannae afterward cannot be recognized with any certainty from the sources. The general circumstances were not more favorable for the Romans but were, in fact, considerably less advantageous than at Cannae. At Cannae they had a significant numerical superiority, on the Trebia little or none. At Cannae they had 6,000 horsemen against the 10,000 Carthaginians, on the Trebia only 4,000. Furthermore, at that time the Carthaginians also had a number of elephants, which supported the attack of the cavalry. And in addition, if one is to believe the account, there was also the ambush by the Carthaginians. Finally, Polybius describes in detail how the Romans, as a result of their crossing of the winter-cold, swollen Trebia, during which they walked through chest-deep water without having eaten in advance, went into the battle physically weakened from the start.

That the Romans in this battle finally escaped more successfully seems only to trace back to the fact that Hannibal here assigned only cavalry and light infantry for the envelopment. His own phalanx was therefore all the stronger, but it was still penetrated at the spot where the Celts and the Africans were placed.

For the very difficult individual questions on the battle I invite the reader's attention to the excellent work by Joseph Fuchs, *The Second Punic War and its Historical Sources, Polybius and Livy* (*Der zweite punische Krieg und seine Quellen Polybius und Livius*), which will be mentioned below (Chapter III). Against Fuchs's viewpoint, however, recently, is Beloch, writing in the *Historische Zeitschrift*, Vol. 114, 1915; moreover, he established again also that Kromayer corrects Polybius' account by contradicting, in the most flagrant manner, his own concept as expressed in other places.

6. The battle on Lake Trasimeno is a surprise attack during a march. It shows the sureness with which the Carthaginian cavalry leaders understood how to command their troops independently, while the Romans were helpless. On the Trebia 10,000 men had broken out of the Carthaginian envelopment, by Lake Trasimeno 6,000, but they did not find a way, on their own initiative, to come to the aid of those units of the Roman army still engaged in battle, whereas we see how the Punic commanders acted independently.

The question as to how Hannibal really moved from upper Italy to Lake Trasimeno formerly seemed very obscure, but it has now been definitively solved, in my opinion, as a result of the study by Joseph Fuchs, "Hannibal in Central Italy" ("Hannibal in Mittelitalien"), *Wiener Studien*, Vol. 26, Book 1, 1904. I do not, however, agree with Fuchs's account of the battle itself, which he does not consider as a surprise attack but as a battle in the open field accepted deliberately by Flaminius.

(*Added in the third edition.*) Among the more recent writings on this battle I also invite attention to: Gärtner, *Berliner Dissertation*, 1911; Gröbe, *Zeitschrift für österreichische Gymnasien* 7 (1911): 590; Caspari, *English Historical Review*, July 1910; Reuss, *Rheinisches Museum*, 1910; Fuchs, *Zeitschrift für österreichische Gymnasien*, 1911; Sadé, *Klio*, 1909; Konrad Lehmann, *Jahresbericht des Philologischen Vereins*, Vol. 41, 1915.

There is no reason for going into the controversy itself here. I simply mention the fact that, as K. Lehmann particularly has proved, Kromayer here once again places himself in strong contradiction to Polybius. That is, of course, no reproach, but it only serves to establish again that Kromayer may not be considered as the defender of the authoritativeness of Polybius.

NOTES FOR CHAPTER I

1. The average depth was naturally considerably smaller, since the intervals, which had become irregular during the approach ·

march, had to be filled up before the impact with the enemy by having rearward troops spring forward. In earlier editions I still admitted the possibility of a doubled length with correspondingly lesser depth. But I have now become convinced that a front of nearly 2 kilometers would no longer have been capable of forward movement in orderly fashion. One can grasp this more clearly by imagining a street like "Unter den Linden" in Berlin, which is almost 1 kilometer long and about 90 paces wide. The Roman infantry front at Cannae would therefore have reached about from the monument of Frederick the Great to the Wilhelmstrasse and would have overflowed to some extent in its depth the width of this street.

2. Polybius says that the Iberian and Gallic cavalry were on the left flank, the Numidians on the right, and he later characterizes the fighting of the latter as simple skirmishing. In the battle on the Trebia he makes a distinction between the heavy cavalry and the Numidians. By that account, then, the Iberian cavalry were the heavy units—a fact that does not necessarily eliminate the possibility of Hannibal's also having had African cuirassiers, only *a potiori* may the light cavalry have been called the Numidian.

Chapter II

The Basic Strategic Problem of the Second Punic War

A basis for consideration of the strategy can only be gained through a determination of the tactical relationships on both sides. The Carthaginians were unquestionably the tactically superior side. They had a military commander, whereas the Romans each year elected two governing mayors who also commanded the army. The mayors had so little understanding of the principles of large-scale command that they either had the consuls divide up the legions between them or, if they were together, the two of them bore the command alternately, a day at a time. Some have tried to soften the monstrousness of such a situation face-to-face with a Hannibal by saying that the alternation only meant daily changes of the chairmanship of the council of war. Actually, that would be a sharper charge, for in that case the command would not have been by an individual at all, but by a council. We are more accurate if we remain with the idea of the expression "alternating command"—although, of course, there were councils of war, too. The situation of the commanders was also reflected in the officer corps. On the Carthaginian side, professional officers trained in the school of Hamilcar Barca; on the Roman side, citizen warriors of more or less natural ability. The Carthaginian generals maneuver, as necessary, with the various corps, infantry and cavalry; the Roman legions can only march straight ahead side by side. Finally, the Carthaginian cavalry is also far stronger than the Roman cavalry numerically.

Against all these advantages of the enemy the Romans can bring to bear only the single advantage of an almost inexhaustible mass of militarily competent and reliable men.[1]

This diversity of the strengths on the two sides creates a situation that offers a certain analogy to the relationship of Athenians and

Spartans in the Peloponnesian War. For a long, long time it was impossible to arrive at a definitive decision, because the Athenians were the more powerful at sea, the Spartans on land, and neither was able to come to grips with the other in his own element. In the Second Punic War the contrast was not so sharp and it was only very gradually recognized by the Romans. At first they brashly challenged the enemy to battle in the open field, only finally to learn through a series of frightful defeats that they should turn to other areas. But Hannibal knew from the start his weakness as well as his strength.

Whoever intends to wage war on the basic principle of defeating the enemy must be capable, after he has sought out and defeated the enemy forces in the open field, of pursuing his victory relentlessly, to the point of laying siege to and capturing the enemy capital; and finally, if even that does not yet lead to peace, he must follow through to the total defeat of the enemy. Hannibal was too weak for that, and he was aware from the start of the fact that, despite the greatest victories, he would not be capable of besieging and capturing Rome itself.

At Cannae, then, he had beaten and wiped out only the smaller half of the Roman legions (8 of 18), and the Romans soon replaced their losses through new levies; they did not even have the legions that were stationed overseas—in Sicily, Sardinia, Spain—return home. To have moved against Rome immediately after the battle with a view toward the terrorizing effect would therefore have served no purpose for Hannibal and, passing as a negative demonstration, would have nullified the other morale effects of the victory at Cannae. If the well-known statement by the cavalry leader, Maharbal, that Hannibal understood how to win but not how to exploit his victories, was actually said, it only proves that the brave general who said it was a simple fighter rather than a true strategist. During the lengthy butchery of the encircled legionaries the Carthaginian army had itself sacrificed 5,700 killed, and consequently in addition at least 20,000 wounded, who were not capable of marching again until days and weeks had passed. Had he started out immediately after the battle, Hannibal would have arrived before Rome with hardly 25,000 men, and the Romans would not have given in to such a small force, even at the height of their terror.

Later, after his army had had time for its wounds to heal and replacements to be incorporated, Hannibal may have had enough strength to allow him to consider besieging Rome with, say, 50,000 or 60,000 men. But Rome was a very large, well-fortified city; the so-called Servian wall, probably built at the time of the Samnite Wars, had a circumference of more than 5 miles. Large open areas within the walls could accommodate the refugee inhabitants of the countryside. As a large trading center and capital, Rome was richly provided with supplies of all kinds. If Hannibal had controlled the sea, had first taken Ostia and then been able to supply himself by sea, then it might not appear impossible for him to have thought of besieging Rome with 50,000 to 60,000 men. But here we must not lose from sight the fact that the Romans were the stronger at sea; in order not to divide his strength, Hannibal had concentrated all his forces in his land army. The siege army would, therefore, have had to be supplied by land. Gigantic supply lines would have had to be organized and made to function through a completely hostile countryside and passing by innumerable cities and strongholds that blocked the routes. A very large portion of the Carthaginian troops would have had to be assigned to this duty, and every isolated unit would have been exposed at every turn to the legions and cohorts, both Roman and allied, which were still stationed in the country or were newly organized. The remainder of the army which would have been available for the siege, divided by the Tiber River, would have withstood only with great difficulty the sorties of the numerically far superior garrison. The principal arm of the Carthaginians, their cavalry, could not have been of any assistance.

Hannibal knew very well what he was doing when, after the victory at Lake Trasimeno as well as after Cannae, he did not march on Rome. From the very beginning he had conceived another means of defeating the enemy.

Not in a position to overcome the Romans completely, to destroy them as a world power, he based his conduct of the war on the goal of wearing them down and exhausting them to the point where they would be willing to agree to a negotiated peace. Strategy becomes politics and politics strategy. After the apparently decisive victory at Cannae, the Carthaginian leader nevertheless had it said to the Romans that it was not a war of complete destruction—a matter of national survival—that he was waging with them (*non internecivum sibi esse cum Romanis bellum*—Livy 22. 58), and he offered to discuss peace terms. The Romans rejected the offer, but to persuade an enemy to accept a mutually agreed peace is even possible without great decisive actions, to which the Romans now no longer were exposing themselves, and from the start Hannibal had had this in mind.

As soon as Hannibal had first appeared in Italy, he announced that he had not come to fight against the peoples of the peninsula but to liberate them from Roman domination. After every battle he released without ransom those allies who had been taken prisoner so that they would spread the word in their native regions concerning the political goal and the generosity of the Carthaginian leader. Roman citizens made up hardly a third of the population of Italy; the remainder consisted of more or less independent communities and cantons that could decide to withdraw from the Roman leadership to which they had subjected themselves. They provided independent contingents to the common army of the allied forces. Even communities that had been established as Roman colonies could perhaps find it advantageous to separate their destiny from that of the mother city.

After Cannae defection started on a large scale. Capua—after Rome the largest city of Italy, which even had Roman citizenship *sine suffragio* (without suffrage)—and a large number of cantons and smaller cities, and finally also the third city of Italy, Tarentum, went over to Hannibal; and, just as the Gauls had given their support to the Carthaginians in the north, on Sicily Syracuse, too, went over to their side. If Hannibal had been able to maintain the momentum of this movement through unrelenting pressure and threats, the moment would inevitably have come when the Romans, worn out, would have made peace or when Hannibal's base in Italy would have become so broad and sure that he could undertake the siege of Rome.

After Polybius had recounted the events up to the battle of Cannae, he interrupted his account, spoke first of things from Greek history, and, before taking up the Punic War again, he inserted a discussion of the Roman constitution. This arrangement shows the truly great historian. How little interest the abstract forms of a constitution and the usages of an administration hold in and of themselves! With Polybius, however, they answer the question: How was it possible for a state to withstand a defeat like that at Cannae, following on the heels of those at Ticinus, on the Trebia, and at Lake Trasimeno? The extreme suspense that those events must have produced is carried over to the reader. This question and this answer form the masterpiece of Polybius' art, for it is no superficial artifice that produces the tension, but the very nature of the thing itself, which in this case, through its form, is so ingeniously expressed.

We wish to try to imitate Polybius by breathing life into the dead statistical figures by means of the same reflection. How great was the accomplishment of Rome which permitted her to counterbalance the genius of Hannibal and to hold her own with unbreakable strength despite all the defections of her allies? Let us give the detailed estimates later, but the principal figures, as they can be derived from the historic accounts—not with complete certainty, it is true, but with sufficient assurance nevertheless—are as follows:

The Roman state (leaving aside the allies) had, at the beginning of the Second Punic War, according to the evidence available to us through the official census figures, about a million free persons and at the beginning of the war mobilized some 34,000 men for the land army. To this must be added a supplementary number for the fleet, which we cannot estimate, however, since by far the larger portion of all the crews consisted of allies and slaves.

The 7 to 8 legions of the first year had increased in 216 B.C. to 18, despite the losses on the Trebia and Lake Trasimeno, and the strength of those in the principal army was raised to 5,000 infantry. Eight legions were assigned to the principal army facing Hannibal, 2 in Spain, 2 in Sicily, 1 in Sardinia, 2 against the Cisalpine Gauls, 2 in Rome as garrison troops and replacements, and 1 with the fleet. The last 8 of those listed must be regarded as very much under strength. If we estimate 4,800 men for each of the legions at Cannae, 4,000 each for the 2 legions in Spain, 2,500 for each of the other 8, the total is about 66,000 men, or easily 6½ percent of the free population. If we also consider those killed in 218 and 217 B.C., we arrive at 7½ percent.[2]

Since 2 new legions were formed from the remnants of the Cannae army, we can consider 6 as having been lost; shortly thereafter 2 more legions were destroyed by the Gauls. They were not capable of replacing this loss completely, especially when entire large communities (Capua) of *cives sine suffragio* were going over to the enemy. By going so far as to empty the prisons and levy youths not yet seventeen years old, they formed 2 legions, and 2 additional ones were organized with slaves, who were promised their freedom. Rome therefore once again had 14 legions, which gradually increased to 22 in the next few years as 2 new legions were formed each year of the youths who had just come of age. The highest strength, 22 legions, was reached in the years 212 and 211 B.C. The total number of individuals, however, remained considerably smaller than that of the year 216 B.C., since the actual strength of each legion was much lower. Up to 216 B.C. the prisoners were ransomed in accordance with a specific agreement that had already been in existence in the First Punic War. But the Senate, in order to establish an example, declined Hannibal's offer to sell the prisoners of Cannae back for ransom, preferring to form the slave legions. The prisoners were therefore sold abroad, and as long as half a generation later the Romans found so many of their compatriots as slaves in Greece that, when the Consul Flaminius in 194 B.C. offered to ransom them from the Greeks, the Achaians alone had 1,200 of them to return,[3] and six years later another large number of them were said to have been freed in Crete and returned to their native country.[4]

Although, therefore, the state during the war renounced its citizens, once they had fallen into the power of the enemy, and left them to their fate, we may very well assume that, even though not through official governmental means, nevertheless many prisoners were individually ransomed by their families. The slave traders who took over the prisoners from the Carthaginian camp had no further interest, after all, than to dispose of them for the best possible price, and in 210 B.C. Roman citizens complained of the prices, which they could not afford, saying that they did not have left even enough money for a ransom price (Livy 26. 35). The fact of private ransoming from war prisoner status was therefore a contingency that one took into consideration. Even though in this way the losses of Lake Trasimeno and Cannae may be reduced by several thousands, the effort of the Roman people still remains without parallel. Even the achievement of Prussia in 1813 is estimated at only 5½ percent of the population, and it was not required for even a full year running. From time to time the Athenians probably had a larger percentage of their citizens under arms than did Rome, but always for only a very short time. But here it happened that year after year and in very distant theaters of operations almost the entire service-qualified manpower was under arms. Even a very large percentage of the slaves were requisitioned either for the legions or for service at sea. It is astonishing that the economic life and the financial administration could be maintained during this period. Besides taxes, credits payable after a peace treaty were demanded, especially from purveyors; Sicily is supposed to have been strongly pressed for support, and a lowering of the value of the currency brought relief to debtors and made money more liquid. Only the efforts of the German people in the World War from 1914 to 1918 exceeded those of the Romans.

While the Roman constitution in this way put the full power of its own people at the disposition of the state, the well-thought-out construction of the treaty of alliance, at the head of which stood

the city on the Tiber, also proved itself. True enough, a large portion of the allies defected, went over to the enemy, or at least became very lax in their contributions. But all the Roman colonies, all
the Latins, and a large number of Greek cities remained loyal to
Rome,[5] and it was precisely the progress realized by Hannibal that
changed the conditions of the conduct of the war. Even before the
battle of Cannae, after the experiences of the Trebia and Lake
Trasimeno, the dictator Quintus Fabius Maximus had wanted to
wage war by avoiding a tactical decision. But he stood almost alone
in this concept, and basically one cannot blame the other side too
much for wanting to bring to the test for once the possibility of defeating the terrible enemy by attacking him with Rome's double
superiority. Now the defeat not only led back to the Cunctator's
strategy but also gave to it what was missing before Cannae and because of which it had not been possible to see it through: a positive
goal. It lies in the nature of war that every success, if it does not
lead to the total defeat of the enemy and the restoration of peace,
forms a basis for counteractions and retribution. Hannibal arrived,
according to Clausewitz's expression, at the culminating point of
victory. The Romans no longer accepted large open battles;[6] Hannibal was too weak to undertake large-scale sieges as long as
numerous Roman legions were still in the field and could cut off
his supply lines. On the other hand, however, he was himself not
capable of preventing the Romans, on their side, from laying siege
to the defected cities, subjecting them again, and punishing them.
From this time on these sieges were the central point of Rome's
conduct of the war. To take by storm a fortified Roman camp in
which the consuls took cover during their siege of a city was
beyond the capabilities of the military superiority of the Carthaginian army. In this kind of situation, cavalry shock action and the
tactical coordination of various units and arms were not important,
and the tough courage of the Roman legionaries held the field.[7]
The siege and recapture of Capua by the Romans was virtually the
critical point of the war. This is a completely unique event in military history: the one side was able to carry out a large-scale, wearing
siege, even though the other side possessed the unquestioned
superiority in the open field. We can explain it only through the
unusual division of forces, the fact that the armies were not similarly composed but that each side had its characteristic forces:
cavalry on the one side, the mass of infantry on the other.

Hannibal is supposed to have made an attempt to storm the
Roman circumvallation, while the Capuans made a sortie. This in-

formation, however, stems from the treasury of the Roman victory bulletin! An actual, large-scale, repulsed attack would necessarily have had stronger aftereffects, and Polybius reports nothing about it. Hannibal recognized from the start the impossibility of success—the Romans probably had some 40,000 to 50,000 men in the siege work—and when he failed to lure the enemy out for a battle, he tried to attain his goal through a purely morale effect. He marched directly on Rome and came right up to the gates of the city. But the Romans refused to be intimidated, and Hannibal had to leave Latium again. The only results of this move were a plundering march and a demonstration, and Capua fell.

From this point on, it was no longer possible for Hannibal to conquer Rome. The Romans had already overcome Syracuse before Capua; soon Tarentum fell to them again. Instead of a wider and wider, spreading defection of the Italian states, on which Hannibal had counted for his final victory, a renewed expansion and reinforcing of Roman hegemony set in. Hannibal's fighting forces, however, insufficiently reinforced from the homeland, gradually dwindled; some of his Numidian and Spanish troops even went over to the enemy. In the secondary theaters of operations—Sicily, Sardinia, Spain—where there was no fear of the military genius of Hannibal and the main strength of the Carthaginians, their cavalry, was in part less numerous and in part never proved very effective, the fortunes of war swung back and forth After the largest part of Spain had already been taken once by the Romans, they suffered, in the same year in which they won back Capua (211 B.C.), a crushing defeat, from which, however, they recovered again, brought up reinforcements, and again went over to the offensive. It was still impossible to foresee how the final decision would fall, but the superiority which the Carthaginians had won in the first years of the war in the great field battles gradually slipped away from them, and the opposing forces were again in equilibrium. Neither of the two sides was in a position to force a decision. The Romans would not risk an open battle, and Hannibal was not strong enough to be able to lay siege to Rome.

After we have understood the strategic-political relationships, it is appropriate for us to compare how the popular memory of the people explained these things. Quite rightly it connects the swing of the pendulum with the name of Capua, but with what a motivation! According to the story, in this sensuous and dissipated city the tough warriors of Hannibal became soft and lost their strength and courage. (Livy 23. 18). The legend does not concern itself with the

344 History of the Art of War

question why the Romans nevertheless tolerated this now unwarlike and undisciplined army for twelve more years in Italy. For the legend, objective relationships do not matter; it works exclusively in the realm of personalities and personal motives and in doing so completely distorts the real relationship. "Capua" as a byword for a softened army has entered the vocabulary of all enlightened peoples, as has "Xerxes" for a mass army, and it will endure there. In the Second Punic War, where we have Polybius for a source, it is easy to distinguish between the various mentalities. We have been able to repeat his report about what really gave the name Capua its great importance in this war, and what we have related in this chapter has long been the common property of historians in its important points. For the Persian Wars, where Herodotus reports to us nothing but the legend, it was naturally more difficult to separate truth from legend.

Excursus

1. The accounts of Hannibal's march on Rome differ greatly, but they are in general of but little credibility. Like Livy, Polybius attributes to Hannibal the actual belief that he could take Rome by surprise. It is natural that Hannibal should not have said from the start that he considered the capture of Rome impossible. If he had not created the appearance of a serious attempt, he could not have achieved any effect at all, and chance, after all, sometimes works wonders. But Hannibal can not possibly have deluded himself into thinking he could take a city like Rome by surprise, and when he arrived, he did not even make the effort. Since a large army always moves slowly, the news of his approach had naturally already reached Rome long before he did, and there was in any case time enough to organize the defense of the walls. Even if no field troops at all had been in the city, the *seniores* would nevertheless have sufficed for the time being.

When Polybius tells us, then, that he appeared before Rome totally unexpectedly and the city was saved only through the fact that fortuitously just at that moment the men of two newly levied legions were formed up, this is a natural exaggeration through which the terrible fear of the Romans found its expression and in which it continued to be reflected. Cantalupi has pointed out the probability that also the two older *legiones urbanae* (garrison legions) were still in the city, so that there were in all 4 field legions, 2 of them untrained, at hand for the defense of the city.[8] The reproach that Streit, in his otherwise accurate study,[9] directs against the Roman Senate for having left the capital without a garrison while Hannibal was not far distant, is therefore not justified.

Further, Livy reports that the Romans, informed in a timely way of Hannibal's move, had a corps under Fulvius moved up from the army laying siege to Capua and that it arrived at the same time as the Carthaginians; I see no reason for questioning this report.

According to both these authors, the Roman troops not only garrisoned the walls but also moved out in front of the gates and formed up against the Carthaginians for open battle. This is a patent Roman fiction. An open battle, of the kind he had never failed to win, waged directly before the gates of Rome, would not only have offered the Carthaginian general the highest laurels but also a real opportunity to press through the gates simultaneously with the beaten Romans and to take Rome against all rational odds. And Hannibal supposedly did not accept such a battle? According to Livy, the armies stood facing each other twice, and each time the eager warriors were separated by a heavy rain. In this sign Hannibal realized that the gods were opposed to the battle. According to Polybius, however, Hannibal was intimidated in the face of the unsuspectedly large number of Roman warriors and held back from his planned attack. Polybius does not concern himself with miracles, but he should have gone one step further in his critique of the Roman legend and eliminated the whole formation in front of the walls. Of course, he does not expressly say that it was a formation for battle; we could possibly imagine that it was also an advanced defensive work.

Fulvius' corps, which the Romans had moved up from the siege army at Capua, had not left that army so weakened as to invite an attack. And so Hannibal was forced to fall back and leave Capua to its fate.

2. THE ROMAN EFFORT

With what forces Rome waged the Second Punic War can be estimated to a certain degree through our having at hand in Livy figures on the number of available legions over a period of years, figures bearing the stamp of an official accounting. What strength the legions had, how greatly the actual strength differed from the authorized strength, how many allies or mercenaries were also involved, how many sailors are to be included—on all these points we have little of a definite nature. Furthermore, the number of legions reported often does not agree with the numbers at which we arrive when we add up those which are named individually, so that errors must have crept in during the estimating. Nevertheless, through careful comparison and weighing of all the individual data, a result that is approximately correct can probably be arrived at. The best basis is once again offered by Beloch, not only in his book but also in the postlude he added to the treatise of Cantalupi (*Studi di Storia antica*, I: 42), by which the older study of Schemann, *History of the Legions during the Second Punic War* (*De legionum per alterum bellum Punicum historia*, (Bonn dissertation, 1875) has been superseded.

To the 6 legions with which, according to Livy, Rome began the war are to be added garrison troops in Sicily, Sardinia, and Illyria, which, together, can be estimated at 1 to 2 legions, so that there were altogether some 34,000 men under arms on land.

The sources contain contradictory material concerning the reconstitution of the army after Cannae. The error, however, can be recognized and eliminated.

Livy, 22. 57, recounts first that 4 legions were raised, partly of under-age youths, and then speaks of the levying of 8,000 slaves. In 22. 14 he reports further that 6,000 criminals and imprisoned debtors had been enlisted. That would make a total of 7½ legions, in addition to the 10 already in existence. In the following year, however, he tells us (26. 11) that, in order to attain 18 legions, 6 new ones had to be formed. The question arises: How did the Romans manage this, when in the preceding year they had already had to resort to slaves, criminals, and youths?

If, however, these legions had actually been formed, there would have been not 18 but 23 or 24. These legions, therefore, are either partially or completely duplicates—that is, they include all the units that were formed after Cannae in 216 and 215 B.C. The sequence was probably as follows: first, 2 legions were formed of criminals, the remnants of the preceding levy, and under-age youths, and 2 legions of slaves. And the 2 last ones were not organized until the following year, 215 B.C., when the next year-group had become somewhat older. These legions formed of the very young men are the *urbanae* (city legions), which spent their first year in the city, simultaneously being trained and acting as garrison for the capital.

Of the reported numbers of legions, Beloch believes that the following ones should be eliminated: (1) 1 legion on Sardinia after 215 B.C., when the island was no longer threatened and 2 legions would have been too many; (2) 2 legions on the Gallic border, as duplicates; the same nonexistent legions also appear in front of

Capua; (3) the *legiones urbanae* (city legions). I agree with Beloch on the first two points, and especially the second one, but not with respect to the *legiones urbanae*. Beloch bases his belief on the fact that the account of Polybius (9. 6. 6) concerning the threat to Rome by Hannibal in 211 B.C. eliminates the assumption that the city had a standing garrison. That is correct, but this account itself is of a legendary character and cannot be regarded as conclusive in comparison with the repeated and very definite statement of Livy. There is a very good treatment by Steinwender in *Philologus* 39: 527, concerning the *legiones urbanae* in their triple character as replacement, garrison, and recruit legions, of which aspects now one and now the other predominated.

After the capture of Syracuse and Capua (211 B.C.) a small reduction of the army took place. The oldest year-groups were discharged and a few legions disbanded. When Hasdrubal approached from Spain, in 207 B.C., slaves were once again incorporated in the legions, and after the victory on the Metaurus reductions were again made.

For the mass of Roman citizens we have the reported census figures and the numbers of service-qualified men from the year 225 B.C., as recorded by Polybius. Of the various interpretations to which these numbers have been exposed, I agreed in my first edition with that of Beloch and on that basis came to the conclusion that the military levy amounted to no less than 9½ percent of the population. Eduard Meyer reached the same result in *Conradsche Jahrbücher* 70 (1897): 59, and in the article "The Population in Antiquity" ("Die Bevölkerung im Altertum") in the *Pocket Dictionary of Political Sciences* (*Handwörterbuch der Staatswissenschaften*). In the latter it is stated: "In the war against Hannibal, more than 20 legions, or at least 70,000 men, without counting allies, were maintained under arms for years, that is, almost 30 percent of the adult male inhabitants and almost 10 percent of the total free population."

More recently Nissen in *Study of Italy* (*Italienische Landeskunde*), Vol. 2, Introduction, para. 9, again took up the study of this point and came back to Mommsen's opinion, according to which the reported census figures reflect not the entire citizenry but only the *tabulae juniorum* (registers of the young). This, as well as a few other corrections, leads Nissen to an estimate of the population of Italy at the time of Hannibal as about twice as high as that of Beloch—that is, at 7 million. In an essay in *Klio* 3 (1903): 471, Beloch answered this contention in detail and defended his concept with reasons that were very telling, in my view; he agrees to a figure up to 5 million souls, at the highest, for the peninsula. The weak point in Nissen's argument is that he cannot reconcile the difference between the last available Republican census, that of the year 70–69 B.C.—910,000 individual citizens—with the census of Augustus of the year 28 B.C., which results in 4,063,000.

Nissen contends (p. 118) that there were included in the 4 million, first of all, all the men from the age of majority, second, all independent women, and third, orphans possessing property. But it is clear that this modification of the manner of counting could not possibly have come close to doubling the numbers of *juniores* (young people); likewise, it is just as unlikely that the difference is accounted for by the natural increase of the population and the granting of citizenship to others. There is no other possible explanation than that of Beloch, according to which, since the time of Augustus, not only the men but all individuals were counted,[10] and if this was the case, then the old census figures give not only the *juniores*, but all the men.

My further investigation into the controversy has led me, nevertheless, to an important modification of my estimate on one point, where I had already expressed a certain amount of doubt in my first edition and where Beloch, too, now makes a concession. This has to do with the numerical strength of the Roman army levy, which, corresponding to the number of legions, which were regarded as almost full-strength, I estimated for 216 B.C. at 83,000 men in the land army, a strength which was almost reached again a few years after the battle of Cannae by virtue of continuous enlisting of the youths. In 216 B.C. Rome had 18 legions under arms, in 212–211 B.C., 21 (or even possibly 23).

Even Beloch earlier agreed (*Population* [*Bevölkerung*], p. 383) with the opinion "that between 214 and 203 B.C. something like 20 Roman legions were on active duty is a fact that cannot be disputed in any way." Now he contends, supported by Polybius 8. 3, that the 20 (or even 22 to 23) legions are to be explained as boasting by the Roman writers, and he believes that Rome had no more than 8 legions in the field, only 4 of which were in Italy. Now this is a patent error. Under no circumstances does Polybius say that Rome had 8 legions in the field, but he says that she had two armies in Italy under the command of the consuls, and the possibility that he might have understood in this connection armies of 2 legions each is not only not said but is completely eliminated by the fact that he also applies the word *stratopedon* ("army"*) to the fleet command of Publius Scipio in Spain. Further, how would it have been possible for the Romans to recapture Capua with only 4 legions, since Hannibal certainly still had at his disposal in the years following the battle of Cannae an army of 40,000 to 50,000 men? Moreover, the number of legions given by Livy obviously goes back to an official account, and the account of the levy of the year 212 B.C., which we shall discuss very shortly, very definitely has the stamp of credibility. Nevertheless, Beloch's instinct was right and his opinion, with a few small corrections, can be accepted and can further be supported by means of other very weighty evidence.

If the legions really numbered 22, Beloch asks, why did not Polybius give the number of legions in his Chapter 8. 3, where, after all, he purports to describe the totality of Roman arms, precisely in these years? He probably did not do so because a large part of these so-called legions were small units of garrison troops that were dignified with the proud name of legion only because of the Romans' love for imposing words. I have no doubt that in this sentence there is opened up to us a solution that simultaneously banishes a whole series of difficulties. We can base the strict proof for this on the *legiones urbanae* (city legions).

During the years from 215 B.C. to 212 B.C. Rome formed 2 new legions annually, which were trained in Rome itself and simultaneously formed the garrison for the capital, and in this way she gradually brought the number from 14 legions, the number existing at the start of 215 B.C., up to 22. In filling up the army after the battle of Cannae the totality of available manpower was completely exhausted, so that it was necessary to take the step of enlisting imprisoned debtors and slaves. If now they continued to form two new legions in each of the next four years, there was available for this purpose only the age-group that had just entered its eighteenth year. Compared with our modern concepts, the Romans in doing so went back to an age that is not yet generally considered as strong enough for military duty, much less for combat. From a practical viewpoint it was probably not this way. The Romans maintained no birth registers; the age of young men could therefore not be so easily determined, and it may have happened often enough that unwilling candidates placed their age too low in order to escape service for one or two years longer. This possibility was blocked when they decided that even seventeen-year-olds were liable to drafting, for that meant in other words that the draft authorities could take anybody who seemed to them to be sufficiently developed physically and did not have to worry about the objection that the drafted youth was not yet of the legal age, which would have been easy for eighteen- to twenty-year-olds.

The number of adult male citizens amounted at that time to something over 270,000, of whom some 25,000 are to be counted among the defected Capuans. The year-group of seventeen-year-olds amounts in the German Empire to 3.13 percent of all men over seventeen years old, and in France to 2.45 percent of that group.[11] The age distribution of the Roman citizenry was supposedly more similar to that of France than to the German; assuming the age-group of seventeen-year-olds as 2¾ percent, it amounted to 6,740 persons, or, in order to be on the safe side, let us say 7,000 to 7,500. From that number the physically disqualified individuals must be deducted. In Germany at present the percentage of those who are qualified at the time of induction varies between 52.7 percent (1898) and 59.9 percent (1896). In addition, however, we must include the great number of those who have only quite minor disabilities, are assigned to the replacement reserve, and would be inducted in time of war. In the last decade the number of completely unqualified men has varied only between 8.5 percent (1903) and 6.9 percent (1904). Transferred over to the Roman situation, this would mean a year-group of around 6,500 qualified recruits, or probably fewer. From that number those deferred for special reasons must be deducted. Livy recounts (24. 18) how in 214 B.C. the lists of *juniores* were reviewed and 2,000 men were found who had not served in the last four years, without being able to cite authorized dispensation or illness (*qui quadriennio non militassent, quibus neque vacatio iusta militae neque morbus causa fuisset*). Therefore, even at that time, in addition to illness, there were legal dispensations, and the addition of *quadriennio* in conjunction with the later prescription that a man was obligated for 16, and in case of emergency, 20, campaigns leads to the conclusion that there was a certain diversity of enforcement; in other words, dispensation for economic reasons, as Nissen correctly pointed out, played a considerable role in the levying of troops, a more important one than even I had earlier estimated.

To lead into battle anywhere near the totality of men between seventeen and forty-six would never be possible for more than a few days. On the small farms on which, after all, the great mass of the Roman population lived, it was necessary to leave a man capable of working, or at the very least there had to be some relative on a neighboring farm who could lend a hand, if there was not to be famine and a complete economic breakdown. This situation, of course, also worked to the special advantage of the seventeen-year-olds, since often one would have had to let the father, who was a trained soldier, go home, if one took from the farm wife her growing son who was helping her and in whom the army would have gotten a raw recruit in place of a seasoned warrior. From the economic and family points of view, such an exchange might even have been desirable, of course; but it was not in the best interests of the pursuit of the war. This concept is attested to by the account in Livy (25. 3) that in 212 B.C., in addition to the 2 new city legions that were to be formed, replacement levies were also decided on for the older legions stationed in Italy. Such a decision could only be reached if a good portion of the available recruits from the preceding years had been left over. Livy does, of course, report to us further on that the number of recruits did not suffice for the implementation of this decision and that consequently youths not yet seventeen (that is, those who said they were not yet seventeen), who showed sufficient strength, were inducted. But since the replacement levy for the old legions, which had been opposing the enemy for years, required, after all, at least 5,000 to 8,000 men if it was to have any significance, the need was so great that in every case they must have counted on very considerable carryovers from the last previously inducted year-group. Consequently, from the approximately 6,500 service-qualified recruits who were available, we have to make a very considerable reduction for the actual number called, and since 2 legions with cavalry normally required 9,000 men, it follows, that these legions were organized at a strength far below the normal one and since, because of the extreme youth of the recruits, they had large discharge rates, they probably numbered hardly even half of the normal figure when they moved out on a campaign.

This situation is also reflected in the other legions. Once the Romans had become accustomed to designating as legions units that numbered perhaps only 2,000 men, even at the start of a campaign, we are no longer compelled to assume that the field legions always had a strength approaching the normal; on the contrary, we feel called on from the start, especially with respect to those troops that had already been in the field for a rather long time, to make a very considerable deduction, and Polybius knew what he was doing when he flatly declined to accept the number of legions as the measure of the Roman army strength.

The army Hasdrubal led over the Alps to the aid of his brother in 207 B.C. was certainly only moderately large. Further, Hannibal's fighting strength was surely already greatly shrunken. Why would the Romans have been in such great fear of these two armies if they had had something like 20 actual legions in the field? Why did Nero have to make his famous secret march to reinforce the northern army, if the Romans had had 2 real legions in Etruria, 2 in Rome, 1 near Capua, and, in addition to the field army, 4 more in Lower Italy?

Whereas I assumed earlier that the 22 legions had been about 80,000 strong, I now believe that I can and must reduce that figure to between 50,000 and 60,000. The question is whether also the 18 legions of the year 216 B.C., concerning which it was specifically reported that the strength of those in the main army had increased to 5,000 men, must suffer a larger reduction than we had formerly assumed necessary for them. Of course, they were considerably closer to normal strength than were the legions of the later armies, and particularly the 8 legions that fought at Cannae and the 2 in Spain were probably almost at full strength; for the 8 others, however, we no longer need to make that assumption, since the missions that were assigned to them actually required only moderately strong garrison troops. If we assume, then, a strength between 45,000 and 47,000 for the 10 main legions, the total strength still probably did not amount to more than some 66,000 men.

Consequently, our estimate now brings us to some 6½ percent of the population, and with the inclusion of casualties, 7½ percent, as the measure of the military effort, whereas we previously arrived at the figure of 9½ percent. I confess, however, that I had always felt dubious about this number deep inside me, and I only accepted and passed it on simply because there seemed to be no reason for opposing the estimates. Even 5 percent year in, year out, after the enormous combat losses, is already such a gigantic effort that we could be completely satisfied with it and could well understand the complaints of the Roman citizenry, which have been passed on to us quite fully.

Insofar as the Roman citizenry is concerned, we are, as has been seen, quite accurately informed of the war levy. But the Roman citizens formed only a third of the free inhabitants of the entire alliance. The military burden was distributed in such a way that the allies furnished for the land army a somewhat stronger contingent than did Rome, as well as providing the principal part of the fleet (*socii navales*). At this point our knowledge comes to an end: how much of this obligation was actually carried out and how much not? After Cannae a portion of the allies went directly over to the Carthaginians; but even those who remained loyal to the Romans can hardly have striven with all their strength in the same manner as the Romans themselves; and at any rate, with the defection of so many, the policy that a half of that army was supposed to be composed of allies could not be sustained. How large, then, the Roman armies actually were after Cannae we do not know, since the sources do not include figures concerning the strength of the contemporary allies, and this is an important lacuna for an analysis of the later campaigns, especially the one of 207 B.C.

ADDED IN THIRD EDITION

Since the foregoing was written, the problem has been explored in many ways, especially by Beversdorff in *The Armed Forces of the Carthaginians and the Romans in the Second Punic War* (*Die Streitkräfte der Karthager und Römer im 2. pun. Kriege*), Berlin dissertation, 1910; by Kromayer, *Ancient Battlefields* (*Antike Schlachtfelder*, 3: 476; by E. Meyer, *Sitzungsberichte der Akademie*, 1915, p. 948. Kromayer believes that the number of Roman citizens should be significantly increased because of the assumption that men over sixty years of age were excluded in the census figures and as a result of a few other corrections of the historical accounts. Nevertheless, he agrees with me in believing that very many of the legions reported in Livy were, to be sure, in existence, but were also far below the normal strength. If in doing so he states the opinion that I make too sharp a distinction between consular legions and garrison legions, this point is based on a misunderstanding; in this respect I concur fully with his explanation. On the other hand, I would not agree with his assumption that the men over sixty years of age were not included in the census figures, and I would hold fast to the concept that in 216 B.C. the number of inductable citizens had been completely exhausted for all practical purposes. For, even if a certain number of service-qualified men between seventeen and forty-six years of age were actually available, nevertheless the majority of them were probably so indispensable that they could not be inducted, even in this extreme emergency, and it was preferable to form slave legions. I should therefore like to stick to my estimates and only lessen them a bit in accepting Kromayer's proof that there were many furloughs in winter, even for entire legions.

E. Meyer has modified his earlier estimates (1915) by lowering the land army strength to some extent, but at the same time he assumes among the crews of the fleet something like a third, that is, some 18,000 Roman citizens. Since I assume that this estimate is much too high and that in the fleet at that time not much more than the high command was of national Roman origin, then I may be permitted to retain my estimates that the total levy of Roman citizens amounted to 66,000 in 216 B.C. and to 50,000 to 60,000 men in the following years.

The English *United Service Gazette* published in 1905 (No. 3787) an estimate of the strength of the English armed forces during the Napoleonic period. According to this study, in 1805, with a population of less than 17 million, they numbered about 800,000 men. Concerning the performances of the nations in the World War of 1914–1918 we do not yet have official accounts. The effort of the German people undoubtedly amounted to at least the double of the effort of Prussia in the year 1813.

NOTES FOR CHAPTER II

1. Polybius 3. 89. 9.

2. I am not adding any for the fleet, since at this time they would have left very few Roman citizens aboard ship. Since there was no real sea war taking place, they were able to provide the crews from allies and slaves (except for the one fleet legion).

3. Livy 34. 50.

4. Livy, 37. 60.

5. I do not see fit to agree with the idea that fear of the wild Gauls, who formed such a large percentage of the Punic army, caused the Italians to adhere to Rome; for the defections increased continuously in the years 210 and 211 B.C., although that fear, to whatever extent it existed, must have been getting stronger and stronger.

6. The numerous victories that the Romans are supposed to have won from Hannibal from 216 to 203 B.C. according to Livy, were, as is so excellently explained by W. Streit in *On the History of the Second Punic War in Italy after the Battle of Cannae* (*Zur Geschichte des zweiten punischen Krieges in Italien nach der Schlacht bei Cannä*, Berlin, 1887), patriotic Roman fantasies—frankly, pure lies. Very nicely was Streit able to add up that Hannibal is supposed to have lost

120,000 killed in all these battles from Cannae on. Where it was a question of larger battles, as at Herdoniae and Numistro, victory still went to the Carthaginians. The alleged victories of Marcellus at Nola turn out to be very insignificant engagements.

7. It is precisely this way that Polybius describes the situation (9. 3–4).

8. *Studies of Ancient History published by Jules Beloch* (*Studi di Storia antica pubblicati di Giulio Beloch*), I: 34.

9. *On the History of the Second Punic War* (*Zur Geschichte des zweiten punischen Krieges*), p. 35.

10. In my first edition I rejected with more detailed documentation the objections of Kornemann in *Conradsche Jahrbücher*, new series, 14 (1897): 291, which I have not repeated here.

11. According to the census of 1 December 1900 the number of young men over seventeen and under eighteen in the German Empire amounted to 525,582, and the number of all men above seventeen was 16,806,581 (see also *Statistik des Deutschen Reichs*, 150: 118 ff.). According to the census at the beginning of 1901 in France, the number of men between seventeen and eighteen on 1 January 1901 amounted to 330,318, and the number of all men over seventeen years of age to 13,456,430 (see also *Résultats statistiques du recensement de 1901*, 4: 58).

Chapter III

The Strategic Prelude
to the War in Retrospect

From the position of knowledge that we have now attained let us once again turn back to the prelude to the war on both sides. Recently Joseph Fuchs has published on this subject excellent studies, with which I concur in their important aspects.[1]

Hannibal took the land route because this route led him to that people that was ready to join him immediately against the Romans, the Gauls. If he had, for example, first crossed over from Africa to Sicily, he would have had to rely for a long time solely on his own resources. Furthermore, such an expedition by sea would have been exposed to attack by the superior Roman sea power, and it was also practically impossible to create a cargo fleet large enough to move the army's 10,000 horses. This was probably the final, decisive factor; for on the concept of going in from the very start with unquestionably superior cavalry and winning the first battle with it everything else was based.

Confident that he would be able to establish for himself a new base in Italy itself, Hannibal gave up a continuous connection with the homeland, limited his fleet to the barely essential, devoted all of his means, instead, to the land army, and also provided himself from the start with a well-filled war treasury. If he did not possess an actual superiority at sea, it was of less use to him to have a fleet of mediocre strength than the cash with which he could pay his mercenaries regularly and could show up in the area of the Gauls, as in Italy, without at the same time being too much of a burden for the allies whom he expected to join him. Polybius is correct in making a point of the fact (3. 17. 10) that Hannibal also took money along with him on his expedition.

The concept of the Romans strikes us as less clear than the logic of Hannibal, so that the general feeling, even to include Fuchs, has been to see in the Roman viewpoint hardly anything else than an incomprehensible and completely un-Roman indecisiveness and a purposeless hesitation.

Why did the Romans not seize the offensive from the start and carry the war to Spain, preferably during the time when Hannibal was still occupied with the siege of Saguntum?

Just as the tactical superiority of the Carthaginians later showed itself at Cannae, so would any army, even though as large as his, which the Romans might have sent against him in Spain, easily have fallen prey to him there. The Carthaginians were, after all, much stronger in Spain than in Italy.

If the Romans had, instead, mounted at once a great attack against Carthage itself, Hannibal, crossing over from Spain or even possibly sending only a part of his army, would have brought to this Roman army the same fate that befell Regulus in the first war.

It would have been worse yet if the Romans had divided their forces and attacked Spain and Africa simultaneously, exposing both expeditions, in turn, to the attack of the unified Carthaginian forces. It was, of course, out of the question to think that Carthage could possibly be taken while Hannibal was still fighting with the Roman force in Spain. Carthage was a mighty fortress that would require years to be taken by siege, and Hannibal would have made short shrift of the Roman force sent against him.

One is therefore obliged, along with Fuchs, to agree completely with that party in the Roman Senate that, according to Livy, 21. 6, believed *"non temere movendam rem tantam"* ("such serious matters should not be hastily acted upon"). Compared with the Carthaginian army that the Barcas had organized in Spain, the Romans were not in a position to seize the offensive, and their hesitation, their long period of indecisiveness, the surrender of Saguntum—all of this is very easily explained, even though, as we shall establish below, the Carthaginian army in Spain was not 130,000 men strong, as has previously been assumed, based on the word of Polybius, but rather only some 82,000 men.

It would appear now that there is a contradiction between this idea and the manner in which the Romans, after they had finally entered the war, actually proceeded, and what they planned. They thought they could carry on the war with 6 legions; in fact, at the start, before they became occupied with an uprising of the Cisalpine Boii, they seem to have intended to get along with their normal strength of 4 legions. Of the 4, they sent two under the Consul

Sempronius to Sicily, so that they could cross over to Africa, and the other consul, Scipio, was supposed to lead 2 legions to Spain. If they believed that they would be able to make out against Hannibal in Spain with 2 legions, or a total of 22,400 infantry and 2,000 cavalry (Livy 21. 17), then it was, of course, inexcusable on their part not to have gone to the aid of the Saguntians.

Fuchs has cleared up the matter by drawing the following interpretation from the sources. The Romans suspected and knew Hannibal's war plan from the start. The natural difficulties of the gigantic march through nothing but enemy peoples from the Ebro, across the Pyrenees, to the Alps, seemed to them, of course, still much greater than they did to Hannibal. They counted on the fact that his strength would already have shrunk very greatly before he even arrived at the foot of the Alps. Their idea, therefore, was not to oppose him until this point, perhaps on the Rhone, and to organize the opposition of the natives of the area against him. From the beginning, Scipio's expedition was intended for this area, and Spain was only a secondary objective. Sempronius' expedition was only being readied in Sicily and was not supposed to move on to Africa until it was definitely established that Hannibal was engaged with his army in Gaul and could not suddenly fall on the Roman forces in front of Carthage.

Even in view of these plans, however, the weakness of the two consular armies is still noteworthy. If something like twice the strength, or 4 legions, had been set in motion for each of the two undertakings, then it would appear perfectly clear that the strength of the Carthaginians was known to the Roman Senate and that this body therefore chose a defensive-offensive strategy, left the initiative to Hannibal, sacrificed Saguntum, and entered the war with cautious hesitation.

The explanation for the fact that each of the two consuls was given only 2 legions probably is that it was a question of overseas expeditions. To send out large armies by sea requires huge resources, and the large fleets can hardly be controlled afterwards. There are not enough ports to accommodate them all; the wind drives them out of formation and leaves those that are shaken loose from the formation easy prey to the enemy. The Romans did not yet have the remotest idea of the raging power unleashed by Hannibal in battle, and so while very well knowing that they could not oppose him directly in Spain or Africa, they might nevertheless have been confident that a full consular army on the Rhone, based on the befriended city of Massilia and allied with the Gallic tribes, which could not tolerate the passage of the Carthaginians, could carry on successful combat.

Seen in this light, the conduct of the Romans loses its appearance of weakness, of indecisive, contradictory half-moves. It derives quite naturally from the attitudes that governed the way the Senate directed the fortunes of the Roman state, both before and afterward.

In the first place, Hannibal thwarted the Roman estimates by overcoming the obstacles on his march much more quickly than had been expected. When Scipio with his 24,400 men landed near Marseilles, thinking Hannibal was still held up in the Pyrenees, the latter was already on the Rhone, and he completed his crossing before Scipio could do anything to stop him.

At this point one might well raise the question why Hannibal, apparently worried, avoided an engagement with the Romans instead of welcoming the arrival of Scipio as good news. With his far superior army, both numerically and qualitatively, he would only have had to envelop Scipio in order to cut him down; the finest, most certain victory was offered him by the unsuspecting Romans. This shows the full genius of the young Carthaginian commander, the combination of the highest courage with the calmest calculation, in that he did not pursue the temptation of this prize. Napoleon's saying *"une victoire est toujours bonne à quelque chose"* ("a victory always serves some good purpose"), however indisputable it may appear, is nevertheless still subject to exceptions and limitations. If Hannibal had held up his advance for even only a few days for a victory over Scipio, he would not have been able to cross the Alps that year. However certain the victory was, the Romans still were accustomed to selling their lives dearly in every encounter. The Carthaginians could have taken the losses in themselves, but they could neither have given up the great mass of their wounded in this enemy territory nor succeeded in urging them through the march over the Alps that immediately faced them. It was already late autumn, and in a few weeks the snow would block the passes. If, however, the Carthaginian army had spent the winter in Gaul, in order to descend into Italy the following spring, it could be expected that the Romans, warned and frightened by the defeat of the first army, would be waiting in greatly superior numbers for the Carthaginians as soon as they moved out of the Alpine passes. That was the most dangerous weak spot in Hannibal's strategic plan. If the Romans had from the start held their defensive action for this point and had fallen on the Carthaginians just as they came out of the passes, while their cavalry was half out of action, partly because of fatigue and partly because of the terrain, it is difficult to see how Hannibal could have carried out his invasion. But with his penetrating, psychologically oriented perspicacity, he had foreseen, as Fuchs masterfully explains, that the old bold offensive spirit of the Romans would not allow them to await the arrival of the enemy within their borders. If they did not move out to oppose him as far away as Spain, something he perhaps hoped for at the start, they would certainly go as far as Gaul.

Hannibal may also have had positive information at his disposition. We may assume that he was not without contacts in Rome, where people of all nationalities streamed in, and that he had organized an intelligence service. Even with all the Roman virtues, decisions taken by a body as large as the Senate were hard to keep completely secret, and the concealment of practical preparations was even harder. In 216 B.C. the Romans claimed to have discovered in their city a Carthaginian spy who had been there for two years, and as a fear-inspiring example they sent him out with his hands chopped off (Livy 22. 33).

Hannibal therefore had good reason to expect to find the Romans somewhere along his route, and if he then avoided an engagement or moved immediately after the battle to cross the Alps, he would find on the other side, at the exit from the passes, still no prepared defenses, perhaps even if he fought the battle in Spain. For the fame acquired by this victory would have greatly facilitated for him the march through the Celtic peoples. The march Hannibal made, from the Ebro into the Po valley, amounts to about 550 miles as the crow flies, and he would then perhaps have been able to make it in three months rather than five. But we do not have to exhaust every combination of possibilities; suffice it to say that Hannibal, with good reason, counted on being able to carry out his crossing over the Alps without being stopped by the Romans and that, on the other hand, he eschewed with logical reasoning a victory on the Rhone, in order to carry out with complete certainty his entrance into the Po region, without weakening himself by sacrificing several thousand wounded men, and to create a new base for himself there, in alliance with the Cisalpine Gauls.

Hannibal's estimates all proved valid, whereas those of the Romans were not. But we should not be too critical of them; they happened to be dealing with Hannibal, and in those circumstances it was not easy to come out on top. A senate cannot arrive at decisions through genius-inspired intuition; it cannot act differently or come to decisions in any way except in the manner of its forebears, and that is what the Romans did in this case, fearlessly and in keeping with the dictates of common sense. In many a historical moment, however, that is not enough.

EXCURSUS

ESTIMATE OF STRENGTHS

Before Hannibal left Italian soil in 203 B.C., he had erected in the ancient, highly revered Temple of Hera Lacinia near Croton a brass tablet on which his deeds and triumphs in the peninsula were engraved. Polybius tells us that he saw this tablet himself and that he took from it the entire enumeration of the troops left back in Spain and in Africa by Hannibal, as well as the army's strength on arrival in Italy (3. 33 and 56).

Although there have always been great commanders who were inclined to understate their strength after winning a victory—Caesar, Frederick, and Napoleon even did that to an extreme degree—nevertheless, we may first of all give full credence to the figures stated by Hannibal. There is a question, however, whether Polybius' extract is correct and whether all his numbers come from this source.

Polybius, taking his figures from the Lacinian tablet, states that Hannibal had left behind as garrison troops in Africa 19,920 men (with the missing number of Balearics filled in from Livy), and in Spain 15,200 men (3. 33). Somewhat further on he recounts that Hannibal marched off with 102,000 men. He would therefore have had an army of some 137,000 men.

Of the 102,000 men, he left 11,000 behind for the region north of the Ebro, and he released 11,000 Spaniards in their homeland. He crossed the Pyrenees with 59,000 men. The subjection of the Spaniards north of the Ebro had cost him, then, 21,000 men. For a short campaign against a few barbarian peoples that is an absolutely unbelievable number.

He arrived at the Rhone with 46,000 men (38,000 infantry, 8,000 cavalry). The move up to that point had therefore cost him 13,000 men.

After the crossing of the Alps the Carthaginian army numbered a bare 20,000 infantry and 6,000 cavalry, and for this figure Polybius again depends on the Lacinian tablet. The crossing of the Alps, then, apparently cost the Carthaginians 20,000 men more.

These huge losses have not been considered improbable, since it is well known how greatly marches through enemy territory, even without large battles, can cause attrition in armies, and we are reminded of the losses Napoleon's army suffered during its advance on Moscow. This analogy, however, is not valid. Napoleon's army, and especially the French regiments, were composed in their great majority of very young men and unwilling draftees, who were held in the service only through force. Hannibal's army undoubtedly consisted of warriors who were capable of withstanding every kind of fatigue. Although it is true that the opposition furnished by the Celtic peoples did delay the march to the extent that security measures had to be taken, it cannot possibly have caused very much bloodshed, since, in view of the overwhelming numerical and qualitative superiority of the invaders and the strength of their cavalry, the barbarians could hardly afford to allow themselves to be drawn into combat. We hear nothing of any battle of importance or of any combined resistance of many tribes that might have come close to rivaling the strength of the Carthaginians. Only on very favorable special occasions in limited localities —consequently, especially in the Alps—were the local inhabitants able to exercise a damaging effect of any considerable proportions on the progress of the march. If under such circumstances a seasoned army is to sacrifice as a matter of course far more than half of its strength on a march of about two months' duration,[2] then the marches of Caesar, which were carried out for the most part over the same routes as those of Hannibal, from Italy to Spain and from Spain to Italy, as well as the marches of Alexander in Asia, become completely inconceivable, and it also becomes incomprehensible that the strength of the Carthaginian army in the following campaigns in Italy was so well maintained.

Consequently, there is no other possibility but that the Lacinian tablet did not contain an accounting of the strength of the Carthaginian army as it marched out, that Polybius combined information from other sources with that of the Lacinian tablet and arrived at the huge march losses through the differences. In just the same way, of course, he also arrived at the exaggerated loss of 70,000 men by the Romans at Cannae. Consequently, we do not know how large Hannibal's army actually was when it crossed the Ebro. There is nothing to prevent our assuming, however, that the overall march casualty figures did not exceed, say, 10,000 men—surely in fact, they must have been even much smaller, for in none of the sources is there the slightest evidence to force us to assume losses of more than a few hundred men. Precisely for this reason we can assume that Hannibal listed on the Lacinian tablet only those troops that he left behind in Spain and Africa and those with which he arrived in Italy.

My sharp challenging of the estimates that up to now have unhesitatingly been copied from Polybius concerning the original strength of Hannibal's army and his march casualties evoked contradiction by O. Hirschfeld in *Festschrift für T. Comperz* (Vienna: Alfred Holder, 1902), p. 159. From this controversy I have accepted a correction as to detail, but I repeat insofar as the rest of my argument is concerned the defense of my viewpoint, which I copy here from Volume II [German-language] of the first edition (p. 242).

First of all, Hirschfeld challenges my doubting of the figures of Polybius on a moral basis, as if I were raising "a serious complaint" and were "insulting" that great old historian. In the abstract, it is difficult to argue over an evaluation of this type. I believe, however, that we can very easily come to agreement as soon as Hirschfeld decides to take a position on the analogies that I adduced from the works of Moltke, Sybel, Droysen, and Treitschke in Vol. I [original German edition], pp. 21, 387 and Vol. II [original German edition], pp. 67, 294. As soon as one approaches the subject more closely through such an analogy, one sees at once that an objective doubt in no way constitutes a moral complaint, and then it becomes immediately clear how dangerous it is, even in the case of such highly respected authors, to invest every figure with a kind of infallibility.

In the present case it should have been all the less permissible for Hirschfeld to take this point of departure, since I did not, after all, limit my criticism to this one figure but supported it by means of Polybius' figures on Cannae. In this case it is quite clear that the author does not only repeat the figures from his sources, but that he also establishes new ones through his calculations, and that these calculations are cursory and false. These facts are, I believe, undisputed and undisputable and obviously very important for the evaluation of other figures of this author. Hirschfeld did not devote a single word, however, to opposing this argument, which for me is a very important one. I have considered it superfluous to introduce in this matter still other evidence that Polybius, in his estimates, was in no way very careful but rather went over them quickly. Since this point now seems to be disputed, however, I shall also make reference to his account of the battle of Issus. Since it is a question here of the critical rejection of another author, Callisthenes, one would suppose that Polybius would have been doubly careful. But it is generally acknowledged that his calculations contain errors. I may be allowed to stress this point all the more, since I believe that in this situation I have successfully defended the reasoning of Polybius in the matter, even against the sharp attacks that it has elicited; but his figures are patently incorrect in part and in contradiction with one another. Finally, it is now probably also generally recognized that his figures on the

Roman fleet in the First Punic War were greatly exaggerated and likewise rest on false calculations, that is, the inclusion of *all* the ships, even the small ones, as penteremes. See also Beloch, *Population (Bevölkerung)*, p. 379.

Hirschfeld seeks to support the figures of Polybius by a note in Livy (21. 38), according to which Hannibal himself is supposed to have said to Cincius Alimentus, who had been taken prisoner by him, that he had lost 36,000 men after his crossing of the Rhone. Like all the earlier scholars of this period, I too have left this passage out of consideration, since it seemed worthless to me. Hirschfeld now gives it a new interpretation. The passage reads: "Ex ipso autem audisse Hannibale, postquam Rhodanum transierit, triginta sex milia hominium ingentemque numerum equorum et aliorum jumentorum amisisse." ("From Hannibal himself, moreover, he learned that Hannibal, after he had crossed the Rhone, had lost 36,000 men and vast numbers of horses and other beasts of burden.") Up to now that has been understood to mean that after his crossing over the Rhone—consequently principally on his passage of the Alps—Hannibal lost 36,000 men. Hirschfeld also admits that Livy himself probably also meant it this way, but he believes nevertheless that he is justified in interpreting as the original sense that it was not the march from the Rhone on that was meant, but the march up to the Rhone. Now since Polybius' figures for the losses of this first march phase lead to 35,000 men, the two figures appear to support and corroborate each other.

I cannot concur in any way with this evidence. In the first place, the remaining difference of 1,000 men, though objectively unimportant, is still, however, quite significant from the critical point of view, since, if the two estimates could really be followed back to a common source, they would also have to agree exactly. In addition, however, the relationship to the first march phase is completely excluded both by the context and by the particular reference to the loss of cattle and horses. Livy inserts this note after Hannibal has just arrived in Italy and has the costly crossing of the Alps, with all its terrors, behind him. At this point should there be some special mention of the losses up to the Rhone, but no mention of those in the passage of the Alps? Hannibal, if indeed he honored Cincius Alimentus with information of his great losses, supposedly mentioned neither the overall losses of the march nor the special losses on the crossing of the Alps, but only and particularly the losses up to the Rhone? And at that with special emphasis on the loss of horses and cattle?

Personally, I place no value at all on these kinds of figures; but if one insists, after all, in purging this estimate and somehow eliminating the obvious errors by means of guesses, it seems to me that the only rational conclusion is that the reference is to the losses for the entire period from the crossing of the Rhone up to the moment of the conversation. Cincius was praetor in about 209 B.C. and apparently was not taken prisoner and given the honor of a personal conversation with Hannibal until some time later.

Instead of losing ourselves in similar hypotheses, we would probably do best to point out that in that very same passage Livy also reports that, according to Cincius Alimentus, Hannibal had led 90,000 men over the Alps, counting the Gauls and the Ligurians, and thereupon to add that we attribute no validity at all to numbers given by this author.

It is also a wholly inadequate explanation of the huge losses of Hannibal on the march when Hirschfeld presumes there were "massive desertions" of the Spanish troops. Neither in the sources nor by the nature of things does this assumption have the slightest support. It is completely arbitrary. After all, where would these deserters have gone? Would they have penetrated directly through strange, and often hostile, tribes, wandering and begging their way homeward? In the first place we can assume that, among the peoples of the peninsula, Hannibal found enough warlike elements that were fully inclined, just as were the Africans, to follow his banner in the expectation of pay, booty, fame, and adventure, and that he did not find it necessary to press unwilling men into service; and second, it is clear that, once they had crossed the Ebro, any return was completely out of the question. In this respect Hannibal enjoyed the advantage for which the Russian armies were noted in the eighteenth century, that is, that they had no desertions, because, once over the border, the private soldier could not make out by himself in a foreign country.

And in like manner it is also inadequate when Hirschfeld states that we have heard so little about Hannibal's combat actions on the march only because they were not reported, and not because there were so few of them. Let us realize that it is a question of 13,000 men from an army reportedly of 59,000, and consequently 22 percent, just on the march from the Pyrenees to the Rhone. Let us recall from the entire span of ancient military history, and especially from Caesar, how small the losses were for a well-organized and well-led army against barbarians, as long as the former was victorious, and let us imagine then what frightful battles those must have been when no word about them has come down to us, although the massive losses were not concealed! And with all of this, the entire march distance from the Pyrenees to the Rhone is no longer than 160 miles. If Hannibal had lost 13,000 men on this short march, that would have been many more than in all his great victories over the Romans, on the Trebia, at Lake Trasimeno, and at Cannae taken together. And the historians supposedly took care of such battles with the brief explanation that he opened the way partly by force, partly by bribery?

All of these completely arbitrary insinuations have been made simply because it is supposed to be impossible for Polybius to have ever carelessly followed an unreliable source! The same Polybius of whom it is quite clear in three other passages that something human could very well happen to him in numerical estimates and computations—just as, indeed, in the case of historians in general, attention to the validity, the significance, and the range of figures is a rare characteristic.

Polybius informs us (3. 33) which troops Hannibal left in Spain and in Africa; two chapters later (3. 35), Polybius tells with how many troops he started out and with how many he crossed the Pyrenees. Much later (3. 56), we learn with how many he arrived in Italy, and again, four chapters later (3. 60), how many he still had at the moment of crossing the Rhone. In the first and third passages Polybius indicates the Lacinian tablet as his source. From this, Hirschfeld concludes that this tablet was also the source for the other passages, since otherwise the author "can hardly escape the reproach that, by the twice-mentioned reference to the Lacinian source, he instilled in his readers a completely unjustified confidence, even in the other figures that have emerged from, as Delbrück believes, other, completely unreliable sources." This conclusion is methodologically false. Polybius himself considered his source as sufficiently reliable—otherwise he would not have used it. That modern criticism with its sharper eyes casts doubt on this cannot be fought out as a struggle over Polybius' morality. In fact, the matter has to be turned completely around: if Polybius had taken all of these figures from one and the same source, then it would hardly be comprehensible why he scattered them so much. By their nature, they belong in two groups: for the start of the march, and for the arrival in Italy. For the start, however, the number of those left behind is separated from the number that marched away by an entire chapter. Even if the sequence of the account justifies this separation, it is still most unusual that the number of troops that reached Italy is reported first, whereas the strength of the army while it was still at the Rhone is not given until four chapters later. Instead of concluding that, because Polybius on both occasions took the first number from the Lacinian tablet (which he expressly says), he must therefore also have done the same thing each time for the second figure (which he does not say), we should turn this about; we can be quite sure that the second figures are not derived from the Lacinian tablet.

Finally, Hirschfeld reproaches me for "correcting according to my own discretion" good source evidence. I hope that, the further my work progresses, the more this honored opponent will gradually come to admit that my criticism rests in no way on my "discretion," but on knowledge of the subject.

Since then Konrad Lehmann, in *The Attacks of the Three Barcas Against Italy* (*Die Angriffe der drei Barkiden auf Italien*), pp. 131 ff., has also spoken up in support of my concept with further arguments.

If I believe, for these reasons, that the initial strength of Hannibal's army must be reduced quite drastically, I also believe that there are good reasons for significantly raising the arrival strength of the army in Italy as given by Polybius.

Hannibal is said to have arrived in northern Italy with 12,000 Africans, 8,000 Iberians, 6,000 cavalry. These figures were taken by Polybius from the Lacinian tablet; his repetition of the figures contains, however, an obvious gap.

In the battle on the Trebia (Polybius 3. 72) there is mention of 8,000 Balearics and "lance-bearers" (*logchophoroi*: peltasts),[3] which Hannibal had with him, and in Livy 22. 37, there is a reference in a speech by the ambassador of King Hiero to Moorish and other sharpshooters that Hannibal had with him (see also 23. 26 and 27. 18). The latter are missing in the note of Polybius taken from the Lacinian tablet. It is entirely out of the question that Hannibal should not have provided his army with a significant force of light infantry precisely for the battles that he had to fight while on the great march, and especially in the mountains.

It is also impossible, however, that the 8,000 light infantry should be included, as Konrad Lehmann believes was the case, in the total of barely 20,000 infantry. In that case, Hannibal would have arrived in Italy with only 12,000 hoplites, of whom only some 9,000 to 10,000 could have been left at the time of Cannae. In that battle he mixed the Iberians in units among the Celts in the center, and with the Africans he made the envelopments on the right and the left, but it is impossible to see how either the 3,000 to 4,000 Iberians mixed among the 22,000 Celtic hoplites or the 5,000 to 6,000 Africans assigned to the two flanks could have accomplished the missions that were demanded of them and that they reportedly achieved. The battle does not take on a logical appearance unless we assume that of the 32,000 hoplites, about 11,000 were Africans, 7,000 Iberians, and 14,000 Celts. Only with this assumption is it understandable that in 203 B.C. there still remained such an important portion of the African-Iberian nucleus of the army as to be able to overcome the rebellious Celts.

Now this calculation seems to be contradicted by the fact that Polybius (3. 72) gives the strength of the Carthaginian infantry in the battle on the Trebia, including the Celts who had joined them in the meantime, as only 21,000 hoplites and 8,000 light infantry. Konrad Lehmann points out (p. 134) that Hannibal was already reinforced in this battle with no fewer than some 7,000 Celtic cavalry. We must, however, assume, he believes, that the reinforcements in Celtic infantry were certainly not smaller, but somewhat larger still. This argument does not hold water. What Hannibal needed was not infantry in general, but disciplined infantry; the tactical maneuvers with which he planned to conquer the Romans and in which he succeeded in doing so were feasible only with well-organized tactical units who were under the direct control of their commanders. He was able to form such infantry, as his success shows, during the course of the winter of 218–217 B.C. from the Celtic mercenaries who rallied to him. In the battle on the Trebia he did not yet have them, or at any rate did not have more than some 2,000. It is definitely not only possible but very highly probable that the Carthaginian leader declared to his Celtic friends at the time of his arrival that he did not need any massive reinforcements of their infantry, that they might better protect their homeland on all sides from the Romans; and that, if incorporated into his army, they would complicate the problem of rations too greatly. What he would like to request of them was the addition to his army of their so outstandingly courageous cavalry, and provisions. Only after the battle on the Trebia were Celtic infantrymen also, in large numbers, organized for the offensive into the Apennine peninsula.

This also takes care of the concern that Cantalupi had, that Hannibal's army at Cannae could probably not have been 50,000 men strong, since in that case more than half of its strength would have consisted of Gauls; that this was quite improbable, and that in view of the unreliability of these allies it would have been a mistake, one that Hannibal would not have made.

If Hannibal brought 34,000 men across the Alps, he probably started out with about 36,000. He left some 20,000 in Africa and 26,000 in Spain. All together, then, he had at his disposal not 137,000, but only some 82,000, but even this number is completely adequate to serve as a basis for the strategic conditions developed above.

If one is inclined to mistrust Polybius in general because he was not definite on the point of including or excluding the light infantry and overlooked the 8,000 men in his extract from the Lacinian tablet, there still remains the possibility that Hannibal himself actually omitted them, just as Caesar, Frederick, and Napoleon often stated in their bulletins and memoirs figures that were smaller than their actual army strengths.

ADDED IN THIRD EDITION

The numerous objections that have been raised against the calculations given above have no doubt shown me that there are all kinds of factors in the historical accounts that contradict these figures, but they have not forced me to abandon my concept. The decisive point remains that Hannibal must necessarily have had considerably more than 12,000 heavily armed Spaniards and Africans; Cannae proves this. The opposing figures have less and less weight the more one agrees with Dessau's hypothesis on the Punic source of Polybius.

STRATEGY OF ANNIHILATION AND OF ATTRITION

IN THE SECOND PUNIC WAR

In his work *Rome's Struggle for World Hegemony* (*Roms Kampf um die Weltherrschaft*), Kromayer raised the interesting question as to the extent to which the conduct of the Second Punic War should be classified under the strategy of annihilation or that of attrition. As with so many historians, however, he does not understand this concept, which is studied in the fourth volume of my work. He believes that, up to the battle of Cannae, Hannibal's strategy was one of annihilation and that Hannibal then shifted to a strategy of attrition. Since Hannibal continuously sought battle in the open field, this concept seems the obvious one; but it is incorrect. If the desire for decisive battles marked the annihilation strategist, then Frederick the Great, too, would have been in this category, and Hannibal would have been likewise not only up to the year 216 B.C., but continuing until a much later time. For even after Cannae he definitely did not stop seeking open battle, and the fact that he did not succeed in bringing this about was not of his own doing but rather of the Romans'. Hannibal, then, did not carry out a change in his strategy, but he was and remained, from the start, a strategist of attrition. If he had followed a strategy of annihilation at the start, he would have had to try, after the defeat of the Roman army, to attack and take the city of Rome itself—that is, he would have had to have self-confidence in his power to do so. He apparently never had this in mind and, in fact, could not have had it in mind. With telling effect Kromayer himself points out—and I myself became aware of the significance of these passages only through him, a point which I gratefully acknowledge—that after the victory of Cannae Hannibal sought a negotiated peace with the Romans, and also that his treaty with Philip of Macedon (Polybius 7. 9) presumes the continuation of Rome as a power—we might even say as a great power. Accordingly, Hannibal's strategy was directed toward forcing Rome, by means of the heaviest possible blows, loss of her allies, and laying waste of her countryside, to make certain cessions of territory to Carthage and to limit her own size. His strategy was, consequently, bipolar, just like that of Frederick, but never set up as its goal the complete military subjection of the enemy as did Alexander and Napoleon.

It is therefore also incorrect, however easy it may be, to set up Hannibal and Fabius Cunctator as representatives of the two types of strategy. If Hannibal had been able to be an annihilation strategist, then all of the maneuvering of the Cunctator would have been in vain; Hannibal would simply have besieged and taken Rome, and the war would have been over. The difference between Hannibal and Fabius is not one of principle, but a purely practical one, going back to the dissimilarity of their arms. Hannibal based his actions on deriving the greatest advantage from his strength, that is, his cavalry and his tactical maneuverability, and this inclined him toward the open battle. Fabius recognized the inferiority of the Romans in this area and sought to bring down the enemy by means of the secondary methods of conducting war. Both of them, however, sought not to annihilate the enemy, but to force him, through attrition, to be willing to make peace or to abandon his foe's territory.

NOTES FOR CHAPTER III

1. *The Second Punic War and its Historical Sources, Polybius and Livy, Explained from Strategic-Tactical Viewpoints. The years 219 and 218 B.C., exclusive of the Crossing of the Alps.* An Essay by Joseph Fuchs, Imperial and Royal Professor in Wiener-Neustadt. (*Der zweite punische Krieg und seine Quellen Polybius und Livius nach strategisch-taktischen Gesichtspunkten beleuchtet. Die Jahre 219 und 218, mit Ausschluss des Alpenüberganges.* Ein Versuch von Joseph Fuchs, k. k. Professor in Wiener-Neustadt.) Wiener-Neustadt, 1894. In Kommission bei: Carl Blumrich, Wiener-Neustadt; M. Perles, Wien; T. Thomas, Leipzig.

Hannibal's Crossing of the Alps. Conclusions from Research and Travel, by Joseph Fuchs, Imperial and Royal Professor in Wiener-Neustadt. With two maps and one illustration. (*Hannibal's Alpenübergang.* Ein Studien- und Reiseergebnis von Joseph Fuchs, k. k. Professor in Wiener-Neustadt. Mit zwei Karten und einer Abbildung.) Vienna, Carl Konegen, 1897.

The question of which pass Hannibal used for his crossing of the Alps does not belong in the framework of this book, since no important strategic or tactical conclusions result from the variety of routes. Fuchs has decided on the Mont Genèvre Pass. Konrad Lehmann in *The Attacks of the Three Barcas Against Italy* (*Die Angriffe der drei Barkiden auf Italien*), 1905, has once again, with a very thorough argument, pointed to the Little Saint Bernard. Subsequently, French Captain of Engineers Colin, too, has appeared in this arena with a work entitled *Hannibal in Gaul* (*Annibal en Gaule*), 1904. To date, none of the various theories has been able to win general acceptance.

2. Hannibal is supposed to have left New Carthage at the start of May, but not to have crossed the Pyrenees until the beginning or

the middle of August; at the middle of October at the latest, and perhaps even at the end of September, he descended into the Po valley.

3. Beversdorff, p. 16, criticizes me for conceiving of javelin-throwers as peltasts. I still wish to hold to that idea; since the number of javelins that a man can carry is much smaller, for instance, than the number of arrows or lead balls for slings, which the actual sharpshooters have, the former must then to a certain extent be equipped for close combat—that is, they must be peltasts.

Chapter IV

Rome Wins
the Upper Hand

The Second Punic War had come into a sort of equilibrium through the fact that Hannibal dominated the open field, whereas the Romans prevented the further expansion of his sphere of power through the fortified cities that remained loyal to them or were won back. Then the balance gradually sank more and more in favor of the Romans as they completely won the upper hand in the secondary theaters of war and even in Italy wrested back more and more cities from the Carthaginians. Hannibal made one final magnificent attempt to force destiny by giving up Spain and having the troops that were stationed there led by his brother Hasdrubal on the ancient route over the Pyrenees and Alps to Italy. But before this army could join up with him, it was attacked by the Romans on the Metaurus (207 B.C.), and was beaten and destroyed,[1] and it must be said that, even if Hasdrubal had been victorious on the Metaurus, this victory would not yet have sealed the defeat of the Romans. Even if united with his brother, Hannibal would not have been able to undertake the siege of Rome, in view of the possibility that the Roman fleet could bring home the victorious legions from Spain, Sardinia, and Sicily. Would the Romans then have been willing to seek a negotiated peace? Who can tell?

No matter how favorable, however, the situation of the Romans had now become, they could not win a final decision by following the same old methods. For that, it was necessary that the main Carthaginian army, too, be defeated in open battle and its power broken. As long as they were unwilling to attack Hannibal himself and he remained in Italy, there could be no question of subduing Carthage. There was always the possibility of a sudden swing of the pendulum, as for example through a general uprising of the

Spanish peoples against the Roman domination, the intervention of King Philip of Macedon, or the complete financial collapse of the Roman state. If Rome did not overcome such an eventuality, she could, it is true, possibly finally force Carthage to an unfavorable peace but still could not completely break her independence as a great power, and if Carthage had held her own in this condition of independence, it would have been completely impossible for the ancient world to become unified under Roman domination. In the next generation Rome defeated Macedon and Syria and in doing so essentially established her world hegemony, as Polybius already correctly understood. If Carthage had still been able to intervene in favor of those two empires, there would have been established a sort of balance of power, reminiscent of modern conditions —before 1914—which was, after all, maintained only through the fact that, at critical moments, all the weak powers stood together against the strongest one. The decisive factor of ancient history, therefore, is to be found in the fact that the Romans, in the course of the Second Punic War, finally developed a method of warfare that was capable of defeating Hannibal in open battle, completely breaking the power of Carthage in the process. There is no more important study in world history than the question: What change took place in the Roman military system in the fourteen years between Cannae and Zama?

Our best method of proceeding, once again, is not to assemble chronologically the individual and still uncertain traces as they come to our attention here and there from the sources, but rather that we keep squarely in view and analyze that event in which the change stands before us complete and clear, the last campaign, in which Hannibal succumbs to Scipio, the battle of Zama. The individual intermediate steps we can then either leave aside, where the sources are not clear enough, or they will clarify themselves.

The first difference that comes to view when we compare the Romans at Zama with the Romans at Cannae is—and we may be allowed to use this expression—one related to political law. The Roman army at Cannae was commanded by the two men who were at the moment the highest officials of the Republic, whereas at Zama it was commanded by a general. Hard experience had taught the Romans that, when faced with a Hannibal, the old method of rotating the army command like other offices yearly among the most outstanding senators could not succeed. The solution of naming a dictator, which had been tried after the defeat of Lake Trasimene, was not to be repeated. This position was, by law and the nature of things, one of short duration, six months at most. If the same man had been entrusted with a constantly renewed or permanent dictatorship, that would have led directly to a monarchy. Instead, an alternative had been found through the process of electing as consuls the most successful commanders, like Quintus Fabius Maximus, M. Claudius Marcellus, Q. Fulvius Flaccus, as frequently as possible, against the proscriptions of the law and custom, and of turning over command positions to them as proconsuls and prolonging their period of command after the expiration of their time in office.

But this compromise was not enough. Men who are capable of leading armies are rare, and when one of them is at hand, it is a good idea not simply to place him in some rotation or other or on a year-to-year basis, but to give him command on a lasting basis. When the report came in 211 B.C. that the Roman armies in Spain had suffered an annihilating defeat, the people elected Publius Cornelius Scipio as general with consular powers for that theater of war, and they left him in that position until his final victory and complete expulsion of the Carthaginians from Spain. The breach of the constitution was all the more serious in that Scipio had only been an aedile and he did not even have the legal age for this position. We can consider as a precedent for this innovation the fact that the people after Cannae had bestowed consular powers on the Praetor Marcellus.[2] This irregularity was inevitable, if Carthage was to be defeated, but it meant the abandoning of the republican constitution. The one person whose genius is indispensable stands up above the crowd. The field commander Scipio is the precursor of the commander and sole ruler Caesar. The complaint that the old Cunctator raised against him in the Senate sounds like a prediction, that is, that he handled discipline in the manner of kings.[3] The developments of a century and a half also formed part of this process. The framework of the Roman constitution was strong enough to bear tension for a long time and to give effectiveness to great personalities within the legal forms. When Scipio came back from Spain, he was elected consul and was invested with the command in Africa as proconsul, but a new spirit lived in the old form; no longer can one call this consul or proconsul a burgomaster, and the Roman Senate in 203 B.C. expressly decided that his command status in Africa would not be of limited duration, but would last *"donec debellatum foret"*[4] ("until the war should be finished").

Just as it created a commander, the long war also formed an officer corps, and the army itself was transformed.

The soldiers who went down to defeat at Cannae still had the characteristics of citizens who were called to bear arms. Up to that time the Republic had seldom had more than 4 legions, or 18,000 men (aside from the allies) in the field, and often only 2 legions.

The men who were called up for service in 217 and 216 B.C. probably marched out on campaign with the impression that they would soon again be able to return home. But 14 years later the nucleus of Scipio's army was still formed of the 2 legions that had been organized from the survivors of the army of Cannae and had twice been reinforced by large groups of replacements, in 214 B.C.[5] and 209 B.C.,[6] by recruits or the remnants of other legions. In addition to them, there were units of volunteers.

There exists, it is true, the suspicion that the communities that provided these volunteers had offered them less through goodwill than for the purpose of gaining back the favor of the Romans, which they had lost during the war through indifference and hesitation; but that does not exclude the possibility that these troops were composed, after all, for the most part of recruits who sought service for the sake of the service itself and the booty, once the war had made warriors of them and had weaned them away from civilian life.

Scipio's army, then, had the characteristics of any army of professional soldiers, not only in its virtues, but also in its vices as well, in its insolent mistreatment of its own civilian population.[7]

If the Roman military organization had still been in 204 B.C. the same as it was in 216 B.C. (that is, citizen soldiers, citizen officers, citizen generals), Rome would never have been able to risk sending any army across to Africa and fighting against Hannibal there. They would finally have concluded a peace in which Rome made some kind of concession to the Carthaginians and Hannibal, in return, abandoned Italian territory. The significant result of the Second Punic War from the point of view of world history, however, is that Rome had undergone an internal change that immeasurably increased her military potential. The account of the battle of Zama will clarify this new situation for us.

NOTES FOR CHAPTER IV

1. Raimund Oehler, *The Last Campaign of Hasdrubal Barca and the Battle on the Metaurus*. An historical-topographical Study. (*Der letzte Feldzug des Barkiden Hasdrubal und die Schlacht am Metaurus. Eine historisch-topographische Studie.*) 1897. The significant aspects of

its conclusions were rejected by Konrad Lehmann, *Deutsche Literaturzeitung*, 1897, No. 23, Column 902.

Lehmann himself later treated the battle in detail in his book *The Attacks of the three Barcas* (*Die Angriffe der drei Barkiden*), 1905, and sought to reconstruct the battle, but the result remains subject to serious doubts. I doubt that, in view of the sources available, it will ever be possible to gain a positive insight into the battle. Even the army strengths are very uncertain. Lehmann estimates that Hannibal still had 15,000 men and Hasdrubal 12,000, whereas there were 150,000 Romans under arms in Italy. With numbers such as these, the Romans' conduct would be incomprehensible. See also the critique of Kromayer, *Göttingische gelehrte Anzeigen*, 169, No. 2 (June 1907): 458. Beversdorff gives Hasdrubal 15,000 men on the Metaurus, whereas Kromayer estimates some 30,000.

2. Mommsen, *Political Law* (*Staatsrecht*), Vol. 2, Part 1, p. 652.

3. Livy 29. 19.

4. Livy 30. 1. 10.

5. Livy 24. 18.

6. Livy 27. 7.

7. The Locrians made such a complaint on this score that the Senate conducted an investigation. Livy 29. 8–22.

Chapter V

The Battle of Zama-Naraggara and the Echelon Tactics

Scipio had crossed over to Africa with only a moderately sized army, but as in Hannibal's case earlier in Italy, he had sought and found reinforcements for it in Africa. During the first two years, while Hannibal was still in Italy, he had operated very cautiously, and his principal accomplishment lay in the fact that a portion of the Numidians had deserted the Carthaginians and had gone over to the side of the Romans. The most powerful sheik of the Numidians who were friendly to Carthage, Syphax, was taken prisoner by the Romans, and his rival Masinissa took over his position of leadership. Scipio did not allow himself to be drawn into a decisive battle with Hannibal until Masinissa had brought over to him 6,000 infantry and 4,000 Numidian cavalry. For this reason, at Zama-Naraggara the Romans were far superior to the Carthaginians in this latter arm. Even the Roman reports, the only ones available to us, state that Hannibal had only 2,000 to 3,000 cavalry.

The Carthaginians were probably somewhat stronger in infantry, and moreover, they had a number of elephants, whereas the Romans had none. But in this battle, too, the elephants played no really significant role; in general, these were the same kinds of troops, but allocated in an opposite manner to that at Cannae. The internal structure, however, was completely different.

As at Cannae, both armies had cavalry on both infantry flanks. The cavalry started the battle, and the stronger side—in this case, the Romans—swept the weaker, the Carthaginians, from the field.

In order to win the victory of Cannae, it had not only been necessary at the time that the 10,000 Carthaginian cavalry push

370

back and defeat the 6,000 Romans, but also that, immediately after their victory, they should assemble again and ride into the attack in the rear of the Roman phalanx. Such an action is unusually difficult. We have already become familiar with the number of battles in which a cavalry wing, even under the personal command of the supreme commander, was victorious, but where the conquering cavalry, instead of then attacking the enemy infantry, charged off in pursuit of the defeated enemy cavalry and in doing so nullified their success insofar as the overall outcome of the battle was concerned. That is what happened at Ipsus under Demetrius, at Raphia under Antiochus, at Mantinea under Machanidas; and so it continued in later centuries, for example even with the Austrian cavalry at Mollwitz. To reassemble brave cavalrymen calls for a state of military training that is not easily reached and certainly not accomplished overnight. Consequently, the victory at Cannae was not only a function of numerical superiority but also of the trained officer corps of Hamilcar Barca, which was able to keep the troops under control even in the midst of battle. The Numidians whom Masinissa brought over to Scipio came directly out of the Atlas Mountains and from the oases. According to the Roman reports, Hannibal had, in addition to his cavalry, 80 elephants, and since we know that elephants are used most effectively against cavalry, we could perhaps imagine that Hannibal might very well have sought to counterbalance the Roman superiority by combining his cavalry with the elephants. But he did not do this; perhaps the number of elephants was much smaller than the Romans stated, but at any rate it was too small for Hannibal to have based his hopes on them. Rather, he had the cavalry battle start out in the usual manner on the two flanks, without supporting it, as he had done on the Trebia, with his elephants, and the Romans easily won—with such ease, in fact, that we may assume that the Carthaginian from the start had not planned it any differently; Hannibal had given his men the order not primarily to fight, but, more important, by fleeing to draw the enemy away from the battlefield in pursuit. And so it happened. On both flanks the Numidian as well as the Italo-Roman cavalry charged away in the enthusiasm of their victory behind their enemies and left the point of decision farther and farther behind them.

At the start the light infantry of the two sides had skirmished with each other in the center, and the battle here had become more serious than normally, since Hannibal had placed his elephants at this point this time. Since we know that elephants accomplish nothing against good infantry in close formation, and when wounded, made wild, and pushed back, could become dangerous for their own infantry, we cannot avoid asking how Hannibal determined to use this formation here. I believe that he wanted to gain some time, in order to postpone the start of the infantry battle. The maneuver with which he hoped to win the battle could not take place until the cavalry had moved away. If the enemy cavalry remained close by, it was impossible for the Carthaginians to win the battle. We may be allowed to assume that Hannibal's camp was fortified and so laid out that it could not immediately be encircled. Hannibal would therefore have been able, if he considered it necessary, as long as the elephants were still rampaging about in front of the main line, to break off the battle and withdraw again into his camp. At Cannae he had pushed his center forward in order to come to hand-to-hand combat as soon as possible, from which there no longer exists the possibility of any orderly withdrawal. At Naraggara he ingeniously prolonged the combat of the outposts by mixing in the elephants, in order to keep control as long as possible of the decision whether he should proceed with the actual battle or not. There was one method that could be applied against the danger that wounded elephants, turned wild, would turn about and trample their own troops: the mahouts had a pointed steel wedge which they drove into the neck of the animal if it could no longer be controlled, thus causing it to drop dead.[1]

The overture had corresponded to the master's concept. The cavalry on both sides were off and away, while the combat of the sharpshooters and the elephants was taking place. The phalanxes moved forward, and around their flanks or through their intervals the outposts drew back.

Now we would seem to have the simple old phalanx battle, where the mass and its courage decides the outcome, not the commander. Then there happened something new, unheard of.

Hannibal drew up his heavy infantry in two echelons; in the first stood the Carthaginian citizens, who were personally defending their very existence against their fearful rivals; in the second echelon was the force that Hannibal had brought back with him from Italy, the Old Guard, which had already followed him across the Pyrenees and the Alps and had turned gray with him in the twenty-year war.

Naraggara is the first battle in the history of the world in which we find echelon tactics significantly and decisively applied in the conduct of the battle as a great, newly discovered principle.

In the echelon formation the tactical units are placed one behind the other, far enough apart so that each can move independently, near enough so that they can directly support each other.

As we have seen, the nature of the phalanx rests on the fact that no more than the first few ranks or possibly even the very first rank only really takes part in the battle, and therefore at the most a fourth, perhaps only a fifteenth or a thirtieth or even fewer of the troops. The value of this whole mass stems exclusively from these factors: it facilitates the replacement of casualties, allows the continuity of the line to be maintained, and provides for the bringing to bear of a physical and morale pressure from the rear. If now the rearmost half of this formation is removed and drawn up at some distance from the forward half, much of the advantage of those factors is lost; the physical pressure, especially, is completely removed. On the other hand, however, the second echelon is in a position to make independent movements and therefore to fend off possible flank or rear attacks and, by pulling out of its position, to make flank attacks itself.

Hannibal had his second echelon take position more than a whole *stadium* (that is, over 300 paces) from the first, and he took personal command of it. If the Roman cavalry, instead of pursuing the fleeing Carthaginian horse, had turned immediately against the infantry, the second echelon would have covered the rear of the first. The enemy cavalry would hardly have risked moving in between the two echelons. The Carthaginian army then, forming a solid front on all sides without difficulty, while its elephants held up the Roman phalanx, would, I assume, have taken up a withdrawal into its camp.

Now the enemy cavalry had disappeared, however, and so Hannibal immediately set his second echelon in motion so that, divided in two forces, it could quickly move right and left to the flanks and attack the Romans on their flanks, while the first echelon closed with the Roman *hastati*. It was the same movement that the Africans carried out at Cannae, with the difference that (1) it started later, because this time the troops had a longer distance to cover, (2) the simultaneous attack from the rear by the cavalry did not take place, and (3) this time the Roman infantry was not numerically superior but weaker, perhaps considerably weaker than the Carthaginian infantry. And so the first echelon, the Carthaginian citizens, held their own without difficulty, and if they now had been supported by the double flank attack of the "old-timers," the Romans would necessarily have succumbed. Despite the superiority of the enemy cavalry, Hannibal would have won the battle.

But the genius of Rome, too, had brought forth a man who un-

derstood the signs of the times and, as Gneisenau did with
Napoleon 2,000 years later, was able to oppose the god of war with
his own art.

We are already familiar with the old division of the Roman legion into the three year-groups of *hastati, principes*, and *triarii*, which
were drawn up one behind the other. For the battle formation of
Naraggara, Polybius reports, Scipio drew up the maniples of the
principes and *triarii* "with an interval" (*en apostasei*). Consequently,
the Roman phalanx, too, was divided into two echelons. At Cannae
the *principes* and *triarii* had still stuck closely to the *hastati*; now Scipio, as soon as he noticed the movement of the second Punic echelon, moved his own in just the same way to counter it. A citizen
army and citizen officers are not able to make such a movement;
but the war itself had developed for the Romans not only their
commander, but also officers and soldiers who were able to maneuver on the battlefield just as well as their opponents. Hannibal's
Old Guard, instead of striking the flanks of the Roman phalanx,
met an extended battle line, and the battle remained just what it
had been, a parallel battle.

Nevertheless, the Roman legions had a very difficult time against
the desperate courage of the Carthaginian citizens, the victory-
tempered combat experience of the veterans, and perhaps also
their numerical superiority, and it appears that they were close to
succumbing at the moment when the Roman cavalry returned from
their foolish pursuit and fell on the Carthaginians in their rear.
What a fateful turn in world history depended on these few minutes!

The Carthaginian army was beaten and annihilated in its flight.
Luckily, Hannibal himself was able to escape to Hadrumet.[2]

PRECURSORS OF ECHELON TACTICS

The system of echelon tactics is a discovery of such unusually
great importance in the history of the art of war that one would
like to establish every single moment in its development. On this
point, however, the sources leave us in the lurch. Suddenly, and on
both sides simultaneously, the innovation is there. Precursors of
this are the angled formation of Hannibal's Africans at Cannae and
the small troop units behind Alexander's two wings at Gaugamela.
Still farther back, we can point out the reserve that Xenophon
held out in his combat against Pharnabazus (Book II, Chapter V,
p. 150). On the other side, the Roman organization of the phalanx
in the three lines of *hastati, principes*, and *triarii*, although not a di-

rect predecessor of echelon tactics, was still a formation that aided Scipio and facilitated for him the introduction of the new system.

But there is still a mighty leap from all these analogies to the organic principle. The Roman *hastati*, when for the first time they were not followed directly by the *principes*, no doubt felt that they were halfway betrayed, and only a commander enjoying the highest personal respect and sure of the unquestionable trust of his soldiers could risk such a reform. No matter how obvious the advantages of a second echelon are, we must still realize how much was lost in adopting this formation. Why then did one put these huge masses into the field? We have seen that they were used much less often to extend the battle line than to strengthen the formation in depth. The pressure of the mass was supposed to bring victory. And so, if the rearmost half was removed, that appeared at first as a contradiction of the whole phalanx principle. The filling up of the spaces that developed during the approach march—the purpose for which the manipular formation had formerly been created—was now made difficult by the intervals between the three echelons, and the decisive pressure from the rear was reduced by more than half.

This contradiction was counterbalanced by military training. Just as the Roman manipular formation had once become a possibility because the individual man knew and believed that both the neighboring and following maniples would do their duty, by now the military temper had risen to such a point that the first echelon could get along without the physical proximity and the physical pressure of the rearmost half and was content with the moral certainty that help would not be missing in case of emergency. Citizen soldiers cannot have so much inner certainty; for this, one needs warriors who have become professional soldiers and officers with years of experience. Whether the echelons of the *hastati*, *principes*, and *triarii*—units already long in existence—were drawn up with an interval of a hundred feet or of several hundred feet might seem to be insignificant. Nevertheless, this interval calls for a completely different type of warfare, a completely different military spirit, in the commander as well as in the officers and in the soldiers. A citizen general would not be able to handle echelon tactics; the greatest commander would not be able to make them work with citizen soldiers.

A second echelon and a reserve are concepts which overlap. A reserve remains unconditionally at the disposition of the commander; a second echelon follows the first one so closely that it can either entirely or partially intervene or be drawn into the course of the battle without special order. For this reason, we use the expression *reserve* when it is a question of troop units that are placed somewhat farther back and are consequently smaller, which can, moreover, be formed in just the same way as a second or third echelon.

At any rate, Naraggara was not the first engagement in which Scipio tried out the new method of combat. Of the preceding battle on the "Great Plains," where he defeated Hasdrubal and Syphax (203 b.c.), Polybius also reports (14. 8. 11) that the infantry of the enemy center was surrounded and hemmed in by the *principes* and the *triarii* on both flanks. This means that these units made a movement quite similar to that of Naraggara. The most likely possibility is that Scipio developed the new tactics in Spain, where we are told that he had his soldiers drill very thoroughly. When, because of all kinds of complaints that had come back, the Senate sent a commission to inspect his army in Sicily, before they crossed over to Africa, Scipio had a land and naval maneuver carried out for the inspectors near Syracuse,[3] in order to show the training and state of preparedness of his soldiers. But we do not know anything more definite about how far these maneuver formations went toward being real previews of the maneuvers on the battlefield.

It is not improbable that at this time the Romans also improved the javelin with which the first waves of the maniples were armed in imitation of a type that they found in use by the Iberians. We may therefore perhaps say that the introduction of the *pilum* also belonged to the military system of Scipio.[4]

EXCURSUS

1. I have perhaps presented the sequence of the battle of Naraggara in a somewhat more definite form than the state of the sources actually permits. But I did not want to interrupt the course of the account continuously with critical differences with the sources, so that I could let the outline of the typical elements in the overall event, which is our principal concern, stand out in the clearest possible way. But I can also spare myself the trouble of establishing a critical basis here in detail, since for this purpose I can refer the reader to an excellent study by Konrad Lehmann,[5] who, using the same method as Josef Fuchs did in the works named above, links philological exactitude with military judgment and completely clarifies the course of the battle.

Our information on the battle of Naraggara is much less definite than on the battle of Cannae, because in this case Polybius no longer had the excellent source from the Carthaginian camp but had to rely solely on Roman reports, and we already know how very much Polybius, in spite of his critical approach, is dependent on his sources. No doubt, he eliminated from them that material that is completely fable, and he did not, for example, accept the individual combat between Hannibal and Scipio, which other Roman reports show as deciding the outcome of the battle. But nevertheless a great deal of false and disturbing material did remain, which we must make up our minds to excise with a sharp knife, if we are not to limit ourselves to a simple repetition of the events but are resolved, instead, to arrive at an acceptable picture of the battle, understandable from the military history point of view. It is always very difficult to come to the conclusion that one must declare as objectively incredible and impossible an event reported by Polybius, but I invite the reader's attention to how little satisfaction there is in his Hellenic battle accounts and in what he tells us about the Roman fleet construction and the Roman-Gallic battles. His figures on the strength of the Carthaginian army in Spain are extremely debatable; he passes on to us the silly Roman fable that Hannibal was so afraid of his own Celtic allies that he always disguised himself with different types of wigs; he halfway accepts and repeats the Roman boast that the legions had lined up before Rome in 211 B.C. to offer the Carthaginians open battle.

Despite all of this, Polybius certainly remains an authority of the first rank, but it would be a distortion to put oneself completely in his hands. In the face of the great certainty with which the Roman legend appeared, and in view of the deep inner respect that he held for the Roman political system, he was not able to bring to his critical study the unconditionally penetrating power that scholarship needs in order to arrive at complete truth. Lehmann has shown that it is highly probable that very much of the Polybian report derives from the epic of Ennius. Not that Polybius could have been so naive as to accept as historic reality the accounts of a heroic poem, but in the circle of the Scipio family, in which he lived and gathered his information, the images of the poetic fantasy of Ennius had gradually been blended with the truly historical tradition, so that the writers themselves probably could no longer distinguish with certainty the elements from one another, and through this link, from which undoubtedly, for example, also the individual combat of the two commanders as reported by Appian stems, a purely fictitious element also made its way into the account of the rational analyst Polybius.

2. The principal points that should be observed critically in the Polybian account of Naraggara are as follows:

Polybius does not give any reason for the interval between *hastati* and *principes*; instead, he mentions another change that Scipio ordered in deviation from the Roman custom—that is, that the maniples were not lined up, as they otherwise had been, on the intervals, but on one another. This was supposedly done because of the large number of enemy elephants. This point must be questioned in that, first of all, the Romans could not know that Hannibal would form his elephants this time in front of his infantry, instead of near his cavalry, and second, if there was an appreciable interval between waves, the aligning of the maniples one behind the other no longer served any purpose. Even assuming that the elephants would have done the Romans the favor of always running straight into the intervals, they were still not bound to a straight line and would also have found the openings in the second echelon if they were a few paces—it was not a question of any greater distance—to the right or the left. It is clear that, into the both correct and important historical recollection of the innovation of the interval between echelons, which was of little interest to the minstrel Ennius, there had been blended images from the combat of the elephants, images which he had conjured up in keeping with the free laws of poetic tactics.

Scipio is supposed to have filled the intervals between the *hastati* maniples with *veliti*, who were to charge forward from them. There is no apparent reason whatever as to why in this particular battle the *veliti* should have been placed initially in the intervals. The advantage the intervals offered for an orderly approach march, would, of course, have been lost in this way. Lehmann conjectures that it was only a question of the position in the original formation, before the approach march was taken up, where Scipio gave his speech to his troops and therefore needed as closed a formation as possible.

That Hannibal's first echelon (Ligurians, Celts, Balearics, Moors) consisted of sharpshooters has been proved with certainty by Lehmann. In keeping with our terminology, therefore, we do not term it a true "echelon."

The Romans, too, were lined up, as Lehmann has shown to be extremely probable, in two echelons, by having the *principes* and the *triarii* closed together. With the normal strength of the maniples, there would have resulted from this an incongruous situation in which the second echelon was considerably stronger than the first, whereas the nature of things preferably calls for the opposite. The sharpshooters, who can be counted in with the first echelon, do not, after all, equalize the two echelons. The first echelon always has to be so strong that it can withstand the frontal attack of the enemy under any circumstances. Scipio must have compensated for this in some way or other.

The artificial delaying of the phalanx battle resulted, in the Roman legend, from the Carthaginian citizen echelon's halting out of cowardice, instead of following up the first wave, thus causing the skirmishers to believe that they had been betrayed.

The fact that the Roman *hastati* echelon more or less held its own against the Carthaginian citizen echelon, as taken from the patriotic Roman fiction, is presented by Polybius as follows: The Carthaginians were first of all attacked by their own mercenaries, who faced about and intended to punish them for their cowardly betrayal. In this critical situation they took on new heart, and once engaged, they even threw into confusion the Roman *hastati*, who, strangely enough, had not taken advantage of the battle the Carthaginians were waging among themselves. Finally, they were beaten by the Romans after all, but Scipio had his victorious *hastati* called back by trumpet calls from the pursuit, because the field was so covered with dead, wounded, and weapons, and the ground had become so slippery from the great quantity of blood, that the troops were no longer able to pass through in orderly fashion. That the *hastati*, if victorious, already had to be beyond this blood-covered, slippery field and only a withdrawal would force them to pass through it again naturally did not bother the poet, but it does show us very clearly how little care Polybius took as he trustingly repeated his sources.

Hannibal's decisive movement with his second echelon is not mentioned directly at all by Polybius—a clear indication that we are dealing here only with a Roman report without any real understanding of the historical and tactical aspects. This fact is indirectly clarified for us, however, from Scipio's movement, in which he, too, pulls out his second echelon on the right and the left and so clashes with Hannibal's veterans, who therefore must have made a similar movement from their original positions. As a motive for Scipio's move, however, we are not given the movement of the enemy—that would be too sober, too prosaic—but rather that mass of corpses and blood in the middle, which necessitated turning in a different direction.

3. With respect to the strengths of the armies, on neither side do we have any sure and trustworthy information except for the point concerning the great superiority of the Romans in cavalry. Lehmann (pp. 532, 574) has, with a certain degree of probability, accepted the total strength of the Romans as 35,000 men, including 10,000 Numidians. That Hannibal was superior in infantry follows less from the assertion of the Roman sources as from the plight into which he was able to push the Romans. The claim that he had no fewer than 80 elephants is to be rejected as undoubtedly exaggerated.

4. The two battles of Baecula, the second of which is also called Elinga, Silpia, or Ilipa,[6] shows us highly ingenious maneuvers. On both occasions Scipio outflanked the enemy on both sides, even though in the second battle he is supposed to have had only 45,000 infantry and 3,000 cavalry against 70,000 infantry, 4,000 cavalry, and 32 elephants. Here is undoubtedly another case where Polybius was not sharp enough in his analysis and passed on Roman fables in as rational a way as possible. Ihne, in *Römische Geschichte* 2: 350, 369, is of the opinion that probably both battles, and in any event the first one, are pure fiction. In neither case did the battle have any direct result. Hasdrubal is supposed to have broken off the first one at an appropriate time and to have set out with his beaten army on the road to Italy. The

fearful thunderstorm that suddenly broke out prevented the Romans from taking full advantage of the second battle (as such a storm had twice prevented the battle before Rome in 211 B.C.). From the military history point of view, at any rate, nothing is to be learned from these battles. And just as little from the engagements reported in Livy 28. 33 and Frontinus 2. 3. 1.

The accounts preserved in Livy,[7] of the numerous combats in Italy after Cannae, quite often show an echelon-like formation of legions. None of these reports, however, has the slightest credibility.

NOTES FOR CHAPTER V

1. Livy 27. 49.

2. Why he did not go directly to Carthage is not reported. Perhaps he simply did not want to arrive in the capital with the few survivors of the battle and may have had in Hadrumet some troop reinforcements and supplies of weapons, which, if brought along with him, would still give him a position and the city a possibility to defend itself.

3. Livy 29. 22.

4. See also p. 276, above.

5. *The Last Campaign of the War with Hannibal (Der letzte Feldzug des hannibalischen Krieges)*, by Konrad Lehmann, special extract from the 21st supplemental volume of *Jahrbücher für klassische Philologie* (Leipzig: B. G. Teubner, 1894).

6. Polybius 10. 38, 39; 11. 20–24. Livy 27. 18, 19; 27. 12–15.

7. Livy 27. 1, second engagement of Herdoniae; 27. 2, Numistro; 27. 12–14, victory of Marcellus in Apulia; 30. 18, Mago's defeat in the region of the Insubres.

Chapter VI

Hannibal and Scipio

When Scipio crossed over to Africa from Sicily, Hannibal, still undefeated, was in position with a moderate-sized army in lower Italy. One could raise the question why Scipio did not first attack Hannibal here, where he could easily assemble a greatly superior force, and thus bring an end to the war. The answer can well be that Hannibal would probably have avoided an attack by a truly superior force and would finally have moved to Africa with his army. If he were there ahead of Scipio, however, it would have become very difficult for the latter to get a foothold in Africa and to win the allegiance of the Numidians.[1] We can therefore preferably turn the question about, asking why Hannibal did not willingly leave Italy sooner, a country where he could no longer hope for an outright success. The answer very likely is that Hannibal was now no longer aspiring to the conquest of Rome but rather to a tolerably favorable peace, and he assumed that the Romans would still be willing to pay a price for the evacuation of Italy. Even when Scipio had landed in Africa, Hannibal did not immediately follow him. He knew that his Roman foe would not be able to accomplish so very much, that he would plan least of all to move against the city of Carthage itself, whose fortifications had a circumference three times as great as that of the Rome of that time (26,905 meters). If his countrymen should succeed in overcoming Scipio without him, while the Romans, for their part, could not drive the Carthaginians out of Italy, then the relative strengths would be equal, so to speak, and on this basis a peace treaty could be signed.

Not until Scipio had already been in Africa for two years and, by virtue of several fortunate strokes and undertakings, had won an unexpectedly important position, especially by bringing Syphax under his power and finding in Masinissa a strong ally, did Hannibal leave Italy with the rest of his troops and appear in Africa for the last battle. His appearance encouraged the Carthaginians to break an armistice and a peace treaty that had already been concluded, and it then became a question of who would develop military superiority. In addition to Hannibal's veterans, there had arrived also troops of his brother Mago, Balearics, Ligurians, and Celts; recruiting was carried out among the African tribes, and the Carthaginian citizens themselves took up arms. What was lacking was the great majority, especially, of the Numidian tribes that were camped nearby, which were now summoned by Masinissa to bear arms for the Romans.

On both sides the greatest effort went into preparations. With wise calculation Hannibal set up his headquarters not in Carthage itself, but in a small coastal city five to six days' march south of Carthage—Hadrumet. Here he protected his veterans from the distracting contacts with the capital, here he had better control over his new troops who were still being trained, and from here he would have taken from the rear any movement of Scipio against Carthage itself, and was, for his part, protected by the flanking position of Carthage against any attack by the Romans before his preparations were complete. It appears that close to three-quarters of a year passed before Hannibal,[2] still with a very weak cavalry force, moved out against the Romans. This he did with good reason. Scipio had not yet joined forces with Masinissa; if, therefore, he succeeded in coming to grips with Scipio before this union of forces, or in moving between the two and keeping them apart, the victory of the Carthaginians was assured. Scipio did not yet have even one harbor in his possession, but instead he had installed on a peninsula near Utica, which he had unsuccessfully blockaded, a fortified camp (*castra Corneliana*) as a base. Moving out from there, he had marched for a few days up the fertile Bagradas (Medjerdja) valley into the interior and plundered and laid waste the countryside.

There he received the report that Hannibal had moved out against him from his base at Hadrumet and had arrived near Zama, the more westerly village of that name. Scipio's situation was critical.

If he waited in the Bagradas valley and was attacked by Hannibal before the Numidian reinforcements arrived, his defeat was sealed.

If he returned to his beach camp, he would be cut off there, separated once and for all from Masinissa, and would have, in the face of Hannibal's leadership, no prospect of changing his fate. The expedition would be a failure, and he would have to be con-

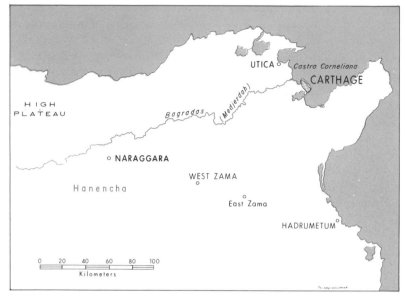

Fig. 3   BATTLE OF ZAMA-NARAGGARA

tent just to be able to move his army back to Sicily reasonably intact.

It is at this moment that tradition would have the famous personal discussion occur between the two commanders, in which Hannibal appears in the role of peace seeker. There is no doubt that, as Konrad Lehmann has pointed out, this meeting is a fantasy painted by Ennius. At that moment nothing lay further from Hannibal's mind than going to the Romans to ask for peace, and Scipio was preoccupied with concerns quite different from a lofty and unquestionable certainty of victory. Three Punic spies who were captured in his camp were reportedly not punished but were released by Scipio with proud confidence, to return to Hannibal after they had been shown everything. This account is taken almost verbatim by Ennius from Herodotus' *Persian Wars*,[3] passed from him into the Roman tradition, and so came to Polybius also and into the definite status of historical writing. We recognize how carefully we must examine the accounts of the sources. We must seek to find the standards for our judgment much more in the character of the actual situation than from these freely formed figures of fantasy. In this process neither Scipio nor Hannibal will lose. It is the same situation that we were already able to observe with respect to the Persian Wars: the heroism of the Greeks has not been lessened as a result of our true understanding, which caused us to reduce so drastically the strengths of the Persian armies. Legend and poetry do not paint falsely when they paint with other colors than does history. They simply speak another language, and it is a question of translating correctly from this language into that of history.

The great decision of Scipio—the decision that aligns him with the greatest commanders in the history of the world and bestows the right of inner truth on all the poetic images that Ennius invented in his honor—was that Scipio, placing his hope in boldness, gave up his contact with the sea and any retreat or possibility of rescue in case of a defeat, and since he could no longer risk waiting for Masinissa, he moved farther into the interior to join him. He must have marched off when Hannibal was already close to him. Near the town of Naraggara, on the border of modern Tunisia and Algeria, his forces made contact with those of Masinissa and here he awaited the arrival of Hannibal, who had no choice but to follow him, for the battle of decision.

We have seen how the pointer of the scale continued to oscillate in this battle up to the last moment. It is difficult to appreciate the entire strength of spirit that went into the order for the march off toward Naraggara as well as into the control of the details of the following battle with unwavering coolness. We cannot appreciate such matters until we have measured both aspects in relation to each other—the battle within the strategic situation and the strategic decision from the viewpoint of the razor's edge on which the balance of the battle stood.

The desperate aspect of the decision by the Roman commander has been very interestingly reflected, up to the present day, in the erroneous name that has been adopted in legend for the battle —Zama. Even after his victory Scipio did not dare to confess, in his report to the homeland, the entire strategic situation, the march away from the coast into the interior; he did not name the location of the battle itself but only the headquarters of Hannibal at his last halt, and so the battle came to be named after the latter and in this way the strategic situation became so confused that there was good cause for doubt as to whether the westerly or the easterly Zama was meant. We may compare this march of Scipio with the marching away of the Silesian army from the Mulde across the Saale in October 1813 and the withdrawal from Ligny toward Wavre in 1815, two operations that were strategically responsible for the defeat of Napoleon. If Scipio, instead of boasting of the unprecedented boldness of his decision, preferred to conceal and cover up the danger he had victoriously withstood, one is reminded of Moltke, who, in the face of the faultfinders, referred to his most ingenious and boldest strategic act, the divided march into Bohemia, as the "remedy for an unfavorable situation."

Even after the victory of Naraggara, Scipio, with his moderate strength, could not consider besieging and conquering Carthage itself. Rome was so exhausted economically and spiritually by the long war that she was neither able nor willing to provide rather large resources, and there were already forming in the Macedonian-Greek group of countries conditions that made an intervention and a new war very likely. Just as the sages of Rome had not been willing to approve Scipio's expedition to Africa and had prophesied disaster, even now, after his victory, they were once again being heard from, but with the opposite tune, finding that the victory had to be pursued to the point of complete crushing of the rival city. But the victor of Naraggara showed that, just as he was able to estimate his strength correctly, so too he could judge the limits of his strength, and today one should no longer repeat the reproaches of those who intended to be cutting while they were nothing more than envious, to the effect that he had made peace so as not to bequeath to a successor the fame of this event. It would have been a long time before a successor of Scipio would have been able to gain fame by continuing the fight against Hannibal and the insuperable wall of Carthage. Scipio knew better what was to the advantage of his home city, and he accepted the offer of peace that was now brought to him on behalf of Hannibal. The conditions did not extend so very significantly beyond those that Scipio had already set up a year earlier, before Hannibal's arrival, and which the Roman people had approved. The significance of the battle of Naraggara does not lie, therefore, so much in the positive, immediate advantage gained by the Roman state, as it does negatively in the fact that Carthage was broken in its last upward surge, and its citizens lost hope in the future. The most important condition that was added to the new peace treaty was that Carthage was not permitted to wage any war without Rome's approval, thereby giving up, in effect, her full sovereignty.

Whether this condition would remain an empty letter or would really bring an end to the independent Carthaginian policies was not known with any certainty at the moment of the peace treaty. Whether the conquered city would subject itself to this condition on a continuing basis depended on world conditions, on the policy of Macedon and Syria, on the inner development of Rome and of

Carthage. History has shown that the defeat of Naraggara broke the power of Carthage definitively. Six years later, in 195 B.C., after the Romans had in the meantime also defeated the Macedonians without interference from the Carthaginians, the Carthaginians, at the demand of the Romans, drove Hannibal out of his native city, and this event now finally gave the peace its definitive confirmation.

Hannibal and Napoleon are the two great commanders of world history who were finally defeated without sacrificing, for that reason, their fame and their historical greatness. Yes, they are so great that history has always been tempted to judge their conquerors more sternly than it judged them, just so that the idea would not arise that the conqueror was greater than the conquered. If the Romans wished to consider Scipio in the same way that the English considered Wellington, everywhere where national pride did not enter the picture there were reservations as to their greatness; in fact, Wellington was no doubt spoken of even with a certain lack of appreciation, and least of all has credit been given to that general who played the greatest role in the strategic defeat of Napoleon: Gneisenau. There can hardly be a question here at all of a comparison with Napoleon, since, of course, not Gneisenau but Blücher was the commander of the Prussians and in the latter's case, again, the claim of being on an equal level with Napoleon as a strategist was not raised at all.

Even if one wishes to favor the conquered generals with this satisfaction in the writing of history, since the others, of course, have been richly rewarded in the victory itself, a study like ours must nevertheless weigh all the aspects more carefully. We shall have occasion to speak of the more modern commanders later. Of Scipio, however, it must be expressly stated, as our entire account has already shown, that he deserves to be placed, certainly not above, but nevertheless, with complete justification, beside Hannibal. The sober Roman system with its strict, authoritative governmental forms does not allow individualities to stand out with such lifelike ebullience as does Greece. The common trait of discipline so dominates every single aspect that one is almost afraid to speak of a genius, who must, after all, always be absolutely individual. But in truth, one may not be stingy with this word in the case of the man who gave the Roman army new tactical forms, who risked the movement to Africa and the march off from the Bagradas valley to Naraggara, who with sureness conducted the battle against Hannibal through the most dangerous crisis, and finally, nevertheless, did not exaggerate his demands but concluded the right peace. But we recognize in Scipio still more than the traits of abstract greatness, as they are revealed to us by the events themselves. We are allowed also to look at this commander face to face, in the picture that Mommsen's descriptive power has created for us from the sources. It is with this picture that I should like to round off this account of the Second Punic War, after I have succeeded, of course, as I hope, thanks to this study, in completing it by the final decisive trait, the proof of the complete greatness of the commander and the statesman. Mommsen portrays the character of Scipio when the latter steps up in front of the Roman people, after the Roman armies were beaten, to seek his appointment to the command in Spain.

The son who was going to avenge the death of his father, whose life he had saved nine years earlier at the Ticinus, the manfully handsome young man with the long hair, who, blushing modestly, offered himself for the post of danger for lack of a better man, the simple military tribune whom suddenly the votes of the centuries lifted to the highest official position—all of this made a wonderful, unforgettable impression on the Roman citizens and peasants. There rests a special magic on this graceful hero figure; with the cheerful and self-assured enthusiasm which Scipio radiated about him, half piously, half cleverly, this figure is absolutely enveloped, as if by a blinding aureole. With precisely enough enthusiasm to warm one's heart, and enough calculation to decide for that which was intelligent and not to lose sight of the commonplace; not naïve enough to share the belief of the masses in his divine inspiration; still straightforward enough to push it aside and yet to be quietly convinced in his mind that he was a man especially favored of God—in a word, the nature of a true prophet; standing above the people and no less outside the people; a man of rockbound fulfillment of his word and royal mind, who believed that by accepting the royal title he would be lowering himself but who could so little understand that the constitution of the Republic was binding on him, too; so sure of his greatness that he knew nothing of envy and hate and cordially recognized the merits of others, sympathetically forgave the errors of others; an outstanding officer and well-trained diplomat, without the detracting special stamp of either profession, joining Hellenic culture with the fullest Roman national background, accustomed to speaking and of graceful customs, Publius Scipio won the hearts of soldiers and women, of his compatriots and the Spaniards, of his rivals in the Senate and of his greater [according to Mommsen; here I differ] Carthaginian opponent. Soon his name was on every tongue and he was the star who seemed destined to bring victory and peace to his country.

EXCURSUS

ADDED IN THIRD EDITION

1. At this point in the first two editions I copied Appian's complete report on the battle, in order to give the reader the opportunity to compare my presentation with this report and so to gain a direct appreciation of the fact that with the authors of antiquity there are battle reports that have no similarity at all to the true events and which must simply be completely discarded. Nobody denies that with respect to this report by Appian, because we are in the fortunate position of being able to arrive at the truth from another source. But that is not enough. We must have the courage to reject obviously legendary accounts even under circumstances where we are not in a position to substitute something better. It is not easy to arrive at this decision, and it is only by a very gradual process that the scholarly world becomes accustomed to the proper criteria. For this purpose I urgently recommend the reading of that account by Appian, but I must omit it here in the interest of saving space.

2. Veith, in the volume (3: 2) of *Ancient Battlefields (Antike Schlachtfelder)* prepared by him, agreed tactically and strategically with the basic features of the campaign of 202 B.C. as developed by me and Konrad Lehmann, and through a thoroughly painstaking geographical and topographical study, also determined the location of the battle as nearly as possible. Specifically, he, too, places the battle not at Zama but at Naraggara and considers the saving points for the Romans to lie in the echelon tactics developed by Scipio in Spain and in the return of the cavalry after it had first been lured away by the Carthaginians. I cannot agree, however, with what he goes on to accept or to work out for himself from the account of Polybius.

Veith considers that Lehmann and I have taken too skeptical a view of the account of Polybius; he holds that the only significant error in it is the contradiction in the report showing that the echelon of Carthaginian citizens was at one point cowardly and at another courageous. But he considers this to be only an *explanation* for their conduct and not a *fact*, and such an error is, after all, excusable. It seems to me precisely the contrary, that an isolated false fact should be more excusable than an explanation, which is bound to be reflected on and is therefore so obviously absurd that it eliminates itself. But be that as it may, the fact that Hannibal was supposedly on the point of winning the battle even though his two echelons were fighting with each other, and the withdrawal of the first Roman echelon because the battlefield was covered with blood and corpses—these things are fables that evidently come from the same armory as the wigs of Hannibal, rowing on the land, the ebb tide that occurs regularly at New Carthage in the afternoon, and so many other things that Polybius, despite his critical viewpoint, has copied unthinkingly from his sources. But the tactical maneuvers that Veith builds up from such source material are nothing more than fantasy forms. All the more so must we regard them as such when we see that the defense against the alleged 80 elephants of Hannibal plays such a large role in this account, whereas Veith himself, in his numerical estimates (p. 681), comes to the conclusion that the Carthaginians did not have more than 15 to 20 of those animals. And because of these few elephants Scipio is supposed to have drastically changed the normal Roman battle formation. This is all the less credible in that the elephants were normally not used against the infantry but against the cavalry. Veith believes (p. 691) that Scipio had been able to realize from a distance

Hannibal's intention to use the elephants in this battle against the infantry, since the elephants were drawn up in front and therefore had been formed up first. I cannot attribute to Hannibal such a lack of caution. If he intended to do something unusual, it was clear that, if done with surprise, it would be doubly effective. Hannibal would therefore have had to order that the elephants be drawn up at first in the usual way with the cavalry and that they trot out in front of the infantry only at the last moment; it was a question, after all, of only a few hundred paces to be covered. If the whole structure does not already reveal it, certainly this consideration would clearly prove that the entire elephant story, with the prearranged lanes in the Roman battle formation for them to run through—lanes that the elephants also used in a most obliging way—is a myth. How Hannibal actually used them—and, by all appearances, effectively—is recounted above.

That there is present here and there in the entire African campaign the conscious invention of a fiction writer was directly pointed out, later, by Konrad Lehmann, when he uncovered as source of the spy story the parallel account of Herodotus (*Jahrbücher für klassische Philologie* Vol. 153, No. 68, 1896). Polybius was critical enough to omit the individual combat between Scipio and Hannibal, which naturally stemmed from the same source; but he did not realize that the spy anecdote, the personal conversation of the two commanders, the battle of the Carthaginians among themselves, and the ground made impassable because of blood and corpses—all of these points are just as incredible. Old Laelius himself, in whose mind was a blurred mixture of actual recollection and pictures from the fictitious account by Ennius, may have recounted this to him, and then his critical approach was hushed. But then, even Thucydides allowed himself to be deceived by his Spartan host with the story of the treason of Pausanias.

A significant deviation of Veith's from my concept lies in the fact that he does not accept the belief that Scipio moved from the area of Zama to Naraggara, in order to reinforce his troops with those of Masinissa, but that he was already in this area before Hannibal's approach. If that were the case, then the strategic accomplishment, not only of one but of both commanders, would be distinctly lowered. Scipio's awesome decision to march off in a direction that offered no further withdrawal falls away, and Hannibal can be reproached for moving out of Hadrumet without an overriding reason and demanding the decisive battle before he had completed his preparations. For if Scipio was in the Zama area at the time the Carthaginians marched out of Hadrumet, Hannibal had the prospect of striking him with superior forces, and his precipitate moving out is justified; but if Scipio were already in the area of Naraggara, it was likely that he would be united with Masinissa, and there was then no reason for Hannibal's not first completing the preparations before undertaking the campaign.

This would-be diminution of the prestige of these two great men of world history is, of course, no basis for rejecting the facts, if they could otherwise be made to appear credible. Such, however, is not the case. The considerations Veith cites (p. 639) are very vague and at any rate they have no kind of strength as proof. It is a similar case to that of the battle on the Lechfeld, where the greatness of Emperor Otto in world history depended very significantly on whether the battle took place on the right or left bank.

Veith (p. 641) states that he must reject as psychologically very improbable my belief that Scipio himself later did not completely confess the unprecedented boldness of his marching away toward Naraggara, since *success* justifies one's actions still more in the eyes of his contemporaries than in following ages. I can support this alleged psychological improbability with historical analogies. When Napoleon in 1800 had marched up in the rear of the Austrians and sought to cut them off, he had the boldness to divide his army up among the various roads that the Austrians could use, in order to come to grips with them under any circumstances. The result was that he fell into the most extreme danger of being beaten at Marengo before Desaix, who had been on a separate mission, arrived. But it did not occur to Napoleon to boast of his boldness after his victory (in which he would have been completely justified), but on the contrary, he even had the battle reports intentionally falsified, in order to substitute for his boldness the appearance of wise prescience. Another example: Moltke's greatest strategic action is undoubtedly his march into Bohemia in two separated armies, with the accompanying danger that one of them could be attacked by the main body of the Austrians before the other arrived on the scene. Although the march succeeded brilliantly, the military criticism of the second-guessers did not at all bow to the success but again and again tried to prove that only unprecedented luck or unprecedented stupidity on the part of the enemy had thrown the victory in his lap, and the field marshal himself took up his pen (1867) to defend himself against this charge.

Saan, in *Studies on Scipio's Campaign in Africa (Untersuchungen zu Scipios Feldzug in Afrika),*[4] p. 24, refutes quite effectively the reasons for which Veith has Scipio move to Naraggara. But what he himself adduces in order to justify Scipio's formation at Zama is no more tenable. He believes, namely, that Scipio in this way wanted to cover the approach of Masinissa. That would have been very distorted. Where then was Masinissa coming from? Out of the west, after all. Instead of exposing the Roman army to the danger of being attacked itself by a superior force while holding its covering position, Scipio would simply have ordered the Numidians to move up to the Roman army on one of the cited more northerly roads.

We shall have to state the controversy in this way. If the battle took place at Naraggara, then Scipio's march into this area can be explained in no other way except that, making a virtue of necessity and seeking salvation and victory in boldness, he drew back before Hannibal to that point in order to join forces with Masinissa. Veith's explanation, that he voluntarily marched there, is insufficient. If the battle took place at Zama, it is hard to see why Hannibal fought there. He had the expectation of receiving a considerable force of cavalry under Vermina, which actually did reach him a few weeks after the battle. His fighting at Naraggara, even though he supposedly knew that Scipio and Masinissa had now joined forces, came naturally after he had already moved so far forward and had brought Scipio into the most unfavorable imaginable strategic position. If, however, the two armies had faced each other in the Zama region, Hannibal would have lost little and gained a great deal by delaying the decision for a few more weeks and being reinforced in the meantime by the cavalry of Vermina, which was so urgently needed. Veith is right, then, to the extent that he rejects Zama as the site of the battle; he is wrong, however, when he suggests an insufficient motive for Naraggara (a plundering expedition into this region).

Veith misunderstands me when he states (p. 658) that Scipio's maneuver to lengthen his front from the second (or third) echelon came, in my opinion, as a *surprise* to the Carthaginians. I myself say that Scipio had already developed his echelon tactics in Spain and had used them in the battle on the "Great Plains." Naturally Hannibal knew that and was consequently also prepared for the movements made by Scipio. Nevertheless, he counted on victory and, to a certain extent, had the right to do so, since he was superior in infantry, and he would, according to the testimony of the Romans themselves, have won the victory by virtue of this superiority if the Roman-Numidian cavalry had not returned and fallen on his rear.

One of the most significant findings of my studies on ancient warfare is the verification of the fact that the Romans did not develop echelon tactics until the Second Punic War, under Scipio. The first person to agree, while Mommsen was still definitely rejecting this idea, was Fröhlich, in his work *The Importance of the Second Punic War for the Development of the Roman Military System (Die Bedeutung des zweiten punischen Krieges für die Entwicklung des römischen Heerwesens)*, 1884. Kromayer and Veith, too, have now come around to this point of view. "Scipio's dividing of the Roman battle formation into three independent echelons, arranged in depth, and his brilliant flank maneuvers, *made possible only by this formation*, were the things which grasped victory from the hands of his great adversary," writes Kromayer.[5] That is absolutely

correct, but it stands in contradiction to the concept that Kromayer adopts elsewhere, that the Romans had always understood the art of maneuvering in very small
tactical units, the maniples. Whoever was familiar with this art would find flanking
movements like those that Scipio executed at Naraggara not only nothing unusual,
but as simple as one's daily bread; in fact, it must even be said that the formation of
Scipio would have represented no progress at all but a step backward; not a refinement, but a coarsening step. Neither Kromayer nor Veith was able to avoid the impression that a fundamental change had occurred between the helpless immobility
of the Roman tactics at Cannae and the maneuvers at Naraggara and that one of the
great deeds of Scipio had to be sought in this fact. But when they hold fast at the
same time to the idea of the wonderful fineness of the supposed ancient Roman
quincunx tactics, they fall into an unsolvable inner contradiction.

When I first published my discovery, as I may characterize it (in the *Historische
Zeitschrift*, Vol. 51, 1883), a principal objection, which I raised myself, was that
Polybius not only did not report any change of Roman infantry tactics in the Second
Punic War, but also obviously knew nothing about it. Today everything has been so
well explained that this objection will probably no longer be raised on any side; even
Kromayer has now adopted my idea on this decisive point. But whoever properly
reflects on the fact that a man like Polybius did not understand such a fundamental
happening as the army reform of Scipio will not close his eyes to the further
methodological conclusion that we must regard all detailed reports and expressions
concerning tactical events in the ancient authors with the most extreme scepticism.
To what little extent contemporaries can be aware of fundamental changes in tactics,
even in the case of specific military authors, can be seen in the fourth volume of this
work (Book IV, Chapter VI) in the observations of the excellent, perceptive Hoyer
on the military system of the armies of the French Revolution. It may also be cited
here that a hundred years after Frederick his strategy was no longer familiar to the
Prussian General Staff (Vol. IV, Book III, Chapter VI).

NOTES FOR CHAPTER VI

1. In the speech that Livy has the elderly Quintus Fabius Maximus and Scipio himself make in the Senate concerning the planned
expedition, this motive does not appear with correct emphasis.
If he pointed this out, Scipio would have been placing too much
stress on the difficulty of the whole undertaking, whereas his
speech was based, and necessarily so, on emphasizing the concept
of the offensive with unconditional confidence.

2. We can assume that Hannibal returned to Africa in the fall of
203 B.C. and that the battle of Naraggara took place in about August of 202 B.C. Lehmann, p. 555.

3. Proved by Konrad Lehmann in *Jahrbücher für klassische
Philologie* 153: 573.

4. Berlin dissertation, 1914.

5. *Rome's Struggle for World Hegemony* (*Roms Kampf um die
Weltherrschaft*), p. 61.

BOOK VI

The Romans
as World Conquerors

Chapter I

Romans and Macedonians

Immediately after the Second Punic War came the victory of the Romans over the armies that can be considered as the heirs of Alexander the Great. Concerning the organization, manner of fighting, and tactics of the troops that Hannibal had led into the field against the Romans, little is reported to us. Since we are told that he gave them Roman weapons, it can be assumed that in general, especially insofar as their armament was concerned, the opposing armies were quite similar.[1]

Hannibal, naturally, did not have the special maniple organization of the phalanx, since his army was made up of barbarian mercenaries of various races with a few Carthaginian officers of higher grade, but he may from the start have had the beginnings of a second echelon or have taken other smaller measures that had the same effect and gave his phalanx the same mobility as that of the Romans, or even a greater one.

In the battles the Romans now waged against the Macedonians, the differences in armament and tactics are particularly noticeable. The Romans had first articulated the old hoplite phalanx by means of the maniple formation, and then had replaced it by the echelon formation, changed the spear into the *pilum*, and fought in close combat with the short, pointed sword. On the other hand, the Macedonians had tightened up the old phalanx even more and had changed the spear into the long spear, the *sarissa*.

The world tensely waited to see which type of warfare would prove the stronger.

Since it seemed doubtful to us whether the *sarissa* and the unique Macedonian phalanx, as we see them in the last battles of Alexander's descendants, were already in use in his time, we delayed our investigation into this subject until this point. Let us first of all acquaint ourselves with the Macedonian manner of fighting,

393

as it is described for us by Polybius, who, as a contemporary, was a classical witness of the battles of Cynoscephalae and Pydna (18. 28–32). In addition to his account, we also have similar descriptions in several manuals on tactics that have come down to us. Nevertheless, the study was very difficult and went astray on a number of occasions, since the sources contain several irreconcilable contradictions, and certain problems, as for example the question of the length of the *sarissa* and its relationship with the width of the files and the interval between ranks both with the Macedonians and the Romans, are intertwined. Rüstow and Köchly have denied the presence of the true long spear (24 or 21 feet) among the Macedonians, and by reading the Greek word as *podes*, "foot," instead of *pecheis*, "ell," of which Polybius speaks, they have assumed that the *sarissa*, in actual practice, was no longer than 14 feet. I confess that I, too, long held this opinion, but a special study by Edmund Lammert, a comparison with the Swiss and the lansquenet pikes, and finally a practical test carried out by the Berlin academic gymnastic clubs at my request, showed me that the larger figures here, for once, have to be considered the correct ones, and so I have formed the following picture:

The *sarissa* was a spear that, according to the regulations, extended up to 24 feet, but which in actuality went up to 21 feet, which the soldier grasped with both hands in such a manner as to hold the point extended far forward. Whenever the phalanx closed up in tight formation, the *sarissae* of five ranks protruded beyond the front and were all effective at the same time, since those of the first three ranks were proportionately shorter.[2]

That the foremost ranks had shorter spears is reported, it is true, neither by Polybius nor by other sources in a specific manner, but it follows indirectly from a note, according to which the couched spears would have formed a circular arch; and further, from the apparent fact that the very long spear would have been useless for the first rank; finally, from the fact that it was reported that the soldiers of the phalanx carried shields. A 21-foot-long *sarissa*—or even only an 18-foot one—cannot be controlled with one hand but requires, as is also expressly stated, the use of both hands. Whoever wields his spear with both hands must do without the protection of a shield. He could, of course, perhaps slip a small, light round shield over his arm, in order to use it in close combat with sword or dagger, after his *sarissa* was shattered, but in the fighting with the *sarissa* itself the shield would be such a burden and, held almost perpendicular to the body, would be of such little help that we may not assume that the *sarissa* fighter even carried a shield. The reports fall into agreement, however, if the first rank or the first few ranks carried a shorter spear, which they wielded with one hand. If then, say, the fifth rank carried 21-foot-spears, the fourth 18-foot ones, the third 15-foot ones, the second 12-foot ones, and the first rank 9-foot spears, the spears could form in front of the line an almost uniform vertical plane or a slight arch inclined to the rear, thus presenting an impenetrable wall of points.

The *sarissa* phalanx is based completely on the mass effect and not on the fighting of the individual man. The contact both with the neighboring file and with the preceding file can therefore be much closer than in the Roman formation, with its throwing of *pila* and its fighting with the sword. Polybius says specifically on this point that against each Roman, who needed an interval of 3 feet, there came 2 phalanx soldiers and since, after all, 5 ranks of the phalanx held their spears out in front simultaneously, 10 phalanx men against each Roman.

The gigantic weight of the shock of the *sarissa* phalanx was further increased through the fact that it was drawn up twice as deep as the old hoplite phalanx, 16 men deep according to the regulations. The rearmost 11 ranks held their *sarissae* up and thereby formed for themselves a certain protection against arrows and javelins.

When this entire mass, bristling with spears, moved forward, it formed, we are told, a frightful sight, and even the Roman commander Aemilius Paullus trembled when he saw it roll forward at Pydna.

Concerning the relative virtues of the Macedonian and Roman tactics, Polybius says: "In the front nothing can stand up to the *sarissa* phalanx; the individual Roman with his sword can neither slash down nor break through the ten spears that simultaneously press against him. But the Roman legionary is adaptable to any place at any time and for any purpose. The *sarissa*-bearer can fight only as a member of the entire phalanx and not even in small units and not as an individual fighter. Furthermore, the phalanx can move only on very level terrain; every ditch, every hill, every hole, every clump of woods causes it to fall into disorder. But if it has fallen into disorder at any place at all or if Roman maniples should fall upon it from the flank, which can be easily done with the echelon formation of the Romans, then it is lost."

This explanation is so convincing and clear that one must raise the question how it was possible that the Macedonian kings themselves did not realize it from the start,[3] and this leads to the further question, since it is already clear that Alexander's phalanx could not possibly have been of such an inflexible nature—the question of how and when the later one developed from the earlier one.

The *sarissa* phalanx of Polybius can also hardly have existed yet under the immediate successors of Alexander. At any rate, it does not appear in the battle accounts, and especially the history of Pyrrhus testifies against it. There cannot very well be any doubt that Pyrrhus, who had such a close relationship with Macedonia, had the idea of conquering the West also with the tactics that enabled Alexander to overcome the East. We are told expressly, however, that in Italy he incorporated into his army Italians with Italian arms, in such a way that there appeared alternately a unit of Epirotes and a unit of Italians.[4] This is only possible with types of armament that, even if different among themselves, are still intended for similar types of combat; it would not matter, for example, whether one unit was armed with swords and the other with spears and whether the spears were of different lengths, provided only that they all uniformly moved into individual combat with their hand weapons.

Now it is possible, of course, as I learned from the practical test, for a small unit also to make an attack at the double with long spears, but there naturally remains a difference of esprit between a unit with long spears and one with short spears, and in such an action the *sarissa*-bearers lose what is absolutely indispensable to them, secured flanks. As long as the *sarissa* phalanx remains in good order, it crushes down everything before it. But the enemy can draw back in front of an individual *sarissa* unit in order to drive with his full force on the alternate units armed with short weapons, and if he can drive one of them out of line, then the *sarissa*-bearers are also at his mercy, since he can then take them from the flank.

The feeling of insecurity that must have been caused by this dependence on the courage of foreigners who were their direct neighbors in the formation would necessarily have tended to undermine such a battle formation. The *sarissa* unit can as a basic principle exercise its full effect only in the great closed mass, which has to be covered on its flanks by other troops. The report of the mixing of units necessarily leads us then to the conclusion that the phalanx soldiers of Pyrrhus were not armed with the truly long spear.

If, then, Pyrrhus did not yet have the Polybian *sarissa* phalanx, there remains for us the choice of whether it developed gradually and the *sarissae*, which were perhaps only a maximum of 12 feet long under Alexander, were lengthened more and more, or whether it was precisely only the impending war with the Romans that persuaded King Philip V to introduce the two-handed long spear in his phalanx. King Philip V was a man of intelligence and energy; at his court, in his military ambiance, the Roman victories over Hannibal must certainly have made an impression. They probably weighed and compared the advantages of the tactics customarily used on the two sides. To adopt the Roman tactics without further ado was impossible for the Macedonians; in fact probably such an idea hardly came under consideration. One cannot suddenly throw aside the customs and viewpoints of a large standing army and a military tradition and replace them with something new and completely unrelated. The Macedonians understood how to fight in close order with a very long spear but not how to throw the spear and fight with the sword. When it was now seen what great successes this method of fighting had achieved, they may very well have come upon the idea of coping with it by increasing still further the strength of their own native method, of bringing it to its highest potential, by lengthening the spears to as much as 21 feet and closing the formation in to 1½ feet per man, while disregarding the disadvantages resulting from such one-sidedness. If this explanation is correct, the decision would offer a certain analogy to the deep formation of the Roman maniples at Cannae; that is, they could in no way match the enemy in maneuverability, and so they sought to subdue him through pressure.

Strangely enough, it never came to a completely fair test of the battle validity of the two methods of combat. The two battles in which the Macedonians succumbed to the Romans, Cynoscephalae and Pydna, were so greatly influenced by fortuitous events that the general validity of their results could be contested, and the third battle, which might also be counted here, Magnesia, where the Macedonian-Syrian empire lost to the Romans, shows no phalanx formation at all, according to the admittedly completely fantasy-like battle reports we have.

CYNOSCEPHALAE

This battle corresponds in all respects with the overall picture we have formed, from Polybius, of the meeting of phalanx with legion. The battle was not planned in advance, however, but developed from a reconnaissance skirmish. Philip, thinking he was taking advantage of a favorable moment, accepted battle, even though the hilly, broken terrain was unfavorable for the *sarissa* phalanx. Furthermore, the latter did not deploy uniformly, and while the right wing moved forward victoriously, the left, still in the process of forming up, was broken through by the elephants of the Romans and then thrown back by the legionaries without difficulty.

Since we find nowhere else in history a verified victory of this kind by elephants, it is important to stress that here, too, it was not a well-ordered force that was broken up by the elephants but that the soldiers of the phalanx, as Polybius clearly reports, were still in march formation and were impeded in forming up by the terrain.

When this flank of the Macedonians was beaten, instead of having them pursued, a tribune led 20 maniples of the victorious legions, presumably from the second echelon, against the rear of the other Macedonian wing and thereby brought the Romans the decision in the battle on this side too.

The history of tactics would be greatly confused if chance had had it that we had received, instead of Polybius' account, only the touched-up version of the battle of Cynoscephalae by Livy. For Livy, in 33. 8, has translated Polybius' Greek passage reporting the command of Philip to the phalanx to attack with couched spears as: "Macedonum phalangem hastis positis, quarum longitudo impedimento erat, gladiis rem gerere jubet." ("He ordered the Macedonian phalanx to put down their spears, whose length was an impediment, and to engage with swords.") This example is extremely valuable in leading us to practice, so to speak, critical decisiveness whenever, as is so often the case, the wording of the report is subject to question from a practical point of view. How many scholars would there be who would consider it as permissible to attribute such a definite statement to a simple misunderstanding, if we were not by chance able to compare it with the original text?[5]

PYDNA

On the battle of Pydna we do not have the report of Polybius himself but only the slightly reliable and also incomplete accounts of Livy and Plutarch. This battle, too, reportedly came about by chance, without having a proper battle formation assumed in advance.

MAGNESIA

In Livy and Appian we have only completely fantastic reports on the battle of Magnesia. The Syrian army was said to be outfitted with scythed chariots, camel riders, the levies of sixteen different peoples, Indian elephants far superior to the African ones. It was more than twice as numerous as the Romans (according to Florus, twenty times as strong), four times as strong in cavalry; although it was drawn up in a very deep formation, the front was still so long that, in the foggy weather, the flanks could not be seen from the middle. Nevertheless, there was no question of an envelopment by the widely extended mass. Not even 400 of the Romans and their allies were killed, whereas the Syrians lost 53,000.

There appears as a special feature of this battle the division of the *sarissa* phalanx into 10 subunits, with 2 elephants placed in each of the intervals. Probably this arrangement, too, belongs among the fantasies of the fiction writer to whom we are indebted for the entire battle account. All foolishness has its limits, even that of a Syrian king who has Hannibal in his service and yet does not understand how to employ him. As we know, elephants are most effective against cavalry. They do not drive in on infantry who are arrayed in close order; on the contrary, it can easily happen that they are driven back by missiles. Or on the other hand they storm forward, and then it is possible to let them pass through the battle line as the soldiers spring aside. In any case, there arises for the soldiers of the phalanx the worst thing that they have to fear, a wide gap in their front, where the Roman maniples can drive in and take them from the flank. This is all the more sure to happen because of the fact that the elephants have difficulty keeping pace with the marching phalanx unit, but, as soon as they begin to suffer from the enemy missiles, they charge against the foe as fast as possible (provided that they do not turn about).

To whoever still believes that it is methodologically permissible and proper to arrive at a historically presentable account from such battle reports by means of critical examination, I would make the request that he try that, first of all, with the two battle accounts by Appian of Cannae and Naraggara, and if that has succeeded, then I shall have no further objection to his trying it also with the account of Magnesia.

EXCURSUS

SOME CRITICAL CONSIDERATIONS CONCERNING THE BATTLE OF MAGNESIA

ANCIENT STRATEGY OF KING ANTIOCHUS

Kromayer in *Ancient Battlefields* (*Antike Schlachtfelder*, Vol. 2) has tried to analyze the battle rationally. He estimates for the Syrians 60,000 infantry and 12,000 cavalry, and for the Romans 27,600 infantry and 2,800 cavalry. To my question as to why the

Syrians, with such a great superiority, did not envelop, he replies that an envelopment on both flanks was intended and did, in fact, actually take place on the one flank, whereas on the other it was broken up and thwarted by a bold offensive blow of the Romans, and because of this the battle was decided in favor of the Romans. This battle account condemns itself; it is not only incredible but absurd. If it were possible to overpower a cavalry force more than four times as large and by no means of inferior quality by such a simple method, the art of war would no longer be an art, but a game.

As for the incorporation of the elephants—to which Kromayer adds sharpshooters—into the phalanx, Kromayer explains this by the fact that the phalanx was supposed to maintain a defensive stance only, and the enemy sharpshooters were supposed to have been fended away from the phalanx by the elephants and the light infantrymen in the intervals. These are concepts that are tactically impossible in every respect. A defensive stance on one side does not, after all, prevent the other from attacking; but a phalanx with elephants and light infantry in the intervals would have fully lost its character and would have been powerless against an attack by the legions, which needed to entice or to drive the elephants and light infantry out of the intervals at only a single spot in order to be able to roll the phalanx up toward both sides from that spot. But the Romans would doubtless even have penetrated simultaneously into many intervals.

Kromayer leans for support on the fact that the reports of Livy and Appian both go back to Polybius. That is still not at all the same as the report of Polybius himself; we have just seen what kinds of errors are possible in Livy, and furthermore there may very well have been elements from other sources mixed in with his. If it should actually be exclusively the report of Polybius that serves as a base for this, one would have to say that the master was just as lax here in his critical analysis as he was also not infrequently in other cases (see also pp. 376, 387, above). Even Kromayer, in his description of the battle of Magnesia, eliminated a few of the fantastic features of the Livian-Appian report, which would also be attributable to Polybius. The supposition that Polybius trusted too strongly an unreliable source and repeated its foolishness may therefore in no way be arbitrarily rejected as inadmissible. It is a quite different situation with the military-political reasoning that springs from the historian's own reflection; here the power of his intellect is at its height, and it would take very strong arguments indeed for one to be willing to risk contradicting his judgment. In my opinion, that is the methodological principle one must follow when utilizing Polybius. What Kromayer really things about Polybius is hard to say. At times he treats Polybius' factual statements in the way an orthodox interpreter does the sayings of the Bible, tries to save things that are obviously wrong by the strangest interpretations, and repulses doubters with hard words as slanderers of religion. (We shall soon have occasion to treat still another of these cases.) At other places he rejects the positive statements and dismisses the military and political judgments of Polybius without any hesitation. We have already seen examples of this (p. 244), and his presentation in the second volume of *Ancient Battlefields (Antike Schlachtfelder)* is based to a large extent on this, especially the wars against Antiochus and Perseus. In the strategic analysis of these wars there are numerous individual good and clarifying observations, but, also leaving aside the fact that the vagueness that I have already deplored concerning the concept of the strategy of attrition lies over the whole question, it is for me, at least, impossible to escape from the suspicion that Polybius' judgment is not only put aside but on a number of occasions is directly reversed. If Polybius, in his judgment of these wars, which he knew so well, is as prejudiced as Kromayer indicates, then the authority that we have previously attributed to him, and justifiably so, despite numerous factual errors of detail, is shaken at its base. A strict, detailed proof cannot be adduced either for or against—for example, whether Perseus, when he received the news of the envelopment of his position at Diun in 169 B.C., was justified in retreating and evacuating Tempe or whether this resulted from a simple lack of true strategic ability. Anybody who feels convinced by Kromayer's critical analyses should realize very clearly that he is thereby rejecting the authority of Polybius, to which we have given credence up to now.

At any rate, the idea of Kromayer that he presented on the so-called "Historians' Day" in Dresden and developed in an essay "Hannibal und Antiochus der Grosse" (*Neue Jahrbücher für das klassische Altertum*, 19 [1907]:681), that the contradiction between the strategy proposed by Hannibal and that followed by Antiochus represented the opposition between Carthaginian and Seleucidian policies and that therefore Antiochus, if he had followed Hannibal, would have been serving foreign interests—this concept is basically false. The opposition is rather the same one that dominated the politics of Europe from 1805 on and still in the winter of 1813–1814 the headquarters of the Allies, where it is a well-known fact that there was also a faction that considered it as completely superfluous to defeat Napoleon completely and reasoned in a manner quite similar to that of Kromayer now with respect to King Antiochus, that it was sufficient if the enemy were deprived of certain areas and provinces. Today nobody any longer questions the fact that Czar Alexander, if with Stein and Gneisenau he insisted on the Rhine crossing and pushing the march toward Paris, was representing not only his Russian interest in freedom, but also that of the European community. In precisely the same manner Hannibal, when he urged a general coalition against Rome and a corresponding conduct of the war, was not representing Carthaginian policy, but he stood for the general freedom of peoples, that is a balance of power between the Mediterranean countries, and with it also the future of the Syrian empire and its dynasty. The defeat of Carthage in 202 B.C. and Macedon in 197 B.C. did not necessarily mean Roman world domination any more than Jena and Wagram meant that of the French. Only by virtue of the fact that the weaker nations never banded together completely against the most powerful one did the world power of antiquity attain victory. We should perhaps not judge King Antiochus too harshly for not understanding his task right away, on the occasion of first clashing with the Romans; the Czar, too, only saw the subject in its true light when Moscow was in flames. To see in Hannibal's efforts at the Syrian court a result of specific Carthaginian policy, however, is just about as justified as the complaints with which Stein, Scharnhorst, and Gneisenau were greeted in 1812 by the wise and the doubting when they tried to woo the European powers, to the effect that they were agents of a special interest.

Since Kromayer's work is built completely on general arguments, we can easily substitute in his writings Napoleon for the name Rome, Alexander for Antiochus, Stein for Hannibal, Prussia and Austria for Macedonia and Carthage, and then any doubt over the level of this method of observing events can quickly be eliminated. Every historian remembers the delightful irony with which Theodor von Bernhardi presents the political-strategic wisdom of Lieutenant Field Marshal Duka—perhaps Kromayer will also espouse the cause of the late Duka and on the next "Historians' Day" (which has already patiently endured many such talks) will defend this gallant fellow against the malice of Bernhardi as he is now doing for King Antiochus the Great against the anger of Mommsen. But I hasten to mention now, along with this criticism, the fact that Kromayer, in his work *Rome's Struggle for World Hegemony* (*Roms Kampf um die Weltherrschaft*), has presented in excellent fashion the political relationships of this period.

CONCERNING THE SARISSA AND THE INTERVAL BETWEEN FILES

We find the long spear not only among the Macedonians but also quite often in the barbarian tribes. Xenophon (*Anabasis*, 4. 7. 16) recounts that the Chalybes carried spears 15 ells long, and that the Mosynoeci (5. 4. 25) had had spears that were so long and thick that a man could hardly carry them. The Aetolians, too, had *sarissae* (Livy 38. 7), and we shall have occasion to find them again among the Germanic peoples, and finally among the Swiss and the lansquenets, and in the case of the latter we shall again observe more exactly the use of this weapon.

Whether the word *sarissa* always had the meaning of a long spear or originally only the idea of "spear" in general, among the many other names (*dory, lonchē, aichmē, kontos, xyston, akontion, saunion, hyssos, palton*: spear-shaft, spear-head, spear-point, pike, etc.), as we, of course, also have in German *Spiess, Speer, Lanze, Pike, Ger, Gleve, Pinne*, is not certain. Strabo 10. 1. 12 (XC 448) says, "For the employment of spears is twofold: either for hand-to-hand fighting or for throwing, just as the pike is used for both purposes. The latter, of course, can be used for close fighting as well as for striking from a distance, as can both the *sarissa* and the javelin."* If this statement is to be interpreted as meaning that the *sarissa* could also be used as a missile, then it can not have been unduly long.

Diodorus (16.3) recounts that it was King Philip II who established the Macedonian phalanx. As its unique quality, however, he points out only the tight formation, not the long spear; but from the tighter formation of the phalanx we can accept the lengthening of the spear as a necessary consequence. If Philip had given his soldiers only the closer formation but with Greek arms, it is hard to see what kind of advantage he would have gained. The Greeks had such long experience with hoplite combat that they certainly had already arrived at the optimal density for this kind of fighting. If the Macedonians formed up more tightly, that is, too closely for individual combat, then their intention must have been focused on a mass, close-order shock or a passive defense, and for those purposes they needed longer spears than those of their enemies. We may assume that a spear of up to some 12 to perhaps 14 feet in length can still be manipulated with one hand, and it is possible that the Greeks, too, at times had already used spears of such length. When Cornelius Nepos describes in *Chabrias*, Chapter 1, how the Athenian commander "*obnixo genu scuto projecta hasta impetum excipere hostium docuit*" ("instructed his soldiers to receive the attack of the enemy with their shields at the knee, their spears held out forward"), then we certainly must think of a longer spear than the usual hoplite arm of hardly 8 feet in length.

How long, however, they actually were made, and particularly at the times of Philip and Alexander, we cannot say with certainty. Arrian never makes a clear-cut reference to the *sarissa* as a long spear, and in his account of the death of Clitus he uses the word in a sense that excludes the meaning "long spear." Alexander, he says, seized, according to one account, the lance (*logchēn*) of one of the aides-de-camp, and according to another the *sarissa* of a sentry, and stabbed Clitus with it. Then, as a few would have it, in despair he leaned the *sarissa* against the wall in order to plunge into it himself. Both of these actions are hardly feasible with a long spear; an 18-to-21-foot pole is such a generally awkward instrument, one needs so much room to manipulate it, so much time to grasp it correctly at its center of gravity that one can hardly manage it in a filled banquet hall.

When, shortly before his death, Alexander accepted barbarians in his army, he gave them, according to Arrian (3. 6. 5) "the spears of the Macedonians in preference to the javelins of the barbarians."* That the source from which Arrian took this information does not here use the expression *sarissa*, but "Macedonian spear" does not seem to me an indication that the difference between the various types of spears was very great.

The only passage in Arrian that seems to indicate that the *sarissa* was a long spear is the description of the moving up of the phalanx in the battle of Gaugamela (3. 14): "And the Macedonian phalanx in close formation and shivering with *sarissae*, had made its advance."* When, however, we read of the infantry in the battle on the Hydaspes, of which it is specifically said that they were *hypaspists* (5. 17. 7), "he [Alexander] gave the signal for the infantry to lock shields, to press together into the closest possible mass, and to attack as a phalanx,"* then the conclusiveness of the first passage seems to be annulled. Polybius, in 4. 64. 6 ff., even uses of peltasts the expressions "to lock shields"* and "to close ranks with their shields."* Under King Perseus there are, as Kromayer verifies in *Antike Schlachtfelder*, 2: 321, peltasts armed with *sarissae*.

Very often (1. 27. 8; 3. 23. 3; 4. 6. 3; 4. 28. 8) Arrian speaks of the "lighter hoplites" ("the lighter equipped of the hoplites," "the lightest-armed men of the Macedonian phalanx," "choosing from the phalanx the lightest-armed but yet best equipped men")* or, on the other hand (2. 4. 3), of the heavily armed ("with such ranks of foot soldiers as were heavily armed").* Since the other differences of armament within the phalanx cannot, after all, have been so significant, perhaps that is principally in reference to the shorter, handy spear of the foremost ranks as opposed to the clumsy long spear.

In the battle accounts of Diodorus we find nothing from which we may draw any information concerning the peculiar character of the *sarissa* phalanx. In the battle on the Hydaspes (16. 88) he recounts how the Macedonians with their *sarissae* felled the Indian infantry stationed between the elephants. Now, since we know from Arrian (see above, the analysis of the battle on the Hydaspes) that there were only *hypaspists* present here, and not *pezetairoi*, one could come to the direct conclusion that the spears of the *hypaspists*, too, were called *sarissae*.

Diodorus (17. 100) describes for us the individual combat between the Athenian Dioxippos and the Macedonian Korragos. Dioxippos was armed, in the manner of Hercules, only with a club. Korragos first threw a lance at him; Dioxippos stepped aside and avoided it: "Then the former leveled his Macedonian *sarissa* and charged, but his opponent shattered the *sarissa* with his club after his attacker got near him."* Here the *sarissa* is undoubtedly conceived of as a long spear.

In the manual on plants written by the philosopher Theophrastus, disciple of Aristotle, we find the note (3. 12. 2): "The male cornel-cherry tree grows to a maximum height of 12 ells, the length of the longest *sarissa*." Theophrastus died in 287 B.C.; he makes mention of historical events as late as the years 307 and 306 B.C.[6] Therefore his book was written during the period of the Diadochi, between 306 and 287 B.C. If the largest *sarissa* at that time was 18 feet long, we may be permitted to conclude that at the time of Alexander and Philip it was at any rate no longer than that. It has not yet been said, however, that even at the time of Theophrastus the phalanx soldiers used 18-foot-long *sarissae*. It might also be possible that the philosopher had in mind, in speaking of the "longest *sarissa*," not a field weapon, but one used in siege warfare, for the defense of the walls, or on shipboard. The fact that the male cornel-cherry tree (from whose wood the knotty "Ziegenhain canes" are made) actually grows to a maximum height of 18 feet in those regions has been confirmed for me by our botanists. Theophrastus proves for us, therefore, that even the closest successors of Alexander still did not have the Polybian *sarissa* phalanx with 21-foot-long spears.

The account Plutarch gives in *Philopoemen*, Chapter 9, of the introduction of the *sarissa* among the Achaeans is not usable. It appears, according to him, as if the Achaeans, up to Philopoemen, had not had real hoplites at all.

Among the Lacedaemonians, Cleomenes is supposed to have introduced the *sarissa* (according to Plutarch, *Cleomenes*, Chapters 11 and 23). In what way they saw an advantage in this is not stated; the Lacedaemonians can, after all, hardly have formed a Polybian phalanx. In the battle of Sellasia it is precisely the Macedonian phalanx and its armament that are said to have overcome Cleomenes (Chapter 28).

The thorough description that Polybius (18. 28–32) gave of the Macedonian phalanx has caused so much difficulty because the length he gives for the *sarissa*—that is, 16 ells according to the regulations, 14 ells in reality—seemed impossible from a practical viewpoint and because, in the second place, Polybius indicated both for the Romans and the Macedonians 3 feet of width for each file but claims at the same time that a legionary occupied twice the width of a phalanx soldier. The answer, which is correct in its main points, is to be found in an article by Rudolf

Schneider in the *Philologische Wochenschrift*, No. 20, 15 May 1866, and in the treatment by Dr. Edmund Lammert, "Polybius und die römische Taktik," Programm des Königlichen Gymnasiums zu Leipzig 1889.

As far as the breadth of each file is concerned, it is clear that one of the two figures given by Polybius has to be discarded. Previously it was the common tendency to assume that it was 3 feet for the phalanx soldiers and, for the legionaries, who needed room for fighting with the sword, 6 feet. Even Stoffel, in his history of Caesar, assumes this. Schneider and Lammert have, however, both through objective observation and critical consideration of all the sources, proved quite clearly that that is false, and if I myself earlier raised the objection that with 1½ feet per man, there was no room left in which to hold the spears, since the man alone, of course, is about 1½ feet wide, experience has taught me that this objection is unjustified. The Berlin academic gymnastic societies were so accommodating as to place themselves at my disposition for a *sarissa* drill. On the large exercise field of Schönholz we first drew up a phalanx equipped completely with poles of some 20 feet in length and attempted to determine in how closed a formation the mass would still be able to march. It resulted that, with lances couched, movement was still quite easily possible with each man having something less than 2 feet. It is true that the poles were very difficult to handle, but they were made of quite green, strong spruce wood. The statement that the phalanx soldiers were aligned at 1½-foot intervals need not be taken, of course, as absolutely accurate mathematically, especially under field conditions. But if we should imagine trained men and lances of seasoned wood, we could justifiably state that the forming-up and movement with 1½-foot intervals is quite possible.

The experiment worked particularly well when, following Lammert's proposal, we armed the foremost ranks not with the full-length spears, but with shorter spears, graduated by rank. Even the points of the sixth rank still protruded beyond the first rank, and the entire mass was able to move without difficulty, even at double time.

Through this experiment we also eliminate definitively the contradiction that Soltau raised in conjunction with his essay in *Hermes* 20: 362, against Lammert's article in the *Deutsche Literarische Zeitschrift*, Vol. 37, 1890. Soltau interprets the passage from Polybius as meaning that the Romans originally lined up with a breadth of 3 feet for each file, but that they left wide intervals between the maniples during the approach march and then filled them up shortly before the attack by having each man take an interval of 5 to 6 feet. When Polybius then speaks once again about 3 feet, in this instance, according to Soltau, the man himself is not counted ("a slackening and a moving apart.")* According to the passage itself, this explanation would perhaps not be completely impossible, if we had no further evidence but the writing of Polybius. But one needs only to have taken a good look at such a formation and to have examined it carefully in order to be convinced that it is completely impossible, from a practical point of view. A formation with widths of 3 feet per file is already so generally loose that it is quite out of the question to refer to it as a close formation; but 6 feet would hardly permit the existence of even any cohesiveness, and the maneuver of taking interval during the approach march in preparation for the attack would be completely impossible of execution. We may therefore continue to accept Lammert's interpretation, which was very carefully arrived at with due consideration given to all the other pertinent passages. And Liers, too, in *Military Systems of the Ancients* (*Kriegswesen der Alten*) p. 45, pointed out well that also the description in Thucydides 5. 71 leads to the conclusion of a close formation of the Greek hoplites.

Lammert is of the opinion, incidentally, that the contradiction in Polybius' account is not attributable to that historian, but that the excerpt that we have at hand was worked over by somebody else. For the details, I refer the reader to this excellent study.

In order to answer the objection of Rüstow and Köchly that the *sarissae*, as described by Polybius, could not have been handled, since the center of gravity was too far forward, Lammert made the assumption that the rear end was counterbalanced with a heavy metal piece, and at first that seemed to me, too, quite plausible. Nevertheless, I have moved away from this opinion as a result of a comparison with the weapon that resembles the *sarissa* most closely—is, in fact, the same thing—the long pike of the Swiss and the lansquenets. Demmin, in *The Historical Development of Military Weapons* (*Die Kriegswaffen in ihrer geschichtlichen Entwicklung*), 3d ed., p. 779, states that these spears were 7 to 8 meters long, "consequently 2 to 3 meters longer than the 5- to 6 meter long Macedonian *sarissa*." These figures are almost certainly incorrect. As we know, the *sarissa* was up to 24 feet long, and therefore more than 7 meters, but there seem to have been no German spears of this length. Wendelin Böhcim, on p. 319 of his *Handbook of Weapons* (*Handbuch der Waffenkunde*), gives as the "average length" of German long spears 4.5 meters (15 feet) and as a maximum 5 meters (not quite 17 feet). As we shall see very shortly, that is once again somewhat too little.

These old German long spears are very rare today, and the Berliner Zeughaus (Berlin Ordnance Museum) formerly did not possess a single one of them. Director von Ubisch was kind enough, however, to secure one at my request. Furthermore, I requested information from the Carolino-Augusteum Museum in Salzburg and the Swiss National Museum in Zurich, which have the largest numbers of long spears, and have been given information in the most obliging manner by the managements of both institutions. Finally, I have received strong assistance in my study of wood types from my local colleague in botany, Privatdozent Dr. Reinhardt.

The Berlin long spear is 17 feet long (more than 5 meters); of the 31 spears in the holdings of Salzburg, the longest one is something over 17 feet long (515 centimeters); of the 18 spears in Zurich, the 4 longest are somewhat over 18 feet (540 to 544 centimeters). Even though this length is still about 3 feet shorter than the *sarissa* of 21 feet that, according to Polybius, was actually used, the weapons are nevertheless similar enough to permit our drawing a conclusion.

Now Lammert informs us of a calculation by which a *sarissa* of seasoned ash wood, 6.5 meters long (about 14 Greek ells or 21 feet), 5 centimeters in diameter below and 3 centimeters above, would have a wood weight of 5.6 kilograms, to which must be added 270 grams for an iron point. On such a spear he considers as probable a counterweight of 2.4 kilograms at the foot.

In like manner I have had calculations made for pine, ash, and cornel-cherry wood, all of which agree with Lammert's calculation. The specific weight of ash wood is 0.59, of the best pine wood 0.63, and of cornel-cherry 0.81. The last-named is, therefore, unusually heavy, but it does not come into consideration for the very long spears. Pine wood varies according to the ground on which it grew; there are some useful types that are lighter than ash. It is conjectured that the Greeks, like the Swiss, grew satisfactory wood especially for the making of spears on barren, not too moist, soil. Ash does not normally grow entirely straight up to this length. Regardless of whether the Macedonians actually used ash or pine, the difference is not particularly significant.[7] As far as the strength of the wood is concerned, the Berlin spear has almost no taper at all and an average diameter of about 3.5 centimeters. The Salzburg and Zurich spears are consistently strongest in the middle; the Salzburg ones have a circumference of 13 centimeters at that point, 8.5 at the foot, and 7.5 at the start of the iron; consequently they have a diameter of somewhat over 4 centimeters at their midpoint. Among the Zurich collection, the strongest one is 4 centimeters in the middle, 3.1 at the point, and 3.2 at the foot. Böheim (p. 312) gives the diameter as 4.5 centimeters. This agrees, therefore, on the average with Lammert's assumption. None of the German spears, however, has a counterweight, not even a sleeve at the foot. Only a number of short spears in the Zurich Museum, which are attributed to the seventeenth century, have such a weight.

If, therefore, the Germans were able to handle their long spears without any counterweight, we may be allowed to assume that the Macedonians could do likewise, and the experiment in Schönholz, mentioned above, also supports this point.

In the course of this experiment, furthermore, I was particularly impressed with how uncomfortable the long spears were to carry on the march; they caused more trouble here than when couched for the attack.

(Added in the second edition:) I have more recently personally studied the long spears in Zurich and also in Vienna and have found everything above to be confirmed. In like manner, repeated little drills with the spears of the Berliner Zeughaus, which I have had carried out by the participants in my seminar on military history, have confirmed the results of the experiment on the exercise field at Schönholz.

Nevertheless, Kromayer has opposed my concept of the Roman and Macedonian phalanxes with one differing from it in principle and has defended his in repeated polemics.[8] He interprets the passage from Polybius that was treated above as meaning that the Macedonian phalanx soldiers fought with 3 feet of space each and the Romans originally with 3 feet also, but that they then opened up their formation after the first impact and, through a process of moving forward and backward, fought with an interval of 6 feet. In his opinion, a formation with only 3 feet of interval does not allow the use of the sword. After the first shock, therefore, the foremost rank spreads out into a thin chain of skilled individual fighters, which is the only rank to carry out the active combat, while the men of the following ranks intervene in the fight only by watching for the moment when they can aim a lance or a missile at the enemies through the gaps between their own foremost fighters, or where they can spring forward beside their own men to protect them by fending off blows or throwing back an enemy who has been able to penetrate too far forward, or when they can carry or drag back and away from the fray their dead or wounded, and finally by replacing those who are killed. (*Historische Zeitschrift* 95: 17). From time to time the individual fighting of the first rank with an average interval of 6 feet per man alternates with the more closed massing.

If this concept were correct, we would have in it a scholarly discovery of prime importance. It is a question here of the very nucleus of ancient infantry tactics, not of some secondary technical feature.

It is the use of the weapons in conjunction with the pressure of the mass that constitutes the character of the phalanx in the presentation of this work, and the development lies in a gradually improved organization. This picture of the development is completely destroyed if Kromayer's theory of the width of the files and the individual fighting of the first rank is correct, a consequence which the author himself, of course, did not appreciate, since he specifically agrees, after all, with my account of the battle of Cannae, which is of course completely based on the concept of mass pressure. But the fact that the author did not himself recognize the consequences of his idea does not remove their potential impact from an objective viewpoint. It is incumbent on us, therefore, not to avoid a thorough investigation.

Kromayer's ideas are false and unrealistic for the following reasons:

1. He considers the interval of 6 feet to have been necessary for the Romans because it would have been impossible to fight with the Roman sword without such an interval. By this theory, then, the Romans would have been deprived of the use of their weapons at the first shock, at which moment Kromayer, too, assumes they had only 3 feet of interval—a very unusual manner of opening a battle, especially if the enemy were maliciously to form his men in such a way as to be able to use their weapons.

2. The 6-foot interval that then results from a spreading out is supposed to be accepted as an "average," since, of course, no exact taking-up of intervals was possible in the fray. "Average" is a saving expression which is useless here. By this concept, some have too much, others too little. At the spots that are too wide the enemy can penetrate, whereas at those which are too narrow the Roman soldier cannot use

his weapon. For this reason Polybius cannot possibly have been thinking of such an "average" in his account.

3. The greater interval for the fighters of the first rank is supposed to be gained by having "individual soldiers or several press more deeply into the enemy, while at another place their comrades are pushed back somewhat." One wonders how the supposedly necessary interval of 6 feet can be assured for the individual in this process of pushing into the enemy and whether the squeeze resulting from enemy contact does not restrict the fighting just as much as that from the neighboring comrades in one's own line.

4. Least of all can one imagine this penetration of individuals into the enemy front in a fight of Romans against a phalanx armed with long spears, the type of battle about which, after all, Polybius is speaking. For the legionary with his short sword who has already passed between the long spears is in such close contact with the pikeman that the latter can no longer defend himself. Polybius reports to us specifically that the *sarissa* front was impenetrable. How can Kromayer believe, then, that on the average of every 6 feet there was nevertheless a Roman who was able to pass through, drawing from this an estimate of the width of the files on both sides?

5. Kromayer imagines that the Roman warrior launched his blow with his arm stretched horizontally toward the side. That he would certainly have done only very seldom, since this kind of blow is very impracticable and ineffective; the most important blow moves from rear to front with a bent arm that then stretches forward. We learn this not only from the modern art of individual fencing but it is also clearly indicated in Vegetius 1. 12, where the legionaries are told not to strike but to thrust, since the latter action is more dangerous for the enemy "and furthermore, while a blow is being carried out, the arm and the right side are left uncovered, whereas a thrust is executed with the body protected." For this thrust, during which the arm is held close against the body, 3 feet of space are therefore completely sufficient. But even for a thrust with the arm extended horizontally it is not necessary to have 6 feet, only 4.

6. Every commander places his soldiers as close together as the manipulation of their weapons possibly allows, for the closer they stand, the more weapons there are along the front. If it were true that fighters with the Roman sword needed 6 feet of room, whereas the old Greek hoplite, for example, with his spear, needed only 3, it follows that the sword would have been a completely useless combat weapon. It would have been possible to have two spearmen attack each man armed with a sword, and then no degree of individual skill would have helped the latter; he would necessarily have succumbed. Consequently, doing battle with the Roman short sword and with the hoplite spear cannot have required any significant difference in interval.

7. If the Roman phalanx had been based not on mass shock action but on the individual fighting of the first rank, with secondary support from the second and third ranks, then in a deep formation like that at Cannae, at least nine-tenths and probably nineteen-twentieths of the army would have been practically superfluous.

8. Kromayer seeks to find a certain activity for the mass of Roman warriors to the extent of picturing a kind of alternation between the individual fighting of the foremost ranks and the pressure of the mass. The individual fighting is supposed to start after the first mass impact has ended with a "natural recoil action" and the masses have consequently been shaken up into a somewhat looser formation. Then, "when the enemy at some point or other seems to be about to resume the mass attack," then "the same living human wall" is supposed to "throw itself against him again, answering blow for blow" (*Historische Zeitschrift* 95: 17). And so the formation supposedly shifts from closed to open not just once, but continuously. In opposition to this concept is the fact that such actions, if they occur at all, would only be imaginable under the assumption that both sides executed both actions—taking interval for individual fighting and pressing together without the possibility of using their weapons—completely simultaneously, for that side which did not take up wider in-

tervals and carry out individual fighting at all, but went ahead with its mass action continuously or even just a moment longer than the enemy, would have had the victory. The thin chain of individual fighters at 6-foot intervals would not have been capable—and Kromayer, too, realizes this—of withstanding, even for a moment, the weight of the enemy mass with a depth of 10, 20, 30, or perhaps even 60 men. And if the ranks behind the chain of individual fighters have drawn back, even for only a very small distance, in order to give the first rank the necessary room for individual fighting, how are they to be brought back into forward motion again? In the huge melee there is neither command nor signal for the entire mass, and even if such a control did exist, a mass formation that has once fallen back before the enemy, even for only a moment, while the latter is pushing forward, is for all practical purposes impossible to set in forward motion again—unless there be special circumstances such as those, for instance, in the battle of Cannae. In a battle between two phalanxes, the first step backward is the decisive one; it gives the advancing side a morale advantage that increases with each passing second and will almost always lead to victory, unless new forces intervene. Kromayer's concept of a "natural recoil" is "natural" only for the inferior side, not equally for both opponents, and with this idea we must also reject the possibility of a constant alternation between a looser and a tighter formation.

9. For his concept of individual fighting in the battle, Kromayer (*Historische Zeitschrift*, Vol. 17) relies on a description of the battle of Mutina by Appian in *Civil Wars (Bürgerkriege)*, 3: 68. But this passage bears no evidence at all in favor of his hypothesis. It is not a question here of a pitched battle but of three independent combats by fractions of legions side by side, which were not at all strong enough for a true phalanx-type pressure, and the situation consequently devolved quite naturally, because of the bravery of the veterans, into toughly fought individual combat on a massive scale. There is no question of a repeated shifting between pressure and individual fighting, and the long individual fight appears to the author so little like the normal, larger-scale type of combat that, on the contrary, he bases his analogy on that of wrestlers, who, in order to catch their breath, move apart for a moment and then have at one another again.

10. For the assumption that the phalanx soldiers had needed 3 feet of space (and consequently, then, the Romans 6 feet), Kromayer depended on the customs of the Swiss and the lansquenets (*Antike Schlachtfelder* 1: 323, and *Historische Zeitschrift* 95: 18). To the fourth volume of this work (Book II, Chapter III), I have added a special investigation, from which it results that the cited passages provide no valid proof. For our question, it is apparent that there is nothing at all to be concluded from them. The phalanx formation that Polybius contrasts with the Roman one is, of course, not to be construed as the old Greek one or the Macedonian, but as a formation whose tightness was brought artificially to its highest degree in that very period and not earlier, and which did not prove itself. It is therefore not at all surprising that the Swiss and lansquenets had a looser formation; even in their cases, however, the close formation is also to be found.

11. Kromayer takes as an example a situation where two phalanxes in close formation are fighting against each other and derives therefrom the impossibility of this whole tactical picture, since the two masses, capable only of pushing forward and not able to parry and to fight individually, would have skewered each other. It is very doubtful that two such phalanxes ever actually stood opposed to each other. If it happened, or if it were to happen, then the various ranks, unable to do much individual fighting, would indeed have pressed into each other's spears, or would have been pressed into them by the following ranks as they pushed forward. The foremost ranks, which had the shorter spears, might, it is true, have retained a certain possibility to parry, but it was very limited under any circumstances. This is no reason, however, for rejecting the whole concept. Even in this manner the stronger and more determined side could win, and necessarily would have. Furthermore,

there has been specifically reported to us and confirmed in the writings of the tacticians (Asclepiodotus, Chapter 4) a formation with 1½ feet of interval, consequently without any possibility of actual individual combat, used for defense. Naturally it is conceivable only in the case of troops armed with the long spear, which, held forward in a mass formation, forms a defense, whereas not only the sword but also the short spear would be almost useless without room for manipulation.

12. Finally, I include the fact that we have in Vegetius (3. 14) the definite proof that the Romans fought with 3 feet of interval, because with such a formation the battle line was uninterrupted and also it provided enough room for the use of the weapons ("Singuli autem armati in directum ternos pedes inter se occupare consueverunt, hoc est in mille passibus mille sescenti sexaginta sex pedites ordinantur in longum, ut nec acies interluceat et spatium sit arma tractandi." ["Each and every armed man was accustomed to occupy 3 feet of space in the rank—that is, in the space of 1,000 paces 666 infantrymen were drawn up, so that the line itself could not be seen through and so that there would be enough room to brandish the weapons"]). Therefore I trust that I may be allowed now to consider as disproven once and for all the concept that Kromayer has put forth with the greatest certainty.

Kromayer's idea of the spreading out of the legion's front into a thin chain of individual fighters becomes all the more fantastic when we later see that he espouses elsewhere (*Antike Schlachtfelder*, 2: 83) the theory of Veith, according to which the Romans maintained wide intervals between the maniples (and cohorts), not only during the approach march but also during the battle. The battle line of legionaries, which otherwise already resembles a very thin line of skirmishers, is now, therefore, still much more weakly manned, since at repeated intervals that are generally as long as the front of the fighters itself, there are no fighters at all. In these small scattered groups, even in the few moments of initial shock action admitted by Kromayer, there can no longer be any question of pressure exerted by the mass.

It appears doubtful whether Kromayer understood that Veith's theory of the intervals in battle and his own concerning the width of the files combined algebraically in thinning the line and thereby completely nullify each other. It is also questionable whether it was consciously or unconsciously that he dropped this theory in the second volume of his *Antike Schlachtfelder* and adopted another one. For in the latter case (p. 83) he speaks of the "custom" of the Romans "to give way a little at the start of the battle and then, through the toughness of their opposition, first to disabuse the oncoming enemy of his illusion of victory, then to wear him down, and finally to overpower him." Instead of the "natural recoil" of the older theory, which was supposed to occur in the same way on both sides in order to make room for the individual fighters, there has now appeared "a custom" only on the Roman side. It is obvious that this new theory is just as impossible as the old one, for if the Romans really had intentionally drawn back a short distance after the first clash and had left only the loose chain of individual fighters in direct contact with the enemy, it is clear that this loose chain could not have withstood the mass pressure of the enemy for a single moment. Kromayer himself realized that earlier, for in *Historische Zeitschrift* 95: 17, he states as the mission of the rearward ranks of the phalanx "when the enemy at some point or other seems to be about to resume the mass attack, to oppose him at once with the same living human wall, answering blow for blow."

It seems remarkable that Rudolf Schneider, in the *Göttingische gelehrte Anzeigen* 169: 445, explains that the question of the interval is still an unsolved problem for him, since the phalanx soldier cannot get along with 1½ feet but can when he is given 3 feet, whereas the double, 6 feet, is apparently too much for the legionary. Why didn't he simply assemble 100 students, arm them with hop poles, and form a phalanx? Whoever has once seen and measured such a phalanx is immediately relieved of any further tortures of doubt concerning the interval between files. Scholars are remarkable people. Here for once we have the rare opportunity of solving a historical problem through a very simple experiment; why doesn't one do it?

Kromayer seems to have been influenced toward his shift of concept from the "natural recoil" to a simple special "custom" of the Romans by having become aware later of the account of the battle between the Romans and the Gauls in 223 B.C., for he supports the new theory with the following note: "This is how Polybius, in 2. 33. 7, describes the manner of fighting of the Romans in an observation that is of the utmost importance for their tactics. Flaminius," he says, "in a battle with the Gauls, made the Roman's peculiar style of fighting impossible by using a formation that allowed no falling back ('ruined the tactic that was peculiar to the Romans by not leaving the cohorts room enough to fall back by foot, maniple by maniple')." The passage, however, continues: "For if it happened that the men were pushed back even the slightest distance during the battle, it would have been necessary for them to hurl themselves into the river, because of their general's error."* The sense of the passage, therefore, is that it was the Romans' custom, even in a battle that was going poorly for them, not to flee, but only to withdraw step by step, but that Flaminius, by drawing up the army with its rear on a river, had made such a withdrawal impossible. If the Romans had had to draw back even a small distance, they would already have fallen into the river, would consequently have become disordered, and would inevitably have suffered a complete defeat. This passage does not contain the slightest new information concerning any special tactics of the Romans.

NOTES FOR CHAPTER I

1. Polybius 18. 28.
2. It was already understood in this way by Johann von Nassau and Montecucoli. Jähns I: 573. Montecucoli, *Writings (Schriften)* 2: 225.
3. See also in this connection Livy 33. 18.
4. Polybius 18. 28.
5. In the second volume of his *Antike Schlachtfelder*, Kromayer has placed the battle somewhat differently than was earlier the case; nothing new has resulted from this change insofar as the actual events are concerned. Whether his account of the strategic relationships of the entire war, which are treated very thoroughly on the basis of specialized topographical research, is to the point, I have not verified in detail.
6. Zeller, *History of Philosophy (Geschichte der Philosophie)* Vol 2, Part 2, p. 640.
7. In Blümner, *Technology and Terminology of Arts and Crafts among the Greeks and Romans (Technologie und Terminologie der Gewerbe und Künste bei den Griechen und Römern)*, 2: 252, 263, 285, 289, source passages are cited that indicate spears (and javelins) also made of beech, oak, stone-pine, and yew. Strangely enough, there is no mention of the use of pine for spears, but fir is cited on p. 289. Concerning the presence of the various woods in Ancient Greece, see Neumann and Partsch, *Physical Geography of Greece (Physikalische Geographie von Griechenland)*, pp. 365 ff.

8. "Comparative Studies of the History of Greek and Roman Military Systems" ("Vergleichende Studien zur Geschichte des griechischen und römischen Heerwesens,") *Hermes*, Vol. 35, Book 2. Answered by me in *History of the Art of War* (*Geschichte der Kriegskunst*), 2: 16 (not repeated in this edition). Kromayer, *Ancient Battlefields* (*Antike Schlachtfelder*) 1: 321 ff. In reply, "Theological Philology" ("Theologische Philologie,") *Preussische Jahrbücher*, 110, (May 1905): 209 ff. Kromayer, "True and False Objective Analysis" ("Wahre und falsche Sachkritik,") *Historische Zeitschrift*, 95 (1905): 1 ff. Answered by me in *Preussische Jahrbücher*, 121 (July 1905): 158 ff.

Chapter II

The Professional Army: Cohort Tactics

The military forces of the Romans that had been formed in the Second Punic War had sufficed to conquer the Eastern powers; two of these, Macedon and Syria, were defeated, and the third, Egypt, as well as most of the smaller countries, voluntarily allied themselves with the Romans and assumed subordinate roles. From now on there was no other country that could have taken the offensive against Rome. But the gradual consummation of direct Roman world hegemony continued to necessitate smaller and larger wars, in which the military tradition was maintained and extended. Fighting went on against the Gauls in upper Italy and in Spain; Macedon was finished off; Greece was kept in check, Carthage destroyed, and war carried on with a Numidian king. It often happened that only after initial defeats and a long period of alternating fortunes did the Romans finally win the upper hand in these wars. The new military system, as created by Scipio, since it had overcome Hannibal, would easily have subjected the *orbis terrarum*, if it could have been incorporated as an organic institution into the body of the Roman Republic. But, as we have seen, it stood as a basic contradiction to the Republic, and from now on Roman military history, and with it Roman history in general, moved within the framework of this innate contradiction. The old constitution, by which the two mayors for the year commanded the armies and the legions were levied according to need from the citizenry and then again dissolved, still existed, but if it had been applied literally, it could neither have fulfilled the missions of Roman policy nor could it have been tolerated. A system of universal military service cannot be applied to a continuous state of war such as Rome now had to maintain, and the soldiers who had to fight in Spain and in Asia, in

Africa and on the Alps, could not be citizens at the same time. It can be estimated that under the legal universal military obligation only about a tenth of the service-qualified Roman youth actually served,[1] but these gradually divested themselves more and more of the aspect of citizen and formed a real soldiery. This professional warriorhood had now become, in effect, a fact, but it was not a constitutional institution, and consequently the machine functioned with the most pronounced lack of regularity. The citizen army time and again infringed on the professional soldiery, especially in the high command.

They were, nevertheless, victorious, since with the gigantic materiel superiority of Rome over all the other nations occasional defeats and rather long-drawn-out campaigns caused little damage and the body of professionally trained warriors—generals, officers, soldiers—remained large enough so that, finally, as soon as a really competent man took the situation in hand, a useful army could be organized and a decisive blow carried through.

In the third century, during the Punic Wars, we may assume that a third of the free inhabitants of Italy possessed Roman citizenship. If, therefore, the Romans comprised the somewhat smaller half of the land army, the *socii* (allies) the larger half, and the *socii navales* (naval allies) the principal contingent for the fleet, the military obligation was quite evenly distributed. During the Second Punic War, however, the Romans themselves had had to carry the principal burden, since a portion of the allies defected and another portion became quite lax in reporting for service. So after the victory the Romans inducted the allies all the more frequently; now the smaller part of the army by far consisted of citizens. Recruiting was carried out in the provinces, too, and all kinds of mercenaries —Numidians, Balearics, Gauls, Iberians, Cretans—were taken into the service, while the Greek allies were called on to furnish auxiliaries. The truly Roman army was as a rule only 4 legions strong, or some 18,000 to 20,000 men. With all the contingents, however, the Republic had some 50,000 men rather constantly under arms, whose number was increased from time to time, whenever an uprising broke out in Spain or it was necessary for the purpose of subduing Carthage while fighting at the same time in Macedon and Greece.

The Republic was faced with a somewhat more difficult test when a new barbarian enemy appeared on the border and threatened to invade Italy—the Germanic tribes. The Romans suffered a series of defeats (113 B.C., under Papirus Carbo, in

Noricum; 109 B.C., under M. Junius Silanus, against the Allobroges; 107 B.C., under L. Cassius, on the upper Garonne; and 105 B.C., under Mallius Maximus, Caepio, and Aurelius Scaurus, near Arausio), until finally C. Marius, with a newly formed army, defeated and destroyed the Teutones and Ambrones near Aquae Sextiae in 102 B.C., and the Cimbri and Tigurini near Vercellae in 101 B.C. We can realize how great the Romans' fear had been through the great fame and the position that Marius won through his victory. For six consecutive times the people had elected him, a noncommissioned officer who had worked his way up, as consul, and after the victory he was hailed as the third founder of Rome, but all the details of the war that have been reported turn out on closer examination to be guard house stories and noncoms' gossip, so that nothing of value for military history is to be derived from them. The war is very important for us, however, in that it marked the gradually achieved shift of the Roman army from a citizen army into a professional army, bringing formal attainment of a new organization. Although it is true that even this point has been handed down to us directly only in part, nevertheless all indications point to the fact that Marius was the creator of the organization that we later see more clearly.[2]

The division of the legions into the three year-groups, *hastati, principes,* and *triarii*, must already have become a pure formality by the time of the Second Punic War. The two *legiones urbanae*, which were formed anew year after year, must have consisted almost entirely of young men who had just reached the age of service qualification, and the *triarii* in these legions were probably soldiers of just as little experience as the Young Guard of Napoleon in 1814, which consisted of nothing but recruits.[3] On the other hand, in the older Roman legions even the *hastati* were no longer so very young; in fact, in the legions of Cannae that were still fighting at Naraggara, even the youngest must have been considerably older than the famous "grumblers," the Old Guard of Napoleon.

Even the sense of the grouping by age, the sparing of the older year-groups, had disappeared since the units had become echelons. Since the *triarii*, who had supposedly been favored, were now freely ordered from the rear echelon to a flank or to face about to the rear or to a detached force, it was possible that they might well be sent to spots that were threatened with the greatest dangers and the highest losses.

If the arrangement in a triple formation nevertheless remained in force for a hundred years longer, that can be explained by the natural stability of any existing organization.[4]

The double role of the *veliti*, as supply train drivers and orderlies on the one hand and light infantrymen on the other, was perhaps already modified, as we have seen, in the Second Punic War.

Marius now did away with all these distinctions. The train drivers and orderlies were no longer counted at all as combatants and were removed from the legion.[5] Light infantry service was now assigned completely to a special corps of archers and slingers. The legion was made up of uniformly armed and equipped hoplites. The number of maniples remained the same, but each maniple was brought uniformly to a strength of 200 men and every 3 maniples were grouped as a cohort.

The cohort of 600 men, which therefore resembled to some extent a modern battalion, formed the basic tactical unit from now on. The legion had 10 cohorts, or 6,000 men.[6]

The new formation was based on the past to the extent that a cohort of 3 maniples already existed. The contingents of allies, which of course were not able to form entire legions but otherwise had to have the same organization as the Romans, had always been called cohorts and were divided into *hastati*, *principes*, and *triarii*.[7] But these cohorts had no tactical significance. In camp they were presumably combined into legions, and in battle formation they were deployed to the extent that the *hastati* moved into the first echelon, the *principes* and *triarii* into the second and third echelons, respectively. The cohorts of Marius are something completely different. They remain together, forming a single, all-important tactical body.

The maniples that were in existence up to this point still did not form a tactical unit; they were too small for that. They did not have any true independence; even if it may have happened in individual cases that a single maniple or several of them together made independent movements or carried out an isolated action, it was, as a rule, the entire echelon or a definite part of the echelon that was executing the action. The old maniple had a strength of only 60, or 120, or at the most 150 men; the new cohort has 600. This unit, thoroughly drilled, could now execute any movement and assume any form that was ordered. The echelons were formed by cohorts. The commander could order the army to form up in 1, 2, 3, or 4 echelons. He could make one echelon stronger, the other weaker. He could form an angled flanking unit or have the cohorts form back-to-back, creating a double front. He could have any cohort move out from the place it was occupying and take position in another location.

The legion continued to be an administrative unit; the original tactical unit was the entire phalanx, whether it consisted of one or several legions. In general, the Greeks and Macedonians retained the phalanx as the tactical unit. The Romans first provided the phalanx with joints, then divided it into echelons, and finally broke it up into a number of small tactical units that were capable now of drawing together into a compact, impenetrable unit, on another occasion of changing formation with complete flexibility, dividing up, turning toward one side or the other. How anxiously the old Greek hoplite phalanx had to remain on guard against a possible flank attack, especially one by cavalry! After the time of Marius the Roman commander could order a few cohorts to take over the mission of flank protection and could feel that he was secure. How simple such an arrangement appears, but to make this simple thing possible—the formation of small masses that held together so firmly that they formed tactical units—was unendingly difficult. It required a development over hundreds of years and the Roman discipline as well. Only this *one* nation of antiquity really succeeded in this, and in doing so it won hegemony over all the others.

First it was discovered that a group of individual warriors fought with the greatest effect when they joined together in a unified and effective mass. But this mass was slow and awkward and highly sensitive on its flanks and rear. The majority of weapons in the mass could not be brought into play.

But in order to establish in the place of one large mass a number of small groups that could compensate for their weakness by helping each other mutually, there was needed a new power, military discipline, which bound a number of individual fighters into a unit spiritually stronger than the sum of its parts, controlled by *one* will, standing fast, so that even the soul-shaking excitement, the melee, the noise, the fear, the danger of death in the battle—none of these things could break it up. The cohort remained firmly under the control of its leader, and the leaders followed the orders of the army commander.[8]

The cohort tactics marked the apogee of the development which the fighting skill of ancient infantry could reach. The task of the artist, the commander, from now on was not to find new formations, but to perfect and to use those he found already in existence.

The prerequisite for the cohort tactics was the professional army, which had now replaced the citizen army.

Up to the time of Marius the old forms of levying the army seem to have been maintained, even though the system had long since changed. The original general military obligation had been administered in a very mild way ever since long before the Second Punic War. During that war it had once again functioned with the greatest strictness and on the broadest scope. From that time on, it became obsolete. The armies that Rome was putting into the field were so small with relation to the number of citizens that only a few year-groups would have sufficed to fill them. But instead of repeatedly inducting and training new recruits, for the sake of equal justice, it was preferable to take experienced warriors, even if they showed little inclination in that direction. Pay, booty, and gifts associated with triumphs were so abundant, however, that often many men enlisted voluntarily. When the war against Perseus of Macedon broke out, according to Livy (42. 32), many old soldiers reported voluntarily for service, since they saw that those who had previously been in the field against Philip and Antiochus had become rich. Theoretically the general military obligation remained in force and was also used from time to time either by having the draftable men draw lots, or through the more or less arbitrary drafting of individuals by the authorities. We may assume that in the lottery those whose names were drawn were not prevented from arranging for a suitable substitute, and with a system of discretionary designation by the authorities, the well-to-do, who were hard to spare from the conduct of their business, were favored or were able to escape service through bribery. To what a large extent the concept of service obligation had already been weakened in the second century B.C. can be recognized particularly from the fact that there are numerous reports to the effect that recruits could not be assembled for campaigns that were dangerous and gave promise of little booty. The men who were called up had all kinds of excuses for escaping induction, and there was a general hesitancy to delve into their reasons. Finally, however, there was nothing else to do but attack the problem squarely.[9]

Repeated efforts were made to bring a certain degree of order into this system of administrative arbitrariness. Although we read in Polybius of the decree that the Roman citizen was obligated to accomplish 16 campaigns, and even 20 in case of necessity, at one place in Appian we find the observation that whoever had participated in 6 campaigns was justified in demanding his discharge. It appears that Caius Gracchus renewed these kinds of limitations on service or instituted still others, all of which, however, had to be removed when the Cimbrian invasion created panic in Rome and the nation was not able to dispense with the services of its tried and thoroughly trained soldiers.[10] To bring true system and dependable order into a levy that demands unlimited justice but has only a limited need is impossible; we shall see this illustrated later in the case of Frederick William I of Prussia. The military principle of having men of long service naturally always overshadows the humane one, which, for the sake of fairness, would divide the burden more or less evenly, and the inclination to remain completely in military status shown by many soldiers who have become estranged from civil life through long service favors this tendency. Thus there developed a contradiction of form and content, a peculiar caricature of a levy that was actually composed of administrative arbitrariness and free recruiting, or "shanghaiing," as it is called in English naval history. If the consuls applied the formal law too strictly, the citizens felt that that was tyranny, and they called on the people's tribunes for help. Livy reports on two different occasions, for the year 150 B.C. and for 138 B.C. (*Epitome*, Chapters 48 and 55), cases of such controversies where the people's tribunes threw the consuls into prison. Marius now ended all the antiquated forms and established a direct system of recruiting. The more capitalism and slavery tended to grind down between them the old middle class and peasant classes, the more material Italy provided for the recruiting officer, and Marius supposedly did not even hesitate to enlist slaves.[11] Even then the general military service obligation was in no way removed legally, and later it again formed the basis for levies, but just as the army organization had already long been characterized by its mercenary aspect, from now on it also had the corresponding forms.

Because of the granting of citizenship a few years later to all Italians, the difference between the truly Roman legions and those of the allies, too, was removed. This difference, of course, had always been only a political, not a military one, somewhat like the troops of the Rhine Alliance, Italians, and Swiss in the army of Napoleon. There was no significant difference in organization or combat techniques. The *auxilia* (auxiliary troops), which appeared in the Roman armies after the end of the Second Punic War, were of a different kind; they were special branches of troops, like archers and slingers, or barbarians classified by tribal types. The cavalry, especially, consisted exclusively of such elements.

EXCURSUS

1. My concept of the history of the Roman military obligation differs in important

aspects from that commonly held up to the present. Whereas I have taken as a point of departure that this obligation was absolutely general in the strictest sense in the small original canton, the prevailing concept holds that the obligation only spread on a gradual basis and finally became general at the time of the Punic Wars. Whereas originally all who possessed less than 12,500 (or 11,000) asses had been exempt from service, according to this concept, the limit was later lowered to 4,000 asses or even less for army duty, and the lowest stratum was conscripted for sea duty. In my opinion, since the military obligation was already general before this time, the introduction of sea duty did not constitute a new obligation, previously nonexistent, which was initiated for the poorer men, but quite the contrary: there was created a saving condition for the well-to-do. Whoever had a fortune of more than 4,000 asses was liable for the draft only for land duty and not as a ship's crew member. In no way, however, did this mean that the lower classes were exempted from army duty. This point follows definitely from the fact that there were even formed after Cannae two legions of slaves. They would certainly not have resorted to this extreme expedient if there had still been available a whole class of citizens that could have been levied. In that case they would, after all, have preferred to give the equipment to the citizens and to assign the slaves as oarsmen. The words of Polybius (4. 17. 1–3) conform very well to this concept. He says that everybody had a service obligation up to the age of forty-six, "with the exception of those men whose worth is assessed at less than 400 drachmas; all of these men are used in naval service."* In the second century, at the time Polybius wrote those words, Rome needed only a part, usually only a rather small part, of the service-obligated men. For army service, it is probable that in most cases volunteers would suffice to fill the positions. The wealthy classes were spared, or they were able to obtain favor for themselves. For the very unpopular seaman's and oarsman's service, the levy had to be stricter.[12] For this service, therefore, it was principally the proletarians that were selected. The limit of 400 drachmas (4,000 asses) given by Polybius, presumably was not based on the law but was an administrative measure, a senate decree that was modified according to the circumstances. And so it will happen that, whereas Polybius names 4,000 as the limit, Gellius closes the class of proletarians and *capite censi* (those reckoned by the head) with 1,500 and 375 asses. That the *aerarius* (citizen of the lowest class) had a military obligation in the period of the Second Punic War, as Mommsen had already correctly realized (*Staatsrecht*, 3: 252), is also directly proved by several accounts in Livy (24. 18; 27. 11; and 29. 37). These accounts are completely convincing and they necessarily eliminate the last possible doubt. It would be entirely impossible for us to be told how people were classified as *aerarii* and simultaneously sent into the field, or that a censor threatened to classify the entire citizenry as *aerarii*, if there had been tied to this status the legal concept of exemption from service.

The prevailing opinion approaches mine to some extent in that it concedes that, in cases of emergency and on exceptional occasions, levies were made without regard to classes and census. As Mommsen expresses it, the reform of Marius consisted of his changing the extraordinary procedure into the regular one. This expedient seems to me impracticable, (1) because I believe I have proven that, even in the earlier period, there did not exist a limitation of service obligation based on "classes"; (2) because in any event, after a general military service obligation had existed on a practical basis throughout the entire Second Punic War and had become a part of the legal consciousness, it seems completely unthinkable that this duty or this right, whichever way one wishes to express it, would have again been limited to the upper classes. It is correct that the land army took on a certain somewhat higher social status, because the proletarians were principally levied for the fleet, and possibly the ability to provide one's weapons also played a certain role, so that a very poor person could not directly become a hoplite.[13] But if a proletarian first went into the army as a *veles* and then applied again as already being a somewhat better-trained and more disciplined soldier, certainly we cannot assume that he was not finally made a hoplite.

If, then, a general military obligation existed in Rome, it is nevertheless clear that it must already have been administered very laxly throughout the entire second century. The census counts of the second century go from 243,704 up to 337,452 (in the year 164–163 B.C.);[14] a year-group of recruits therefore numbered at least 10,000 to 15,000 men. The army that was levied on a regular basis consisted of 4 legions, or some 18,000 to 20,000 men. Since we may surely assume that certainly many, and probably *most* of those who became soldiers at all remained in the army and served their 16, 20, or even more years, in normal times not more than 1,000 to 2,000 recruits needed to be called up yearly—that is, instead of all the eligibles, only about a tenth of their number. The regulation that one needed to have served in 10 campaigns in order to occupy public office was certainly no longer observed. Nevertheless, in a country so militarily oriented it was necessary to have belonged to the army if one wished to play a role in public life, and in addition to those who were attracted by the military profession itself, there were no doubt also more than a few young men who were ready, for this political reason, to bear arms for a few summers. And so it was easy to find sufficient numbers of the most willing and militarily most useful elements. Of course, for the thankless war in Spain against Numantia it was reportedly difficult to get either officers or men—a further proof that it was no longer a question of a real, regular levy as a normal thing.

Polybius (6. 19) describes for us how the entire body of service-qualified Romans assembled annually in Rome for the levy ("If they plan on making an enrollment of soldiers, they announce in the assembly the day on which all the Romans of the proper age will have to present themselves")* and the soldiers were chosen from among them by tribes and were allocated to the legions.

According to the description, that was an ideal, a procedure that in reality must have appeared somewhat different. The entire group of service-qualified Romans would have been 150,000 to 200,000, and they could not possibly have converged on the capital each year from all of Italy.

We must therefore imagine that each tribe was responsible for providing enough men so that the needs could be filled. There was no check, then, on those who were absent, and the whole assembly passed for a muster of all the service-qualified men. If at any time higher demands had to be made and there were not enough volunteers on hand, then there was a true drafting and a drawing of lots among the obligated candidates.[15] In what manner that was done, we do not know. At any rate not in such a way that all the service-qualified men first assembled in Rome, with the most appropriate ones and those who could be spared from other duties selected out and a drawing of lots conducted among them, or in such a way that only precisely that group that happened to be the youngest year-group was inducted. Probably there took place ahead of time, in the tribe, a preliminary examination and a designation of those who were qualified, so that at the moment of the real levy in Rome only a manageable number appeared.

These remarks could possibly be accommodated to the prevailing concept. But the significant question remains whether in the second century the replacements for the Roman army were basically limited to the sons of the middle class or whether it was already in effect a professional army, which in fact retained (to the extent that the proletarians entered the navy, in case there was a levy for the latter) only a certain citizen-peasant character. In the former case Marius' reform would have placed the army on a completely different basis and would have created something completely new; in the other case it would have given to something that already existed only a corresponding form, for that remnant of citizen-peasant characteristic was not completely eliminated, even with Marius, but only quite gradually died off.

With this explanation of mine, based on the figures for the population and the army handed down to us, there is another source that cannot be reconciled, a source on which the prevailing opinion is strongly based and which up to now has been regarded as a real cornerstone and base for the history of the Roman military constitution. This is the account that Sallust (*Bellum Iugurthinum*, Chapter 86) gives of the army reform of Marius: "Milites scribere, non more majorum neque ex classibus, sed uti cujusque lubido erat, capite censos plerosque." ("He enrolled soldiers, not from the classes, in the manner of our forefathers, but at each man's pleasure—for the most part from among those 'reckoned by their head.'") By a natural and literal interpretation, we would have to conclude that up to that point the levy took place according to classes—that is, by the ancient Servian classes based on wealth—and the proletarians (*capite censi*) had no service obligation. That this was not accurate has now long been recognized. Polybius, who certainly must have known, reports nothing of a levy according to classes, and he has only those evaluated under 4,000 asses going to the fleet. This has been explained by claiming that the original Servian census of the fifth class had been lowered from 12,500 to 4,000 asses and that Sallust did not mean a levy according to the 5 different classes, but he considered the "classes" as a whole on the one side, the proletarians on the other.

I consider that to be a forced distortion of the sense of the passage. Sallust really believed what he said, that up to the time of Marius there still existed some vestige of the levy according to the Servian classes, but as small as the levy by the Servian class system might have been, just as small, of course, was the levy by the system of classes created in 179 B.C. We are confronted here with nothing more than the fact that Sallust, just as did Cicero, lived under the illusion created by the "Commentaries of King Servius" concerning the older Roman constitution, and that he pondered the question of what had become of this ancient arrangement, when and under what circumstances it had been eliminated, and found no other answer than that it must have happened under Marius, when, of course, a great reform took place. That such errors are possible in the works of very important historians I can document at once with very illustrious examples.

Everybody will believe that Heinrich von Sybel or Heinrich von Treitschke knew the history of the development of the Prussian army, and whenever the two say precisely the same thing, future generations will consider it as presumptuous to doubt such a statement. Both of them, however, place the idea of universal military service in the regime of Frederick William I, although it is known not to have been introduced until the regime of Frederick William III, in the Wars of Liberation. Sybel *Founding of the German Empire* (*Begründung des Deutschen Reiches*, 1: 32) calls the canton regulation of 1733 the "first step toward universal military service," and Treitschke, *German History* (*Deutsche Geschichte*, 1: 75; see also 153), finds that as early as in the regime of Frederick the Great "one of the pillars that support the national structure, the concept of universal military service, had slowly started to waver." In this case even the source of the error can be established. Max Lehmann, in his early work *Knesebeck und Schön* (p. 284) had written that Frederick William I "had seen the idea of universal service, even if not in its full glow, at least in a half-light." This comment made a very strong impression at the time; Sybel and Treitschke certainly believed they needed only to repeat it, but they made the mistake that it contains much more serious still than it was originally, because of the expressions they use. No other than Max Lehmann himself has recently done the most to bring about a better recognition of the situation. It is the basic concept of his *Scharnhorst* that the universal military service obligation was not the continuation but the diametrical opposite of the Old Prussian army constitution and of the entire Old Prussian nation. What Frederick William I wanted was the sharpest possible distinction between the status of citizen and soldier. In his eyes the universal military service obligation meant absolutely nothing different from what likewise existed in all the other nations of his time—France, Austria, Russia—namely, that the ruler had the right to levy his subjects for military service according to his discretion. Today, however, we understand as universal military obligation not only an abstract principle, but a practical system such as Prussia, and Prussia alone among all nations, has possessed since 1813.

In the other sense of the expression we would have to say that France and Austria, too, had already had a universal military obligation before 1870, which would amount to a play on words. It was obviously the possibility of this ambiguity, however, that deceived two such great scholars as Sybel and Treitschke into their error—one that, if it had been called to their attention, they would naturally have realized immediately themselves and would have admitted.

The reader will, I hope, excuse the lengthy explanation of this analogy, but it is of the greatest importance from the methodological viewpoint. Again and again in the course of this study I have found myself in a position where I was forced, on the basis of critical analysis, to reject definite statements of the ancient authors concerning performances and organizational arrangements of their nations, as with Herodotus' 8-*stadia* run at Marathon, Livy's description of manipular combat, Thucydides' figure on the number of Athenian citizens, and now Sallust's statement concerning Roman recruiting. However firmly tied together my conclusions may seem to me, I can still at times hardly avoid concern about whether the high-towered structure will be capable of withstanding all the storms of contradiction, and I must consequently seek to give the Gothic walls of my building an unshakable strength by means of buttresses formed on the firmest stone of the latest indisputable facts.

The concept of the later generation concerning the original classes has also given rise to the account by Livy 10. 21 to the effect that, during the terror caused by the Gauls in 295 B.C., there was ordered before the battle of Sentinum, "*omnis generis hominum dilectum haberi*" ("that a levy be made from every class of man"), or Orosius 4. 1. 3, from Livy, that, when Pyrrhus was approaching in 280 B.C., the legions were brought up to strength with proletarians, who were actually always supposed to have remained in the city in order to provide offspring.

2. The transition from citizen status to soldier status seems to have been provided by the *evocati* (veterans recalled to the colors), concerning whose nature it is difficult to come to a clear understanding. The solution probably is that the name had various meanings in the different periods. Such men supposedly already existed in 455 B.C. (Dionysius 10. 43). Historically, we find them, as one might expect, from the end of the Second Punic War on; they are former soldiers who voluntarily returned to active duty. When, however, was a former soldier an *evocatus*?

The legal service obligation lasted, of course, up to one's forty-sixth year and covered, for the infantryman, 16 years—in case of emergency, 20. According to this, an *evocatus*, even with uninterrupted service, would have always been a man of thirty-three, at the very least, and normally more like a minimum of forty years old. In this case, however, their number could have been only very small.

We may therefore picture in the second century the *evocatus* as a man whom, even though still legally obligated to serve, the replacement authorities would really no longer have been allowed to take, for reasons of fairness, but who voluntarily signed up for duty. When in 200 B.C. the Roman people decided on the war against Philip of Macedon, it was at the same time definitely established that nobody from the ranks of the veterans who had served in the Second Punic War could be forced into service, and that only volunteers might be taken (Livy 31. 8). Such volunteers, "*rengagés*" (reenlistees), "*Kapitulanten,*" formed the nucleus of the new army. In the following year, however, they mutinied, saying they had been embarked for Macedon against their will, and demanded their discharge. When, later on, there existed for a while the provision that 6 years of service gave one the right to request discharge, all those who served longer than 6 years would have been considered as *evocati*.

As a purely mercenary status now gradually permeated the system, recognizing no other limitation on length of service than that imposed by fitness, there was no longer any place for *evocati* in the previous sense of the word, and whenever and however we find them mentioned, it is always a question either of temporarily levied troops,[16] or they are of another type. Now they form a unique troop,[17] they have their own commander,[18] they have horses:[19] a man who has been *primus pilus* (centurion of the first maniple of the *triarii*) is later an *evocatus*.[20] For this reason I prefer to assume that it was a question of a kind of staff guard into which the oldest and those with the best records of service were transferred.[21] When Caesar reports that at Pharsalus Pompey had 2000 *evocati* whom he distributed along the entire line of battle, this number may be strongly exaggerated; for the indicated purpose, however, it would be quite appropriate. The *evocati* were no longer, as in the second century, the veterans who formed the framework of every maniple, but a small elite unit that no longer needed to perform ordinary service but took their places in the formation on the day of battle. At Thapsus, not only the generals (*legati*) but also the *evocati* were gathered around Caesar, demanding that he give the order for the battle. Later, Octavian is supposed to have assembled 10,000 veterans around him as a bodyguard,[22] obviously a stratagem to persuade old soldiers to reenter the service, so that they could be called to the colors in a different form from that of the ordinary legionary service, with granting of the privileges that were normal for the *evocati*.

The passages where *evocati* are mentioned in the sources have been assembled in Marquardt's work, 2: 387, and in Fröhlich, *Caesar's Method of Waging War* (*Kriegswesen Cäsars*), p. 42, where also the indication as "staff guard" is articulated.

3. The essay by G. Veith, "Tactics of the Cohort Legion" ("Die Taktik der Kohortenlegion") in *Klio* 7 (1907): 303 and in *Ancient Battlefields* (*Antike Schlachtfelder*) 3: 701, is based, in its polemics against me as well as in its positive conclusions, on nothing more than misunderstandings and contradictions. The author explains (p. 312) that a long, continuous front is the opposite of a mobile, elastic body and is the most cumbersome formation in existence. The presentation of proof is superfluous, however, since it is, after all, the same that I, too, presented by developing the value of the intervals between the maniples and the cohorts. The difference is that, by my concept, the intervals are filled up at the moment of impact, the beginning of the fight, by having individual men of the same maniple springing forward from the rear into the small gaps, while whole units (centuries, maniples, cohorts) move up from the second echelon into the larger intervals, whereas, according to Veith's idea, rather large intervals remain between cohorts even during the fight, for the sake of maneuverability. At the same time, however, Veith himself remarks (p. 328) that "dangerously large intervals" were not to be permitted; (p. 324) that, once troops are engaged in hand-to-hand combat, one can no longer control their movement, and (p. 328, note) that the closer the battle came to the decisive point, the more limited the intervals became (by having men move up from behind) and the more cohesive the whole front became.

One need not reflect long to realize that what Veith postulates for the decisive moment of the battle—the cohesive front—is necessary for the battle in general. For, wherever there was a gap in the front at any time during the battle, the side that had a continuous front had the capability of attacking the opponents from both front and flank. Or are we to imagine that those warriors who as they came upon a gap in the enemy's line as they drove forward, came to a standstill in front of it? The enemy's penetration into the gaps could not be prevented from the second echelon, for before help could arrive, the damage was already done, both the physical and, even more importantly, the spiritual. And afterward there was not much that could be done to help the situation, since obviously the soldiers who had penetrated straight into the line could hold toward the front, whereas the flanking files behind them sufficed to cut off from the flanks the enveloped ranks of the enemy, which, of course, had to defend themselves from the front. Those who were attacked in this way from their right, the unshielded side, were particularly defenseless. Veith believes that those, too, who had penetrated into the gaps were, for their part, attacked from three sides. To what extent? Those who up to that point had been fighting toward their front could, after all, not suddenly ignore the enemy there and turn toward the flank? There is a great difference in whether a unit penetrates the enemy front and thereby drives into the midst of enemy troops or whether a unit is enveloped on both sides and thereby becomes surrounded by the enemy on three sides. The first-mentioned unit pushes forward and the following ranks naturally follow up precisely at that point; the second-mentioned unit, however, is being pushed and within a very short time it is crushed. Veith is right when he concludes that a penetration into a gap that has intentionally been left open is not as dangerous as when the enemy has created the gap by putting a unit to flight. That is quite obvious, for that would already amount to a partial defeat. But that does not eliminate the fact that any gap occurring during a battle between two front lines fighting with close-combat weapons is highly dangerous and can become decisive. Even if the aid that the second echelon is supposed to bring does not arrive too late to do any good at all, it can at best only succeed in throwing back the soldiers who have made the penetration and in filling the gap—that is, in establishing the condition that Veith has told us is disadvantageous! In so doing, the creator of these astonishing battle scenes constantly refers to the fact that he is an experienced military man!

In order to prove his thesis, Veith even goes to the extent of claiming (p. 313) that the various units, if they had taken advantage of the terrain during the approach march, would not have been capable at the moment of impact of suddenly joining together in a continuous line and closing all the intervals. There is no reason in the world why not, as soon as one realizes that the second echelon is following at a slight distance behind the first, and the third closely behind the second. The *legati*, for whom Veith has trouble finding a battle assignment, have the mission, as obvious as it is important, of seeing to it that, whenever gaps open up in the first echelon during the approach march that are too large to be filled by individual soldiers from this same echelon, the appropriate unit from the second, or, if necessary, even from the third echelon is alerted and led forward to fill the gap.

There is, naturally, no question of Veith's producing documentary source proof. Everything that seems to prove his point is based on the constant confusing of intervals in the approach march with intervals in battle. Or on the other hand, for example, when the author draws for this purpose on the battles that Caesar describes in 5. 15, and 5. 34, he loses sight of the fact that in Caesar's account it is not at all a question of pitched battles.

Consequently, I repeat: I am completely in agreement with Veith that there were intervals between the maniples (or, as appropriate, the cohorts) and that such intervals have to exist, because the colonels and generals cannot otherwise control the individual tactical units. And, on the other hand, Veith is also completely of the same opinion as I, that, once the troops are engaged in hand-to-hand combat, they can no longer be controlled. So, when Veith concludes from Polybius 15. 15. 7 that intervals did exist, he is correct; but when he concludes that the intervals were also present during the hand-to-hand combat, this conclusion is inadmissible.

4. (Added in the third edition.) It is generally accepted that the Roman citizen cavalry disappeared after the Second Punic War and was replaced by barbarian mercenaries. Nevertheless, in the *Zeitschrift für österreichischen Gymnasien* 22 (1911): 385, 481, 577, Soltau has pointed out that one must be more careful in making distinctions in this area. As actual cavalry, the citizen mounted groups were indeed replaced by foreign mercenaries; they continued to exist on a modest scale, however, as units for the sons of senatorial and well-to-do citizen families and served as Horse Guards, couriers, and in other similar duties. (See below, Book VII, Chapter I, Comment 3.)

5. Oehler, in his "New Studies on the Battle of Muthul" ("Neue Forschungen zur Schlacht bei Muthul") *Jahreshefte des österreichischen archäologischen Instituts* 12 (1909): 327 and 13 (1910): 257, describes a combat situation from which I can only con-

clude that the sources present nothing which might have any military history value.

6. On the question of the individual load carried by the Roman soldier, I simply accepted, in the first editions of this volume, the findings of Stoffel, and only in the second volume (Book IV, Chapter IV), in discussing feudalism, did I treat this subject more thoroughly. Stoffel rejects as impossible the suggestion that the legionary carried provisions for 16 or even possibly 30 days. More recently there has appeared the very significant study by Stolle. *The Roman Legionary and his Equipment* (*Der römische Legionär und sein Gepäck*) (Strasbourg, 1914), in which the author seeks again to prove that, although the 30-day figure was indeed false, the 16-day estimate was definitely corroborated by the sources, and not as an exceptional situation nor on the basis that the load became smaller each day, but simply as the normal thing.

He reduces somewhat the weight of the flour that was carried by showing that the soldier had some of it in cracker form. His estimate is as follows:

Bread, crackers, flour	11.369 kilograms
Meat	1.910 "
Cheese	0.436 "
Salt	0.327 "
Wine or lemonade	0.327 "
Total provisions	14.369 kilograms
Equipment	5.278 "
Tools	7.149 "
Total baggage	26.796 kilograms
Weapons (minimum weight)	14.463 "
Total load (minimum)	41.259 kilograms

Stolle does not overlook the fact that this load is a very heavy one, and he seeks to explain it by showing that the Romans made only short daily marches. (See below, Book VII, Chapter III, Conclusion.)

One must concede, of course, that under special circumstances the soldier can carry 41¼ kilograms, and even more; but it is a question here of the *normal* load. In my discussion in the second volume, which, unfortunately, Stolle was not familiar with, I have pointed out how drastically a load of more than 31 kilograms reduces the soldier's march capabilities. Is it to be supposed that, in order to eliminate the need for 300 mules for a legion, the Romans actually deprived their armies of the possibility of making longer marches—say over 15 kilometers? Statements by Cicero and Ammian are not sufficient to make this point credible—in Cicero's case because he can be suspected of rhetorical exaggeration, and in Ammian's case, even though he was militarily knowledgeable, because by his time the disciplined troops had long since disappeared and barbarian mercenaries were the least willing of all to have themselves heavily burdened. Consequently, I consider as completely worthless any evidence from the period following the fall of the Severians. Even at the time of the Roman Republic, when the discipline had already become lax, the legionaries were so anxious to lighten their load that they privately secured an orderly or a pack animal (Sallust, *Bellum Iugurthinum* 45. 2; Plutarch, *Marius*, Chapter 13). The evidence of Cicero and Ammian is all the less convincing in that it is directly contradicted by the evidence in Josephus, *History of the Jewish War* 3. 5. 5, according to which the soldier himself carried provisions for only *three* days. Stolle did not see fit to ignore this evidence, even if he did interpret it falsely. Even with only three days of provisions, the legionary was already quite heavily burdened.

NOTES FOR CHAPTER II

1. J. J. Müller, in *Philologus* 34 (1876): 125, has already observed that the four regular legions could not possibly have absorbed the entire mass of service-obligated young men. He believes therefore that, depending on need, the youngest year-groups—e.g., ten —were inducted. But even that would give much too large a number.

2. Fröhlich, in *Caesar's Method of Waging War* (*Kriegswesen Cäsars*) pp. 13–14, effectively raises doubts whether the definitive introduction of the cohort tactics should really be ascribed to Marius. Madwig believed that it did not occur until the War with the Allies. On the other hand, it is perhaps possible to prove its existence as early as the Jugurthine War. It is my opinion, however, that every probability points to the fact that Marius was the reformer. The cohorts that are referred to in the Jugurthine War (Sallust 51. 3; 100. 4) need not be considered as tactical units but merely as parts of the legion, and if, according to a Sisenna fragment, there was still on one occasion in the War with the Allies a battle by maniples, there is little to be concluded from that, since, after all, there were maniples in existence both before and after that event.

3. Nitzsch, in *History of the Roman Republic* (*Geschichte der römischen Republik*) (published by Thouret), 1: 181, has already drawn attention to the fact that if, after Cannae, legions appeared formed up one behind the other, that was related to the fact that in the newly formed legions the differences of age did not play the same role as in earlier days.

4. When we read in Livy 7. 34 (for the year 340 B.C.) that the *hastati* and *principes* of a legion were detached, or in 10. 14 (for the year 297 B.C.) the *hastati* of a legion, that point has, of course, no historical value, but it may be cited here as a reflection of the experience of the second century B.C.

5. In the Livy *Epitome*, Book 67, it is stated that in the battle of Arausio 80,000 soldiers, 40,000 supply train drivers and campfollowers (*calones et lixae*) were killed. These figures are certainly very exaggerated, but it is perhaps worthy of note that at this time a strength amounting to 50 percent of that of the combatants was attributed to the supply train. We could conclude from this that even before the time of Marius the *veliti* had disappeared for the most part, or at times perhaps completely, out of the legions, and the orderly and supply train system had been organized differently, on a practical basis.

6. Stolle, in *The Romans' Camp and Army* (*Das Lager und Heer der Römer*) (1912) opposes the idea that the number 6,000 is to be regarded as normal for the legion, and therefore 600 for the cohort, and we must agree with him that it is not as well founded as had been believed up to now. Nevertheless, it seems quite plausible to me, and the differences can, at least for our purposes, be ignored.

7. Of course, that has not been proved directly, but as Marquardt has remarked (2: 339), it is very probable. See also Polybius 11. 23, where it is stated that three maniples were called a cohort.

8. The passage where Polybius describes this quality of the Roman battle formation—that it was at the same time impenetrable (consequently in close order) and capable in all its individual units of turning in any desired direction (15. 15. 7)—is unfortunately somewhat obscure in its wording, but according to the sense quite clear and very valuable. The two characteristics of impenetrability and mobility can only be united by having intervals between the cohorts and keeping these intervals as small as possible. The large intervals that Veith (in Vol. 3, Part 2, p. 701) uses this passage to support are not only not proved by it, but are in fact contradicted, since a battle formation with intervals in its front is not impenetrable. The small intervals, as I conceive them, do not remove the quality of impenetrability, since they are closed up at the moment of impact by the press from the rear.

9. Livy 43. 14. Polybius 35. 4.

10. See the source citations in Mommsen, *Roman History* (*Römische Geschichte*) 2: 107 and 175; Marquardt, *The Roman National Constitution* (*Römische Staatsverfassung*), 2: 381.

11. Plutarch, *Marius*, Chapter 9.

12. That it was a question of this kind of service, and not that of a marine infantryman, is correctly pointed out and documented in Marquardt, *The Roman National Constitution* (*Römische Staatsverfassung*), 2: 380, note 10.

13. According to Polybius 6. 39. 15, the nation provided clothing and weapons if necessary but deducted their cost from the soldier's pay. This was supposedly discontinued by Tiberius Gracchus (Mommsen, *Roman History* (*Römische Geschichte*) 2: 107); but according to Tacitus (*Annales* 1. 17), it occurred again also under the empire, and the soldiers complained about it.

14. The figures 394,736 and 394,336 for the years 125 and 115 B.C. have been questioned by Beloch, with good reason.

15. Appian, *De Rebus Hispanorum*, Chapter 49, for the year 149 B.C.

16. Caesar, *Bell. Gall.* 3. 20. 2.

17. Cicero, *Ad familiares* 15. 4. 3.

18. Cicero, *Ad familiares* 3. 6.-5.

19. Caesar, *Bell. Gall.* 7. 65.

20. *Bell Civ.* 3. 91.

21. Nevertheless, I do not believe that the volunteers who offered their services to the consul and, according to Polybius 6. 31. 2, had their own area in camp, were meant under the term *evocati*, but rather that the former were more important men. The *evocati* of that period were not yet a privileged group in the sense in which Marquardt (2: 338, footnote 1) conceives of them.

22. Appian, *Bell. Civ.* 3. 40.

Chapter III

The Centurions

The real key man of the new Roman military system was the centurion. In reality, the status of each person had changed, from the army commander to the private soldier and the train orderly, and in the final analysis one position is as important as another, but in the new army system it was the centurions who formed the truly *Roman* aspect of the organization. The generals and higher officers of Rome were similar to those we see in other nations, and the soldiers were not significantly different from other mercenaries. But the centurions were a completely individual phenomenon.

To date, nobody has succeeded in establishing a completely clear picture of the social structure of the Roman people in the last century of the Republic. We may see clearly enough in our mind's eye the aristocracy, possessing great riches, who resemble the Greek pattern and rule the country through the Senate and the offices they hold. This group does not form a closed caste; it is not impossible for a person of marked talent of one or another kind from the common people to move up into the ruling circle and even eventually to find a warm welcome and high position there. Nevertheless, this kind of upward mobility remains very infrequent. The spirit of the ruling aristocracy is that of an inherited status.

No less clear to us is the status of a class of rich merchants, who, as such, are excluded from the high offices and the Senate and are filled with a certain political envy of the ruling aristocracy. Dating from the time of the class division according to property, these merchants are called the "riders," a title that, since it had become a status symbol, has tended to be translated as "knight," a designation by which, one must add, we should be careful not to let ourselves be deceived.

Finally, we can recognize at the other end of the social scale a large urban and rural proletariat, minor citizens and small farmers.

In the middle lie the positions that are not clear to us: how large, how formed, how situated economically, how articulated class-wise, and how educated were those social levels that we designate today as the real middle class? It is this middle group, still more than the highest and the lowest groups of the free citizenry, that was dislocated socially by the institution of slavery and which, consequently, is the hardest to compare with modern conditions. However this may be, and regardless of what may be discovered in future research, it is sufficient for us to establish this point, because this group, socially weak as it was under any circumstances, had no place at all in the organization we are discussing, the Roman army.

Up to a certain point, this situation is inherent in the nature of every mercenary army: either the army has no special social distinctions at all, or the lowest and highest layers of society are brought together in it, but the middle class, the social layer which, of course, may be broader or narrower or may be considered to be broader or narrower, is completely missing.

The marked distinction between officer corps and men that characterizes modern armies (up to 1914) and which we did not yet find in ancient Greece first appears with the Romans, but with a different system of levels from that which seems natural to us today in Germany. The officer corps, in the modern sense, was composed in Rome only of generals (*legati*) and field-grade officers (*tribuni militum*). These field-grade officers, however, were the young gentlemen of the two aristocracies, the hereditary and the "knights' group," who had chosen the military profession. On the average, their military capabilities were small,[1] but their aristocratic education had nevertheless provided them with so many of the prerequisites for their profession that they could become good officers, and whenever one of them was gifted with natural military talents, he could easily reach high command positions while still in the best years of youthful elasticity and could develop into an excellent general. The experience of all periods teaches us that there is a psychological rapport between aristocracy and military command, that the former is a particularly favorable soil for the growth of the latter.

There was only a gradual development of a firm relationship between the Roman senior officers and the tactical units of the army; the generals (*legati*) first took command of a legion because of a special mission, and the tribunes did likewise with the cohorts. The tribunes, in rotation as determined by lot, simultaneously exercised supervision over the laying out and the policing of the camp and the guard duty and provided for military justice and the execution of the higher punishments.[2]

Of a completely different type from these aristocrats were the men who carried out the duties of the present-day company-grade officers, the centurions. They came from the ranks of the common soldiers, who, in turn, were recruited principally from the lowest, uneducated layers of the population. The centurions received no more than twice the pay of a private, which Caesar raised from 120 *denarii* (90 marks) to 225 (165 marks) per annum. The centurions, therefore, corresponded in status to our noncommissioned officers, but their functions were those of our captains. They exercised discipline; the maniples and the men were in their hands.

Polybius makes the specific point (6. 24) that they were not selected simply because of their courage, but especially on the basis of their leadership ability and their steadfastness ("as leaders, steadfast and deep of mind").*

Their situation should be clearest for our purposes if we compare them with our first sergeants. The closest analogy is offered by those French captains who have been commissioned from the ranks of noncommissioned officers, always with the difference, however, that through their promotion into the officer corps they move up to a higher social level, many of the characteristics of which they naturally assume. The Roman centurion, on the other hand, remained socially what he had always been, and it was against this background that this particular position formed and maintained its unusual character. He had a proud awareness of his ability but still laid no claim to belonging to the ruling group. The centurion was a Roman patriot, brave and strict, but his field of vision was limited. He needed a higher commander above him, and he realized this. According to tradition, he was subordinate to the constitutionally elected magistrate—an election in which he, too, played a role—and the Senate. But the more he ceased to be a citizen and considered himself only a soldier, the more this concept of constitutional authority must have disappeared from his thinking, being replaced by the army commander, who had himself grown away from the forms of the old constitution.

The closest analogy to the army of the world-conquering Roman Republic is probably provided by the English army of the eighteenth century. The senior officers came from the aristocracy, and after a short period of study, started their careers as field officers; Wellington was a lieutenant colonel at the age of twenty-four. The mass of the army was recruited and was held together under the sternest discipline, but the basis was a national English one. Foreigners, who were enlisted in large numbers to fill up the ranks, formed their own units. The difference between this army and the Roman one lay in the company-grade officer corps, which in England was recruited from gentlemen, the poorer nobility and the higher bourgeois, and which was clearly distinct from the noncommissioned officer corps, whereas the Roman centurion simultaneously fulfilled the functions of both of these corps.

We hear remarkably little of the noncommissioned officers, who (together with first-class privates) were designated as *principales*. The most important noncommissioned officer is the *optio*, who seems, however, not to have been involved in actual front-line service but was used for administration, paper work.[3] The squad leaders were the *decani*, later called *caput contubernii*,[4] whom we never find mentioned, however, in the battle accounts. The burden of company command rested on the centurion, whose century was, it is true, somewhat smaller than a German company but still amounted to 100 men. But we should keep in mind that the soldiers, except in the case of newly formed legions, were almost all experienced veterans who only had to be kept in order and no longer needed training and instruction.

Besides the *optio*, we also read of the *tesserarius*, the man who received the countersign, and the *signifer* (standard bearer). We are not told, however, whether these men played any role as troop leaders.[5]

The Second Punic War had, for practical purposes, given Rome a professional army, but it was not simply as a matter of form that it remained a citizen army; the actual transition continued for a very long time.

The intermediate position between citizen army and professional army in the second century B.C. is also emphasized by the fact that, in the continuing formation of new legions and their officer corps, the individual was always assigned anew each time to a position; consequently, there still did not exist the concept of regular promotion. No doubt, the centurions were ranked among themselves in a well-defined order: the second centurion of the tenth maniple of the *hastati* was the lowest, and the first centurion of the first maniple of the *triarii*, the *primus pilus*, was the highest, but assignment to such a position had no permanent character. The consuls and war tribunes, who were also constantly alternating, assigned positions anew with each reorganization in accordance with their discretionary judgment. As long as the citizen character of the legion was predominant, there was nothing disturbing about that; even the consul for this year had, after all, to obey another one next year, and in the case of the Athenians a citizen could serve one year as army commander and might find himself the following year a private again.

The Roman centurions, however, gradually became too militarily sensitive not to regard as a grievance a demotion, which of course was often dictated by pure chance or whim. On one occasion they opposed this system, and the account that Livy (42. 33 ff.) has given us is so characteristic of the Roman state and of the life and viewpoint of the centurions that I want to insert it here verbatim.

When, in 171 B.C., war was declared against Perseus of Macedon, the Senate ordered that as many veteran centurions as possible be called to active duty, and many of them also volunteered. Twenty-three former centurions of *primus pilus* rank, however, appealed to the people's tribunes and demanded that, if they were to be called up again, they be given their former status. Since each legion had only one *primus pilus* and at first only four legions were to be organized, to be followed by four more reserve legions, it is hard to see how their demand could be fulfilled. It appears that, with this call, even a limitation of the levy itself was intended. But however that may have been, the most interesting thing for us is the account itself, which reads as follows:

> The consuls carried out the levy with much greater care than usual. Licinius also called up many veteran soldiers and centurions, and many volunteered, for they saw that those who had served in the earlier Macedonian War or against Antiochus in Asia had become rich. Since the war tribunes saw fit to call up those who had been centurions, twenty-three *primi pili* appealed to the people's tribunes after receiving their summons. Two of the latter, Marcus Fulvius Nobilior and Marcus Claudius Marcellus, referred them to the consuls, saying that those who had responsibility for the levy and prosecution of the war would have to decide. The others explained that they would look into the question of why these men had been called up, and, if any injustice had been done, they would help their fellow citizens.
>
> The matter was heard before the people's tribunes. There appeared the former consul Marcus Popillius, who was called as a legal adviser, the centurions, and the consul. Since the consul then demanded that the matter be brought before a

citizens' assembly, the people were called together. Speaking for the centurions, Marcus Popillius, who had been consul two years earlier, said: "Soldiers who have accomplished their normal service and whose physical capacities have been dulled by age and constant exertion still do not refuse to give their services for the common good; they only wish to request that they not be given a lower grade than that which they had during their previous service."

Consul Publius Licinius ordered that the Senate's decrees be read: first, the one declaring war against Perseus and then the second one, in which the Senate had ordered that as many former centurions as possible be levied for the war and had not exempted from service anyone who was not older than fifty. Then he requested that in this new war, so close to Italy, they neither hinder the war tribunes in their conduct of the levy nor prevent the consul from assigning to each man the rank which would best serve the interests of the Republic.

After the consul had spoken, Spurius Ligustinus, one of those who had appealed to the people's tribunes, asked the consul and the people's tribunes that he be allowed to address a few words to the people. With permission from all concerned, he is said to have spoken as follows: "Citizens, I, Spurius Ligustinus, come from the Crustumerium district of Sabine province. My father left me an acre of land and a small hut, in which I was born and brought up, and there I still live today. As soon as I was of the proper age, my father gave me his brother's daughter as my wife, and she brought with her nothing but freedom, chastity, and a fertility which would have been enough even for a rich home. We have six sons and two daughters, both of them already married. Four of our sons are already wearing the toga of manhood, two still wear the boy's skirt. I became a soldier under Consuls Publius Sulpicius and Caius Aurelius. In that army, which was sent to Macedon, I was a private soldier for two years, fighting against King Philip. In the third year, as a reward for my bravery, Titus Quinctius Flaminius gave me the tenth *hastati* maniple. Since, after the defeat of Philip and the Macedonians, we were brought back to Italy and discharged, I immediately volunteered and was sent to Spain with Consul Marcus Porcius Cato. Those who came to know him and other commanders through long service in the field know that, among all the living commanders, none was a sharper observer and judge of bravery. This commander considered me worthy enough to be assigned the first *hastati* century. For my third period of service I was once again a volunteer, for the army that was sent against the Aetolians and King Antiochus. I was given the position of first centurion with the *principes* by Manius Acilius. After King Antiochus had been driven away and the Aetolians defeated, we were brought back to Italy, and after that I served twice in the legions that did one year of service. Then I served twice again in Spain, once under Quintus Fulvius Flaccus and once again under the Praetor Tiberius Sempronius Gracchus. I was brought along by Flaccus with the others from his province whom he took to his triumph because of their bravery. I was asked by Tiberius Gracchus to go with him to the province assigned him to govern. Four times within a few years I was *primus pilus*; thirty-four times I was rewarded by my commanders for bravery; I was given six civic crowns. I spent twenty-two years of service in the army, and I am older than fifty. Even if I had not completed all these years of service and were not exempt because of my age, it would still be easy for me to avoid service, since I can provide four soldiers in my place. But I want to make this point clear: I will never seek exemption as long as any commander who is forming an army considers me a worthy soldier. It is up to the war tribunes to decide what position they consider me worthy of. I will do my best to see that nobody in the army excels me in bravery; that I have always done so can be testified to by my commanders as well as by those who served with me. You, too, comrades, even if you succeed in having your rights recognized through this appeal, must, since as youths you never did anything against the authority of the officials and the Senate, justly subject yourselves now to the power of the Senate and the consuls and consider as honorable any position in which you can be useful to the common good."

After he had spoken thus, Consul Publius Licinius praised him extensively and led him from the assembly into the Senate. There, too, he was thanked with the full approval of the Senate, and because of his courage the war tribunes gave him the first maniple of the first legion. The other centurions gave up their appeal and obediently followed the call to service.

Unexplained in this little story is the reason why Ligustinus, who at the start seems to speak very forcefully in favor of the centurions, finally comes out against their demand. The situation seems to place the character of Ligustinus in a questionable light. But whether the event took place in this way or somewhat differently, Ligustinus' speech—sincere or feigned—is at any rate an expression of the attitude that the ruling Roman aristocracy wanted to see among the centurions.

NOTES FOR CHAPTER III

1. Correctly noted and solidly documented but expressed somewhat too strongly by Fröhlich in *Caesar's Method of Waging War* (*Kriegswesen Cäsars*), p. 19.

2. Polybius 6. 34. One would expect that, corresponding to the 10 cohorts of the legion, 10 tribunes would be assigned; however, even under the empire, there were only 6. Vegetius 2. 12, states, "*Cohortes a tribunis vel a praepositis regebantur*" ("the cohorts ought to be commanded by tribunes or others set over them"). The contradiction in the fact that the cohort appears as the basic tactical unit but the centurion is the key leader stems from the development of the army from a general citizen levy. For a long time already, the tribunes had had the character of magistrates, whereas the centurions had become soldiers pure and simple.

3. See also the passages in Marquardt, 2: 545; Festus, p. 198, says that he had moved into the position of the old *accensus* (orderly) and on p. 184 that the centurion had chosen him "*rerum privatarum ministrum*" ("the one who attends to private affairs").

4. Vegetius 2. 7.

5. During the period of the Empire we see many titles of men with special functions who, in our system, would probably be designated as privates first-class or as noncommissioned officers with administrative functions. See I. H. Drake, *The principales of the Early Empire*, 1905, and Domaszewski, *The Rank Structure of the Roman Army* (*Die Rangordnung des römischen Heeres*) 1908.

Chapter IV

Mithridates

Fierce conflicts among the different parties, the defection of allies, and a civil war that raged back and forth through all of Italy seemed to be breaking up the Roman Empire before it was even completed and gave a Cappadocian prince the courage to rise up against Rome in order to wrest the Greek Orient away from her and unite it under his hegemony. Mithridates was by origin a Persian, perhaps a relative of the Persian royal line of Achaemenidae, by education and manner a Greek, a true product of the blending of nationalities by Alexander the Great. Through wise and powerful politics he had extended his empire beyond the shores of the Black Sea, and the Greeks, driven to despair by the Roman officials and tax collectors, shifted for the most part over to his side, notably the Athenians.

The Roman nation seemed to be in complete disorder, whereas Mithridates was uniting and controlling the strengths of his countries with royal authority. Economically and financially the Orient was undoubtedly stronger than the Occident; the Greek world and even the body of Roman emigrants made available to the Pontic King military and political talents and wise minds in abundance. The armies on both sides had essentially the characteristics of mercenary units. From all of these points it would seem that Mithridates, who was himself undoubtedly a significant personality, might well have been a match for the Romans.

Nevertheless he was defeated. After all, only part of the Greeks went over to his side; a few states, particularly Rhodes and also the Macedonians, stood by the Romans, and the base of the Roman power was too much broader and too much more militarily oriented than was the King's. Even though the Greeks gave him commanders and he was able to recruit mercenaries not only from his own subjects but also, as far as his finances allowed, from warlike barbarian peoples, he still lacked that one thing that was at the base of Rome's power, the military position with the concept of discipline resting on the national-political base of the Roman citizen concept, the centurion. With all its internal confusion, the Roman state still had enough solidity to keep it from falling apart. A man of genius, Sulla, became the commander of the army, and with that step the superiority of the Roman arms was assured. We do not know in detail how the war was fought out, since our sources have no more validity than the reports of Appian on Hannibal's battles or the accounts of the war with the Cimbri and the Teutones. The memoirs of Sulla himself, which were used by Plutarch and others, must have been boastful and vague. In the battle of Chaeronea Sulla is supposed to have defeated 120,000, or, to take the more modest figure, 60,000 Asiatics with only 15,000 infantry and 1,500 cavalry of his own. Either 100,000 or 50,000 of the enemy were reported to have been killed, whereas only 14 Romans were missing, 2 of whom were found later. Presumably the entire account of the battle is a fantasy and the battle itself amounts (as one of the sources reports)[1] to a surprise attack, for a short time later, at almost the same place, near Orchomenus, Sulla again had to meet and defeat an Asiatic army of 70,000 or 80,000 men, supposedly sent by Mithridates by ship, along with 10,000 cavalry, after he received the news of the first defeat.[2]

Later the armies of Mithridates increased to 500,000 men. It is very possible, however, that the Romans had not only qualitative but also numerical superiority. It goes without saying that a man like Mithridates was wise enough not to lead into the field incompetent masses, which would have to be supplied and would accomplish nothing worthwhile on the battlefield. To maintain experienced mercenaries in the field for many years is, however, extremely expensive, and Mithridates had to support not only a land army but also an important fleet. Sulla crossed over with an army of 30,000 men and first lay siege to Athens. If it appears incomprehensible that the great royal army, which was supposedly stationed in Macedon, made no attempt to relieve the city, which was defending itself with extreme stubbornness, the explanation probably is that that army existed only in the fantasy of our sources and that in reality only a very small force was at hand, a force that would not risk engaging the Romans until the arrival of reinforcements. In view of the kind of source materials we have, there is nothing to be gained from going into the details of these wars.

It might be appropriate to raise at this point the striking similarity between the account of Marius' war against the Cimbri and

Teutones and that of Sulla against Mithridates. Certain portions of the two accounts are completely parallel. In both cases the soldiers suddenly became afraid at the view of the great masses of the enemy; in each account a particularly descriptive report is given of how the enemy warriors filled the air with their noise and shouts and mocked the Romans behind their camp fortifications. Marius had his soldiers dig a canal in order to harden them; Sulla had his men deflect the course of the Cephisus so that the hard work would drive them to prefer fighting. Marius' soldiers finally demanded a battle, after they had become accustomed to the terrifying sight of the barbarians; Sulla's men sought the battle because they had become fed up with their digging. Why Archelaus, Mithridates' field commander,[3] did not attack the Romans while they were busy digging receives no more explanation than does the inactivity of Marius, who allowed the Teutones to march by in front of his camp for six days without taking advantage of the opportunity to destroy a sixth of them each day.

When the Cimbri were defeated and were pouring back into their camp, they were met and killed by their own wives wielding axes. When the Asiatics were fleeing, Archelaus ordered the gates of the camp closed in order to force them to turn back into the battle, and, helplessly squeezed together, their mass was cut down by the Romans. In order to heighten the impression, the Cimbri women even found time to put on black clothes; the soldiers of Mithridates had so much gold and silver on their clothing that the fear the Roman soldiers felt when facing them was increased all the more. Not only a hugely superior force was conquered by the Romans, but also an outstandingly courageous enemy; the Cimbri chained together the men composing their first rank, and the archers of Mithridates kept fighting to the very end, using their arrows as swords.

The parallel aspect of these accounts is not to be traced back to some possible imitation of one source by the other, but rather it stems from a psychological process. For the sake of attaining the greatest possible degree of glorification the writers have almost completely suppressed the truly historical events and so finally arrived at such general types and descriptions as to make the one leader and the one war look almost exactly like the other leader and the other war. Only at times there comes through the impression that we are here dealing with Marius, the coarse trooper, and there with the blasé aristocrat, Sulla; here with the rough sons of the North, there with the Asiatic king, Mithridates.

It is the same psychological process that provided the Swiss account of the Burgundian Wars with precisely the same scenes and characters as are found in the Greek accounts of the Persian Wars, but with the difference that in these latter cases we have a popular fantasy that, with all its freedom, is still complete enough and basically truthful and interested enough in the events themselves not to let the actual facts disappear, even though they are transformed and embellished. On the other hand, the Roman accounts of the victories of Marius and Sulla were the products of the inadequate fantasy of vain rhetoricians who were completely indifferent to the events themselves.

The sources on the campaigns in which Lucullus and Pompey, after the war had broken out anew, finally conquered first Mithridates and then King Tigranes of Armenia are of entirely the same type and for our purpose, at any rate, are without value.[4] The King of Armenia, who, as he looked at the Roman army, made the famous statement "Too many for a diplomatic mission, too few for an army," was himself the ruler of only a medium-sized area, which, mostly mountainous, could not provide food for a large population and therefore could not have raised a large army, and the Armenians have rarely been known for particularly warlike qualities.

NOTES FOR CHAPTER IV

1. Memnon, who also says not a word about the second battle. *Episodes of the History of Greece (Fragmenta historiae Graeciae)* (ed. Carolus Müller), 3. 542.

2. Kromayer, *Ancient Battlefields (Antike Schlachtfelder)* Vol. 2, has tried to reconstruct at Chaeronea a full-fledged battle, something that has just as little corroboration in the sources and is objectively just as impossible as the same author's battle of Magnesia. It would be superfluous to give detailed proof for this.

3. That the largest part of the army had spread out to plunder is not a sufficient reason, for if the remainder was much weaker than the Romans, we must ask ourselves again why Sulla did not take advantage of this opportunity to attack.

4. K. Eckhardt, *Die armenischen Feldzüge des Lucullus*, Berlin dissertation 1909, *Klio*, Vols. 9 and 10. The military-objective analysis is not incisive enough. Nor does Gröbe, in *Deutsche Literaturzeitung*, Vol. 47, 1910, agree with him.

Chapter V

Romans and Parthians[1]

The campaign against the Parthians undertaken by Crassus as governor of Syria forms a continuation of the wars against Mithridates and Tigranes. The Parthians were a people closely related to the Persians, and their methods of fighting were precisely those of the ancient Persians. They fought as cavalry and archers, but as the Persians had done, these mounted men also carried close-combat weapons, principally spears, in addition to their bows.

On the basis of certain expressions in the sources, writers have tried to establish the distinction that the great mass of Parthian warriors was composed of lightly armed bondsmen, whereas a quite small number of freemen were armored knights. This concept may not be completely without a thread of fact, but there is really nothing specific on this point, and there are no further conclusions concerning the events that might be drawn from this.

The Roman army had a strength of seven legions, 4,000 cavalry, and 4,000 light infantry. These appear to be very significant numbers, but since the legions were not at full strength, the total estimate must be limited to 36,000 men, whereas Alexander's army is said to have numbered 47,000 men. Further, Alexander's army was more favorably composed for the impending battle than was the Roman army: it had 7,000 cavalrymen whereas the Romans had only 4,000. We cannot establish with certainty how many of the Macedonian infantry are to be considered as lightly armed men.

In Plutarch's *Crassus* we have a quite thorough, though anecdotal, description of the events of the Roman campaign, and there is also an account in Dio Cassius. The following basic facts can therefore be established with a certain degree of probability.

It is not clear from the sources just where Crassus eventually intended to conduct his march; perhaps to Seleucia. The Parthians did not await the Romans on the other side of the Tigris but came out to meet them on the Mesopotamian plain, and the encounter took place after a few days' march. The Parthians succeeded in luring a portion of the Roman cavalry into an ambush and destroying them. This force was under the command of the younger Crassus, son of the army commander, who had distinguished himself in Gaul under Caesar and had brought 1,000 Gallic cavalry to join his father. The Roman army was now no longer in a position to continue its offensive but had to turn back. If we compare its situation with that of the 10,000 Greeks after the battle of Cunaxa, the Romans do not yet seem to have been in so much danger. Mounted archers cannot really do so much damage to a closed infantry formation with good protective weapons, and the plaintive accounts in our sources concerning the awesome shooting by the Parthians, who were accompanied by whole camel loads of reserve arrows so that they would not run out of ammunition, should not be allowed to deceive us into thinking that these mounted archers were anything other than those whom we already know from our study of military history and principally from the ancient Persian-Greek battles. To oppose them the Romans still had, after all, a certain mass of light infantry, who could shoot much more accurately on foot than the Parthians on horseback, and also the remainder of their cavalry, which could make sorties if the enemy pressed in too closely.

In addition, it was reported of the Parthians just as it had been of the Persians that in the evening they moved off to a position far from their foe, so as not to be exposed to a night attack, thus giving the Romans the possibility of making undisturbed night marches. Finally, the withdrawal that the Romans had to make was quite short, certainly not to be compared with the march of the Ten Thousand. Their encounter with the Parthians took place one day's march south of Carrhae, southeast of Edessa, only some 45 miles from the Euphrates.[2]

If, nevertheless, the Greeks had escaped while the Roman army was almost wiped out during its retreat, the reason should not be sought in any special courage of the Parthians, for the Persians, too, had not been lacking in personal courage. And we are also not inclined to attribute larger numbers to the Parthians than to the Persians (even after reducing greatly the exaggerated numbers given by the Greeks). The sources make much of the treachery of a ruling prince of this region; it is not clear, however, just what harm he really caused the Romans except for reportedly giving them false advice and fleeing with his troops before the battle. At the particular place where we would expect it, the account of the defeat of the Roman cavalry, there is no mention of him or his treachery, so that the Roman loss cannot be attributed to this betrayal. I prefer to believe that the distinguishing factor is to be found in the fact that, in the earlier situation, the Persians under Tissaphernes did not consider it necessary to overpower the Greek army through their own bloodshed; they hoped that the invaders would be completely wiped out in the Cadusian Mountains, and if the Cadusii had to suffer losses in the process, so much the better from the Persian viewpoint. The Parthians, however, had to base their actions not only on driving the Romans back but also on making it impossible for them to renew their advance later, and their success in doing this is attributable to the great mass of the Roman army. Xenophon's Greeks numbered 13,000, or, with all their orderlies, probably not more than 20,000, without a large supply train. The Romans, even after the defeat of their cavalry, still numbered 30,000 combatants, with very large supply trains, for a total certainly amounting to between 50,000 and 70,000 individuals. This great mass was unable to escape from the enemy by means of fast marches, particularly night marches, which had been so helpful for the Greeks.

The Romans did split their forces, it is true, after reaching Carrhae and taking up the continuation of their march from there. One corps, with the army commander himself, instead of moving westward toward the Euphrates, turned toward the north in order to seek cover in the Armenian mountains, but its situation was worsened by spreading demoralization. The final catastrophe was not brought on by a general battle but by negotiations, in which Crassus showed the weakness of allowing himself to participate personally and in which, whether because suspicion caused misunderstandings or the Parthians carried out an intentional betrayal, he was killed.

Two legions which were formed from the remnants of Crassus' army fought later at Pharsalus under Pompey against Caesar.

ANTONY

It is appropriate at this point to follow up the account of the defeat of Crassus by our observations of the campaign in which Antony undertook seventeen years later (36 B.C.) to avenge the dishonor of Carrhae. It appears that he prepared his campaign very carefully. His army was more than twice as large as that of Crassus,[3] including no less than 10,000 cavalry, and it had slingers whose shots carried farther than the Parthian arrows and could even penetrate armor.[4]

Antony crossed the Euphrates at the same point as Crassus (near Zeugma) and took the same direction and even approximately the same route that Alexander had once followed, directly from west to east, where the Armenian-Cadusian Mountains level off into the plain, the direction in which the cities of Edessa, Nisibis, Tigranocerta lie (or used to lie). The Parthians did not risk attacking this army. Antony crossed the Tigris, and, holding his easterly direction, he drove into Media (Atropatene), which formed a Parthian vassal state under King Artavasdes. Here the Romans were supposed to be joined by their ally, the king of Armenia, who was also named Artavasdes, with an important force. Antony's plan apparently was to depend on Armenia as a base and first of all to win Media over from the Parthian side to the Roman. The question has been raised: Why didn't he move down along the Euphrates into the fertile area of central Mesopotamia, where the large Greek city of Seleucia was awaiting the Romans as liberators? The Parthian kings lived in Ctesiphon, a suburb of Seleucia, so driving them out would already have constituted a great success. The answer probably is that it was no easy matter for a large army to continue the offensive from Seleucia over the mountains to Parthia. If Media was successfully persuaded, however, to join the Romans, the Parthians would have been forced to give up Mesopotamia anyhow, and the Romans would have been in a good position to continue the war in any direction. Antony therefore took the route to the Median capital, Phraaspa, today probably Tachti Suleiman (190 miles east of Gaugamela), where King Artavasdes kept his family and his treasure. The Romans probably estimated that, once they had taken this city, Artavasdes, to whom they could offer favorable conditions, would subject himself to them just as his namesake from Armenia had done. In order to carry out the siege with imposing speed, the Roman army was carrying along its siege engines, including an 80-foot battering ram, for no hard wood grew in Atropatene. These engines, which could be moved only very slowly, were protected by two legions, while Antony himself moved ahead with the main body in order to appear quickly before the fortress and initiate the siege.

Then it happened that the following train, under the command of Oppius Statianus, allowed itself to be attacked by surprise by the Parthians, and it was wiped out and the siege engines were destroyed. We do not know the details of this engagement, but it is unimaginable that this could have happened without the Roman general's having committed the most serious errors. To defend his long wagon trains with two legions against the Parthian cavalry army was of course impossible, and an attack by the Parthians moving up from the south was to be foreseen, since the Romans were, in fact, making a kind of flanking march across their front. It is impossible, however, that Antony did not assign some cavalry to this force, which would have been both able and also obliged to observe and report promptly the approach of the Parthians. Then the Romans would necessarily have prepared a fortified camp, in which they would have been able to defend themselves very well against the enemy cavalry until Antony came to relieve them. But regardless of who bore the blame for this carelessness, the backbone of Antony's campaign plan was broken by this defeat—all the more so, in fact, when the Armenian King Artavasdes, frightened by this news but presumably, deep in his heart, not so very unhappy over it, turned about with his army, which had not yet joined up with the Romans, and returned into his own country in order to defend it and to save himself.

Antony had enough toughness, however, not to give up yet, and he tried to take Phraaspa with improvised siege engines and also moved a bit farther into the country, hoping to lure the Parthians into a battle. One might well ask why he did not divide up his still mighty army, which the Parthians did not dare to face. The circumference of Tachti-Suleiman is only 1,330 paces; a moderate-sized corps would therefore have sufficed to surround the fortress and carry out the siege. It could have defended itself against the Parthian cavalry with a circumvallation while the main body continued on toward Ecbatana or to Hyrcania. But presumably nothing would have been accomplished by doing that. Everything depended on whether they took Atropatene away from the Parthians. From that base they would have been able to continue the war; to continue pressing forward into enemy territory without that base would have been extremely dangerous. After the brilliant victory of the Parthians against Oppius Statianus, certainly the King of Atropatene would not have been persuaded to change sides by anything less than the capture of Phraaspa. But Antony had the further unhappy experience, after he had moved away from the city once, of having the beleaguered garrison make a successful sortie and burn up his approach causeway (*Annäherungsdamm*). Enraged, the commander sentenced two cohorts, which were blamed for not having fought well enough, to the ultimate punishment, decimation. Finally, when foraging produced no further provisions from the surrounding area and there seemed to be no prospect for the early capture of the fortress, there was nothing left to do but take up the withdrawal.

Probably less because his army would have been no longer capable of fighting than because he could no longer hope to find provisions along the invasion route which he had followed, Antony took another route. Instead of crossing the Mesopotamian plain, he took the road into the mountains, toward the north, through Armenia, where the King, his ally, would have to provide him with victuals.[5] On this retreat the Parthians still caused him considerable losses, and even though the Romans were victorious in each actual battle, repulsing and driving off the Parthians, the army's morale was still strongly shaken, and Antony considered it advisable not to break camp in the morning, as was customary, but at midday, in order to gain as much time as possible for an undisturbed march toward evening.[6]

The campaigns of Crassus and Antony direct our attention both to the future and the past. We shall have occasion to refer back to them when we explore, in the next volume, the reasons why Mesopotamia continued to be the limit of the Roman area of influence and no Roman commander was able to repeat Alexander's expedition.

But here again we ask how it was possible for the King of the small country of Macedon to subdue all of Asia to the Indus, whereas Roman armies just as large and much larger than his failed in the attempt and were wiped out. Alexander's genius is not a sufficient explanation; in the meantime the occidental art of warfare had been developed so greatly in the Roman cohort tactics and the military organization of the Romans had become so much more massive than that of the Macedonians that Alexander's personality alone can not have counterbalanced these developments.

The strategic form of Antony's campaign has an even greater similarity to Alexander's Gaugamela campaign than is at first apparent. After a certain period of time following the Parthians' defeat of Crassus, they had gone over to the offensive again, but they were finally beaten by one of Antony's lieutenants in northern Syria. This defeat can be compared with that of Issus: about the same provinces that Darius still held after Issus formed the Parthian empire of King Phraates IV, against whom Antony took the field. As we have seen, the Roman took almost the same route as Alexander through upper Mesopotamia, also probably crossed the

Tigris in the same area, and, like Alexander, had no enemy encounters before this crossing. What would have happened if
Darius, instead of taking up a battle position near Gaugamela, had
avoided battle as Phraates did and had limited himself to the defense of his fortified places, cutting off the supply of provisions to
the Macedonians?

In order to be able to carry out this kind of strategy, a people
and a state must have a strong will to resist. Even after their defeat
at Gaugamela the Persians could have defended themselves in the
manner of the Parthians, but all the large cities—Babylon, Susa,
Persepolis, Ecbatana—opened their gates to the Macedonians without any opposition; in fact, the local commanders even invited
them to come, and soon the fugitive King was dethroned and mur-
dered by one of his satraps. Darius Codomannus himself stemmed
from a secondary branch of the Achaemenidae and had only come
to the throne through a palace revolution, one of many. We must
not overlook this inner weakness of the Persian Empire when we
consider the incomparable successes of Alexander. The Parthian
empire represented an Asiatic reaction against the Hellenic-
Macedonian hegemony but still not one of pure barbarism; rather,
it was marked by a certain blending of Hellenic cultural elements.
On the day the victory at Carrhae was celebrated, a tragedy of
Euripides was presented at the court of the Parthian King. When
Antiochus III of Syria extended his empire once again as far as
India (209 B.C.), he was nevertheless unable simply to subdue the
Parthians and Bactrians but had to grant them the status of semi-
independent vassal nations. When Antiochus VII again undertook
to restore the Greater Syrian Kingdom and had driven victoriously
into Media, his soldiers, divided up among various winter quarters
for convenience in supplying them, were attacked and killed by the
inhabitants (129 B.C.). Nowhere did Alexander the Great encounter
this kind of resistance. The Persian Empire which he destroyed
was, to be sure, very large, but it was internally decayed and unsta-
ble. This observation is in no way to be interpreted as a belated de-
traction of the personal importance of Alexander, just as Napoleon
loses none of his laurels when we recognize how weak the monarchy of Frederick the Great had become in 1806. Persia was already
undergoing a sort of internal dissolution when the Macedonian attack approached. This unquestionable fact makes all the Greek accounts of the arrogance and the confidence of the Persian court
appear very doubtful, and from this point of view it is also most
improbable that Darius would have been able to raise two strong

armies, one after the other. To accomplish that one must have not only a tight national organization, an efficient administration to assure the supply of provisions, but also good will from below. All of these things were already lacking in the Persian Empire; and so we also have here an additional argument to the effect that Darius' armies were not only not large but were even numerically smaller than the Macedonian armies.

EXCURSUS

I have established a significantly different picture of Antony's campaign from that which has been painted up to now, especially by Gutschmidt in his *History of Iran* (*Geschichte Irans*) (1888) and Gardthausen in *Augustus and his Times* (*Augustus und seine Zeit*) (1891).

We assume that all our reports go back to a single source, a companion of Antony, Dellius. From this source some historians have taken this, others have taken that, and each has colored his account with his own subjective treatment. The point of view in Plutarch is favorable to Antony, whereas that in Dio Cassius and in the lesser Latin writers who refer back to Livy is hostile toward him (Gutschmidt, p. 97, footnote 3). The basic point, however, is that Dellius, although he was quite well informed concerning the events themselves, apparently either knew nothing or understood nothing of the real relationship of these things. His principal interest lay in anteroom gossip about the commander who forgot the principles of warfare because he was pining for Cleopatra and in rhetorical embellishments. The Parthians' horses were supposed to have been frightened by the clanking of the weapons of the Roman legions and therefore took to flight. When Antony was about to start out on his withdrawal, a wise man had to come to him, a former soldier of Crassus who had been a prisoner of the Parthians for seventeen years, and inform the Roman commander that the Parthian cavalry was less dangerous in the mountains than on the plain. The Romans formed an overhead cover of joined shields against the Parthian arrows, and the Parthians took that for a sign that the Romans were finished, but suddenly the Romans stormed out on them again. All of these stories as well as all the figures given for the army strengths of the Parthians must naturally be completely rejected.

Concerning Antony's march forward at the start of the campaign, Gardthausen (Vol. 2, Part 11, p. 153) says that the route cannot be understood but that there is also no doubt of it, since the sources indicate that Antony marched through Armenia. Armenia, however, like Arabia, is a much too indefinite geographical expression and our sources are exposed in such details to much too many misunderstandings for us to ascribe to a commander like Antony something completely nonsensical, simply on the basis of a few such words in the accounts; and least of all when we consider that the report in Plutarch (*Antony*, Chapter 37) reads as follows: Antony marched (from Zeugma) "through Arabia and Armenia." From the objective point of view, however: why should he have avoided the plain? He was certainly strong enough in all arms to offer the Parthians battle, and he sought to do so.

Gardthausen himself (Vol. 1, Part 1, p. 295) points out quite correctly that Antony crossed the Euphrates near Zeugma and marched through Osrhoëne and Mygdonia to the Tigris and then continued south of Lake Urmia. That is the straight line that continues on to Phraaspa. Armenia cannot be pushed into that area, and it is either to be eliminated completely or to be considered in its broadest interpretation, which includes upper Mesopotamia.

And with this there disappears, too, the idea that Antony planned to invade Parthia from the north; further, this concept is contradicted by the statement (Gardthausen, Vol. 1, Part 1, p. 295) that he marched south of Lake Urmia.

We must also eliminate the idea that Antony deceived and surprised the Parthians with his campaign plan; the route he followed was the quite normal one, and furthermore the approach of such a huge army can be noticed so long in advance that King Phraates did not have to take any particular pains to learn of this in plenty of time.

The retreat was, of course, not without its difficulties and losses, but with the strong cavalry and the excellent slingers that the Romans still had available, the Parthians cannot possibly have harmed them so very much. The descriptions of the suffering and dangers, as well as that of the despair of the commander, are rhetorical exaggerations.

(Added in the second edition.) The study of this campaign by Kromayer, in *Hermes*, Vol. 31, 1896, was not yet known to me when I wrote the foregoing. I cannot agree with it even now, however, but consider it as erroneous in its decisive point. Kromayer believes that Antony did not feel strong enough with the army he had assembled at Zeugma to confront the Parthians on the Mesopotamian plain and therefore took the route through Armenia, making a huge circle toward the north, in order to be able to find protection from the mountains while on the march and to draw in reinforcements: the Roman troops under Crassus, who had fought in the Caucasus in the previous year, and the army of the Armenian Artavasdes. The source-based proof, however, that he seeks to cite for this march fails to make the point—one only needs to read again in context the passages he cites—and from the objective viewpoint it is completely incredible that Antony, who, even if a few corps had not yet joined him, still had a huge army at hand, should have avoided a battle with the Parthians. In the preceding years his lieutenant Ventidius had already defeated the Parthians a number of times in large battles, and Antony had no less than 10,000 cavalry. Of course, the account of the 16,000 heavy cavalrymen that the Armenian Artavasdes was supposed to add to the Roman numbers is pure fable. The reinforcements that Antony would have gained on his northern march in the form of Artavasdes' contingent and perhaps Crassus' corps would have been largely counterbalanced just by the march losses in men and materiel which would have resulted from the detour of more than 450 miles through mountainous country. When Kromayer points out that Caesar, too, intended to march against the Parthians through Little Armenia, he does not consider that Caesar came from Rome, whereas Antony's army came from Syria; consequently, what would have been the direct route for Caesar was a detour for Antony.

NOTES FOR CHAPTER V

1. The changes I have made in this chapter are based on the painstaking work of Francis Smith in the *Historische Zeitschrift*, Vol. 115, 1916.

2. Regling, "Crassus' War Against the Parthians" "Crassus' Partherkrieg," *Klio*, Vol. 7, 1907.

3. According to Gardthausen, Vol. II, Part 1, p. 150, footnote 6, the figures for the strength of the Roman army vary between 13 and 18 legions. The Armenian reinforcing troops should also be added to that number.

4. Dio Cassius 49. 26.

5. Plutarch, *Antonius*, Chapter 49, conclusion. Dio 49. 31.

6. This is how Frontinus, *Stratagemetos* 2. 13. 7, is to be understood.

BOOK VII

Caesar

Chapter I

Introduction

Up to this point we have preferred to follow the method of setting aside the strict chronology of events in order to gain, either systematically or through the treatment of a particular battle, a firm concept of the tactics of the period and only then, proceeding from this definite base, to go into our study of the strategy. With Caesar it is not necessary to proceed in this way. All the individual elements of his art of generalship are already known to us; we have only to show how through his application of them he brought the art of ancient warfare to its apogee and must therefore be regarded as the greatest military artist of antiquity.

As thoroughly and excellently as we are informed of Caesar's campaigns through his own writings, however, we still suffer from the lack of source material on the other side. Even in the case of the civil war, the reports from Pompey's and the Senate's side are insignificantly meager and vague in comparison with the broad account of Caesar and his supporters, and on the Gallo-Germanic wars we have simply nothing except the reports of the victorious Romans. We must not forget that for a moment, and we cannot say the scholars have forgotten it in the past, but they could do nothing, so to speak; they were helpless. Immeasurable as the completeness of descriptive writings is on the wars of Caesar, critical analysis has still not really broken through. Such studies lacked means of coming to grips with the great commander, who was his own historian and no less a great one for that, and of coming to the root of things through their understanding of him. That required tools that could only be created gradually, in long, successive steps: a knowledge of the organization and tactics of the troops, of the meaning of technical expressions, geographical and topographical studies, and the establishing of definite statistics on the strengths of the armies. Today all of these prerequisites have been so broadly developed through the work of generations of philologists, archaeologists, historians and military men and through travels, excavations, and methodical comparisons that critical scholars may risk taking up the confrontation with the titan, looking him in the eye and forcing him to reveal his real self.

EXCURSUS

1. Of the older works on Caesar's methods of warfare the two most important ones, which are still of value today, are W. Rüstow's *C. Julius Caesar's Military Organization and Conduct of War* (*Heerwesen und Kriegführung C. Julius Cäsars*) 2d ed. (1862), and that of Baron August von Göler, Major General of the Grand Duchy of Baden, *Caesar's Gallic War and Parts of his Civil War* (*Cäsars gallischer Krieg und Teile seines Bürgerkrieges*) 2d ed., edited by E. A. von Göler (1880). A new working over of all the material, with careful consideration of the entire body of newer publications, is offered by Franz Fröhlich in *Caesar's Method of Waging War* (*Das Kriegswesen Cäsars*) (1889 and 1890). A few criticisms of this book, though not very important ones, have been made by F. Cauer in the *Historische Zeitschrift* 64: 123 and 66: 288. Colonel Stoffel, in the *Revue de Philologie*, Vol. 15, 1891, made some thorough and sharply critical observations against a series of points in Fröhlich's work.

The Life of Caesar, by Napoleon III, got no further in its two volumes than the Gallic War, ending with Caesar's crossing of the Rubicon. Even if it does not rate particularly high as a literary accomplishment, it is still valuable from the scholarly viewpoint and it has contributed greatly through the geographical research, the excavations, and the experiments to which it led. Of much higher quality, however, is the sequel, *History of Julius Caesar, Civil War* by Colonel Stoffel (*Histoire de Jules César, guerre civile, par le colonel Stoffel*) 2 vols. in large quarto (1887). As aide-de-camp to the Emperor, Colonel Stoffel had already participated extensively in the preparatory work that the Emperor had carried out, and from 1866 to 1870, during his stay in Berlin, he had continued to work on this project. After the events of the war had interrupted the work and had brought an end to the official life of the colonel as well as that of his imperial master, Stoffel took up the work once again in 1879 and saw it through to completion, visiting every theater of operations and every battlefield of Caesar's. Step by step this work represents the most significant progress. Stoffel is just as much a true scholar, untouched by the slightest tinge of dilettantism, as he is a campaign-hardened soldier. If, nevertheless, I differ with him quite often, these points of contention probably all go back to a single basic difference, namely, the degree of skepticism and of criticism which I feel bound to apply to Caesar's own accounts and which I hope to base on a factor neglected by Stoffel, the statistical one.

In addition to the civil war Colonel Stoffel also published as a further sequel to the Emperor's work a very valuable monograph on the first two campaigns of the Gallic War, *The War between Caesar and Ariovistus and Caesar's First Operations in the year 702* by Colonel Stoffel (*Guerre de César et d'Arioviste et premières opérations de César en l'an 702 par le colonel Stoffel*) (Paris, 1890), 164 pp.

Just as I was putting the finishing touches on this chapter before sending the manuscript off to the printer, there came into my hands *Caesar's Conquest of Gaul* by T. Rice Holmes, (London: 1899), 845 pp. It is a book that is just as scholarly as it is perceptive and which also has the additional advantage of blending charming humor with its criticism and which brings together everything in any way relating to the *bellum Gallicum*. I am in agreement with Holmes on the high esteem we both have for Stoffel's works and judgment. In those places where I differ from him—and, as in Stoffel's case, that is quite frequently—I shall take particular pains to justify my position.

For further literature on this subject I refer the reader not only to Jähns's *History of Military Science* (*Geschichte der Kriegswissenschaften*) but also the same author's very thorough study *Caesar's Commentaries and their Literary and Military Science Consequences* (*Cäsars Kommentarien und ihre literarische und kriegswissenschaftliche Folgewirkung*) Vol. 7, Supplement to *Militärisches Wochenblatt* (1883), to which I am indebted for several important citations and observations.

In 1906 there was added to the literature on Caesar the work of the Imperial-Royal First Lieutenant G. Veith, *History of C. Julius Caesar's Campaigns* (*Geschichte der Feldzüge C. Julius Cäsars*) (Vienna: L. W. Seidel). Impressive as the layout of the work is, it still does not represent any scholarly progress. The writer is still convinced that the Roman cohorts in the front line left intervals of a cohort's width between them, and he finds his "proof" for this point (pp. 48, 486) in the "military technical term *quincunx*," a military *terminus technicus* that stems, however, not from Livy but from Lipsius. (See also the review by R. Schneider in the *Göttingische gelehrte Anzeigen* 169 [June 1907]: 419.) The statement of the author (p. 483) that he "goes back exclusively to the original sources on all important points" therefore rests on self-delusion, no less so than his belief that his position as a first lieutenant qualifies him to enter the field of military history as an expert.

2. For the details and the source writings related to Caesar's method of warfare, German readers would do best to rely on Fröhlich's book (276 pp.). While I recommend this work in general, I should like to mention briefly here a few points on which, principally in agreement with Stoffel, I differ from Fröhlich. In addition to Stoffel's criticism already referred to above, we should also take into consideration principally the "Remarques générales" that Stoffel added to his life of Caesar.

On page 9 Fröhlich doubts that the Thirteenth Legion, with which Caesar crossed the Rubicon, was 5,000 men strong, as reported by Plutarch, since it had been in the war for many years and had never received any replacements. In the *Revue de philologie*, (p. 140) Stoffel correctly opposes that point of view by saying that Caesar undoubtedly brought in replacements to keep his legions up to strength. If on one occasion we read of a "*supplementum*" that was not incorporated but, rather, had a special organization (*Bell. Gall.* 7. 57), that was only a transitory situation. Now if, despite this system of gradually replacing the losses, there was always a distinction made between old and young legions and finally the old legions, instead of simply releasing the older men in their ranks, were completely disbanded, that point can be explained by the fact that the losses in killed in ancient battles were, as a rule, quite small—except in case of a defeat, where the entire body of troops could easily be wiped out. In old legions, therefore, the number of veteran soldiers was so large, or at any rate the number of very young men so small, that *a potiori* the legions themselves could be distinguished as old or young ones.

Nevertheless, Stoffel would place the strength of Caesar's legion very low and he even rejects the concept of the "normal strength of the legion," which, according to him, has no more justification than if one wished to speak today of the "normal strength of a division." A division is something different, however, from a legion of Caesar's times. The older Roman legion, which still had its definite allocation of cavalrymen and light infantry, can well be compared with a modern division, to the extent that it consisted of a blend of the various arms. In Caesar's time, however, that situation had long since ceased to exist; consequently, one can compare this legion more readily with the modern infantry brigade, in that it has about the same strength, or with the regiment through the fact that it forms an administrative unit. But all of these comparisons do not really help. The decisive point is that, according to a definite scheme, the legion was made up of 10 cohorts, each consisting of 3 maniples of 2 centuries each. These smallest units must necessarily have had a definite strength. Drill, camp, supply, and the transmission of commands would all become unbearably complicated if the subordinate tactical units were not approximately equal in size. If, then, the centuries and maniples had a prescribed strength, the legion, too, had a definite size, and the passages quoted in Fröhlich leave no doubt that this normal strength for the legion was 6,000 men, for the cohort 600, for the maniple 200, and for the century 100.

The principal objection that can be raised against this assumption will be eliminated in the computation of the strengths for the battle of Pharsalus.

On page 17 Fröhlich says that the centurions are to be compared with modern first sergeants, not captains. That is true, as explained above, only with respect to their social status; with respect to their functions, however, they do correspond to modern captains, and it is of decisive importance precisely for Caesar's history that the fundamental function of the "captain and company commander" in the Roman army was in the hands of men having the social status of noncommissioned officers.

On page 19 Fröhlich points out the low military ability of Caesar's war tribunes. The nucleus of this idea is correct, but it is too strongly colored, as Rice Holmes proves on his page 570, where he shows how many important functions these tribunes did in fact carry on.

In his *War between Caesar and Ariovistus (Guerre de César et d'Arioviste)* (p. 127) Stoffel states that in the course of the Gallic War, the legates, who of course originally were only high officers at the disposal of the commander, had been brought into a more definite relationship with the individual legions and had become their regular commanders. Holmes (p. 568) believes, and very probably correctly so, that this was not the case. Under Caesar the relationship of the legates to the individual units remained just as it had been in the Roman army up to that time; accordingly, the sphere of activity of the tribunes was not narrowed by Caesar.

Concerning the *antesignani* (those in front of the standard), discussed by Fröhlich (p. 29), I have already made the necessary observations on p. 275, above.

On page 38 Fröhlich agrees with the opinion of Schambach that Caesar once again, as in earlier times, assigned a definite unit of cavalry to each legion. Schambach's explanations do not appear very convincing to me. That point is not, however, very important. Holmes, too (p. 583), rejects the opinion of Fröhlich.

Fröhlich's chapter on the *evocati* (starting on p. 42) should be supplemented, in keeping with my discussion on p. 415 above, with the fact that one must distinguish between the *evocati* of the second century B.C., who were simply reenlisted veterans and were very numerous, and those of the first century, who formed an honor guard or life guard for the commanders. From this there follows also a simple and clear interpretation of the controversial chapter of *Bell. Civ.* 3. 91 (from R. Menge, *Berliner Philologische Wochenschrift*, 1890, p. 273). The chapter reads as follows:

Erat Crastinus evocatus in exercitu Caesaris, qui
superiore anno apud eum primum pilum in legione
X duxerat, vir singulari virtute. Hic signo dato:
Sequimini me, inquit, manipulares mei qui fuistis,
et vestro imperatori, quem constituistis, operam
date. Unum hoc proelium superest; quo confecto et
ille suam dignitatem et nos nostram libertatem
recuperabimus. Simul respiciens Caesarem: Faciam,
inquit, hodie, imperator, ut aut vivo mihi aut mortuo
gratias agas. Haec cum dixisset, primus ex dextro
cornu procucurrit, atque eum electi milites circiter
CXX voluntarii eiusdem centuriae sunt prosecuti."

("There was in Caesar's army an *evocatus* named Crastinus,
a man of remarkable courage, who, in the previous year,
had served under Caesar as the first centurion of the

Tenth Legion. When the signal was given, Crastinus
addressed the men who had been his companions, and
said, 'Follow me, and give me as your commander the
kind of service which you normally do. There's only
one battle left; when it's over, we shall recover both
his [Caesar's] dignity and our liberty.' At the same time, he looked at Caesar and
said, 'General, today I'll present you the opportunity to thank me, whether I'm
alive or dead.' When he had thus spoken, he ran forward
out of the right wing and about 120 picked men from the
same cohort ran out voluntarily with him.")

The century which Crastinus is addressing here is a century of the life guard,
formed of *evocati*, that was stationed on the right wing. We may assume that, at the
start of the civil war, Caesar had, as a spur for the entire army, named as *evocati* the
men with the longest service, principally those of the Tenth Legion. Since Crastinus
had been *primus pilus* in this legion, most of them had been in his maniple, and he
could therefore address them as his former manipular comrades. As *evocati* they
were considered as men whose period of service had actually expired, who had voluntarily reenlisted once more, for this war only, and had recognized Caesar as their
commander, but who were released from their obligation at the end of the war and
"won their freedom again."

On page 72 Fröhlich states the opinion that the legions had kept on their armor
while they were digging fortifications. That point has been rejected, quite properly,
by Stoffel in the *Revue de Philologie*, p. 142.

Likewise, Stoffel correctly rejects the opinion (Fröhlich, pp. 75 and 127) that the
soldier himself carried enough flour for sixteen days.

With respect to the Romans' marching (Fröhlich, pp. 104 and 200), see Chapter
III below.

We cannot accept Fröhlich's opinion (p. 105) that the legionaries also used the
bow, a point that is not proved by the passage he cites.

Stoffel criticizes the passage on page 121, where Fröhlich speaks of a *pilum* with
amentum; the *pilum* was never thrown with an *amentum* (strap); the latter was only
used with lighter missiles.

The interval between towers in the contravallation line around Alesia was 80 feet.
Fröhlich (p. 145) regards this as the width of a manipular front. Stoffel explains it
better as related to the range of the Roman missiles.

On page 169 Fröhlich takes from Vegetius certain false ideas concerning the
cuneus (wedge formation), which we shall discuss in our next volume.

On page 183 Fröhlich describes the maneuver that Caesar had the Seventh and
Twelfth legions carry out in the battle with the Nervii as if the legions had fought
back to back. Giesing has more correctly understood this as meaning that the rear
ranks of the two legions faced about. (*Neue Jahrbücher für Philologie*, 145 [1892]: 493.)

3. THE MOUNTED TROOPS

A special chapter should really be devoted to Caesar's cavalry, or more properly, a
history of the cavalry, parallel to the development of infantry tactics, should have
been carried through from the start. As early as the Persian Wars, then with Philip
and Alexander, and from Hannibal on in the course of Roman history, the cavalry
proved itself of the utmost value or even the decisive factor. In the case of the infantry we have observed a systematic development of the battle forms; should not
something of a similar type be established for the cavalry?

It is a matter principally of two questions: to what extent did the ancients develop
the actual shock action, the closed attack carried out at high speed? And secondly,
how are we to conceive of the mixed battle of cavalry and light infantry?

Despite a carefully worked out monograph by Schambach, *The Cavalry in Caesar's*

Army (*Die Reiterei bei Cäsar*) Mühlhausen Program 1881, which can be compared with Fröhlich, Book 3, Chapter 5, there still remains many an uncertain point, and we ourselves shall not go into this particular study at this point but shall take it up later, after we have gained enough material for comparisons from much later periods.

Chapter II

The Helvetian Campaign

We can assume that Caesar's account of his campaign against the Helvetii is well known and proceed at once to a testing of the improbable points, the gaps, the contradictions, and the impossibilities it contains.

According to Caesar, the Helvetii decided to emigrate, with wife and child, bag and baggage, in order to win for themselves the mastery of all Gaul (1. 30. 3); their own country was too small for them.

We can disregard the erroneous estimates Caesar made concerning the size of the Helvetian region, but we ask how the motive that Caesar ascribes to the emigrants can be reconciled with the manner in which they carried it out. If the Helvetii intended to subject the rest of the Gauls, it was not necessary for them to move out with families, herds, and household goods; on the contrary, that necessarily limited drastically their military action.

The area on which the Helvetii had cast their eyes as a substitute for their own was that of the Santones, lying along the Atlantic Ocean between La Rochelle and the mouth of the Gironde. Neither is this region particularly appropriate to serve as a base for the conquest of Gaul, nor was it necessary, if the Helvetii were seeking a new area in which to live because of overpopulation of the previous one, for the entire people to emigrate and leave empty the splendid region they had been occupying. Assuming that the Helvetii, instead of extending their control of their homeland somewhere into neighboring areas, actually did have the plan to move to the ocean, drive out or destroy the peoples already living there, and settle anew, this intention, difficult enough to carry out in itself, cannot possibly have been combined with a plan to seek at the same time to establish their hegemony over all the other Gallic peoples. This combination of plans is all the more impossible in that Gaul, as we do not yet know in this connection but learn soon afterward from Caesar himself, already had a ruler, the Germanic prince Ariovistus, who had conquered the Gauls and had forced them to send him hostages and pay him tribute. It is true that we do not get a very clear idea as to how broadly the hegemony of Ariovistus really extended, since at times it seems to be only the Aedui and the Sequani with their vassals who were subjected, whereas at other times it is envoys from almost all of Gaul (Chapter 30) who ask Caesar for help against him—but however that situation might have been, any plan of the Helvetii to win the mastery of Gaul had to take into account first and foremost Ariovistus and would necessarily collide with him. Caesar mentions not a word on this subject. As long as he is recounting the Helvetian War, it is as if Ariovistus did not exist.

Among the preparations that the Helvetii made for their great war of conquest were included peace and friendship alliances with their neighboring states. Our question is: With which ones? Those in the west would have belonged to those to be conquered, Ariovistus was in the north, the east does not come into the picture, and the south belonged to the Romans.

Only by two routes, Caesar continues, could the Helvetii leave their country: either on the north bank of the Rhone, through the region of the Sequani, or on the south bank, passing by Geneva, through the Roman province. This should be completed by adding the clause "if they intended to march in the direction of the region of the Santones," for otherwise quite a number of other routes across the Jura or north of the Jura would have been available to the Helvetii if they wanted to conquer Gaul.

Although, according to Caesar, the Helvetii had already been making their plans for two years, which must therefore have been widely known, it nevertheless appears that the Romans not only knew nothing about an intended march through their province but also had no concern about it. For in this endangered border territory only one legion was stationed when Caesar arrived, and he had to gain time through a ruse to lay out hastily a defensive line some eighteen miles long from Geneva to Fort l'Ecluse, where the Rhone is fordable at a few spots, and to garrison the defensive line with his legion and the home guard levied from the local inhabitants.

The Helvetii are reported to have made vain attempts to break through this line.

We must look on this assertion with the strongest doubt. The Helvetii were a very warlike people, and their army, even if, as we shall see, it was not 92,000 men strong, was nevertheless certainly quite significant in size. Militarily, the home guard which Caesar had levied hardly came into consideration. How could it have been possible to defend an 18-mile line with the forces of a single legion? From the military point of view, that is absolutely impossible. A hastily constructed, 18-mile-long field fortification attacked simultaneously at three places by a force several times larger than the defenders would (before the most modern developments in weapons) always and under all circumstances be penetrated, if the attacker was in earnest. Caesar states that after his victory over the Helvetii tablets were found in their camp listing the number of persons belonging to each tribe; these gave a total of 368,000. Since we can arrive at an approximate estimation of the size of the region occupied by the Helvetian tribes (18,000 square kilometers),[1] it follows from these figures that there was a population density of 20 per square kilometer. Beloch has correctly declared that to be impossible. But Caesar gives us still a second figure; when he sent the Helvetii back to their region, he had a census taken that resulted in 110,000 persons. Now since, by Caesar's own account, the losses of this people during their migration and in the battles cannot have been so very great, Beloch took this figure as a point of departure, added 40,000 for losses, and arrived at a population density of 7.5 per square kilometer.

There would be no important objection to this conclusion, if we could fully depend on the fact that Caesar actually carried out the census and that all the Helvetii really had left their country. In this case, since the loss figure of 40,000 still seems to be very high, one might even arrive at a somewhat smaller number than Beloch's. In view of the uncertainty of our basic figures, however, about which we shall have further occasion to speak, let us drop this line of investigation. We must determine more definitely only the negative aspect, that the original total cannot have amounted to anything approaching 368,000 persons, and we have the means to do so.

Caesar states that the move of the Helvetii was made by a total of 368,000 individuals, who carried along with them provisions for 3 months. Estimates which Napoleon III caused to be made resulted in a figure of 6,000 wagons, each drawn by 4 animals, which would have been necessary to transport flour alone; and assuming 15 kilograms of baggage per person, 2,500 additional wagons would have been required. A total of 8,500 wagons on one road, 15 meters to the wagon, would cover some 77 or 78 miles.[2] These figures are based on an assumed load of 500 kilograms per draft animal. I have more recently become convinced, however, and have stated my proof for this point in Vol. II, Book IV, Chapter IV, Excursus, "Provisions and Train," that this load is between two and three times too high for the conditions existing in ancient times. The assumed wagon train would therefore have been not 77 or 78 miles long, but some 180 miles. As we imagine the roads in the Gaul of those days, it would have been very seldom that the wagons could travel in several parallel lines abreast of each other. If there were a narrow stretch at just one place along the route, the column would necessarily be held up, even if it were possible elsewhere to spread out across the fields. March discipline was certainly minimal, accordion action frequently caused jams and extended intervals, and the wagons were drawn principally by oxen. Such a movement certainly requires at least from 40 to 55 minutes to cover a mile. Even in midsummer, when it would be possible to start the march at 3 A.M. and the end of the column would not need to arrive in camp before 9 P.M., and even if the day's march is limited to about 4½ miles, not more than 2,500 wagons could make that march. Fifteen hours would be available (from 3 A.M. until 6 P.M., when the last wagons would have to start the march), and in each 3-hour period 500 wagons would move out. Even if we reckoned with only slightly over 25 minutes to the mile, still only 250 wagons could start out each hour, so that with a total march time of 16 hours (from 3 A.M. until 7 P.M.) 4,000 wagons could move about 4½ miles forward.[3] Now our column, however, does not consist merely of wagons—and surprisingly Napoleon does not speak of this—but we also have the entire mass of persons, including women and children, and in addition to the draft animals also the herds, the young animals, and the smaller domestic animals.

According to Caesar's account, the march column of the Helvetii, decreased somewhat by the splitting off of the Tigurini at the Saône,[4] moved in some 15 days from their crossing point (somewhere between 9 and 18 miles north of Lyons, near Trévoux or Montmerle) to the vicinity of Bibracte (near Autun). That is a straight-line distance between 63 and 72 miles and consequently meant a daily march rate between 5 and 7 miles. Only at the start did the route follow the broad Saône valley; thereafter the movement was through the mountainous region of the Maconnais and the Charolais, where certainly the carts would often have been forced to travel in single file. Even if some of the provision wagons were already emptied, the Helvetii undoubtedly still did not drop them off; wagons are valuable articles, and they needed them for the booty that they were gathering and for replenishing their provisions. Since the column was moving through enemy territory, it was not possible, for example, to send the women and children a day's march ahead, thus dividing up the column. Caesar's description leaves no doubt that the mass remained as a unit and marched along together, but this leads to the conclusion that it cannot possibly be a question of an original mass of 368,000 souls. Even reduced to a half, to a quarter—to an eighth—the wagon train with the accompanying people and animals would still be much too long to move in a single column on a single road. Caesar's figures, then, like those of Herodotus concerning Xerxes' army, are not simply to be reduced but absolutely rejected.

While Caesar was moving up five additional legions, two of which were newly levied, from Northern Italy, the Helvetii were marching across the Jura to the Saône and crossing this river above Lyons. After Caesar had attacked and broken up their rear guard as it was crossing, the others moved northward along the river.

Caesar gives no kind of reason for their taking this direction. After all, they intended, as he tells us, to go to the region of the Santones, that is, toward the west. Scholars have filled this gap in various ways. Mommsen, Göler, and Napoleon III believed that Caesar drove the Helvetii away from their intended route, and Napoleon III added that there would have been almost impassable mountains on the direct route toward the Santones, via Roanne, pointing out that even in the nineteenth century the post route from Lyons to La Rochelle still went by way of Autun and Nevers.

This explanation, however, is simply not sufficient. According to the generally accepted assumption, Caesar was in the region of the Segusiavi near Lyons, in the angle between the Rhone and the Saône, when with three legions he attacked the Helvetii as they were crossing the Saône somewhere in the Trévoux-Villefranche area. He had left the other three legions behind. Even if we assume that the latter were on the right bank of the Saône, from there they would in no way have cut off the route of the Helvetii either southward into the province or westward into the mountains. Two of the three legions were the recruit organizations that had just been levied; under no conditions could the Romans afford to go into battle against the Helvetii with them. The Helvetii could not have wished for anything better than to be able to attack a part of the Roman army here, just as Caesar had fallen upon a part of theirs the preceding day. Probably that portion of Caesar's army was not on the other bank at all, and if it was, it was certainly in position behind a fortification from which it could not dare move out.[5] The Helvetii had at least one day's lead on the legions of Caesar himself, while he was occupied building a bridge over the Saône. The mountains directly to the west may well be steep, but they are not impassable, contrary to what Napoleon III stated.

In his book *Chemins de la Gaule* (p. 289 ff.), Bial believes it possible to show several routes leading across the Cévennes, and Maissiat in his *Jules César en Gaule* (1: 349) points out that one can very easily cross the Cévennes through the valley of the Azergues, which flows into the Saône near Trévoux-Villefranche, and that to descend into the Loire valley one has not only one valley but a choice of three tributary valleys (via Chauffaille, Tarare, and Sainte-Foy). This route would have had the double advantage of allowing the Helvetii to cross the Loire and the Allier near their sources and of avoiding from the start any possible Roman attack. Once they were in the mountains, a small rear guard would be able to hold off the Romans. Instead of this they moved along the convenient Saône valley, where Caesar could easily overtake their slow-moving column, did not reach the protection of the mountains until considerably later, and shortly thereafter again had broad streams to cross.

Even if we are willing to assume that the Helvetii did not reach a decision as to their withdrawal quickly enough and left Caesar enough time to cross the Saône downstream and block the entrance to the valley of the Azergues, there still remains no explanation of why they did not move down directly from the Monts du Charolais into the Loire valley and seek to cross near Briennon or Digoin. We can, in fact, conclude definitely that Caesar himself expected no different move by the Helvetii than that they would march along the river, since, as we hear later, he moved his provisions by ship and had not provided a wagon pool.

Judging from all of this, we can reasonably doubt that the Helvetii had the serious intention of moving into the region of the Santones.

When Caesar had denied the Helvetii the possibility of marching through the province, Dumnorix, prince of the Aedui, made possible for them a peaceful move through the area of the Sequani. From the Sequani the Helvetii reached the territory of the Aedui—and from the foregoing we would have to assume as friends. But they actually appeared as enemies and laid waste the land, and the Aedui appealed to the Romans for help against them.

In this situation there must have taken place certain background incidents which Caesar does not relate to us.

Caesar goes on to tell us that, after their partial defeat on the Saône, the Helvetii offered peace and said they were ready to move into any area that Caesar might indicate to them. The negotiations broke up over the fact that the Helvetii refused to turn over the hostages Caesar demanded. Are we to assume that Caesar did not give them any reply, however, to the principal question? He must, after all, probably have said to them: "Since you promise to move into the area which I assign to you, I call upon you to return to your own former region." The fact that this sentence is missing makes the whole negotiation, or the context in which it is placed, highly suspect.

Caesar does not specifically tell us in which direction the Helvetii then moved off; we can only come to a conclusion on it through Caesar's statement that he was not able to supply himself via the Saône because the Helvetii, whom he was following, turned away from the river, and from the fact that the battle was finally fought in the vicinity of Bibracte (Mont Beuvray, 20 kilometers west of Autun). At one point Caesar made an attempt, by means of a detour, to attack the Helvetii from two sides, and when that failed because of a fortuitous incident, he broke off in order to move on to Bibracte. He says that he had to do that because of the supplies that the Aedui had promised him when they called for his help against the Helvetii but were not delivering. His turning away brought on the battle, however, since the Helvetii either interpreted this as fear on his part or wanted to cut off the Romans from their provisions, and so they went over to the attack themselves.

Are we really supposed to believe that the Helvetii could have interpreted the move of the Romans toward Bibracte as prompted by nothing other than fear? And that this same people, who a short time previously had offered to accept from Caesar's hand a new homeland and who had sought to escape from him through a 15-day march, were now so emboldened by this turn of events that they suddenly faced about and attacked him? And on the other hand, how are we to understand the other motive, that of cutting the Romans off from their supplies? If the Helvetii wanted to cut Caesar off from his previous line of communications and his base, neither an attack nor a battle was necessary for that purpose. Did they want to cut him off from Bibracte? Cutting off supplies and waging a battle are mutually exclusive concepts in this situation: if the Helvetii were victorious, no Roman would need any more supplies; if they were defeated, then nothing was any longer cut off from the Romans. Why had the Helvetii continued to march on? If they were intending to move to the territory of the Santones, we must assume that their march up to this point had been in a northwesterly direction and that they were already quite close to the Loire, so that now, as the Romans turned eastward, they could continue their move unmolested. If they wished to avenge their defeat on the Saône, why only at this late point? Why had they not selected a good defensive position along the way and waited to see if the Romans would attack?

The short reports and piecemeal statements on these campaigns which we find in the works of other Roman authors add no clarification, and it might appear hopeless to try to gain a correct picture of the events if we had to rely exclusively on an account in which the truth is shaded over in many passages, apparently intentionally. But after all we cannot simply stop our study by throwing out Caesar's account without replacing it with something else. It is a recognized fact that we cannot simply accept and repeat what Caesar has said. Napoleon I once said that the Helvetian campaign was simply incomprehensible,[6] and even those historians who place the greatest trust in Caesar still feel it necessary to fill in and correct his accounts in some very important points. Mommsen adds as a motive for the migration the fear of Ariovistus, a point that is probably not compatible with the desire of winning hegemony over Gaul; furthermore, Caesar states, as if Ariovistus did not exist, the exact opposite: the Helvetii, hemmed in by mountains and streams, had found it painful not to be able to invade their neighbors' territory. Mommsen, moreover, simply omits any mention of peace negotiations on the Saône. Napoleon III, for his part, treats the migration and the desire to subject Gaul not as chronologically simultaneous but rather as successive plans, and he omits from the peace negotiations the offer of the Helvetii to let Caesar assign a region to them. Finally, Holmes believes, as does Mommsen, that the Helvetii, pressed by the Germanic tribes, had decided to seek a new homeland, and he pictures the plan for the subjection of Gaul merely as an intrigue of Prince Orgetorix. This is exactly the opposite of what Caesar tells us. But all of these corrections still are not satisfactory. There is still missing an explanation of what stance the Helvetii intended to take vis-à-vis Ariovistus in the course of their conquest of Gaul. There also remains the impossible situation of trying to defend a hastily built field fortification line 18 miles long with a single legion and simple home guard against a large army. There is missing a motive for the march off toward the north from the Saône crossing and for the sudden turning about for the battle. We must seek also to eliminate these errors and fill in these gaps in order to arrive at a picture that, even if not provable, at least has the advantage of being conceivable and possible.

Let us try to do this with the following outline:

Central Gaul was under the mastery of the Germanic prince Ariovistus.[7] Only grudgingly did the Gauls endure this yoke and pay their annual tribute. In complete secrecy a prince of the Aedui, Divitiacus, had already turned to the Romans and had asked for their help, as Caesar tells us—not in his first book, to be sure, but incidentally, in a later book (6. 12). In Rome they were not inclined to go along with this but had, on the contrary, sought to get along well with Ariovistus; during Caesar's own consulate they had hailed him as king and had bestowed on him the honorary title of Friend and Ally of the Roman People. Nevertheless, the Aedui refused to give up the idea of being liberated. Another faction, under the leadership of Dumnorix, a brother of Divitiacus, had conceived the idea of freeing Gaul through the power of the Gauls themselves.[8] There was still a powerful and warlike people in this region who were not under the domination of Ariovistus, the Helvetii. An alliance was made with them. A simple uprising, with the hope that the Helvetii would send help, was not possible, since almost all of the prominent families of the Aedui as of the Sequani and other peoples were tied by the hostages in Ariovistus' hands. A ruse was to help the situation. The Helvetian leader Orgetorix proposed to his people that they migrate. Perhaps he spoke of overpopulation, or perhaps he pointed out that in their own land they would soon have to subject themselves, like the other Gauls, to the Germanic peoples. Under the pretense of a migration to the ocean, to the area of the Santones,[9] the Helvetian army was to appear in the territory of the Aedui before the suspicions of Ariovistus were aroused, and, with the support of the Helvetii, the patriotic faction hoped to overcome all hesitation and to bring about the general uprising against the Germanic peoples. Naturally, women and children also accompanied the march, as was later the case with the peasant armies, and in this case there were perhaps still more than usual for such columns, in order to increase the deception. Even the sudden death of Orgetorix did not stop the move.

Caesar was accurately informed of all these things in Rome by

Divitiacus and the Roman faction among the Aedui. Under no circumstances did he want this scheme to be carried out, for it was his
plan that the Gauls should be freed from the yoke of the Germanic
tribes not by their own strength but with the help of Rome, so
as to exchange that yoke for the Roman one. An inquiry by the
Helvetii about whether they could move through the province was
enough to cause him to strengthen his army and move it to the
border. The Helvetii had only made the request in order to maintain as long as possible the fiction that they intended to move to the
region of the Santones. In keeping with the same plan, they still
took the most southerly possible route after Caesar had turned
them away, in order to head for their real goal, the region of the
Aedui, once they had crossed the Saône. Under the pretense that
they had violated the border, Caesar attacked their rear guard as it
was crossing the Saône. In the meantime the Roman faction among
the Aedui, presumably supported financially by the Romans, had
won the upper hand and persuaded the Aedui to call for Caesar's
help against the invaders instead of welcoming the Helvetii as
liberators. The Helvetii now found themselves in a very embarrass-
ing situation and they sent to Caesar, asking him to assign them an
area, that is, to return to their own territory. The agreement, just
as Caesar explains it, fell through only because of the question of
turning over hostages. Caesar, however, insisted on this condition,
not so much because the Helvetii were not to be trusted, but because, after all, this undertaking was to be for him the start of the
subjection of all of Gaul. The Helvetii were not willing to accept
the dishonor and so they moved northward in order to move back
in a broad circle across the upper Saône and into their own land.
They did not remain, however, in the river valley, where the
Romans could have made short shrift of them, overtaking their
column and attacking from all sides, but rather they moved as soon
as possible into the mountains, where a strong rear guard could
hold up the Romans from defile to defile. Caesar followed them,
reinforcing his own troops with the Aedui cavalry. But in the first
engagement, while still in the plain, this cavalry failed to carry out
its mission, taking flight in the face of the Helvetii, and Caesar
suspected that this was not only due to unfavorable terrain but that
ill will was also involved, since Dumnorix was in command.

Although Caesar could have attacked the Helvetian rear guard
daily and involved it in combat, he did not do that but only followed at a certain distance, exercising the greatest caution and remaining alert for any opportunity to deliver a heavy blow.

Finally this occasion seemed to be at hand; an envelopment of the Helvetii by two legions under Labienus was successful, but a chance incident, a false report, caused things to go wrong and saved the enemy. Caesar thereupon moved away from the Helvetian column and headed directly for the capital of the Aedui, Bibracte, which was by now not far away. As he himself says, he was forced to this by supply difficulties. We may perhaps also assume that it was distrust of the Aedui that forced him to make this move. The Roman commander could not continue to move farther into the country without assuring himself of a firm base of operations. This turn, however, brought on the decision.

The Helvetii could, of course, have continued on undisturbed and have returned into their own country by passing through the territory of the Sequani, with whom they were on friendly terms. But if they had done that, they would have left Bibracte and the Aedui, and with them all of central Gaul, at the mercy of the Romans. The patriotic faction of the Aedui, which itself had called in the Helvetii and was presumably in constant secret contact with them, undoubtedly brought the strongest pressure to bear on them, implored their help, possibly even held up the prospect of going over to them during the battle. Since Caesar, even though he had stayed so close to the Helvetii day after day, had not yet initiated an attack himself, the Helvetian leaders may have entertained the hope that he would finally move off and leave them alone. As they learned from their Aedui friends, his supply of provisions would soon be exhausted, and the Aedui were not delivering any to him. But now his turn toward Bibracte dashed all these hopes. And at any rate, there may very well have been from the start among the Helvetii a faction that held it to be shameful to return to their own country without having avenged their brothers who had been insidiously attacked and slaughtered by the Romans on the Saône. This faction now prevailed, and it was decided to turn about and attack the Romans on the march.

The point that Caesar wished to conceal in this account is the purpose the Helvetii had in mind on this undertaking, the struggle against Ariovistus. Consequently, the name of Ariovistus is not mentioned by him anywhere in this entire campaign. He imputes to the Helvetii the desire of becoming masters of Gaul, as if Gaul did not already have a master in the form of the frightful German warrior prince, and coupled paradoxically with this concept of hegemony there appears again the innocent migration with women and children to the region of the Santones. Caesar has to give as a pretense a violation of the border, has to suppress the shift of alliance of the Aedui, has to leave the peace negotiations in shadowy form, has to leave the Helvetii's march toward the north with no plausible motivation, and he searches in vain for their motives for the sudden decision to fight—all of this because of the single point, that he does not want to state the true intention of the whole military operation of the Helvetii. Once we have straightened out this point, however, everything else falls automatically into place.

Here let me repeat once more: I am not claiming that things took place exactly as I have just recounted them. I am simply claiming that Caesar's account does not stand up under critical appraisal and is in itself impossible, and I have wished to propose in its place another account, possible and imaginable, which also differs basically less from Caesar's account of events than do the interpretations by Mommsen, Napoleon III, and Holmes. In doing this we have had to go more deeply into the truly political aspects than our mission in itself requires, but that was necessary because in this case the military is inseparably related to the political and because we wished to show from the start the degree of caution that History must apply in using Caesar's *Commentaries*.

THE BATTLE OF BIBRACTE

We have already had to conclude from general considerations that the number of 368,000 individuals that Caesar gives for the Helvetian migration is extremely exaggerated. Consideration of the political character of the undertaking stimulates further doubt about whether it was really the entire Helvetian people, with their allies, that moved out. Surely a certain number of women and children went along—that was required by the plan—but it is very hard to believe that the Helvetii actually loaded up their families and all their household equipment and burned their hamlets and villages behind them. The daily marches which they made were, to be sure, not unusually short,[10] but they were also not long, and they seem to indicate the presence of a certain wagon train; the account of the battle shows that it can not have been so very large. Caesar, who had camped some 2 to 3 miles behind the Helvetii, gave up the idea of continuing to follow them closely and turned in the direction of Bibracte. A few deserters brought this news to the Helvetii, who faced about and started the battle toward the seventh hour, that is between noon and 1 P.M. The Helvetii were followed by all their carts, with which they formed a wagon barricade. Consequently, the Helvetii had first started their march, with all their carts, in one direction and then faced about and followed Caesar in the other direction. The wagon train must nevertheless have traveled some 7 to 9 miles that morning; we know what that means, even if Caesar naturally does not say that all the wagons were once again in place when the battle began. We cannot estimate specifically, but it is clear that a group that makes such movements cannot, after all, be of more than moderate size.

Caesar had 6 legions and native auxiliaries, including 4,000 cavalry (Chapter 15). Normally 6 legions would be 36,000 men strong; of that number, Caesar may have had 30,000 on hand, including 2 legions of recruits, which he placed in a rear position and did not use in the battle. Caesar therefore had, including his native auxiliaries,[11] between 36,000 and 40,000 men, and consequently a considerable numerical superiority on the spot.

As soon as Caesar noticed that the Helvetii were approaching, he sent his cavalry against them to hold them up as long as possible, had his 4 veteran legions form up in 3 echelons on the slope of a hill, and used the 2 legions of recruits, with all the native auxiliaries, to establish and occupy a fortified camp behind the line of battle, into which the entire train was driven.[12]

The Helvetii drove up against the very favorably selected position of the Romans and were thrown back. When the Romans pushed forward in pursuit, they were attacked on the flank by the Boii and the Tulingeri, either because the latter forces were only just arriving on the battlefield or because the Romans had had their flanks protected by the terrain in their initial position, from which they had intentionally been lured out by the Helvetii. The flank attack also encouraged the front of the Helvetii to move forward again, and the situation would have become precarious for the Romans, in view of the extraordinary courage with which the Gauls were fighting, if the Roman echelon tactics had not proved themselves against the double attack. Caesar had the third echelon swing around against the Boii and the Tulingeri and on both sides he moved over to the offensive (*"Romani conversa signa bipartito intulerunt"* ["The Romans wheeled about and attacked in two divisions"]). The Gauls slowly gave way, and not until nightfall did the Romans succeed in storming the wagon barricade. Caesar did not order a pursuit but remained on the battlefield for three days, because of the wounded, as he says, and to bury the dead. The Helvetii fled to the east (northeast) into the region of the Lingones and surrendered a few days later.

It is curious that Caesar did not use his two recruit legions at all but had the flank attack of the Boii and Tulingeri thrown back only by the third echelon. He tells us with great emphasis how hard the Helvetii contested the victory of the Romans and that they had only been pressed back, that not a one of them had turned his back and fled. Why then did he not move his reserve into the battle?

The explanation probably is that Caesar, on seeing the Helvetii moving up so suddenly, suspected that the Aedui were planning a betrayal and that, while he was fighting the Helvetii, he might suddenly be attacked in the rear by a force of Aedui. He did not wish to say that, not only because it did not occur, but also because he was, after all, trying to obscure as much as possible the Aedui's entire relationship to the Helvetii. He continues to tell us only about Dumnorix, who misled the people. According to our concept, however, this faction was much stronger, and we find further corroboration of this idea in the fact that it also provides an explanation for the otherwise incomprehensible holding back of all the sharpshooters and a full third of the hoplites.

Excursus

1. According to our concept of the nature of the whole campaign, the Helvetii must have moved by on the east of Bibracte, whereas those scholars who maintain that the goal of the migration was the region of the Santones would place the battlefield to the west of the Aedui capital. That the Helvetii, if they intended to return to their homeland, still moved so close to Bibracte—that is, so far westward—does not contradict our concept, since they no doubt continued to count on a political shift on the part of the Aedui. A very strong argument in favor of the correctness of our reconstruction, however, is Caesar's statement that they took up their withdrawal in the direction of the Lingones, that is, eastward. How are they supposed to have gone there if, as other scholars assume, they had fought the battle facing eastward? A fully defeated army flees in the direction of its defeat and under no circumstances in the exactly opposite direction. If the Helvetii, however, as I believe, fought the battle facing westward, they cannot have been on the way toward the Loire, and, beyond that, the region of the Santones.

Napoleon III and Stoffel, in *Guerre de César et d'Arioviste* (p. 78), seek to show the possibility of this situation by having the Helvetii, after the battle near Luzy, southwest of Autun, had been fought with their front toward the south, take up their withdrawal via Moulins-Engilbert, Lormes, Avallon to Tonnerre, consequently northward. To make this plausible, however, one has to assume that near Tonnerre they were already in the region of the Lingones, a point which hardly seems credible, since the latters' territory reached southward as far as the Saône and their principal town was Langres.[13] This assumption also stands in direct contradiction to Caesar's statement that the Helvetii arrived in the area of the Lingones on the fourth day of their withdrawal. From Luzy to Tonnerre it is a distance of 120 kilometers as the crow flies, a stretch that the Helvetii could not have covered in four days under any circumstances, even if they marched day and night.[14]

From the fact that Caesar still had to make a rather long march to Besançon after the capitulation of the Helvetii (*Bell. Gall.* 1. 38) we cannot conclude anything of a definite nature, since it is possible that in the meantime he had made a further movement that was not reported by him.

Stoffel believes that, through excavations, he definitely found traces of the battlefield between Montmort and Toulon-sur-Arroux, about nine miles southeast of Luzy, directly south of Mont-Beuvray. But the objects found there do not show any kind of direct relationship to this period or, in fact, even to a battle, so that no proof can be drawn from this. According to Holmes (p. 619), there were later found in the area of the excavated fortifications remains of swords, javelins, and helmets, but that still does not constitute real proof.

A direct counterproof, however, is provided by a passage in Caesar's text. He says that the Boii and Tulingeri had enveloped the Romans "*a latere aperto.*" According to the normal concept, "*latus apertum*" means the right side, the one not protected by the shield. But it is clear that, if the column of the Helvetii proceeded westward and finally turned its front toward the south, as Stoffel claims, their rear guard could only have struck the Romans in their left flank. Stoffel therefore produces very detailed evidence to the effect that *latus apertum* does not necessarily mean the right flank, but, in general, the unprotected one. Holmes, however, has vitiated this evidence through reference to the passages in *Bell. Gall.* 5. 35. 2 and 7. 4, where "*latus apertum*" obviously is used as a technical expression for "right flank." Holmes himself, since Stoffel's explanations otherwise appear to him to be so convincing, is still unwilling to speak out with absolute certainty on this point. I myself would like to say just the opposite, namely, that with this point we have definite proof that the battle was fought east of Bibracte. For if the Helvetii retired westward and finally made their withdrawal toward the north, then they must have deployed toward the left flank and must have had their front facing southward during the battle. The Boii and Tulingeri, then, who moved up from the west, could only fall upon the Romans' left flank. If the battle took place east of Bibracte, however, and the Helvetii fled approximately toward the northeast, then the Helvetii had their front facing southwest or south, and consequently the Boii and Tulingeri, as they moved up, could attack the right flank of the Romans. This would be conclusive if Holmes had not established that Caesar's manuscript reads only "*latere aperto*" and not "*a latere aperto,*" which can perhaps be interpreted as "while their flank was uncovered." Nevertheless, "*latere aperto*" applies with much greater probability to an attack by the Boii into the Roman right flank and therefore supports a determination of the position of the battlefield as east of Bibracte as well as the concept that the Helvetii were not on their way toward the region of the Santones.

2. Many of the necessary objections to Caesar's account have already been brought forth quite correctly in the rather crude pamphlet *The Struggles of the Helvetii, Suebi, and Belgae against C. Julius Caesar*: New Looks at Old Stories, by Max Eichheim (*Die Kämpfe der Helvetier, Sueben und Belgier gegen C. J. Cäsar*: Neue Schlaglichter auf alte Geschichten, von Max Eichheim.) (Neuburg A. D. Selbstverlag, 1866), but in view of the obvious scholarly dilettantism of the author and his wild sallies to right and left these points have either been ignored or rejected by the scholarly world. Later H. Rauchenstein attempted, in a Jena dissertation, *Caesar's Campaign against the Helvetii* (*Der Feldzug Cäsars gegen die Helvetier*) 1882, to present Eichheim's analysis in a logical light, so to speak, and to reformulate the latter's objections, pointing out their value in a scholarly and methodical manner. Nevertheless, he did not win any supporters either, since he attempted to manipulate the external facts in too bold a manner. The logical conclusion of his concept of events forces him in the end to assume that Caesar was not victorious at Bibracte but, on the contrary, was driven back into his camp. The fight at the wagon barricade, as he sees it, was not at the Helvetii's train but rather at Caesar's, and since the Helvetii were not strong enough to defeat the Romans, they finally came to an agreement with them.

The point where Rauchenstein goes astray is right at the start, with respect to the purpose of the Helvetian march. Probably every student of the Gallic War, without exception, has felt that the two purposes stated by Caesar, migration and the winning of hegemony over all the Gallic peoples, are incompatible with each other. Rauchenstein recognizes that but, like all the others, he takes the wrong direction in arriving at his correction; he disregards the aspect of conquest and concentrates on the migration.

It is true, of course, that Caesar himself also does this, although he expressly says that the Helvetii, even after the death of Orgetorix, adhered to the decision they had formerly made (migration *and* conquest), but nevertheless, from that point on, he speaks only of the migration. He could not avoid leaving this lacuna, since of course he does not want to admit to us the real reason for the Helvetian march, the intended fight against Ariovistus, which would have made the intervention of the Romans in these Gallic affairs unnecessary and impracticable. If we read his account with this true purpose in mind; that is, if, of the two purposes that he gives and one of which must under any circumstances be eliminated, we drop the migration—or rather, reduce it to a simple politico-military pretense—everything becomes completely clear.

Rauchenstein emphasizes the point that, despite his victory, Caesar neither pursued the Helvetii nor moved to Bibracte, whereas he had told us earlier that his soldiers had no more provisions. The explanation is that Caesar's victory already gave him everything that he needed. He did not pursue the Helvetii because he had no desire to destroy them but, on the contrary, wanted to spare them after they were defeated. After all, he now intended to appear on the scene as the champion of all the Gauls against Ariovistus. This agrees very well with the fact that the Roman commander—a point he does not mention but which Mommsen points out in *Hermes* 16: 447—granted the Helvetii a very favorable treaty. On the other hand, to have marched off immediately in the opposite direction, to Bibracte, would have been unwise, for it could have given the impression that the victory had not been so very clear-cut. As for provisions, the Aedui undoubtedly brought them to the Romans on the spot right after the victory.

3. The study by H. Klövekorn, *Caesar's Battles against the Helvetii in 58 B.C.* (*Die Kämpfe Cäsars gegen die Helvetier im Jahre 68*) (Leipzig, 1889), I know only through Ackermann's review in the *Wochenschrift für klassische Philologie*, 1889, Section 1392.

I have heard of a study on the same subject by Bircher but have not been able to obtain it.

4. The attitude of Napoleon III and Stoffel toward Caesar's reports of numerical strengths forms a remarkable proof of how hard it is to free oneself from the authority of the written word. Napoleon gives us an estimate of the length of terrain over which the Helvetian wagon train would have had to stretch if Caesar's figures were correct. But neither he nor even Stoffel carried this process out to its logical conclusion and rejected Caesar's figures, and, basing his position on theirs, Holmes too explains (p. 224) that Caesar's figures could not be challenged, since, after all, Stoffel was a man who knew what he was writing. But here it is not a question of authoritativeness but rather of the nature of things that forces the decision, and the single objective explanation that Holmes found is unusable. He refers to the fact that the Helvetii did not need to have all their wagons travel in a single column but were able to form several columns. That can certainly be done, but only as long as the march is crossing smooth terrain. If there is but a single narrow spot along the way, such as a bridge, a ford, a narrow pass, that has the same effect as if the whole route were narrow. With very good equipment and thorough discipline one could possibly manage to have the wagons pass the narrow spot at double speed and thereby neutralize the effects of the obstacle. But this method is not feasible for a train composed of carts drawn by oxen and occupied principally by women and children. This recourse also breaks down at every spot where soft, or rain-soaked, or uneven ground prevents the carts from moving temporarily at a trot. We can therefore assume that the migrations of the peoples (*Völkerwanderungen*) in cases where they really occurred, were carried out principally with a single line of wagons and were limited to very short daily movements.

5. That Caesar's figures were too high was also recognized in Rome at that same

time by thoughtful individuals. We may draw that conclusion from the fact that we find in Orosius 6. 7. 6 another report, according to which the column making the move had a strength of only 157,000, of whom 47,000 died on the way. This information probably stems from Asinius Pollio, one of Caesar's generals in the civil war.

But although Pollio apparently accepted the figure of 110,000 as the strength that the Helvetii were supposed to have had on their return to their own land, nevertheless this figure, too, must still be too high. This count is presumably more an estimate or an overall reckoning based on the statements of the aldermen (*Altermänner*: the leaders of the hundreds), who did not go about it as accurately as in the case of a real census. When I think of all the movements the column made, I cannot imagine that it ever amounted to anything even approaching 110,000 individuals, and I therefore suspect that this total also includes those who remained in the homeland. In Strabo 4. 3. 3 we find the report that the number of survivors was 8,000. Should we assume that this figure is taken out of thin air? If we relate this number only to the warriors themselves and assume that, in view of the heavy losses and of the breaking away of the Boii, who remained in the territory of the Aedui, the number was originally half again as large, it would then seem to be basically very probable. A total of 12,000 courageous barbarians might very well have felt themselves capable of engaging four Roman legions, and with a column of this order of strength, which perhaps counted a total of 20,000 individuals, the reported movements would no longer evoke skepticism on our part.

The study by Wachsmut in *Klio* 3 (1903): 281, is based on an acceptance of the credibility of the movements of the hundreds of thousands as related by the ancient authors.

6. Veith, in *Caesar's Campaigns* (*Feldzüge Cäsars*), repeats Caesar's account in the text of his work and supplements it with my concept, with the reservation that Caesar did not intentionally distort the facts but failed to perceive all the relationships of the overall picture.

7. In contradiction to my concept, several newer studies have sought to defend the credibility of the main points of Caesar's report, particularly holding to the migration plan of the Helvetii, and, as a result, placing the battle not to the east but to the southwest or south of Bibracte. Some of these, specifically, are Ziehen, *The Latest Attack on Caesar's Credibility* (*Der neueste Angriff auf Cäsars Glaubwürdigkeit*) *Berichte des freien deutschen Hochstifts zu Frankfurt a. M* (1901); F. Fröhlich, *Caesar's Credibility in his Report on the Campaign against the Helvetii* (*Die Glaubwürdigkeit Cäsars in seinem Bericht über den Feldzug gegen die Helvetier*) (Aarau, 1903); H. Bircher, *Bibracte* (Aarau, 1904).

The critical point is whether the Helvetii really intended to migrate to the mouth of the Garonne or whether this plan was only a pretense for bringing up a reinforcing army for the Aedui patriotic faction against Ariovistus.

If we accept the second assumption, the turning off of the column northward after the Saône crossing as well as the facing about for the battle can be very simply explained; with the first assumption, both of these points remain plainly inexplicable.

Ziehen says, "I must now say first of all that in the year 1900 advice concerning routes which one can choose can be given very easily on the basis of excellent maps; for the poor Helvetii 2,000 years ago, however, this knowledge was not so easy to obtain, particularly since they had the Romans behind them. Furthermore, how does Delbrück know whether the routes that have been discovered by the French scholars were at that time already really usable? But even if we assume that they were and that the Helvetii knew about them, it is still entirely possible that their use was blocked by the mountaineers living in the area. We know from the negotiations with the Sequani at the start of the move how important the Helvetii considered it to avoid difficult defiles, and Delbrück himself says precisely on this point that the Helvetii could easily have held up the Romans with a small rear guard on those mountain roads. But what works to the advantage of the Helvetii can also work against them; consequently they could only risk taking this route if the local population caused them no difficulty, and the possibility that this did occur, after all, can be disputed by nobody."

My answer to this: It goes completely without saying that there were roads leading through the mountain valleys in this well populated region, which was in no way lacking in towns and movement between them. Furthermore, the Helvetii were familiar with them. They had planned their move for a long time and were not so careless as to march off into the blue. Their announced intention was undoubtedly to take the direct route toward the Santones; otherwise, why would they have crossed the Saône so far to the south and not already have turned toward the northwest much sooner, either from Geneva or as soon as they entered the plain? What purpose was served by their right-angled detour? It appears conceivable that the mountaineers might unexpectedly have sought to close the passes to them. This motive is not strong enough, however, to justify such an important measure as the drastic change in the direction of the march. The occupation of passes in mountainous country of such moderate altitudes does, of course, cause delays, but it is possible to move around them, and the resulting difficulty is not to be compared with the danger to which the Helvetian column was exposed in the river valley, as it was being followed by the Romans. Most important of all in this context, however, is the fact that the animosity of the mountaineers, which is considered so possible in this argument, is a completely groundless presumption; Caesar does not say a word about it. Not only does he give us no reason for the surprising change of direction by the enemy column, but it is also clear that he himself had from the start expected nothing other than the march northward along the Saône. For the reprovisioning of his army that he had arranged was to follow him on the river, and when he turned away from the Saône, he did not have the necessary wagon train to move his provisions up behind him. If the Roman commander had initially foreseen the campaign as going over the mountains into the Loire valley, he would necessarily have had to provide for an adequate train. Caesar gives us no reason for the turning off to the north of the Helvetii because he himself never believed in the march to the region of the Santones, and the shift of the Helvetii toward the north was the more natural and obvious move.

The same points apply to the Helvetii's sudden facing about for the battle. If they intended to move to the Santones, why in the world did they become involved in a battle with the Romans just at the moment when the latter were turning away from their pursuit and heading off in another direction? Up to now, nobody has undertaken to answer this question in even a partially logical manner.

On the other hand Fröhlich has eliminated the last remaining doubtful point in the report by Caesar itself. I have written above that the attack by the Boii and the Tulingeri "*latere aperto*" must be the decisive point if this Latin expression, even without the addition of the preposition "*a*," means "the right flank." Now Fröhlich cites (p. 29) two passages from the *Bellum Alexandrinum* (20. 3 and 40. 2), from which it is clear that the addition of the preposition is, in fact, meaningless. If then the Boii and Tulingeri attacked the right flank of the Romans, the withdrawal of the Helvetii must, in keeping with the positions of the armies, logically have taken place toward the east or northeast, and therefore on the right of Bibracte, and Stoffel's interpretation has become impossible, since he has to have the attack coming from the left. It is true, of course, that Bircher opposes this argument by having both armies make such a drastic wheeling about as they took position (the Romans facing southwest) that the flanking attack could, after all, still take them from the right. I consider that to be fully impossible; principally also for the reason that the main body of the Helvetii could not then have taken up their withdrawal toward the Lingones. Bircher himself adds that the events following the battle remained "extremely vague," especially the dashing flight, 30 kilometers a day. All vagueness disappears, however, if the battle took place east of Bibracte, that is, not very far from the borders of the Lingones' region.

8. A. Klotz, in "The Migration of the Helvetii" ("Der Helvetierzug,") *Neue Jahrbücher für das klassische Altertum*, Vol. 35 and 36, No. 10, 1915, seeks again to rescue Caesar's report by simply skimming over the difficulties.

9. Konrad Lehmann, in *Sokrates* 69, No. 10/11, 1915: 488, defends Caesar, agreeing in general with my concept, against the attacks of Ferrero.

NOTES FOR CHAPTER II

1. According to Beloch. Hubo, in *Neue Jahrbücher für Philologie* 147 (1893): 707, estimates 25,000 and seeks to justify Caesar's own figure by eliminating a "C" from the latter's number for the width.

2. Clausewitz, too, estimates in this way (10: 66). A useful comparison is provided by "The War Journal of Albrecht von Brandenburg" ("Das Kriegsbuch Albrechts v. Brandenburg") in Jähns's *History of Warfare* (*Geschichte des Kriegswesens*) 1: 521.

3. The trains that followed the Prussian army at Olmütz in 1758 were made up of almost 4,000 wagons, most of them drawn by 4 horses, and had a length of almost 2 days' march. *General Staff Publication* (*Generalstabswerk*) 7: 93.

4. Not by a full fourth, as is often said; the quarter of which Caesar speaks refers only to the Helvetii in the narrower sense. The allies were already across, and Caesar also does not say that the quarter was still there when he attacked, but rather, when his scouts observed it. See also Stoffel, *The War between Caesar and Ariovistus* (*Guerre de César et d'Arioviste*) p. 75.

5. If Maissiat should be right in distinguishing between the "Segusiavi" and the "Sebusiani," placing the latter in the southern Jura, north of the Rhone, on the Ain, and thereby having Caesar not camp near Lyons but follow the Helvetii from Fort l'Ecluse through Bourg-en-Bresse, with the result that Labienus with his three legions was waiting one day's march to the east during the battle on the Saône, then the Helvetii would indeed have had full freedom of movement from Montmerle, where they were attacked, to take the route either directly westward or southwestward.

6. Las Cases, *Memoirs from Saint Helena* (*Mémorial de Sainte-Hélène*) 2: 445.

7. H. Bender, in "Caesar's Credibility on the War with Ariovistus" ("Cäsars Glaubwürdigkeit über den Krieg mit Ariovist,") (*Neue Korrespondenzblätter für die Gelehrtenschulen Württembergs*, 1894), shows how very exaggerated Caesar's account of the hegemony that Ariovistus exercised in Gaul actually is, but the fact itself that Ariovistus was master of a part of central Gaul is not to be doubted.

8. Caesar has this thought expressed specifically by Liscus (1. 17) in the form that they would prefer to obey other Gauls rather than Romans—which presupposes that these other Gauls had first broken the mastery of the Germans.

9. The fact that the Helvetii announced precisely this area as the goal of their migration has been explained very brilliantly by O. Hirschfeld in his study "Aquitania in the Roman Period" ("Aquitanien in der römischen Zeit") (*Sitzungsberichte der Berliner Akademie*, 1896, p. 453), where it is shown to be highly probable that the Helvetii, and perhaps also the Boii, who were accompanying them, were related to tribes already settled on the lower Garonne. In that connection Hirschfeld, too, makes the observation that such a migration was not so easy to imagine. With only one step farther along this train of thought we arrive at the hypothesis presented above in the text.

10. The long time they are supposed to have taken crossing the Saône is no proof, since we cannot know to what extent Caesar exaggerated here also.

11. I consider it as impossible that, as is often assumed, Caesar had with him, in addition to cavalry, a considerable force of other Gallic allies, either from the province or from the Aedui or other tribes. His six legions were strong enough to oppose the Helvetii in battle, and allies whose reliability is questionable are of no use but only create problems through the difficulties they cause in the matter of rations. The *auxilia* of which Caesar speaks are mainly the Numidians, Balearics, and Cretans whom he has with him (2. 7).

12. The passage describing the formation has not been passed down very clearly in handwriting and has been read and corrected in a variety of ways by the different editors. All, however, have interpreted its meaning in the same way.

13. Strabo 4. 1. 11. In the north the region of the Lingones is supposed to have extended still farther than that of the Mediomatrici. Strabo 4. 2. 4.

14. Scholars have disagreed as to how Caesar's expression "*nullam partem noctis itinere intermisso*" ("the march was not interrupted for any part of the night") is to be interpreted. Meusel puts it in parentheses, and it does, in fact, look very much like a side comment. The meaning can neither be that they marched only at night nor that they marched continuously, day and night, for four days, but this can only be a hyperbolic expression for the fact that, in their haste and fear, they also took advantage of darkness for some of their marching.

Chapter III

Ariovistus

After the subjection of the Helvetii Caesar had delegations from the Gallic princes appear before him, and they asked him to liberate them from Ariovistus' hegemony. Caesar moved out and came upon the Germanic army in the region of Belfort or in upper Alsace.

It is not possible to determine the definite location. Ariovistus did not move directly into the decisive battle but marched around the Roman camp and set up his wagon barricade about two miles away, in conformity with the mountainous terrain, so that he could send his cavalry out from there and cut the road along which the Romans were bringing up their provisions. Since Ariovistus cannot have thought of taking care of the situation without fighting a battle and also cannot have had in mind maneuvering Caesar back perhaps some fifteen or twenty miles, the purpose of his maneuver must have been to force Caesar into a withdrawal because of his supply situation and then attack him on the march. The strength of his army lay in the coordinated functioning of his cavalry and lightly armed foot soldiers, who were well drilled and greatly feared. The Gallic cavalry that Caesar had with him was afraid to move out against this force.

This relationship of the fighting arms, the superiority of the Germanic army in its own special mixture of weapons, must also serve as an explanation of the success of Ariovistus' maneuver. Otherwise it would be difficult to imagine (unless we concluded that Caesar as a strategist was greatly inferior to Ariovistus) how Ariovistus succeeded in setting up his wagon defensive position so close to the Roman camp, and in doing so, marched by and around the camp. Even if Caesar's account is very exaggerated, if it was not really whole Germanic tribes with their women and children who made this movement but a relatively much smaller group of mobile

479

warriors with a small train of supplies and women following, even a few hundred carts are still a heavy burden and cannot be exposed to an orderly enemy attack while on the march or forming up the wagon defenses. This action only becomes understandable if we assume that Ariovistus was able to cover his circling movement simultaneously by clever utilization of the terrain and his light infantry. After this passing movement was successful, Ariovistus dominated the plain and intercepted the supplies coming up, and if the Roman army started to march in any direction whatever, it could not help being hard put to defend itself and its train against the sudden attacks, now from this direction and now from that, by these barbarians who scorned death. Ariovistus had maneuvered with complete dexterity, but Caesar was superior to him. First Caesar repeatedly challenged him to come out for battle by having his army deploy on the plain. Ariovistus warily declined to move out from his wagon defenses, and that raised the morale of the Roman soldiers, who interpreted the reluctance of the Germanic army as cowardice. But the most important thing was to open up the supply route again. Caesar moved with his army in battle formation to a position that blocked off the Germanic troops' entrance to the plain in the direction of Caesar's supply road and had his two forward echelons remain in battle order while the third echelon, behind them, established a fortified camp large enough for two legions, the force which was then assigned to occupy it. As soon as the main body of the Romans had moved back into their principal camp, Ariovistus tried in vain to take the smaller camp by storm in a dashing attack. Caesar was so confident of his fortification and its garrison that he did not even bother to move his main body out to their relief. On the following day, however, he deployed his entire army again for battle and moved up close to the Germanic wagon defenses. Ariovistus finally decided to accept the challenge. Caesar was now in a better position to hold out than he; he had secured his supplies, and the Germanic army had nothing more to gain by delaying. Certainly Ariovistus must have been prepared for many weeks or even months for the start of the war, and he had surely gathered all the available forces before moving against the Romans. Otherwise, he could, of course, have withdrawn a long distance and drawn Caesar along behind him without difficulty or any significant losses. But certainly that possibility lay far from his thoughts. On the other hand, the Romans would surely not have allowed themselves to be lured into an attack on the wagon defenses, and a longer period of waiting would have heightened their morale, since they were the side laying down the challenge, whereas it would have weakened that of the Germanic army. Ariovistus therefore moved out of his wagon defenses and drew up his warriors for battle in tribal groups.

Once again the echelon tactics of the Romans proved their worth. When their left flank became hard-pressed, young Crassus, who actually commanded the cavalry, led the third echelon toward this side and through this reinforcing action won the upper hand there, just as Caesar had already done on the other flank.

In Caesar's account we find no mention of the position or the action of the cavalry. Where were the dreaded Germanic double fighters? Why, after they had driven off the Gallic cavalry, did they not fall on the flanks and rear of the Roman legions, as Hannibal's cavalry did at Cannae? It is completely impossible that some unusual situation might have caused them not to be on hand, since in that case Ariovistus would not have moved out of his wagon defenses on that same day.

Everything depends, of course, on the answer to this question. Caesar is silent on the subject. I believe that the answer is to be found in the writings of his most highly qualified commentator, Napoleon I, who, in his dictation on St. Helena concerning Caesar's wars, states, against all the concepts of his time, that the Germanic army cannot have been numerically superior to Caesar's. We take the liberty of going one step farther: For the failure of the Germanic cavalry in the battle there can be only *one* explanation: that Ariovistus was so weak in infantry and he had to incorporate with his regular infantry the lightly armed foot soldiers who normally accompanied the cavalry. This reduction in strength made it possible for the Gallic cavalry to stand up to the Germanic to a certain extent and to prevent them from attacking the flanks of the legions. Caesar has told us nothing about this because he did not want to report either the numerical superiority of his army over that of the Germanic army or the cooperation and accomplishments of the allied Gallic cavalry.

A welcome corroboration of the assumption that Ariovistus' army was only very small is to be found in Caesar's report (1. 40) on the manner in which the Germanic King had gained his mastery over the Gauls. For months, Caesar says, Ariovistus remained in a camp protected by swamps ("*cum multos menses castris se ac paludibus tenuisset neque sui potestatem fecisset*" ["he had kept his forces in their camps and in the marshes for many months and did not offer the Gauls a chance to fight him"]). Even if these months should only have been weeks, this point still conclusively eliminates the possibility that the army might have numbered several tens of thousands, all the more so in that, of course, there were women and children accompanying the army and, in addition to the horses, certainly also herds of cattle to be fed. We can imagine, improbable as it might seem, that the Germanic army carried along with it even much more grain than the Helvetii carried on their carts, for the Helvetii were on the move and took their forage from the countryside, whereas the Germanic warriors, in their camp, had to feed their horses from their accumulated supplies. It is certain that the army that Ariovistus led against the Romans was larger than the one with which he first gained his hegemony, but the nucleus was nevertheless still the same; we can perhaps imagine a doubling of the original strength, but certainly not a tenfold expansion.

The corroboration of the fact that the Romans probably enjoyed a very considerable numerical superiority now enables us, as we look back, also to understand better Ariovistus' maneuvering and clarifies another well-known episode of this war.

When Caesar had gone as far as Besançon on his advance against Ariovistus, his troops mutinied and refused to follow him farther against the fearful Germanic army. Caesar spoke to them reassuringly, told them about that earlier campaign of Ariovistus and closed his speech with the announcement that, if the others were unwilling to do so, he would continue the march with the Tenth Legion alone.

If the Germanic army had really been stronger in numbers than an army of six legions, Caesar's announcement that he would wage the war with *one* legion would, after all, hardly have made a good impression on the soldiers; they would have had the impression that their commander was a *miles gloriosus* (braggart soldier). Caesar probably added one more sentence, however, which he did not mention in his commentaries: that is, that the Germanic forces were so small in numbers that he was confident of beating them with the Tenth Legion alone. That was probably confirmed for the Roman soldiers by the Gauls, and the Romans then summoned up their courage and consented to follow their commander into the distant, unknown wilderness to fight against the uncouth Germanic warriors.

We would be able to discuss this campaign at much greater length and with greater certainty if we were in a position to determine with any degree of accuracy the marches of the two armies and the battlefield. That would be desirable not only for Caesar's sake and that of the Roman art of war, but also for the sake of his opponent. Ariovistus must have been not only a strong personality but also one endowed with strategic genius. He encountered one stronger than he and went down to defeat, but in the period halfway between the Cimbri and Arminius he is a strong witness for the original warlike qualities of the Germanic people. We know practically nothing of the Cimbri except that they defeated Roman armies and in the end were themselves defeated. It would be imaginable that they possessed no other quality but raw strength, but since we see how cleverly and boldly, even ingeniously, Ariovistus maneuvered and how soon after Ariovistus Arminius comes to our attention, we cannot doubt that from the very beginning the Germanic spirit possessed not only the savage factor of warfare, so to speak, but also its higher, intellectual aspects, and we can only regret that we cannot gain a more complete and more definite picture of Ariovistus' leadership.

Excursus

1. In Dio Cassius there appear now and then expressions that are in agreement with the concept of the Helvetian and Germanic campaigns presented above. They cannot, however, be valued as true source material, since J. Melber pointed out convincingly in a Munich program (1891), *The Report of Dio Cassius on Caesar's Gallic Wars* (*Der Bericht des Dio Cassius über die gallischen Kriege Cäsars*), that this report is nothing more than a rhetorically exaggerated excerpt from the commentaries. But even this author, in his reworking of the original, did not completely overlook the gaps and contradictions in Caesar's account, and from time to time he filled them in in the right direction from his own concept.

2. Even back in his time Napoleon I deplored in his précis the fact that Caesar's battles in Gaul "without names" cannot be fixed topographically and consequently cannot be fully judged.

Countless attempts have been made to establish the location of the battle against the Germanic army, but none of them has won general acceptance. The possibility of varying combinations is multiplied especially in this case through the fact that one of the most important passages is indefinite. Caesar's manuscripts agree in stating that the Romans pursued the defeated Germanic army 5,000 paces (*passus*), up to the Rhine, that is, between 4 and 5 miles. Plutarch, who took his information from Caesar, says, however, that it was 400 *stadia*, which would be 50,000 paces, and we read this same number in Orosius, who also used Caesar as his source. It is therefore possible, in fact probable, that the number in Caesar's manuscripts was corrupted and that the flight of the Germanic forces did not cover 4 to 5 miles but some 45 miles to the Rhine. This is all the more probable in that the maneuvers of Caesar and Ariovistus, if they took place only 4 or 5 miles from the Rhine, and therefore in the middle of the Alsatian plain, would not be at all understandable; what is needed here is an area that is in some respects limited and narrowed by the mountains.

This would be convincing if the Rhine River Control experts had not coincidentally come to the conclusion that in former times an arm of the Rhine flowed through the area of the present-day Ill River. On the basis of this determination,

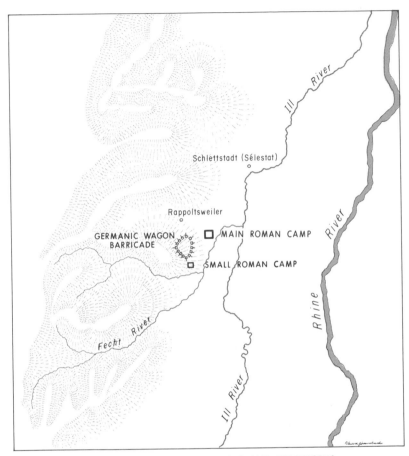

Fig. 4   BATTLE BETWEEN CAESAR AND ARIOVISTUS

Göler has held fast to the 5,000 paces and has sought the battlefield on the southern edge of the Vosges near Sennheim (Cernay), northeast of Belfort.

Napoleon III placed the battle in the same region, but with the maneuvering of the two sides turned about.

Colonel Stoffel places the battlefield 40 kilometers farther to the north, at the foot of the Vosges between Colmar and Schlettstadt (Sélestat), near Rappoltsweiler. According to the description of this perceptive soldier and outstanding scholar of Caesar's military actions, there is an area near the village of Zellenberg in which the maneuvers recounted by Caesar fit perfectly. The Germanic wagon train could have been moved by at some 3 kilometers' distance from the Roman camp over the foot-hills of the Vosges, where the legions, moving uphill, could have attacked it only with great difficulty, and again the small Roman camp finds its position somewhat to the south, where it blocks the Germanic forces from entering the plain.

Against this hypothesis Wiegand has stressed the point that the Germanic army could not have made a withdrawal to the Rhine from a battle in which it was facing eastward.[1] The objection is justified, but it can be clarified. It is very possible that the Germanic army did not accept battle directly in front of its wagon defenses near Zellenberg but rather made a movement in advance so that its front faced toward the south. While Caesar does not make any direct mention of such a move, it can nevertheless be inferred from the statement that the Germanic troops had surrounded their battle formation with their wagons and carts; they did therefore actually make some kind of movement with their wagon defenses before the battle. The purpose of this, as stated by Caesar, "so that there would remain no hope for flight," belongs in the same category of reports as that of the ranks bound together with chains in the battle with the Cimbri, and furthermore, as we learn later, the Germanic troops did nevertheless take flight.

Not so easily eliminated is another objection, raised by Colomb and Stolle.[2] Caesar says that on the seventh day of his march from Vesontio he received a report of the approach of Ariovistus and set up the camp near which the battle later took place. He did not, however, take the direct road but, in order to march through open terrain, made a swing (*circuitus*) of 50,000 paces, that is, about 45 miles. Now Stoffel, like most other scholars, considers the *circuitus* to have been only a part of the entire route, and he believes that the Roman army marched in the 7 days up to the region of Rappoltsweiler, which means an average daily march of 27 kilometers. That is certainly not an out-and-out impossibility, but it is still such a strenuous accomplishment that we would at least have to be able to find some special motive for such an effort. But there does not appear to be such a reason. It is impossible that Caesar can have driven his troops on in the hope that by gaining 2 or 3 days of marching time he would be able to fall upon Ariovistus while the latter was still unprepared. If Ariovistus was waiting for reinforcements, he would only have needed to remain in place or at most to move back a day's march, instead of going forward to meet Caesar, in order to put the situation back in balance. If Caesar had had such an idea, it would also be incomprehensible why, when he was informed that Ariovistus was still 36 kilometers away, he halted and established a camp instead of driving on against the enemy. Consequently, Colomb and Stolle are right in believing that under the prevailing circumstances Caesar cannot have moved from Besançon to Rappoltsweiler in 7 days.

Nevertheless, I should not like to give up Stoffel's hypothesis. We have been relying on the fact that Caesar's statement that he marched for 7 days was absolutely correct. But is this really so certain? The account was not written out until 8 years after the events. It is possible, of course, that he referred to some kind of written notes made at the time of the campaign; but it is also possible that no such notes were used or that they did not contain a specific statement about the time element. When we have occasion in a later volume to discuss the memoirs of Frederick and Napoleon on their campaigns, writings that we can corroborate through original documents, we shall see how many and how serious errors have crept into them, even without a biased intent. It is not at all impossible that Caesar was mistaken in his recollection and that the march had lasted not 7 but 9 or 10 days, and that would remove the objection to Stoffel's concept.

I place even less weight on the other objection, that the pursuit could not have extended some 45 miles from Rappoltsweiler to the Rhine. The direct, nearest route to the Rhine would, of course, have amounted to only some 11 miles, but if the battle was fought with the Germanic army facing southward, it could arrive at the Rhine only by moving off at a very acute angle, and it is also not impossible but is, in fact, highly probable that once again Caesar's statement is greatly exaggerated.

In the face of such extensive skepticism there will be some perhaps who bring up the question as to how we could risk explaining anything at all about the Persian Wars. In Caesar's case we have the account of an individual who was perhaps prejudiced and one-sided but was a professionally skilled and participating witness of the highest order—in the other case the account of a writer completely lacking in professional knowledge who repeats what was being said by people half a century after the events. Certainly Caesar is an infinitely better source than Herodotus, and

I should like first of all, turning the situation about, to emphasize for those who believe that they may repeat what Herodotus has written that, if even in Caesar's case such great caution is called for, Herodotus must still appear much more suspect. Nevertheless, we need not despair about attaining historical knowledge of the Persian Wars, for it is precisely here that we possess a tool of objective analysis that is so painfully lacking in Caesar's case: the battles of the Persian Wars can be definitely established topographically, and the terrain forms such an important part of every battle that, where we have reliable testimony in this respect, many vague points of the accounts handed down to us can thereby be eliminated.

The earlier hypotheses concerning the location of the battle with Ariovistus all had the weakness of offering inexplicable objective difficulties. Göler's concept, which also requires the injection of a march by the legions that was not reported by Caesar, especially fails to provide a suitable location for the smaller Roman camp and its purpose. Napoleon III has the Germanic army making its march by the Romans through the Alsatian plain, where the terrain would have provided it no protection whatever against a Roman flanking attack. Stoffel's hypothesis removes all objective difficulties. It is also entirely understandable that Ariovistus, knowing that his strength lay in his cavalry-light infantry combination, first allowed the Romans to move completely into the Alsatian plain before he confronted them. But it cannot be denied that the specifying of the location of the battle simply cannot be reconciled with the wording of the text of the commentaries as we know it.

The latest hypothesis by Colomb and Stolle,[3] according to which the battle was fought near Arcey, 10 kilometers east of Mömpelgard, has the advantage of corresponding exactly to the two definite space and time indications of Caesar (more than 50,000 *passus* with the *circuitus* from Besançon and 50,000 *passus* from the Rhine). On the circuitous route approximately via Voray, Pennesières, and Villersexel, Arcey is something over 45 miles from Besançon and just the same distance from the Rhine in a straight line. The objection that just a little over 45 miles is too short a distance for a march of 7 days is justifiably rejected. The Romans had to make their march with great caution and fortify their camp each evening; they had no reason for unusual haste, and it is of course also imaginable that bad weather deteriorated the roads and delayed the march.

Nevertheless, the points to be made against this hypothesis are as follows:

First: We cannot understand why Caesar halted, when he received the word near Arcey that Ariovistus was 36 kilometers away. If he were already deep in Alsace, this halt would be understandable and natural; the Roman commander did not want to overextend his line of communications unnecessarily and complicate his resupply. A halt near Arcey, still in the middle of the Sequani's area, far from the enemy, would have given the impression of fear; at Rappoltsweiler they would already have progressed so far toward the enemy that there could no longer be any such question.

Second: In the vicinity of Arcey we can understand neither the purpose nor the feasibility of the Germanic circling maneuver. Stolle did not push his study this far, and Colomb's conclusions are tenable neither from the critically analytical point of view nor from that of source interpretation. He assumes that Caesar's camp was between Sesmondans and Désandans and that Ariovistus, coming from Mömpelgard, blocked his supply route near Arcey. This, however, would neither have really cut off the Romans' supplies, since they could have them come up from the Lingones and the Leuci, nor would the Germanic army have been able to pass around the Roman camp through the plain, for in doing so they would have been attacked not only by the Gallic cavalry but also by the legions.

Fröhlich, in *Caesar's Method of Waging War* (*Cäsars Kriegswesen*), p. 206, has already rejected as being considerably too high the opinion of Rüstow, based on Vegetius, that a normal Roman day's march "*justum iter*" ("an appropriate march") was 30 kilometers. Colomb and Stolle, the latter in a very painstaking and scholarly study, now seek to show that such a march in wartime in enemy country amounted to not more than 12 to 14 kilometers. Stoffel assumes 25 kilometers, a distance that would still be greater than what has been considered normal up to our time, even though the Roman soldier still has to establish the fortified camp each evening. In a more recent study, *The Camp and Army of the Romans* (*Das Lager und Heer der Römer*, Strasbourg, 1912), Stolle successfully defended his opinion.

3. Winkler, in *The Location of the Battle between Caesar and Ariovistus* (*Der Cäsar-Ariovistsche Kampfplatz*, Colmar, 1907), believes that he has established the fact that the area determined by Stoffel cannot be reconciled in some of its points with Caesar's description, and he seeks to place the battlefield 23 kilometers still farther northward. Fabricius, in *Zeitschrift für die Geschichte des Oberrheins*, checked on the various topographical studies and found that a good deal was confirmed but that other portions were not.

4. C. Ebert, in *On the Origin of the Bellum Gallicum* (*Ueber die Entstehung des Bellum gallicum*, 1909), attempts to prove that Caesar wrote and published each of his books immediately after the events. He has not succeeded in convincing me; but even if he should be right, my knowledge of military history memoirs leads me to the belief that an error such as the one I have assumed and pointed out above (p. 485), that a march lasted not 7 but 9 days, is in no way impossible.

NOTES FOR CHAPTER III

1. *Mitteilungen der Gesellschaft für Erhaltung der geschichtlichen Denkmäler im Elsass*, Vol. 16, 1893.

2. G. Colomb, "Caesar's Campaign against Ariovistus" ("Campagne de César contre Arioviste") in *Revue archéologique*), Series 3, Vol. 33, 1898. Franz Stolle, *Where did Caesar Defeat Ariovistus?* (*Wo schlug Cäsar den Ariovist?*), (Strasbourg, 1889). Colomb carried out the topographical studies that led him to Arcey; Stolle complemented his work in the philological area. His treatment is extremely painstaking and in many respects valuable, but unfortunately it is rendered almost unreadable by a contrived system of formulas and abbreviations. At the end he gives an overall tabulation of the various concepts that have been formulated and a complete bibliography, which I should like to refer the reader to. Winckler's works were not available to me. One should compare Stolle's work with the review by Konrad Lehmann in *Deutsche Literaturzeitung*, No. 44, 1899, para. 1682.

3. Stolle has now dropped this pinpointing of the battlefield (*Camp and Army of the Romans* [*Lager und Heer der Römer*], 1912, Introduction).

Chapter IV

The Subjection of the Belgae

As liberator of the Gauls from the Germanic hegemony and as their leader, Caesar had conquered Ariovistus and had thereupon established in the latter's place his own mastery throughout the country. In the very next year he moved on farther in order to subject also the northern regions, whose inhabitants he himself collectively designated under the name of Belgae.

The Belgae had a premonition of their impending danger, united their forces, and when Caesar crossed their borders, moved out against him with a large allied army.

But civilization has means of warfare that are lacking to barbarians. The Belgae were no doubt capable of assembling a large army but not of holding it together and feeding it. Just as the Cimbri and Teutones had had to split up on their campaign into Italy and then were defeated individually by Marius, Caesar, instead of moving immediately into a decisive battle against an army of the same size as his or perhaps considerably larger, found the means of splitting up the allied army so that he could then deal with only individual tribes. In the meantime Caesar had organized 2 new legions, so that he now had a total of 8; with his auxiliary troops of Numidians, Cretans, Balearics, and Gallic cavalry, his army may well have numbered 50,000 combatants and a grand total of 80,000 to 100,000 souls. In order to feed such a mass in one place for a rather long time, one must have a very strong and reliable organization, transport, suppliers, and finance system. The Romans had such means, whereas the Belgae did not.

But Caesar had still other means at his disposal. He set up a camp on the north bank of the Aisne, and his army was so well equipped with tools and his soldiers so well disciplined and so well trained in their techniques that within the shortest possible time an

488

impregnable fortress stood there. Napoleon III had excavations made at a spot indicated by Göler and found and confirmed near the village of Berry au Bac, a crossing point that also played a role in the events of 1814, very significant remains of a military installation. The moats were 18 feet wide and 9 to 10 feet deep; the rampart, a combined palisades and breastwork, was 12 feet high, and consequently 21 to 22 feet above the bottom of the moat. Along the front of the camp, which lay on a long ridge, ran a marshy brook, the Miette.

Up to this point everything fits into the picture. But the description that Caesar gives in detail of the direction of the moats and the relationship of the deployment for battle to the camp cannot be reconciled with the excavation. A number of scholars have therefore assumed that Caesar himself, when he wrote his account, no longer had the situation clearly and definitely in mind,[1] whereas others have indicated as the camp and battle location a place some 5 miles downstream (westward), near the village of Chaudardes,[2] where, however, no excavations have yet been carried out either to confirm or to contradict this presumption. Basically, the question has no real importance. The important points remain: (1) Caesar took up his position on the north shore of the river; (2) he covered the crossing behind him (and somewhat off to the side) with a bridgehead; and (3) he also established a stronghold on the south side of the river that was occupied by six cohorts and served to cover the supply roads.

Caesar took up his position on the side of the river facing the enemy. In case of a battle he would have had the river behind him, but the fortified camp gave him such great security that he could afford to risk that, and from this point he himself was in a position to go over to the offensive at any moment.

The Roman camp was in the territory of the Remi, a tribe of the Belgae that had, however, already gone over to the Romans. The allied army of the Belgae at first invested the Remi border town of Bibrax (Vieux-Laon or Bièvres), no doubt with the hope of thereby luring Caesar out of his camp, since the conquering of this small town would, in itself, have been no great task for a large army nor would it have had any particular significance. Caesar succeeded, however, in reinforcing the garrison with sharpshooters and slingers from his army, so that the town held fast and the Belgae gave up the siege. Now they moved up directly against the Roman camp itself, and Caesar had his army move out and deploy in battle order. Beyond this demonstration, however, nothing happened, since justifiably neither of the two sides was willing to decide to attack through the swampy valley.

The Belgae then attempted to cross the Aisne farther downstream with a small body of lightly armed troops in order to cut off the Romans' supply line, but Caesar had the river bank well patrolled and on receiving the first report of this attempt he was able to send his own cavalry and sharpshooters back across his bridge and thus prevented the crossing. If the Belgae had crossed with the main body of their army, the Roman lightly armed troops would of course have been unable to prevent the move, but that was too much for the strategic capabilities of the Belgae. In this event they would, it is true, actually have cut off the line of communications of the Romans and interrupted their supplies, but to the same extent they themselves would have been cut off from their territory and would have laid it open to attack by the Romans. What then should they do? Since the Romans did not move out for a battle in the open field, the Belgae would have had to surround their camp on all sides and starve them. Since the area was crossed by the Aisne and the swamp, they would have had to form a very wide circle. According to Caesar's figure (he gives the Belgae 306,000 men),[3] their numerical superiority would have sufficed for this purpose. It is possible that they had no such superiority at all, but even if they did have, the difficulties of feeding such a large army surpassed their capabilities. They had reached the end of their military skill, and when they now also received the news that the Aedui, allied with the Romans, had invaded their land at another point at Caesar's behest and were laying it waste, they decided to return home. There was nothing else they could do. Their promise to come to the mutual aid of one another if Caesar invaded their territory was nothing more than a face-saving disguise for their complete defeat. Caesar's military skill had enabled him to apply the superior organization of the Roman army over the mass levy of the barbarian tribes in such a way that the mass was first of all split up almost without any bloodshed and then the individual parts were easily defeated. His success was so great that Caesar himself was at first taken by surprise and thought that the withdrawal of the enemy hordes was only a ruse. The Belgae had started their retreat during the night, and it was not until morning that the Roman-Gallic cavalry took up the pursuit and brought hard pressure to bear on the fugitives.

Even the fortified positions of the Belgae now surrendered to the

Romans as soon as the latter brought up their elaborate siege engines.

A single group consisting of three tribes, the Nervii, the Veromandui, and the Atrebates, combining courage with a stratagem, made one last effort to save their freedom. They fell upon the Romans, whose patrols had not been alert enough, just at the moment when they were setting up their camp in a wooded area on the Sambre. The allied Gallic cavalry, the lightly armed troops, and the train took to flight, but the Roman legionaries had enough discipline not to allow themselves to be caught up in the panic, and they quickly took up an orderly formation again. As soon as the fight was brought to a deadlock, it was already won, since the Romans were dealing with only three Gallic tribes and therefore, even without the allied troops that had fled, still enjoyed a large superiority under any circumstances, perhaps even a twofold preponderance. Two legions, which were for a while in a dire situation,[4] were soon disengaged by the others, which had already been victorious, and by the two last ones, which were still on the march and hastened forward.

First in the battle with the Helvetii, again in the battle against the Germanic army, and now for the third time in the battle with the Nervii, we have reached the opinion that the numerical superiority lay on the side of the Romans. In the case of the Helvetii we arrived at that conclusion from the movements of the army before the battle; with the Germanic army the indication came from its earlier campaign against the Gauls and from the events of the battle itself; for the Nervii, it is the population statistics that will give us this proof. Whoever might wish to regard these bits of evidence only as probabilities must nevertheless recognize the ever-increasing weight of the probability through the fact that it is not each time simply a repetition of the same kind of evidence but rather a completely different relationship each time that leads us to the same result. At the same time we have now come to one of Caesar's numerical statements which, as nobody has failed to recognize for a long time now, can be shown through his own statement to be a monstrous exaggeration. When the Nervii surrendered, they supposedly reported that only 3 of their 600 captains were left and only 500 of their 60,000 service-qualified warriors. Nevertheless, three years later Caesar has them appearing on the scene once again with an important army (5. 39), and two years after that they send 5,000 men to Alesia, not as their whole levy but simply as a partial detachment of their army. If it is methodologically false to believe unquestioningly the strength figures given us by the author who reports to us obviously false loss figures, we are in a position here to oppose those figures with a positive counterestimate.

Through the Roman census we have an excellent, reliable basis for estimating the population of Italy at the time of Caesar. The peninsula itself, without any of the islands, had at that time some 3½ to 4 million inhabitants, or between 25 and 28 per square kilometer, Upper Italy (*Gallia cisalpina*) had 1½ to 2 millions, or between 14 and 18 per square kilometer. The Roman Province must have had a somewhat lesser density of population than Cisalpine Gaul, since it had not participated as long in the civilized economic life, and free Gaul, where the tribes were continuously at war with each other, would have had still fewer inhabitants. The upper limit of population density for free Gaul must therefore have been some 9 to 12 persons per square kilometer.

A lower limit can be determined through a comparison with Germania. The great military accomplishments of the Germanic tribes necessarily postulate a certain mass, not too small in size. As we shall point out more specifically in the next volume, we cannot go below some 5 persons per square kilometer (13 per square mile). Under any circumstances, Belgium was already more densely populated than Germania, and central Gaul more so than Belgium. The lower limit for the average population density of Gaul would therefore be found somewhere between 7 and 8 individuals per square kilometer. The region of the three tribes which fought on the Sambre can be estimated between 18,000 and 22,000 square kilometers (8,250 square miles), of which some 11,000 belonged to the Nervii; consequently, their total population at the most was 150,000 souls or 40,000 adult men, of whom, after subtracting slaves, the aged, the ill, and the handicapped, there could have been at hand at the very most 30,000, and presumably very many fewer, whereas the Roman army numbered at least 40,000 men in its legionaries alone.

Excursus

1. It could appear curious that the Apennine peninsula should have had only 25 to 28 inhabitants per square kilometer toward the end of our period of reckoning, whereas we have already estimated around 60 for the Roman canton in the year 510 B.C. If, however, there should be an error in these figures, it would necessarily be that the second one was too high rather than the first too low, since the latter, because of its relationship to the completely reliable numbers of the Roman census, can absolutely be regarded as true, and if we had to show above that Rome cannot have had more than 60,000 inhabitants in the year 510 B.C., then we must also at-

tempt here to show that it is credible that there really can have been so many. But this actually is the case, since we may assume that: (1) in the half-millennium between Tarquinius and Caesar there was no very important increase in the population of Italy; (2) almost the entire slave population and also between a fourth and a third of the entire population of the canton of Rome lived in the city in 510 B.C. and received their provisions from outside; (3) the countryside, too, was relatively very thickly populated, not only because of its fertility but also because it stood under the mighty protection of the great city and enjoyed a relatively high degree of security in comparison with other regions.

2. The bases for our estimates are once again taken from Beloch, who has somewhat modified the figures of his book and thoroughly defended them in an essay in the *Rheinisches Museum*, New Series, 54 (1899): 414, to which I refer the reader for the details. See also p. 346, above. His evaluation of the numbers that Caesar gives for the large relieving army before Alesia I can, however, agree with only partially. That is, he estimates according to the strength of the individual tribal contingents, since Caesar, after all, presumably had his figures agree to a certain extent with the relative sizes of the different peoples, a density of population gradually decreasing with increasing distance toward the north from the Roman province. That is a very valuable statistical confirmation of a fact that we could otherwise establish only through the general relationships. Nothing further, however, is to be derived from these numbers, since we of course have no clue at all about how the strength of the levy was related to the total number of available men or about the degree of care or negligence with which Caesar made his estimates. Only in the opposite way, since we have of course gained an idea of the population of Gaul, can we arrive at the probability that the stated strength of the Alesia army amounted to something like a third of all men qualified for military service, a twelfth of the entire population.

In the final analysis I am inclined, on the basis of a comparison with the Germanic tribes, to accept a somewhat higher estimate of the total population of Gaul than Beloch gives, that is, between 7 and 12 individuals to the square kilometer instead of 6.3, which would then give for all of free Gaul (523,000 square kilometers) 4 to 6 million persons.

3. Beloch, *Rheinisches Museum*, estimates the region of the Nervii (southern half of the "Nord" *département*, Antwerp, Hennegau, half of Brabant) at 11,000 square kilometers; the area of the Atrebates and Morini together (Pas-de-Calais *département*) he puts at 7,000 square kilometers. The Veromandui (County Vermandois, Aisne *département*) receive no particular mention in Beloch, since they are not named by Caesar at Alesia. It is not to be assumed that precisely these three peoples should have had a density of population significantly exceeding the average, even though their territory was very beautiful and fertile. The Nervii were considered to be the most savage, "*maxime feri*" ("extremely ferocious") of the Belgae and had no towns at all (when the Romans approached, they hid their families in places protected by swamps). These are sure signs that their economic life was still very underdeveloped and therefore that their production of crops and their population density were also small.

4. On the basis of the information that we have now gained let us take another look at the Helvetii, whose migration column is given a total strength of 368,000 by Caesar, supposedly according to a census.

The territory of the Helvetii and their allies has been estimated, as we have seen on p. 461 above, at 18,000 to 25,000 square kilometers. If we take the smaller of these figures, which includes less mountainous area, their density of population can have been greater than that of the Belgae. By this reckoning the Helvetii could have numbered between 180,000 and 250,000 souls.

Their army column cannot possibly have been that large; consequently not the whole nation but only a part of that people took part in the march. But if only a part of the population went on the march, this gives us a supplementary confirmation of the assumption that it was not at all a question of the migration of a whole nation but rather a military campaign followed by a certain number of families in order to maintain the political pretense.

NOTES FOR CHAPTER IV

1. Dittenberger in the new edition of Kraner's publication of Caesar.

2. Konrad Lehmann, *Neue Jahrbücher für das klassische Altertum* 7, No. 6 (1901): 506, and *Klio* 6, No. 2 (1906): 237.

3. Strictly speaking, Caesar does not say—and Konrad Lehmann has called attention to this point—that the 306,000 men were actually on hand, but he only says that the Romans had reported to him that they knew exactly how many each tribe at their assembly had promised to provide.

4. Concerning the maneuver that they carried out, see p. 457, above.

Chapter V

Vercingetorix

Caesar conquered Gaul in a bold and rapid sequence of events, but his movements were accompanied by great care, in fact downright caution. Strategy and politics went hand in hand. From the very start he was allied with a part of the Gauls themselves, and he was able to divide up the others before he fought with them. In the three battles that made him the master of the whole great area, he undoubtedly had at his disposal each time—against the Helvetii as well as against Ariovistus and against the Nervii—a significant numerical superiority.

After his first victories, not only did he not reduce the strength of his forces but he continued to increase it very considerably. He had led out 6 legions against the Helvetii; in conquered Gaul he eventually had 10 legions,[1] and in addition he had 2 legions and 2 cohorts for the defense of the province and presumably in Cisalpine Gaul 8 more cohorts, for a grand total of 13 legions.[2]

We do not need to follow through either with the partial battles that ensued or with the daring moves to Britain and over the Rhine, but instead we now turn directly to the decisive battle, which did not take place until the seventh year of his governorship, when all the Gallic tribes rose up together and united against him under the leadership of the Arvernian Vercingetorix.

One would think that, since Gaul certainly contained a million men fit for battle, it could not have been very difficult for Vercingetorix to assemble a huge army and crush the Romans with it in one decisive battle. But that did not occur. Rather, Vercingetorix recommended to his compatriots the use of their superiority in cavalry to cut off the Romans' flow of supplies and even to lay waste their own land all around, in order by this method to force the Romans to withdraw. Had that been the total of Vercingetorix' strategic wisdom, we would have to consider him a very inadequate

495

intellect—for, after all, what would the advantage have been to the Gauls if the Romans had withdrawn temporarily into their province because of the problem of provisions? They would have returned very soon. The liberation of Gaul could not be attained simply through maneuvering; if they really wanted to get rid of the Romans, they would have to defeat their army so decisively that they would lose any desire to return, or, if possible, destroy it, just as the Cherusci did later in the Teutoburger Forest. As a matter of fact, Vercingetorix, too, had this in mind. Caesar tells us that—not the first time, it is true, but the second time that he has occasion to speak of the Gallic war plan (7. 66)—and since he himself describes Vercingetorix to us as an extremely remarkable personality, we may and must assume that the Gallic national hero had the proper strategic insight from the start, that is, that everything depended not on forcing the Romans to withdraw but on defeating them. We should understand the action to cut off the supplies only as a preparatory measure, intended to create favorable conditions for the battle.

These favorable conditions for which Vercingetorix was striving were two in number: first, the winning over to the national cause of those Gallic tribes that were initially still on the side of the Romans, especially the Aedui, and second, the opportunity for a surprise blow, an attack against the Roman army on the march.

The first goal was attained. Since the Gauls did not assemble to offer him battle, Caesar had to resort to sieges, first taking the capital of the Bituriges, Avaricum (Bourges), with a full-scale attack, and then dividing up his army in order to subject the tribes individually and to conquer their towns. He sent Labienus with 4 legions against Paris, and with 6 legions he himself moved out to besiege the principal center of the Arverni, Gergovia. But these forces were too weak for their missions. Caesar himself, in attempting a surprise attack in front of Gergovia, suffered a setback, and only with difficulty did Labienus succeed in fighting his way through the Gauls who were blocking his route, in order to join up again with Caesar (in the area of the Seine), who was moving toward him. Encouraged by this success, almost all of the Gallic tribes now joined the Arverni.

Although Caesar reinforced his reunited army still further with newly recruited Germanic cavalry, he was nevertheless still not capable of maintaining himself in central Gaul but was forced to seek to base himself on the Roman province to assure his provisions. He directed his march through the territory of the Lingones (near

Langres), who remained allied with him, toward the region of the Sequani. Göler believes, as did Napoleon III, that he intended to march to Besançon to use that town as a fortified base.

From there, Göler believes, he could more easily have gone to the assistance of the Roman province than if he had remained farther to the north in the territory of the Senones, and in this way he would at least not completely have evacuated all of Gaul. Napoleon adds that he could not have considered taking the direct route through the area of the Aedui, the focal point of the insurrection. If that were correct, then we would have before us the remarkable spectacle of the two opposing armies both attempting equally and directly to avoid battle.

Was the situation really so bad that Caesar not only had to evacuate Gaul but also, without having suffered a defeat in the open field, avoided the enemy? Even if he had to move back to the borders of the province, it would still have been a quite different situation if he made his march right through the enemy's territory and, while the enemy avoided the challenge, thus asserted his superior morale, than if he stole away, so to speak, as Göler and Napoleon would have it.

The interpretation of Göler and Napoleon, however, is undoubtedly incorrect. The region of the Sequani was just as hostile to the Romans as that of the Aedui, and there is absolutely no statement to the effect that Caesar intended to move directly to Besançon. That town was by its location very well protected, and we cannot assume that it had a Roman garrison. It would therefore first have had to be laid siege to and captured, if Caesar intended to establish his strong point there, a function, moreover, for which it offered no particularly favorable conditions, but would, in fact, have been particularly unfavorable.

Caesar's march to the Sequani's area, then, has to be explained in some other way. He himself says that he took this direction so that he could all the more easily have brought assistance to the province. For Vercingetorix had not been content with operating against the Roman army directly but had also had raids made into the province, hoping in this way to maneuver Caesar out of Gaul. For Caesar, however, still more important than the help that he was to bring to the province was the help that the province was to provide him, that is, regular resupply, which the few Gallic tribes that had remained loyal to him could not possibly continue to provide for his large army in the long run. What Caesar needed now was a position where he could feed his troops and protect the province while exercising at the same time continuing pressure on the Gauls. Consequently, he directed his march not on Besançon but on the Saône, and specifically across the more open terrain east of the Côte d'Or across the plateau of Langres, where an ambush could not easily be laid for him. On the Saône he would be able to repeat the maneuver that had enabled him to subject the Belgae. If he established a fortified camp on this river, somewhere near Auxonne or farther downstream, where the Doubs flows into the Saône, the Gauls would not be capable of driving him out of it. Situated on the right bank, he could keep the neighboring tribes, and especially the Aedui, in constant fear of a sudden invasion, while a few detached legions again subjected the tribes on the left bank, the Sequani and Helvetii. Vercingetorix could not have brought them any help, since he could not have risked either sacrificing the territory of the Aedui or of crossing the Saône and Doubs and thus exposing himself on the other side to an attack by the entire Roman army. If then the entire left bank was once again pacified, Caesar would have a secured road for his line of communications with the province; indeed, he would have been able, with a few security measures, to move up his provisions in the most convenient possible way, by water on the Saône, which is navigable as far as Gray.

I believe there can be no doubt that this was Caesar's strategic intention, and Vercingetorix had a premonition of this, feeling that the moment was now at hand where he had to bring on the decision by attacking Caesar on the march, before he reached the Saône. He believed that he could break up the enemy's march column with cavalry attacks.[3] But these attacks failed because Caesar used his closely formed infantry to support his cavalry, which had been recently reinforced by the addition of the newly recruited Germanic units, whereas Vercingetorix kept his infantry out of the battle. The Gauls were completely defeated. Instead of continuing its march to the Saône, the Roman army now turned to pursuit. Vercingetorix was able to stem the flight of his troops in no other way than by taking cover in a fortified place, the town of Alesia (Alise Sainte Reine, on Mont Auxois, between Nuits and Dijon). Caesar immediately encircled the place, in order to besiege it. Since the Gauls had evacuated the countryside, he had space and time to secure provisions for the siege army, even if only with difficulty.[4]

There now came about a great assembling of all the Gallic tribes in order to relieve the army under siege in Alesia. The great battle, without which there can be no great decisions, had to be fought now. Buf if Vercingetorix had not been willing earlier to pit his infantry against the legions in the open field, victory now for the Gauls would be all the more difficult.

Caesar had used the interval of five to six weeks between the encircling of the garrison and the arrival of the relieving army to establish fortifications on both sides. Napoleon III had excavations made that uncovered almost the entire trace of these fortifications and are in complete accord with the account in *Bellum Gallicum*. The contravallation line was some 16 kilometers long, the circumvallation line 20 kilometers. Where it extended over the open field, any possible attack was made difficult by artificial obstacles of all kinds: caltrops, pitfalls with 8 rows of sharp stakes arranged in checkerboard fashion, and finally fallen trees.

For our judgment of the decisive battle we are unfortunately lacking here even more so than in earlier battles the important factor of relative strengths. Caesar had 11 legions, Numidian and Cretan sharpshooters and Germanic cavalry and light infantry, for a total of perhaps 70,000 men. For the Gauls, Caesar says there were 80,000 in Alesia and 250,000 infantry plus 8,000 cavalry in the relieving army. Since we are already familiar with his exaggerations in stating enemy strengths, here again we cannot trust the accuracy of his figures, and many scholars have already expressed doubt, especially over the 80,000 supposedly under siege; 20,000 men were sufficient for the defense of the place, and it would have been very unwise of Vercingetorix to have kept more there, since he had relatively few food supplies. Since Caesar tells us, moreover, that Vercingetorix, in his reliance on the superiority of his cavalry, had not by any means assembled all the available infantry and that, before the completion of the Roman fortifications, he still had room to send his cavalry out of Alesia, we may therefore assume with certainty that, in the matter of infantry, too, he had kept with him only the necessary number, consequently some 20,000 men at the most.

At first appearance the numbers given for the relieving army, 250,000 infantry and 8,000 cavalry, do not seem to be unreasonable. Almost all of Gaul, forming a total mass of at least 4 million souls, and perhaps even 8 million, with from 1 to 2 million men, was involved in this struggle. For the final, decisive battle for national liberation they could well have put 250,000 warriors in the field.

But let us just consider what an army of a quarter of a million men means. It would have been three times as large as the largest army ever previously assembled and confirmed for us in world history up to that time, that is, the Roman army at Cannae. If a Gallic commander had been capable of operating with an army of 250,000 men, it would remain an unpardonable, completely incomprehensible error on the part of Vercingetorix not to have assembled this army from the start and with such superiority to have sought the open battle.

We feel obliged, however, to go one step farther and say that not only would 250,000 men have been an army so large that no Gallic commander could have operated with it, but also that the idea that such a large mass of peoples as the Gauls could easily have called up 250,000 warriors is false. For the number of warriors that a people can assemble depends—and we have already noticed this point in the case of the Persian armies—not only on the number of available men but also on the nation's military attitude and its social conditions. In the medieval kingdoms, whose history is now quite well known to us, we can no longer establish any relationship between the strengths of their armies and their numbers of service-qualified men. The strength of an army is determined not by the overall population but by a special warrior class. But it is precisely this military tradition and organization for war that Caesar reports to us in the case of the Gauls. He tells us (6. 13) that the common people lived in a condition approaching slavery; the warrior group was composed of the knights with their followers. We should assume that that did not apply equally to all the Gallic tribes. Among the Helvetii and all the Belgae the mass of common men had probably not yet lost the warrior spirit to such a great degree. In other respects, too, we should not push too far the analogy between the attitude toward war of the medieval countries and that of the Gauls, but we must rather keep in mind that very important differences, though not always clearly recognizable in their details, prevailed. The basic fact, however, of a special warrior group dominating the mass of the people, who were therefore unaccustomed to the use of weapons, cannot be doubted.

In order to raise the gigantic Gallic army reported by Caesar, we must therefore imagine that the local guard forces (Landsturm) were called up. But such local levies composed of men unaccustomed to battle are worthless for full-scale war, unusable in battle and a definite hindrance in the matter of their need for provisions. For this reason the medieval armies, as we shall see later, were very small, even in the most decisive battles.

But at Alesia the situation was now somewhat different in that here everything depended on an imminent decision. The problems of providing supplies over an indefinite period, therefore, as well as the control of a variety of operations, were eliminated, as were the tactical maneuvers of the battle. A certain mass levy, even of *Landsturm,* could therefore appear to be of use here. But the sequence of events of the battle does not reveal in any way a numerical superiority on the part of the Gauls. That point has already been made by Napoleon I, with his sharp perspective for everything practical; he too assumes that Vercingetorix had no more than 20,000 men in Alesia, and he says that the relieving army did not camp and maneuver like one that greatly outnumbered its foe, but rather like one of equal strength. From the course of the battle itself, then, we must also try to gain an idea of the probable strength of the Gauls.

On the day of the arrival of the relieving army, which established camp to the southeast, a cavalry battle took place in which, according to Caesar, once again his Germanic cavalry, supported by Roman cohorts, was victorious. Presumably the intention of the Gauls in this battle was simply to cover the approach of their infantry.

Then, after they had spent a day in preparations, they attempted a night surprise attack against the Roman works on the plain of Laumes, which is some three kilometers wide. When this attack was thrown back, on the next night they sent a column up Mount Réa, which lay on the north side, where the Roman circumvallation had had to be extended along the downward slope and was therefore particularly exposed to attack from above. Then at noon the assault began simultaneously from both sides, while Vercingetorix, as on the preceding days, stormed the contravallation at the same time from his interior position. On Mount Réa the Gauls pushed forward so strongly that the Romans seemed to be on the verge of defeat; then Labienus, on Caesar's orders, led a number of cohorts and a cavalry force from the fortified area farther up the mountain, perhaps along Rabutin Brook, and attacked the assaulting columns in their flank and rear.[5] This push carried the day. The Gauls first took flight in this area and then also on the plain of Laumes. Vercingetorix turned back into the town with his force and surrendered.

The circumference of the contravallation and the circumvallation together amounted, as we have seen, to some 36 kilometers. If then

Caesar's army was 70,000 men strong, the occupation of the entire breastworks with a man to every half-meter would have taken up the entire army to the last man.

The first time the Gauls attacked only on the plain of Laumes, which is 3 kilometers wide. If they had really been 250,000 men strong, they would probably have made the assault with a front of 2,000 men and a depth of 120, covered on the right and left by their cavalry. If we could in any way imagine such a mass as being at all capable of movement, they would probably have been able to take any entrenchment, for the following ranks, hardly touched by the enemy missiles, would press the front ranks forward, fill up any moat with them, flow over every obstacle, and would eventually penetrate the defenses over a causeway of corpses. This fantasy, however, cannot be accomplished; a closed mass of a quarter of a million men simply would be unable to move. The natural, logical use of such a mass is rather through multiple, divided attacks, and that is particularly the appropriate maneuver at night, since the enemy cannot distinguish between an attack in force and a mere demonstration.

Not until the second day did the Gauls hit upon the idea of dividing their forces, but even then they limited themselves to two points instead of storming in simultaneously from all sides of the periphery, wherever there was a possible approach, or at least conducting demonstrations.

This is the proof beyond any doubt that they did not enjoy a superiority of numbers but were, in fact, probably the considerably weaker of the two forces. If they had only had an additional 10,000 men available to employ in the Rabutin valley, they would have covered the flank of their attack on Mount Réa, and Labienus would not have been able to strike the decisive blow. It was in no way simple negligence that was to be blamed for this apparent oversight, for Caesar himself reports that the Gauls had finally broken off their first night attack at sunrise, since they feared that the Romans would move out and attack them in the flank.

Napoleon's observation that the foes must have been of about equal strength is very probably correct, unless it be that this puts the Gauls' strength somewhat too high. We must always keep in mind the fact that Caesar could not risk leaving a single point of his miles-long lines completely unguarded and without having a reserve within easy reach. He had no other choice but to split up his troops, whereas the enemy could choose the points where he wanted to concentrate his massive attacks, and wherever he at-

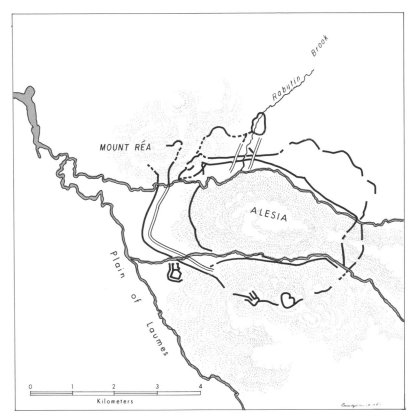

Fig. 5 SIEGE OF ALESIA

tacked there was certain to be a corresponding sortie by the beleaguered force from the other side, so that the Roman soldiers
stood under the mental pressure of threatened attack from their
rear. The defense of a siege army against a relieving army therefore belongs among the most difficult strategic missions, even with
equal forces, and many field commanders have rejected the idea of
accepting battle under these circumstances as being basically wrong.
In the later volumes of this work we shall have many more occasions to speak of this.

If it is true that the opposing forces at Alesia were of approximately equal strength, that consequently, if Caesar had 70,000

men, some 20,000 men were besieged in the town and 50,000 Gauls moved up to relieve them, we are still attributing to the army of the Gauls a size that the actual warrior class even of such a large region can certainly not possibly assemble. But we may assume that the knightly class had strengthened its forces in this final, most extreme emergency, just as the Saxons did in their struggle against Henry IV, by recruiting brave young men from among the common people, the serflike peasantry. Many knights dismounted and fought among the infantry, as we may conclude from Caesar's figure of 15,000 cavalry belonging to Vercingetorix but only 8,000 cavalry for the relieving army. The military history of the Middle Ages gives us many examples of cases where knights dismounted to lead the infantry or the people into battle.

If this is an appropriate description of the strength and composition of the Gallic relieving army, then Vercingetorix' conduct in the preceding campaign now becomes completely understandable. We have now solved the apparent contradiction that at Alesia the Gallic infantry went into action, storming the Roman entrenchments with the most extreme courage, whereas Vercingetorix did not risk sending his infantry against the Roman legions in the open field.

We can regard the army at Alesia as representing the largest number of troops that the Gauls were able to assemble at one point. It only approached or, at most, equaled the Roman army in strength. But the Romans were superior to the loosely organized bands of the Gauls in every kind of maneuvering, as well as in their battlefield movements.[6] Their thoroughly trained, well-organized units and their strict discipline also enabled them to maintain their supply of provisions, where the poorly organized masses composing the Gallic army had soon dissipated their supplies. Vercingetorix therefore had to renounce any idea of reaching a decision through an open battle. He did not have at hand a numerical superiority that might have guaranteed victory for him, and if he had achieved such superiority for a moment, Caesar would not immediately have accepted a decisive battle any more than he had done in the second year of the war in the case of the Belgae, but he would first have obliged the large Gallic army to split up again, through his own temporizing. Consequently, Vercingetorix did not initially assemble the overall, reinforced Gallic levy but limited himself to perhaps from 20,000 to 30,000 infantry and placed his principal hope in the assembled Gallic knighthood, which was both numerous and effective. Even when the opportunity came for the sudden attack he had been planning, he still did not bring up his infantry, not wishing to expose it to an attack by the far superior Romans. This whole concept was not at all bad, but the excellent order of the Roman army, which understood how to protect its train in its march column and at the same time to give its cavalry the support and active cooperation of the infantry, brought the plan of Vercingetorix to naught. Now there was nothing else for him to do but make a last desperate attempt to succeed through the combination of the siege and the action of the relieving army, a course that did have the advantage of allowing the Gauls to bring larger masses to bear while Caesar could no longer maneuver, necessarily had to give the Gauls the choice of places to attack, and was himself taken between two attacks, in return for which, however, he established the awesome fortifications against which their courageous assault broke down.

NOTES FOR CHAPTER V

1. Caesar himself says (7. 34) there were 10 legions, that is, the Seventh to the Fifteenth, and the First. In addition, after the siege of Alesia, the Sixth appears. In this connection, see the comment by Napoleon III (in *Uebersicht*, 2: 282). Göler, p. 333, rejects the "Sixth Legion" and names instead the "Third." Both Meusel and Kübler, however, have correctly accepted the "VI" version (8. 4). See also Domaszewski, *Neue Heidelberger Jahrbücher* 4 (1894): 158. In this connection, see also Chapter VII, below, first paragraph.

2. *Bell. Gall.* 7. 65.

3. After careful examination of all the various hypotheses that have been advanced concerning the location of this battle, Holmes decided (p. 780) that it was impossible to arrive at a definite answer but that the most likely possibility was the concept of Gouget, who seeks to place the battlefield near Dijon, on the Ouche. Under any circumstances, the place favored by Napoleon III, some 25 miles farther toward the northeast between the Vingeanne and the Badin, south of Langres, is incorrect.

4. See also *Bell. Civ.* 3. 47. It is not easy to imagine how an army that numbered all together surely 100,000 souls, and probably considerably more, could have fed itself and all its horses for almost six weeks in one location in the middle of enemy territory (see also Ilerda). Great quantities of supplies necessarily had to be brought up over long distances. How did they manage to get through the enemy areas? My concept is that supplies were already stocked in

Vienne and were transported up the Saône to a point only some 45 miles overland from Alesia. Later we find the Sixth Legion joined up with the main army; perhaps this legion, escorting the supply transport, pushed its way through during the siege. It may already have started on its march when Caesar moved down toward it from the north. In the period immediately following his victory, while the Gauls were still occupied with their preparations and the assembling of their army, this legion, marching along the left bank of the Saône, was undoubtedly able to bring up the supply train with relatively little danger, and on the final stretch Caesar may have sent out troops and vehicles to meet them. But of course it is still surprising that, even if the supply train was protected to a certain extent against the main force of the Gauls by the river, the Sequani in league with the Helvetii did not attempt to intercept the supplies. After all, up to that point the whole strategy of the Gauls had been directed toward cutting off the Romans' food supplies. Could it possibly be that the Sequani, contrary to what Caesar reported, did not take part in the rebellion at all? However that may be, no army as large as the Roman one before Alesia could feed itself simply from the immediately surrounding countryside. The execution of the siege of Alesia is inconceivable without envisaging that large supply trains of food and forage made their way through successfully, and these trains must have been accompanied by troops who protected them. The reader is reminded of the difficulty of supplying rations for the German army that was besieging Metz in 1870—despite the close proximity of the German border and the availability of the railroad net. This situation is presented in my lecture "Mind and Mass in History" ("Geist und Masse in der Geschichte"), *Preussische Jahrbücher* 174 (1912): 193.

5. According to the manuscripts, Labienus carried out his sortie with 39 or 40 cohorts. As has long been recognized, this number is too large; it is impossible that more than one-third of the entire force of heavy infantry could have been available at one spot for a sortie. For this reason it has been conjectured that "XL" should read "XI," and the more recent editors, Meusel as well as Kübler, have placed "XI" in the text. If this number were definite, we could conclude from it that the Gallic assault columns cannot have been as strong as Caesar reports; but since this number is based only on conjecture, we cannot go any further in evaluating it.

6. Veith, p. 177, recounts that Vercingetorix spared neither time nor effort in continuously training his army according to the Roman pattern. Not only does Caesar make no mention of this, but

also this report is based on a false concept of the nature of the training. Closely associated with training is a discipline that cannot be improvised, even by means of the most extreme strictness, but which can only be developed very gradually, through habit and tradition. What Caesar says (7. 4) is that Vercingetorix assembled and dealt with his army with the most extreme severity and cruelty and (7. 29–30) that he forced them, against their custom, to fortify their camp in the Roman manner.

Chapter VI

The Roman Art of War Against the Barbarians

Caesar's strategy in Gaul was based on the fact that he knew how to avoid meeting the Gauls in their full strength and always knew how to match the strength of the Romans against the weakness of the Gauls. The strength of the Gauls lay in their great number of more or less militarily competent peoples. If Caesar had divided up his legions in order to fight them all at the same time and then to provide their fortresses and capitals with garrisons, in order to keep them under control, the Romans would certainly have gone down to defeat. Once in the fourth year, when Caesar, as a result of a poor harvest, had split his army up into various winter quarters out of concern for supplies of food, 1½ legions were suddenly attacked by the Eburones, and since their leaders could not agree and conducted themselves incompetently, these troops were completely destroyed. With their auxiliaries and cavalry, this force of 1½ legions was probably some 9,000 combatants strong.

In the war against Vercingetorix, when Caesar saw that the Gauls were avoiding an open battle, he once again sought a solution by dividing up his troops; and once again the result was a defeat. Caesar himself, with the principal army, was not strong enough to besiege the Gauls in Gergovia, and a sudden attack failed with heavy losses. The besieging of Alesia was only made possible through the fact that the entire Roman army was united.

After Alesia had fallen, however, it was not difficult in the course of the following year to subject the individual tribes that were still offering resistance. The masterpiece of Caesar's strategy, however, was probably the conquering of the Belgian area, in the second year. If the Nervii had not attempted their sudden attack, all of these warlike tribes would have submitted to the heavy hand of the

Romans practically without a fight—not so much because Caesar would have avoided battle as such, but because, before accepting battle, he created for the Romans, through the splitting up of the enemy forces, such advantageous conditions, that is, such a great numerical superiority on the spot, that the Belgian tribes no longer dared to let the situation develop into a battle.

When modern peoples come into conflict with barbarians, the outcome is determined from the start by the differences in weapon technology. In antiquity this relationship was not so simple.

Here we may wonder in what manner the Roman military system was really superior to that of the barbarians. Vis-á-vis civilized peoples, barbarians have the advantage of having at their disposal the warlike power of unbridled animal instincts, of basic toughness. Civilization refines the human being, makes him more sensitive, and in doing so it decreases his military worth, not only his bodily strength but also his physical courage. These natural shortcomings must be offset in some artificial way. Scharnhorst was perhaps the first one to state that the main service of the standing army consisted of making civilized peoples, through discipline, capable of holding their own against the less civilized. If a given group of Romans normally living as citizens or peasants had been put up against a group of barbarians of the same number, the former would undoubtedly have been defeated; in fact, they would probably have taken flight without fighting. It was only the formation of the close-knit tactical body of the cohorts that equalized the situation.

From Caesar we cannot learn directly with certainty the stage of development of the Gauls during his time.[1] For generations they had not been an exclusively warlike barbarian people. They had cities, industry, trade, and commerce. The national priesthood of the Druids had become a kind of hierarchy. The people, Caesar says (6. 13), were treated like slaves: through indebtedness, taxes, and harassment those in power brought the common man to regard himself as a serf. These men in power were the warrior class, the knights with their vassals, and a special warrior class standing apart from the masses cannot raise a mass army. But what we have taken away in numbers we must credit in quality. Caesar draws distinctions between the various peoples; he names the Helvetii, the Nervii, and the Bellovaci as outstandingly courageous. Certainly such distinctions did exist, but the warlike virtues had not disappeared among the Arverni, the Bituriges, or the Carnutes, either, and those forces that finally opposed the Romans in the field must undoubtedly be regarded as personally irreproachable warriors, forming a warriorhood that was based partially on the concept of honor of a special warrior class but also in part on the still surviving warlike instincts of the barbarian condition.

Nor did the Roman army, either, consist of those elements of the body of Roman citizens that had become the most refined through their culture. Caesar's legions, levied or recruited principally in Cisalpine Gaul and the Narbonnese province, surely consisted for the most part of romanized Celts. If the army had formerly been composed of Roman citizens, this situation had by now practically been completely reversed; entry in the army was the way to attain Roman citizenship, and the Roman army, for its part, was also not deprived of contact with the basic source of uninterrupted natural strength.

But this was still only a point of contact, except where purely barbarian elements, principally for example the feared Germanic cavalry, were attached to the Roman army; in comparison with the legionaries, the Gauls were still complete barbarians, and as an individual the Roman legionary was not superior to these warriors. There is no reason to assume that a Roman cohort of 600 men would have conquered a Gallic group of the same strength under otherwise similar circumstances. We have seen how Caesar avoided fighting against a numerically superior force, making sure, on the contrary that he himself enjoyed numerical superiority. The refinements of the Roman cohort and echelon tactics were consequently not so significant in counterbalancing the fierce boldness of the barbarian hordes whenever the latter were also numerically superior. This is a point of fundamental significance for the immediately following period, and we shall have occasion to refer back to it again in completely different periods of world history.

This primary point is that the superiority of the Roman art of warfare was based on the army organization as a whole, a system that permitted very large masses of men to be concentrated at a given point, to move in orderly fashion, to be fed, and to be kept together. The Gauls could do none of these things. It was not so much the courage of the Romans, which was in no way greater than their own, but the Roman mass power that subdued them —and again, not that their own mass, of itself, would not have been much greater, but their mass was an inert one, incapable of movement. It was the Roman civilization which conquered barbarism, for imparting the capability of movement to a large mass is a work of art that only a higher civilization can achieve. Barbarism cannot do it. The Roman army was not simply a mass, but an organized mass, and it could be a mass only because it was organized and formed a complex and living entity. Not only soldiers and weapons went into its makeup, cavalry and infantry, and not only legates, tribunes, centurions, legions, cohorts, maniples, centuries, discipline from below, leadership from above, advance guards, rear guards, patrols, reports, the laying out of camps— but also the quaestor and his army of officials, controllers, engineers with their tools, capable of skillfully building bridges, ramparts, blockhouses, battering rams, engines to hurl missiles, ships; quartermasters with their pools of wagons; army suppliers with their agents; doctors with field hospitals; magazines, ordnance depots, portable forges; and finally the head of the whole organization, the commanding general, in whom inherent fundamental strength must be blended with the flexibility and the refinement of a mind developed in the atmosphere of the highest culture so that he might intellectually embrace everything and provide direction for the whole from a single point and through a single will.

The recognition of all of these factors is hidden and obscured by the idea that the Gallic armies that Caesar conquered were always several times larger than his own. The fact that Caesar himself presents his victory to us in this light should not, to repeat again here a point we have already made, be held too strongly against him, for victory of a small force against a vastly superior one is simply the basic manner in which the crowd pictures heroic deeds and strategic genius. It is the task of scientific knowledge to break through this outer shell to the heart of the matter, and the result is in no way a diminution of the greatness of Roman and other historical army commanders, but rather it is only in this way that this greatness comes to be truly recognized. As long as we have 70,000 men defeating 300,000, we may arouse in the public a vague concept of bravery and generalship, but a rational recognition of the situation still does not exist. Not until we tell ourselves that the individual Gaul was fully capable of standing up to the individual Roman and even 10,000 Gauls to 10,000 Romans do we arrive at an idea of the immensity of the strategic mission that Caesar faced, and now we also see once again that not only did Caesar conquer Ariovistus and Vercingetorix, but Rome conquered the Germanic peoples and the Gauls, and civilization conquered barbarism.

In order to arrive at this realization, Caesar's own authority as a reporter had first to be limited, and there will be many a scholar who will be even less willing to accept this criticism than that concerning Herodotus and who would like with mistrust to oppose as a matter of principle the critical analysis that brings such results to light. Consequently we must consider as a kind of good luck the fact that we have at hand at least *one* passage in which Caesar himself gives away the true numerical relationship and thereby helps the cause of critical analysis. In the case of the worst defeat that his army suffered in Gaul, the destruction of the 1½ legions by the Eburones, he himself adds the statement that the two opponents were equal in courage and numbers but that the Romans had been left in the lurch by their leadership and by fortune (5. 34). Scholars have long felt that this sentence stands in irreconcilable contradiction to all his other battle accounts. Heller (in *Philologus* 31 (1872): p. 512) calls this statement "senseless." "How?" he exclaims, "how? The Romans were supposed to be numerically as strong as the Gauls? And the Eburones, without putting a considerably stronger army in the field, were supposed to have attacked a most strongly fortified camp, they were supposed to have dared attack a Roman army of the same strength as theirs, in spite of their unhappy experiences in five years of war? No military man can be persuaded of that; only schoolboys can be deceived in such a matter."

Instead of *"erant et virtute et numero pugnando pares nostri; tametsi ab duce et a fortuna deserebantur"* ("they were our equals in courage and in numbers of combatants; nevertheless, our men were deserted by their leader and by fortune"), Heller, basing his argument on the fact that the manuscripts show *"pugnandi"* ("for fighting"), prefers to read *"virtute et studio pugnandi"* ("in courage and in zeal for fighting"), and in the latest edition Meusel could find no better solution than to eliminate completely *"erant et virtute et numero pugnandi."* For our part, we now recognize that it is precisely this sentence that contains the truth, that is, that the Eburones were able to bring up, with cavalry, home guard, and some reinforcements, a total of about 9,000 men, consequently about the same strength as the Roman corps, and that we now are no longer faced with the prospect of simply throwing out Caesar's strength figures but rather of choosing between his own conflicting estimates. We accept Heller's arguments but turn the point in the other direction: since Caesar himself reports here that a numerically equal band of Gauls was able to defeat the Romans, as soon as the latter's leadership failed, then the Romans cannot in other battles always have conquered forces that were from two to four times as numerous as they. If Caesar himself has explained it to us in this way, he was actually writing for his compatriots, and the Romans were accustomed to receiving reports of victories like those of Sulla, who claimed to have defeated at Chaeronea an enemy force of 120,000 men with 16,500 of his own, losing only 12 men, or Lucullus, who at Tigranocerta supposedly defeated a force of 250,000, including 55,000 cavalry, with his 14,000 men,[2] suffering losses of 5 dead and 100 wounded. Of course, that is still very modest compared with the 900,000 Persians, who, according to Xenophon or his interpolator, were defeated by the 13,000 Greeks at Cunaxa, but it nevertheless shows that the Romans, like the Greeks before them, lived in a kind of numerical hypnosis insofar as barbarian armies were concerned, a condition that obscured the discriminatory powers of even the wisest. If in this case Caesar likewise lived more or less under the spell of this concept or consciously made concessions to it, at any rate, of all his figures for the strengths of Gallic and Germanic armies, only those concerning the Eburones can be accepted, and the relationship between Roman and barbarian military accomplishments can be judged on the basis of approximately equal military qualities of the individual soldiers.

The point that we have discovered is so important that I should like to formulate it once again, with the opposite approach.

The concept handed down in the sources is that barbarian armies were mass armies. We have found that, on the contrary, barbarians were not capable of assembling mass armies. Even where a mass of militarily qualified men was undoubtedly available, as in Gaul, it was impossible to marshal a large army. They were unable to move it or to operate with it. The capability of moving large masses of men is a product of civilization. Masses of men are not a lifeless material that raw power can assemble at will. In order to form masses, men need articulation, organization. Victory by a mass, which at first glance seems to mean victory through pure natural power and can actually mean this under certain circumstances, must mean, quite to the contrary, victory through an organizing and leading mentality, when the mass becomes very large.

Excursus

Since writing the above I have developed these ideas still somewhat further and supported them with more recent examples in an academic lecture, "Mind and Mass in History," ("Geist und Masse in der Geschichte") which appeared in the *Preussische Jahrbücher* 147 (1912): 193; and I continued this theme in a series of lectures in the English language given at London University in 1913, which were published under the title *Numbers in History* (London: Hodder and Stoughton, Warwick Square).

NOTES FOR CHAPTER VI

1. The description by Diodorus, in 5. 28 ff., is also colorful, to be sure, but it is nevertheless of no significance for us.

2. Theodor Reinach, *Mithridates Eupator*, trans. by Goetz, pp. 355 and 358.

Chapter VII

The Civil War
in Italy and Spain

Strategy, as we have come to know it in Gaul through Caesar, consists of avoiding the enemy's strength and pitting one's own strength against the enemy's weakness. Caesar did the same thing in the Civil War, but the same principles called for another kind of execution, since the military conditions were different. Laying out fortified camps, providing systematically for resupply, occupying favorable positions, maneuvering—Caesar's Roman opponents understood all these activities just as well as he did. The materiel superiority of the existing government over the autonomous general was so great that the rulers in Rome could not really accept the idea of the war until the last minute. Of his 13 legions, Caesar had given 2 over to Pompey, and so he still had 11.[1] Pompey had 7 veteran, competent, war-hardened legions in Spain; in Italy, in addition to the 2 he had received from Caesar, he had a third in training; and behind these forces, which in themselves were almost equal to Caesar's, he had the whole mass of the Roman Empire with all its resources, so that it was possible to form new legions at will, so to speak. The single advantage that Caesar had on his side (apart from the lively sympathy among broad segments of the population for him and the democratic principles that he represented) was that the enemy forces were not yet united. Once they had joined their forces, there would be no hope of separating them by maneuvering, as he had previously done with the Belgae. And even less could he count on Pompey's not being able to assemble his superior forces at a given point, if he were given enough time to do so. Caesar's only chance for victory, therefore, was by striking the enemy forces before those already available could be united and before the newly formed ones were capable of measuring up to

515

the existing legions. If in Gaul the strategic art had consisted of keeping the enemy forces separated from the viewpoint of space, now it was a question of separation in time.

Caesar carried out negotiations while he was at the head of but a single legion in northern Italy, so that Pompey did not yet see any urgent need to prepare himself. But in short order Caesar had brought up 2 additional legions, and with this force he launched his campaign. These 3 legions, which, with their auxiliary troops, numbered some 20,000 men, were sufficient for the time being to give Caesar the preponderance of strength in Italy. To be sure, Pompey also had 3 legions on the peninsula, but they included the 2 that were previously under Caesar's command, which Pompey could not risk pitting directly against their former commander, and a newly formed legion hardly ready for combat. Caesar drove through Italy almost without opposition. Pompey's newly formed cohorts broke up and went over to Caesar or, having been taken as prisoners, later entered his service. The Optimate senators, with Pompey at their head, fled to Greece.

Pompey has been blamed for not having gone to the relief of an Optimate force under Domitius Ahenobarbus that was besieged by Caesar in Corfinium. Colonel Stoffel has pointed out very nicely and effectively that that would have been the same error that MacMahon committed in 1870 when he tried with insufficient forces to relieve Bazaine at Metz. In doing so, he only succeeded in bringing disaster on himself. Pompey had enough strategic understanding and sense of consistency to recognize this situation, and so he left Domitius Ahenobarbus to his fate and thereby saved the nucleus of the army for the final decisive battle.

Now Caesar turned to Spain. He could also have followed Pompey directly and could have brought up his legions from Gaul overland through Illyria. Then, without any significant opposition, he would have brought under his power the entire Orient, where preparations for the war were only just beginning. In the meantime, however, he would have sacrificed the Occident to the republican legions in Spain. Pompey undoubtedly would have fled there himself, would have placed himself at the head of the troops, and would have taken up the offensive. By the time Caesar would have arrived in Antioch, Pompey would perhaps have been back in Rome. Caesar followed the basic principle that the first and most important task was to seek out and destroy the enemy army, wherever it was.

Several legions newly formed in Italy were sent to Sardinia, Sicily, and Africa; others stood ready to defend Italy proper. Of the 9 veteran legions accustomed to victory in Gaul, 3 were assigned to the siege of Marseilles, which had gone over to the side of the government, and 6 were sent to Spain.

Pompey had 7 legions in Spain, but under 3 different legates. Two of them, Afranius and Petreius, joined forces in northern Spain against the attack that was threatened from the north, whereas the third, Varro, no other than the famous historian and philologist, remained in the southern part of the country with his 2 legions. Guischard has expressed the suspicion that Varro, who was later reconciled with Caesar and was highly honored by him, perhaps intentionally avoided the decisive confrontation. At any rate, it is impossible to find a military reason for his not having united his forces with those of the other two legates. Southern Spain could not have been better protected than by a successful defense against Caesar's forces at the Pyrenees.

From the very start Afranius and Petreius, with their 5 legions, felt themselves to be weaker than the attackers. Even though at first only 3 of Caesar's legions were approaching, the Pompeian generals still envisaged a purely defensive stance. Perhaps the 5 legions, which had in fact had little to do in Spain, had not exactly been carefully kept up to strength. Caesar speaks of 80 cohorts of Spaniards that the Pompeians were also supposed to have had; we may regard this figure, like those for the strength of the Gauls, as very exaggerated. It is certain that Caesar's army, with a strong force of Germanic and Gallic cavalry and other Gallic auxiliaries, was the significantly stronger of the two.

Consequently, the strategy of the Pompeians could not be based on a decisive battle but only on holding Caesar up and gaining time until Pompey himself could have completed his preparations in the East and likewise appeared in the Spanish theater of operations or caused Caesar to turn back through an attack on Italy.

In the passes of the Pyrenees Caesar's forces encountered but little opposition. Probably the Pompeians did not even have enough time to occupy them; but even if they had had enough time, we already know from the battle of Thermopylae how unpromising and how dangerous it is to try to block mountain passes. The Romans, too, were familiar with this principle; once when the Cimbri were moving down from the Brenner Pass, the Roman general Catulus had, as Plutarch reports to us (*Marius*, Chapter 23), renounced from the start any idea of occupying the passes, because in doing so he would have split up his forces, and he preferred to await the enemy in the plain. Afranius and Petreius, too, showed that they understood the art of war.

Some 90 miles (150 kilometers) south of the Pyrenees passes, between 22 and 27 miles north of the Ebro, on the right bank of the powerful Sicoris (Segre) River, there stands on a ridge the city of Ilerda, with a stone bridge over the river. A short distance south of the city there rises, beside the river, another ridge, which was very well suited for a Roman camp site. Afranius and Petreius took up their position there. It was such a naturally strong position that no attack in force could hope to overcome it. To bypass it was not possible for Caesar, since in doing so he would have left the route open for the enemy army toward Massilia and Italy. Finally, it was very difficult to lay siege to the position, since the Sicoris was a very treacherous stream that would suddenly rise and sweep away the bridges in its savage swirling. In that way a besieging army would be pulled apart into two separate forces, while the besieged army with its firm stone bridge could move its forces from one bank to the other as needed. A large stock of supplies was assembled in order to assure provisions for a long time.

They could perhaps also have found a similar position on the Ebro itself, on the north bank, from which they would have been able to seize the offensive at any moment, with a firm bridge behind them, so that they could also have dominated the other bank, just as Caesar had once done on the Aisne. But Afranius and Petreius presumably did not consider it necessary to move back quite so far. At Ilerda they were still covering a considerably larger portion of their province; and if they should eventually be forced to decide on a further withdrawal, it could be assumed that they would be able to open up a route on one side or the other of the Sicoris. They dominated the south bank of the Ebro and could erect a floating bridge at any time they wanted to. The enemy could not possibly react so quickly, and therefore they would immediately gain a new sector on the Ebro and a cover that would guarantee them free movement.

Since Afranius and Petreius took up the position at Ilerda after an emissary from Pompey, Vibullius Rufus, had come to them, it is quite possible that Pompey himself, who of course knew Spain in detail, specified the campaign plan and the camp location.

The position at Ilerda gave the Pompeians everything that can be expected of a position. After the first 3 legions to arrive, under Fabius, had already been there for 4 weeks, Caesar's entire army camped before the position for almost 6 weeks (from about 17 May to 24 June, 49 B.C.) without accomplishing anything.[2]

Fabius had laid out his camp about 2½ miles north of Ilerda, on the same bank, and had built two bridges across the river, 6 kilometers apart. On one occasion the river swept the lower bridge away, just at a time when 2 legions were foraging on the other side. Afranius and Petreius immediately led 3 legions across and were threatening to overpower them when Fabius came to their aid just in time with 2 additional legions over the other bridge, which had held fast, and he was able to disengage them.

Another time, after Caesar himself had already taken over the command, the river tore away both bridges simultaneously. Now the Pompeians occupied the left bank and, aided by the high water, prevented Caesar from replacing the bridges. Caesar was just expecting a large supply train from Gaul, which was now unable to cross the river, was cut off and was driven back again into the mountains by the Pompeians. The resources of the area surrounding the camp were exhausted and no further foodstuff was to be found there; farther westward the crossings of the rivers were also destroyed by the floods and so Caesar was hemmed in as if on a kind of island. His troops began to suffer very serious shortages whereas the Pompeians enjoyed plentiful rations from the supplies that had been stocked in Ilerda long in advance.

Since the Pompeian legates did not dare, however, to move out too far from their camp and to pursue Caesar's supply train into the mountains to destroy it, Caesar finally succeeded in bringing it up. More than 18 miles upstream, at a position beyond any enemy outposts, he erected a new bridge, which enabled him to reestablish contact with his base of operations, Gaul.

This link was too distant to allow Caesar to besiege the Pompeian camp on both banks. A bold attempt that Caesar had made immediately after his arrival, to drive between the enemy camp and the city of Ilerda itself by means of the bridge, had failed. The Pompeians still seemed to be exposed to no direct danger. Nevertheless, they now decided to move out. As distant as Caesar's new bridge was, it still enabled him to send his superior cavalry over to the left bank of the Sicoris and to prevent the Pompeians from foraging. Several Spanish tribes, including the Iacetani and the Illurgavonensi on the two banks of the lower Ebro, went over to Caesar. Finally, it could be foreseen that, when the flood conditions had subsided, a ford across the Sicoris just above Ilerda would become passable and would allow Caesar's troops to move directly from one bank to the other, thus facilitating the complete encircling of the position. Caesar even made an attempt, by means of wide ditches that he had his men dig, to lower the surface of the water artificially in order to make the ford passable.

Very calmly, without any special precautionary measures except that they started during the night, in the third night watch (between midnight and 3 A.M.), with their entire train, the Pompeians took up their withdrawal to the Ebro, across which they had had a floating bridge built near Octogesa, at the confluence with the Sicoris. No doubt the column was attacked and harassed by the enemy cavalry, so that it moved forward only at a slow pace; but once the more open, rolling terrain was left behind them and the mountainous area of the Ebro, some 23 miles south of Ilerda, was reached, this plague, too, would stop, and nothing would any longer be able to prevent the crossing over the Ebro. They had already marched some 18 miles when they suddenly saw the enemy legions moving up on a forced march.

The water of the Sicoris had fallen to the extent that it was still higher than a man's chest at the Ilerda ford. Consequently, the ford was not yet really passable for infantry. But as Caesar tells us, he had, at the request of his soldiers themselves, risked making the crossing; horsemen stationed below the ford fished out those legionaries who were swept off their feet by the stream, so that nobody was lost. Arrived on the other side, the legions took up the march and, without a train and taking no break to prepare for battle, they succeeded in overtaking the enemy late in the afternoon. If Afranius and Petreius did not want to sacrifice a large part of their force in a rear-guard action, their only alternative was to halt the entire army and have it take position. As it was, of course, the day's march had already been a very long one.

The situation still did not seem desperate; after all, they had only 4½ more miles to cover before reaching the protection of the mountains and then only 4½ more to the river and the bridge. They gave up the idea of attempting a night march, for fear of being attacked en route. Finally, it was not necessarily impossible to cover the remaining short distance even in the view of the enemy.

Then Caesar's troops, as a result of their extraordinary zeal, succeeded in marching around the Pompeian forces, crossing almost impassable terrain, and beating the latter, who were again held up by the attacks of the cavalry, to the defile and the commanding terrain features, thus blocking their route to the Ebro.

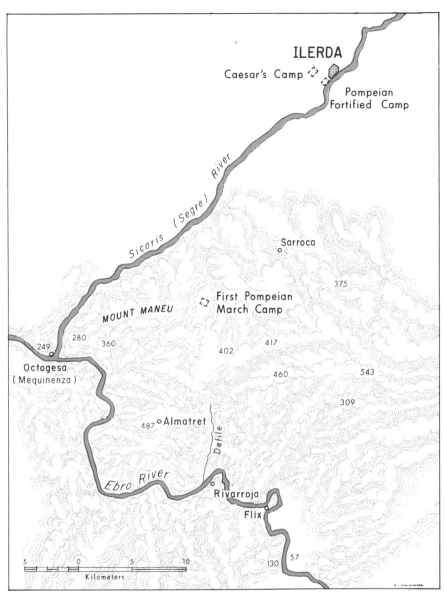

Fig 6. SIEGE OF ILERDA

Caesar's energy and speed, together with the goodwill and the outstanding capabilities of his troops, had accomplished what would appear to be impossible by normal military estimates. The Pompeian army, which intended to move back from one impregnable position to another, was brought to a standstill in the course of this short move and was blocked off from its goal. Now it had either to fight or to surrender within a short time. The constant, determined offense had shown itself superior to a defense that was just as strongly based. The Pompeian army, no doubt the weaker of the two but after all not so very much weaker, had kept the enemy occupied for a few months but only at the price of its final complete defeat. There still remain many doubtful points concerning the detailed maneuvers, and it is no doubt possible that in the end a difference of opinion between Afranius and Petreius facilitated Caesar's victory. In such a crisis, where everything depends on the decision of the moment, the need for coordination between two generals has a particularly detrimental effect. It is particularly curious that, when they were overtaken by Caesar, the Pompeians remained motionless for an entire day and only sent out reconnaissance patrols. If they believed at all that they could still carry out movements within view of the enemy, it is hard to understand why they did not try to move directly forward on the road to Octogesa. They no doubt could not expect that Caesar would allow them to break away;[3] he had moved out without baggage and rations, but the columns were naturally already on the march to bring up the most necessary supplies. It was this one day's halt that plunged the Pompeians into disaster, and it can hardly be explained by anything other than indecisiveness and a difference of opinion in the Pompeian headquarters. But the accomplishment of Caesar and his troops is barely diminished by this point. The error that the Pompeians made was, after all, already a result of the morale superiority of the enemy, which was exerting its pressure. In such a situation a general who would not have made any mistake would have had to be a very great commander indeed.

When the enemy turned back again toward Ilerda, Caesar felt so certain of the final complete victory that he no longer considered a battle to be necessary. His soldiers demanded a battle, in which victory could not escape them, but Caesar contented himself with deploying his army in the open field and leaving it up to the enemy as to whether he wanted to attack. Even the brave Petreius, who was determined to hold out to the end, had to realize that the battle itself would be a purposeless slaughter, and so finally there was nothing else to do but capitulate.

This victory of Caesar's undoubtedly stands alone in world history through the fact that absolute success, the complete destruction of the enemy army, was accomplished without a battle, simply through maneuver and a few moderate-sized skirmishes. The Roman army at Lake Trasimeno and at Cannae, the Prussian army in 1806, and three French armies in 1870–1871 were all completely destroyed, but only after stubbornly fought battles. Nevertheless, one should not confuse Caesar's strategy with that of Pericles, for example. The latter, fully aware of the inferiority of the Athenian land army, avoided from the start and as a matter of principle any large land battle, and since the enemy, on the other hand, declined to accept a decisive sea battle, he sought to end the war through a process of attrition. Nothing would have pleased Caesar more than to have Pompey's legates immediately accept a tactical decision, so that, having finished them off, he could turn as quickly as possible against Pompey himself. It was only because the legates, for their part, avoided a tactical decision that the war became a war of maneuver and that, only at the very end, when a battle had become unnecessary, Caesar himself also renounced such action—but let it be noted that it was the battle itself that he forwent, and not the purpose of the battle, the destruction of the enemy forces.

Battles would hardly ever be fought if the commanders were able to estimate with certainty the opposing strengths, the physical and the spiritual as well. He who is certain from the start of being defeated (unless it be a situation like that of Leonidas) seeks to avoid battle. In the campaign of Ilerda we have the rare example of a situation where the decision could be reached without a battle, because both sides analyzed the situation so well and correctly that there was no necessity for testing their estimate.

The two legates, aware of their numerical inferiority, avoided battle and selected a position where they could not be attacked and could be besieged only with great difficulty. Recognizing the impregnability of the enemy position, Caesar prepared for the siege. The legates slipped away from it, and they were already on the march when Caesar won a position that in effect amounted to a closed siege. Since once again both sides recognized the situation, the one realizing that he no longer needed a battle, the other that there was no longer a chance of success, the outcome was the destruction of the weaker side without any further bloodletting.

1. The campaign of Ilerda has already been treated very thoroughly by Guischard in *Critical and Historical Commentaries on Several Points of Ancient Military History (Mémoires critiques et historiques sur plusieurs points d'antiquités militaires)*, Vol. 1. Then it was studied by Göler and in a special research project by Rudolf Schneider, *Ilerda* (Berlin, 1886). All of these works, however, have been overtaken and made obsolete by the work of Colonel Stoffel, who produced a map that was very significantly different from the previous ones and who also personally studied the terrain. Stoffel (*Guerre civile*, 1: 256) states that Napoleon III in 1863 asked the Spanish government to have general staff maps drawn up of the region of Ilerda and Munda, and that by 1865 these maps, of excellent quality, were turned over to him. He says that his own maps are reduced reproductions of them. These Spanish maps must have remained unknown in Germany, since even the map that Schneider placed in his book, coming from Heinrich Kiepert, did not take them into consideration.

Under these circumstances it is unnecessary to go into the discrepancies between Göler and Schneider on the one hand, and Stoffel on the other; we are inclined to go along completely with Stoffel, who is in every respect the most outstanding expert. Nevertheless, I am unable to brush aside a few points of hesitation and for that reason, as in the campaign against Ariovistus, I have limited my account to the more general features.

It can hardly be doubted that Octogesa is the present town of Mequinenza. I should like to risk adding one more point to Stoffel's reasons. If the legates had had their floating bridge built near Almatret (Göler) or Flix (Schneider), they would have had to take the chance that Caesar would immediately move his entire army to the left bank of the Sicoris and would block their route. If then they had wished to withdraw along the right bank, they would first have had to move the bridge upstream to a point above the confluence with the Sicoris. The position selected for building the bridge was therefore just slightly downstream from the mouth of the Sicoris, which allowed them freedom of action, even at the last minute, depending on Caesar's course of action, to withdraw from Ilerda along either the right or the left bank. If, however, Octogesa was situated at the mouth of the Sicoris, it is not sufficiently clear why the Pompeians did not march along the left bank of the river. Stoffel assumes that they had avoided the level terrain along the river, since they foresaw that the enemy cavalry would harass them on the march. Of course, the route via Sarroca does lead through hilly terrain, but as the outcome proved, it was still open enough not to prevent the action by the cavalry. If they had taken the route along the river, at least one flank would always have been covered, and furthermore this route was considerably shorter, a point that took on great importance. Are we perhaps to assume that the Pompeians feared that, if they were to march directly along the river, they would be exposed to the arrows and slungshot of the sharpshooters from the other bank?

It is also not clear why the legates, when they were overtaken by Caesar, decided to take the route through the defile of Rivarroja, as Stoffel assumes they did. We can suppose that at the same time they sent an order to the officer in charge of the bridge to move the bridge to Rivarroja. But we cannot discern a reason for the change of the march route, and all the less so in that, after all, at the last minute the march was supposed to be resumed once more toward Octogesa. The route along Mont Maneu, too, must have had some stretches with the characteristics of a defile, where they could have found cover against Caesar's troops.

Finally, it is particularly curious that the legates, when the apparent withdrawal of Caesar toward Ilerda began, and especially when they saw that the march was on the Rivarroja road, did not immediately take up their march via Mont Maneu toward Octogesa.

All of these uncertainties would be removed if we could assume that Caesar had in mind the actual front and not the momentary position of those who were looking at the front, when he wrote, *"ubi paullatim retorqueri agmen ad* dextram *conspexerunt"* (Chapter 29) ("where they caught sight of the column gradually turning back to the *right"*), which would mean that the column of Caesar was turning to the *left*, or westward. After studying this situation again, I no longer have any doubt that such was the case and that, consequently, the whole series of details in the middle of the account, telling of the Pompeians' turning toward Rivarroja, is to be eliminated. They never had any other objective than Octogesa (Mequinenza), and Caesar blocked this route to them by moving in between their march camp and the Sicoris, in the direction of Mont Maneu.

2. Caesar's account of his efforts to create an artificial ford in the Sicoris seems very strange. First of all, one wonders why he did not preferably build a bridge. Even if the flood waters had swept away his bridges on several occasions, a ford would still be much more vulnerable, and the work that went into the ford was, by Caesar's own description, greater than that which would have been required to construct many bridges. Since Caesar already dominated the left bank with his cavalry, the enemy could not have prevented construction of a bridge.

We can find no other reason except perhaps an absolute lack of wood, but this would again prompt the question whether it would not have been possible to float the wood down from the Pyrenees on the Sicoris.

The main question, however, is whether it is, in fact, at all possible to create a ford in the manner intended by Caesar. There are greatly varying opinions as to just how the ditch-digging procedure is to be understood. Schneider, basing his concept on that of Guischard, assumes a full-fledged diversion of the river, a work of such gigantic proportions that it seems impossible to me, since, after all, hardly more than ten days could be devoted to the project. Stoffel's idea is much simpler. He takes as a starting point the fact that, 2 kilometers above Ilerda, the river splits and forms islands; he would have Caesar's men digging several 30-foot-wide ditches through these islands, thus widening the bed of the river to that extent and thereby lowering the surface. To what extent this is technically possible and correct is beyond my judgment.

NOTES FOR CHAPTER VII

1. See also pp. 495 and 499 above. Even if these numbers have not been directly handed down to us in the sources, I believe that one can still give them with certainty. Domaszewski, in his valuable essay "The Armies of the Civil Wars in the Years 49 to 42 B.C." ("Die Heere der Bügerkriege in den Jahren 49 bis 42 v. Chr."), *Neue Heidelberger Jahrbücher*, Vol. 4, 1894, has pointed out that Caesar had 11 legions at the outbreak of the civil war. Since, however, only 10 are mentioned in the campaign against Vercingetorix and 11 in the following winter quarters, but Caesar had given up 2 legions, he could really only have had 9 remaining. Domaszewski explains the difference by saying that Caesar, as soon as he saw the conflict coming on, immediately formed 2 new legions as replacements for those he had given up. But it seems to me that there is a still better explanation. In the year 52 B.C., in addition to the above-mentioned 10 legions, Caesar also had 22 cohorts that were

defending the province (7. 65) and that had been levied in the province itself, so that they were not all composed of Roman citizens. The Fifth Legion, Alauda, was such a legion of noncitizens. According to Suetonius (*Caesar*, Chapter 24), Caesar had already formed it during the Gallic War and not, as Domaszewski believes, as late as the year 50 B.C. There is nothing more natural than for us to assume that it belonged to those 22 cohorts of the year 52 B.C., and the same for the Sixth Legion, although of course Suetonius speaks of only *one* such barbarian legion. If we consider, however, that the Sixth Legion now appears in the *Commentaries* for the first time; that, as Napoleon III has already remarked, it arrived before Alesia as part of the main army; that Caesar cannot possibly have still had a veteran legion in Cisalpine Gaul at that time; that nothing would be more natural than for Caesar, after he had defeated Vercingetorix and the province was no longer in need of protection, to order up to his main force a part of the garrison there, in preparation for the decisive battle—under these circumstances we can hardly reach any other conclusion than that this legion was also a part of those 22 cohorts "*praesidia ex ipsa coacta provincia*" ("the garrisons drawn from the province itself").

In opposition to this it could be argued that in the *Bellum Alexandrinum*, Chapter 69, it is said that the Sixth Legion had been reduced to 1,000 men as a result of hardships and battle losses ("*crebritate bellorum*" ["the frequency of the wars"]) and that it was deactivated in 45 B.C. as a veteran legion. Even if it was not formed, however, until the winter of 53–52 B.C. (but perhaps also earlier), it had still participated in the battles in defense of the province, the battle against the relief of Alesia, and later the entire civil war and therefore had at least six years of intensive battle experience behind it when it followed Caesar from Egypt against Pharnaces. In a footnote on his page 171 Domaszewski, even on the assumption that the Fifth, Alauda, Legion was not formed until 50 B.C., cites it as a veteran legion in 48 B.C.

(Added in the second edition.) Gröbe (*Festschrift für Otto Hirschfeld*, 1903, reprinted in the 2d ed. of Drumann's *Römische Geschichte*, 3: 702), in a study concerning Caesar's legions, likewise came to the conclusion that the Fifth Legion had been formed from the cohorts that had been mentioned as being in the province in 52 B.C. But he fixes the organization of this unit as not occurring until 51 B.C. The Sixth Legion that participated in the civil war was supposedly not formed until 50 B.C., after the older Sixth Legion had been transferred to Pompey (and was designated as the First Legion in his army).

The 8 cohorts that I assume to have been in Cisalpine Gaul are not considered by Gröbe. Consequently, he gives Caesar only 10 legions in the year 52 B.C. The difference, however, is smaller than it appears, since it is only a question of whether legions were formed from the 22 cohorts somewhat earlier or later and whether the 8 cohorts in Cisalpine Gaul were already in existence in 52 B.C. Cicero's letter to Atticus in December 50 B.C., cited by Gröbe, seems to point to the formation of a considerable number of new units in 50 B.C.: (7. 7. 6) "Imbecillo resistendum fuit et id erat facile; nunc legiones XI, equitatus tantus, quantum volet, Transpadani." ("Resistance was weak, and the task was easy; now there were 11 legions and as much cavalry as he might wish, levied from the region north of the Po.") But there is not really anything to be learned from this passage, since under any circumstances Caesar had had in 52 B.C., in addition to his 10 legions, the 22 cohorts.

2. The cited dates are in accordance with Stoffel's calculations, based on the estimates of the astronomer Leverrier, which were requested by Napoleon III. According to Ideler, Mommsen, Matzat, Soltau, and Unger, the events occurred some three weeks earlier.

3. When Caesar moved out on the following day and initially took the route back toward Ilerda, the Pompeian soldiers naturally believed that a lack of provisions was forcing the enemy to retire. This does not contradict the sentence above, however.

Chapter VIII

The Campaign in Greece

The victory in Spain gave Caesar the upper hand over his enemies on land. Besides the 11 legions with which he started the war, he had gradually formed 17 new ones, principally from Pompey's soldiers, who, after being defeated, came into his service.[1] Two of the new legions under the command of Curio he had lost on a move to Africa, and another 1½ legions under C. Antonius in the Adriatic Sea, on the coast of Illyria. Of his remaining forces he assembled about half, 12 legions and 10,000 cavalry, near Brundisium in order to cross over to Epirus and carry the war to Pompey; the rest of his forces were divided up among Italy, Sicily, Gaul, and Spain.

At first Pompey had available to oppose the army that was to sail across to Epirus only 9 legions, which were to be joined by 2 additional ones from Syria under the command of Scipio. These troops were not a match for Caesar's either in numbers or in quality. Two of the legions were those that had formerly belonged to Caesar's army, and they were not absolutely dependable; the others were either newly formed units or older cadres that had been filled out with levies in Greece and Asia. After the destruction of his actual main army in Spain, Pompey would have had to give up any hope of success if he had not had absolute superiority at sea, just as Caesar had it on land. To the available Roman ships he had joined those of the eastern subject nations. Caesar had, to be sure, also ordered the construction of ships, but he lacked the nucleus of a fleet. The most important seaport of his original area, Massilia, had gone over to his enemies and had had to be conquered again, but only after a hard siege. The fleet in the Adriatic Sea was defeated and destroyed by the Pompeians. The advantage that Pompey won through these circumstances and events was so great that Caesar

528

could not overtake him. When he came to Brundisium, there were not even enough ships on hand to transport in a single voyage the army with which he intended to take the offensive.

Today it is considered strategically impossible for an army to move overseas without controlling the sea at least temporarily. Caesar decided to make the move even though his transport ships were not even sufficient. If he had waited long enough to assemble sufficient ships to move the entire army across, their great mass would still have made the move very difficult; even more important, in the meantime the enemy fleet, which was still quietly lying at anchor in the harbors, would have been alerted. Pompey himself had not yet arrived in Epirus with his army; the coastal cities, where great stocks of supplies had been stored, were without the protection of land forces. Speed promised the greatest successes. By reducing the supply train, Caesar was able to embark about half of his army, 7 legions and a cavalry force, and they made the crossing successfully, since at that time, in midwinter, the enemy was not prepared to cope with it.[2] It has been observed that a change of wind direction from south to north regularly occurring at this time of year, which was normally followed by several days of quiet weather, must have worked very favorably for Caesar's undertaking. The north wind brought his fleet in 12 to 15 hours to a part of the coast that is well protected precisely against this wind and which offered an excellent beach for the quickest possible debarkation.[3]

Only now did they encounter the real difficulty. It is true that a few of the coastal cities of Epirus, particularly Oricum and Apollonia, were quickly captured, but the principal town, Dyrrhachium, had been reached and secured by Pompey with his army just before Caesar arrived, and the Pompeian naval vessels overtook and burned a part of Caesar's transport fleet on its return trip and thereafter through increased alertness prevented the crossing of the second part of Caesar's army. Cut off from his base, Caesar with half of his army was paralyzed in Epirus. Nevertheless, this did not yet bring him into any direct danger. Although Pompey was stronger in infantry by 2 legions and very considerably stronger in cavalry, he still did not dare to attack directly Caesar's veterans with his inferior troops or to besiege them in their fortified camp.

And so the two commanders stood fast, confronting each other without fighting. Pompey was waiting for Scipio's legions in order to gain a sure superiority and for the summer in order to make use of his fleet. Caesar hoped that his generals would bring over to him the second half of his army from Brundisium.

One might well ask why Caesar did not bring up the necessary reinforcements by land, through Illyria, and this leads to the further question of why he did not have his legions take this route in the first place, when they came from Spain and Gaul, which would have avoided the dangerous sea crossing and was actually shorter. The answer probably is that the movement of a large army through the mountainous and hostile countryside of Illyria in winter would have posed insuperable supply difficulties. At the least it would have been necessary to make very extensive preparations, whereas the march through Italy to Brundisium could be made with security and without delay. Even the sea crossing was, as we have seen, no doubt a bold and daring act but in no way an unreasonable one. It does seem astonishing, however, that Caesar risked ordering that part of the army that had been left behind to proceed with the crossing and that the latter succeeded. We must understand that the ancient warships with their massive and tightly packed crews of oarsmen were not able to stay at sea continuously for a very long time.

Consequently, they could not, for example, blockade Brundisium. True enough, the Pompeian admiral, Libo, made an attempt to do this, and for this purpose he occupied a small island situated in front of the harbor. But the island did not have enough water, and Mark Antony, who was in command in Brundisium, through the use of widely spaced cavalry patrols prevented the ships' crews from going ashore on the mainland to obtain water. And so the Pompeians had to give up the blockade and content themselves with keeping a close watch on the sea from their ports in Epirus, in order to attack, if the situation arose, Caesar's approaching fleet of transports. If, however, a strong wind favorable to Caesar's forces was blowing, the oar-propelled warships could not do much against the sailing transport vessels. The voyage still remained very risky, since it was completely at the mercy of the whims of the wind. A full two months passed before Antony and the other generals decided, after receiving repeated orders from Caesar himself, to undertake the venture; and fortune was so favorable to them that not only did their entire fleet cross over without loss but it even happened that the enemy fleet, which hoped to intercept them, was driven on the rocks by a sudden change of the wind.

It appears that Caesar, in view of the uncertainty of the sea transportation, had also started reinforcements moving toward him via Illyria, but, held up by the hostile mountain tribes, they did not arrive in time for the decisive battle.[4]

Antony brought over to Caesar 4 legions and cavalry, so that he now held unquestioned superiority. But what was he to do with it? By one of his sudden forced marches he succeeded in moving his army between Pompey and Dyrrhachium, but he gained little in doing so. Pompey dug in directly on the beach, and thanks to his ships he was able to maintain continuous contact with his main supply point, the richly stocked Dyrrhachium, and with the rest of the world. He could feed his army without difficulty via the sea route, whereas Caesar had to rely on supplies brought up with great difficulty overland from an area whose resources were already partially exhausted. Despite his superior strength, Caesar was not in a position to force a decision.

He decided to divide up his army. Almost all of the reinforcements that had finally joined him, 3½ legions, he sent into the interior of the country. Two legions went in search of Scipio, with the mission of pinning him down, if possible, and defeating him. One and a half legions turned toward Hellas in order to subject or to win over to Caesar's side as many cities and country regions as possible. With the main body of his army, Caesar undertook to besiege the army of Pompey. The terrain favored this operation so that, for the time being, it was only necessary to steepen somewhat the natural slopes of the hills by digging and to lay out individual redoubts. But the work was still a massive undertaking, and the expected gains were small. Caesar himself states that he had three goals in mind through the siege: He wanted to protect his own supply route from the superior cavalry of Pompey; he wanted to harm and weaken this cavalry by cutting it off from the possibility of foraging; and finally he wanted to exert pressure on the morale of the enemy side by letting it be widely known that Pompey was besieged and did not dare join battle. Caesar himself does not state the belief that he could have brought Pompey to capitulate through the siege or could even have forced him to treat for peace, and these possibilities were also completely out of the question. Nothing could prevent Pompey from embarking his army whenever he wanted to and moving it somewhere else.

The question is why Pompey did not simply move over to Italy, as a number of his friends advised. He had a good reason for not doing so. In that case Caesar would also have led his army back to

Italy, through Illyria, which he would have succeeded in doing sooner or later with at least a portion of the army, and then, even if Italy had fallen into Pompey's hands in the meantime, it would be necessary at once to fight the decisive battle, which offered Pompey no prospect of success, for he had only 9 legions with him, whereas Caesar had 11 and more than as many as that again in Italy, Gaul, Spain, and the islands.

The best plan for Pompey would probably have been not to move out at once directly back to Italy and Rome, but first, with the help of King Juba of Numidia, to take back Siciliy, Sardinia, and Spain from Caesar, and only then, after significantly increasing his forces from those in these provinces, to accept the decisive battle. With the help of his fleet all of these undertakings could be carried out simultaneously or in very quick succession. The 4 legions that Caesar had in Spain consisted primarily of former soldiers of Pompey; perhaps it was possible to win them back to his side. We do not know whether Pompey considered such plans. We do not have any source that provides us with a reliable insight into the more intimate estimates of his headquarters.[5] Since it is reported on all sides, however, that Pompey wished to avoid a battle and we have no reason to assume that his strategy was purely negative, we are justified in attributing to him ideas approximately of the kind developed above.

Caesar's actions, however, probably gave Pompey the idea that there were still greater chances of success offered him here. The army with which Caesar was carrying out the siege was smaller than Pompey's army. With the help of his ships, the latter could attack the besiegers in their rear at any time. We may give such an experienced commander as Pompey credit for recognizing what advantages were offered him by Caesar's excessively daring venture and for deciding, instead of that other far-reaching plan, to make the most, first of all, of the present situation and keep his army and fleet together. All the ability of Caesar's veterans still did not finally prevent a large-scale attack by the Pompeians with the help of their ships from succeeding. Caesar's army was attacked simultaneously on three sides, from Pompey's camp, from the beach, and from the rear, suffering a defeat with heavy losses, and its fortifications on the south side, where they extended down to the beach, were broken through.

This result seems so natural that one is inclined to consider as a serious error Caesar's attempt to besiege from the land a larger, undefeated army that had control of the sea. Under the best circumstances he had but little to win but very much to lose. But in war both chance and fortune play a role, and Caesar left the outcome up to fate, not through arrogance, but because there was no alternative for him. Furthermore, he also hoped, through connections that he had made in the city, to have Dyrrhachium fall into his power. If, instead of conducting the siege, he had marched into the interior with his whole army, he would not have accomplished any more than his detached legions were able to do. Neither would the seaports have surrendered to him nor would he have defeated Scipio, who naturally would have kept a safe distance between himself and the main enemy army. In the meantime, however, Pompey would have been able to send his legions on expeditions with the fleet that presumably would have resulted in greater successes than Caesar's marches with his army. The enemy's superiority at sea, which enabled him to avoid a decisive battle, would then have proven itself to be still more valuable by far.

The siege of Pompey's army led, it is true, to nothing at all, and in fact to something even worse, a defeat. But it was precisely this blow that brought on the desired counterblow.

Puffed up by this success, the Pompeians would now have been ready to accept the decisive battle on the spot, but Caesar, wisely estimating that he must give his troops some time to recover from this blow to their morale, avoided the battle. Through a clever maneuver he got a head start and took up the march toward Thessaly in order to join up again with his detached troops. The latter had won for him a large portion of the interior; the principal force, under Domitius, was maneuvering around Scipio, but without success, since he avoided a battle.[6]

The safest thing now for Pompey would still have been not to move directly into a decisive battle but rather, on the strength of the morale success of his victory at Dyrrhachium, first of all to win over the western provinces again and only then, with doubled strength, to attack Caesar himself. But even if Pompey did think along these lines, as indeed Caesar reports, saying that he was still inclined to avoid a decisive battle, nevertheless he was still not sufficiently in control of his party to force its acceptance of such a long-drawn-out plan. Caesar reports that, for his part, he considered three possible enemy courses of action: that Pompey would move over to Italy; that he would besiege the ports in Epirus where Caesar had garrisons and which formed his depots; and that he would pursue Caesar directly. Of these three possibilities, the second one would undoubtedly have been the best for Pompey.

Caesar says that in that case he, for his part, would have besieged Scipio, thus forcing Pompey to come to his relief. But Scipio had the possibility of withdrawing to a seaport, perhaps Thessalonica, or to Byzantium, where Caesar, without a fleet, could not have caused him any harm, whereas Pompey could have attacked Caesar's fortresses by land and by sea. The strengths of the two sides were consequently similar in no way. But the Pompeians were now much too self-confident to work up to victory gradually by such devious ways. First of all they tried to see if they could cut off Domitius' corps, which was maneuvering against Scipio in Macedon, and when that attempt failed just at the last minute and Domitius with his 2 legions managed to escape and join Caesar, they followed him onto the plain of Thessaly and offered battle. Each of the commanders now had at his disposal in the theater of operations a total of 11 legions; Caesar had left behind 8 cohorts in the ports of Epirus that he occupied, whereas Pompey had 15 cohorts in Dyrrhachium. But Caesar did not yet have back the detached force of 1½ legions that he had sent to Hellas, so that the Pompeian army, just as it enjoyed strengthened morale from its recent victory, also had a considerable superiority in numbers.

Caesar himself states that he had only 22,000 infantry and 1,000 cavalry, whereas Pompey on the other hand had 45,000 infantry and 7,000 cavalry. If we immediately add to this the point that Caesar claims to have won his victory with a loss of only 200 men, whereas 15,000 Pompeians are supposed to have remained on the battlefield, then one could give credence to such strengths, as long as one is still willing in general simply to repeat the numbers in the sources without questioning them; it is somewhat astonishing, however, that these numbers even today are still zealously defended. Impossible as they are in and of themselves, they also stand in contradiction to Caesar's further statement that Pompey, up to the last minute, actually did not want the battle and that it was only through the blind trust in victory and the constant pressure of his retinue that he was finally driven to it. What kind of personality must Pompey have been, if with more than twice as many infantry and seven times as many cavalrymen as his enemy, he wanted to avoid the decision? How could he hope ever again to encounter Caesar under such favorable circumstances, when we know, of course, that Caesar was greatly superior to him in the total number of his land troops? To judge from the movements that Pompey made, we may assume that he enjoyed a certain superiority of numbers but that this advantage was still not significant enough to give him the confidence to engage in an open battle against the qualitative superiority of Caesar's veterans right in the Dyrrhachium area. Now for the first time, after the morale of his troops had been increased greatly by the successful attack on the enemy camp near Dyrrhachium, and that of the enemy, as he could easily believe, had been weakened, he came to the decision to risk the decisive battle, but he still sought up to the last minute to gain further small advantages for himself in the terrain, and he thereby delayed the battle. If we take into consideration the other reports that have come down to us, which perhaps go back to Caesar's general, Asinius Pollio, who also wrote a work on the civil war, then we may—with the reservation that it is not very definite—estimate Pompey's army at perhaps 40,000 legionaries and something like 3,000 cavalry, and Caesar's at a good 30,000 legionaries and perhaps 2,000 cavalry. Pompey was also probably stronger in light infantry forces, which were present on both sides.

We cannot give any credence to the point that Pompey even now still had reservations about going into the battle. Once he had followed Caesar into the interior, any hesitation could bring no further advantage. He could not prevent Caesar from marching through the fertile countrysides from the Black Sea to the isthmus and having these areas furnish provisions for his troops. The supply advantage that the Pompeian army had in being able to bring up ships from a distance through its close contact with the seaports was still not great enough to counterbalance the disadvantage that a long delay would cause by nullifying the gain in morale provided by the campaign to date. Furthermore, Caesar could then expect to be joined by the 1½ legions from Hellas and probably also the 2 legions that were coming from Italy via Illyria.[7] If Pompey actually did express any reservations, that must have been while he was still in the Dyrrhachium area, before deciding to follow Caesar, or at the latest when the blow against Domitius' corps had failed—and no longer at the time when he finally stood facing Caesar in Thessaly. That the battle still did not develop at once, when the two armies were again in sight of each other, was due only to the fact that each side, thinking that the enemy was now at last ready for battle, was seeking for itself a favorable position and hoping that the enemy would allow himself to be drawn into battle there.[8]

Finally Pompey moved out from his camp so far onto the plain that he no longer had any terrain advantage, and Caesar, who was already about to march off, thereupon decided to await his reinforcements no longer but to accept the challenge, and so he moved in on the enemy.

Let us try to establish a picture of this fateful day of decision. It will differ in a not unimportant way from the accounts that have been accepted up to now, since I believe that Caesar's own account, which has normally been accepted, requires rather incisive corrections, on the basis of the descriptions of the other sources, just as in the case of his numerical strengths.

NOTES FOR CHAPTER VIII

1. Perhaps even a few more. Gröbe, in Drumann's *Roman History* (*Römische Geschichte*), 2d ed., 3: 710.

2. 28 November 49 B.C., according to Stoffel; 5 November, according to Mommsen.

3. These observations and the confirmation of these points had already been made by a commission sent out by Napoleon III in 1861 in a work published by L. Heuzay, *Julius Caesar's Military Operations, studied on the Terrain by the Macedonian Commission (Les opérations militaires de Jules César, étudiées sur le terrain par la mission de Macédoine)* (Paris, 1886), which was confirmed by Stoffel in *Life of Caesar (Vie de César)* 1: 138.

4. Domaszewski, in *Armies of the Civil Wars (Heere der Bürgerkriege)* pp. 171–172, considers it impossible for legions to have come from Italy to Illyria, since the Pompeians controlled the sea. This reason is not convincing, since the land route was open.

5. Up to the present this point has probably not been sufficiently emphasized. Ranke, in his *World History (Weltgeschichte)*, even states the opinion that we have descriptions of the battle of Pharsalus that stem from supporters of the Senate and of Pompey. Such is the case only to the extent that Livy wrote from the Pompeian point of view and Lucanus, particularly, presented the civil war with this bias. But these two were already significantly dependent on written sources, and since, despite their bias, they have practically nothing that does not go back to either Caesar or Pollio, that is a sure proof that a truly Pompeian original source containing unique information either did not exist or had already disappeared at that time. Lucanus apparently did do his best to find such a source but it is downright astonishing how little of a positive nature his work contains which would not be known from other sources. Plathner, in *On the Credibility of the History of the Civil War (Zur Glaubwürdigkeit der Geschichte des Bürgerkrieges)* (Bernburg Programm, 1882), has compiled these points very well and has shown that Lucanus used Livy as a source. And so the two of them were able to express their sympathy for Pompey's cause only through the material handed down from the enemy side.

6. Appian and Dio Cassius write of important defeats suffered, in

turn, by these detached corps. These reports probably have to stem from Asinius Pollio, but if they were true, there would have had to be in some way or other more significant consequences. We must therefore prefer Caesar's report; Pollio must have been taken in by the exaggerated accounts of persons who took part in those battles.

7. Plutarch, *Caesar*, Chapter 43.

8. That is the sense of *Bell. Civ.* 84. 2 and 85. 1.

Chapter IX

The Battle of Pharsalus

Pompey's right flank rested on a deep ravine with a brook flowing through it. With this base the commander decided to vary his battle formation in an important point from the usual plan. Trusting that the brook would provide his legions sufficient flank protection on that side, he moved almost his entire cavalry force with his light infantry, under the command of his best general, Labienus, who had gone over from Caesar to the aristocratic party, to the other, the left, flank. If the cavalry got the upper hand here and drove from the field those of Caesar's troops that were directly opposing them, then they were immediately to fall on the enemy legions in their flank and rear; and in order to hold off the infantry battle as long as possible before this moment, Pompey's legions were not to charge forward at the assault pace against the enemy in the usual way but were to await the enemy's attack. In this way Pompey presumably also hoped to gain a particular advantage in that Caesar's troops, expecting the enemy to come out and meet them halfway, would take up the run too soon and would arrive at the point of hand-to-hand contact out of breath and in disorder.

Caesar does not specifically report whether he too assigned all or almost all of his cavalry to the flank on the plain, but we can probably assume so, since he could of course already see the enemy formation from a distance and cavalry on the flank by the stream, who would only have infantry to attack in front of them, would not be able to accomplish anything.

In view of the superiority of the enemy cavalry, Caesar had assigned to his own cavalry selected soldiers from the younger men of his legions and from the most agile of the *antesignani* (men before the standard), in light equipment, who fought in coordination with the cavalry in the manner of the *hamippen*, as was also customary among the Germanic tribes, and who a few days before the battle had already engaged in a

538

successful skirmish using these coordinated tactics. But he went still further. While the 2 armies were still engaged in the approach march, he pulled 6 strong cohorts, totaling 3,000 men, from his third echelon, moved them to an angled position on his right flank in support of his cavalry, and instead of having the rest of his third echelon move up with the two leading ones, he held this force back as a general reserve. Pompey's 3 echelons were each 10 men deep, for a total depth of 30 men, and it was against this formation that Caesar's men, initially only about half as deep in their formation without their third echelon, clashed. But Caesar was justified in trusting his tried legions, even under these circumstances, to stand up to the enemy for a rather long time, and Pompey's arrangement to delay the infantry battle somewhat was of direct assistance to him.

When Pompey's cavalry with its sharpshooters, somewhat in advance of the phalanx, moved into the attack, the Germanic and Gallic horsemen, following their instructions, did not accept the attack but moved back. But when the Pompeian forces then followed them up, they were attacked in their flank by the 6 cohorts from the angled flanking position. Caesar's cavalry then swung around and moved in on the Pompeians with its light infantry; the Pompeians were thrown back, and Caesar's troops pursued them.

Although none of the sources reports it specifically, we may be permitted to assume that generals like Pompey and Labienus knew what they had to do against the envelopment with which they were now threatened by Caesar's cavalry. They moved up supporting troops from the third echelon of infantry and attempted to form a flanking angle against the envelopment. But the situation was developing too quickly; there is a difference between having the support from the third echelon foreseen, as Caesar had done, and on the other hand, not having it ordered until the moment when the fleeing mass and behind it the pursuing enemy are already pouring back, at which time the difficult change of front is supposed to be carried out. At this time, too, the phalanxes had just made contact with each other, and the hand-to-hand combat of the first echelons had started.

Under these circumstances the Pompeians' strength was not sufficient to mount against the enveloping cavalry and cohorts a counterattack that would have thrown them back again. Despite the flight of their cavalry and sharpshooters, the Pompeians were still numerically equal or even superior to their opponents, but the manner in which the latter were now fighting, with their envelopment and their combination of arms, was the more effective. Caesar reinforced his phalanx from the rear with his third echelon, and under the pressure of the double attack from front and flank, deprived of the support of their own cavalry and sharpshooters, at first the left flank of the Pompeians gradually gave way and finally the whole army.

The battle was set up in accordance with the old, well-known plan for the flank battle, but it was immeasurably refined through the combination with the arrangement of the echelons and the defensive-offensive action. Both generals designated their corresponding flanks for the offensive. Pompey very appropriately made his flank as strong as possible through the concentration of all his cavalry with the light infantry and, according to the normal course of things, would necessarily have been stronger than the opposing force. But Caesar, foreseeing the development of events, gave his cavalry wing an extraordinary degree of reinforcement and at the same time held the cavalry back until the favorable moment. If he had simply had his 3,000 legionaries move forward with his cavalry, they would not have been of much help and would perhaps have been swept back with the cavalry as the latter, as might be foreseen, was pushed to the rear. For this reason Caesar drew them up in an angled position, in an ambush, as one of the sources expresses it; from this position they first let their own cavalry move back by them and then finally fell upon the enemy cavalry in its flank while their own cavalry wheeled about again and took up the battle.

This support of cavalry by heavy infantry that moves forward offensively against the enemy cavalry is the highest imaginable accomplishment of cohort tactics. Only completely trained tactical units led with absolute confidence—not entire phalanxes but only cohorts, which are flexible because of their small size—are capable of operating in this way.

Caesar had previously conquered the cavalry of Vercingetorix, which had no infantry echelon with it, by using the same combination of arms, but at Pharsalus the partial victory immediately developed into a complete victory over the enemy infantry as well. As complicated as the entire army organization had become, nevertheless the sentence that Polybius had once written (35. 1) still held true—a single factor decides the outcome of battles.

Like Hannibal's center at Cannae, Caesar's phalanx had borne the pressure of the far larger enemy phalanx until relief came through the flanking action; but this accomplishment was even greater than that at Cannae because the flanking action did not start at once but had to develop gradually from the initial defensive over into the offensive.

Like the legions, Caesar's cavalry and its accompanying light infantry must also have had excellent morale and been filled with
complete confidence in the leadership of their commander and
their officers. This is evident in the fact that, after they had given
way during the initial attack, it was possible to have them swing
around again at once, as soon as the intervention of the cohorts
had reversed the balance. The cavalrymen were Gauls and Germanic warriors.

And so a smaller force defeated a considerably stronger one of
essentially similar troops by virtue of their better quality, which the
leadership of their commander knew how to utilize in the most brilliant manner.

Pompey's order that delayed the start of the infantry battle was
of itself not badly conceived, but it necessarily turned to the advantage of the enemy commander when the latter took his countermeasures, facilitating for him the formation of a fourth echelon
and through it victory in the cavalry battle.

A battle like that at Pharsalus is a matter of life and death, survival or destruction. Of what good would it be to the Pompeians if
they then made an orderly withdrawal and defended their camp?
They would have been besieged in it, as was Vercingetorix at Alesia
or Afranius and Petreius at Ilerda, and since there was no relief
possible, they would sooner or later have been forced to capitulate.
Such was the situation for the army, but not for the leaders. The
cause of the aristocratic party was not yet finally lost as a result of
this battle; there were still in many places strong forces opposed to
a monarchy, and Caesar still had to fight two great battles to make
his mastery complete. The sources are unanimous in blaming Pompey for breaking down completely under the pressure of the defeat, running away from the battle prematurely and rushing to his
camp but taking no steps there for its defense. Caesar only reports
that Pompey retired to his tent, awaited the outcome there, and
when the enemy soldiers were pressing into the camp, he discarded
the commander's standards and left the camp on horseback.
Plutarch and Appian paint a more detailed picture, showing him
sitting silent and dazed in his tent until the approach of the enemy
soldiers swarming in over the camp parapet frightened him away.
It may perhaps have happened that way, but it is also necessary to
point out that, as soon as the battle was decided, there was nothing
more for Pompey to do. The army could no longer be saved, but
the leaders, by saving themselves, still had the possibility of continuing the conflict in other places. From the purely military point of

view, Pompey's conduct, as described by Plutarch, seems to indicate that he had forgotten that he was Pompey the Great and that Zeus had confounded his senses, as he had once done with Ajax. Politically his conduct is explainable through the fact that the interests of the army and of its leaders no longer coincided. Appian reports that Caesar sent out heralds among the combatants, calling out that his soldiers should spare their fellow countrymen and should turn only against the allies. This account cannot be literally accurate, since it is impossible to spread such orders in the midst of the melee and furthermore, one could not distinguish among the Pompeian legionaries (since it was now a question only of them) between those who were Roman citizens and the foreigners who were mixed in with them. But even if this point cannot be accepted as realistic, it is a valid indication of the nature of the situation. Something like a third of Pompey's legionaries was formed of soldiers who a short time earlier had honored Caesar as their commander, and even the other two-thirds had no inner tie to the faction for which they were fighting. Loyal to their oath and in keeping with the law of military discipline, they fought the battle through bravely; there was nothing in their situation, however, that called for a further, hopeless resistance.

Thus ended the battle, with Pompey fleeing, his camp given up after a brief defensive action, the defeated army at first fleeing into the mountains to save itself, where, relentlessly pursued and encircled by Caesar's troops, it surrendered on the same night without any further resistance.

Excursus

1. For the army strengths in the campaign of 48 B.C. we have greatly varying reports, two groups of which come into consideration: that of Caesar himself, and a second one that includes Plutarch, Appian, Eutropius, and Orosius and which goes back to Asinius Pollio. Up to now it has been customary to give the preference to Caesar's figures and simply to accept them, but that cannot be justified.[2]

If we have seen in the Gallic War that Caesar exaggerated the strengths of the defeated opponents to a massive degree, that still does not allow us to draw any conclusion about the unreliability of his figures for the civil war. The public for which he was describing the Gallic War would not have understood him at all if he had given the correct figures; these were barbarian armies which he had conquered and, according to both Greek and Roman concepts, barbarian armies had to be mass armies. We must therefore see if there are figures given in the account of the civil war itself that will allow us to check on the reliability of the author.

In the Spanish War Caesar gives Afranius and Petreius 80 cohorts of allies, in addition to their legions (*Bell. Civ.* 1. 39). Stoffel has already pointed out (1: 265) that that cannot possibly be correct, and he proposed that the figure "XXX" be read in the account instead of "LXXX."

In *Bell. Civ.* 3. 37. 7, we hear of a fight in which the Pompeians lost 80 killed, Caesar's forces 2.

In 3. 45–46, there is an account of a very hard-fought battle, with alternating success on the two sides, involving the Ninth Legion in front of Dyrrhachium, in which that legion finally lost a total of 5 men while the enemy lost *"complures"* ("several").

In 3. 54, we are told how six different combat actions took place on one and the same day around Dyrrhachium. One portion of the account of these fights has been lost; the manuscripts of the *Bell. Civ.* have a gap here that, however, can be filled in to a certain extent from the other sources. At any rate, it was a bloody day and, according to Caesar, the total losses of the Pompeians amounted to 2,000, whereas his own troops lost no more than 20 men.

At Pharsalus, according to Caesar's own account, his cavalry was initially pushed back, the legions had a tough fight in the hand-to-hand melee, and it was only the moving in of Caesar's third echelon in coordination with the flanking movement that forced the Pompeians to give way. Finally, too, the camp was courageously defended for a while, although it is true that this was less by the Pompeian legionaries than by the Thracian and other barbarian allies, and it was finally taken by storm. Nevertheless, Caesar claims after the battle that he had no more than 200 soldiers missing, whereas the Pompeians are supposed to have had 15,000 killed.

It is impossible to clarify all these figures in the manner in which Stoffel sought to do so in the case of the Spanish cohorts, through corruptions in the text. But it is just as impossible to accept them. I myself have pointed out several times (pp. 359, 455) how small the losses of the victors usually were in ancient battles, but what we are told here goes completely too far beyond the realm of probability. The troops fighting on both sides, even if they were not of equal quality, were still as Roman legions of such a similar type that we are obliged to reject the great differences in the loss figures as simply impossible.

We are not the first ones to do that. As we already observed above, in the case of the figures for the Gauls, Caesar's contemporaries in Rome knew very well that the figures he gave were not to be trusted. The principal source, from which the majority of reports by far which have come down to us, except for Caesar's own accounts, have stemmed, was undoubtedly the work of Asinius Pollio, which we have already mentioned several times, I do not have the impression that Pollio was a truly critical and objective historian, although one is inclined to believe so when one sees that, even though he was one of Caesar's generals, he often contradicts Caesar and rejects his exaggerations. Rather, it appears to me that these contradictions are attributable not so much to objectivity but more likely to a certain supercilious attitude of envious rebelliousness against the great man, of a type not infrequently found in the retinue of such heroes and which also comes to light in the memoirs of several of Napoleon's and Frederick's generals.

We may therefore not conclude that whenever Pollio, as one of Caesar's generals, says something unfavorable about Caesar, this point is a guaranteed fact; similarly, there is just as little reason to believe that whenever he agrees with Caesar, the reliability of the report is confirmed by that fact. When we find, however, that Pollio consistently refuses to accept the numerical estimates given by Caesar, then the criticism that we have arrived at through objective analysis at any rate receives from this fact a very important corroboration, even when we find that on one occasion Pollio himself overshot the mark. I believe that we have such a case at hand. Caesar states as his losses in the last defeat in front of Dyrrhachium 960 men and 32 officers; in Orosius—that is to say, undoubtedly Pollio—we read 4,000 men and 22 (erroneously copied for 32) officers. For any army of some 30,000 men, a figure of 4,000 killed would (since we would after all also have to figure on from 12,000 to 20,000 wounded) mean a lack of battle readiness for a rather long time. The figure of almost 1,000 killed, which Caesar gives, is already such a large loss that I should not like to raise any objection to it from an objectively critical viewpoint. Apparently in this case Pollio's general suspicion that Caesar was unreliable in his statement of strength figures ran away with him, so to speak, and he repeated some exaggerated rumor or other without giving it any further thought.

Let us turn now to the strength estimates.

According to his own statement, Caesar had 80 cohorts at the front at Pharsalus while 2 guarded the camp. Since he had detached 23 cohorts (15 in Greece, 4 in Apollonia, 3 in Oricum, 1 in Lissus), there were missing 5 cohorts from his total command of 11 legions or 110 cohorts. Stoffel emended the text at this point, as Heller had already done before him, and probably with good reason; he found that 2 cohorts were not enough for the defense of the camp, and he chose to read 7 instead.

According to Caesar, the 80 cohorts at the front accounted for 22,000 men, so that the cohorts averaged 270 men each. Furthermore, Caesar had assigned a number of *antesignani* to his cavalry. The overall infantry strength of the legions would therefore have been, by his account, some 24,000, and the cohorts could then be estimated around 300 men on the average.

Orosius (6. 15) and Eutropius (6. 20), however, give Caesar's infantry as something under 30,000 men, and Appian (2. 76) and Plutarch (*Pompey*, Chapter 71) estimate Caesar's fourth echelon, which by his figures was 6 cohorts strong, at 3,000 men, which would give each cohort not 300, but 500 men. To draw a general conclusion on the whole army from this and to estimate the legions at 500 times 80, or a total of 40,000 men, would be unreliable, since of course it is possible that Caesar took from his third echelon the 6 largest cohorts, which may well have been very unequal in strength. But even if we may not simply multiply, it is still clear that, even if there were only 6 cohorts in the third echelon with as many as 500 men, the average can still not have fallen below 300. Furthermore, we read in Plutarch's *Antony* (Chapter 3) that the 4 legions that Antony brought over to Caesar, along with 800 cavalry, were 20,000 men strong (in hoplites). Even if we deduct considerable losses for the fighting around Dyrrhachium, not only in killed but also wounded, who probably remained behind in Apollonia and Lissus, and we assume that the legions that came up later were numerically stronger, it is still impossible that 80 cohorts at Pharsalus would have been only 24,000 men strong when 4 months earlier 40 cohorts were 20,000 men strong.

Since we have now sufficiently determined the unreliability of Caesar's strength figures in other passages and we have here not, for instance, the estimate of an opponent but of one of his own generals who was present in the battle, we shall not hesitate to give our preference to his own general. Whether it be that Caesar pulled his figure quite arbitrarily out of the air or whether instead of using an average strength figure he based his multiplication on the lowest figure that he had in memory at the time, under any circumstances we must raise his figure considerably, and I do not doubt that even the "less than 30,000" figure from Pollio is still too low and that this latter figure should at least be increased by the number of *antesignani* who were pulled out of the cohorts and assigned to the cavalry.

Caesar states that the Eighth and Ninth Legions were so weak that together they would actually only have formed one legion. If we take this expression literally, it means that together they numbered about 6,000 men, that is, that each cohort was some 300 men strong.

With this point we have now found cues for the numerical strengths of both the strongest and the weakest cohorts in Caesar's army: 500 men and 300 men. If we accept as the average for the whole army 400 men, the 80 cohorts at the front numbered 32,000 men, from which perhaps 2,000 may be subtracted to account for the *antesignani* assigned to the cavalry. This estimate gains a certain credibility through the fact that it is in agreement with the total that goes back to Pollio, 30,000.

We arrive at a somewhat higher number still if we go along with M. Bang, who in *The Germanic Warriors in the Service of Rome* (*Die Germanen im römischen Dienst*), 1906,

p. 27, states as "completely beyond doubt" that Caesar also had at Pharsalus a strong contingent of Germanic foot troops at the front. He bases this belief on *Bell. Civ.* 1. 83 and 3. 52. These passages, however, do not provide complete proof of the point. In the first one there is specific mention of Germanic *"levis armaturae"* ("lightly armed troops"); these are presumably the infantry assigned to coordinated fighting with the cavalry (see also Book VII, Chapter III, above). These same men may also be meant in the second passage, the interpretation of which is not quite clear.

Caesar states the strength of the Pompeian infantry as 110 cohorts totaling 45,000 men; in addition, 2,000 *evocati* are specifically mentioned, and a further 7 cohorts guarded the camp.

Orosius-Pollio gives only 88 cohorts at the front, and there can be no doubt that this number is the correct one.

Caesar himself tells us (3. 4) that Pompey initially had 9 legions, to which were added the 2 under Scipio. In accordance with these calculations, he gives Pompey 110 cohorts at Pharsalus. He forgot to subtract, however, the 15 cohorts that Pompey had left behind as garrison for Dyrrhachium under Cato, and he himself says that 7 cohorts remained in the camp. There have been various proposals for filling in these numbers. Stoffel (1: 343) assumes that it was not legion cohorts of Roman citizens that were left in Dyrrhachium; Göler (2: 163) claims that the 15 cohorts of Caesar's troops that were captured in the Adriatic and were then incorporated in the Pompeian army are to be added to the 11 legions. Both of them explain the additional 7 cohorts as those that had made their way to Pompey after the army in Spain had been dissolved. But all of these details fail to ring true. According to Caesar's own specific statement (3. 4. 2), the 15 cohorts taken as prisoners were not formed as individual troop units but were divided up among other units, and it is completely impossible that 7 complete cohorts moving on their own should have made their way through Italy to Pompey without being stopped by Caesar's commanders. If a few hundred men undertook such a venture and succeeded, that is already very many.

If we did not have Pollio's testimony, we could still believe that at least one or two individual cohorts were formed out of these veterans, since Caesar states it so positively and even makes particular mention of them in the battle formation, and that the rest of them, too, had been brought to the army in some manner or other possibly mentioned by Caesar in some passage that has been lost. Since Pollio knew the figures given by Caesar, however, and consciously stated his own in opposition to them, and his number agrees with the situation if we subtract from the overall army of 110 cohorts the 22 that we know to have been detached, then there can be no doubt that Pompey never had more than those 110 cohorts and that of that total 88 stood in the battle formation at Pharsalus.

To be consistent, we shall also prefer for the strength of the cohorts, as we did for their number, the figure that goes back to Pollio (in Eutropius and Orosius), that is, 40,000 men, in preference to Caesar's figure. Pompey's cohorts, therefore, were somewhat stronger on the average (some 455 men) than Caesar's. That is only natural, since, as Caesar reports (3. 4), and we may believe him. Pompey had filled up his legions by means of levies in Thessaly, Boeotia, Achaea, and Epirus and had incorporated all of the 15 captured cohorts into his army.

Appian states (2. 70) that, according to the lowest estimate, Pompey had half again as much infantry as his opponent and that, according to some, 70,000 Italians participated on the two sides in this battle, whereas according to others it was fewer than 60,000. We can allow this statement to stand by itself.

Everything considered, the numerical relationship was probably some 40,000 to a good 30,000, and consequently, even if not 47,000 against 22,000, as Caesar would have it, still a very great superiority.

Most difficult of all is the question of the cavalry. Caesar himself states that he had only 1,000 horsemen, whereas Pompey had 7,000.

Of the 7,000 Pompeian cavalry, Caesar (3. 4) enumerates the following contingents:

600 Gauls under Dejotarus
500 Cappadocians
500 Thracians
200 Macedonians
500 Gallic and Germanic troops from Egypt
800 Shepherd slaves
300 Galatians
200 Syrians

Besides these 3,600, also Dardani, Bessi, Macedonians, Thessalians, and other peoples. What other kinds of peoples are those supposed to be who formed a full half of the cavalry and still could not be named?

Even to assemble a cavalry force of 7,000 men was a very difficult matter in those times. Of course, Alexander the Great had crossed the Hellespont with 5,100 cavalrymen and had still left 1,500 at home. Three years later, at Gaugamela, he even had 7,000 horsemen. At the time of the Diadochi, too, and later, up to the disappearance of the independent nations of the East, we find important masses of cavalry. But in the meantime more than a hundred years had passed, and peoples emerging from a state of continuous warfare lose very quickly the capability of activating a cavalry force. We need only remember of what significance it was to the Romans at Cannae that their cavalry was so weak; they had prepared themselves with the most massive effort and had mustered an unprecedented mass of infantry, but they were still able to put into the field only 6,000 horsemen against Hannibal's 10,000. In the second century B.C. the Roman citizen cavalry gradually faded away completely, whereas the legions were constantly developing greater technical skill and effectiveness. In order to have cavalry it was necessary to recruit among the barbarians, who were not always so easily and quickly available in sufficient numbers. Proof for this is to be found in Crassus' Parthian campaign, which, as we have seen, failed because of his weakness in cavalry. Although Caesar had sent him 1,000 Gallic cavalry under the command of his son Publius, Crassus still had only slightly over 4,000 cavalry all together. It is impossible that this arm was allowed to become so weak simply as a matter of negligence and convenience; they knew very well, of course, that they were waging war against a people of horsemen and that their march would be crossing broad plains. Crassus also had enough time to organize his army; it was not until the second year of his command that he crossed the Euphrates. If, in spite of all of this, he had no more than 4,000 cavalry in an army totaling 45,000 men, there can be no other reason than that usable horsemen were simply extremely hard to find. Caesar had his Germanic and Gallic cavalry; Pompey did not have similar sources available to him. It is characteristic of the situation that he, who had the remainder of Crassus' army among his troops, sent to the Parthian King to request his support, that is, to seek cavalry.[3]

Caesar himself claims to have had only 1,000 cavalry and in order to be able to pit these 1,000 against Pompey's 7,000, he tells us (3. 84), he attached to them specially selected young men and *antesignani* on foot with light equipment, and they worked together with such excellent coordination that the 1,000 were not afraid to stand up to the 7,000 in the open field, and shortly before the general battle they waged a successful skirmish against them.

In the battle itself, to be sure, Caesar's horsemen are said to have fallen back before the mass of their opponents, but then 6 cohorts, which, according to Caesar's further statement of strengths, numbered hardly 1,800 infantrymen, reportedly not only repelled the Pompeian cavalry but, by taking up the offensive against them, put them to flight and drove them completely from the battlefield. To anybody with any understanding of military history this account is incredible, even if the 6 cohorts had a total of 3,000 men rather than 1,800. Nor is it imaginable that a general like Labienus would have led a cavalry force so lacking in any kind of fighting spirit or that even a mediocre cavalry—and in this force were, after all, Gallic and Germanic warriors, Thracians, Macedonians, Thessalians—would have fled into the mountains (*altissimos montes*) when faced with a relatively small mass of heavy infantry. And Caesar does not even indicate that his own cavalry, which was initially pushed back, turned around and participated in the attack.

After all of this we are undoubtedly already inclined to consider the 7,000 figure for Pompey's cavalry as a very gross exaggeration. But we are confronted with a picture that is not only changed but completely different when we read in Eutropius (6. 20) and Orosius (6. 15), that Pompey had 500 cavalry on his right flank and 600 on his left.

If these figures were actually reported by Asinius Pollio, that would destroy not only our whole previous understanding of the numbers involved but also the entire concept of the tactical development that we have had until now, for the latter was based on the concentration of the cavalry of both opponents on a single flank.

The problem that the sources present to us here has long occupied my attention and, I must say, irritated me. The statements are so far apart that they can in no way be reconciled, but one of the two must somehow be rejected. It is impossible simply to ignore the reports in Eutropius and Orosius, as has been done until now, especially since under any circumstances there is still some grain of truth in them.

Caesar himself and Plutarch, in his *Caesar*, expressly state, it is true, that the entire cavalry of both sides was placed on the *one* flank. But Appian has the Pompeian cavalry stationed on the flanks (Chapter 75) and he later (Chapter 76) has the best—and therefore not all—move over to the left flank, and in like manner Plutarch reports in *Pompey* (Chapter 69) that "almost all" of Pompey's cavalry was assigned to the left flank. It is therefore beyond doubt that Pompey also had a unit of cavalry on his right flank that Caesar did not consider deserving of particular mention but which Pollio specifically recorded.

Two solutions seem possible to me. One of them is to assume that there is a corruption in the text. Although it is true that the figures are doubly attested to, nevertheless neither Eutropius nor Orosius drew directly on Livy (who, for his part, used Pollio) but rather on one and the same lost epitome.[4] It would therefore be thinkable that in this epitome the digit for thousands in front of the "600" on the left flank had been dropped or the number was corrupted in some other way and that both authors passed on the same error. Pollio, for example, perhaps wrote: "Pompey had on his right flank only 500 horsemen, on his left X thousand 600." From this, Appian and Plutarch, in his *Pompey*, expressed it in such a way as to show that he had "almost" all of his cavalry on the left flank, without actually giving the numbers; Livy's epitomist took over these same numbers but corrupted them in doing so.

The second possibility is that Pollio really did attribute to Pompey only 1,100 cavalry, and consequently only a minimal numerical superiority; and that these horsemen were initially assigned to the two flanks in groups of 500 and 600 and only later, as Appian reports, was the great bulk of the cavalry moved to the left flank, but that this shift was lost in the account somewhere between Pollio and Livy's epitomist.

This second solution is difficult to accept because the exaggeration of which Caesar would have been guilty in the relative strengths (7,000 against 1,000 instead of 1,100 against 1,000) would be much too monstrous, but from the objective point of view it is not impossible. Undoubtedly we must assume that the Pompeians did have a significant numerical superiority; but a superiority of 10,000 men in heavy infantry, some preponderance in the sharpshooters, and a still noticeable preponderance in cavalry would still be sufficient to explain the decision of the Pompeians to accept battle, especially in view of their raised morale resulting from success in the battle of Dyrrhachium.

My principal objection to this solution really lies on the other side; the mere 1,000 horsemen that Caesar claims to have had do not seem to me to be a very credible figure, even though all the sources, including those stemming from Pollio, give this number.

Caesar himself tells us that he had had his whole cavalry force assembled at Brundisium, and Appian gives their number as 10,000. Caesar reportedly transported only 600 of them overseas with the first convoy and 800 in the second. Since he had lost a few from this total of 1,400, and had detached others, and since a few had gone over to the enemy, it seems very consistent that 1,000 should appear at Pharsalus. We must ask, however, why Caesar had not yet had still more of the large number at Brundisium cross over to join him. There had, after all, been months and months in which to do this, and if it had been too dangerous at Brundisium, individual units, embarking at any number of ports, could have crossed the sea either to the north or south, landing on the coast of Illyria or Epirus, and could have moved to join their commander while he had the Pompeian army surrounded. Even if many transport ships were destroyed, new ones could be obtained from Tarentum or Syracuse or the Adriatic ports; Caesar had two squadrons of considerable strength at anchor at Messina and at Vibo in Bruttium.[5] If Antony had previously succeeded in crossing over with his large convoy despite the enemy ships, then all the more easily could small units of cavalry risk it. It even needed to be only individual ships that, to be safe, could land at any point on the eastern shore, since Pompey's entire army was fixed in place at Dyrrhachium. Even if the transportation of horses is always difficult, there can be no question of its impossibility.

Finally, the situation of the light infantry is also unclear. Caesar does not name them at all. Appian (2. 70) says that Caesar had Dolopes, Acarnanians, and Aetolians. The tendency has been to conclude from this that he had not brought any light infantry at all with him overseas but had filled this need through recruiting in the neighboring regions. But during the storming of Pompey's camp after the battle, against the energetic defense of Thracians and barbarian auxiliaries, Caesar tells us that the defenders were driven from the breastworks by the hail of missiles. Among these missiles (*tela*) we must understand primarily the *pila*, or heavy javelins of the legionaries, since at this large camp it was a question of very large masses of men. The range of these weapons was short, however, and the barbarian defenders of the camp were certainly sharpshooters, whether archers or slingers, who would necessarily have caused very heavy losses among the assaulting legionaries before the latter came close enough to throw their javelins, unless the assaulting troops themselves were accompanied by numerous sharpshooters who even from a distance suppressed and held down the fire of the defenders. For this reason Caesar uses the general expression *tela* and not *pila*. Consequently, even if the events at Dyrrhachium show that the Pompeians were considerably stronger in sharpshooters, it is still hardly believable that Caesar had only the recruited Greeks and had brought none at all overseas with him. In this connection, he did not identify the cavalry, either, that crossed in the first convoy; we know their number, 600, only through Plutarch and Appian.

Finally it becomes decisively important to consider the fact that Pompey was so hesitant in deciding to join battle. Up to the last moment he sacrificed still a few more days in hopes of gaining a small advantage from the terrain, and in the speech, too, that Caesar has him give at the last moment, there is no kind of reference to an overwhelming superiority. If Pompey had actually had 45,000 infantry against 22,000, 7,000 cavalry against 1,000, and also a superior number of sharpshooters, his conduct would have been absolutely incomprehensible. Not even the cavalry sergeant, whose attributes Mommsen would still ascribe to him, would remain of the man whom Rome had nevertheless called the "Great Pompey," because of his military deeds

To all these calculations one could offer the objection that, if Caesar's figures really varied from the truth so very much and especially in the case of the decisive arm, the cavalry, a rather strong protest would have been raised on the Pompeian side and some trace of it would have come down to us, as for example in Cicero's letters or in the work of Lucanus. Even if, as is pointed out above, no account really stemming from the Pompeian side has been known, such a fundamental fact would still have been retained for a long time in the oral tradition. We have here, however, one of those rare cases where on both sides the interest in hiding the truth for various reasons coincided, or at least did not mutually conflict. If the Pompeians had blamed their defeat on the excessively small size of their fighting force, then the reproach would have fallen with double weight on the leadership, not only on Pompey alone but on the whole group of leaders, that they had accepted the battle when it was not necessary. The qualitative superiority of Caesar's veteran legions was beyond any question. Even the Pompeians therefore needed for self-justification the statement that they were numerically superior and presumably explained, as is usually the case, that the defeat was due only to false leadership or to treason.

With such uncertainty and unreliability in our sources, we must either completely abandon the idea of arriving at accurate numbers, or, in order to make the account and the description of the battle clearer, we establish a number that seems to correspond best with the train of events, with the reservation that, as such, it has been arrived at according to subjective impressions, and therefore arbitrarily. On the basis of such a computation, I have adjusted the numbers above to something approaching 2,000 cavalry for Caesar and approximately 3,000 for Pompey. One can disagree with this by pointing out that, in Caesar's case at any rate, the figure of 1,000 cavalry is also attested to by Pollio. But first of all, it is not really so completely sure that Pollio is repeating Caesar's figure here without any reservation, that possibly some original deviation from Caesar's figure has not disappeared in the works of those using him as a source, and in the second place, after all, not even Pollio's testimony would in any way be completely final. In such statements of figures, accidental errors and misunderstandings play a role often enough, as we learn from the military history of more modern times. Against the number of 1,000 for Caesar's cavalry, however, we must weigh not only the very strong influence that it had on the battle in any event but also Caesar's habit, which we have already sufficiently established, of understating his own strength.

2. The question of the strength of the cavalry on both sides leads us to the principal point concerning which I believe that Caesar's account of the course of the battle must be corrected. According to his account, the Pompeian cavalry was defeated solely by the 6 cohorts of the fourth echelon. These cohorts then slaughtered the light infantrymen who had accompanied the cavalry and finally fell on the flank and rear of the infantry and decided the outcome of the battle. According to the account I have given, based on Appian (2. 78), it was the cavalry, on the other hand, which, together with its attached light infantry and the cohorts, fought to victory and made the flanking attack on the enemy legions.

Modern scholars have up to now accepted Caesar's account to the extent that the editors of Appian's works have even inclosed the word *"hippeis"* ("mounted men") in parentheses, taking into consideration the fact that there is no further word of them in Plutarch, either. The nature of things, however, so clearly calls for the participation of the cavalry that it would have to be assumed, even if Appian did not expressly speak of it.

Caesar himself tells us how, by assigning *antesignani* to the cavalry, he made the latter capable of standing up to their opponents. This account would be beside the point if the cavalry had done nothing in the battle but take flight.

Caesar himself recounts how the defeated sharpshooters who accompanied the Pompeian cavalry were all slaughtered. Why did they not flee? Certainly the heavily equipped legionaries could not overtake them? This account makes sense only if Caesar's cavalry and light infantry turned about and once again fell on their enemies.

Finally, the overpowering of the Pompeian legions themselves requires the participation of these troops. A flank attack by only 6 cohorts would not have been able to exert such a strong effect on the far larger mass of Pompeian infantry. Even the time that the 6 cohorts needed to accomplish their wheeling movement would have been too long; the enemy generals would in the meantime have taken their countermeasures. The situation was quite different if it was the cavalry and the sharpshooters who first quickly completed the movement and were followed by the closely formed cohorts.

But Caesar had a good reason for attributing the credit for the decision not to the cavalry but to the cohorts. In the battle against Ariovistus we have already noticed the lack of mention of the part played by the Gallic cavalry in the victory. Now public opinion in Rome was reproaching him for leading barbarians against the Republic.[6] Should he also be obliged to them for the decisive victory? The origin of these barbarians is revealed to us only too clearly in a little story that Appian has provided for us. When the army marched into Thessaly, the small town of Gomphi was taken by storm and plundered, and the soldiers had taken full advantage of the wine supplies; to this account Appian adds (2. 65): ". . . the most laughable of all, however, were the Germans in their drunkenness." It was the Germanic cavalry, which had already played the decisive role in the victory of the Romans over Vercingetorix. Still another bit of evidence—still legible even though half eradicated —has been preserved for us on this point. Florus (2. 13. 48) says, "Germanorum cohortes tantum in effusos equites (Pompei) fecere impetum, ut illi esse pedites, hi venire in equis viderentur." ("The German cohorts made so violent an assault on his [Pompey's] cavalry, which was then rushing out, that the latter looked as if they were mere infantry, the former as if they had arrived on horseback.") Did Caesar ever have Germanic cohorts? Had he incorporated Germans into his legions? Hardly. It can hardly be anything except the fact that here Caesar's account that his 6 cohorts had beaten the enemy cavalry has somehow run together with another account to the effect that it was his Germanic warriors that had secured this victory. By separating once again this false mixture into its two parts, we restore the picture of how the joint attack of the cohorts and the Gallic and Germanic cavalry and the "double fighters" won the engagement.

We can recognize from still another point how greatly Caesar's account was governed by political motives. In his *Commentaries* Caesar gives the laurels exclusively to the 6 cohorts. In Appian 2. 79, however, we read that Caesar had written in his letters that the Tenth Legion, which was stationed on his extreme right flank, had enveloped the enemy wing, which had been left uncovered by the cavalry, and had attacked it from the flank. ("The Tenth Legion under Caesar himself surrounded Pompey's left wing, which had lost its cavalry, and from all sides assailed its flank, where the men remained unmoved; until, at last, the attackers threw it into confusion by force, and so began to win their victory.")* This is, at any rate, a very unusual deviation, the origin of which, however, has already been guessed by Schweighäuser. When Caesar wrote and published his *Commentaries* on the civil war, in the fall of 47 b.c., before he went from Rome to Africa, the Tenth Legion had mutinied and had thereby most seriously offended its commander. Now it was no longer the unit that had decided the victory at Pharsalus but was replaced by the fourth echelon, composed of the cohorts of 6 different legions. But we conclude from this that it was not until later that the commander came to this particular presentation, that the main role in the decision cannot possibly have been played by these troops but was artificially attributed to them because the commander, for good reasons, did not want to acknowledge to whom he principally owed the victory, that is, the brave barbarian cavalry.

The longer I have spent studying Caesar, the more definite has my opinion become that his *Commentaries* are not to be evaluated historically any differently than the *Mémorial de Sainte-Hélène*. Like the latter, they are a wonderful fabric of interwoven realistic, penetrating truth and fully deliberate and intended deception. Whoever is familiar with the Napoleonic writings knows that precisely the trait of giving the fame for a victory to this or that troop unit or general, according to the political motives of the moment, even when there was no basis for it, was characteristic of the great Corsican.

3. Along with the shifting of the accomplishments of the various troop units there is also a very important temporal shifting in the account in the *Commentaries*. Caesar first has the two infantry phalanxes clashing, and then he recounts the cavalry combat, starting with the expression *"eodem tempore"* ("at the same time").

But Appian says expressly (2. 78) that the cavalry moved out somewhat before the infantry, and it follows from Pompey's battle plan, in which, of course, he intentionally held back his infantry, that it must have occurred in this way. Caesar, however, could not tell it that way, because then the heroism of the *evocatus* Crastinus, which now introduces the battle so effectively and gives such a splendid picture of the relationship of these old soldiers to their commander, would not have had its full effect. In his *Caesar* Plutarch follows the latter's account; in *Pompey*, where he used Pollio as a source, he explains the situation by following each author with half of the army; in accord with Caesar, he has the battle start with the infantry, and following Pollio's account he has Pompey hold back his right wing, since it cannot be the whole line that is withheld.

4. If Pompey had an interest in delaying the clash of the phalanxes until his cavalry had been victorious, we could believe the same thing of Caesar, who, of course, also hoped to win by means of a flanking movement, and this would have applied all the more strongly to Caesar, when he counted on winning the victory on the cavalry flank only through the counterattack. Nevertheless, we do not hear that Caesar held his legions back, and with good reason. For Caesar, everything depended on Pompey's not developing, for his own part, a countermovement from his third echelon after his cavalry was thrown back, a move that would again disengage his flank and would resist Caesar's enveloping movement. That could have happened all the more easily in that, of course, the decision in the cavalry battle took place at quite some distance from Pompey's infantry. It would be made more difficult, however, if in the meantime the battle had already broken out along the whole line, demanding Pompey's attention and also involving the third echelon in the melee. As we know, Caesar had taken the precaution of also holding back the rest of his third echelon, to have it ready for any eventuality. Pompey, trusting firmly in the victory of his cavalry, had presumably not done that. For this reason, the mass of the Pompeian infantry, under any circumstances much more numerous, was at the start probably twice as strong as Caesar's two forward echelons, which opened the battle. But Caesar trusted his veterans to withstand for a long time under all circumstances even the pressure of a force twice as strong as his, and in the meantime he carried out the envelopment.

After me, Veith and Kromayer have treated the battle of Pharsalus, both with sharp polemics against my version of the battle but without presenting any reasons that could have persuaded me to change anything (with the exception of the considerations concerning the strength of the cavalry). Most of their objections are of such a nature as to make it appear superfluous to offer for the careful reader any specific rebuttal. I discuss below the points that perhaps still need a special explanation.

Kromayer doubts whether the conflicting strength estimates go back to Asinius Pollio, since it is not shown that Livy, the link between the events and Orosius, Eutropius, Lucanus, and Dio Cassius, actually used Pollio. True, they could by no means stem from Pollio, since the sources that definitely go back to Pollio, that is, Appian and Plutarch, bring us Caesar's numbers. I cannot see in what way a conclusion can be reached from this. But even assuming that Plutarch and Appian had not used Caesar himself, that they had taken their figures from Pollio, that the latter therefore had Caesar's figures, and that the conflicting figures, going back to Livy, had stemmed from some other source that he regarded as trustworthy—what would have been changed by all of this? I have, after all, in no way cited Pollio as a very special authority (a point Kromayer accuses me of); on the contrary, I have estimated his authority on this point as quite mediocre. The only important point is that the second, conflicting, account does actually exist. But since we know (Appian 2. 82) that Pollio gave strength estimates on the battle differing from those of Caesar, then it is very probable that the questionable variants are to be attributed to him. For, as I have specifically pointed out, the independent reports that we have in addition to Caesar's are so scanty and are so particularly lacking in any kind of information from Pompey's camp that a significant source of this kind no longer existed even at the time of Livy and Lucanus, and even Livy, for whom of course a certain possibility still existed, can no longer have sought out and recorded a significant oral tradition.

In this matter my two opponents are not willing to consider Caesar capable of the false figures for which I reproach him. There is a very certain method of coming to the realization that I have in no way been unjust to Caesar with my objections. Just as one finds the correct approach to Herodotus with the greatest certainty by making a critical study of Bullinger's history of the Burgundian Wars, in the same way it is an infallible means of understanding Caesar correctly if one studies the memoirs of his great colleagues, Frederick and Napoleon, and the related critical literature. Then one will find that these are mere bagatelles that I have criticized in Caesar's writings and eliminated. Even in the case of Frederick, whom we justly praise for his very high degree of truthfulness, the weakness of shifting the army strengths somewhat to the higher glory of the Prussians is established on many occasions,[7] and in other respects, too, there is no lack of errors and contradictions, both biased and unintentional. Scharnhorst, to cite also this illustrious name, in his "Report on the Battle of Auerstadt and Jena" ("Bericht von der Schlacht bei Auerstadt und Jena"), states the strength of the Prussians as 96,840 combatants; later Höpfner, working from the official documents, arrived at a strength of 141,911 men. I have already cited above (p. 43) an example from Moltke. With respect to Napoleon, everybody knows and has always known how indifferent he was to historical accuracy. For a special study of this subject, however, I now recommend the history of the official report on the battle of Marengo, which Hüffer has recently given in his introduction to *Sources for the History of the War of 1800 (Quellen zur Geschichte des Krieges von 1800)*. In this way one can also become convinced as to how little weight lies in the objection that contemporary publications must necessarily be completely accurate because otherwise they could be disavowed by persons knowing the facts who are still living. As an authority for how one maneuvers and how one goes about winning battles, certainly Napoleon cannot be surpassed, and I believe that I was right in supporting my judgment of the events at Alesia through his opinion. But when Kromayer cites Napoleon's authority because Napoleon believed Caesar's statement of the losses at Pharsalus, I believe that Kromayer has overlooked the point that here Napoleon the bulletin-composer would have overstepped somewhat in the area of the military historian and that a certain subconscious self-defense influenced his accounts of ancient battles, accounts that are in other respects very much to the point. Judging from my knowledge of military history, and on the basis of the one-sided testimony of the victorious commander, I cannot regard as credible either the victory of 1,000 cavalry and 6 cohorts over 7,000 cavalry and many lightly armed men, or the victory of 22,000 Roman infantry over 47,000 Roman infantry, or the winning of such a victory with a loss of 200 killed.

The reproach that can be made against Caesar because of such biased, erroneous numbers is, subjectively, no very crushing one, first of all because it is a question of a common human weakness, but more importantly for the reason that the Romans were, after all, accustomed to hearing even more strongly contrasting figures. The Caesarian officer who later described the African war evoked no particular objection to his report that in the battle of Thapsus Caesar's forces had slaughtered 50,000 of the enemy and in doing so had themselves lost only 50 men.[8] When Hannibal at Cannae had his troops cut down the 50,000 encircled Romans, that still cost him at least 5,700 dead from his own force. After all of this, it is hardly necessary to go into all the tricks of interpretation with the help of which Kromayer tries to do away with the testimony in Livy, Appian, and Plutarch. According to Kromayer, the 85 cohorts (instead of 110) that Livy says Pompey had in the battle are to be considered only as the cohorts of Roman citizens, whereas there were 22 additional cohorts at hand. He arrives at these numbers, however, by interpreting Caesar's own statement (3. 4)—to the effect that Pompey had filled out his legions with men from Thessaly, Boeotia, Achaea, and Epirus and had also incorporated the Caesarian soldiers under Antony's command who had been taken prisoner—as meaning that he had formed special filler cohorts. The passage in Caesar (3. 6) reads: "Praetera magnum numerum ex Thessalia, Boeotia, Achaja, Epiroque supplementi nomine in legiones distribuerat, his Antonianos milites admiscuerat." ("Besides, he had distributed a large number of reinforcements from Thessaly, Boeotia, Achaea, and Epirus by name to the legions, and to these he had joined Antony's soldiers.") That replacements form special units before they are assigned is natural and is occasionally reported; but that permanent replacement cohorts should have been assigned to the legions, instead of bringing the existing cohorts as close as possible to normal strength, is neither objectively credible nor does it correspond to the sense of our passage. This point is not contradicted by the fact that, according to Caesar's report, the soldiers of the Spanish army, who after being discharged by Caesar had gone over to their old commander, Pompey, formed their own cohorts. The loyalty of these warriors was honored by leaving them together instead of distributing them as newcomers among unfamiliar troop units. But the newly recruited men and the prisoners had to be blended into the old units in order to make them more or less usable; that is, they were "incorporated" (*"unterstecken"*), as it was called in the eighteenth century. It would have been too dangerous to form them into their own battalions.

Kromayer has attempted to give a new solution for the topographical question, which, however, was immediately considered as suspect by R. Schneider in the *Göttingische gelehrte Anzeigen,* 169 (June 1907): 438; Victor Dusmanis, Major on the Greek General Staff, in *Beihefte zum Militär-Wochenblatt*), 7th issue, 1909, "Observations on the Determination of the Location of the Thessalian Battle Between Caesar and Pompey" ("Bemerkungen zur Bestimmung der Oertlichkeit der Thessalischen Schlacht zwischen Cäsar und Pompejus"), claims, on the basis of a book on *History and Geography of Thessaly from the Military Viewpoint (Geschichte und Geographie Thessaliens in militärischer Beziehung),* that the battlefield is located not at all in the vicinity of the town of Pharsalus (which Caesar does not name at all) but some 40 kilometers farther to the west, near Karditsa.

At first glance genuine criticism and arbitrary treatment of the sources, true professional knowledge and mere playing with military concepts are not so easily distinguished. Kromayer and Veith base their concepts mutually on each other; the scholar calls for support on the authority of the military man, the military man on the authority of the scholar. That appears to be the most favorable imaginable cooperation; nevertheless, as we have seen throughout this volume, nothing has resulted from this but distorted and confusing ideas. Why this is we may learn from two series of conclusions that the two authors develop with respect to the battle of Pharsalus. The contrast may well serve as a prime example of how easy it is to deduce the opposite meaning from an historical source when a person has at his disposition only a certain cleverness and has not become accustomed to strict objective analysis.

In Kromayer 2: 431, we read: "We have no statement as to whether the hand-to-hand combat of the legions lasted for a long time. At noon everything was already decided *(Bell. Civ.* 3. 95), whereas in the morning Caesar had already packed up in order to march to Scotussa (*Bell. Civ.* 3. 85), when suddenly the prospects for a battle assumed a favorable form. Only then did he move out for the battle—the distance required almost an hour (p. 405)—and the deployment is also to be estimated as requiring several hours. This leaves by no means very much time for the battle, but particularly the decisive action on the flank itself must have taken place very quickly."

"The withdrawal of Caesar's cavalry, the flanking attack of the six cohorts are things which are to be counted as lasting minutes, or at most, quarter-hours. And if one still assumes, like Delbrück, that the attack of the Pompeian cavalry took place before Caesar's attack with the legions, then the time for the close combat of the latter is still further shortened."

Kromayer therefore claims that the battle was very brief, and specifically so in order to prove that Caesar's statement that he lost only 200 men in the battle can be considered as completely credible.

But Veith writes (*Klio* 7. 332): "The battle of Pharsalus lasted—without counting the fight for the camp and the pursuit—from morning until noon. . . . The reported length of the battle can only be explained if we assume a fight varying in times and locations, consisting of numerous localized and brief phases. . . . And in this way, of course, the battle of the main bodies near Pharsalus could last for several hours."

Veith, therefore, holds that the battle lasted for a long time, and specifically so in order to prove that the Roman battle order did not form a simple, cohesive line, even in the battle, but that it was based on much more complicated tactics.

Let us note also that Veith claims that Caesar's *antesignani* did not participate in the cavalry combat of the battle and that Kromayer contradicts him on this point; that Veith explains that even a victory by his cavalry would not have brought Pompey victory in the battle, whereas Kromayer takes the opposite viewpoint—thus the cleavage between the two becomes wider and wider, and we arrive at the pressing suspicion that it is here not just a question of differences of detail, such as those that always occur even between scholars who hold the same overall opinions from the objective viewpoint, but that we have here a deeper, organic disorder. This suspicion will become a certainty when we now realize that the two of them with their conclusions not only contradict one another but that each of them contradicts himself, and that they themselves have not even noticed this. Veith is completely right in believing that a long-drawn-out fight is appropriate to his concept of a Roman battle with small, separated infantry units—but then a loss of only 200 men at Pharsalus is impossible, and Caesar's credibility insofar as numbers are concerned, which Veith otherwise supports very strongly, is badly shaken. Kromayer is correct when, because of the small losses, he postulates a very short duration for the battle, but with this point Veith's concept of cohort tactics, which, as we have seen, Kromayer has accepted (pp. 408, 423, above) falls by the wayside. This self-contradiction is the decisive point, and it arises from the basic error in method, namely, that each question is treated only in isolation but is not seen in its relation to military history in general and is not thought through to the end and thoroughly worked out in its consequences on all sides. Only he who has accomplished this task is capable of true objective analysis. Kromayer, despite his broad readings of modern military writers, has not done this and is therefore just as little qualified for military critical analysis as is Veith for philological source criticism. For each of these scholars the sources form only a kind of wax that they shape to their own ends in one way or another according to the needs of the moment. The professor who has a phalanx of 15,000 men move 600 meters backwards and the first lieutenant who proves his concept of the Roman tactics "according to the sources" by means of the "*terminus technicus quincunx*" ("technical term: chessboard form"), which stems from the sixteenth century—the two of them are not to be found in the temple of learning, but only in its vestibule.

(Added in the third edition.) Here, too, I again copy this polemic explanation, but at the same time I refer the reader to what I have said above, on pp. 313, 331, and 389, where I have noted in the cases of both authors considerable progress in their understanding of ancient warfare, and I point out even more specifically what I have to say below, on Caesar's African campaign.

NOTES FOR CHAPTER IX

1. Frontinus 2. 3.

2. Much has already been written concerning the credibility of the *Commentaries*. As particularly effective in this regard I should like to cite Pfannschmidt "On the History of the Pompeian Civil War" ("Zur Geschichte des Pompejanischen Bürgerkrieges"), Weissenfels Program, 1888.

3. Dio Cassius 41. 55. *Bell. Civ.* 3. 82.

4. Zangemeister, in the preface to his edition of Orosius, p. xxv.

5. *Bell. Civ.* 3. 101.

6. Dio Cassius 41. 54. 2.

7. A. Ritter, *On the Reliability of the Place, Strength, and Time Indications in the Military History Works of Frederick the Great (Über die Zuverlässigkeit der Orts-, Zahl- und Zeitangaben in den kriegsgeschichtlichen Werken Friedrichs des Grossen)*, Berlin dissertation, 1911 (Wernigerode: Rudolf Vierthaler).

8. According to Plutarch. The manuscripts of the *Bellum Africanum* give X instead of L, which has been retained, apparently incorrectly, by the more recent editors.

Chapter X

The Last Campaigns
of the Civil War

The campaign in Greece and the battle of Pharsalus, the combat of Romans against Romans under the command of their two most famous leaders, form the high point of the art of war in antiquity. While it is true that Caesar's following campaigns are rich in individual events, they offer nothing new in principle, no further development. If up to now the sources have also seemed to be too uncertain to warrant their evaluation from the viewpoint of military history, we may say that this shortcoming has now been removed. By linking topographical research with careful analysis of the sources, Veith has succeeded in producing a very clear and completely plausible picture of the African campaign. The only point to which I take exception in his excellent presentation is his repeated polemic against me, which is groundless, since I agree completely with his opinion except that I believe he has occasionally highlighted his picture too sharply.

After Pharsalus, Caesar himself, of course, did not describe any of his further campaigns for us, but this was done, rather, by a few of his officers of varying talent and much grosser bias than Caesar himself. The *Bellum Africanum* comes to us from a line officer of limited perceptiveness, whose work, however, we can fill out by reference to the accounts of Dio Cassius and Plutarch, which have retained the description of Asinius Pollio, an author adept at recognizing the strategic relationships.

Caesar intended to besiege Thapsus, which was situated on an isthmus between the sea and a lake. Scipio attempted to block the isthmus on both sides. And although it is true that Caesar dominated the sea, nevertheless, since this action took place at the beginning of February, this formed a very uncertain base. If his contact by land was completely cut off, he could have fallen into a most precarious situation. Caesar's intelligence service was so alert, however, that he learned of the approach of the enemy in the north, attacked him before he could complete his fortifications, and threw him back. Immediately after this blow to half of the enemy army, Caesar drove out against the other half, 10 kilometers away at the southern entrance to the isthmus, reached it before the defeated army from the north could again link up with it, and caused it to break up without any further fighting.

The reader is referred to Veith for the details. Of the greatest general interest is his supposition, which has assumed a very high degree of probability, that Scipio, about whose lack of ability Caesar himself joked, was only nominally the commander in chief and that the real leadership was exercised by Labienus. If then the Pharsalus campaign appears as a duel between the two most famous commanders of their time, the African campaign is interesting in that here Caesar was opposed by his own top general from the Gallic War. Veith has determined, apparently with complete justification, that Labienus proved himself a thoroughly worthy disciple of his master. His operations were extremely energetic, well thought out, and decisive. If, nevertheless, he did finally go down to defeat, it was not that he was facing only Caesar but also Caesar's troops, against whom his newly formed African legions could not measure up. The defeat at Thapsus was, at first, from the tactical viewpoint, not much more than an unsuccessful undertaking, and it only turned into a catastrophe because the unbeaten troops were panic-stricken, abandoned their camp, and took flight. When those who had been beaten in the north then arrived on the scene, expecting to find a refuge, they discovered that their comrades were gone, whereupon they wished to surrender, but they were cut down by Caesar's battle-roused legionaries. They were Roman legions on both sides, but their character was that of mercenaries, and, as we shall see again in the later volumes, mercenaries in no way spare each other mutually. At Ilerda Caesar had still been able to prevent a massacre, but here he could no longer do so.

EXCURSUS

1. THE BATTLE OF RUSPINA

This battle needs to be considered, for the reason that it gives the impression —and it has been so understood by modern scholars—that Caesar's tactics here really did accomplish something completely new, that is, that they provided a means of escape from the kind of situation in which Crassus in Mesopotamia and Caesar's general Curio, one year earlier, in Africa, had perished with their entire armies. The relationship, however, must be conceived of differently.

With three legions and a small accompanying force of cavalry and sharpshooters Caesar had made a foraging march into the interior from his camp near the port city of Ruspina, in eastern Tunis, when he was attacked in the open plain by the Numidian cavalry and sharpshooters under the command of Labienus. He had his infantry take up the shallowest possible formation, facing in all four directions, and repelled the enemy attacks by having the cohorts, with the support of the small number of cavalry present, storm out from time to time and drive back the enemy skirmishers with a volley of javelins. According to the account of the Pseudo-Hirtius, as we shall call the author of the *Bellum Africanum*, the engagement ended in a victory as the cohorts, summoning up their last ounce of strength, finally drove the nimble enemy away over the nearest hills. According to Appian (2. 95), however, Caesar was beaten, and it was only because of sluggishness that the enemy did not complete their victory. Since with men like Labienus and Petreius such a reason does not seem acceptable, we are at a loss for a satisfactory explanation. Nevertheless, it is to be found without difficulty in the account of Pseudo-Hirtius himself, if we remember what Xenophon reports in the *Anabasis* concerning a similar situation of the Ten Thousand. It was nightfall that saved the hard-pressed infantry from the arrows of the mounted sharpshooters. Antony, too, when he was pressed by the Parthians during his retreat, was helped out of this situation by the night, as we have seen in the account of his campaign of 36 B.C. The account in the *Bellum Africanum*, to the effect that the cohorts finally drove off the enemy with their offensive, is incredible because we cannot understand why they did not do that at the very start, if they were capable of doing so. Their real accomplishment—presumably with considerable losses, if Appian's source was able to picture the engagement as a defeat for Caesar—consisted of holding out for the entire day, until the fall of darkness. During the night the enemy horsemen moved far back, in order not to expose themselves to a surprise attack, and since Caesar was only 3,000 paces (*passus*)—4½ kilometers—from his camp, he was now able to pull back to it without difficulty. He still accomplished the military feat of maintaining the morale and the good order of his troops in this painful situation and, by forming them in a kind of square with the longest and thinnest possible lines, provided the largest possible operating space for the use of the *pilum*, the only effective weapon in this situation, while giving the least possible chances for the effectiveness of the enemy arrows and javelins. Since there is always something uncertain about a thin formation, this shows how much confidence Caesar had in his troops and how excellent their conduct was under his leadership. The decisive point, however, was the closeness of the camp, and, since this was in winter, also the shortness of the day, which prevented the crisis from lasting too very long. Curio, who had been wiped out in the previous year in the same kind of situation, had marched out while it was still night (about the fourth night watch [*Bell. Civ.* 2. 29]) and had covered 16,000 paces (*passus*)—24 kilometers—fighting numerous skirmishes under way, when he encountered the enemy main body. His cavalrymen even had a night march behind them already and were completely exhausted. Even if they had held out until evening (the battle took place in midsummer), they would still have had no possibility of returning to their camp during the night. And so the soldiers were overcome with despair, they gave up the resistance, and were cut down.

The tactical movements which Caesar had his men make in order to defend against the enemy skirmishers have been interpreted in greatly varying ways; the three most important military men who have studied the account in recent times, Göler, Rüstow, and Stoffel, have all given very different pictures of the battle, and the only solution that the philologists have found has been an altering of the text.

The following explanation seems to me the most natural one: When Caesar suddenly got the report that the enemy was approaching *en masse* and the cloud of dust could already be seen coming closer, he first had his three legions form up in one echelon with his weak cavalry on the two flanks. This unusual formation in a single echelon seemed to be called for because it offered a certain protection against enemy outflanking action and for its own part threatened the enemy with an envelopment. As a normal procedure, this was not permissible, because one could never be sure of being able to throw back the enemy infantry with the first echelon; hence the second and third echelons in the rear, to be employed, as needed, either to reinforce the front or for flanking movements. In this case, however, where they were not dealing with heavy infantry but with massed bands of lightly armed soldiers, it was possible to rely on the fact that the line would need no reinforcement from the rear, and the front could therefore be made as long as possible.

The enemy, however, did not allow the situation to develop into a regular battle but contented himself with a sharpshooting combat, while his cavalry simultaneously enveloped the Roman front, long as it was, and, by driving back the few opposing horsemen, threatened the line from the rear. Now the Romans had to face in both directions, and that would have broken up all the tactical units as they made sorties, now in this direction, now in that. In order to prevent that, Caesar ordered every second cohort to face about and to place itself behind its neighboring cohort, fighting back to back with the latter. The intervals were filled by having each cohort spread out within itself and thereby occupy a doubled width. If then the cohorts had at first stood 8 ranks deep, let us say, now they were only 4 ranks in depth. In the middle, between the two fronts, there was naturally left a certain space in which the vehicles that were possibly on hand were placed, into which the unhorsed cavalrymen could retire, and where the higher officers could move back and forth freely. Individual soldiers were forbidden to spring out of ranks, in order to attack, for example, an enemy sharpshooter who might have approached too boldly. Entire cohorts, however, and especially the cohorts on the flanks, in conjunction with the cavalry, made sorties which now and then broke the circle of the surrounding attackers, and Pseudo-Hirtius puffed these momentary successes up into full-fledged victories. But since the cohorts making these sallies always had to fall back again promptly on the main body, for fear of falling into an ambush, we may be allowed to presume that the fleeing foes, too, immediately turned around again, for the author tells us himself that the fight lasted until sunset, when it automatically had to break up.

The principal passage (Chapter 17) reads: "Caesar interim consilio hostium cognito iubet aciem in longitudinem quam maximam porrigi et alternis conversis cohortibus, ut una post alteram signa tenderet, ita coronam hostium dextro sinistroque cornu mediam dividit." This is to be translated as follows: "Caesar, after recognizing the enemy's plan [to encircle him], orders the battle line to stretch out as much as possible and every other cohort to face about and place itself behind its neighbor, from which position he breaks through the enemy ring with his right and left wings." The change which has been proposed—"ut una post, altera ante signa contenderet"—says the same thing in the final analysis but drops the movement behind one another of the cohorts and thereby obscures the action instead of clarifying it. It is therefore to be rejected, as has been done by Stoffel, with whose concept I also agree, in the main, in other respects, with the difference that I do not assume any intervals between the cohorts, but rather, as Göler has already understood it, I interpret the stretching out of the front in length as a lessening of the number of ranks. Furthermore, Stoffel himself has already explained, in the Revue de philologie 1: 154, that he did not mean such large intervals as are shown on his sketch but had in mind only the small intervals that have to be left quite naturally between the tactical units for the sake of good order. When he reproaches Fröhlich for this misunderstanding, that is really not justified, since in his book he did not state in what manner he thought the holes were filled that had been caused by the pulling out of the 15 cohorts.

See also Rüstow, *Caesar's Military Organization and Conduct of War* (*Heerwesen und Kriegsführung Cäsars*) 2d ed., p. 133. Göler, (*Cäsars gallischer Krieg*) 2d ed., 2: 272. Stoffel, *Civil War* (*Guerre civile*), 2: 284. Domaszewski, *The Banners of the Roman Army* (*Die Fahnen im römischen Heer*) p. 3. Fröhlich, *Caesar's Method of Waging War* (*Kriegswesen Cäsars*) p. 194.

(Added in the third edition.) Veith, in *Ancient Battlefields* (*Antike Schlachtfelder*) Vol. 3, Part 1, p. 784, has the same concept as I; when he, nevertheless, as he says, "enters a sharp protest against my source-contradicting reconstruction," that can only be based on a very hasty reading, since the differences that he so strongly opposes simply are not there, unless Veith evaluates the success of Caesar's counterblows more highly than I do. I have not changed a single word of the second edition.

3. Nobody has yet succeeded in establishing a credible picture of the battle of Munda from the reports. A few authors show Caesar personally deciding the battle in a completely fantastic manner. But it is perhaps noteworthy that, as at Pharsalus, not only did the cavalry (in which Caesar had the superior strength at Munda)[1] force the decision on the one flank, but our sources also obviously went out of their way to attribute to that arm only indirect credit, while giving the real palms of victory to the legions. The author of the *Bell. Hisp.* tells us that the Tenth Legion pressed its opponents so strongly that it was planned to bring a legion to their aid from the other flank. Caesar's cavalry took advantage of this opportunity to attack and thereby prevented the planned maneuver. Dio Cassius (43. 38) recounts that the decision was brought on by the fact that, although neither of the phalanxes would yield to the other, the Numidian King Boguas, outside the battle line, attacked the Pompeian camp, whereupon Labienus pulled five cohorts out from the front and sent them to the aid of the camp. The other soldiers had presumably believed that their marching out of the line was the start of a flight from the battlefield and had lost their courage. Are we to believe that the best general of the Caesarian school, in the moment of crisis, withdrew troops from the battle in order to protect the baggage? I believe that it would not be too bold to assume a more direct influence on the course of the battle by the Numidian cavalry, an accomplishment that the jealousy of the various branches of the arms among themselves, and of the Romans vis-à-vis the barbarian allies, has sought to hide from us.

NOTE FOR CHAPTER X

1. *Bell. Hisp.*, Chapter 30, can probably not be interpreted in any other sense; it would also be surprising if the superiority which Caesar naturally had in this arm had not proven itself in any of the three great battles of the civil war. At Munda, in addition to his Gallic and Germanic cavalry, he also had Numidian horsemen.

Chapter XI

The Elephants

The last battle of antiquity in which elephants were used was the battle of Thapsus. It might therefore be appropriate at this point to consider everything that we have learned now from our observation of the military use of these animals in antiquity in all the battles in which they appear.

The battle on the Hydaspes gave us occasion to remark that it must have been quite difficult for the Macedonians to overcome the elephants, since we see later to what pains they themselves went to adopt this instrument of warfare. If we now consider, however, the question of success, we seem to arrive at the opposite conclusion, since we do not find a single corroborated battle in which the elephants accomplished something of importance; on the contrary, usually the side that was stronger in elephants was defeated. It is unfortunate that the reports on the most famous elephant battles have all come down to us more or less in only legendary or anecdotal form. The only one for which we can establish an historically useful picture is still the first one, the battle on the Hydaspes. The battles of the Diadochi, the battles in which Pyrrhus participated, the battles of the First Punic War—all offer us no reliable gain in this respect. At Zama-Naraggara and Thapsus we may well be told that elephants were on hand in supposedly large numbers, but we learn nothing of their accomplishments, and their commanders were defeated. If we take all of the reports, as they stand, the balance of victories and defeats speaks against the elephants. They are involved in the victories of Ipsus, Antiochus I over the Gauls, of Heraclea, Asculum, Tunis, Hamilcar over the Mercenaries, on the Tajo (Hannibal over the Spaniards),[1] on the Trebia, at Cynoscephalae and Pydna. But even though they were present on the one side only, or in great preponderance on one side, they did not prevent defeat on the Hydaspes, at Paraetacene, at Gabiene, Gaza,

561

Beneventum, Agrigentum, Panormus, Raphia, Himera,[2] Baecula, Metaurus, Zama, Magnesia, Muthul,[3] Thapsus. No example whatever is reported of an occasion where elephants penetrated closed infantry formations. On the only occasion that could come into consideration, at Cynoscephalae, it is expressly said that the Macedonians were not yet drawn up in battle formation when the Romans attacked them and the elephants scattered them.

At Zama the Romans are reported to have left intervals between their maniples, so that the elephants could go through these passages. At Tunis they were drawn up, on the contrary, in a very deep formation, and Polybius (1. 33. 10) specifically praises this arrangement as one suitable for use against elephants. As we know, both of these reports go back to unsatisfactory sources; the most valuable point is probably the judgment of Polybius, who approves the deep formation and consequently does not credit the elephants with the power to break through it. According to his own account, however, the elephants had nevertheless caused considerable havoc in the foremost ranks of the Roman phalanx, but this account must after all have been exaggerated, since otherwise we would necessarily have heard similar accounts rather often in the later battles.

The really well-confirmed effectiveness of elephants is only that against cavalry, where they frighten the horses, and against light infantry.

The best testimony for their usefulness in combat still remains, however, the fact that even the great commanders always used them again and again, especially Hannibal and also Caesar, who at least, Cicero says once (*Philippics* 5. 17. 46), procured elephants for the Parthian War. In reality, he did not use them. After the Second Punic War, when the Romans had established close relations with the Numidian kings, who provided them with these animals, they used them during the entire second century B.C., although of course only in conjunction with allies and in small numbers.[4] They used them not only against the Macedonians but also in Spain,[5] and against the Gauls. Although they are supposed to have performed very well against the northern barbarians,[6] strangely enough they no longer appear even in the Cimbrian War or in Caesar's Gallic War. When the Numidian King Juba used elephants against him in Africa, Caesar had animals sent to him from Sicily in order to accustom his soldiers and horses to their appearance and to train them to fight with them.

If we consider the entire experience of the military history of antiquity, we may say that the usefulness and the actual use of elephants for battle may under any circumstances not be rated too highly. Against peoples who were still not at all familiar with them and against cavalry and sharpshooters they had some successes, which were, however, as in the case of the battles against Pyrrhus, for example, very greatly exaggerated by the losers in order to find an excuse for their defeat.[7] Troops who are familiar with them and do not fear them, who know how to avoid them and how to attack them properly, are able to deal with them, as Alexander had already done on the Hydaspes, not through some kind of ruse or flaming arrows or by frightening them, but by skillful use of their weapons. We can recognize what this expert use of their weapons must have been like when we consult the works on natural sciences describing the characteristics of these animals.

According to these works, the elephant is not at all invulnerable but even has a rather sensitive hide, and even if spears and arrows do not kill him outright, they still penetrate so deeply that they remain imbedded in his body,[8] and the pain makes the animals uncontrollable and causes them to shy away. It is reported often enough that they then penetrate into the ranks of their own troops, throw them into confusion, and bring about defeats, as, for example, on one occasion for the Romans in front of Numantia.[9] As the ultimate means of dealing with such cases, the mahouts, as we have already mentioned above (p 372), each had a sharp steel wedge, which they drove with a hammer into the animal's neck in order to kill him and render him harmless.

EXCURSUS

The statement appearing again and again in the writings of the ancients, that the Indian elephant was superior to the African (also in Livy's account of Magnesia, 37. 39), we have likewise already rejected above (p. 246) as a mere fable.

The authors on the subject of tactics, Asclepiodotus, Aelian, and Arrian, make no mention of the employment of elephants.

All the reports from antiquity on the use of elephants are collected in the work of A. W. Schlegel appearing in the *Indian Library (Indische Bibliothek)*, 1: 129, and especially in the very useful work of P. Armandi, knight of the Legion of Honor, former colonel of artillery, *Military History of Elephants from the Earliest Times to the Introduction of Firearms (Histoire militaire des éléphants depuis les temps les plus reculés jusqua'à l'introduction des armes à feu)* (Paris, 1843).

See also p. 221, above, and the notes 8 and 9 to Book III, Chapter VII.

NOTES FOR CHAPTER XI

1. Polybius 3. 14.
2. Livy 25. 41.

3. Sallust, *Jugurtha*, Chapter 53.

4. According to the observation by Fröhlich in *The Significance of the Second Punic War* (*Die Bedeutung des zweiten punischen Krieges*), p. 20.

5. Valerius Maximus 9. 3. Appian, *Iberia*, Chapter 46.

6. Orosius 5. 13. Florus 1. 37.

7. Schubert, in *Pyrrhus*, p. 222, calls attention to the fact that in the account of Pyrrhus' campaign in Sicily, which goes back to Timaeus, hardly any mention is made of the elephants.

8. J. Chr. D. Schreber, in *The Mammals* (*Die Saugetiere*) (Erlangen, 1775), 1: 245, which is still today the authoritative work on descriptive zoology, strongly emphasizes this point and says that the elephant is even sensitive to the bite of a fly. In Volume 6 of the same work, by J. A. Wagner (1835), p. 265, it is recounted how the javelins of hunters remain imbedded in the body and gradually kill the elephant. Baker, in *The Albert Nyanza*, 1: 284, tells how skilled hunters can kill an elephant directly by a stab with a spear from below.

9. Appian, *Iberia*, Chapter 46.

Conclusion

The art of war in antiquity reaches its peak with Caesar. Not that we would place him personally above Miltiades or Alexander, Hannibal or Scipio—an observation or comparison of this type would be just as preposterous as it was fruitless—but among all these great artists he is the one who had at his disposition simultaneously the most complete and the vastest means. The cohort of his time is an immeasurably finer instrument than the old, simple phalanx or even the triple-wave phalanx.

The cohorts working in organic coordination with effectively trained sharpshooters, strong cavalry, field fortifications, and systematic supply procedures—that is the army Caesar controlled with the personal courage of the soldier and the strategy of the accomplished commander. In the army itself there is nothing new; before his time we are familiar with all the individual elements as well as with their coordination. To this extent it could be said that Caesar did not play a decisive role at all in the history of the art of war. Miltiades, Pericles, Epaminondas, Alexander, the manipular phalanx, Hannibal, Scipio, Marius—all stand for particular innovations, original thoughts in the manner of leading an army. Caesar finds everything, the means as well as the ideas, already at hand, but he brings them to their ultimate expression and the acme of coordination in the richest variety, to the greatest degree, and in the most perfected form.

A favorite saying of his has come down to us in the writings, that he would rather conquer by means of hunger than with iron,[1] and the tendency has been to interpret that as meaning that he preferred to subject the enemy not by defeating him but by a mere process of attrition. Every step of his career as a commander shows that this saying must be understood differently. The strategy of attrition can only be pursued justifiably in a situation where, according to Clausewitz' expression,[2] the will and the power are not sufficient for a great decision. But Caesar's circumstances were always of such a kind that both his strength and his will were appropriate for a complete defeat of his enemy, and the natural means of

565

doing this is by attacking the enemy's main force, the decisive battle. Caesar always had this in mind, but his saying can nevertheless,
for this very reason, quite well be true. The manner of bringing on
a great decision does not consist of a blind charging in but of the
skillful provision of favorable conditions. To this end the difference
between hunger and adequate rations has played a principal role in
every period, but in Caesar's case to an unusually high degree. Indeed, his concern for supply procedures is not to be evaluated as a
weakening but rather as a strengthening of the concept of destruction, and this is the viewpoint that we must take if we wish to
characterize him as a strategist.

In Gaul it was the superiority of the Roman supply system that
enabled Caesar to avoid fighting against the great Gallic masses and
to win the decision by pitting his entire force against fractions of
the enemy forces. To this extent he could say that he conquered
primarily by means of hunger rather than by iron.

In the civil war it was different. Here it was the field fortifications that gave the characteristic stamp to the strategy. Caesar obviously had a natural inclination toward the technical; he was a born
engineer. We can see with what affection his works and installations
are described in the *Commentaries*: the fortifying of the bank of the
Rhone against the Helvetii, the camp on the Aisne, the invention of
the long sickles in the naval war against the Veneti, the Rhine
bridges, the siege engines at Aduatuca, Avaricum, Massilia, the obstacles around Alesia, the water conduit at Uxellodunum, the artificial ford across the Sicoris, the gigantic installation for the encircling of Pompey at Dyrrhachium. But it is not just the personal talent and inclination of this commander that give these things so
much emphasis in his conduct of war; rather, it is the natural
course of events that brings this about. The old Roman campcraft,
like every technical subject, tended to perfect and broaden itself
through new inventions. This campcraft gave such a degree of
superiority to the defensive that even the smaller force could hold
its own in the open field. If no mistake was made, it was impossible
for a battle to develop unless both sides wished it so. If the weaker
side avoided a decision and sought to prolong the war, the coun-
termeasure for the stronger side was the besieging of the enemy
camp—and thus, once again, the conduct of war by means of
hunger: in the one case as the expression of the cultural and organizational superiority of the Romans over the barbarians, in the
other the expedient of the offensive against the technical superior-

ity of the defensive. In neither case, however, does this method of warfare contradict the strategy of total victory but rather it only forms a means for carrying out that strategy in the most certain, energetic, and complete possible manner. The dissolution of the army of the Belgae through the camp on the Aisne and the starving out of the Pompeian forces at Ilerda were both great strategic successes that outwardly resemble each other to a certain extent but nevertheless, in the final analysis, stemmed from different causes. On the Aisne Caesar was not willing to risk an open battle against the assembled forces of the Belgae, and he recognized in the superiority of the Roman campcraft and supply system the means of first obliging the enemy to split his forces. At Ilerda it was he who had the superior force and his enemies who avoided the battle; for this reason he threatened them with a siege, fought against the reprovisioning of their troops, and in this way managed to bring the situation to the point where finally, when the opportunity for a battle offered itself, it was no longer necessary.

If Hannibal, in his time, had been able to operate in this way and had he been able to besiege and starve out the Roman armies that avoided his attack, the ancient world would not have become a Latin one. But Hannibal's means of conducting war were not sufficient for this; he came right up to the culminating point of victory but then slowly slipped back again. Caesar's offensive power was still superior to the strongest defensive and was able to break it. He won one victory after another; it was as if his wars knew no time; his strategy was lightning-like; through his combination of sword and hunger he brought every war, in the theater of operations where it took place, to an end with a single campaign. His originality lay in this gigantic enhancement of the art. We can no doubt establish a parallel in a development of the most recent period. The improvement of firearms seemed at first to work to the advantage of the defensive; against modern infantry and artillery fire an attack over open ground is no longer possible—just as little so as it was possible for Roman legions to make an attack against a Roman field fortification. But the increased effectiveness of weapons allows the modern attacker, on his side, to extend his lines at will, even to move to the attack in widely separated columns from different directions and by means of envelopment to win fire superiority for himself. And thus the advantage of the defense is shifted over into an advantage for the offense—like the Roman field fortification, which first protects the army that is not willing to fight but then gives the enemy more than ever the possibility of forcing the final decision by a siege, thus turning to his advantage. (Written in 1908.)

The World War showed that even this development could once again be surpassed. Something occurred that no theorist had been able to foresee: the battle lines were extended until they stretched to the obstacles of absolute borders and could not be enveloped by any further operations: from the English Channel to the Swiss border; from the Baltic to Romania. And thus it was necessary to turn back again from the tactics of envelopment to the frontal attack, the penetration, from the superiority of the offensive to that of the defensive. (Written in 1920.)

Caesar's was a constantly active intelligence; he had studied in Rhodes and for a while had concerned himself with studying and writing about questions of grammar. There is no doubt that he also took pains to familiarize himself theoretically with the whole realm of the art of war; in incidental remarks here and there it is reported that he had read Xenophon's *Cyropaedia*,[3] and writings concerning Alexander the Great.[4] In his own works, however, theoretical reflections are hardly to be found at all, so that Frederick the Great was able to make the remarkable statement that the soldier could not really learn anything from him,[5] and Napoleon, much as he recommended the study of Caesar, also still complained on one occasion about his lack of clearness, saying that his battles had no names—and it is, of course, obvious that strategic study can derive little from a campaign as long as its geographical location is not established. And in addition to these points we also have all the impossible numerical relationships. But those are defects that are explained by the political purpose that Caesar was pursuing with his books, shortcomings that nevertheless detracted but little from the effectiveness of his writings. These deficiences, moreover, are susceptible to filling in and correcting by the progress of research and have actually been so emended. If Frederick expressed himself much more strongly on this subject than did Napoleon, there are good reasons for that, which we shall have occasion to explain when we discuss this master himself. In his works Caesar did not intend to present his subject from a didactic viewpoint dealing especially with the military, and he therefore omitted the details, motives, and reflections that would have been necessary for such a purpose. It is from the facts themselves that we learn, and not from the words. On a few occasions, however, the philosophical mentality of the thinker still breaks through the easy flow of the account and reveals theoretical understanding of a kind that we do not yet find in the case of the reflective military writers of antiquity, Xenophon and Polybius. When Caesar reports in his account of the battle of Pharsalus how Pompey had commanded his soldiers to await the attack on the spot, he condemns this viewpoint and emphasizes, as we would express it today, the morale value of the offensive. In the clearer manner of expression of the language of antiquity, his words were:

> It seems to us that Pompey was not wise in doing this, for the reason that in each man there is a certain innate passion and spiritual stimulus that is sparked by the excitement of battle. Commanders should not suppress these feelings but should strengthen them; and it is not for nothing that the custom has come down to us from olden days that the trumpets blow and the battle cry is raised from all sides, because it was believed that the enemy was frightened by this and one's own men were emboldened.
>
> (Quod nobis quidem nulla ratione factum a Pompeio videtur, propterea quod est quaedam animi incitatio atque alacritas naturaliter innata omnibus, quae studio pugnae incenditur. Hanc non reprimere, sed augere imperatores debent, neque frustra antiquitus institutum est, ut signa undique concinerent, clamoremque universi tollerent: quibus rebus et hostes terreri et suos incitari existimaverunt.)

We can see another theoretically significant reflection in the fact that Caesar particularly liked to emphasize what a role chance plays in war. The comparison of strategy with chess, which has often been made previously, is therefore the opposite of the correct one, because this game is based on the most all-inclusive and refined estimations, whereas strategy also depends on mastery of that which is beyond estimation. For this reason, exercise of the art of command demands not only the intelligence but also the entire personality of the man, who even pits himself against chance, counters it continuously with new information, and thereby masters capricious luck and ties it to his chariot. We must look upon Thucydides as the first one to clarify this aspect of the conduct of war. We have already cited above the words that he places in the mouth of Pericles: "that opportunities in war do not wait." But he also has the Corinthians saying (1. 122), ". . . War proceeds only in the smallest way in accordance with definite laws; its principal part it creates for itself by itself, depending on the circumstances that arise," and, on another occasion, King Archidamus of Sparta (2. 11. 3): ". . . The course of war is hidden, and much comes about from very small things, and passion brings about accomplishment."[6] These are the basic thoughts of Clausewitz' philosophy of war that are appearing here for the first time, the recognition that there is an irrational element in war, to which the commander must dare to trust his fate. Already in Cicero's writings we find that, in addition to *"scientia rei militaris, virtus, auctoritas"* ("knowledge of military things, courage, authority"), he also calls for *"felicitas"* ("good fortune") as a quality of the great leader,[7] and Caesar writes *(Bell. Civ.* 3. 68): "Sed fortuna, quae plurimum potest quum in reliquis rebus tum praecipue in bello, parvis momentis magnas rerum commutationes efficit." ("But fortune, which influences many a thing, both in other matters and especially in war, produces the greatest changes with small impulses.")

Caesar has quite often evoked the opinion that he trusted altogether too much to luck, that he challenged it like a gambler, and it is certain that he did believe in his star, like Napoleon. The account as to how, in the midst of the stormy sea, he consoled the sailor with the information that he was transporting Caesar and his luck, may be literally true, even if he himself has not recounted this to us. It would be incorrect, however, just as in Napoleon's case, to see nothing but boldness in him, whether it be to praise or to condemn. We have convinced ourselves that, step by step, this quality was always paralleled by wise awareness and weighing of the situation. The ancients, too, already realized this. Suetonius praises him (Chapter 58)—". . . *in obeundis expeditionibus dubium cautior an audentior"* ("in entering upon his expeditions it was a question as to whether he was mainly cautious or bold")—and just as in the case of modern commanders, his strategy was based principally on the decisive point of having numerical superiority on the battlefield. We have pointed out that he always had such superiority in Gaul and at Ilerda in Spain. Thapsus was not a pitched battle; on Munda we have no reliable figures, but there can hardly be any doubt at all that Caesar, who was then already emperor, levied more men than his enemies, who only had a single country at their disposition. If we overlook the completely strange circumstances in Egypt and the five-day campaign against Pharnaces, which comes but little into consideration, then the battle of Pharsalus is the only one in which Caesar was victorious with presumably considerably smaller forces. He could still have avoided this battle and awaited the arrival of reinforcements, 1½ legions from Hellas and 2 from Illyria. But if he had done that first, Pompey would surely no longer have accepted battle, but thanks to his ships, would have transferred his army and the war to some other area. After all, the enemy's superiority at sea had also prevented Caesar from the very start of this campaign from taking advantage of the superiority in land troops that was theoretically at his disposal. He had to use the larger half of his manpower, though admittedly the less effective portion, the newly formed legions, to protect Italy, Gaul, Spain, and Sicily, and as early as at Dyrrhachium, in order to accomplish anything at all of a positive nature, he had detached so many troops that against Pompey himself he was in the minority. From every point of view it is important to establish clearly the fact and the reason that Caesar fought specifically the decisive battle, and this battle alone, with numerical inferiority. The sea power of the Pompeians, through its indirect effects, imposed such strong fetters on Caesar's conduct of operations that he did not have a free choice between alternatives; but Caesar personally shows up all the greater here in that, as highly as he estimated the importance of numbers, based on consideration of the situation, he put that concern aside and trusting only in the quality of his troops and his own leadership accepted the decisive battle.

The Roman art of war, as it appears to us in Caesar as the matured fruit of a development that had lasted for centuries, did not die out again with him but lived on in the Roman world as his bequest. After him great areas, particularly the Alps, the countries south of the Danube, and England were conquered for the Roman Empire. Finally two nations set the limits for the world conquerors; of the one people, the Parthians, we have already previously spoken. The others were the Germans. We shall start the second part of our work with the Germans' military system and conduct of war. Of what type was this power that was able to stand up to the Roman art of war?

NOTES FOR CONCLUSION

1. Frontinus, 4. 7. 1. Similarly, *Bell. Afric.*, Chapter 31.
2. *Vom Kriege*, Book 7, Chapter 16.
3. Suetonius, Chapter 88.
4. Plutarch, Chapter 11.
5. In the preface to his treatment of the *Commentaries* of Folard on Polybius, 1755.

6. The excellent bringing together of the three citations in the work of Adolf Bauer, "Thucydides' Views on the Conduct of War" ("Ansichten des Thucydides über Kriegführung"), *Philologus* 50: 416.

7. In the oration "Pro lege Manilia" in the year 66 B.C.

Index

573

train with siege engines, 444-45; attempt to capture Phraaspa, 445; decimation of two cohorts, 445-46; forced to withdraw, 446; question as to route followed into Media, 448; exaggerated report of losses, 449; fallacious aspects of Kromayer's study, 449; command of Caesar's residual forces at Brundisium, 530; successful crossing of Adriatic, 530-31

Apollonia: captured by Caesar, 529

Appian: false account of battle of Cannae 328-31; "four stratagems" at Cannae, 331; fictitious report on individual combat between Hannibal and Scipio, 377; account of battle of Magnesia, 398-99; opposing strengths at Pharsalus, 544-49

Aquae Sextiae: victory of Marius over Teutones and Ambrones, 414

Archelaus, 439

Archers: respected in Greece, 55; of secondary importance to spear, 55; importance in Persian army, 67; range of, 89 n.6; action at Plataea, 114; auxiliary aspect of, in Greek tactics, 124; Delbrück opinion of Athenian, as elite, well trained corps, 124; qualities required of, 124; units of, created by Spartans, 132 n.1; Hercules as prime example of, 158; mounted, in Alexander's army against Darius, 177; inactivity of Persian, on Granicus, 188; Briso's, in Alexander's army at Gaugamela, 215

Archidamus (king of Sparta): belief in chance in war, 570

Aretes: command of Paeonian cavalry at Gaugamela, 215

Argives: elite unit of 1,000 men among, 146

Ariovistus: domination of Gaul by, 460, 467; not mentioned by

Caesar in account of Helvetian campaign, 460; Roman policy to get along with, 467; held hostages from Gallic tribes, 467; Caesar's intention to defeat, 469-70, 477 n.7; campaign against Caesar, 479-87; coordination of cavalry, light infantry, 479; setting up of wagon defenses, 479-80; battle against Caesar, 480-81; army not larger than Caesar's, 481-82; forced to use light infantry with regular infantry, 481; uncertainty as to location of battle, 482-87; capabilities of, 483

Aristobulus: source for Arrian, 302

Ariston: command of Paeonian cavalry at Gaugamela, 215

Arms: *arma antesignana*, 282 n.9; *arma postsignana*, 282, n.9

Army Organization and Conduct of War by the Greeks: Dr. H. Droysen, 28; basis for scholarly knowledge of Greek military art, 28

Army strengths: starting point for military-historical study, 33; critical treatment of historical accounts impossible without concept of, 33; false impressions of, 33-35, 70; Greek, at Plataea, 36, 112; Greek, at Marathon, 37, 64, 70; Athenian, reported by Thucydides in speech by Pericles, 39-42; Athenian, at Delium, 41; garrison troops in Athens, 42-44; Greek, estimate of, 63; misstatement of, at Gravelotte-Saint-Privat, by Moltke, 43; popular legend concerning, 69; Persian, at Marathon, 72, 82, 87; of Alexander and Persians on Granicus, 185-86; commanders' tendency to understate, 357; Caesar's numerical superiority in battles in Gaul, 471, 481-82, 491; Caesar at Alesia, 499, 505 n.1;